Connecticut River
Hadley Meadows
Aqua Vitæ
Goodman's Ferry
Elwell's Is.
Water Street
Bridge
Toll Hs.
Old Rainbow
Young Rainbow
Strong's Farm
Walnut Tree Division
Venturer's Field
Nook
Webbs Hollow
Second Square
First Square
Third Square
King's Bottom
Shepherd's Farm
Bark Wigwam
Meadow
Middle
Hockanum Ferry
Hockanum
Hockanum Meadows
Hunts Tavern
Prospect Street
Alms House
Round Hill
Wolf Pit Swamp
Elm Street
Phelp's Meadow
Mills
West Street
South Street
Fort Hill
Pancake Plain
J. Strong
Clark
North Street
King St.
Hampden Canal
Burial Ground School
School
American Hotel
Fort Brook
Sheep Pastures
Pine Brook
F. Marsh
Great Swamp
Patson's Swamp
Fish Place
Triangle
Hulberts Pond
Hog's Bladder
Indian Massacre 1704
Rock Ferry
Line between Hadley
Nashawannuck
Manhan
M O N S
H A D L E Y

A PLACE CALLED PARADISE

A PLACE CALLED PARADISE

Culture and Community in
Northampton, Massachusetts,
1654–2004

EDITED BY

KERRY W. BUCKLEY

HISTORIC NORTHAMPTON
Museum and Education Center

Published in association with
University of Massachusetts Press
Amherst and Boston

Printed in the United States of America

LC 2004019705
ISBN 1-55849-485-5

Designed by Dennis Anderson
Set in Sabon and Adobe Garamond
Printed and bound by The Maple-Vail Book Manufacturing Group

Library of Congress Cataloging in Publication Data

A place called paradise : culture and community in Northampton,
Massachusetts, 1654–2004 / edited by Kerry W. Buckley.
p. cm.
Essays commemorating the 350th anniversary of Northampton, Mass.
Includes bibliographical references and index.
ISBN 1-55849-485-5 (cloth : alk. paper)
1. Northampton (Mass.)—Civilization. 2. Northampton (Mass.)—History.
3. Northampton (Mass.)—Social conditions.
I. Buckley, Kerry W. (Kerry Wayne) II. Historic Northampton
Museum & Education Center.
F74.N86P58 2004
974.4'23—dc22
2004019705

British Library Cataloguing in Publication Data are available

This publication was made possible, in part, by a grant from the
Massachusetts Foundation for the Humanities, a state-based affiliate of the
National Endowment for the Humanities.

For

Stanley Elkins

"Gladley would he learn, and gladley teach"

CHAUCER, "The Clerk at Oxenford,"
from, *The Canterbury Tales*

Contents

	Acknowledgments	ix
	Introduction	1
1	Peter A. Thomas, Into the Maelstrom of Change	5
2	Margaret Bruchac, Native Presence in Nonotuck and Northampton	18
3	John Putnam Demos, "Hard Thoughts and Jealousies"	39
4	Kevin M. Sweeney, The River Gods in the Making	75
5	Ronald Story, Jonathan Edwards and the Gospel of Love	91
6	Marla R. Miller, The View through the Eye of a Needle	107
7	Gregory H. Nobles, Revolution in the Neighborhood	137
8	Leonard L. Richards, The Revolution That Failed	168
9	Christopher Clark, The Roots of Rural Capitalism	197
10	Martha Hoppin, Arcadian Vales	231
11	The Look of Paradise	245
12	Jill A. Hodnicki, The Literary Landscape	257
13	Stephen Nissenbaum, Sylvester Graham and Health Reform	282
14	Christopher Clark, The Communitarian Moment	301
15	Nell Irvin Painter, Sojourner Truth: A Life, a Symbol	343
16	David W. Blight, When This Cruel War Is Over	365
17	Dean Flower, The View from Prospect House	395

18 Helen Lefkowitz Horowitz, Smith College and Changing Concepts of Educated Women 403

19 Kathy Peiss, Love across the Color Line 419

20 Kerry W. Buckley, The Man Nobody Knew 459

21 Barry Werth, The Scarlet Professor 493

Notes on Contributors 513

Index 517

Acknowledgments

THIS ANTHOLOGY is the product of a collaborative effort that has benefited from the talent and generosity of many. I am grateful to the contributors and their publishers, who kindly granted permission for their work to appear in this book. Bruce Wilcox and Clark Dougan, at the University of Massachusetts Press, provided crucial guidance and editorial advice that carried the enterprise forward.

Neal Pogue, Michael Messinger, Ann Schuyler, and Joyce Capper assisted in the laborious task of preparing the original manuscript. Marie Panik's careful oversight of this process and her many hours of dedicated work made the timely completion of the project possible.

It has been my good fortune to work with a team of skilled professionals, who transformed this assembly of documents into a book. I owe a great deal to Jack Harrison, who managed the overall design and saw the project through the labyrinth of production. Dennis Anderson designed the graceful typography that is, in itself, a pleasure to behold. Kay Scheuer's skillful copy-editing brought order and consistency to a welter of editorial styles.

I am indebted to the Smith College History Department and especially to Neal Salisbury for co-sponsoring the lecture series which brought many of the contributors to this volume to Northampton during its 350th anniversary year. Without the generous support of the Massachusetts Foundation for the Humanities, this book and the lecture series upon which it is based would have remained only an idea.

A PLACE CALLED PARADISE

Introduction

Eighteenth-century travelers to the Connecticut River Valley of western Massachusetts observed a distinct culture that set the region apart from other places. "The inhabitants of this valley," President Timothy Dwight of Yale remarked in 1790, "possess a common character. . . . even the beauty of the scenery, scarcely found in the same degree elsewhere, becomes a source of pride as well as enjoyment." Those who struggled to climb the heights of Mount Holyoke were rewarded with a panorama that unfolded before them at the summit. "The view here," wrote Reverend Peter Coffin in 1760, "exceeds all I ever had before . . . a beautiful garden, variously yet elegantly laid out." It was, said President Dwight, a "Beautiful" prospect.

Dwight was describing the environs of Northampton, Massachusetts, a place that epitomized eighteenth-century ideas about the natural world and man's place in it. The beauty of this place was in its proportions—the balance between natural beauty and the cultivated landscape. It was, as Swedish soprano Jenny Lind later described it, a "paradise": that is, a garden for the delight and edification of those who dwelled there.

For others, Northampton embodied equally powerful visions. Jonathan Edwards's Northampton was the stage upon which was enacted God's drama of saving grace and redemption. For Henry James, Northampton symbolized the willfulness underlying American innocence. In the roaring 1920s, Northampton became Main Street USA—a reassuring backdrop for the Coolidge presidency. But for literary critic Newton Arvin, it was the dark side of small-town America that surfaced in mid-twentieth-century Northampton.

Since Timothy Dwight wrote his *Travels in New England*, writers and historians have concurred with his assessment of a distinct regional culture along the mid-Connecticut River Valley. It has been characterized as the first American frontier settled by Europeans during the Great Migration of the 1630s, after the Pequot Wars and smallpox had diminished, but not destroyed, the native population. Research has shown how the river and its tributaries linked the Northampton region with global trade networks independent of the Atlantic Coast ports overland to the east. Here, historians have discovered important regional social, economic, and cultural patterns that helped shape both the American and the Industrial Revolutions. The distinct material culture that emerged in the seventeenth century and flourished through the nineteenth is embodied in the artifacts and built landscape that characterize the region. From the seventeenth-century verse of Edward Taylor to the poetry of Sylvia Plath, from the fiction of James Fenimore Cooper and Henry James to that of Brett Lott and Paul Theroux, and from the essays of George Washington Cable to those of Tracy Kidder, this region has produced a literature of its own. Likewise, a regional school of neorealist artists like Jane Lund, Randall Deihl, and Scott Prior follow the paths of Winthrop Chandler, Ralph Earl, and Thomas Cole.

This rich cultural broth nourishes the vitality of Northampton's history, but the history of a place or a community is not a history without conflict. In fact, the terrain of local history is itself often-contested territory. Scholars, antiquarians, civic boosters, and community factions often differ on which story to tell. The stories themselves, told and retold over generations, shift in voice and perspective over time. Each generation rewrites its own history, not because the facts change, but because the questions change. Each community, each group, each generation asks its own questions of history. The history that we write today will, no doubt, reveal much about our time to future generations. Northampton, Massachusetts, celebrates the 350th anniversary of its European settlement in 2004. This occasion affords a community with a long and distinguished past an opportunity to ponder new questions, to enrich a new generation's historical imagination, and to preserve its historical legacy for posterity's questions.

It is also an opportunity to highlight the significance of local history in approaching questions of wider historical import. Local history has often been considered provincial by scholars seeking broad historical themes, or seen merely as a backdrop by those painting portraits of historical figures. In one sense, to paraphrase Tip O'Neill, all history is local. It is at the local level where history happens and where historians can see larger forces at work. In American history, this has been especially true since the end of the nineteenth century when specialized empirical studies began to replace sweeping narrative in the nation's academic circles. Focusing more on social change and process than on great events, wars, and calamities, the new history sought to understand the lives of ordinary people through demographic studies, institutional records, and vital statistics. More recently, historians have tried to recover the "voices" of those marginalized by conventional accounts of the past by unearthing narratives of everyday experience long hidden in letters, diaries, and writing fragments and by deciphering the "texts" embedded in the artifacts of material culture.

The first historian to practice his craft in Northampton was the great romantic historian George Bancroft, who founded the Round Hill School here in 1823. Though he wrote in the shadow of Solomon Stoddard's Manse and Jonathan Edwards's church, Bancroft conceived his history as a grand narrative that swept up merely local events in the unfolding of America's national destiny. At mid-century, antiquarians like Sylvester Judd began to compile local historical documents and records. Based largely on Judd's notes, a vast tome on Northampton history was compiled by newspaper editor James Trumbull in 1890. Though comprehensive through 1800, it was decidedly Whiggish in tone, reflecting Gilded Age sensibilities of Providence and progress. In 1954, a commemorative volume was commissioned for Northampton's Tercentennial. First published as newspaper articles, its essays included contributions from Smith College scholars such as Daniel Aaron, Harold U. Faulkner, and Oliver Larkin.

Since then, especially during the last twenty-five years, a significant body of scholarship on local and regional history has accumulated, reflecting new insights and discoveries. To name but a few, these studies include Christopher Clark's Turner Prize–winning book *The Roots of Rural Capitalism*, John P. Demos's *Entertaining Satan*, Nell Irvin Painter's *Sojourner Truth: A Life, a Symbol*, David Blight's *When This Cruel War Is Over*, Stephen Nissenbaum's *Sex, Diet, and Debility*, Helen Horowitz and Kathy Peiss's *Love Across the Color Line*, and Gregory Nobles's *Divisions Throughout the Whole*. William Hosley's *The Great River*, and Martha Hoppin's *Arcadian Vales* have profiled the distinctive fine art and material culture produced by regional artisans and craftsmen. These scholars and many others from around the globe have found this region fertile ground for their research. Their work has defined a growing body of scholarship based on regional issues and themes.

A Place Called Paradise brings together for the first time a diverse selection of this scholarship connected by theme and region into one volume. During Northampton's 350th anniversary year in 2004, Historic Northampton and the Smith College Department of History brought many of these scholars to Northampton for a series of public lectures. This book not only contains the articles upon which these lectures were based, but includes a number of additional articles that enlarge the scope of the commemorative lecture series.

A Place Called Paradise seeks to "bring history back home" by making this overview of recent scholarship accessible to the regional community, the community of scholars, and the community of readers for whom these studies illustrate, in microcosm, the dynamics at work in the course of American history. The mythology and iconography of small-town America are still abiding symbols in the mass culture that defines the present. Looking at the historical development of a community like Northampton reveals a great deal about the impact of cultural continuity. But the reality of experience for those who lived there was also marked by profound change, change that did not happen in a vacuum. One of the objectives of publishing *A Place Called Paradise* is to help define and promote continued studies in the history of this region. Ultimately, however, the larger goal is to illustrate the extent to which local history resources are an important touchstone for exploring larger issues in American history and culture.

In the twenty-first century, urbanized Americans still seek to replicate a vanished village culture with malls and planned communities. Yet these sanitized substitutes reflect only a one-dimensional concept of community. The paradox of small-town life is a persistent theme in American art and letters. The American village has been characterized on the one hand as a pastoral refuge, a symbol of moral and political virtue, and on the other, as a provincial backwater, a bastion of intolerance and suspicion. All these elements have surfaced at one time or another in Northampton's long history. Yet the frictions sparked by these contradictions fire the crucible out of which a community like Northampton is formed. This dynamic between factions—newcomers and old-timers, Yankees and immigrants, young and old—has always been part of the creative tension that, at its best, has enlarged the community's capacity for tolerance. Over three and a half centuries there have been times of consensus and times of conflict and there have been moments when contending parties become reconciled to their shared destinies, realizing that for better or worse, their fates are intertwined.

Returning to the summit of Mount Holyoke today, Thomas Cole would find the vision largely unchanged. Sylvia Plath spoke of "the high hush" at the top. "All's peace and discipline down there," she wrote. It is a place that has been called "paradise" by some, but perhaps above all, it is a place that many could call "home." In his book *Hometown,* Tracy Kidder captures the view of Northampton at the beginning of the twenty-first century, on the eve of its 350th anniversary:

> From the summit, the cornfields are a dream of perfect order, and the town seems entirely coherent, self-contained, a place where a person might live a whole life and consider it complete, a tiny civilization all its own. Forget the messiness of years and days—every work of human artifice has a proper viewing distance. The town below fits in the palm of your hand. Shake it and it snows.

The view from Mount Holyoke will continue to provide perspective on a region whose culture has been defined by its sense of place.

KERRY W. BUCKLEY
Northampton, Massachusetts, 2004

1

To THE English of the seventeenth century, the place they called Northampton was a vacuum domicilium*—a vacant wasteland on their maps, an unredeemed wilderness. It was a place to tame, to plant, and, for the Puritans, to establish the City of God on earth. But these spaces were not empty. To the native peoples who had lived here for ten thousand years this place was called* Norwottuck, *or* Nonotuck*—the place in the middle of the river. It was the midpoint, the balance point on the Connecticut, "the long tidal river."*

For William Pynchon in 1636, it was a meeting place, a convenient location to barter trade goods for valuable hides and furs. But by mid-century the beaver were gone, and land was all the native peoples had left to trade. So it was that on September 24, 1653, title to the land that became the English town of Northampton was conveyed to John Pynchon of Springfield by "Chickwallop, alias *Wawhillowa, Neessahalant, Nassicohee, Riants, Paqualant, Assellaquompas and Awonusk the wife of Wulluther all of Nanotuck" for the "consideration of one hundred fathum of Wampum by Tale and for Tenn Coates."*

Peter Thomas examines Indian-white relations in this region during the contact period. Thomas dispels some of the commonly held myths about New England's Indians and characterizes the transformations that took place in the native villages between Agawam (Springfield) in the south and Squakheag (Northfield) to the north.

Into the Maelstrom of Change*

PETER A. THOMAS

FROM the time the English arrived in the New World until the present, most writers have described Indian "tribes" in southern New England as well-defined, stable political units with recognizable leaders and identifiable territorial boundaries.[1] If one reviews specific chains of historical events during the seventeenth century, however, it becomes apparent that persistent tribal unity is a figment of the historian's imagination. George Sheldon's Pocumtuck Confederacy, for example, never existed.

For seventeenth-century New England, it seems that, as social, political, and economic entities, most Indian groups fall within a type of "egalitarian society" that anthropologists have defined as "segmentary tribes."[2] In any

* From Peter A. Thomas, "Bridging the Cultural Gap: Indian/White Relations," in Stephen C. Innes et al., *Early Settlement in the Connecticut Valley* (Boston, 1984).

description of a New England segmentary tribe, emphasis should be placed on the reality of segmentation and not on the unity of "tribe." As such, the primary political, social, and economic unit was the village, which rarely numbered more than 300 to 500 people. The "tribe" as such was episodic. What defined a segmentary tribe at all was the intermittent cooperation between communities to meet outside pressures.[3] As the notion of "segmentary tribe" suggests, community units, particularly in noncoastal areas, were relatively small and had populations numbering between 150 and 500 people. In the early years of the seventeenth century, groups may have maintained a dual settlement system in which small hamlets were occupied by extended families surrounding a centrally located village which was the focus of political and religious activities.

Between 1630 and 1640, the size and perhaps the distribution of Indian villages underwent a radical change. While discussing potential English expansion into the Connecticut Valley in 1633, the leaders of the Massachusetts Bay Colony decided against such a move because they thought "the place not fit for plantations, there being three or four thousand warlike Indians."[4] If these figures for the number of warriors are approximately accurate, they suggest a total population of 12,000 residing in the Connecticut River watershed. In that same year, however, a smallpox epidemic swept through southern New England. William Bradford's vivid description of conditions between the summers of 1633 and 1634 leaves a marked impression on any reader. An unidentified village which lay well to the north of the Dutch trading post at Hartford had a reported population of one thousand in early 1634. During the winter, some 950 died. "Many of them," commented Bradford, "did rott above ground for want of buriall."[5] The lower valley Indian towns were severely hit. Bradford described the gruesome scene:

> This spring, those [Indians] that lived about [Plymouth's] trading house at Windsor fell sick of ye small poxe, and dyed most miserably; for a sorer disease cannot befall them; they fear it more than ye plague; for usually they that have this disease have them in abundance, and for wante of bedding lining and other helps, they fall into a lamentable condition, as they lye on their hard matts, ye poxe breaking and mattering, and running one into another, their skin cleaving to the matts they lye on; when they turne them, a whole side will flea of at once, and they will be a gore blood, most fearful to behold; and then being very sore, what with could and other distempers; they dye like rotten sheep.[6]

The radical drop in population and subsequent dislocation virtually removed any significant impediments to English expansion into the lower Connecticut Valley. We will probably never know what effects this epidemic had on the communities at Woronoco, Agawam, Norwottuck, Pocumtuck, and Squakheag, but repercussions are likely to have been profound.

Map of New England (detail from "The White Hills Map"). William Hubbard (ca. 1621–1704) and John Foster (1648–1681). From William Hubbard's *A Narrative of the Troubles with the Indians in New-England . . .* Engraved by John Foster. Boston, 1677. Woodcut. H: 12 ⅛ in. (30.9 cm); W: 15 15/16 in. (40.5 cm). Inscribed: *A Map of New England. Massachusetts Historical Society, Boston.*

This detail is from a bold woodcut map of New England. It depicts a landscape largely empty except for European-style villages, most with English names. In fact, most of these towns were settled on or alongside existing Indian settlements that continued to be occupied, though with diminished populations, by Native Americans with strong kinship ties throughout the region. The map, regarded by its makers and acknowledged by scholars as the first ever to be engraved and printed in America, appeared in William Hubbard's *Narrative of the Troubles with the Indians in New-England, from the First Planting Thereof in the Year 1607, to this Present Year 1677,* published in Boston.

In 1636, the town of Springfield was established as a northern English outpost on the Connecticut River. Within a decade of the town's settlement, the types of social and political interaction between the Indian and the English community began to take on a recognizable form. Social boundaries were rather closely prescribed. Indians were prohibited from visiting English towns at night, entering private houses, or handling or purchasing European guns. Moreover, settlers were prevented from falling prey to the natives' corrupting influence by being forbidden to "take up their abode with the Indians in a prophane course of life." Failure to comply with this policy of social isolation meant that a colonist faced the prospect of three years' imprisonment and a fine, or "corporall punishment as the particular Court shall judge meet to inflict."[7] Interracial marriage was, of course, prohibited.

In the aftermath of the Pequot War of 1638, the Puritan colonies initiated various policies which they hoped would secure favorable relations between themselves and their Indian neighbors. Only in rare instances, and never from a purely legal standpoint, was their approach based on a recognized autonomy of native communities. Rather, all individuals within a colony's boundaries were officially considered subjects of the Crown and, as such, were held responsible for their actions under British law. It was ordered that any native community located near an English village should

> declare who is their Sachem or Chiefe and that the said Chiefe or Sachem shall paye to the saide English such trespasses as shal be comitted by an Indian in the saide plantacon adioyninge, either by spoilinge or killing of Cattle or Swine either with Trappes, dogges or arrowes and they are not to pleade that it was done by Strangers unlesse they cann prduce the prty and delivr him or his goodes into the Custody of the English.[8]

There were, however, gross discrepancies between the "assumed" and the "real" extent of English authority or power.

In 1646, for example, the Commission of the United Colonies was presented with a complaint from Windsor that some Indians, particularly Wahannor, had set fire to about one hundred pounds worth of pitch, tar, tools, and a cart. This incendiary had been captured, but had been rescued by his friends. The magistrates were annoyed by this action and by the considerable abuses leveled against their deputies, especially by Chickwallop, a sachem from Norwottuck who had joined in the fracas. John Gilbert and an armed party were dispatched to Woronoco after the escape. Chickwallop and Wahannor could not be found, and the reception given the constable was anything but friendly. Gilbert seems to have been amazed at the Indians' effrontery when he reported:

> The Sagamores and Indians at Waranoco carryed it insolently towards the English vauntinge themselves in their armes, bowes and arrowes, hatchets, swords, some with their guns ready charged before and in the presence of the English Messengers, they primed and cocked them ready to give fire, and tould them that if they should offer to carry away any man thence, the Indians were resolved to fight.[9]

During the following year, a raiding party from Norwottuck attacked a small village of Indians near Quabaug and killed three residents. The Quabaugs sought redress not from the English, but from an eastern sachem named Cutchamaquin to whom they owed nominal allegiance. Cutchamaquin, a close ally of the Massachusetts Bay Colony, induced a missionary, the Reverend John Eliot, to intercede with the colonial government on the Quabaugs' behalf. The Governor's Council sent a letter to William Pynchon, their chief magistrate in Springfield, instructing him to pursue the Norwottuck murderers. Pynchon agreed that if Quacunquasit, a Quabaug sachem, or others could get the suspected Norwottucks to Springfield he would seize them and ensure that they stood trial. It is likely that Pynchon felt that the Indians would never succeed in doing that, and his reply to the Massachusetts Bay authorities was candid. He cautioned:

> If ye Lord should let loose the reynes to their malice . . . it may be of ill Consequence to ye English that intermedle in their matters by a voluntary rather than by a necessary calinge, for they and their friends stand uppon their inocency,

> and in that respect they threaten to be avenged on such as lay any hand uppon them; and our place [Springfield] is more obnoxtious to their malice than the Bay be farr, especially the Naunotuck Indians are desperate Spirites.

Pynchon further warned that even though Norwottuck was within the lines of the Massachusetts patent, its inhabitants must be "esteemed as an Independent free people." They had never signed a treaty recognizing British domination nor had the colonists bought their land. The Springfield magistrate made his point, and he was instructed to let the matter drop.[10]

By mid-seventeenth century, Indian villages throughout southern New England were faced with a number of regional and local issues that threatened their political integrity. Within thirty years, marginal English plantations centered in the Cape Cod Bay region had mushroomed into over forty towns which were inhabited by more than twenty thousand immigrants. Other Europeans, notably the French and Dutch, also began to extend their economic and political spheres of influence. Even more significantly, intervillage feuding among the Indian communities was intense, and raids were common. No individual, whether Indian or white, could escape the political and economic shock waves reverberating throughout the northeast.

After 1636, although they were not likely to encounter problems brought about by close social and religious interaction, Valley Indians were repeatedly confronted with specific issues involving land, trade, and political independence as English settlements multiplied. Increasing Indian-English contact meant that repeated accommodations had to be made in both cultural systems if open ruptures between the two societies were to be avoided. How were people with conflicting points of view and goals to settle their differences? Where was the arena of resolution? The events just presented indicate that the points where compromise was likely were extremely limited. Trade held out the one hope. Trade was the only significant area where interdependency frequently existed.

A brief look at the trading system which developed in the Connecticut Valley may help to explain this point.[11] Once Springfield was established in 1636, its leading citizen, William Pynchon, found a ready market for the wampum, cloth, and other items he had transported from the coast. From its inception, barter between Indians and settlers involved two commodities—horticultural produce and furs. Until English grains could be grown in the valley in sufficient quantities to feed English families, a local traffic in native horticultural produce was crucial for the immigrants' survival. As long as the colonists were dependent upon their Indian neighbors for a portion of their food supply, the English could not adopt a hostile attitude without significant risk to their own security. Until mid-century, therefore, residents at Woronoco, Norwottuck, and Pocumtuck were able to utilize this bargaining position to thwart unwanted political and economic encroachment.

The dispersal of European goods, which were funneled through a small number of colonial traders to Indian villagers, performed a significant bridging function between the colonial and indigenous societies. Along with the manufactured commodities went information—a vital resource for strategy planning. To ensure this flow of information, Indian spokesmen (clients) within the Connecticut Valley established commercial connections with well-placed Englishmen, who were not only major merchants (brokers), but frequently the Bay Colony's executive and judicial representatives as well. This gave several influential colonists the potential, at least, to function as patrons.[12] Economic transactions kept political doors open, and as long as mutually satisfactory business ties could be maintained, there was less potential for "hard line" actions to be taken by either side.

This system worked particularly well because trade, whether for corn or pelts, was not open to all colonists, but was monopolized by a few individuals. The pivotal character in this slowly emerging system was William Pynchon, the founder of Springfield. For the most part, Pynchon functioned more as a merchant/broker than as a patron. On rare occasions, however, he did function in typical patron fashion by forestalling colonial intervention in Indian political affairs, and, as magistrate, by acting as judicial arbiter in local English-Indian disputes. After 1652, he was followed by his son, John Pynchon, who truly became an entrepreneur with executive and judicial power, as well as by several minor patron-traders, such as David Wilton and Joseph Parsons in Northampton, who constantly dealt with a number of Indian clients and made the system a practical reality.

In the middle Connecticut Valley, the period between 1650 and 1665 was marked by considerable uncertainty in some Indian villages. At a local level, the potential for increased Indian-English conflict intensified as the English population at Springfield expanded and as new towns sprang up to the north. Growing interest in the Westfield River valley and the establishment of Northampton (1654), Hadley (1659), and Hatfield (1661) had profound implications. This growth of colonial populations and the reduction of geographic proximity between English and Indian towns resulted in several personal confrontations. As in the past, there was an obvious need to resolve situations of conflict between Indian villagers and their colonial neighbors. The fur trade and the development of a number of patron/broker–client relationships continued to be one means of compromise around which other strategies could be developed.

As indicated, the fur trade provided a "bridging mechanism" between the English and Indian societies.[13] Continued participation in the fur trade, however, became increasingly difficult due to the incessant warfare among the Indian communities themselves. Two forces were at work. The first was a centrifugal force generated from recurring attempts to consolidate or expand

Land deed. From James Trumbull, *History of Northampton, from Its Settlement in 1654*, vol. 1 (Northampton, 1898).

On September 24, 1653, title to the land that became the English town of Northampton was conveyed to John Pynchon of Springfield by "Chickwallop, *alias* Wawhillowa, Neessahalant, Nassicohee, Riants, Paqualant, Assellaquompas and Awonusk the wife of Wulluther all of Nanotuck" for the "consideration of one hundred fathum of Wampum by Tale and for Tenn Coates."

native and colonial power, which threatened to tear the trading system apart. The second was a centripetal force generated from the recognition that trade was important for sustaining good intersocietal relations and for acquiring foreign commodities.

The amount of disruption to which the fur trade was subject was directly conditioned by the successes or failures of various segmentary tribes throughout the northeast in maintaining or expanding their political influence. One fact which John Pynchon's trading ledgers make abundantly clear is that there were gross fluctuations in the number of skins valley hunters could secure each year. Annual variations ranged between 3,723 pounds of beaver pelts exported during Pynchon's most successful year, 1654, to only 191 pounds of furs in 1664. A review of historical events makes it abundantly clear that such fluctuations in the volume of beaver furs were directly related to the political climate in the middle Connecticut River Valley and the surrounding region. Virtually every peak year corresponds to a year of relative peace, every trough to a period of strife among the New England segmentary tribes.[14]

Over a period of fifteen years, from 1650 to 1665, the fur trade lost its vitality. The processes involved in the decline were complex, yet two basic causes seem apparent. The first may have been a natural decrease in beaver and otter populations as exploitation overtaxed their reproductive limits. Second, and probably more significant, the incessant warfare that characterized the period, the eventual constriction of the power domains of Indian communities in the valley, and the complete elimination of the Squakheag and Pocumtuck villages in 1664 and 1665 after Iroquois raids precipitated a crisis for which there was no easily achieved solution. As a consequence, various strategies were attempted, but none produced the desired results—social, economic, and political stability.

While political strife was effectively undermining the trading system, other factors worked to keep it operating. Several detailed studies of economic transactions between Valley Indians and English traders, particularly John Pynchon, make it apparent that European goods were distributed unevenly in the Indians' societies. When one remembers that tremendous fluctuations occurred in the yearly returns from the beaver and otter hunts, it must be concluded that there were periods in which items could simply not be replaced if they were lost or broken. Therefore, any Indian who could control the flow of the available pelts in his own community, or who could provide an alternative resource for exchange, could achieve a considerable advantage over less enterprising individuals. This ability is particularly important because the manipulation of resources for redistribution to one's followers was employed to validate or reinforce any community leader's prestige and authority. Wampum and European trade goods that circulated in the Indian society also functioned as gifts between friends, as validations of social relationships, as tokens of peace tendered to potential enemies. A limited number of

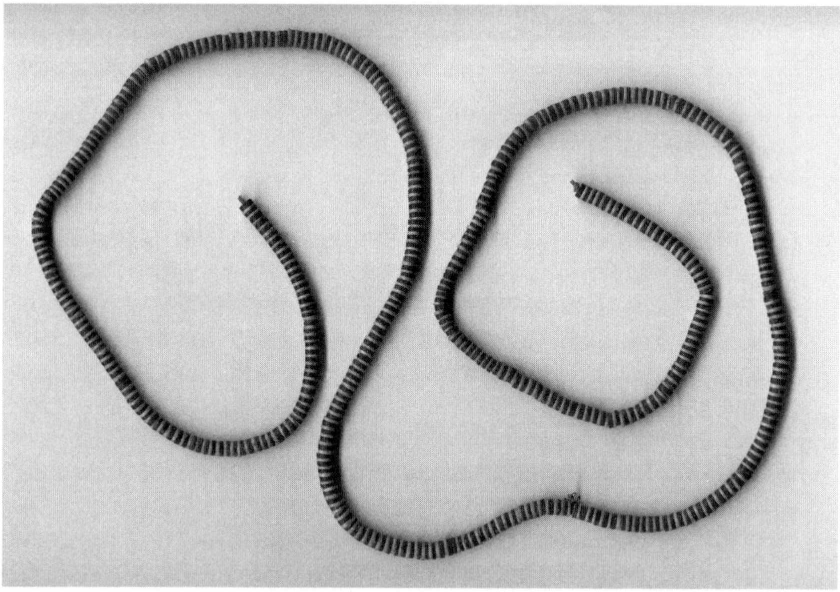

Wampum, c. 1660. Gift of Martha Woodruff. *Historic Northampton.*

No other single aspect of Indian material culture attracted as much of the attention of whites as wampum. There is some controversy among historians and anthropologists regarding the exact origins and functions of wampum before contact with white traders, but the available historical and archaeological evidence strongly suggests that it was not widely produced before the fur trade was established and that it performed restricted functions, such as in the regalia of sachems and in treaty negotiations in the form of belts. Only after white traders discovered that wampum woven in standard lengths could be used as a currency unit in the fur trade did various coastal tribes begin to increase production of wampum, and the control of the centers of production became the underlying issue in power struggles between tribes and between various groups of whites interested in controlling the tribes.

Indian men or women who could manage furs or other resources and maintain community harmony became prominent figures in the Indian-English trade.

It was the slow but steady development of a credit system that provided a number of Indians with influence, resources for distribution, and a means for maintaining Indian-white communications. On a short-term basis, the practice had considerable advantages. Native Americans, after all, relied on two major resources for their trading endeavors—horticultural products and pelts—both of which were highly seasonal in nature. English goods and wampum could be obtained throughout the year only if one's "credit rating" was maintained. In order for such a system to work in a balanced fashion, however, at least two conditions had to be met. Consumption had to be kept at levels commensurate with the amounts of corn or pelts that could be acquired annually for trade, and for rational planning to occur, quantities of corn and pelts had to be predictable. Were such commodities predictable? The answer proved to be an emphatic NO!

Between 1652 and 1657, the annual returns of beaver amounted to 2,290 pounds. Between 1658 and 1663, annual returns averaged 953 pounds, a drop of 59 percent. Indian leaders who relied on the fur trade for many reasons found themselves faced with a monumental predicament. They needed an alternative resource to pelts and horticultural produce. Increasingly, land seemed to provide the answer, if only for a short while and not without the prospect of considerable stress. By 1660, land and the fur trade had become inexorably tied together. The connecting link between them was the English traders' use of credit. From this period, land became the demanded collateral for English goods, which were received on the promise that pelts would be forthcoming the following season. As may be surmised, within less than fifteen years, the loss of the Indians' land base in the middle Connecticut River Valley was nearly complete.

The following is but one example among many land transactions that occurred in the early 1660s. On April 2, 1661, Samuel Marshfield of Springfield exacted a deed of mortgage for all native land holdings remaining within the borders of Springfield from Cuttonis, Coe, Mattaquallant, Menis, and Taqualloush—leaders of the Agawam community who had interacted with the settlers for years. These individuals were to balance their accounts in beaver if possible. Marshfield was also willing to take wampum, corn at two shillings per bushel, or moose, otter, or deerskins. Sufficient resources could not be found by any of these signers, and the lands transferred to Marshfield.[15]

Repercussions from this loss of land were severely felt within the Agawam community. The amount of horticultural acreage became so restricted that families had extreme difficulty in meeting subsistence needs. The Indians complained so bitterly against Samuel Marshfield that in May 1665, a petition was submitted to the Massachusetts General Court by Elizur Holyoke and others in an attempt to solve the problem. On their own behalf, Cuttonis and his neighbors made it clear that "by virtue of a deed of mortgage" which Samuel Marshfield "hath gotten into his hands," they had become "impoverished," had "little or nothing left to plant on," and were forced to rely on the English for support. At least some concessions on the part of the English court did occur. Marshfield was ordered to provide fifteen acres for the use of the Indians. With this done, Cuttonis and Taquallоush, as well as Coe and his sons, agreed to desist from further complaints.[16] This theme of overtaxing landholdings was a common one throughout this period.

By the mid-1660s, various factors, then, had combined to produce a crisis for the native communities at Agawam, Woronoco, and Norwottuck, and to a lesser extent, for those at Pocumtuck. Tremendous English expansion had occurred in the valley. From eight men in 1636, Springfield's population had grown to ninety-one families with over 450 members. Northampton had been founded in 1654. By 1660, fifty-seven men had received homelots for themselves and about 250 members of their families. Hadley had been established in 1659, and five years later, 211 settlers were in residence.[17] Thus, by 1664, approximately nine hundred immigrants had staked out their claims in the middle Connecticut River Valley, where they were probably employing over 12,000 acres of land, divided between agricultural fields, houselots, woodlots, and open pasture.

Concurrently, the Indian populations had grown after the ravages of the smallpox epidemic of the early 1630s. By 1664, the population of the villages between Agawam and Norwottuck (about 754) was nearly identical to that in the English towns (951). However, the land base had become grossly restricted. Although many of the transfer deeds to Indian lands contained specific clauses that allowed the Indians to hunt, fish, gather wild plants, collect wood, and build their wigwams on the town commons, prime horticultural land was scarce. Agawam families were probably restricted to fewer than twenty acres. Fields at Pojasick on the Westfield River had not as yet been mortgaged, but stress may have been felt as former Agawam residents joined their kinsmen up-river. At Norwottuck, the village on the Hadley side still used between twelve and twenty acres of adjacent cornfields, but this could hardly have been sufficient to support its inhabitants. Residents on the western side of the Connecticut River were faced with worse conditions.

Not only were subsistence resources extremely taxed, but the potential for harvesting surplus crops for exchange in the English communities had been virtually eliminated. If the erosion of one resource base were not bad enough, Mohawk raids in northern New England, the uncertain truce that existed among the segmentary tribes in southern New England, and the resultant depression in the fur trade compounded matters. Indian spokesmen who now relied on the Indian-English exchange network to meet a variety of needs were faced with the prospect that the system might collapse entirely. "Free-will" sales of land during the late 1650s, the mortgaging of territorial reserves beginning in 1659, and the slight rebound in the fur trade that occurred between 1661 and 1663 kept hopes alive. At this point, Iroquois raids into the Connecticut Valley brought about the abandonment of Squakheag during the spring of 1664 and the destruction of Pocumtuck in February 1665. Norwottuck and villages to the south began to witness a steady flow of refugees into their midst. In particular, a number of former Pocumtucks found sanctuary at Norwottuck. With their resources already severely strained, the future must have looked exceedingly bleak.

Thus, within about thirty years, one may view the establishment, expansion, and virtual collapse of a trading system which facilitated the exchange of native American products, particularly pelts and crops, for manufactured goods brought by English immigrants. More significantly, the network of exchange had a far broader function. Trading posts became the points through which both societies could resolve differences. In the early days, the resultant amicability was a positive feature of trade. The export of beaver pelts was a vital part of the Massachusetts Bay economy, and the supplies of corn and beans from native villages proved critical for newly established English towns. So long as this reciprocal relationship could be maintained, colonial entrepreneurs, particularly the Pynchons who monopolized economic and political power in the valley, were fairly consistent in serving Indian interests.

For their part, leaders of the valley's segmentary tribes were probably divided in their attitudes concerning the most useful economic and political strategies. Nonetheless, individuals and their families who maintained contacts with the English obtained goods for consumption and for the development of prestige, secured commodities, particularly wampum, to be used for political transactions to build native alliances, and found the articulation critical for gaining information about a markedly alien society. By 1650, both societies had become dependent upon the trading system for several reasons. Within a decade, the smooth functioning of the system was threatened. The growth of both the indigenous and immigrant populations produced a high degree of stress. Competition for land increased. When the fur trade became depressed and warfare among Indian segmentary tribes intensified, settlers began to question the policy of having native villages within close proximity to their homes. At this point, the lack of flexibility in either economy and the decreasing amount of reciprocity between the two systems produced a significant change in attitudes. The strategies which had once been central to Indian-English relations grew increasingly unproductive. It would only take another ten years and the ravages of King Philip's War to complete the rift that had begun to develop.

Historians have tended to explain Indian depopulation and the forced migration of New England's Indian communities before and after King Philip's War as a product of long-standing, unscrupulous colonial aggression focused against less powerful indigenous communities. Acts of aggression can be easily documented, but the end results of aggression do not explain why historical events unfolded as they did. To a large extent the segmented political structure of New England's Indian tribes contributed to their inability to effectively oppose English expansion. There was no central authority to force conformity. One must also realize that within any Indian community considerable factionalism developed. This factionalism is particularly evident in the "economic" transactions between the English traders and some Indians in the middle Connecticut River Valley. Here, Indian families controlled resources, whether the commodity was corn, furs, or land. A case can be easily made that at Norwottuck, Woronoco, and Agawam, families who consistently found it to their advantage to deal with the English traders for pelts, and ultimately for land, were acting at cross-purposes with other residents of their own towns. In short, to speak of Indian tribal policies without recognizing fragmentation, factionalism, and shifting family and village alliances may lead one to misinterpret a good deal of "political" action during this period. It is inaccurate to speak of "Pocumtuck" motivations, or "Norwottuck" strategies as if all community members were in agreement.

These factors are significant, because in trying to understand the processes of Indian-white interaction, it is crucial to be aware of the roles played by individuals or extended kin groups within the Indian communities. Without this recognition, it is incredibly easy to see Indians as simply acting or reacting as pawns of the English, without any motivation, except that of self-preservation from colonial encroachment. Some Indian leaders were no less culpable than some English in seeking self-aggrandizement at the ultimate expense of other members of their own society. Individual motives on both sides molded the processes of change. Human action is the stuff of which history is made, and the means by which societies and cultures are transformed. Native Americans in southern New England were not passive witnesses to their own demise. Rather, for better or worse, many were active participants in shaping their own destinies.

NOTES

1. See, for instance, Alden T. Vaughan, *New England Frontier: Puritans and Indians, 1620–1675* (Boston, 1965).

2. Marshall Sahlins, *Tribemen* (Englewood Cliffs, NJ, 1968).

3. For an extended discussion of political organization among these Indians, see Peter A. Thomas, "In the Maelstrom of Change: The Indian Trade and Cultural

Process in the Middle Connecticut River Valley, 1635–1665" (Ph.D. diss., University of Massachusetts, 1979), 33–44.

4. James K. Hosmer, ed., *Winthrop's Journal, "History of New England," 1630–1649* (New York, 1908), 1:103.

5. William Bradford, *Bradford's History of Plimoth Plantation* (Boston, 1898), 387.

6. Bradford, *History*, 388–389.

7. James H. Trumbull, ed., *Public Records of the Colony of Connecticut, 1636–1776* (Hartford, 1850), 1:72.

8. Trumbull, *Public Records of Connecticut*, 1:19.

9. Ebenezer Hazard, ed., *Records of the United Colonies of New England*, in *Historical Collections, consisting of State Papers, and other authentic documents, intended for materials for America* (reprint, Freeport, NY, 1969), 2:63.

10. Josiah H. Temple, *History of North Brookfield, Massachusetts* (Boston, 1887), 37–38.

11. For extended discussions, see Thomas, "In the Maelstrom of Change," 155–193 and 261–333.

12. For further discussion of patron/broker–client relationships, see Arnold Strickton and S. M. Greenfield, eds., *Structure and Process in Latin America: Patronage, Clientage, and Power Systems* (Albuquerque, 1972).

13. J. A. Barnes, "Networks and Political Process," in Marc J. Swartz, ed., *Local-Level Politics: Social and Cultural Perspectives* (Chicago, 1969).

14. Peter A. Thomas, "The Fur Trade, Indian Land, and the Need to Define Adequate 'Environmental' Parameters," *Ethnohistory* 28 (1981): 359–379.

15. Harry A. Wright, *Indian Deeds of Hampden County* (Springfield, MA, 1905), 46–47.

16. Nathaniel B. Shurtleff, *Records of the Governor and Company of the Massachusetts Bay in New England*, vol. 4, part 2 (Boston, 1853–1854), 156; Probate Records of Hampshire County, ms. in Hampshire County Registry of Probate, Northampton, (1660–1820), 1:63; Waste Book of the County Court, 1663–1677, ms. in Connecticut Valley Historical Museum, Springfield, 26–28.

17. Henry M. Burt, *The First Century of the History of Springfield; The Official Records from 1636 to 1736, with an Historical Review and Biographical Mention of the Founders* (Springfield, 1898–1899), 1:40–45; James Trumbull, *History of Northampton, from its Its Settlement in 1654* (Northampton, 1898–1902), 1:88.

2

STEADY pressure from English settlements reduced the traditional homelands of Native Americans and destroyed the populations of game and fur-bearing animals. The defeat of Metacom in King Philip's War of 1675–1676 put an end to large-scale armed resistance to English settlement in Northampton, but not to Indian habitation. Though many Native peoples sought refuge elsewhere, some never left their homelands, choosing to make themselves less visible by moving beyond the fringes of colonial settlements. This strategy of avoidance helped ensure a continued Indian presence in the valley up until the present day, but that presence often went unrecorded and unnoticed by whites. Margaret Bruchac chronicles the struggles of Nonotuck peoples as they coped with social upheaval and environmental change while sustaining cultural identity and kinship ties.

Native Presence in Nonotuck and Northampton

MARGARET BRUCHAC

THE first English colonists to arrive in the middle Connecticut River Valley identified the indigenous inhabitants by the Algonkian Indian[1] terms for the places where they lived: *Agawam*, the "landing place" that is now Springfield, *Woronoco*, the "winding land" at Westfield, and *Pocumtuck*, the "shallow, sandy river" at Deerfield. The region around the oxbow, at the geographical midpoint of the river, was called *Nonotuck*, a term which has been roughly translated to mean either "the middle of the river" (Noah-tuk), or the "far away land" (Nauwut-ucke) in the Massachusetts dialect.[2]

Three hundred and fifty years after the Euro-American settlement of Nonotuck (now called Northampton), the Native American[3] history of this place may seem elusive. Much of the early archaeological record has been destroyed, if not by colonial settlement, then by the search for the relics and remains of the earliest Indian inhabitants. Lithics, pottery shards, beads, and bones from the distant past have surfaced in the plow zone and emerged in washouts, to land in both public and private collections of Indian relics.[4] Woodlands era (c. 4000 B.C. to the present) site features, like storage pits, post holes, and corn planting mounds, that remained visible well into the twentieth century, have now been supplanted by housing developments and industrial parks.[5] The locations of Native gravesites, like those of the Maminash family on Hospital Hill, or the unidentified burials salvaged from the meadows beside the river, have long since been forgotten by all but a few anthropologists and Native historians.[6] Even the landscape itself has been reshaped, particularly rivers, like the Cappawonganick (Mill River), which once wove its way alongside wigwam villages set on terraces, and now slips over the falls below Paradise Pond to hide in culverts beneath the main streets of town.

Northampton once had an Indian fort, but it never had an Indian reservation, and it does not have a resident tribal community today. Smith College once had a museum devoted to Indian history, but those antiquated displays of plaster-covered skulls and mute lithics have been dismantled and are patiently awaiting repatriation.[7] A handful of exquisite artifacts on display at Historic Northampton, including quilled moccasins trimmed with silk ribbon, woven ash splint baskets stamped with floral designs, and a single strand of disk-shaped shell wampum beads, testify to the complex intercultural relations between Nonotuck's Indians and Northampton's English inhabitants.

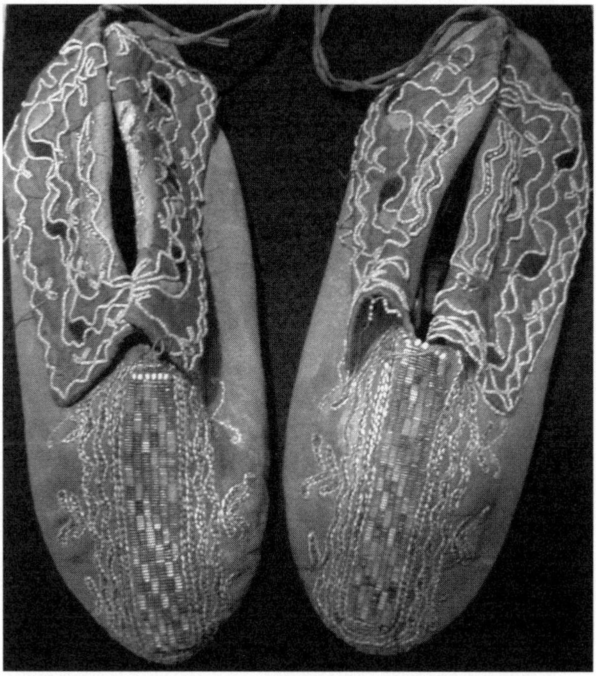

Moccasins, c. 1682. Gift of Martha Woodruff. *Historic Northampton.*

This pair of moccasins represents a fusion of native technology and European style. The lining is cotton tape and the ties are silk, both trade goods. The porcupine quill embroidery is executed with traditional techniques, but the design of a meandering vine and flowers probably derives from European embroidery patterns.

On the streets of the town today, Native history can be viewed as a series of locative snapshots, from the farm fields called "Bark Wigwams," to a street named "Fort Hill," to a fading downtown sign for "Nonotuck Savings and Loan." But these snapshots do not tell the whole story. In the following pages, I offer a few glimpses into Northampton's Native past, by commenting on some of the sources that reference local Native history and reflecting on the lives of some of the Native peoples who continued to inhabit Nonotuck long after it became known as Northampton.

Remnants of Once Powerful Tribes

During the early nineteenth century, a series of historical myths were created and embellished by American historians in order to disconnect contemporary Native communities from their history and landscape. In western Massachusetts, those myths took four basic forms, which reflected popular interpretations of pre-contact Native history: 1) Before colonial settlement, this area was a wilderness; 2) All nonfarming Native sites were temporary, nomadic camps; 3) Algonkian peoples were developmentally inferior to, and less industrious than, their Iroquoian neighbors; and 4) Local Indians had abandoned these lands and moved on, thereby justifying permanent resettlement by non-native colonists.[8]

Local archaeologists of the late nineteenth and early twentieth centuries, such as Edward Hitchcock, Harry A. Wright, Harris Hawthorne Wilder, William J. Howes, William S. Fowler, and Walter S. Rodiman, incorporated these myths into their interpretations of the Native sites they found. Amateur and professional archaeologists in the region contributed to the disconnection of local Native history as they systematically disinterred graves, disarticulated bodies, separated grave goods from gravesites, and traded desirable collections around the region. Many worked in the footsteps of earlier collectors, tapping into the same local sites repeatedly in their search for particular kinds of artifacts.[9] As just one example of the bias prevalent in the minds of collectors, Harry A. Wright suggested, in 1940, that stylistic similarities between Nonotuck and Mohawk pots implied that the local Native woman "must have recognized the inferiority of the pottery she was producing" and thus imitated the Mohawks. Recent tests show that some of the most ornate local pottery actually predates similar designs in New York, so the styles may well have originated here.[10]

Throughout the nineteenth and most of the twentieth centuries, Native gravesites were widely regarded as archaeological sites rather than sacred or private property. Deerfield's Memorial Hall, established in 1870, was dedicated to housing "such memorials, books, papers and relics as would illustrate and perpetuate the history of the early settlers, and of the race which vanished before them," including exhibit cases of Indian graves.[11] Similar exhibits were set up at local colleges for regular viewing by students.[12] In an 1820 address to the American Antiquarian Society, Worcester historian Isaac Goodwin articulated the sense of entitlement to Indian lands and Indian remains that was common among American intellectuals: "We tread upon their graves without emotion. With unconcern we build our streets and erect our edifices upon their sacred enclosures. . . . with sacrilegious hands we scatter to the winds alike the bones. . . . the land they once defended is ours. . . . these hills, are all our own."[13]

Local historians like Sylvester Judd, James Russell Trumbull, and George Sheldon built on these ideas as they fashioned town histories that recounted the details of Indian warfare and raids, with the prevailing assumption that the Indian was doomed to disappear in the face of expanding civilization. Historians in the Connecticut River Valley gave little attention to the oral traditions attached to local sacred sites, the domestic pursuits evidenced in the landscape, or the intricate networks of intertribal relationships across New England, unless those details could be seen as contributory factors to warfare. The focus on warfare carried with it a corresponding focus on male leaders and Euro-American gender stereotypes, without sufficient consideration of the complexities of Native family and kinship relationships and roles.

These practices and beliefs were supported by the prevailing sense that colonial victory in Indian warfare had justifiably dispossessed Native peoples of any claims to the past. In 1873, local historian William S. Tyler wrote: "There is scarcely a town in the valley whose soil was not sprinkled with blood in the early wars with the Indians." In 1837, when the town of Deerfield had erected a monument to a 1676 event known as the "Bloody Brook Massacre," Massachusetts Governor Edward Everett had stepped in to deliver the oration, since "the commemoration of an Indian catastrophe was thought of as an occasion capable of being turned to good electioneering purposes."[14]

Although there was not a large Native community in Northampton, a number of local Native families and individuals continued to circulate within their traditional homelands, marketing baskets and brooms, hiring out as day labor, and dispensing traditional Native medicines to their white neighbors. Many were frequent travelers, tracing intertribal connections and kinship networks within a broad homeland.[15] Certain kinds of work—particularly basket-making, chair seat-weaving, administering Native medicines, and crafting splint brooms—were regular occupations of Native itinerants. Sylvester Judd personally knew the Sampson family, local Indians living in Amherst and Hadley, who made baskets and brooms and hunted: "Joseph Sampson had a hut near Smiths mill. . . . He was an excellent marksman, and could shoot a swallow flying."[16] Mrs. Newton of Hadley told Judd in 1859 that only "Indians and squaws peddled brooms and baskets in Hadley when she was young and after. She does not recollect that white people made or peddled brooms."[17]

In 1861, Massachusetts Commissioner John Milton Earle summarized the general public's view of Native peoples when he wrote:

> Much ignorance and misapprehension prevail in the community at large, among those who have not had the opportunity of personal observation relative to these remnants of their race. They seem to suppose that they have hardly emerged from their aboriginal state, although the painted face may not now be seen, nor the war whoop, the tomahawk, or the scalping knife . . . and the questions: "What sort of people are they?" "Do they dress like white folks?" "Can they speak the English language?" "Do they live in wigwams?" or other of like nature are often asked.[18]

The popular media often depicted Indians as exotic outsiders, dubbing those who still lingered around the outskirts of Yankee villages as "the last of their kind." In 1838, one such group was depicted in disparaging terms by the local newspaper:

> The Miserable Remnants of a tribe of Indians from Canada, squatting in the woods a mile or two from town have been, and continue to be, the lions in this vicinity. Strange how demoralizing the contact of civilization with that of savage life, where it is but partial and of a loose and anti-Christian character. . . . They are a slothful, ragged, dirty, squalid race, appearing to have adopted the vices of the whites without seeming to emulate any of their virtues. The lofty bearing and noble demeanor of the primitive Indians are gone, and nothing is left but the abject and debased exterior of the red man. . . . Altogether considered, they are merely a wretched remnant of a race of noble and proud Red men, who once tenanted this fair valley, and whose stealthy tread and uplifted tomohawk, carried death to hearts terrified by their appalling war-cry.[19]

Later historians perpetuated these biased representations of local Native peoples in historical texts, children's stories, speeches, and pageantry.[20] During Northampton's Quarter Millennial Commemoration, in 1904, Smith College President L. Clarke Seelye intoned:

> How different the scenes which greet us from those which greeted her [Northampton's] infancy. Above are the same heavens; the same majestic river flows through the meadows; our horizon is bounded by the same picturesque mountain ranges; but how changed the inhabitants and their environment! No longer unbroken forests stretch as far as the eye can reach, concealing in their unexplored recesses wild beasts and savages; no longer men fear lest a sudden Indian raid may massacre the few inhabitants. . . . In place of a rude and contracted society, we behold a prosperous and highly civilized community.[21]

By 1916, a Rhode Island newspaper wrongly declared that the Nonotucks had utterly vanished: "In regard to the Nonotucks . . . there is almost no historical account except the mark of a few of them upon local deeds." This report praised the exhibits created by Smith College Professor Harris Hawthorne Wilder, noting that this "restoration has thus a special interest, as it supplies data that were supposedly lost forever."[22] Wilder's craniometric studies and his collections promoted scientifically flawed and prejudicial beliefs about race and intelligence. Natural differences in cranial measurements were used to "prove" that the "real" Indians were all dead, and that their living descendants were inferior specimens. In the 1950s, a *Daily Hampshire Gazette* reporter wrote about Indian remains that were still on display: "What stands behind this case . . . and perhaps what lies unknown beneath the local soil is all that remains of the peaceful, agriculturally inclined Nonotuck Indians who have long since been replaced by the citizens of Hampshire County."[23]

Museums across America had evolved from curiosity cabinets into historical exhibits that aimed to display narratives of colonial progress vis-à-vis the Indians, while generally ignoring or misrepresenting the stories of Native communities.[24] Local museums and colleges often took their lead from prominent historical organizations like the American Antiquarian Society, which depicted the surviving New England tribes as degraded, racially mixed remnants, compared to their noble, but now extinct, progenitors.[25] The disconnection that was implied between living populations of northeastern Indian peoples and legitimate versions of northeastern Indian history became part of what contemporary historians have termed the "discourse of disappearance." That discourse directly affected the ways in which Northampton's early Native history was recorded and interpreted. By way of demonstration, let's take a step back in time to the founding era of Northampton.

Planting at Cappawonke and Weekwassuck

The documentary records of correspondence among the English leaders of the United Colonies indicate that the Nonotuck and Pocumtuck peoples were initially regarded as sovereign nations, savvy trading partners, and formidable enemies. For example, in a 1648 letter to Massachusetts Governor John Winthrop, William Pynchon wrote:

> I grant they are all wthin ye line of yr pattent, but you cannot say that therefore they are yr subjects nor yet within yr jurisdiction untill they have fully subjected themselves to yr government (wch I know they have not) & untill you have bought their land: untill this be done they must be esteemed as an Independant free people, & so they of Naunotak do all account themselves, & doubtless wch ever goes with strength of men to disturb their peace at Naunotuk they will take it for no other than a hostile action.[26]

William Pynchon began trading with the Nonotuck Indians in the 1640s. By May 1653, twenty-four petitioners from the Connecticut colony and three settlers from Springfield had requested permission from the General Court of Massachusetts to "plant, possess and inhabit Nonotuck."[27] They intended to measure out plantations at Cappawonke, the meadows beside the river. Since trade relations were good, the Nonotuck were initially willing to allow the English to settle a small town, on the condition that: "Pynchon shall plow up or cause to be plowed up for the Indians sixteene acres of land on ye east side of Quinnoticott River . . . the Indians have liberty to plant their present corn fields. . . ."[28]

It must be noted that the earliest English settlers moved into a long-inhabited, carefully managed landscape. Early town records note that the forests and fields had been so efficiently cleared by Indian burning "that many large tracts were almost destitute of timber, and in some place covered with high coarse grass. This grass and other wild herbage furnished pasture for the cattle of the inhabitants of Northampton, Hadley, Hatfield, etc. for many years."[29]

Indian deeds are often cited as evidence of the sale of land, but it's doubtful that these documents were ever viewed by Native signers as quit-claims. In practice, they were negotiated like treaties and temporary joint use agreements, confirmed by the exchange of gifts, and reserved Native rights to hunt, plant, set up wigwams, etc. on land that was supposedly "sold."[30] Although they were clearly misled, Native participants intended to reserve their traditional rights. A 1666 deed for parts of Deerfield noted that the sachem Chauk "doth reserve Liberty of fishing for ye Indians in ye Rivers or waters & free Liberty to hunt deere or other wild creatures, & to gather walnuts . . . on ye Commons."[31] The Nonotuck Indians had planted corn on both sides of the river for generations, and their actions suggest that they never intended to vacate the premises.

Maize, which had been imported from the southwest during the first millennium A.D., had become an important component of Native life in the valley, but it was not the primary food source. Just as they had done for countless generations, Algonkian peoples continued to seasonally gather resources from hunting territories in the hills, fishing places at the falls, and other gathering habitats.[32] In the homelands model, corn cultivation is just one of many food procurement strategies that does not require permanent residence near the planting fields.[33]

Corn served a dual purpose as a valuable trading commodity, since the early colonists were, at first, dependent upon Native foods for their survival. In one dramatic instance, in 1638, the Indians at Pocumtuck accepted payment of 300 fathoms (six-foot lengths) of wampum for 500 bushels of corn, and delivered it by canoe to supply the starving English settlements below Hartford.[34]

Wampum, from the Narragansett word *wauompeg*, "white shell," indicating tubular or disk beads strung on hemp or leather,[35] had long been used by Native peoples for ceremonial purposes, to carry messages and condolences, as tribute, and as decoration. Awonusk, one of the female signatories of deeds for land around Fort River, signed her mark with a symbol that seems to represent a woven strip of wampum.[36] The production and distribution of shell beads increased dramatically after the importation of metal drills and the mass production required for the Indian trade. Between 1645 and 1668, John Pynchon employed a number of Northampton men in stringing fathoms of wampum for the Indian trade.[37]

Indigenous foods and substances quickly became staples of Euro-American economies and foodways. The one surviving fragment of Connecticut River Valley language collected by fur trader John Pynchon, a list of names of the moons of the year and a few words for fur-bearing animals, may, for example, reveal his need to schedule a ready supply of food and furs. His compilation of terms referencing the names for the full moons of the year begins with the following information:

1. *Squannikesos*	When they set Indian corne (pt of Aprill & pt of May)
2. *moonesquan nimockkesos*	when women weed their corn (pt of May & pt of June
3. *Towwakesos*	when they hill Ind corne (pt of June & pt of July)
4. *matterl lawawkes*os	when squashes are ripe & Ind beans begin to be eatable
5. *micheeneekesos*	when Ind corne is eatable
6. *pah quitaqunkkesos*	ye middle between harvest & eating Ind corne[38]

The main resource that fed the fur trade was not corn, but beaver, and when the beaver population started to plummet from over-hunting, Nonotuck and other valley peoples found themselves unable to pay their trading debts.[39] John Pynchon and his agents had become thoroughly enmeshed in political relationships with the valley tribes, and Native leaders, in their turn, had become indebted to these savvy English traders for trading cloth, coats, and a whole host of trade goods that were now feeding intertribal gifting networks.

In 1660, the Nonotuck sachem Umpanchela was forced to part with two tracts of river land at Nattacous and Wequittayyag in order to pay off his debt to John Pynchon, a debt that included a fine of two fathoms of wampum for being drunk. Pynchon was well aware of the fact that the beaver had been depleted, and had noted in his account book just before Umpanchela left on a hunting trip, after three months of purchasing coats, cloth, knives, wampum, and a gun on credit: "Decembr 25 60 Trusted him [Umpanchela] on the same acot one red cote 2 knives. . . . If I am not pd in Bever when he comes from Heakeg [Squakheag, Sokoki hunting territory] all his land is to be mine."[40]

Shifting Homelands

The first English efforts at trade and settlement with the Indians of Northampton seem to have started off peacefully, but over time, ancient intertribal relationships and land tenure systems were dramatically altered by European disease, warfare, and politics. In 1664, a group of Nonotuck built a fortified enclosure named Fort Hill, close by the town of Northampton, across the Mill River. Natives at Fort Hill were compelled to comply with a list of conditions imposed by the town that forbade, among other things, working on the Sabbath, drinking, hosting visitors, and holding the religious observances known as pow-wows.[41]

In times of stress, Native communities shifted residence, moving away and returning when situations calmed.[42] For much of the first two centuries of contact, the fluidity of social boundaries created a great deal of confusion among Euro-American observers, particularly whenever Native peoples traveled to the north. It now appears, from the documentary records and oral traditions of Native families who have been poorly understood by historians, that tribal identities persisted, even after families relocated outside the valley.[43]

Several events contributed to the large-scale diaspora of Indians from the Connecticut River Valley. One potential cause resulted from an event in 1667, when three Northampton youths—Godfrey Nimms, James Bennet, and Benoni Stebbins—broke into several homes on the Sabbath day to secure the money to pay a Nonotuck man named Quequelatt to escort them to Canada. The boys, and eventually Quequelatt as well, were all apprehended and whipped.[44] Pynchon used this incident as justification for appointing a Nonotuck leader who would ensure obedience to English law. Chickwalloppe's trust in the English was seriously damaged a few years later, when his (Chickwalloppe's) son was arrested for a murder in Albany, and hanged, despite Pynchon's assurances that diplomacy would prevail.

Relations had become increasingly strained in the region by 1675, when a Wampanoag leader named Metacom, baptized Philip, and popularly called "King Philip," started a rebellion against English settlement that quickly spread across southern New England. John Pynchon endeavored to secure neutrality from local Indians, but many of them joined Metacom in attacking Northfield, Deerfield, Hatfield, Hadley, Northampton, and Brookfield. In May 1676, the English retaliated with the massacre of nearly 400 Native refugees, including elderly men, women, and children who had gathered at Peskeompskut, now Turner's Falls. King Philip's War eventually became, in the shaping of American historical memory, a marker for the supposed end of Native occupation of New England, and a justification for later Indian removals.

In 1676 Governor Andros of New York invited Connecticut River Indians to settle in the village of Schaghticoke, near the Hoosic and Hudson Rivers. In the succeeding decades, Pocumtuck, Nonotuck, Woronoco, Sokoki, and a few Mahican peoples moved back and forth between the Connecticut River, Schaghticoke, and Canada. A few families joined the Catholic Mohawk mission at Caughnawauga, now Kahnawake, south of Montreal.[45] Native peoples nonetheless maintained ties to the valley in a variety of ways. In 1693, during a rout of "Canada" (former Connecticut River Valley) Indians at Quabaug, Major John Pynchon wrote, in his account to Governor Phipps, "What I much wonder at, one of the soldiers a Smith [blacksmith] of Northampton, says that one of their hatchets he knows well that he made it about a year ago."[46]

Schaghticoke, New York, became an active trading post, a stopping point on the way to French missions in the north, and a rallying place for former Connecticut River Valley Indians who traveled back and forth between their original homelands, the Hudson River Valley, upstate New York, Canada, and Vermont.[47] In the spring of 1674, "most of the Indians on the Westfield River at Woronoco and Pojassick had moved to Albany for reasons unknown to the English at Springfield."[48] The move to Schaghticoke was rarely a one-way passage. For example, in 1691, John Pynchon received a letter from Captain Partridge, who wrote: "the Indians that are come down are about 150 of them, men, women, and children, and are settled at Deerfield under the side of the mountain southerly from the town, living in the woods about a mile out of the town, the men plying hunting and leaving their women and children at home."[49] Connecticut River Valley Indians allied with their northern neighbors in the subsequent imperial conflicts between England and France for control of the American colonies. These wars were dubbed King William's War (1689–1697), Queen Anne's War (1702–1713), King George's War (1744–1748), and the French and Indian War (1754–1763). During these wars, hundreds of captives were taken from valley towns, and many of these were incorporated, even if temporarily, into Native kin networks.[50] Titus King from Northampton, who was held prisoner between 1755 and 1758 by former Connecticut River Valley Indians now living among the Abenaki in Canada, recalled his adoption ceremony, when:

> The Famely that I was adopted into gave my Indian master that took me a Sute of Cloths came & took me by the hand lead me away to his house now I was in New Famlly & in a nere Relation: to them: became brother to the old Indian &

> Squaw being in the place of an indian that was Killd the Last War I being in the Same Relation as he was to them I became a Grandfather they Said there Grandfather was come to life again.[51]

Titus King eventually escaped and made his way back to Northampton, where he became a popular schoolteacher. Mary Sheldon of Deerfield formed more lastig attachments with her former captors. She had been taken captive from Deerfield during the 1704 raid on that town, and adopted by the Canadian Indians, who "became very much attached to her." On her release, she remarried and moved to Northampton, where history records:

> In after years these Indians came to visit her at Northampton. They always came when Clapp's corn was green, and would devour it in large quantities, roasting the ears at a fire under an apple tree. On one occasion she received a visit from two squaws. Leaving their papooses in the bushes on Pancake plain, they came into the street, and found the house where Mrs. Clapp lived, by means of the step stones which had been described to them. They asked permission to bring their children, which was readily given.[52]

Over time, despite the raids, white communities tightened their hold on the valley, supplanting Native homelands with large towns situated at the most desirable locations alongside the river.[53] Although the vast majority of Native peoples from the valley relocated to live with their Native neighbors in surrounding communities or northern mission villages, a few Native families remained in valley towns.

Sally Maminash—Last of the Indians Here

Sally Maminash (alternately spelled Mammanash, Mammanache, etc.) is buried in Northampton's Bridge Street Cemetery, where her gravestone, situated in the family plot of Warham and Sophia Clapp, reads: "Sally Maminash. The last of the Indians here. A niece of Occum. A Christian. Died in the family of Warham & Sophia Clap. Jan. 3, 1853. Aged 88."

A collection of fading newspaper clippings from the *Daily Hampshire Gazette* adds a few more tragically cryptic details to Sally's story—her father Joseph's gravestone stolen from a "lonely grave on Pancake Plain," her mother Elizabeth "stoned to death by local boys," her dying brother "neglected and alone," her grandmother "old, lousy and lame," and Sally herself, a "wild, passionate, wilful" girl who worked as an itinerant spinner and weaver, transformed into a "sweet, saintly Christian," sitting peacefully in her chair reading her Bible.[54]

Almost every town in New England had an individual who was described as "the last of the Indians," a popular, if somewhat misleading sobriquet. Molly Ockett, an Indian Doctress who was survived by several daughters and an ex-husband, was called "the last of the Pequawkets" when she died in 1816. In 1859, Eunice Mauwee, a Schaghticoke elder who is the direct ancestor of many members of the Schaghticoke tribe today, was erroneously called "the last of the Pequots."[55] Paine Henries, the so-called last of the Nipmucks, who died in 1936, was survived by two brothers, a sister, and several nieces and nephews.[56]

Sally Maminash's gravestone. Bridge Street Cemetery, Northampton.

The inscription on Sally Maminash's gravestone reads "last of the Indians here." This epitaph tells much more about nineteenth-century New England than about Sally because she was not the only Indian in Northampton and was certainly not the last. She was an accepted and skilled member of the local community, working as an itinerant spinner and weaver. Sally's mother, Elizabeth, came from the community of Mohegan in southeastern Connecticut. Her brother, Joseph Maminash, was a Revolutionary War veteran. Her uncle was Samson Occum, Mohegan preacher, fundraiser for Moor's Charity School (later Dartmouth College), and founder of the Brotherton Community of Christian Indians in New York.

In Northampton, the largest concentration of Native peoples seems to have centered around Pancake Plain and Hospital Hill, where the Maminash gravesites were located. Through much of the twentieth century, the site was home to a mental hospital, rural fields grown up to brush, and homeless shelters. Charles Dean wrote, in a 1958 article for the *Daily Hampshire Gazette:*

> Hospital Hill, the beginnings of which are either distorted or utterly lost in the mists of legendary lore . . . became the end of the trail for the last Native Americans, whose ancestors roamed the forests and fished the streams hereabouts before the coming of the white man. . . . perhaps the most reasonable explanation for the retarded development of this part of Northampton was its remoteness . . . a narrow flat strip of land lying between the foot of the hill itself and the southern bank of Mill River . . . but even as late as the 1830s only seven or eight houses were located there, devoid of elegance or comfort, and occupied by person noticeable for the peculiarities, habits, and dress which makes them known as characters. . . . "Ratty Clark" and family . . . made a somewhat precarious living as potters. . . . But the most colorful inhabitant of the plain perhaps, was "Aunt Nab" whom a contemporary once described as a "maker and vendor of cornhusk mats" and as having a "cracked voice and garrulous manner."[57]

Sally Maminash lived in the center of town, where she was well known to many Northampton residents as an itinerant weaver. In 1816, she joined First Church along with seventy-six other people, including several other Indians and African Americans and a Nipmuc family named Bakeman. By 1819 large numbers of people had left First Church to join new congregations—Edwards Church, the Unitarian Society, Methodists, Baptists, and others. Reverend Solomon Williams recorded Sally Maminash's name on a "List of Church Members 1819 who were living or have not taken a dismissal" after religious controversy split the congregation.[58] Decades after her death, when Solomon Clark compiled his Historical Catalogue, Sally Maminash was described as follows: "Sally Maminash. The last of the Indian race in Northampton; long and tenderly cared for, under the infirmities of age, by Mrs. Warham Clapp, and her son Edward and his wife."[59]

Sophia Clapp, who sponsored Sally's membership in the church, had offered Sally a home in her old age. Although the Clapps treated, and buried her, as a family friend, later writers seem to have embellished the earlier accounts to make Sally appear more simple, more destitute, and more alone than she was in real life. In the Northampton of the late nineteenth century, Sally seems to have been cast as a token civilized Indian, an icon of what was romantically believed to be a vanishing race. The Maminash family were not uncivilized remnants of vanishing tribes—they served as soldiers, weaved in local homes, attended local churches, and participated in the social milieu of Northampton much like their white neighbors. They were, however, vulnerable to racial prejudice and danger from their less tolerant neighbors.

Sally's father, Joseph Maminash, was identified in colonial records as Podunk, Nonotuck, and/or Pocumtuck Indian, listing places of residence in Norwich and East Windsor, Connecticut, and Southampton and Northampton, Massachusetts.[60] The Maminash men, like many Native men in New England, mustered in alongside their white neighbors in local regiments for military service. When Mohegan men from Connecticut were recruited for the English campaign against Louisbourg in 1745, Joseph Mammanash[*sic*], Sally's father, joined Nathan Whiting's 11th company, along with a number of Indian men in this and related companies, including members of the Uncas, Dick, Nanapau, Quaquequid and Wetowomp families.[61] When he died in 1767, Joseph was buried on Hospital Hill, in a grave marked with a brown stone bearing the mark of the turtle, the clan totem of the family. During the 1860s, the stone was stolen, and has never been found.[62]

Sally's mother, Elizabeth, who was identified as the sister of the Mohegan minister Samson Occum, apparently came from the community of Mohegan Indians in southeastern Connecticut. In 1779, then sixty-year-old Elizabeth met an untimely, as-yet-unexplained death. Some traditions say she was stoned to death by a gang of Northampton boys; others that she died in liquor.[63] She was buried beside her husband, and her children took up residence among their Native neighbors.

Sally's brother, Joseph, served in the military during the American Revolution, and is listed in Massachusetts Soldiers and Sailors as follows:

> Mamanash, Joseph, Hadley. List of men raised to serve in the Continental Army from the 4th Hampshire regiment as returned by Capt. Samuel Cook; residence, Hadley; engaged for town of Hadley; joined Capt. Shay's co., Col. Putnam's regt,; term 3 years; also, Private, Capt. Daniel Shays co., Col. Rufus Putnam's (5th) regt.; Continental Pay accounts for service from Jan. 15, 1777 to Aug, 31, 1778; reported died Aug. 31, 1778; also, same co. and regt.; return dated Albany, Feb. 9, 1778; mustered by Col. Woodbridge.

He, too, is buried in an unmarked grave on Hospital Hill. Among the few artifacts remaining from the Maminash family are Sally's Bible, stored at Forbes Library, and her favorite chair, a low ladder back with its original ash-splint seat, still in the hands of a Clapp descendant.[64]

The Maminash family, although a Native family with deep roots in New England, had "arrived" in the records of Northampton toward the end of the French and Indian wars and the beginning of the American Revolution, the very era when American history was being re-scripted to write Indians out of the picture. Indian deeds had long since been signed, and Northampton's settlers refused to see the cornfields in the meadows, the graves on Pancake Plain, the basket-makers on the streets, or the houses on the edge of the river as evidence of Native persistence. The neighbors of the Indian graves on

Hospital Hill today include homeless shelters, empty homes, a crumbling mental hospital, and the Smith playing fields, on the backside of town. Mary Brewster foreshadowed their present obscurity:

> The field where the Indians were buried, now owned by the state hospital, was owned by W. F. Arnold who left standing the group of gaunt pines that long guarded the "Indian Grave" in picturesque and poignant contrast to the spot today where, in sunny bleakness below a stone-covered ridge, gone is the last trace of a historic burial place, unmarked and generally unremembered.[65]

In 1920, Harris Hawthorne Wilder wrote of his delight at discovering the survival of Indian corn-mounds, near the oxbow of the Connecticut River, close to traditional Native village sites, on, apparently, the very same grounds that Pynchon agreed to plow for the Nonotucks in 1654. Wilder plotted out the locations of at least three associated sites: for village locations, on bluffs

Plaited baskets, pre-1830. Gift of Amelia Clark. *Historic Northampton.*

Native Americans continued to live throughout the region, keeping alive their traditions while sometimes having to submerge their identities. Evidence reveals that Indian peoples continued to make a life for themselves. Plaited baskets, woven by native Americans from carefully prepared and painted wood splints, were prized items of exchange throughout the nineteenth century. Made for kitchen use, home storage, or farm work, splint baskets represent some of the ways in which native and non-native peoples interacted from the seventeenth century onward. As such, this basketry was part of a world in which native peoples continued their artistic traditions while also living as farmers, hired laborers, and artisans in nontraditional communities.

overlooking the Mill River along present-day South Street; for burials, in the fields beside the river; and for planting fields, in a sunken meadow shut off by a railroad embankment.[66]

Recovering Northampton's Native Past

By the 1970s and 1980s, as both a corrective to the prevailing sense of erasure, and a deeper investigation into the social dynamics of Native communities, a new generation of scholarship emerged that continues to inform our understanding of Northampton's Native past.[67] Between 1956 and 1983, ethnohistorian Gordon Day patiently worked on Abenaki research with tribal informants and archivists across New England, publishing writings that directly addressed Connecticut River Valley Indian history, such as "English-Indian Contacts in New England" (1962), "The Identity of the Sokokis" (1965), "An Agawam Fragment" (1967), and "The Identity of the St. Francis Indians" (1981), a text that reveals the names of many former Pocumtuck, Nonotuck, and Woronoco peoples who had relocated to northern Abenaki villages. A selection of Day's essays, now compiled as a volume titled *In Search of New England's Native Past*,[68] serves as an excellent introduction to the complex political and social relations of central and northern New England.

The following texts represent just a few of the recent writings on Northampton's Native history that have broken new ground. William R. Young's 1969 volume for the Springfield Science Museum, *The Connecticut Valley Indian: An Introduction to Their Archaeology and History,* stands as a good introduction to the state of research in archaeological sites by that date, and also introduces some of the questions that later works have tried to answer. Peter Thomas's 1979 dissertation on Pynchon's trading arrangements with local Indians, "In the Maelstrom of Change," revealed details about the individual transactions, economic debts, ecological changes, and political shifts that unbalanced Native communities. Following in that trend, James Spady, in his 1994 senior thesis, "In the Midst of the River: Leadership, Trade and Politics among the Native Peoples of the Connecticut River Valley: 1635–1700," and in the article "As if in a Great Darkness: Native American Refugees of the Middle Connecticut River Valley in the Aftermath of King Philip's War" brought out the character of individual Native peoples caught up in the machinations of Euro-American conflicts played out on the American stage. Evan Hafeli and Kevin Sweeney's 1997 work "Revisiting the Redeemed Captive: New Perspectives on the 1704 Attack on Deerfield" helps to both clarify and complicate the identities of Native peoples involved in eighteenth-century raids on Connecticut River Valley towns. In 1992, Historic Northampton made a significant contribution to inspiring the development of new local curriculum with *Native Peoples and Museums in the Connecticut River Valley—A Guide for Learning*, edited by Dorothy Krass and Barry O'Connell.

Lest one think that New England's historical scholarship resides exclusively in the hands of Euro-Americans, it should be noted that many Algonkian Indian elders and scholars have made dramatic contributions to regional history, by sharing Native perspectives and traditions that improve our understandings of Native peoples, past and present. Local museums, like the Pocumtuck Valley Memorial Association and Historic Northampton, have created new exhibits, Web sites, and guidebooks. The Five College Native American Indian Studies Curriculum Committee also encourages Native elders, students, and faculty to develop new methods for teaching Native history. The college exhibits that once displayed Indian bodies have been dismantled, and the colleges themselves are coming to terms with their own legacy vis-à-vis Native peoples by founding new intertribal and interinstitutional partnerships. In sum, the year 2004 may represent three hundred and fifty years in which Euro-American settlement and history overwhelmed Native presence in Northampton . . . but it also marks an opportunity to do justice to all of our interwoven histories, by finding ways to work with Native peoples, respectfully recovering Native histories that have not vanished, that are still so close at hand.

NOTES

1. The term "Algonkian," alternatively spelled "Algonquin" or, by linguists, "Algonquian," describes a broad cultural and linguistic grouping that includes all the non-Iroquoian Native peoples of New England (i.e., Abenaki, Mohegan, Narragansett, Nipmuc, Nonotuck, Pequot, Pocumtuck, Schaghticoke, and Wabanaki, Wampanoag, and others). It seems to have originally derived from a French adaptation of a Malecite word. For further explanation, see Gordon Day, "The Name Algonquin," in Michael K. Foster and William Cowan, eds., *In Search of New England's Native Past: Selected Essays by Gordon M. Day* (Amherst, 1998), 123.

2. Letter from Reverend Edwin Benedict from Odanak, Canada, to C. Alice Baker of Deerfield, MA, February 17, 1890, Collections of Pocumtuck Valley Memorial Association, Memorial Libraries, Deerfield, 1; Harry Andrew Wright, *Indian Deeds of Hampden County*, (Springfield, 1905), 28–29; James Hammond Trumbull, *Natick Dictionary*, Bulletin 25, Smithsonian Bureau of Ethnology (Washington, DC, 1903), 87.

3. Since this discussion relies on so many early documents, I will use the generic terms "Indian," "American Indian," and "Native" (with a capital "N") to refer to the indigenous peoples of the North American continent, rather than rely exclusively on the relatively modern term "Native American." Even though the term "Indian" is technically a misnomer, no insult is implied or intended by its usage here.

4. Elizabeth S. Chilton, "In Search of Bark Wigwams: Archaeological Investigation of an Early Contact Period Site in the Connecticut Valley" (paper presented at the

Northeastern Anthropological Association Meeting, South Burlington, VT, March 1990). Eric S. Johnson and James W. Bradley, "The Bark Wigwams Site: An Early Seventeenth-Century Component in Central Massachusetts," *Man in the Northeast* 33 (spring 1987): 1–26; Harris Hawthorne Wilder and Ralph Wheaton Whipple, "The Position of the Body in Aboriginal Interments in Western Massachusetts," *American Anthropologist* new series, 19 (1917): 372–287; William R. Young, "A Survey of the Available Knowledge on the Middle Connecticut Valley Indians—Prehistoric and Historic," in *The Connecticut Valley Indian: An Introduction to Their Archaeology and History* new series, 1, no. 1, Springfield: Museum of Science (1969): 33–61.

5. E. B. Delabarre and Harris H. Wilder, "Indian Corn Hills in Massachusetts," *American Anthropologist* 22 (1920): 203–255.

6. Margaret Bruchac, "The True History of Sally Maminash," *Weathervane*, Historic Northampton (December 1997); Chilton, "In Search of Bark Wigwams."

7. Margaret Bruchac, "Collecting Indians for the Colleges: Constructing Native Invisibility in the Connecticut River Valley," Research report for Five College Repatriation Committee, work in progress 2003b.

8. Russell Handsman and Trudie Lamb Richmond, "Confronting Colonialism: The Mahican and Schaghticoke Peoples and Us," in Peter R. Schmidt and Thomas C. Patterson, eds., *Making Alternative Histories: The Practice of Archaeology and History in Non-Western Settings* (Santa Fe: School of American Research Press, 1996), 87–117; Neal Salisbury, "The Memorial and Indian Rooms, Memorial Hall, Deerfield," in Dorothy Krass and Barry O'Connell, eds., *Native Peoples and Museums in the Connecticut River Valley—A Guide for Learning* (Historic Northampton, Five College Public School Partnership Program, 1992).

9. Young, *Survey of the Available Knowledge*, 33–61; Bruchac, "Collecting Indians for the Colleges"; Margaret Bruchac and Elizabeth S. Chilton, "Where Have All the Indians Gone: Reconsidering Historical Memory in the Connecticut River Valley" (paper presented at the Northeastern Anthropological Association Meeting, University of Vermont, Burlington, March 2002).

10. Wright, *Indian Deeds of Hampden County*, 8–9. Elizabeth S. Chilton, "One Size Fits All: Typology and Alternatives for Ceramic Research," in *Material Meaning: Critical Approaches to the Interpretation of Material Culture* (Salt Lake City: University of Utah Press, 1999.)

11. George Sheldon, *A Guide to the Museum of the Pocumtuck Valley Memorial Association* (Deerfield: Pocumtuck Valley Memorial Association, 1908).

12. Bruchac, "Collecting Indians for the Colleges."

13. Isaac Goodwin, "Address to the American Antiquarian Society," 1820, in *American Antiquarian Society Proceedings*, Worcester, MA (1812–1849): 161A.

14. Harriet Martineau, *Society in America* (London, 1837), 126–127.

15. Donna K. Baron, J. Edward Hood, and Holly V. Izard, "They Were Here All Along: The Native American Presence in Central New England in the 18th and 19th Centuries" (research summary for Old Sturbridge Village, Sturbridge, MA, 1994); Margaret Bruchac, "In Search of the Indian Doctress," in *Old Sturbridge Village Visitor* (Old Sturbridge Village, September 1999); Thomas L. Doughton, "Unseen Neighbors: Native Americans of Central Massachusetts, a People Who Had Vanished," in Colin G. Calloway, ed., *After King Philip's War: Presence and Persistence in Indian New*

England (Hanover, NH, 1997); Handsman and Richmond, "Confronting Colonialism," 87–117.

16. Sylvester Judd, The Sylvester Judd Manuscript, "Miscellaneous," vol. 19:141, Forbes Library, Northampton.

17. Judd, "Miscellaneous," vol. 19:159.

18. John Milton Earle, *Report to the Governor and Council Concerning the Indians of the Commonwealth* (Boston, 1861).

19. Anonymous, *Northampton Courier*, June 6, 1838.

20. Angela Goebel Bain, "Historical Pageantry in Old Deerfield: 1910, 1913, 1916," in Peter Benes, ed., *New England Celebrates: Spectacle, Commemoration, and Festivity* (Dublin Seminar for New England Folklife 2000; Boston, 2002), 120–136.

21. City of Northampton, *The Meadow City's Quarter Millennial Book: A Memorial of the Celebration of the Two Hundred and Fiftieth Anniversary of the Settlement of the Town of Northampton, Massachusetts* (Northampton, 1904), 155.

22. Anonymous, "Indian Princess Restored," *Providence Sunday Journal*, section 5, March 16, 1913.

23. Betty Eudene, "Burton Contains Oddities," *Daily Hampshire Gazette*, Northampton, no date [1950s].

24. Ruth B. Phillips, "Why Not Tourist Art? Significant Silences in Native American Museum Representations," in G. Prakash, ed., *After Colonialism* (Princeton, 1994), 98–125; Richard Slotkin, *Regeneration Through Violence: The Mythology of the American Frontier, 1600–1860* (Middletown, CT, 1973); Alden Vaughn and Daniel K. Richter, "Crossing the Cultural Divide: Indians and New Englanders," *American Antiquarian Society Proceedings* 90 (1980): 23–99.

25. Thomas L. Doughton, "Like the Shadows in the Stream: Local Historians, the Discourse of Disappearance, and Nipmuc Indians of Central Massachusetts" (paper presented at the American Antiquarian Society, Worcester, MA, May 1999), published by Quinsigamond Band of Nipmucs, Worcester, MA, Nipmucnet, on-line at http://freepages.genealogy.rootsweb.com/~massasoit/shadows.htm 1999, 10.

26. William Pynchon to Governor John Winthrop, 1648, in Josiah H. Temple and George Sheldon, *A History of the Town of Northfield, for 150 Years, with an account of the prior occupation of the territory of the Squakheags* (Albany, NY, 1875), 35–38.

27. James Russell Trumbull, *History of Northampton* (Northampton, 1898), 1:8.

28. Wright, *Indian Deeds of Hampden County*, 27.

29. Sylvester Judd, Centennial Issue, *Daily Hampshire Gazette,* September 6, 1886.

30. Wright, *Indian Deeds of Hampden County*, 27.

31. Wright, *Indian Deeds of Hampden County*, 61.

32. Elizabeth S. Chilton, "Towns They Have None: Diverse Subsistence and Settlement Strategies in Native New England," in J. Hart and C. Reith, eds., *Northeast Subsistence-Settlement Change: A.D. 700—A.D. 1300* (New York State Museum Bulletin, 2002); Dena Dincauze, "A Capsule Prehistory of Southern New England," in Lawrence M. Hauptman and James D. Wherry, eds., *The Pequots in Southern New England: The Fall and Rise of an American Indian Nation* (Norman, OK, 1990).

33. Bruchac and Chilton, "Where Have All the Indians Gone."

34. George Sheldon, "The Pocumtuck Confederacy," 1890, in *The Connecticut Valley Indian,* 113.

35. Trumbull, *Natick Dictionary,* 194.

36. Sylvester Judd, *History of Hadley: Including the Early History of Hatfield, South Hadley, Amherst, and Granby, Massachusetts* (Northampton, 1863), 111.

37. Stephen Innes, *Labor in a New Land: Economy and Society in Seventeenth-Century Springfield* (Princeton, NJ, 1983), 454–458.

38. Gordon Day, "An Agawam Fragment" (1967), in Foster and Cowan, *In Search of New England's Native Past,* 99.

39. Peter Allen Thomas, "In the Maelstrom of Change: The Indian Trade and Cultural Process in the Middle Connecticut River Valley, 1635–1665" (Ph.D. diss., University of Massachusetts, 1979).

40. Carl Bridenbaugh, *The Pynchon Papers,* vol. 1, *Letters of John Pynchon, 1654–1700* (Boston, 1982), 288.

41. Trumbull, *History of Northampton,* 1:176–177.

42. Colin G. Calloway, *The Western Abenakis of Vermont, 1600–1800: War, Migration, and the Survival of an Indian People* (Norman, OK, 1990); Gordon Day, *The Identity of the Saint Francis Indians,* National Museum of Man, Mercury Series Paper, No. 71, (Ottawa, 1981); Evan Haefeli and Kevin Sweeney, "Revisiting the Redeemed Captive: New Perspective on the 1704 Attack on Deerfield," in Calloway, *After King Philip's War,* 29–71. James Spady, "As if in a Great Darkness: Native American Refugees of the Middle Connecticut River Valley in the Aftermath of King Philip's War," *Historical Journal of Massachusetts* 23, no. 2 (summer 1995): 183–197; Thomas, "In the Maelstrom of Change."

43. Bruchac and Chilton, "Where Have All the Indians Gone"; Day, *The Identity of the Saint Francis Indians.*

44. Henry M. Burt, *First Century of the History of Springfield, the Official Records from 1636 to 1736,* 2 vols. (Springfield, 1898–1899), 1:70–71; Sylvester Judd, "Northampton and Westfield," in Gregory H. Nobles and Herbert L. Zarov, eds., *History of Hadley: Selected Papers from the Sylvester Judd Manuscript* (Northampton, 1976), 157–160.

45. Day, *The Identity of the Saint Francis Indians;* Haefeli and Sweeney, "Revisiting the Redeemed Captive," 29–71.

46. Trumbull, *History of Northampton,* 1:437.

47. Calloway, *The Western Abenakis of Vermont*; Day, *The Identity of the Saint Francis Indians.*

48. Day, *The Identity of the Saint Francis Indians,* 19.

49. Partridge, quoted by Pynchon to Bradstreet, December 2, 1691, Bridenbaugh, *The Pynchon Papers,* 1:236.

50. Haefeli and Sweeney, "Revisiting the Redeemed Captive."

51. Titus King, *Narrative of Titus King of Northampton, Mass.: A Prisoner of the Indians in Canada, 1755–1758* (Hartford, 1938), 13–14.

52. Trumbull, *History of Northampton,* 1: 485.

53. Spady, "As if in a Great Darkness"; Thomas, "In the Maelstrom of Change"; Peter Allen Thomas, "Bridging the Cultural Gap: Indian/White Relations" in Stephen C. Innes et al., *Early Settlements in the Connecticut Valley: A Colloquium at Historic Deerfield* (Deerfield, 1984) [chapter 1 of this book].

54. Bruchac, "The True History of Sally Maminash"; C. Keith Wilbur, "Land of the Nonotucks" (Northampton, 1987).

55. Trudie Lamb Richmond, "A Native Perspective of History: The Schaghticoke Nation, Resistance and Survival," in Laurie Weinstein, ed., *Enduring Traditions: The Native Peoples of New England* (Westport, CT, 1994), 103.

56. *Worcester Telegram*, 1936.

57. Charles J. Dean, "Hospital Hill and Its Riddles of Yesterday," *Daily Hampshire Gazette*, November 15, 1958.

58. First Church Records, Book 1 and 2, 1819, First Churches Archives, Main Street, Northampton, 43.

59. Rev. Solomon Clark, *Historical Catalogue of the Northampton First Church 1661–1891* (Northampton, 1891), 121.

60. Bruchac, "The True History of Sally Maminash."

61. Nathan Whiting, List of Soldiers, 1745, from *Collections of the Connecticut Historical Society* 13:76–80.

62. Sidney E. Bridgeman, "Sally Mammanash Is Recalled Here: Daughter of Indian Woman Who Was Stoned to Death Lived with the Bridgemans," *Daily Hampshire Gazette*, August 25, 1936.

63. Dean, "Hospital Hill and Its Riddles of Yesterday"; Bridgeman, "Sally Mammanash Is Recalled Here"; Wilbur, "Land of the Nonotucks."

64. Ruth Strong, "Cherished Family Heirloom," photograph of Sally Maminash's ash-splint chair, *Daily Hampshire Gazette*, December 17, 1968.

65. Mary Brewster, "Last Indian of Northampton," chapter 46: Historical Miscellany, in Harry Andrew Wright, ed., *The Story of Western Massachusetts* (New York, 1949).

66. Delabarre and Wilder, "Indian Corn Hills in Massachusetts," 218–219.

67. Krass and O'Connell, *Natives Peoples and Museums in the Connecticut River Valley.*

68. Foster and Cowan, *In Search of New England's Native Past.*

3

THE first permanent English settlers arrived in Northampton in 1654, most having moved from earlier settlements in Springfield and Hartford. Many had first come to New England during the "Great Migration" of the 1630s from the regions of Mid-Essex and East Anglia in southern England. Craftsmen and farmers transplanted a variety of local English traditions in handicrafts, carpentry, and farming to the banks of the Connecticut. Most of the families were of modest means, headed by yeoman farmers. Some settlers were young men coming of age, drawn by reports of fertile meadow lands. The first streets were laid out in parallel rows along the river terraces. Common fields contained lots apportioned according to social rank and wealth. Many of these lots—Venturer's Field, Bark Wigwam, Old Rainbow, Young Rainbow—still retain their seventeenth-century names.

Daily life in early Northampton was plain and at least outwardly modest. Most households contained little more than a bedstead, perhaps a chest, a few utensils for eating, and some ironware for cooking in one or, at most, two multipurpose rooms. Many made do with considerably less. But despite the appearance of an orderly community, outward conformity sometimes masked tensions that lay below the surface. Social position was often hotly contested. Court documents reveal claims and counterclaims about property and debts. Occasionally "hard thoughts and jealousies" erupted into charges of witchcraft and slander. In 1656, and again in 1674, Mary Bliss Parsons, an outspoken and strong-willed woman, was accused of "having entered into familiarity with the Devil" in trials that divided the community.

In this classic study of witchcraft in New England, John Putnam Demos examines the recorded testimonies of the Mary Bliss Parsons cases, revealing the social dynamics underlying everyday life in seventeenth-century Northampton.

"Hard Thoughts and Jealousies"*

JOHN PUTNAM DEMOS

THE story of witchcraft in early New England spotlights very sharply the power of local gossip. Behind the court proceedings—the formal "presentments," the gathering of depositions, the trials themselves—one invariably finds a thick trail of *talk*. Of course, the ultimate source for all this lay in the minds and hearts of the people involved, but the outlet was words—for the

* From John Putnam Demos, *Entertaining Satan: Witchcraft and the Culture of Early New England* (New York, 1982).

most part, spoken words. The fear of supernatural evil sustained a vocabulary both rich and compelling.

This vocabulary was used in many different settings, some of them quite mundane and limited. Thomas Cooper, while arguing with Goodwife Phillips, called her "a blare-eyed witch."[1] Goodwife Holman was presented at court for making "opprobrious speeches" against Elizabeth Hooper; the speeches included such terms as "spiteful old witch" and "base old whore."[2] Mathew Farrington was charged with saying of Thomas Wheeler that "he was the Devil's packhorse, to do the Devil's drudgery."[3] Francis Urselton, in the midst of a lengthy quarrel, "railed on Goodwife Clark, saying she was a devilish woman, and the devil was in her and would have her."[4] Sarah Allen, presented for "keeping company" with her sweetheart on the Sabbath, "wished that the devil had the heart blood of all that spoke against it."[5] John Fosket came to blows with his neighbors, the Mousalls; to Goodwife Mousall he said "that she was a liar . . . and when she was going to the magistrate . . . the devil was at her left hand"—and to her husband "that all that he had was the devil's, for he stood by his bedside and caused his members to rise."[6] John Pinder was notorious for bitter threats and curses; one witness deposed that "I have heard him use the devil in his mouth often times."[7]

To use the Devil in one's mouth was clearly wrong; but the circumstances were not always those of conflict, and the motive was sometimes other than insult. Occasionally such talk had the look of simple bravado. Thus John Long, a "boy" from Cambridge, was brought to court in the summer of 1668 on various counts of "untoward carriage." For example, "Seeing a mare drinking a long time near Benjamin Switzer's house, [he] swore 'by God, I think the devil is in the mare.'" And "upon the hill, going to play, [he said] I will camp the ball to the devil." And "being asked . . . whether he would go home, he replied, 'what should I go home for, the devil is threshing barley in the cellar.'"[8] Words like these made a near approach to blasphemy; in other instances they crossed the line. Goodwife Hannah Hackleton pleaded guilty to a charge of "uttering direct, express, presumptuous, high-handed blasphemy" and confessed "that she had said there was as much mercy in the devil as in God."[9] In still other cases the Devil's name was invoked as a way of gaining influence in some personal or domestic situation. Thus, a servant to the Reverend John Hale of Beverly was accused of threatening another "maid" as follows: "She said she had a book in which she could read and call the devil to kill Sarah." (She also "said if Sarah would do what she bade her, the devil should not catch her.")[10]

"Opprobrious speeches" were serious enough, and blasphemy was (in theory at least) a capital crime. But full-fledged slander made an important category of offenses all its own. Like the inhabitants of small, premodern communities almost everywhere, the New Englanders were vitally concerned with matters of reputation. Whenever their good name was threatened, they were quick to seek legal recourse; actions for slander and defamation appear all through their court records. And among the many imaginable forms of slander, those that touched on witchcraft seemed especially bad.

The slander cases involving witchcraft, however, were themselves quite various. Some of them seem, on balance, the direct extension of personal controversy. Thus, in the county court at Hartford in 1678, Edward Messenger filed suit against Edward Bartlett "for defamation . . . for saying that the said Messenger's wife was an old witch or whore or words to the same purpose"; at the same court Messenger also sued Bartlett for debt "to the value of thirty-four shillings."[11] And at Kittery, Maine, in 1660, a peculiar case unfolded around a preacher named Thorp. It seems that the Reverend Thorp had been boarding in the house of a certain Jonas Bailey, when his fondness for drink aroused the indignation of his landlady. Goodwife Bailey "gravely told him his way was contrary to the Gospel of Christ, and desired him to reform his life or leave her house." Eventually "he departed from the house, . . . turned her enemy," and sought to have her "questioned for a witc"—whereupon the Baileys filed suit for slander.[12] According to subsequent testimony, Thorp had frequently declared that Goody Bailey "was a witch . . . a rotten, damned witch as ever held bread . . . a stinking, rotten witch," and the like.[13]

Katherine Messenger and Goodwife Bailey may have been marked as suspect by more than a lone antagonist, but if so the evidence has not survived. There were other slander cases that involved small cliques of neighbors, and at least a few where suspicions ran very wide. The latter produced, by way of trial proceedings, material quite similar to that which supported the prosecution of witchcraft itself. The defendant might wish to "justify" the purported slander by showing (in the words of one court) "that [the plaintiff's] carriage doth . . . render her suspicious of witchcraft."[14] The plaintiff, on the other hand, sought to present the same material in another light. It was her aim to play down the elements of menace and mystery, and to play *up* the gossip that had prompted her suit in the first place.

Either way, the depositional record ran a familiar gamut from odd behavior and sayings, through the petty details of personal dispute, to unexplained (and seemingly occult) forms of mischance. When the widow Marshfield complained against one of her Springfield neighbors "for reporting her to be suspected for a witch," witnesses came forward with the particulars. The defendant's child had died, and also her cow—"and I am persuaded, said she, that they were bewitched." The same person had lost a pound of wool—"and she said she could not tell except the witch had witched it away." Moreover, "she said . . . that there were diverse, strong lights seen of late in the meadow that were never seen before the widow Marshfield came to town . . . and that it was publicly known that the devil followed her house in Windsor" [where the widow had earlier resided].[15]

Stories of this kind often circulated on a second- or thirdhand basis. The nub of an early slander case in Essex County, Massachusetts, was as follows: "John Caldwell testifies that being in Goodman Bridges' shop, Goodman [Marshall] being present, he heard him say that a woman and her daughter, gathering berries, saw four women . . . [sitting] upon the ground, but when they came near the women vanished."[16] In another case suit was brought not by the supposed "witch" herself, but by the man to whom such supposition had been attributed: "Thomas Crawley, plaintiff, against Robert Hall, defendant, in an action of slander for saying that he called Robert Sayward's wife witch."[17] Along with the gossip went a certain amount of prying and spying: for example, "Mistress Godman charged Hannah Lamberton . . . [with saying] she lay for somewhat to suck her . . . Hannah said she and her sister Elizabeth went up into the garret above her room, and looked down, and said 'look how she lies, she lies as if somebody was sucking her.'"[18]

A few particular unfortunates were obliged to rebut such charges again and again. Thus, Jane James of Marblehead filed three suits for slander over a period of almost twenty years. The first was against Peter Pitford, who had declared "that Goodwife James was a witch and that he saw her in a boat at sea in the likeness of a cat." The second identified Goodwife Gatchell as the source of a similar rumor, "that she [Goody James] was seen going . . . on the water to Boston when she was at the same time in her yard at home." The third charged Richard Rowland with saying that the specter of Goody James "came in at a hole in the window in Rowland's house and took him by the throat and almost choked him as he lay in his bed."[19]

In many such cases, the plaintiff had motives beyond the desire to clear her name. She knew that local sentiment was building against her, and she feared that she might herself become the target of criminal proceedings. An action for slander was, then, a tactic of forestalling, which allowed the supposed witch to confront her accusers before they were ready to bring their own complaint to court. However, the tactic was not without risk. If the case for the defense seemed credible, the court's interest might abruptly reverse itself—with the plaintiff moving over to the prisoner's dock.[20] The decision to file for slander must, therefore, have been a difficult one. The strategic advantage of seizing the initiative was balanced by the danger of bringing into full view problems that might otherwise resolve themselves.

The immediate outcome of these actions was usually favorable to the plaintiff: the court would (with rare exceptions) sustain the charge of slander, and require from the defendant some suitable form of redress.[21] But the long-range effects were mixed. Local suspicion could not be dissipated by legal fiat, and at least a few successful plaintiffs were subsequently tried for witchcraft anyway. A notable case in point was one Mary Parsons of Northampton, Massachusetts. By a relatively early age Goody Parsons had acquired the reputation of witch among certain of her neighbors and peers; and try as she might, over many years, she could never entirely shake it. Indeed, it hung on long enough to touch the lives even of her children and grandchildren. But this is a story that merits retelling—and study—in all of its considerable detail.

ON THE docket of the Middlesex County Court, for its session of October 7, 1656, is found the following entry: "Joseph Parsons, plaintiff, against Sarah, the wife of James Bridgman, defendant, in an action of the case for slandering her [Parsons's wife] in her name. This action, by consent of both parties, was referred to the judgement of the Honored Bench of Magistrates." A separate document records the magistrates' finding in favor of the plaintiff and their order that the defendant make "public acknowledgement" of the wrong she had done. The acknowledgment was to be a dual performance—once in the town of Northampton, and again at Springfield. Failure to fulfill either part of this requirement would result in a fine of £10.[22]

These few lines do not even hint at the substantive nature of the case. The penalty invoked was moderate, and quite standard for slander suits. The "consent of both parties" on the procedural question implies a spirit of accommodation—even, perhaps, a shared wish to have done with the matter. Yet the file papers from the same court convey a different impression.[23] Numerous and detailed as they are, they show very clearly that Parsons vs. Bridgman was no routine case. The issue at hand was witchcraft, or rather, the supposition of witchcraft. The proceedings antecedent to the court hearing were long in duration and complex in structure. The level of feeling, on both sides, was high.

The depositions included in the file papers come to 33 overall. They comprise the testimony of 24 different witnesses (some deposed more than once). Thirteen additional persons are mentioned at one point or another in the papers, yielding a grand total of 37 who had some connection with the case. The 37, in turn, represented 22 different households. Fifteen of the households belonged to the town of Northampton (whose total complement of households at the time was only 32), the remaining 7 to Springfield. These figures suggest a very considerable degree of local interest and involvement.

Taken individually, the depositions seem puzzling—or even, at some points, contradictory. But when sorted in reference to time and place (that is, when and where given) they acquire an unmistakable meaning. In effect, they group themselves into four major sets, corresponding to distinct phases in the slander case itself. They reveal, moreover, the taut lines of a power struggle with effects reaching well beyond the interests of the two principals.

The first set of testimonies was recorded at Northampton on or about June 20, with two of the local selectmen officially in charge. For example:

> Robert Bartlett testifieth that George Langdon told him the last winter that Goody Bridgman and Goody Branch were speaking about Mary Parsons concerning her being a witch. And the said George told to the said Robert that my [Langdon's] wife being there said she could not think so—which the said Goody Bridgman seemed to be distasted with. As also [according to Langdon] they had hard thoughts of the wife of the said Robert [Bartlett] because she was intimate with the said Mary Parsons.[24]

The other depositions in this early group enlarged on the gossip theme. The same Hannah Langdon mentioned in Bartlett's statement testified that "Sarah Bridgman . . . told her that her boy when his knee was sore cried out of the wife of Joseph Parsons." Bridgman had also alleged widespread "jealousies that the wife of Joseph Parsons was not right." For a time Langdon herself had entertained suspicions of Mary Parsons, but recently "it hath pleased God to help her over them . . . and [she] is sorry she should have [had] hard thoughts of her upon no better grounds." Bridgman had also talked with Margaret Bliss, the mother of Mary Parsons, saying "she had heard there was some discontent between the blind man at Springfield and her daughter . . . and then the child of the blind man had a sounding [?] fit." Hannah Broughton remembered a time when Bridgman had quoted Mr. Pynchon as saying that "if that were true which he had heard, Goody Parsons could not be right." And so on. These depositions converged on the issue of what Goody Bridgman had *said*. As such, they constituted an opening salvo in the effort to prove her a slanderer. At the same time they implied a spirit of antagonism toward Mary Parsons which ran wider than any single person.[25]

The second major group of papers in the case carries a date several weeks later. They were taken before a different official, and probably in a different place (Springfield). And they expressed a different viewpoint, as the recorder noted at the top of the opening page: "Testimonies Taken on Behalf of Sarah, the wife of James Bridgman, the 11th day of August, 1656." There are six separate depositions here, and five more which can probably (though not certainly) be associated with the same occasion.

The Bridgmans themselves supplied lengthy testimony on the events that had caused them to suspect Goody Parsons. The previous summer their eleven-year-old son had suffered a bizarre injury while tending their cows: "In a swamp there came something and gave him a great blow on the head . . . and going a little further he . . . stumbled . . . and put his knee out of joint." Subsequently, the knee was "set," but it would not heal properly—and "he was in grievous torture about a month." Then the boy discovered the cause of his sufferings: "He cried out [that] Goody Parsons would pull off his knee, [saying] 'there she sits on the shelf.' . . . I and my husband labored to quiet him, but could hardly hold him in bed for he was very fierce. We told him there was nobody. . . 'Yea,' says he, 'there she is; do you not see her? There she runs away and a black mouse follows her.' And this he said many times and with great violence . . . and he was like to die in our apprehension."

At about the same time the Bridgmans had also lost an infant son:

> I [Sarah] being brought to bed, about three days after as I was sitting up, having the child in my lap, there was something that gave a great blow on the door. And that very instant, as I apprehended, my child changed. And I thought with myself and told my girl that I was afraid my child would die. . . . Presently . . . I looking towards the door, through a hole . . . I saw . . . two women pass by the door, with white clothes on their heads; then I concluded my child would die indeed. And I sent my girl out to see who they were, but she could see nobody, and this made me think there is wickedness in the place.[26]

The Bridgmans were joined by other witnesses giving parallel forms of testimony. A couple named Hannum had also suffered grievously—so they thought—at the hands of Goody Parsons. Honor Hannum had "this past winter . . . spun for the said Mary Parsons," and her yarn had invariably proved defective. Parsons had complained, and Hannum had "spun some more . . . to recompense this defect"—but with the same result. This seemed perplexing since Hannum had successfully performed similar work for many others. In the meantime the Hannums rebuffed a request from Goody Parsons to hire one of their daughters as a maidservant. ("Considering what rumors went about of her, I told my daughter she should not go thither to dwell if she might have ten pounds a year.") A few days thereafter the same daughter, "though formerly healthy," became "very sickly." She had remained so, "and very unhelpful to me," through much of the current summer.[27]

William Hannum had his own part in these dealings. He had argued one evening with Goody Parsons about his wife's spinning—"and the next morning one cow lay in my yard, ready to die, as I thought." (In fact, the cow died some days later.) On another occasion he was chided by Mary Parsons for "abusing her brother's oxen." Hannum rejected the charge, "and she went away in anger"—and shortly thereafter one of his own oxen was fatally bitten by a rattlesnake. Yet a third time he had incurred her anger, by "jesting" with neighbors at Mary's expense. And "she dealt with me about it, showing her offense"; a day later his sow died suddenly. "These things," Hannum concluded, "do something run in my mind, [so] that I cannot have my mind from this woman, that if she be not right this way she may be a cause of these things, though I desire to look at the overarching hand of God in all."[28]

Several other Northampton residents offered testimony designed to show Goodwife Parsons not as a witch but as a liar. ("Goodwife Wright saith that . . . Goody Parsons . . . told her that Goodwife Holton said she would make her candles for her." But, "Goodwife Holton was spoken to about this business . . . and denied it.") There were also some revealing allegations about pressure exerted by supporters of Goody Parsons to block the testimony against her. Goodman Elmore, a local official responsible for "swearing some witnesses" in the case, "urged them . . . and [told] them what they should say . . . and did jostle the meaning of the words and writ down what he thought good." Moreover, he "said . . . that he stood for them and would stand for them, meaning Goodwife Parsons."[29]

Finally, two witnesses from Springfield opened up a new line of testimony, bearing on Goody Parsons's *past*. She was herself a former resident of Springfield, having arrived there at least as early as 1646. Even then she was a controversial figure. There were reports, for example, that she had walked on water "and was not wet." Her own husband had gossiped about her extraordinary intuitive powers. ("He said, . . . 'whenever I hide the key of my door, my wife will find it.'") And "old Mr. Pynchon"—the founder and leading magistrate at Springfield—was said to have "wondered" when these stories were brought to his attention.[30]

The depositions of August 11 were designed ostensibly to defend Sarah Bridgman; but in fact they went far toward indicting Mary Parsons. They carried the threat, implicit in most such slander suits, of reversing the positions of the principals. As such they were bound to call forth a vigorous response from the plaintiff and her supporters. And within a scant few days that response had entered the official record.

Eleven new depositions comprised the third major set, taken at Northampton from August 15 to 18. Several were intended as direct rebuttal to the evidence presented for the other side. Was there any strong ground for suspecting that Goody Bridgman's baby had died from witchcraft? Three women who had attended the birth were skeptical: "The child . . . was sick as soon as it was born," and the mother herself "thought it had taken cold," and suffered from "looseness . . . at the first." (So much, then, for her story of a child born healthy and subsequently "changed" by a sudden "clap on the door" as two mysterious figures passed by outside.) Was there anything strange about the death of William Hannum's ox? Several other men "were present when the ox . . . was stung with the rattlesnake, and they did conceive nothing but what might come to pass in an ordinary way." The same was true for Hannum's cow: a neighbor who had skinned it "found a great quantity of water in the belly of the cow." Moreover, upon observing this, "William Hannum called to his wife and told her they need not fear, but the cow died of the water." Two witnesses recalled the Hannums saying quite specifically "that they had nothing against Mary Parsons."[31]

The Hannums themselves now joined in the plaintiff's case. Apparently reversing their stance of the week before, they charged James Bridgman with pressuring them to testify against Mary Parsons. Still another witness described Sarah Bridgman's insistent "jealousies and suspicion." ("She said . . . she could not be satisfied unless . . . Mary was searched by women three times.") And two more recalled how she had turned aside a request that her son's injured knee be subjected to impartial examination.[32]

There was one final group of depositions, taken at Springfield in late September. Three of them, clearly by Bridgman supporters, were designed to discredit Mary Parsons by deepening the shadows in her Springfield past. In 1652 Springfield had been the site of a separate prosecution for witchcraft. The children of the local minister, the Reverend George Moxon, had succumbed to fits, as had "others"—including Mary Parsons. An eyewitness remembered that "as Mr. Moxon's children acted, so did Mary Parsons—just all one." Indeed, she and they were together "carried out of the meeting, it being the Sabbath day." But there were some aspects of Parsons's fits that raised special doubts and suspicions. It was then that "she went over the water and . . . was not wet." She was, moreover, a grown woman, and this by itself set her experience apart from that of the afflicted children.[33]

The relation of Mary Parsons and her husband, during their Springfield years, formed yet another subject of testimony. One man, "being at Joseph Parsons' house, making barrels," had observed a quarrel between the two of them:

> He said to his wife that she was led by an evil spirit. Thereupon she said he was the cause of it by locking her into the cellar and leaving her. . . . She said also that when her husband locked her into the cellar, the cellar was full of spirits, and she threw the bedstaff at them and the bedclothes and her pillow, and yet they would not be gone. And from this time, she told me, it was that she fell ill into her fits some few days after. She . . . said . . . the spirits appeared to her like poppets, as she was washing her clothes at the brook, and then she fell into her fits.[34]

But the author of this last deposition (John Mathews) soon had second thoughts about it. In fact, within days he offered another statement, disavowing any "jealousy from himself of Mary Parsons," and declaring that his first testimony "was [given] upon the earnest importunity of James Bridgman and his brother." At the same time magistrate John Pynchon repudiated a comment attributed to him months earlier by Sarah Bridgman herself: "Being requested by Goodwife Parsons to declare whether I said . . . [she] could not be right, I accordingly declare that to my remembrance I never said any such word, neither do I remember any reports that I have heard which have given me occasion to speak any such words of Goodwife Parsons."[35]

With this the file papers in Parsons vs. Bridgman were complete. (At least no others have survived.) The date of the final depositions was September 30. One week later the magistrates of Middlesex County rendered their decision, as previously noted. The gathering of evidence had taken an entire summer, but this was, after all, hardly a random process. Each of the first three sets of testimony expressed a unified purpose; only the last was of a mixed character. One set followed another, thrust and counterthrust, as each side sought to gain the upper hand. In a sense both Bridgman and Parsons were on trial—the former officially so, as a slanderer, the latter by implication, as a witch.

The records afford at least a glimpse of intense maneuvering behind the scenes—of pressures and pleadings that certainly shaped the development of the case and may well have decided its outcome. Goodman Elmore, a Northampton selectman, had openly declared his allegiance to the plaintiff and had tried to alter the testimonies accordingly. (Or so one witness alleged.) The names of two Springfield magistrates (the Pynchons, father and son) were invoked on the side of the defendant; but Mary Parsons herself "requested" John Pynchon to repudiate this connection—and he obliged. John Mathews, apparently regretting his first line of testimony, declared that it was given "upon the earnest importunity" of the defendant's husband and brother. William and Honor Hannum, while executing a similar change of position, also mentioned pressures from James Bridgman.

The shifting allegiance of the witnesses bears particular consideration. Of the 24 persons who deposed in the case, 11 were associated (initially) with the plaintiff's side and 13 with that of the defendant. However, in 5 instances (2 and 3 respectively) this reflected a family link, making a shift most unlikely. Of the remaining 19 witnesses, 9 for the plaintiff and 10 for the defendant, 5 seem to have changed sides. And all of these 5 moved in the same direction, from defendant to plaintiff; thus a 9–10 split was converted to 14–5. (There was, in addition, one witness for the plaintiff who admitted having had "hard thoughts" of her during a period *before* the trial.)[36]

Geography was also a factor here. With minor exceptions the depositions for the plaintiff were taken entirely in Northampton itself, and those for the defendant at Springfield. Moreover, five of the (ten) defendant's witnesses were residents of Springfield at the time of the trial, and of the remaining five (i.e., those who lived at Northampton) four subsequently switched to the plaintiff. As a result the final alignment of witnesses expressed a marked Springfield vs. Northampton division.

From all this the plaintiff derived an increasingly strong position. Her support was solidly based in Northampton, the home of both principals and the official center of the proceedings. The local leadership seems to have sided with her—and even to have obstructed the efforts of her opponent. By contrast, the defendant's case was made entirely at Springfield, where half of her witnesses were officially resident. As events went forward, all but one of her Northampton supporters went over to the other side. The movement of these witnesses served, in turn, to forecast the ultimate result. Of course, we cannot discover just how and why the county magistrates decided as they did, and it may be that the plaintiff's evidence seemed compelling on its face. But the evidence itself reflected a summer-long contest for strategic advantage. And by the autumn of the year that contest had clearly tipped in favor of Mary Parsons.

FROM the outcome of Parsons vs. Bridgman, and the struggle which immediately preceded that outcome, inquiry moves backward to the matter of origins. What was there about Mary Parsons to invite "hard thoughts" in the first place? Why might the gossip which connected her with witchcraft seem plausible to at least some of her local peers? And what can be said about the peers themselves? Why, in particular, did Sarah Bridgman assume a leading role here?

The evidence from the slander trial supplies at least part of the answer to such questions. Mary Parsons had experienced "fits" in a witchcraft case at Springfield some five years earlier, and this was unusual in persons fully adult. Moreover, some of her "actings" in this condition had elicited suspicion rather than sympathy: perhaps she was less a victim than a perpetrator of magic. Her own husband had lent credence to these suspicions, in conversations with their Springfield neighbors. Indeed, Mary herself (according to one informant) had spoken of confronting "spirits" on various occasions.

There were other things to be said against her as well. She and her husband were frequently and notoriously at odds with one another. During part of their time at Springfield he had sought to confine her to their house. (Otherwise, he said, she "would go out in the night and . . . when she went out a woman went out with her and came in with her.") When this tactic failed, he locked her in the basement. (It was then, she claimed later on, that she had first encountered her "spirits.") There was at least one quite public episode—again at Springfield—that amounted to a family free-for-all. Joseph was "beating one of his little children, for losing its shoe," when Mary came running "to save it, because she had beaten it before as she said." Whereupon Joseph "thrust her away," and the two of them continued to struggle until he "had in a sort beaten [her]."[37] It was also alleged that Mary Parsons paid little heed to truth. (Several of the trial depositions were designed to catch her in a "made lie.") And her manner could be harsh, or openly accusatory. ("Mary Parsons came and challenged me about the yarn I spun for her.". . . "Mary Parsons came to me and did chide with me for abusing her brother's oxen.")[38]

These events, this reputation, invited unfriendly gossip. But would they by themselves have prompted the very special antagonism—the hatred, the envy, the fear—that was usually implicit in an accusation of witchcraft? Just here there are other factors to consider, involving the entire shape of Mary Parsons's career.

She was born in England in about the year 1628.[39] Her parents were Thomas and Margaret Bliss; she was, probably, their first child. However, Margaret seems to have been Thomas's second wife, and there were at least three older children (presumably from her father's previous marriage). There would, in addition, be seven younger ones (after Mary) born to her mother.[40]

The particulars of this family's arrival in New England are not known—though tradition has preserved a date of 1635.[41] Evidently they lived first at Mount Wollaston (then a part of Boston, now belonging to Braintree).[42] Quite soon, however, they removed to Hartford, where in 1640 their lands were officially recorded.[43] Hartford would remain their home until the death of Thomas Bliss roughly a decade later, but they made little impression on the public life of the place. Thomas held no public office (though belonging at the time of his arrival to the age-group most liable to civic responsibilities). He had not been among the first comers, and hence held no regular rights of proprietorship.[44] He pleaded but one minor court case, and was himself presented once only—"for not training."[45] The amount of his lands was slightly below the local median.[46] The inventory of his estate, taken in February 1651, depicts the household of (at most) an average yeoman. (For example: "his house and a lot belonging to it . . . meadow and upland . . . 2 cows and 2 year-old calves . . . one bedstead . . . a trundle bed . . . a flock bed . . . one loom . . . 2 axes and 4 old hoes . . . 2 brass pots, 1 iron pot, 2 kettles, 1 skillet . . . 2 old bibles.") The total value of his property was £86, another modest figure.[47] The estate passed to the widow "for her use and [for] the education of her children." In making this arrangement the court followed Thomas's own wish, expressed "as he lay on his deathbed." (His daughter Mary was recorded as being "ready to testify" to the same.)[48]

The New England experience of this man appears, in sum, undistinguished. However, his earlier life may well have been very different. Such at least is the burden of a remarkable story of the Bliss family during the years just prior to their departure from Old England. Unfortunately, the story comes to us without firm documentation: it stands therefore as a provisional addendum to the main threads of the current chapter.[49]

Thomas Bliss, the emigrant, was by this account the son and namesake of a well-to-do, locally influential citizen in the village of Belstone, county Devon. In the opening decades of the seventeenth century the father had become a determined advocate of the Puritan cause and had participated with like-minded neighbors in acts of protest against religious "oppression." On one particular occasion he and three of his sons (George, Jonathan, and Thomas, Jr.) had accompanied a party, led by the local member of parliament, in riding up to London to engage both king and archbishop in direct confrontation. The upshot was their imprisonment and the levying of heavy fines (said to have been in excess of £1,000) in lieu of their freedom. Payment of the fines required the virtual liquidation of the family estate, and even then there was not enough money to free all four Blisses. Thus one of the sons—Jonathan—remained in jail some while longer, was severely whipped in the public square at Exeter, and never thereafter recovered his health.

Impoverished and broken in his own health, Thomas, Sr., subsequently returned to Belstone and lived in the household of his daughter, Lady Elizabeth Calcliffe. She was the wife of a knighted "gentleman" who had remained a regular communicant of the Anglican church (thus avoiding persecution). As the crisis of the realm deepened, the father summoned his sons, divided among them what patrimony he still retained, and advised them to remove to New England. Thomas, Jr., and George left soon thereafter; Jonathan was too ill to join them, but sent at least one of his sons in their care. During the years that followed, Lady Calcliffe sought to temper the privations of her relatives across the sea by sending them periodic shipments of clothing and food. And it was in her personal correspondence—regrettably, long since lost—that this part of the Bliss family history was remembered for succeeding generations.

Assuming the reality of all (or most) of this, we must try to imagine its effect on Mary [Bliss] Parsons. She would have been only a small child when the fortunes of her family hit their lowest point—father and grandfather in prison, the rest brought near to poverty. She was perhaps eight years old when her parents took her off to the New World. She was eleven or twelve when they decided on still another move, to the rude little settlement at Hartford. There for a time life stabilized, and Mary grew to womanhood as an average member of an ordinary New England community. But in 1646 she married Joseph Parsons and went to live in Springfield. And this was another turning point. Henceforth her life would be increasingly set apart from the average.

Joseph Parsons had been born in about the year 1619; like his bride he seems to have come originally from Devonshire.[50] His first appearance in any extant records dates from the summer of 1636, when he witnessed a deed transferring Indian lands near Springfield to William Pynchon and two other men.[51] Joseph was unusually young to have an official part in such an important transaction, and this circumstance (among others) has caused genealogists to infer familial ties between the Parsonses and the Pynchons. There is no sure evidence to prove such ties, but they remain a real—and intriguing—possibility.[52] William Pynchon and, later, his son John were truly preeminent figures in the early history of the Connecticut Valley. And Joseph Parsons was for many years their business associate, their friend, and perhaps their kin.

The earliest references to Joseph in the Pynchon family account books include credits for various small services: "a day's work in hay-time," [more] "work in hay-time," and "bringing up my goods" (transport from one location to another).[53] So perhaps he began as a simple farmer, who (like many of his local peers) was at least occasionally in the employ of others. However, there are hints—on the debit side of the Pynchon ledger—of a second, more distinctive, orientation. When Joseph purchased rugs, iron, and wampum, it may have been for the purpose of entering the Indian trade.[54]

In any case, by the time of his marriage to Mary Bliss, Joseph was already launched on the road to prosperity. A tax-list showed him in the top third of local property-holders, while still two or three years away from his thirtieth birthday.[55] He began to hold local offices: highway overseer in 1645 and 1646, fence-viewer in 1650, and then selectman in 1651 and 1652.[56] In 1654 Joseph moved his family to Northampton (while retaining, however, most of his holdings at Springfield). He assumed at once a position of leadership in the new settlement. He served on numerous town committees, including the one which arranged the building of the first meetinghouse. He was selectman three years running (1657–1659) and again at intervals thereafter. (In 1656, wishing to concentrate all his energies on his personal affairs, he asked to be "freed from any office . . . for this year" and offered to pay the town 20 shillings for such exemption; his terms were accepted and the request granted.) He became "clerk" of the local "trainband" and later "cornet" (lieutenant and standard-bearer) of the Hampshire County militia.[57]

But it was as a merchant that Joseph made his greatest mark. In about 1654 he obtained from the Pynchons a share in their chartered monopoly of the Connecticut Valley fur trade. This was without doubt a highly profitable activity for him—just how profitable can be seen, once again, in the pages of the Pynchon account books. In 1655 Joseph purchased from the Pynchons some £25 worth of "trading cloth"; by the 1660s his line for that item had multiplied by four or five times. Meanwhile he was bringing out, and selling to the Pynchons, furs in commensurate quantities (e.g. "331 lbs [and] ½ of winter beaver . . . 19 lb. of beaver . . . 5 otters . . . and raccoon skins . . . 2 moose skins").[58] One incidental result of the trade was a growing familiarity with Indian ways and customs. Often thereafter the settlers would call on Joseph to take the lead in official dealings with the native population.[59]

From furs he moved on to other forms of commerce. He seems to have maintained a retail store in Northampton, supplied at least in part by the Pynchons' own business in Springfield. He sold and shipped large quantities of wheat, peas, butter, and cheese; and the range of his enterprise extended through all the Connecticut River towns, and eastward to Boston. He was part owner of the first gristmill in Northampton and sole owner of its first sawmill. He was licensed, beginning in 1661, to "keep an ordinary" and also to "sell wines or strong liquors, as need shall require." He bought and sold lands through the whole length of the valley, becoming, among other things, the largest property-holder in the town of Northfield—even though he never lived there. In 1675 he bought a warehouse and ships' wharf in Boston, and gained the privileges of a merchant of that city. When he died in 1683 he owned land and other properties in six different towns, and his total worth was well over £2,000. Moreover, he had by that time provided several of his older children with handsome "settlements" of their own.[60]

Like other successful merchants of this era, Joseph Parsons was often in court—usually as a plaintiff, but at least occasionally as a defendant. Civil

Anvil, Eastern Massachusetts, c. 1640–1660. Cast iron. H: 11 ¾ in. (29.7 cm); W: 12 ½ in. (31.7 cm); D: 7 in. (17.8 cm). *Historic Northampton.*

Joseph Parsons made his fortune through personal connections and trade. Skilled craftsmen were also a rare commodity in the seventeenth century, highly valued and sought after by frontier communities like Northampton. Descending in the Pomeroy family before being given to Historic Northampton in 1953, this anvil has been identified as that granted to Medad Pomeroy in 1660. Medad (1638–1716), whose father Eltwood (1585–1673) is also believed to have worked as a blacksmith and/or gunsmith, left his boyhood home in Windsor, Connecticut, for Northampton apparently already trained as a blacksmith at age twenty-one. The settlement of skilled craftsmen who would ply their craft for the town was encouraged and rewarded by Northampton as well as other New England towns. In 1661 the town made grants of land to Medad and other craftsmen on the condition that they continue to practice their craft for the town's benefit.

actions filed by or against him—for debt, for "unlawful distraint," for "nonperformance of covenant," and the like—are scattered through the records of several different courts. At least a few of the charges involving Joseph were more serious. In 1664, for example, he was presented and "admonished" in court for his "lascivious carriage to some women of Northampton." A few months later he was fined £5 for his "high contempt of authority" in resisting a constable's efforts to attach some of his property in another case. (Witnesses reported some "scuffling in the business, whereby blood was drawn between them." Joseph publicly acknowledged his offence, and the court abated part of his fine.) A year later Joseph was fined again "for contemptuous behavior toward the Northampton commissioners and toward the selectmen, and for disorderly carriage when the company were about the choice of military officers." These cases suggest something of his character and personal style. Defined by his own achievements as a man of authority, Joseph did not easily brook the authority of others. Energetic, shrewd, resourceful as he evidently was, he displayed a rough edge in dealings with others. He was, on all these grounds, a figure to be reckoned with.[61]

Measured from start to finish, the career of Joseph Parsons was a success story more commensurate with the milieu of the nineteenth than of the seventeenth century. His estate was the largest one probated before 1700 in all of Hampshire County. Yet there were always some reminders of his modest beginnings. For example, no public record ever identifies him with the honorific "Mr." And his two brothers, also migrants to New England, remained firmly in the ranks of average folk. Thomas Parsons was a long-time resident of Windsor, Connecticut, while Benjamin—like Joseph himself—lived first at Springfield and then at Northampton. Both were farmers, both achieved positions of respect but not preeminence in their local communities, both held property in the middle range.[62]

Of course, Mary Parsons shared the fruits of her husband's extraordinary career. Its precise effect on her cannot be discovered from any evidence now extant; however, local tradition has remembered her as being "possessed of great beauty and talents, but . . . not very amiable. . . . exclusive in the choice of her associates, and . . . of haughty manners."[63] This tradition may well reflect the antagonism of her detractors as much as the reality of her own disposition. But there are, as noted, some hints of a parallel sort in the trial testimonies themselves. And when, years later, there were renewed charges against her, Mary responded with remarkable vigor and directness. (Of this, more below.)

She was not, moreover, the only strong woman in the family: her mother, the widow Margaret Bliss, also deserves notice here. When Thomas Bliss died (in 1650), Margaret was left with the sole care of seven children still in their minority. She promptly sold her home at Hartford and moved upriver to Springfield, where daughter Mary and a grown stepson, Nathaniel, were already resident. Margaret's widowhood would last for another three decades. Her resources at the outset were relatively meagre, but she managed—*more* than managed—with what she had. She made particularly effective use of the courts. She filed, and won, lawsuits on a variety of counts and charges: for example, "for detaining her cow wrongfully"; "for damage done in her Indian corn by [the defendant's] swine"; "for [defects in] ditching and quick-setting a hedge in her meadow"; "[for] debt to the value of 35 shillings"; and (this one against the town of Springfield) "for the annoyance she receives by the passage of the water to the mill."[64] She served as guardian to at least two of her grandsons (and sometimes went into court to protect *their* interests). Her estate, when probated in 1684, came to £278—an increase of more than threefold over her husband's inventory.[65] It made an unusual record by any standards—and, for a widow, perhaps a unique one.

It seems possible, moreover, that Margaret Bliss and Mary [Bliss] Parsons were specially identified with one another. When Thomas had died intestate, it was Mary who could testify to his deathbed wish that the widow receive his estate. When the widow herself died, Mary received a personal bequest from her of "wearing clothes, bedding, and household stuff." And when Mary was first accused of practicing witchcraft, her mother undertook a direct role of support. (She may indeed have sought out the principal accuser, Sarah Bridgman, in a spirit of face-to-face challenge.)[66]

There is one additional record to consider from Mary Parsons's life—the record of her own motherhood. Here, too, her achievements were noteworthy. She bore the first of her children within a year of her marriage, and the last some twenty-five years later when she was already a grandmother. She had two sets of twins, no one of whom survived infancy, but nine of her remaining ten children reached adulthood. And so the totals read: 12 pregnancies, 14 babies delivered (and named), 9 children raised to maturity; two and one-half decades of child-bearing, and four and one-half of child-rearing. No other woman in seventeenth-century Northampton could match these figures overall.[67]

THE experience of Mary Parsons bears comparison with that of one other Northamptonite, in particular. Sarah Bridgman was the sole object of Mary's slander suit—and clearly was at the center of the suspicions, the rumors, the gossip that had associated Mary with witchcraft. The personal histories of these two women exhibit both parallels and contrasts, which reflect suggestively on their confrontation of 1655–1656.

Sarah [Lyman] Bridgman was born in the parish of High Ongar, county Essex; the record of her baptism, on February 8, 1620, is still preserved there. She was the sixth of nine children of Richard and Sarah [Osborne] Lyman. (However, three of her older siblings had died young, before she was born.)[68] In 1629 her father sold his properties in Essex, evidently having decided to emigrate from England.[69] The family did not actually leave until the summer of 1631, when they joined a group of "about sixty" passengers on the ship *Lyon* bound from London to Massachusetts Bay. This was, from the New England standpoint, a very important sailing. The ship carried Mrs. Margaret Winthrop, John Winthrop, Jr. (wife and son of the Massachusetts governor), and the Reverend John Eliot (subsequently famed as the "Apostle to the Indians")—among other notables. Its arrival in Boston occasioned salutes, celebrations, and general thanksgiving.[70] Like many of their fellow passengers the Lymans settled first in Roxbury, where Eliot was soon installed as pastor. In 1635 Richard was recorded a freeman of the Bay Colony. However, just a few weeks later he joined one of the earliest settlement parties to Connecticut. And in 1636 he was listed as a proprietor of the town of Hartford.[71]

The social position of the Lymans seems, at least initially, to have been rather high. Genealogists have attempted to give them an elaborate aristocratic pedigree; and while much of the evidence is too thin to be convincing, one impressive link—to Sir John Leman, knight, merchant, and in 1616 Lord Mayor of London—has been established by extant correspondence.[72] Tradition asserts that Richard Lyman came to New England "with considerable estate, keeping two servants." The terms of his Hartford proprietorship provide more solid evidence on this point. His share in the "undivided lands" was fixed at thirty acres, which placed him in the top quarter of all local householders. (Thomas Bliss, by contrast, was down for six acres, a bottom-quarter figure.)[73]

Yet his several changes of place and circumstance took a toll on Richard Lyman. The Reverend Eliot composed a record of early members of the Roxbury church, which included the following:

> Richard Lyman . . . came to New England in the 9th month, 1631. He brought children: Phyllis, Richard, Sarah, ——, John. He was an ancient Christian, but weak; yet after some time of trial and quickening he joined the church. When the great removal was made to Connecticut he also went, and underwent much affliction; for going toward winter, his cattle were lost in driving, and some of them never found again. And the winter being cold, and [the settlers] ill-provided, he was sick and melancholy. Yet after[ward] he had some revivings through God's mercy and died in the year 1640.[74]

Elsewhere in Eliot's list are found the names of Lyman's wife and his eldest daughter Phyllis. There was special adversity in the life of the daughter as well: "God wrought upon her heart in this land [and] she grew deaf—which disease increasing, was a great affliction to her."[75]

As Eliot noted, Richard Lyman died in 1640. His wife died about a year later—initiating for their children a period of domestic reorganization. Phyllis had already left the Lyman household in order to marry another Hartford yeoman. Before her death the widow Lyman had prepared a "note" directing that Richard, Jr. (at twenty-three, the eldest surviving son) "perform her husband's will" and take charge of his two younger brothers, John (age eighteen) and Robert (twelve).[76] Precisely how these events affected Sarah (now about twenty-one) is not clear, but her marriage to James Bridgman occurred in about 1642. Bridgman first appears in the Hartford records as the purchaser, in 1640 or 1641, of a small home-lot on the south side of town. Significantly, the land of Richard Lyman was only one lot away.[77]

The Bridgmans did not long remain at Hartford. The year 1644 found them resettled in Springfield; there they would live for an even decade. James Bridgman filled several local offices at Springfield: fence-viewer, highway overseer, constable, "presenter." Twice he was punished for small "breaches of town orders."[78] His work was divided between farming and the occasional practice of carpentry.[79] A tax-list of 1646 displays him as an average sort of property-holder—as does the record of his lands.[80]

In 1654 the Bridgmans moved once again, to join the fledgling community at Northampton. The outward manifestations of their life seem to have continued much as before: minor offices for James (constable, fence-viewer, sealer of weights and measures), scattered appearances in court (twice for debt, once for "contempt of authority" in obstructing the county marshals), a middle position in the local wealth hierarchy.[81] Meanwhile there was the usual brood of children, though with a quotient of early mortality that was higher than usual for New England families. The records of Springfield and Northampton mention eight Bridgman births, spanning the years 1643 to 1658. But only four of these children (three girls and one boy) survived infancy; the others (three boys and one girl) died at ages of two weeks, four weeks, six weeks, and nine months, respectively. Sarah Bridgman herself died at the age of about forty-seven, in 1668. A few years later James was freed from training obligations with the local militia, because of "weakness of body," and death claimed him in 1676. When his estate was probated, the inventory yielded a total value of £114.[82]

There are other threads to follow in the story of this family. In marrying James Bridgman and moving to Springfield, Sarah had separated herself from her three Lyman brothers (as well as her older sister). The brothers remained in Connecticut, leaving only modest traces in the public record, until 1655; then they removed, evidently together, to Northampton. Two of them, Richard and John, were married by this time—and well married, too. Their wives had come from substantial Connecticut families; their fathers-in-law were recognized local leaders. Richard and John Lyman would themselves assume leadership roles in Northampton. Both became selectmen, and were frequently chosen for important town committees. Both became wealthy, at least by village standards. Richard died somewhat prematurely in 1662, leaving an estate worth some £500. John lived on until 1690, when his wealth amounted to more than £900.[83]

However, the life of Robert Lyman, the youngest of the three brothers, made a strikingly different story. As a young man, Robert was frequently in court: for debt (several times), for living alone (contrary to law), for breaking into the "common pound" at Hartford. On one occasion he was indicted, convicted, and heavily fined for "gross, lascivious carriage and misdemeanor": he had tried to lure another man's wife into an adulterous relation. Eventually he married—his wife was from a Northampton family of little distinction—and fathered nine children. He continued right along to be a frequent litigant (both as plaintiff and as defendant); once he sued for slander, citing gossip that had linked him with the Devil. Robert was remembered later as a restless sort—a man unwilling to settle into regular occupations. He enjoyed hunting and fishing, and his chief contribution to the local economy was the discovery of a lead mine. He moved for a time to New Jersey, then returned to Northampton. In 1680 three of his children were taken from him by court order and placed in other families, on account of his "very low condition." Still later he was described as being in a "state of distemperature" and unable to manage his affairs. His end was not recorded; but according to family lore he froze to death on a winter's day, having wandered deep into the woods on one of his customary "rambles."[84]

Considered overall, the experience of the Lyman family presents a number of interesting variations on a theme. The theme was profound social and geographic dislocation; the variations were expressed in the eventual destinies of the individual family members. The career of Richard Lyman, the father, seems after his arrival in New England to have spiraled downward into misfortune, shrunken resources, and "melancholy." Presumably his children shared in this descent, at least for a time. Soon before and just after Richard's death his two daughters had taken husbands of very average social credentials; and their lives thereafter were generally undistinguished. Two of Richard's sons—Richard, Jr., and John—found a direct route back to wealth and local prominence. But the third son, Robert, followed a roundabout, troubled, and essentially descending course of his own making. It was as if the older pair had reclaimed the social elevation to which the Lymans were previously accustomed, while the youngest extended the slide of the father's last years. The daughters—to pursue the metaphor—had simply moved sideways.

The sequence must be further considered from the standpoint of the one Lyman who particularly concerns us here. When Sarah was nine, her parents gave up the familial home in county Essex, and when she was eleven they set sail for New England. When she was fifteen they moved, once again, to Connecticut. From this wilderness journey the family emerged with damage both to their property and to their morale (at least to the father's morale). When Sarah was twenty her father died; and a year later her mother was gone as well. She married at about twenty-two, and soon removed with her husband to Springfield. As a woman of thirty-four she made her fifth (and final) move, to Northampton.

We should remember at this point that the lifeline of Mary [Bliss] Parsons was also quite discontinuous. Like Sarah, Mary had (probably) experienced severe dislocation as a child.[85] Like Sarah, she was moved about repeatedly once her family had arrived in the New World. And also like Sarah, Mary had lived through a time when the family fortunes were much diminished and its prestige reduced. But *unlike* Sarah, Mary had effectively recovered and recouped—by marrying Joseph, and sharing in the fruits of his remarkable rise to wealth and power. It is interesting, in this connection, that local remembrance of the Parsons case has emphasized the factor of *envy*: Mary Parsons is said to have "excited jealousy" by reason of her social position, her beauty, and her "haughty" manner.[86] If jealousy is founded in embittered comparisons of self and other, then Sarah Bridgman was uniquely situated to make such comparisons—and to feel their full sting. Despite all the similarities in the early lives of these two women, their ultimate destinies were radically different. And the advantages—at least from Sarah's viewpoint—must have seemed to fall entirely on one side.

Of course, it took many years for the social distance between the Parsonses and the Bridgmans to widen to its full extent, but the trend was abundantly clear by at least 1656. Joseph Parsons was already marked as a town leader—so much so that he paid a fee in that year to avoid office and concentrate on his business affairs. And he was already prosperous, thanks in no small part to an alliance formed with the region's most eminent family, the Pynchons.

There were other points of comparison as well. On May 1, 1655, Mary Parsons gave birth to a son, Ebenezer—who was in fact the first English child born in Northampton. On the thirtieth day of the same month Sarah Bridgman also bore a son, and named him James after his father. But James Bridgman, junior, died two weeks later—under circumstances that were fully remembered in the subsequent witchcraft/slander trial. Moreover, in that same summer the Bridgmans' only surviving son (John) was stricken with a mysterious ailment of the knee. (And this, too, would be drawn into the trial proceeding.) Meanwhile Ebenezer Parsons survived and would eventually grow to adulthood—as did the three older Parsons boys.[87]

The concurrent arrival in Northampton of Sarah Bridgman's brothers—Richard, John, and Robert Lyman—should also be noticed here. Their presence might well have affected her, but in two rather different ways. On the one hand, they added familial support and strength of a sort which had been missing from her life hitherto. Perhaps at some level this made her feel emboldened

Joined chest with drawer. Possibly Northampton, Massachusetts, 1699–1720. Oak and hard pine. *Historic Northampton.*

Household furnishings of most seventeenth-century households, even those of wealthy families like the Parsonses, were sparse. Chests like this one were highly prized. About sixty-five "Hadley" chests still exist. These chests are decorated with shallow carving laid out with templates, in the form of the generic motif composed of a leaf and tulip, along with a variety of freehand carved motifs used as embellishments or fillers. Histories of ownership of these Hadley chests are poorly documented, and although various hands can be recognized on the basis of carving quirks and drawer construction, only this example and five related chests have been convincingly traced to a single town or origin, Northampton. Four of the chests are carved with the full name of the girl or young woman for whom they were made. The "Sarah Strong" chest was made for a girl born in Northampton between 1695 and 1698. In addition to the repeated generic motif, this chest displays large *fleurs-de-lis* on the drawer fronts and outer facade panels with strange quatrefoil designs. The maker also tended to fill voids and compensate for poor spacing of lettering with an odd calligraphic, an incised squiggle.

to act on her suspicions of Mary Parsons. On the other hand, the evident prosperity and distinction of the two eldest brothers may also have called attention to Sarah's far more humble circumstances. They were in the process of reclaiming the Lyman birthright, but what of *her*?

THE birthright issue can hardly have applied in the case of the other trial participants. There was no one else, among all the Northampton settlers, whose experience of social dislocation approached that of Sarah Bridgman, her Lyman brothers, and Mary and Joseph Parsons.[88] Hence, it would be misleading to construe the entire episode from this standpoint. Each side in the dispute had its own cast of supporting players, and they, too, merit some consideration.

As noted earlier, the trial proceedings expressed a sharp contest for advantage lasting through the summer of 1656. At the outset the two sides were almost evenly matched; by the end the plaintiff had pulled well ahead. But to say this is to deal only with numbers; what, in addition, can be learned about the distribution of social quality, about rank and prestige? Twelve persons joined initially with Sarah Bridgman, and when studied in relation to a social profile of the entire citizenry they divide as follows: nine came from the lowest status-group (bottom third), and three from the middle (second third); there were none at all from the top (first third).[89] The pattern for Mary Parsons supporters was notably different. The largest number—five of nine—represented the topmost group; there was also one from the middle and three from the bottom.[90] As the proceedings developed, five of those who had initially witnessed for Bridgman switched to Parsons; and all five were bottom-third. An important element of social process is thus quite clearly suggested. The weight of rank was on the side of the plaintiff from the beginning. And it may have tipped the balance for several lesser participants.

We must consider, second, the special role of women on the defendant's side. Honor Hannum, Joanna Branch, and Hannah Langdon had all for a time supported Sarah in her suspicions of the "witch": together they formed the gossip-group from which particular allegations moved out to the larger community. As noted, Sarah Bridgman's concern with witchcraft ran strongly to illness and death in children, hence the parental status of her allies is also of some interest. In 1656 Honor Hannum was a woman in her early or middle forties, married, and the mother of five children (the youngest being about five years old). Hannah Langdon was approximately the same age, and had at least five children of her own (the youngest being about four). Joanna Branch was in her late thirties, married—and childless.[91] In short, each of these women had reason to be preoccupied with the matter of child-bearing. In two cases child-bearing had recently ended; in the third it had never materialized at all. There was the basis here for some personal resonance to the claims and charges that Sarah Bridgman would ultimately bring forward.

We should reemphasize, finally, the ambivalent setting of these events in a geographic sense. Both the plaintiff and the defendant had come to Northampton after several years' residence in Springfield. Six of the defendant's supporters still lived in Springfield, and two others had done so previously. By contrast, all but one of those on the plaintiff's side were Northampton residents, and all but that same one had come to Northampton from towns and villages in Connecticut. (The exception was John Pynchon, friend and business partner of Joseph Parsons.) The Springfield connections of this entire case seem, therefore, abundantly clear.

In fact, Springfield had experienced a protracted period of agitation about witchcraft going back at least seven years. The apparent start was a slander case in 1649, mentioned briefly earlier in this chapter: the widow Marshfield vs. Mary Parsons (no kin to the Northampton "witch"), "for reporting her to be suspected for a witch."[92] Two years later the court heard formal charges of witchcraft against this same Mary Parsons and against her husband Hugh.[93] It seems, moreover, that there were additional suspects whose identity can no longer be discovered. The contemporary chronicler Edward Johnson included in his *Wonder-Working Providence* the following note about Springfield: "There hath of late been more than one or two in this town greatly suspected of witchcraft, yet they have used much diligence, both for the finding them out, and for the Lord's assisting them against their witchery: yet they have, as is supposed, bewitched not a few persons, among whom [are] two of the reverend elder's children."[94] And a correspondent "from Natick in New England," writing for a London newspaper in 1651, described "sad frowns of the Lord upon us, chiefly in regard of fascinations and witchcraft. . . . Four in Springfield were detected, whereof one was executed for murder of her own child, and was doubtless a witch; another is condemned, a third under trial, a fourth under suspicion."[95]

Mary [Bliss] Parsons was herself deeply affected by these proceedings. She suffered fits (though beyond the usual age for such experiences); she roamed about in a distracted manner; she talked of encounters with evil "spirits." This was, assuredly, a difficult period in her life. She had borne twin sons in the summer of 1649 and seen both of them die soon thereafter. Her father, Thomas Bliss, had also died, apparently during the succeeding winter. Her relation to her husband was somewhat troubled. And her neighbors—judging from their later testimony—regarded her with a certain wariness. The records do not reveal Sarah Bridgman's impressions of all this, but presumably she followed it with interest. And she did not forget it upon moving to Northampton.

MARY PARSONS was successful in the trial of 1656, but the animus which had prompted this proceeding would not go away. Her name was cleared, but only from the legal standpoint. In the years that followed, her husband prospered ever more greatly, her children grew in number and (mostly) flourished, her mother and brothers sank the Bliss family roots deep into the Connecticut Valley. But her reputation for witchcraft hung on.

In 1674 the whole matter was renewed in court—with the important difference that now Mary Parsons was cast as defendant. Unfortunately, most of the evidence from this later case has disappeared. All that survives is the summary material from the dockets of the two courts involved. Still, it is possible to reconstruct the sequence of events in at least a skeletal form—and to discover some important lines of connection to the witchcraft/slander action of eighteen years previous.[96]

In August 1674 a young woman of Northampton, Mary Bartlett, had died rather suddenly. She was twenty-two, the wife of Samuel Bartlett, and the mother of an infant son. More important in the present connection was her family of origin: she was a daughter of James and Sarah [Lyman] Bridgman. Her husband and father jointly believed, as they later testified in court, "she came to her end by some unlawful and unnatural means, . . . viz. by means of some evil instrument." And they had distinct ideas about the *person* most likely to have used such means.

On September 29 the Hampshire County Court received "diverse testimonies" on the matter. Samuel Bartlett came forward "to show the grounds of his fears and suspicion." James Bridgman sent a statement "entreating that diligent inquisition may be made concerning the death of . . . his daughter." And Mary Parsons was also there—on her own initiative: "She having intimation that such things were bruited abroad, and that she should be called in question . . . she voluntarily made her appearance in court, desiring to clear herself of such an execrable crime." The court examined her, considered all the evidence, and deferred further action to its next meeting in November. There followed a second deferral "for special reasons" (about which the court did not elaborate).

On January 5, 1675, the county magistrates conducted their most extended hearing of the case. The previous depositions were reviewed, and (apparently) some new ones were taken. Both Samuel Bartlett and Mary Parsons were present in person once again. Mary was "called to speak for herself, [and] she did assert her own innocency, often mentioning . . . how clear she was of such a crime, and that the righteous God knew her innocency—with whom she had left her cause." Bartlett, meanwhile, produced testimonies both "many and various, some of them being demonstrations of witchcraft, and others sorely reflecting upon Mary Parsons as being guilty that way." The magistrates decided that final jurisdiction in such matters belonged not to them but to the Court of Assistants in Boston. Still, considering "the season" and "the remoteness" (i.e., of their own court from Boston) and "the difficulties, if not incapabilities, of persons there to appear," they determined to do their utmost "in inquiring into the case." Among other things, they appointed a committee of "soberdized, chaste women" to conduct a body-search on Mary Parsons, to see "whether any marks of witchcraft might appear." (The result was "an account" which the court did not disclose.) Eventually, all the documents were gathered and forwarded to Boston, with a covering letter from "the worshipful Major Pynchon to the governor." Joseph Parsons was ordered to pay bond "for his wife's appearance . . . if required . . . before the governor or magistrates or Court of Assistants."[97]

At the same court, and apparently as part of the same proceeding, "some testimony" was offered "reflecting on John Parsons." John was Mary's second son; he was twenty-four at the time, and as yet unmarried. How and why he should have been implicated in the charges against his mother cannot now be discovered; but the evidence was in any case unpersuasive. The court did "not find . . . any such weight whereby he should be prosecuted on suspicion of witchcraft" and discharged him accordingly.[98]

Meanwhile the case against Mary Parsons moved toward its final round. On March 2, Mary was taken to Boston, "presented" at the Court of Assistants, and formally indicted by the grand jury. Thereupon the court ordered her commitment to prison until "her further trial." The trial came some ten weeks later (May 13, 1675). An imposing roster of Assistants lined the bench: the governor, the deputy governor, and a dozen magistrates (including her husband's old associate, John Pynchon). However, her fate rested with "the jury of trials for life and death"—twelve men, of no particular distinction, from Boston and the surrounding towns. The indictment was read one last time: "Mary Parsons, the wife of Joseph Parsons . . . being instigated by the Devil, hath . . . entered into familiarity with the Devil, and committed several acts of witchcraft on the person or persons of one or more." The evidence in the case was also read. And "the prisoner at the bar, holding up her hand and pleading not guilty, . . . [put] herself on her trial."

The tension of this moment must have been very great, but it does not come through in the final, spare notation of the court recorder: "The jury brought in their verdict. They found her not guilty. And so she was discharged."[99]

The social underpinnings of this later trial are largely obscured, since the depositional evidence is gone. We do know of the key roles played by James Bridgman and Mary [Bridgman] Bartlett, and this by itself establishes an unmistakable connection with the proceedings of two decades previous. The participation of Samuel Bartlett is on its face more difficult to explain. Samuel's father, Robert, had helped in the earlier case to *defend* Mary Parsons. On the other hand, there is evidence of conflict between the two families in the interim; and Samuel's "great grief" over the loss of his wife must have exerted an influence all its own.[100]

Otherwise we can simply update our picture of the "witch" herself. She was now, for one thing, a woman in her middle years. She had borne her last child (two years previously), and her eldest had already reached maturity. She had thus joined the age-group most frequently associated with witchcraft. Her social and economic rank was, of course, fully established: there was no longer the aspect of rapidly increasing advantage. In wealth alone the

Parsonses stood far above all their Northampton neighbors. Indeed, the magistrates who presided in Mary's trial were no more than her peers. Some of them knew her personally, and the rest would surely have known *of* her. To see such a figure held for many weeks in prison, and then standing "at the bar" as defendant, must have been highly affecting.

And yet, perhaps there remained some doubt about her qualifications for high rank. She was still the daughter of Thomas Bliss, erstwhile "inhabitant" of Hartford, Connecticut. She was still Goodwife—not Mrs.—Mary Parsons.[101] She seems to have been illiterate, or at least unable to write (even her name).[102] She was not a member of the Northampton church. (By contrast, her husband Joseph had been admitted to membership when the church was founded in 1661. So, too, had most of her antagonists in the 1656 trial—not excluding Sarah Bridgman.)[103] And was there also some lingering antipathy to her on more personal grounds? Her impulse, for example, to confront her accusers directly and "voluntarily" in the 1674 trial seems courageous in retrospect; but it may have left a different impression among her own peers. Perhaps, *in context*, this was a woman too assertive for her own good.

OF MARY'S life subsequent to 1674 there is little direct information. She and her husband would eventually give up their home in Northampton and move (back) to Springfield. Joseph Parsons would die in 1683, and Mary—like her own mother—would enter a very long widowhood. She remained thereafter in Springfield, completed the rearing of her numerous progeny, and saw her sons—and then her grandsons—assume positions of prominence in several Connecticut Valley towns. Death claimed her in January 1712, when she was about eighty-five years old.[104]

She was not again tried for witchcraft, but neither was she free from local suspicion. Some writers have surmised that she was blamed for the death, under mysterious circumstances, of a Northampton neighbor in 1678. (The court investigated this death but returned no indictments.)[105] And there is one last, indirect—but telling—sign of her vulnerability to gossip of witchcraft. It comes from the record of the local court for a session held on January 9, 1702:

> Mr. Peletiah Clover complaining against Betty Negro for bad language striking his son Peletiah, who came and was present—charging Betty that she told him that his grandmother had killed two persons over the river, and had killed Mrs. Pynchon and half-killed the Colonel, and that his mother was half a witch. To which Richard White and Tom Negro gave in evidence that she said on Monday night, the fifth of this instant January, when then Betty owned it [that] she had so said, etc.
>
> We find her very culpable for her base tongue and words as aforesaid. . . . We sentence said Betty to be well whipped on the naked body by the constable

with ten lashes well laid on: which was performed accordingly by constable Thomas Bliss. . . .

Present: John Pynchon, Justice [of the] Peace; [Joseph] Parsons, Justice [of the] Peace.[106]

There are some familiar names here. The first of the justices was the same John Pynchon who had joined Joseph Parsons in many business ventures—and who had participated directly in both of the trial proceedings around Mary Parsons's witchcraft. The other justice was the first Joseph Parsons's son and namesake—and a man of great prominence in the affairs of Northampton during the opening decades of the eighteenth century.[107] The constable, Thomas Bliss, was the grandson of the emigrant Thomas; he was also, therefore, Mary Parsons's nephew.

But who were the Peletiah Glovers, father and son? And who was the grandmother alleged to have "killed two persons over the river"? The answer is easily discovered—and, at this point, is hardly surprising. Mr. Peletiah Glover was a Springfield merchant of much wealth and prominence; his son, Peletiah, junior, was a boy of fourteen. The wife and mother in this family was Mrs. Hannah Glover— née Hannah *Parsons*.[108] And she, in turn, was the daughter of (the first) Joseph Parsons. It was Hannah's maternal inheritance that made her, in Betty Negro's words, "half a witch." By this reckoning Mary Parsons still counted as a full-blooded specimen.

NOTES

1. Essex County Court Papers: Original Depositions and Other Materials from the Proceedings of the Quarterly Courts of Essex County, MA (Essex County Courthouse, Salem), XXVII, leaf 128.

2. Essex County Court Papers, XXVII, leaf 121.

3. *Records and Files of the Quarterly Courts of Essex County, Massachusetts* (Salem), 1911–1978, 2:157.

4. *Quarterly Courts of Essex County,* 2:246.

5. New London County Court Records, III, leaf 38 (Connecticut State Library, Hartford).

6. Middlesex Court Files: Original Depositions and Other Materials from the Proceedings of the Quarterly Courts of Middlesex County, MA (Middlesex County Courthouse, East Cambridge), folder 34, paper 2300.

7. Essex County Court Papers, VI, leaf 33.

8. Middlesex Court Files, folder 45, paper not numbered.

9. Connecticut Colonial Probate Records, III (County Court, 1663–1677), paper 35 (Connecticut State Library, Hartford). For additional materials in this case see Connecticut Archives: Crimes and Misdemeanors, Series I (1662–1789), I, part one, papers 8, 9 (Connecticut State Library, Hartford).

10. *Quarterly Courts of Essex County*, 7:46, 49.

11. Connecticut Colonial Probate Records, III (County Court, 1663–1677), paper 128.

12. See Charles Thornton Libby, ed., *Province and Court Records of Maine*, 4 vols. (Portland, 1929–1958), 2:86.

13. James Phinney Baxter, ed., *Documentary History of the State of Maine*, 2nd series (Portland, 1869), 4:168–169.

14. Mrs. Elizabeth Godman vs. Mr. Stephen Goodyear et al. (August 4, 1653), in Charles J. Hoadly, ed., *Records of the Colony or Jurisdiction of New Haven* 2 vols. (New Haven, CT, 1857–1858), 2:30.

15. Noted in the Pynchon Court Record in Joseph H. Smith, ed., *Colonial Justice in Western Massachusetts* (Cambridge, MA, 1961), 219–220.

16. *Quarterly Courts of Essex County*, 1:301, 325.

17. County Court, Norfolk: Records, 1648–1678, leaf 22.

18. Hoadly, *Records*, 2:34.

19. County Court, Salem: *Records*, 1648–1655, leaves 28, 33; Essex County Court Papers, I, leaf 71; Hoadly, *Records*, 12: leaves 86–87.

20. See, for example, Godman vs. Goodyear et al., in Hoadly, *Records*, 2:30. Another such case occurred in Cambridge, MA, in 1659–1660, in connection with widow Winifred Holman. (See Middlesex County Court Records, 1:165; Middlesex Court Files, folder 25, papers 1468–1480.)

21. Twenty-six cases of witchcraft/slander are noted in records still extant from early New England. Six were terminated short of a verdict ("nonsuited"). Fifteen were decided in favor of the plaintiff. And the remaining five were decided for the defendant.

22. Middlesex County Court Records, 1:91, 92.

23. Middlesex Court Files, folder 16, papers 626, 646–674.

24. Middlesex Court Files, folder 16, paper 658.

25. Middlesex Court Files, folder 16, papers 666, 662, 672.

26. Middlesex Court Files, folder 16, paper 665.

27. Middlesex Court Files, folder 16, paper 665.

28. Middlesex Court Files, folder 16, paper 665.

29. Middlesex Court Files, folder 16, paper 664.

30. Middlesex Court Files, folder 16, paper 665.

31. Middlesex Court Files, folder 16, papers 673, 659, 661, 660, 668.

32. Middlesex Court Files, folder 16, papers 669, 673, 663.

33. Deposition by Simon Beamon, September 19, 1656 (Autograph File, Houghton Library, Harvard University); Middlesex Court Files, folder 16, paper 674.

34. Middlesex Court Files, folder 16, paper 674.

35. Middlesex Court Files, folder 16, papers 646, 672.

36. The reference here is to Hannah Langdon; see Middlesex Court Files, folder 16, paper 666.

37. Middlesex Court Files, folder 16, papers 665, 674.

38. Middlesex Court Files, folder 16, paper 665.

39. There is no extant document which directly establishes a birth date for Mary Parsons. However, the medical journal of John Winthrop, Jr., in a reference from the year 1666, calls her "about 40." (See the extracts from the journal printed in the *American Genealogist* 24 [1948]: 45.) This estimate is consistent also with the year of her marriage (1646) and the year of the birth of her last child (1672).

40. The most recent genealogical account of the Bliss family is found in the *American Genealogist* 52 (1976): 193–197. For earlier accounts (also useful) see Mary Lovering Holman, *Ancestry of Colonel John Harrington Stevens and His Wife Frances Helen Miller* (Concord, NH, 1948), 345–347; Mary Walton Ferris, *Dawes-Gates Ancestral Lines*, 2 vols. (n.p., 1931), 2:123–127; and John Homer Bliss, *Genealogy of the Bliss Family in America* (Boston, 1881).

41. Bliss, *Genealogy of the Bliss Family*, 22.

42. In February 1640 "Thomas Blysse" of Mount Wollaston was granted lands in proportion to his family of "9 heads." (See *Second Report of the Record Commissioners of the City of Boston, Containing the Boston Records, 1634–1660, and the Book of Possessions* [Boston, 1881], 50.) Some genealogists have been disposed to regard this as referring to a second Thomas Bliss, who was subsequently settled at Rehoboth. However, the date and the indicated family size seem to make a better fit with our Thomas (the father of Mary).

43. Connecticut Historical Society, *Collections*, 14:256–258 (Hartford).

44. The names of Thomas Bliss, Sr., and Thomas Bliss, Jr., were included in a list of "such inhabitants as were granted lots to have only at the town's courtesy, with liberty to fetch wood and keep swine or cows by proportion on the common." This list was entered in the Hartford Book of Distributions, immediately after the names of the regular proprietors ("such inhabitants as have rights in undivided lands"). See Connecticut Historical Society, *Collections*, 6:16–20. There is reason to think that members of the non-proprietary group were subsequently accorded some rights in undivided lands, for their names appear on a list of grantees receiving "lots" on the east side of the Connecticut River in 1641. (See Connecticut Historical Society, *Collections*, 6:49–53.) There was also a special grant to Thomas Bliss, Sr., made in March 1641 (Connecticut Historical Society, *Collections*, 6:48).

45. The court case is noted in the records of the Particular Court for May 21, 1647: "In the action of Bliss, plaintiff, against Lyman and Arnold, the defendants are to pay 20 shillings and costs of court." (See *Records of the Particular Court of Connecticut, 1639–1663*, 22:46 [Connecticut Historical Society, *Collections*].) The defendants are not further identified, but the Lyman name is of obvious interest here. At a minimum, this case shows direct (and adversary) involvement between members of the Bliss and Lyman families almost a decade before Mary [Bliss] Parsons opposed Sarah [Lyman] Bridgman in the witchcraft/slander trial at Northampton. On the prosecution of Thomas Bliss for failure to attend military training, see *Records of the Particular Court of Connecticut, 1639–1663*, 45.

46. The lands of Thomas Bliss are listed in full in Connecticut Historical Society, *Collections*, 6:256–258. His share in the special division of lots on the east side of the town was 6 acres. He was, in fact, one of 24 persons to receive a 6-acre portion. There were 110 other Hartford inhabitants who received lots larger than this, and only 12 with smaller portions. (See Connecticut Historical Society, *Collections*, 6:49–53.)

47. For the inventory of Thomas Bliss's estate, and the actions of the court in dealing with it, see Colonial Records of Connecticut, 55:28 (Connecticut State Library, Hartford).

48. Mary [Bliss] Parsons was by this time living at Springfield. Apparently she had returned to visit her parents during her father's last illness. See Colonial Records of Connecticut, 55:28.

49. This story is fully recounted in Bliss, *Genealogy of the Bliss Family*, 16–20—where it is described as belonging to "the ancient traditions of the Bliss family." Genealogists have not been willing to accept it without some documentary confirmation; indeed they have advanced at least two alternative theories of the Bliss origins. One of these links the family with the parish of Daventry in Northamptonshire; however, the Thomas Bliss found there was almost certainly the Rehoboth—rather than the Hartford—settler. A more recent study proposes a connection to the village of Redborough in Gloucestershire—yet here, too, there are difficulties. (On these points, see Charles Arthur Hoppin, *The Bliss Book* [Boston, 1913]; and Myrtle Stevens Hyde, "Thomas and Margaret Hulins Bliss of Hartford Connecticut," in *American Genealogist* 52 (1976): 193–197.) The case for holding to the "traditional" account (preserved by succeeding Bliss generations) depends on the very richness and intricacy of that account; it is hard to imagine so much information having been put together so elaborately with no historical foundation at all. (On the other hand, it is equally hard to feel confident about particular details.) There is the additional, and intriguing, point that a Belstone link for the Blisses would bring their origins and those of Joseph Parsons into very close proximity. Not only do Belstone and Great Torrington belong to the same county (Devon); they also belong to the same part of that county. It is thus not improbable that Joseph Parsons and Mary Bliss should have formed their relation (at least in part) on a feeling of common origins—and not impossible that their families were previously known to each other in Old England.

50. The basis for this supposition is a letter from a great-nephew of Joseph's, the Reverend Jonathan Parsons, dated October 20, 1769. Addressing his own son, the Reverend Jonathan writes as follows about the family origins: "I will tell you as near as my memory enables me (as I have no record of the matter but what I heard from my parents). I suppose my great-grandfather Parsons came from Great Torrington about 20 or 30 miles from Tiverton and not far from Exeter. He came over and brought my grandfather, Benjamin Parsons, and other children, about 130 years ago, perhaps 140." This letter is published in the *New England Historical and Genealogical Register* 12 (1858): 175. The year of Joseph Parsons's birth is inferred from his testimony in a Northampton court case of 1662. He stated therein that he was about seventeen at the time of witnessing William Pynchon's land purchase of 1636. On this point, see Holman, *Ancestry of Colonel John Harrington Stevens*, 338.

51. On this transaction, see Ferris, *Dawes-Gates Ancestral Lines*, 2:625.

52. The most exhaustive extant study of the Parsons genealogy has established a connection by marriage between an Essex branch of the family and a first cousin of William Pynchon. However, the link between the Essex and the Devonshire Parsonses remains problematic. See Henry M. Burt, *Cornet Joseph Parsons* (Garden City, NY, 1898), 93.

53. Pynchon Account Books, 1:100 (Manuscript volume in the Judd Manuscripts, Forbes Library, Northampton).

54. Pynchon Account Books, 1:100.

55. The list is printed in Henry M. Burt, *The First Century in the History of Springfield*, 2 vols. (Springfield, 1898), 1:190–191.

56. These details of Joseph Parsons's life are more fully explored in Burt, *Cornet Joseph Parsons*, 13–15.

57. On the public life of Joseph Parsons at Northampton, see Burt, *Cornet Joseph*

Parsons, 43–44, 49–51, 56–57; and Ferris, *Dawes-Gates Ancestral Lines*, 2:627ff. For original material see the Town Records of Northampton, 1: passim (manuscript volume at the Town Hall, Northampton).

58. Most of the extensive Parsons-Pynchon dealings, as noted in the Pynchon Account Books, have been excerpted and printed in Burt, *Cornet Joseph Parsons*, 18–42.

59. As noted in Burt, *Cornet Joseph Parsons*, 57, and Ferris, *Dawes-Gates Ancestral Lines*, 2:629.

60. The inventory of Joseph Parsons's estate, as presented to a county court on March 25, 1684, is printed in Burt, *Cornet Joseph Parsons*, 66–68. The decedent had left no will, and so the court was asked to ratify an elaborate settlement formulated by his survivors; this, too, is in Burt, *Cornet Joseph Parsons*, 68–71. Of his business activities the fullest record is found in the Pynchon Account Books. His role as proprietor of a "store" at Northampton is evidenced by the scope and bulk of his orders from Pynchon—many of which had nothing to do with the fur trade (e.g., "6 lbs. sugar . . . 1 lb. pepper . . . 3 doz. gr[ea]t silk buttons . . . 1 doz. awl blades . . . 3 inkhorns . . . 3 doz. small scissors . . . 200 of 8d. nails . . ." and an enormous variety of fabric types). The geographical range of his dealings is clear from occasional references, in his account with Pynchon, to other persons and communities (e.g., "Received for what I allow you [Joseph Parsons] for fetching your goods from Hartford"; "Paid for you to Goodman Bissell [of Windsor]"; "Joseph Parsons, debtor: 10 shillings in money at Boston"). On these points, see the extracts from the Pynchon Account Book, in Burt, *Cornet Joseph Parsons*, 18–42. On Parsons's role as ordinary-keeper, mill-owner, and land speculator, see Ferris, *Dawes-Gates Ancestral Lines*, 2:628–630.

61. A number of the court cases involving Joseph Parsons are described in Burt, *Cornet Joseph Parsons*, 51–56. See also the Pynchon Court Record, in Smith, *Colonial Justice in Western Massachusetts*, 221–222, 238, 295; *Records of the Particular Court of Connecticut, 1639–1663*, 79–80; Hampshire County Probate Records, (manuscript volumes in the Town Hall, Northampton), 1:34, 39–40, and passim.

62. For brief summaries of the careers of Benjamin and Thomas Parsons, see Burt, *Cornet Joseph Parsons*, 78, 105.

63. See Ferris, Dawes-Gates Ancestral Lines, 2:634.

64. Pynchon Court Record, in Smith, *Colonial Justice in Western Massachusetts*, 96, 230, 290, 250.

65. Smith, *Colonial Justice in Western Massachusetts*, 234, 298. The will of Margaret Bliss is printed in Holman, *Ancestry of Colonel John Harrington Stevens*, 346–347. The manuscript copy of her inventory is in Hampshire County Probate Records, 2:22.

66. Colonial Records of Connecticut, 55:28; Holman, *Ancestry of Colonel John Harrington Stevens*, 346; deposition by Margaret Bliss, June 20, 1656, in Middlesex Court Files, folder 16, paper 662.

67. On the names and birth-dates of Mary Parsons's children, see Ferris, *Dawes-Gates Ancestral Lines*, 2:636. The comparison with other Northampton families is based on a variety of genealogical works, and on family reconstitution carried out by the author.

68. The most concise, and most reliable, source of genealogical information about the Lyman family is Holman, *Ancestry of Colonel John Harrington Stevens*, 383–387.

69. See Holman, *Ancestry of Colonel John Harrington Stevens*, 384. The sale of Richard Lyman's properties covered "two messuages, a garden, orchard and diverse lands arable, also a meadow and pasture." At about the same time Richard's brother, Henry Lyman, sold property in a neighboring village; hence it appears that the two of them had decided to emigrate together. But Henry died soon after arriving in New England.

70. A partial list of passengers for this sailing is found in Charles Edward Banks, *The Planters of the Commonwealth* (Baltimore, 1972), 94–95. The ship's arrival was noted in the journal of Governor Winthrop himself. See J. K. Hosmer, ed., *Winthrop's Journal*, 2 vols. (New York, 1908), 1:70.

71. Connecticut Historical Society, *Collections*, 6:18–19.

72. The most ambitious attempt to provide the Lymans with aristocratic connections is found in Coleman Lyman, *Genealogy of the Lyman Family in Great Britain and America* (Albany, NY, 1872), part one. Other genealogists have noted errors in this work which undercut many of its conclusions. (See, for example, L. E. deForest and A. L. deForest, *Moore and Allied Families* [New York, 1938], 348.) However, there are some letters, still extant, in which Elizabeth Lyman, the widow of Henry (and thus a sister-in-law of Richard), addresses Sir John Leman as "kinsman." See Holman, *Ancestry of Colonel John Harrington Stevens*, 383.

73. Lyman, *Genealogy of the Lyman Family*, 36; Connecticut Historical Society, *Collections*, 6:22–23. There is one other point of comparison between Richard Lyman and Thomas Bliss with respect to property. Richard's "home-lot" was three acres large; Thomas's was two roods, i.e., approximately one-half an acre. See Connecticut Historical Society, *Collections*, 14:256, 271.

74. This passage is quoted in Holman, *Ancestry of Colonel John Harrington Stevens*, 384.

75. Holman, *Ancestry of Colonel John Harrington Stevens*, 384.

76. Richard Lyman's estate yielded a total value of about £83. His will, the inventory of his estate, and the "note" left by his wife before her decrease, are printed in J. Hammond Trumbull and Charles J. Hoadly, eds., *The Public Records of the Colony of Connecticut*, 15 vols. (Hartford, 1850–1890), 1:442–444.

77. The earliest references to Hartford lands belonging to James Bridgman are in Connecticut Historical Society, *Collections*, 14:297, 570. The proximity of Bridgman's home-lot to that of the Lymans can be inferred from the descriptions of their respective boundaries; see Connecticut Historical Society, *Collections*, 14:271, 570.

78. A short summary of this part of James Bridgman's life as reconstructed from scattered references in the town records of Springfield and elsewhere is found in Burt Nichols Bridgman and Joseph Clark Bridgman, *Genealogy of the Bridgman Family* (Hyde Park, MA, 1894), 9–12. See also the Pynchon Court Record, in Smith, *Colonial Justice in Western Massachusetts*, 215, 220, 221, 229.

79. Antiquarians and genealogists have long supposed that James Bridgman was by trade a carpenter. This idea finds confirmation in the Pynchon Account Books, where James is credited with services such as "the making of 2 bedsteads"; "sawing planks for the mill"; and "5 days in joiner's work." See Pynchon Account Books, 1:69–71.

80. The tax-list is printed in Burt, *The First Century in the History of Springfield*, 1:190–191. The lands owned by James Bridgman at the time of his death are described in the inventory of his estate, as printed in Bridgman and Bridgman, *Genealogy of the Bridgman Family*, 13–14.

81. Bridgman and Bridgman, *Genealogy of the Bridgman Family*, 11–13. For original materials, see the Town Records of Northampton, 1: passim, and the Pynchon Court Record, in Smith, *Colonial Justice in Western Massachusetts*, 219, 239, 261. The assessment of James Bridgman's wealth, in relation to that of his fellow townsmen, is based in part on the list of proprietary holdings in James Trumbull, *The History of Northampton, Mass.* (Northampton, 1898), 145–147.

82. On these points see Bridgman and Bridgman, *Genealogy of the Bridgman Family*, passim.

83. Scattered material on the experience of the Lyman brothers during the period 1642–1656 is found in the *Records of the Particular Court of Connecticut, 1639–1663*, 18, 46, 83, 120, 122, 136, 151, 158, 161. A list of the mill-rates paid by Hartford inhabitants between 1655 and 1657 finds all three Lymans included for the first of these years, but not for the other two. This dates their departure for Northampton in a definite way. (See Connecticut Historical Society, *Collections*, 14:495–497.) On the brothers' marriages see Holman, *Ancestry of Colonel John Harrington Stevens*, 385–386. On the public careers of Richard and John Lyman at Northampton, see deForest and deForest, *Moore and Allied Families*, 348–354; Lyman, *Genealogy of the Lyman Family*, 35–40; and original materials in the Town Records of Northampton, 1: passim. For the inventory of Richard Lyman, see Hampshire County Probate Records, 1:14–17; on John Lyman's inventory, see Lyman, *Genealogy of the Lyman Family*, 40–41.

84. Robert Lyman's court cases are noted in *Records of the Particular Court of Connecticut, 1639–1663*, 22:136, 211, 256; the Pynchon Court Record, in Smith, *Colonial Justice in Western Massachusetts*, 248; and Hampshire County Probate Records, 1:68 and passim. There is a good short account of his life in Lyman, *Genealogy of the Lyman Family*, 42–44. Court orders for putting out his children, and ensuring his own subsistence, are found in Hampshire County Probate Records, vol. 1.

85. Of course, the early parts of this sequence—as recounted here, from Bliss family "traditions"—lack documentary confirmation. However, even if one sets aside their story of suffering in the face of religious persecution, the themes of "dislocation" for Mary [Bliss] Parsons, and of contrast between her experience and that of Sarah [Lyman] Bridgman, remain intact. There was, in short, sufficient dislocation in her *New* England experience to support the central argument of this essay.

86. See Trumbull, *The History of Northampton, Mass.*, 51–52; Ferris, *Dawes-Gates Ancestral Lines*, 2:634; Judd Manuscripts, Northampton volumes, 1:47; 2:170.

87. The sense of ill fate concerning her motherhood may have continued to reverberate in Sarah during the succeeding winter and spring. Her next child, born in January 1657, must have been conceived in April 1656. This implies an interval of some ten months between the death of the one infant and the start of the next pregnancy. Was Sarah, during this period, perhaps doubtful about her prospects of conceiving again—and, if doubtful, then doubly resentful against Mary Parsons? She must, moreover, have discovered her new pregnancy in May or June of 1656—a discovery which could well have excited new anxieties. (Would *this* baby survive any more easily

than the previous one?) The summer of 1656 was, of course, the time when the crisis in her relation to Mary Parsons reached its ultimate stage (at least from the legal standpoint).

88. This conclusion is based on extensive work in family reconstitution, covering the entire population of Northampton in the settlement years.

89. These totals, it will be noticed, do not precisely conform to some of the figures presented earlier in the chapter (see Middlesex Court Files, folder 16, papers 665, 666, 674). The discrepancy reflects a slight shift of viewpoint. The first set of figures embraced actual deponents in the 1656 court case. This second set involves all persons who can be identified as taking one or the other side; it thus includes a few who did not, so far as we know, actually testify in court. Note, too, that *both* sets exclude persons related to the two principals by blood or marriage.

90. The status rankings summarized here are based on a method of analysis more fully described elsewhere. (See Demos, *Entertaining Satan*, 242–245.) Once again, members of the principals' families are not included.

91. Family reconstitution by the author.

92. See note 15.

93. There is a useful summary of this earlier Parsons case in Mason A. Green, *Springfield: 1636–1686* (Springfield, 1888), 101–109. Many original depositions survive, and are found now in the manuscript holdings of the New York Public Library; they are also printed in Samuel G. Drake, *Annals of Witchcraft in New England* (New York, 1869), 219–258.

94. Edward Johnson, *Wonder-Working Providence*, ed. William F. Poole (Andover, MA, 1867), 199.

95. This letter, published in the *Mercurius Publicus* on September 25, 1651, is quoted in Justin Winsor, *Memorial History of Boston, including Suffolk County, Massachusetts, 1630–1880* (Boston, 1880–1881), 1:137.

96. Summaries of the hearings held by the county court in this case are found in Hampshire County Probate Records, 1:158–160. A slightly edited version is published in Trumbull, *The History of Northampton, Mass.*, 230–231.

97. See Trumbull, *The History of Northampton, Mass.*, 231.

98. Hampshire County Probate Records, 1:160.

99. The actions of the Court of Assistants in this case are summarized in John Noble and John F. Cronin, eds., *Records of the Court of Assistants of the Colony of Massachusetts Bay, 1630–1692*, 3 vols. (Boston, 1901–1928), 1:31, 33.

100. The evidence of conflict between the Bartlett and Parsons families comes from court records for the 1660s and 1670s. In 1664, for example, Joseph Parsons was prosecuted—and convicted—at court on a charge of "opposing and resisting the constable of Northampton in [the] execution of his office and work." The constable in question was Robert Bartlett; and the evidence showed "some scuffling in the business, whereby blood was drawn between them." In the end Bartlett, too, was judged responsible—apparently for being over-zealous in his efforts to subdue Parsons—and both men were ordered to pay fines. For another case, involving an (unspecified) slander, between the two families, see Parsons vs. Bartlett, Hampshire County Court Records, 1:26 (American Antiquarian Society, Worcester, MA).

101. There is one extant reference to Mary Parsons which does include the prefix "Mrs."; however, it comes from the very last years of her life—long after the period

of her court cases around witchcraft. See the Pynchon Court Record, in Smith, *Colonial Justice in Western Massachusetts*, 374.

102. The inference of her illiteracy was made by Sylvester Judd, in preparing his detailed notes on Northampton history. See the Judd Manuscripts, Northampton volumes, 2:170. There is apparent confirmation in the Pynchon Court Record, in Smith, *Colonial Justice in Western Massachusetts*, 374.

103. A list of members of the Northampton church is printed in Trumbull, *The History of Northampton, Mass.*, 106–107.

104. The date of her death is given in Holman, *Ancestry of Colonel John Harrington Stevens*, 338.

105. The death in question was that of John Stebbins of Northampton. For the court's action in the matter, see Hampshire County Probate Records, 1:201. An argument that Mary Parsons may have been a suspect in this case as well is made in a short article by Alice Manning, "Witches in the Connecticut Valley: A Historical Perspective," in *Daily Hampshire Gazette*, December 15, 1976, 35.

106. The Pynchon Court Record, in Smith, *Colonial Justice in Western Massachusetts*, 375. It is interesting to find that the defendant had charged the boy's grandmother with having "killed Mrs. Pynchon and half killed the Colonel." Mrs. Amy [Willys] Pynchon had, in fact, died three years previously. Her husband Colonel John Pynchon would himself die another year hence—and perhaps he already seemed much weakened. (He was at the time more than eighty years old.)

107. On the career of this Joseph Parsons, see Holman, *Ancestry of Colonel John Harrington Stevens*, 340.

108. For information on the family of Mr. Peletiah Glover, see Burt, *The First Century in the History of Springfield*, 1:110–111.

4

THE stability of the half-century following King Philip's War was a marked contrast to the turbulent period of settlement. This era was characterized by the long and influential reign of Solomon Stoddard as minister to the congregation at Northampton. Solomon Stoddard preached his first sermon in Northampton in 1669. From then until his death sixty years later in 1729, he maintained a position of influence that went far beyond the boundaries of Hampshire County and left a lasting imprint on New England Puritanism. A graduate of Harvard College and its first librarian, Stoddard entered the ministry in a time of crisis for the Puritan community in New England. The first generation of church members was passing away, and their children showed little interest in meeting the rigorous requirements for church membership. Since church membership was a prerequisite for citizenship, the foundation for a New England theocracy was undermined. Stoddard was champion of the "Half-Way Covenant," a means by which children of members could be baptized and remain as half-members until they were able to demonstrate religious conversion. But Stoddard went even further. By 1677 he was no longer recording whether his parishioners were full members or half-way members, thereby opening the privileges of membership, including citizenship, to all who would join.

When Stoddard came to Northampton, he married Elizabeth Mather, the widow of the former minister. In 1684, they built their house on Round Hill at the site of what is now known as "The Manse." The Stoddard family maintained its influential role in valley affairs through intermarriage within a select circle, including the prominent Williams family. By the end of the seventeenth century, a pattern of alliances developed throughout the region as ministers and their offspring married into the families of well-connected merchants and magistrates. These powerful families, who came to be known as the "River Gods," dominated the social, economic, and political destinies of Northampton and the Connecticut River Valley for the next hundred years.

Through his study of the Williams family of Hatfield, Kevin Sweeney shows us how this extensive kinship network developed and sustained its influence in Northampton and throughout the valley.

The River Gods in the Making*

KEVIN M. SWEENEY

DURING the eighteenth century, the towns along the Connecticut River in western Massachusetts produced a succession of imposing aristocratic leaders, who came to be known as the "river gods." These men were part of a self-conscious gentry elite that embodied the region's clerical, political, and military leadership. Between 1733 and 1774, seven interrelated families—the Ashleys, the Dwights, the Partridges, the Porters, the Pynchons, the Stoddards, and the Williamses and their in-laws—led the Hampshire Association of Ministers, controlled the county courts, commanded the local militia regiments, and represented the region in the general court in Boston. They owed their near monopoly of county offices to their families' prestige and influence; holding public offices, in turn, enhanced their own prestige and power. It was an almost self-perpetuating system, and by the 1760s the youngest members of these gentry families could look back on three unbroken generations of leadership in Hampshire County.

The most prolific and versatile of these gentry families were the Williamses. The Williams family's rise to prominence in the river towns of western Massachusetts embodies the story of the entire elite's rise and eventual fall. Marriage bound the Williamses closely to the six other gentry families; and three generations of public service tied the fate of the Williams clan to the changing fortunes of the ministry, the military, and the magistracy—the three institutional bases of the gentry's power in Hampshire County. The Williams family's story also makes clear the intimate relationship between the region's development and its elite, for the gentry class of which the Williamses were a part was the product of a distinctive region, a region that was for much of the colonial period both a relatively isolated military frontier and a cultural crossroads where the Bay and the River met. The gentry families that succeeded in this region, as the Williamses did, did so by identifying themselves with the region's particular religious outlook, by acting as intermediaries who preserved ties with both eastern Massachusetts and the Connecticut Colony, and by satisfying a need for military leadership.

The lives of the first Williamses to settle in the Connecticut Valley were shaped by choices made in Roxbury in eastern Massachusetts by the two initial generations of the family. Early Williams family patriarchs built up ample estates and preserved them for succeeding generations by devising settle-

* From Kevin M. Sweeney, "River Gods in the Making: The Williamses of Western Massachusetts," in Peter Benes, ed., *The Bay and the River: 1600–1900*, vol. 6, *Annual Proceedings of the Dublin Seminar for New England Folklife* (Boston, 1981).

ments that successfully balanced the desires of numerous sons with the needs of elderly parents. Williams fathers gave elder sons land, money, or an education as they came of age. Middle sons were given college educations or lands in eastern Connecticut. The youngest sons usually remained on the family homestead to care for aging parents and to inherit the family patrimony.[1] This apparently conscious practice of ultimogeniture minimized friction between generations and among siblings and preserved the family's cohesion and wealth across generations. The skillful maintenance of family patrimonies ensured the inner continuity of the lineal family over time and gave individuals a basis for attaining positions of leadership. The pattern of residency resulting from the family's estate practices also provided the Williamses in western Massachusetts with useful connections in both Connecticut and eastern Massachusetts.[2]

The first Williamses to settle in western Massachusetts, the Reverends William and John Williams, established themselves in Hatfield and Deerfield in the 1680s. The Reverends Williams won recognition throughout New England as pastors and preachers: John Williams's account of his sufferings after the 1704 Deerfield massacre, *The Redeemed Captive Returning to Zion* (1707), became a New England "bestseller." The two cousins also made the most of their family legacies and of their clerical offices to lay the economic foundations for the clan's eventual position of pre-eminence in Hampshire County. Though rural ministers often had a hard time collecting their rather modest salaries, they did receive from their towns such capital assets as generous land grants, houses and barns, and, on occasion, slaves bought at public expense. In time such assets accrued in value. Between 1725 and 1750, ten ministers died in Hampshire County, and at least seven of them left estates that ranked among the top 10 percent in the county in terms of wealth.[3] Included among these seven ministers were the Reverends John and William Williams, both of whom, in the words of a descendant, "with mean Sallarys, brought up 4 sons Each, to College, and left them and their other Children something pretty to remember Them [by]."[4] Williams offspring who settled into pastorates in western Massachusetts and eastern Connecticut also did well financially for themselves and for their children.[5]

In addition to putting their families on a sound economic footing, the Reverends Williams allied themselves by marriage to the Reverend Solomon Stoddard of Northampton. The marriages bound the Williamses to an important network of Connecticut Valley clergymen and attested to their support for Stoddard's style of clerical leadership, which was both authoritarian and prophetic, presbyterian in substance yet evangelical in content. Stoddard made his reputation as a "soul winner," but he maintained throughout his life that "authority must be kept up—and that we [ministers] must take heed that we don't Suffer people to trample upon us."[6] The impact of Stoddard's ideas on the region and the Connecticut Valley's affinity for revivalism were due in part to the loyalty, intellectual conviction, and fervor with which the Reverends Williams and their offspring and in-laws followed Stoddard's lead.

After Stoddard's death in 1729, William Williams was recognized as Hampshire County's clerical leader and spokesman for the network of Stoddard kin and in-laws that defended the county's commitment to a modified presbyterianism and evangelical Calvinism.[7] Foes in Boston gave him a backhanded compliment by calling him the bishop of the "see of Hampshire," while at the same time admitting that his intellectual powers often outshone those of

Embroidered picture. Esther Stoddard (1738–1816). Boston, possibly completed at Northampton, c. 1750–1760. Wool and silk on linen ground. H: 21 in.; W: 17 in. *Historic Northampton.*

Esther Stoddard's beautifully worked picture is typical of a large group of canvas-work pictures embroidered in Boston in the mid-eighteenth century by the daughters of prominent and prosperous New England families. The pictures are all meticulously worked in tent stitch on fine linen canvas and are linked together by a number of characteristic motifs which are repeated many times, often rearranged within each picture in fresh and individual ways. Some of the motifs were also used in more traditional samplers made at late as 1800.

Esther would have arrived in Boston after the death in 1747 of Mrs. Susannah Condy, who has long been associated with the design of many Boston canvas-work pictures. She returned to Northampton and died there, unmarried, in 1816. This may not have been Esther's only attempt at stylish embroidery, for there are also a splendid silk embroidered coat of arms of the Stoddard family and an embroidered silk apron both at Historic Northampton, probably worked by either Esther or her sister Prudence.

his father-in-law Stoddard.[8] In 1735 William Williams and his son Elisha Williams, rector of Yale, mobilized their kin to block the ordination of Robert Breck, who was suspected of holding Arminian views. Six of the seven Hampshire ministers opposing Breck were part of the extended network of Stoddard's relatives and in-laws which included the Williamses.[9] Additional support came from the Williamses and their kin in eastern Connecticut, who raised money, wrote letters, and lobbied to block Breck's Springfield ordination.[10] Two offspring, the Reverends Warham and William Williams, junior, who had settled in eastern Massachusetts, did not sympathize with the efforts to prevent Breck's ordination and were upset by Boston ministers' criticism of their kinsmen's actions.[11] Geographical distance and the attraction of competing cultural values could strain the bonds of kinship.

The campaign to keep Breck and his ideas out of Hampshire County eventually failed, but the effort demonstrated the Williamses' commitment to Calvinistic orthodoxy and helped to prepare for the evangelical revival that started in western Massachusetts and spread to eastern Connecticut during 1735. Several historians have noted the connection between the revival's beginning and the opposition to Arminianism;[12] it can also be argued that the mobilization of opposition to Breck in Windham County explains, in part, the rapid spread of the revival into eastern Connecticut. It is evident that several of the Williamses and their kin in Hampshire and Windham Counties followed the Reverend Jonathan Edwards's lead and preached to encourage conversions.[13]

The Williamses in western Massachusetts and Connecticut also promoted revivalism during the Great Awakening of the early 1740s. They followed the progress of George Whitefield, the itinerant revivalist, and invited him to Hampshire County.[14] In the wake of the "Grand Itinerant's" visit to the valley, they preached, exchanged pulpits, organized revival meetings, and comforted those under distress.[15] And when the legislatures of Massachusetts and Connecticut selected election day preachers during the spring of 1741, they both called upon Williamses to explain the surprising work of God.[16]

At the same time, the Williamses strove to uphold Solomon Stoddard's commitment to open communion in church admissions. When their cousin the Reverend Jonathan Edwards publicly changed his views on the question of church admissions and denied Stoddard's legacy by attempting to end open admission practices in the Northampton church, the Williams ministers and their clerical and lay kin actively challenged Edwards's position and encouraged those who worked for his dismissal.[17] Though it is clear that Edwards's parishioners needed no outside encouragement,[18] the Williamses did provide important intellectual and political support and once again affirmed their adherence to the entirety of Solomon Stoddard's legacy of open communion and evangelical Calvinism.

The Williamses' adherence to Stoddard's views on ecclesiology and theology and the family's own clerical background in Hampshire County influenced the membership and character of the county's political leadership. Beginning in the 1730s, Colonel John Stoddard, the Reverend Solomon's son, used his ties to royal governors and his patronage powers to fashion a political elite

Small bowl. China, 1745–1760. Porcelain. *Historic Northampton.*

Prior to the Revolution few valley inhabitants owned expensive porcelains imported from China. References to chinaware or "cheney ware" in seventeenth-century and early eighteenth-century estate inventories are rare and confined exclusively to the estates of the wealthiest. In this class was the Northampton lawyer, Major Joseph Hawley (1723–1788), the original owner of this bowl. As the eldest son of Lieutenant Joseph and Rebecca Stoddard Hawley and the grandson of Northampton's powerful minister, the Reverend Solomon Stoddard, Hawley was assured high rank in Northampton society. Hawley studied theology under his cousin Jonathan Edwards, and served as chaplain during the French and Indian War. He was actively involved in civic affairs, serving as Northampton's representative to the General Court and in other lesser offices. Although the inventory of Hawley's estate does not survive, his will from 1788 records a gift of about one thousand acres of land to the inhabitants of Northampton for use to support a school. This small bowl or slop dish is decorated with blue under the glaze and red over the glaze. It was probably used to contain wasted tea leaves. Waste bowls, or slop dishes, begin to appear with some frequency in estate inventories about 1745 and reflect the increased interest in tea drinking in the Connecticut Valley. This bowl was probably part of a larger tea service used by Hawley to entertain guests, and is the earliest known porcelain form with a history of ownership in the Connecticut Valley in Massachusetts, a reflection of the rarity of this precious material at the time.

that was suited to his conservative political temperament and in agreement with his father's views on religious matters.[19] While members of seven interrelated families shared the colonel's favors, Stoddard's in-laws and the Williamses were especially favored, and they looked upon Colonel Stoddard as the "great benefactor."[20] When Stoddard died in 1748, Colonel Israel Williams assumed his uncle's role as chief distributor of gubernatorial patronage in Hampshire County. Colonel Israel advanced his kinsmen in office and encouraged the continued growth of an elite whose members were distinguished from their Hampshire neighbors by their family backgrounds, education, wealth, and commercial interests. From 1733 to 1774 members of the seven families and their in-laws filled 91 percent of the posts in the upper echelons of the county magistracy, provided half of the representatives who sat for the county's towns in the general court, and provided five of the six county residents elevated to the Governor's Council.[21] In the House of Representatives, the Hampshire County delegates constituted a recognizable voting block favoring a tight money policy and supporting military spending.[22]

While power groups comparable to the river gods of Hampshire County existed elsewhere in rural New England, a quick glance at the upper echelons of the magistracy in the neighboring counties of Worcester and Hartford underscores the special regional characteristics of the river gods' style of leadership. In both neighboring counties a relatively small group of interrelated families obtained a majority of the appointments as county judges, probate judges, and justices of the peace and quorum. Four families—the Chandlers, the Wards, the Wilders, and the Willards—and their in-laws accounted for fifteen of the nineteen appointments made in Worcester County between 1731 and 1774; and these families and their in-laws provided the six county residents who sat on the Governor's Council during the period.[23] In Hartford County, Connecticut, six interrelated families—the Allyns, the Chesters, the Pitkins, the Talcotts, the Wellses, and the Wolcotts—and their in-laws provided sixteen of thirty-one individuals who were chosen as county judges, probate judges, and justices of the peace and quorum and eight of the sixteen Hartford County residents elected to the Court of Assistants.[24] Wealth, college educations, family backgrounds, and commercial interests set these Worcester and Hartford justices apart from their neighbors and allied them to gentry families in Hampshire. Williamses from Hatfield and John Stoddard married into the Chester family of Wethersfield, Connecticut; and two generations of Porters from Hadley married into the Pitkin family of East Hartford, Connecticut.[25] Because of the similarities among the gentry elites, members of these families were able to retain their status and access to office while moving from one county to another, even across colony borders.[26]

Yet despite the connections and despite the obvious similarities among the gentry elites in the three counties, it is possible to distinguish the river gods from their colleagues and kin in the neighboring counties. The family backgrounds of the elite groups differed significantly during the period from 1732 to 1774. Worcester's gentry families initially sprang from yeoman farmers who became large landowners or merchants; half of Hartford County's magistrates could trace their ancestry directly to the colony's founding magistrates; Hampshire County contained gentry families that could trace their origins to yeomen and seventeenth-century magistrates and, most significantly, to clergymen, which is not surprising given John Stoddard's role in choosing county magistrates.[27] In fact, neither of the six leading families in Hartford nor the four prominent families in Worcester were founded by ministers; and throughout the period under study, Worcester's gentry families had few close ties by either blood or marriage to the local clergy.[28] The close ties of Hampshire's magistrates to the clergy help explain their involvement in such matters as the effort to block Robert Breck's ordination in 1735 and the dismissal of Jonathan Edwards in 1750 and probably account for the allusion to divinity in the term "river god."[29]

Another pattern distinguishing the Hampshire elite from the gentry in the neighboring counties was educational background. Hampshire's leading magistrates were more likely to have college degrees: 52 percent had college degrees in Hampshire County; 42 percent had college degrees in Worcester County; and only 32 percent had college degrees in Hartford County.[30] Hampshire County's college graduates were equally divided between the alumni of Harvard and Yale, and this pattern continued when they sent sons off to college. Even during the 1760s the Williamses sent sons to Harvard. Worcester's magistrates and their sons went almost exclusively to Harvard, and Hartford County's preference was, not surprisingly, for Yale. In each case the choice of colleges reflected the region's broader cultural orientation, and the divided preferences of the Hampshire magistracy reflected the dual cultural orientation and the need to maintain ties with both eastern Massachusetts and Connecticut.

Finally and most significantly, Hampshire County's magistrates were much more likely to hold military commissions and to participate actively in military affairs during the 1740s and 1750s. In Hampshire County almost three quarters of the gentry elite held field grade commissions—the rank of colonel, lieutenant colonel, or major—in the militia or the expeditionary forces raised to invade Canada; in Worcester County two-thirds held similar commissions; and in Hartford County only one-half of the higher magistrates held commissions, and most of these commissions were in the militia.[31] Active participation in Connecticut's expeditionary forces could actually hurt one's political career. Joseph Spencer, probate judge for the Haddam district, was temporarily replaced because of his participation in a military campaign; and General Phineas Lyman of Suffield probably lost his seat on the Court of

Assistants in 1759 as a direct result of the absences caused by his active military service.[32] Just the opposite was the case in Worcester and Hampshire Counties, where members of the gentry maintained and advanced their political careers by military service; failure to accept the responsibilities of military command could diminish one's stature. When Eleazer Porter of Hadley hesitated to assume command after Colonel Stoddard's death in 1748, he was ridiculed by Hampshire residents and replaced by Israel Williams, who had acted decisively.[33]

For Colonel Williams and his kin, control of the county militia regiments and control over the expeditionary forces raised and stationed in western Massachusetts gave the river gods their distinctive claims to leadership and the resources to sustain the claims. As long as Hampshire County remained an endangered military frontier, many of its residents depended for their survival and economic well-being on the colony's military establishments. Unlike militia officers in eastern Massachusetts and Connecticut, the colonels and captains who commanded Hampshire County's militiamen performed as active military officers, organized frontier defenses, raised expeditionary forces, mobilized logistical support for provincial troops, and on occasion led them in the field. Military rank was coveted, and in western Massachusetts successful officers were looked up to and respected. When the citizen soldiers in the militia and expeditionary forces, particularly those in Hampshire's exposed frontier towns, answered the call to arms, turned their backs on their homes and families, and marched off to face an uncertain fate, they in a very real sense voted with their feet. When the freemen of Hampshire County voted with ballots or with their hands for selectmen and representatives, they tended to vote for their commissioned and noncommissioned officers.

Military commissions brought their holders other rewards and advantages. Commissions in expeditionary regiments and in garrison companies stationed in forts along the Hampshire frontier gave officers a steady income and a financial incentive to raise troops.[34] Merchants who secured appointments as sub-commissaries received ready access to government bills of credit and the use of much-needed operating capital. During the 1740s and 1750s, four Williamses and two of their in-laws served as sub-commissaries. Military commissions and commissary contracts offered holders the opportunity to reap financial rewards beyond those allowed by the government. In addition to such mundane practices as inflating accounts submitted to the government, members of the Williams family concocted some rather imaginative schemes to use underemployed soldiers and unspent government funds for personal gain.[35]

Their control of the county's militia and of the expeditionary forces raised in Hampshire County gave the river gods extensive patronage powers. Acting as sub-commissaries, members of the Williams family decided which producers

Side chair. Central Hampshire County, Massachusetts, 1770–1800. Cherry and maple. H: 38 ½ in.; W: 20 ½ in.; D: 16 ½ in. Gift of Mina Wood. *Historic Northampton.*

Patronage of the valley gentry supported regional artisans. Framed chairs, or chairs with rectangular mortise-and-tenoned seat rails, were the most fashionable and expensive seating furniture made in the Connecticut Valley during the eighteenth century. This example, made to be upholstered over the rails, is possibly the product of an anonymous Northampton cabinetmaker. The construction of the seat rails seems experimental and suggests that the maker was unfamiliar with the standard construction of framed chairs. A secondary rear seat rail is mortised into the side rails. The upholstery is affixed to it instead of to the rail between the stiles and covered with the shoe at the base of the splat. The donor of the chair, Mina E. Wood (d. 1944), was a descendent of John Wood (1753–1832) of Buckland and Colrain, northwest of Deerfield, and was also related to the Lyman and Wright families.

would sell goods to the troops. They also decided where the troops would be billeted. In the especially favored towns of Deerfield and Hatfield, the direct and indirect beneficiaries of the favors bestowed by the Williamses at government expense included a substantial portion of the population. Self-interest thus reinforced existing patterns of deference and brought artisans and humble yeomen into a network based on favor and reciprocal services.[36]

Control of military offices enabled the river gods to influence matters beyond their hometowns. The Reverend Jonathan Edwards, a man who knew well the power of the Williams clan and its reach, claimed that Colonel Israel Williams's influence on "the principle [*sic*] men in the neighboring towns" could be traced directly to his being the "chief Colonel of the regiment, [for] all other military officers are dependent on him."[37] In fact some 150 officers in the Hampshire militia regiments and recipients of 250 to 300 commissions in the provincial forces that went to Hampshire County men during the 1740s and 1750s were indebted to Colonel Israel Williams or his predecessor Colonel John Stoddard.[38] In the most exposed frontier towns, residents whose survival depended on outside military assistance referred to Colonel Williams as "our father," and usually adopted a deferential attitude when dealing with him.[39] Because of their ability to direct the disposition of soldiers, military disbursements, and officers' commissions, Colonels Stoddard and Williams were able to consolidate the Williams clan's dominance in the towns of Deerfield, Hatfield, and Stockbridge and to extend its influence beyond the boundaries of the family bailiwicks and throughout the county.

This system of deference and reciprocal relations was severely strained during the later 1750s as warfare dragged on and stirred up opposition to the clique of Williamses that directed and often profited from Hampshire County's war effort. Foes of the Williamses formed alliances with opposition factions in the Massachusetts General Court and for a time won the assistance of the royal governor, Thomas Pownall. The disputes did not irreparably damage the Williams family's prominent position, but the contention did carry with it intimations of the river gods' political mortality. The political power of the river gods ultimately rested on their roles as intermediaries between the river towns and the authorities in Boston. When they lost support in Hampshire County while authorities in Boston simultaneously withheld their support, there were no parties to mediate between; the Williamses and their allies became irrelevant and vulnerable.[40]

The termination of the fighting in North America in 1760 ended the political conflict engendered by the war, and during the early 1760s the Williamses assumed an apparently unassailable position in Hampshire County. After some difficulties adjusting to the loss of their roles as defenders of the western frontier, most family members prospered. Income from farming and commerce added to the family's wealth. Family members speculated in undeveloped lands and spent money on houses and furnishings that set them apart from their neighbors and affirmed their identity with gentry families throughout the Connecticut River Valley.[41] They continued to act as power brokers who served as intermediaries between local residents and authorities in Boston. The Williamses and their kin enjoyed a near monopoly of appointive offices in the county; family members and in-laws accounted for eight of eighteen justices of the peace in the county and for three of four places on the common pleas bench in 1768.[42] Colonel Israel Williams sat on the Governor's Council, presided over the court of quarter sessions and over the county court of common pleas, and served as county probate judge. The colonel's political opponents in Boston invested him with the title "monarch of Hampshire."[43]

The story of the Williams family does not end with the achievement of unchallenged power. The political power accumulated by members of the clan slipped through their hands not long after they secured it. Close ties with the royal government in Boston turned into a deadly embrace in the 1770s. Because of the family's dependence on and support of royal authority, the Williamses lost the favor of voters in local elections; and when the royal government was swept away, they lost their hold on the county magistracy.[44] With the loss of office and the taint of loyalism went the loss of power, influence, and prestige; and some Williamses experienced financial hardship as well.[45]

It would be wrong, however, to attribute the Williams family's ultimate demise solely to the Revolution. In a sense the family's position had begun to decline before the Revolution, and the process continued into the early 1800s. The end of the French and Indian wars had removed the river gods' chief source of power and prestige. The waning of the clergy's influence undercut another institutional prop of the rural gentry class. Changes in the county magistracy brought about by the 1780 constitution of the newly independent state of Massachusetts prevented the recreation of the ruling clique that had controlled the county magistracy during the colonial era. Williamses of the fifth generation and their sons gained local political prominence and usually prospered, but the collective influence of the family and of the gentry class of which they were a part faded. Israel Williams's sons and grandsons never had the opportunity to establish themselves as river gods.

NOTES

1. Will of Robert Williams in Harrison Williams, *The Life, Ancestors, and Descendants of Robert Williams of Roxbury, 1607–1693* (Washington, DC, 1934), 44; will of Isaac Williams, 1708; Middlesex County Probate Records, 112:335–338; wills of Stephen Williams, 1719, and Isaac Williams II, 1738, Suffolk County Probate Records, 21:322–324, 43:119–200.

2. Bruce P. Stark, *Connecticut Signer: William Williams* (Chester, CT, 1975), 9–11; Francis S. Drake, *The Town of Roxbury: Its Memorable Persons and Places* (Boston, 1905), 20–30, 92–93, 115–120, 227–230, 235, 384–386.

3. In Ronald K. Snell, "The County Magistracy in Eighteenth-Century Massachusetts" (Ph.D. diss., Princeton University, 1971), Appendix 4, 378–379; Hampshire County Probate Records, 5:18–21, 51–61, 153–156; 6:115–117, 120–121, 129–130; 7:231–232, 262–264.

4. William Williams to William Pitkin, April 12, 1759, Williams Papers, Box 1, Connecticut Historical Society, Hartford.

5. See for example: Ebenezer Williams of Pomfret, d. 1753. *Public Records of the Colony of Connecticut* (Hartford, 1877), 10:379–382; Eleazer Williams of Mansfield, d. 1742, Windham Probate District, Docket no. 4177, Connecticut State Library, Hartford; Chester Williams of Hadley, d. 1753, Hampshire County Probate Records, 8:111–112.

6. Diary of Stephen Williams, August 10, 1721, Longmeadow Historical Society.

7. For a reassessment of William Williams's importance, see Philip F. Gura, "Sowing the Harvest: William Williams and the Great Awakening," *Journal of Presbyterian History* 56, no. 4 (winter 1979): 326–341.

8. William Cooper to Benjamin Coleman, November 25, 1735, Coleman Papers, Massachusetts Historical Society, Boston; Charles Chauncey to Ezra Stiles, May 6, 1768, *Proceedings of the Massachusetts Historical Society*, 1st series, 10 (1809): 157.

9. Diary of Stephen Williams, August 25, 1735; Elisha Williams to Stephen Williams, December 1735, Williams Papers, Beinecke Library, Yale University; Elisha Williams to Stephen Williams, June 30, 1736, Whetmore Collection, Yale University Library.

10. Diary of Stephen Williams, April 14, 1736; Eleazer Wheelock to Stephen Williams, August 26, 1735, Eleazer Wheelock Papers, no. 735476, Dartmouth College; Eleazer Wheelock to Stephen Williams, November 3, 1735, Wheelock Papers, no. 735603; Elisha Williams to Stephen Williams, November 9, 1735, Stokes Manuscripts, Yale University Library; Elisha Williams to Stephen Williams, February 7, 1737, Williams Papers, Beinecke Library, Yale University.

11. Diary of Stephen Williams, December 19, 1735, February 4, 1736, and February 28, 1736; Warham Williams to Stephen Williams, March 20, 1735, photostatic copy at Massachusetts Historical Society; Warham Williams to Stephen Williams, February 24, 1736, Gratz Collection, Historical Society of Pennsylvania, Philadelphia; Warham Williams to Stephen Williams, August 4, 1736, Gratz Collection.

12. Jonathan Edwards, *The Works of Jonathan Edwards*, ed. C. C. Goen (New Haven, CT, 1972), vol. 4, *The Great Awakening*, 17–18; Mary C. Foster, "Hampshire County, Massachusetts, 1729–1754: A Covenant Society in Transition" (Ph.D. diss., University of Michigan, 1967), 87–92.

13. Diary of Stephen Williams, February 16, 1735, and February 23, 1735; William Williams, *Directions to Such as are Concerned to Obtain a True Conversion* (Boston, 1736); Eleazer Williams, *Sensible Sinners Invited to Come to Christ* (New London, CT, 1735).

14. Diary of Stephen Williams, September 23 and 26; October 11, 14, 15, 1740; William Williams to Benjamin Coleman, July 1, 1740, Coleman Papers II, Massachusetts Historical Society.

15. Diary of Stephen Williams, June 28, July 7–9, 1741; Stephen Williams to Eleazer Wheelock, March 16, 1741, Wheelock Papers no. 741216; Solomon Williams to Eleazer Wheelock, May 8, 1741, Wheelock papers no. 741308.2; Solomon Williams to Eleazer Wheelock, May 22, 1741, Wheelock Papers no. 741322.2; Eleazer Williams to Eleazer Wheelock, December 8, 1741, Wheelock Papers no. 741658; Joseph Macchain to Eleazer Wheelock, July 20, [1742], Wheelock Papers no. 742423 Chester Williams to Jonathan Edwards, February 14, 1742, Boston Public Library.

16. Solomon Williams, *A Firm and Immovable Courage to Obey God, and An Inflexible Observation of the Laws of Religion, the Highest Wisdom and Certain Happiness of Rulers* (New London, CT, 1741), and William Williams, *God the Strength of Rulers and People, and Making Them to be so, To Each Other Mutually* (Boston, 1741).

17. Jonathan Edwards to Thomas Foxcroft, February 19, 1750, Boston Public Library; Jonathan Edwards to Sir William Pepperell, January 30, 1753, Edwards Manuscripts, Andover Newton Theological Seminary, Newton, MA.

18. Patricia Tracy, "Jonathan Edwards, Pastor: Minister and Congregation in the Eighteenth-Century Connecticut Valley" (Ph.D. diss., University of Massachusetts, 1977), 170–194.

19. Snell, "The County Magistracy in Eighteenth-Century Massachusetts," 268–285.

20. Will of Ephraim Williams, junior, 1755, in Wyllis E. Wright, ed., *Colonel Ephraim Williams: A Documentary Life* (Pittsfield, MA, 1970), 157.

21. Computed from information in the *Journals of the House of Representatives*, 50 vols. (Boston, 1919–1981); William H. Whitemore, *The Massachusetts Civil List for the Colonial and Provincial Periods, 1630–1774* (Albany, NY, 1870), 54–63.

22. Robert Zemsky, *Merchants, Farmers, and River Gods* (Boston, 1971), 32–33, 265.

23. Based on information in Kevin MacWade, "Worcester County, 1750–1774: A Study of a Provincial Patronage Elite" (Ph.D. diss., Boston University, 1974), 21–64, especially list of justices of the peace and quorum on 40–41. In my analysis I have added to the list county judges William Ward and William Jennison, who also sat during the period being analyzed.

24. Based on list of judicial office holders compiled from *Public Records of the Colony of Connecticut*, 15 vols. (Hartford, 1850–1890), vols. 8–14; H. Franklin Andrews, *The Hamlin Family: A Genealogy of Capt. Giles Hamlin of Middletown, Connecticut, 1654–1900* (Exira, IA, 1900); Bruce C. Daniels, *Connecticut's First Family: William Pitkin and His Connections* (Chester, CT, 1975); A. P. Pitkin, *Pitkin Family in America* (Hartford, 1887); S. V. Talcott, *Talcott Family Pedigree in England and America from 1558 to 1876* (Albany, NY, 1876); Chandler Wolcott, *Wolcott Genealogy: The Family of Henry Wolcott* (Rochester, NY, 1912); and Sherman W. Adams and Henry R. Stiles, *The History of Wethersfield*, 2 vols. (New York, 1904).

25. Adams and Stiles, *Wethersfield*, 2:213–214; "Family Genealogies," comp. Lucius M. Boltwood, in Sylvester Judd, *History of Hadley* (Springfield, MA, 1905), 113.

26. Joseph Dwight served as a county judge in Worcester, Hampshire, and Berkshire Counties. Elijah Williams served as a justice of the peace in Hampshire County, Massachusetts, and Hartford County, Connecticut. He also sat in the Massachusetts House of Representatives and the Connecticut General Assembly.

27. MacWade, "Worcester County, 1750–1774," 45–64; Allyns, Chesters, Hamlins, Pitkins, Talcotts, Wadsworths, Wellses, and Wolcotts all sat on the Court of Assistants during the seventeenth century; for sources see n. 24.

28. MacWade, "Worcester County, 1750–1774," 45–64; other Hartford County magistrates—John Bulkley, Joseph Buckingham, Samuel Mather, Solomon Whitman, and Elisha Williams—came from families with strong ties to the clergy.

29. In 1735 William Pynchon, junior, Colonel John Pynchon, and John Worthington brought a civil action against Breck before judges John Stoddard, Ebenezer Pomeroy, and Timothy Dwight I. Foster, "Hampshire County, Massachusetts, 1729–1754," 69–72; in 1750 Israel Williams and Oliver Partridge actively supported Jonathan Edwards's Northampton opponents; see n. 17. For the term "river gods," see "Reminiscences of Samuel D. Partridge," in Daniel W. Wells and Reuben F. Wells, *A History of Hatfield, Massachusetts* (Springfield, MA, 1910), 278, and "Recollections of Childhood" in Mary B. Dewey, ed., *Life and Letters of Catharine M. Sedgwick* (New York, 1871), 49.

30. MacWade, "Worcester County, 1750–1774," 68–69; Franklin Dexter, *Biographical Sketches of the Graduates of Yale College with Annals of College History*, 6 vols. (New York, 1885–1912); Clifford Shipton, *Biographical Sketches of Graduates of Harvard University in Cambridge, Massachusetts* (Cambridge, 1933–1975), vols. 5–17; John L. Sibley, *Biographical Sketches of Graduates of Harvard University in Cambridge, Massachusetts* (Cambridge, 1873–1885), vols. 1–3.

31. MacWade, "Worcester County, 1750–1774," 40–43; compiled from *Public Records of the Colony of Connecticut*, 6:534; 8:279–280, 441; 9:84, 213; 10:198; 11:95, 96, 336; 12:88.

32. *Public Records of the Colony of Connecticut*, 11:247, 248.

33. George Merriam, "Israel Williams: Monarch of Hampshire, 1709–1788" (Ph.D. diss., Clark University, 1961), 27–33.

34. Michael Coe, "The Line of Forts: Archeology of the Mid-Eighteenth Century on the Massachusetts Frontier," *Annual Proceedings of the Dublin Seminar for New England Folklife* (1977): *New England Historical Archeology*, 44–55.

35. William Williams, Fort Anson Account Book, 1754, William Williams Papers, Berkshire Atheneum, Pittsfield, MA; William Williams to Ephraim Williams, junior, October 25, 1754, in Wright, *Colonel Ephraim Williams*, 81; Arthur L. Perry, *Origins of Williamstown* (New York, 1894), 245–248.

36. Kevin M. Sweeney, "War on the Homefront: Politics and Patronage in Hampshire County, 1754–1760" (paper presented at Historic Deerfield Colloquium on Recent Research in Western Massachusetts History, Deerfield, MA, 1978; copy at Historic Deerfield Library), 6–11.

37. Jonathan Edwards to Thomas Foxcroft, February 19, 1750, Boston Public Library.

38. Sweeney, "War on the Homefront," tables 2 and 3.

39. Quoted in Shipton, *Graduates of Harvard*, 8:309; see also Inhabitants of Huntstown to Israel Williams, May 27, 1757, Israel Williams Papers, Massachusetts Historical Society.

40. Sweeney, "War on the Homefront," 11–28.

41. Robert Taylor, *Western Massachusetts in the Revolution* (Providence, 1954), 11–51; Kevin M. Sweeney, "Mansion People: The River Gods and Material Culture"

(paper presented at Historic Deerfield Colloquium on Material Culture in the Connecticut Valley, Deerfield, MA, 1982; copy at Historic Deerfield Library).

42. Based on Whitemore, *Massachusetts Civil List*, 92–93, 140.

43. Oxenbridge Thatcher to Benjamin Pratt [1762] in *Proceedings of the Massachusetts Historical Society*, 1st series 20 (1884): 47.

44. Taylor, *Western Massachusetts*, 52–74; Bruce G. Merritt, "Loyalism and Social Conflict in Revolutionary Deerfield, Massachusetts," *Journal of American History* 57, no. 2 (September 1970): 277–289.

45. See, for example, the fate of Israel Williams's son William, in John Williams Memoirs, Williams Papers, Box 15, Pocumtuck Valley Memorial Association, Deerfield, MA, 1.

5

SOLOMON Stoddard's handpicked successor to succeed him in the Northampton pulpit was none other than his grandson Jonathan Edwards. Jonathan Edwards is often caricatured as the stern Puritan who preached fire and brimstone sermons, such as his notorious Sinners in the Hands of an Angry God. *Yet Edwards was also America's preeminent genius of the eighteenth century. Besides being a moving force in the Great Awakening, Edwards was a relentless speculative scientist, an acute psychologist, and a world-famous theologian and philosopher.*

Edwards has inspired or provoked an enormous and ever-increasing flow of scholarly commentaries and highly specialized studies—the volume of which almost equals his own prodigious output. Some scholars, following Perry Miller, have seen the lingering shadow of Edwards's influence largely in the writings of Emerson and the transcendentalists of the mid-nineteenth century. Though most traces of Edwards's Calvinism in mainstream Protestantism were buried by the materialism of the Gilded Age, cultural historians such as Joseph Conforti show how Edwards became an icon in the "colonial revival" of the late nineteenth century, especially in Northampton, as nativist Victorians sought a usable "Puritan" past to defend Yankee traditionalism from cultural assaults. In the post–World War II era, neo-orthodox theologians resurrected Edwards from his burial by Progressive Era historians. But historians have argued that their portrayal of Edwards as an isolated genius tragically victimized by irrational forces of his own unleashing mirrored their own fears of populist politics in the McCarthy era.

In one of the most recent contributions to Edwards studies, Ronald Story examines Edwards's legacy and how it has been constructed and reconstructed over the last two centuries. Story argues that an essential element of Edwards's thought and work has been filtered out by theologians and historians alike. The "real" Edwards, Story contends, must include not only his jeremiads and his Enlightenment reflections but also his neglected writings that suggest that love of beauty, harmony, and humanity as well as fear of God have a place in the firmament.

Jonathan Edwards and the Gospel of Love

RONALD STORY

JONATHAN EDWARDS is by now almost certainly Northampton's most illustrious resident. A Yale graduate and the grandson of Solomon Stoddard, who had filled the Northampton pulpit with power and distinction for several decades, Edwards was already reasonably well known when at age twenty-three he became pastor of the town's Congregational church in 1727. But he soon made his own mark. Within a few years he was one of the foremost preachers of New England. He played a signal role in fomenting the religious enthusiasms known as the Great Awakening, which may be said to have begun in its eighteenth-century form in Northampton. He then produced numerous pamphlets and polemics that described, defended, and critiqued it. In 1741 he preached the most famous of all American sermons, *Sinners in the Hands of an Angry God*. He built up a correspondence with British divines that spread his fame. And he wrote. By 1751, when he relinquished his pulpit, he had published seven significant theological and pastoral volumes, plus many sermons and other pieces. Other theological treatises would appear before his death of smallpox at Princeton in 1758.[1]

Edwards's influence as a thinker and preacher was formidable for the next 150 years. His biography of the young David Brainerd was one of the most popular books of the nineteenth century. His great work, *Freedom of the Will*, was a major influence on generations of theologians, as was his evangelical example on generations of revivalists. New editions of his writings appeared at least every fifteen years. Nor has the pace slackened of late. After a slump in the early twentieth century, the last fifty years, and especially the last thirty, have witnessed an avalanche of biographies, critical studies, and literary appreciations and a major new edition of his collected writings from Yale University Press, which now stands at twenty-two volumes, each with the full panoply of modern scholarly and editorial support. The historical profession, the whole Protestant world, and to some degree Christendom itself, know of Jonathan Edwards—and perforce of Northampton.[2]

But if Edwards is the best known of Northamptonites, he is also the most protean and multifaceted. Perry Miller, whose 1949 biography of Edwards inaugurated the recent wave of study, saw him as the quintessential lonely Intellectual, a frontier pastor nurtured in the Calvinist tradition who also read Locke and Newton, saw the need to reconcile their insights to Calvinist precepts, and spent his life attempting to do precisely that. Having lived through a ghastly global depression and ghastlier global war, Miller admired Edwards's skepticism about the banal American faith in intrinsic goodness and inevitable progress. A Harvard scholar awash in a culture of Babbittry and materialism, Miller also admired Edwards as an exemplar of the life of the mind against all odds, struggling for understanding, grappling with non-utilitarian Ultimate Questions. And it must be said that Miller seemed especially impressed that Edwards led the life of the mind in a hick town like Northampton rather than in, say, Cambridge. Despite many revisions, this view of Edwards has largely endured. The modern Yale edition of his writings treats him first and foremost as a thinker and scholar. In the words of George Marsden, his latest and arguably finest biographer, Edwards "challenges the commonsense view of our culture that the material world is the 'real' world." Marsden calls Edwards's effort to reconcile Augustinian themes with a post-Newtonian universe "breathtaking."[3]

Others have admired not Edwards the Intellectual but Edwards the Calvinist, the "last Puritan," struggling to uphold the cardinal doctrines of the faith of the fathers—God's omnipotence, original sin, Christ's atonement, the absolute primacy of Scripture, free grace through the influx of the Holy Spirit, sanctification. It was to preserve and protect this set of beliefs that Edwards tried to reconcile Calvinism with Enlightenment thought. He spent much of his life fighting both Arminians, the Boston-centered pastors who increasingly preached salvation through good works and human will, thereby denigrating God's power, and Antinomians, the revival-inspired pastors who preached salvation through emotional experience, thereby denigrating God's expectation of saintly behavior. "To the Arminians," writes William Breitenbach in a useful formulation, "Edwards said that virtue to be true must be gracious. To the Antinomians he said that grace to be true must be virtuous." This rigorous Calvinism—its Biblicism, hostility to priestly hierarchy, opposition to earning one's way to heaven through alms—accounts in part for Edwards's pronounced anti-Catholicism. Repugnant though it is to nonbelievers (including Perry Miller) and those religious seeking a God of compassion and warmth, it was precisely his devotion to this unflinching doctrine that earned him the presidency of the College of New Jersey (Princeton) just before his death and that appealed to so many nineteenth-century followers and neo-orthodox of our own time. A sympathetic scholar calls him "the most imposing apologist for Calvinism and human depravity in United States intellectual history."[4]

Edwards the Intellectual and Calvinist. But also, and perhaps foremost, Edwards the Evangelist, progenitor of American revivalism. This persona has two sources: his role in fomenting the Great Awakening, which he described and analyzed in detail; and his extraordinary sermon, *Sinners in the Hands of an Angry God*. His famous contemporary John Wesley, whose Methodist followers set the American backcountry on fire in the nineteenth century, read Edwards's account of the Northampton "awakenings," followed their progress, imitated their methods, and acknowledged Edwards as one of the fountainheads of Protestant revivalism. So did Charles G. Finney, Presbyterian architect of the "Second Great Awakening" in the early nineteenth century, who spoke of Edwards's evangelical writings "with rapture" and called him "a great man who was famous in his day for new measures" such as the "physical agony of prayer" and a reliance on lay exhorters. These claims were much exaggerated, but they suggest Edwards's reach across the years, as do the 171,000 copies of Edwards on colonial revivals that the American Tract Society distributed between 1833 and 1875. For nineteenth-century evangelicals, he was, in Joseph Conforti's words, the "father of the Great

Awakening and of American revivalism, and embodiment of a lofty standard of evangelical piety." And while Wesley and Finney preached the unEdwardsian exercise of free will, Calvinsts even of our own day also flock to Edwards's evangelical banner, explaining the great waves of American revivalism, including that of Edwards, as the consequence not of historical conditions but of the working of the Holy Spirit.[5]

As for *Sinners*, its fame is vast. An "awakening" sermon of a type occasionally used in New England to remind dull parishioners of God's anger and the reality and danger of hell, the sermon showed how sin would doom everyone to eternal damnation except for the pleasure of God to keep them from it:

> The God that holds you over the pit of hell, much as one holds a spider, or some loathsome insect, over the fire, abhors you, and is dreadfully provoked; his wrath towards you burns like fire; he looks upon you as worthy of nothing else, but to be cast into the fire; he is of purer eyes than to bear to have you in his sight; you are ten thousand times more abominable in his eyes as the most hateful venomous serpent is in ours. . . . Oh sinner! Consider the fearful danger you are in.

An implacable and terrible imagery and message. "Before the sermon was done," wrote one attendee, "there was a great moaning and crying out throughout the whole house. What shall I do to be saved. Oh I am going to Hell. Oh what shall I do for Christ." Such "shrieks and cries" arose that Edwards had to ask for silence to continue. It was pure terror preaching, deliberately designed to coerce the wicked back to pious behavior and fear of the Lord. Isaac Watts, who printed the sermon in Britain, called it "a most terrible sermon, which should have had a word of Gospel at the end of it," and even some of Edwards's modern admirers consider it "infamous." Even so, it became much beloved of generations of hellfire revivalists who used versions of it to terrify guilt-ridden congregations into getting right with God.[6]

We have, then, Edwards as Intellectual, as Calvinist, as Evangelist. We also have Edwards as Scold—which plunges us squarely into the middle of colonial Northampton. A primary duty of a Puritan minister was to correct the sinful ways of his parishioners. They expected it, and Edwards, with his belief in original sin, high standards of piety and propriety, and willingness to invoke the threat of damnation, did not disappoint. Three episodes make the point. In 1737 Northampton built a new meetinghouse. Previously, church officers assigned seats according to age, estate, and "usefulness"—community service, military rank, and the like. In the new building, pews were assigned, after some controversy, principally by wealth—which implied, says Patricia Tracy, that property was "more respectable than old age" and worldly achievement "more laudable than experience as a humble Christian."

Edwards disagreed with this new dispensation, preached against the contentiousness and pride that underlay it, and warned the congregation: "Consider it is but a very little while before it will be all one to you whether you have sat high or low here."

In 1744 some girls in town told Edwards that young men had been reading a midwifery book, joking about the explicit descriptions and diagrams, and taunting the girls for being "nasty creatures." Long concerned about the potential waywardness of Northampton youth, about, for example, "night frolics and lascivious behavior," Edwards now preached against this instance of "lewd" sinfulness, then read a list of the names of the miscreants publicly from the pulpit. Three of them openly resisted his and the church's authority. One said he would not "worship a wig" and cared not a "turd" or a "fart" for the church authorities. Edwards afterwards expended much time and energy addressing such disrespect and "corruption."

Again in 1744 Edwards quarreled with the town about arrears in his salary. Only after bitter debates did the taxpayers agree to settle and fix the salary according to certain commodity prices. Edwards had a large family and many visitors. More urgently, he believed that the minister should have elevated status in any community calling itself Christian, and that it was "anti-ministerial" and therefore "anti-spiritual" to withhold salary. He naturally said so, both in Northampton and when he preached to surrounding congregations about their own ministers. In all three cases the community was reflecting long-term American trends—stratification in the pew controversy, landless youth beyond parental control in the "dirty book" episode, secularism in the salary squabble. Edwards saw them all as expressions of impiety and did his ministerial duty—to scold.[7]

BUT Edwards was more than just intellectual, Calvinist, evangelical, and scold. He was these, but to stop here would be misleading as to his full nature and the fullness of his mission in Northampton. For example, he preached far less about fire, as in his notorious *Sinners* sermon, than about light. This metaphor was common among New England divines, who stressed saving grace through the influx of the Holy Spirit, but Edwards, who knew his Newton and had been curious about optics as a boy, carried it to special heights. *Jesus Christ the Light of the World* (1723) was a poetic early effort. His first important published sermon (1734) was *A Divine and Supernatural Light, Immediately imparted to the Soul by the Spirit of God*, followed shortly by, among others, *Jesus Christ is the shining forth of the Father's glory*; *False Light and True*; and *Light in a Dark World, a Dark Heart*. Unlike fire, light connotes sight and insight, brightness and illumination, frequently in Edwards's sermons something of "sweetness" and even rapture, personal and collective hope rather than anxiety and dread. And light connoted Christ:

"That beauteous light with which the world is filled in a clear day is a lively shadow of [Jesus Christ's] spotless holiness and happiness."[8]

A brief passage from a 1744 ordination sermon in the poor country village of Pelham, just east of Northampton, might serve to convey just how stunning Edwards's "light" preaching could be. Note the imagery and the rhythm of the language, particularly when read aloud:

> When divine light and heat attend each other in ministers of the gospel, their light will be like the beams of the sun, that do not only convey light, but give life; and converts will be likely to spring up under their ministry, as the grass and the plants of the field under the influences of the sun; and the souls of the saints will be likely to grow, and appear beautiful as the lily and to revive as the corn, and grow as the vine, and their scent to be as the wine of Lebanon; and their light will be like to the light of Christ, which is the light of life.

This was presumably a sermon of less consequence to Edwards because it was not delivered in a significant place, either Northampton or another notable venue. It was more or less tossed off—making its power and beauty all the more remarkable and leaving an entirely different impression from the "awful" fire-and-brimstone *Sinners* sermon. "No one," says George Marsden, "looked more intensely at the biblical meaning of light for his day than did Edwards." This 1744 effort was Edwards at his most typical—and best.[9]

The standard representations likewise fail to capture the importance of beauty for Edwards. This, too, was everywhere in his thought, preaching, and writing and at every level from the ordinary to the sublime. Early on, he found the physical world—nature in the woods or fields, the stars at night, thunderclouds by day, rainbows, flowers—beautiful in its own right: "That sort of beauty which is called 'natural,' as of vines, plants, trees, etc., consists of a very complicated harmony; and all the natural motions and tendencies and figures of bodies in the universe are done according to proportion, and therein is their beauty." He appreciated that the sweetness of honey, the harmonies of music, and the excellence of a building could, like the grace, countenance, and shape of a person, be beautiful. His wife Sarah, after all, was reputed to be one of the "beauties" of the Connecticut Valley, a view that her portrait supports. Edwards wrote of "a beautiful body, a lovely proportion, a beautiful harmony of features of face, delightful airs of countenance and voice, and sweet motion and gesture," all probably with Sarah in mind. So, too, with fine mental work. There was something, he noted, "in the ideas and conceptions of great philosophers and statesmen that may be called beautiful." And perhaps of theologians as well.[10]

Music deserves a word of its own. Edwards always loved music, especially "harmony of voices." One of his major British correspondents was Isaac Watts, whose popular new hymns Edwards helped introduce to the Connecticut Valley churches in place of the cacophonous and "discordant" psalmody that still characterized provincial services. He and Sarah loved to sing, and he thought people could communicate best through music. "The best, most beautiful, and most perfect way that we have of expressing a sweet concord of mind to each other, is by music. When I would form in my mind an idea of a society in the highest degree happy, I think of them as expressing their love, their joy, and the inward concord and harmony and spiritual beauty of their souls by sweetly singing to each other." He preached on "The Sweet Harmony of Christ" amidst the early Northampton Awakening, held "singing meetings," and in one of his most affecting sermons, rhapsodized at length about the "New Song" that Christ teaches and that the saints will sing together with Christ in Heaven: "This must draw your heart, and put it into tune, and fill it with love and joy, which is the excellent harmony and heavenly melody of the soul." He used singing in Stockbridge among his Indian pupils following his dismissal from his pulpit for the same reason he fostered it in Northampton, because "sacred music has a powerful efficacy to soften the heart into tenderness" and to "harmonize the affections."[11]

But music, like other forms of worldly beauty and like light, gave a mere glimpse of the "spiritual harmonies" that accompanied grace. "Natural beauties," Edwards insisted, "only point to those higher spiritual excellencies." The beauty of human love was limited compared to that between Christ and his saints, "where new beauties are continually discovered, and more and more loveliness, and in which we shall forever increase in beauty ourselves." In *The Nature of True Virtue*, one of his major treatises, he equates virtue with "something *beautiful*, or rather some kind of *beauty* or excellence." Virtue, he says, "is the beauty of the qualities and exercises of the heart, or those actions which proceed from them." And the less self-contained and more general the beauty, the closer it comes to the whole "universal system of existence," so that to love beauty of this vast and general kind, whose traits are "consent and agreement" rather than "discord and dissent," is to love benevolence to everything and all. Such "disinterested benevolence" is the essence of virtue. And since such beauty stems from and is coterminous with the Divine Being, virtue is ultimately absolute love of the infinite beauty of God and his works and creatures. Consciousness of self is a natural part of the beautiful whole, therefore validating self-love. But "genuine virtue," he concludes, "prevents that increase of the habits of pride and sensuality," habits that were a special preoccupation of the Northampton years. The "principle of general benevolence" that Edwards spins out from his notions of the infinite beauties of God and God's world instead "softens and sweetens the mind" and makes it susceptible of "proper influence."[12] What he saw around him needed, at the very least, softening and sweetening. Beauty, in any case, is the key concept for Edwards on virtue, as it was a leitmotif in his life.

Light and Beauty, then, but also, and even more, Charity. No virtue was more important to Jonathan Edwards than charity. His Grandfather Stoddard had been known as a minister of the poor and the lowly. The grandson followed suit. "They that do good to others," Edwards preached, "shall be rewarded, whether to their souls or bodies." Doing good to others' souls was obviously a priority. But "they that do good to others' outward man shall not lose their reward, especially in ways of charity to the poor. He that gives to the poor lends to the Lord." No one claiming to be a Christian should be "backward and strait-handed towards his poor brethren," but should "abound in deeds of charity" and perform them with "cheerfulness and joyfulness." Charity and justice, argued Edwards, citing the Sermon on the Mount and the dicta of Paul and of John the Baptist, always trumped external worship as a virtue. Bowing or kneeling before God is of no use except as a sign of inner reverence. Not so with charity, the Christian's duty to the widow, the fatherless, the stranger, and the poor, which is always "significant in itself, for it is to do good." In a sermon on the occasion of a call for donations to support Northampton's poor (preached, interestingly, immediately prior to the *Sinners* sermon, which suggests a link between stinginess and the prospect of eternal damnation), Edwards showcased the generosity of the Virgin Mary, which should inform "public contributions for pious and charitable uses." Edwards himself gave much, though usually anonymously, and by his will ordered what remained of his estate after obligations and expenses distributed "to charitable uses."[13]

When charity was insufficient or niggardly, Edwards was not loath to chastise his parishioners. He scolded them for this more than for licentiousness. Although no leveler, he was "uncomfortable," says George Marsden, with the "increasingly individualistic acquisitive modern culture" that characterized New England, including Northampton, and believed that free enterprise brought out the worst in human nature. "Greedily hoarding up material wealth" seemed un-Christian, an impediment to spirituality and an obstacle to charity. Property alone would avail nothing; only the Holy Spirit arriving through undeserved free grace could get people to Heaven. The best use of property would be to help "the meek, the broken-hearted, the captive, the imprisoned"—plus, to be sure, one's minister, to free him from "worldly cares." Should the "great ones" of a congregation not respond, they should be chastised for wickedness and sin. He assailed magistrates who were "governed by their Private Interest," buying and selling "places of publick trust for private gain," and merchants who took advantage of "poor indigent people," thus committing the "violent" sin of "oppression." He assailed "wicked, debauched men" who conducted their business out of "covetousness and pride."[14]

By what measure should we judge Christian behavior? By how many poor there are in a place, Edwards preached in 1743. And how many would that be? "None." Towns had not done enough if there were any "objects of Charity suffering in pinching want." Rich men should give away one-quarter of their estates, and even that would be only "a little" in the eyes of God. For though Christ is not on earth, "yet he has left others in his room to be his receivers; and they are the poor. . . . God hath been pleased to make our needy neighbors his receivers." In 1742 he drew up a Town Covenant for his parishioners to sign. They promised, among other things, not to overreach or defraud their neighbor or cheat him, and not to rest "till we have made that restitution, or given that satisfaction, which the rules of moral equity require." (Even Perry Miller, no admirer of commercial civilization, calls this a "hard oath" for an expanding economy to observe.) In 1743 he persuaded the congregation (tantamount, remember, to the whole town) to collect funds for the poor at every Sabbath service, and he urged a "public stock"—that is to say, an early welfare system—for the poor. His message on charity therefore had significance for what passed then for public policy. As one model, he held up a pietist German whose stress on charity had produced invaluable orphanages and schools for poor children. Similarly, "rich men" should establish and support schools "in poor towns and villages."[15]

Charity, moreover, implied not only succor for the needy but reaching out, even incorporating them into the fold of the parish. This, too, had started with Stoddard, who criticized how congregations admitted the children of members to communion automatically but required newcomers and outsiders, many of them poor, to narrate their conversion experiences. Reaching out to the excluded was a hallmark of the Great Awakening, in which Northampton played a vital part. Edwards reflected that intent in his ministry. God's grace could descend on anybody, low or high: "They that are . . . not much accounted of, you see that your judgment of things is not much regarded, what you say in conversation is not so much taken notice of, your voice is not so much heard as others in publick affairs." But do not be dismayed: "Christ himself, when he was upon earth, confined himself to your condition. He did not appear in the world in the circumstances of a man of note, but in the state of the poor and despised. He was of low parentage; his mother was a woman of low degree, her husband Joseph . . . an obscure person."

Which groups would this doctrine have touched in the mid-eighteenth century? Those without place, including those without a voice and a vote in town and church affairs—the socially marginal, youth without family or property as yet, perhaps especially women. Urging the town "worms" of high station and property to be inclusive, he preached: "If one worm be a little exalted above another, by having more dust, or a bigger dunghill, . . . what a distance does he keep from those that are below him! . . . Christ condescends to wash our feet; but how would great men (or rather the bigger worms) account themselves debased by acts of far less condescension!" When Northampton voted to dismiss Edwards in 1751, only male church members voted, and not all of those. Edwards himself wrote afterwards that "many more, especially women and youths," would have supported him "if they dared." Charity involved inclusion as well as giving and fairness.[16]

LIGHT. Beauty. Charity. And underlying everything and above all, Love. Whatever his reputation, Jonathan Edwards was a powerful preacher of the gospel of love. This is almost never acknowledged or discussed, presumably because he also believed in depravity and the terrors of hell and frequently said so. But the Edwards of love leaps from the pages of his great work, *Charity and Its Fruits*, which expands upon a group of sermons he preached throughout much of the year 1738. These were commentaries on verses from 1 Corinthians, one of Edwards's favorite books of the New Testament. The sermons do two things. They instruct us to lead loving Christian lives in this world as best we can. And they offer us a picture and a definition of Heaven as a place of pure love.[17]

Edwards urged his congregation in their daily lives to an imitation of Christ. Christ loved his enemies, Edwards says, Jews and Samaritans and Romans as well as Christians. He loved people so much that he felt one with them; he made them a part of "his flesh and his bone." He so loved us all that he gave everything he had and became poor for us and traded ease and honor for suffering and degradation. Christ loved us as he loved the poor, the maimed, the halt, the blind, the empty and needy and vagabond, without ever expecting to be repaid. He was, in spite of the great injuries done to him, "meek and gentle."

And so, preached Edwards, should we love. Christian love, he said, is contrary to a selfish spirit. We must consider not only our own circumstances and necessities but those of our neighbors; regard not only our own desires but others' desires, too. We should love even those of "hateful dispositions," even the proud, the greedy, the hard, the profane, the unjust. We should not only help the poor. We should do it lovingly, "with our hand open wide" and with a charitable heart, "expecting nothing in return." Christian love will dispose us to mercy toward a neighbor who suffers "affliction or calamity." We will in this way "bear one another's burdens and weep with those that weep."

It is love, moreover, said Edwards, that will check and restrain "bitterness and heated spirits" and prevent "broils and quarrels." Love will help us to "suppress wrath, rage, resentment, revenge, bitterness" and all the monstrous passions that stir up "hatred, strife, and violence." "We do not live in heaven, or a world of purity, innocence and love," Edwards wrote. "We dwell in a fallen, corrupt, miserable, wicked world" full of malice and injury. Even so, Christian love will dispose us to peace.

Most people know Jonathan Edwards for his preaching on the fiery terrors of hell, as in the *Sinners* sermon. But this great series of love sermons, *Charity and Its Fruits*, coming between the mini-Awakening of the mid-1730s and the larger one of the early 1740s and immediately after the new meetinghouse controversy, enabled him to define hell more precisely. Hell, he argued, is a place where there is no love. It is a place deluged not with fire but with wrath and hatred and rage, a place of pride and contention and strife, of spite, treachery, fickleness, hypocrisy, and deceit, without friendship or pity or mercy. It may be the best definition of hell any minister ever offered: Hell is the place without love. Once heard, it is a difficult definition to forget.

Heaven, by contrast, is a world of perfect love. Edwards showed us his vision of Heaven in the last of these great sermons on Corinthians, entitled *Heaven Is a World of Love*. In Heaven, said Edwards, we may love God, Christ, and one another perfectly, without envy or malice or revenge or contempt or selfishness. In Heaven no one will ever be grieved that they are slighted by those they love. Nor will the joy of Heavenly love be interrupted by jealousy. "Heavenly lovers," in Edwards's words, "will have no doubt of the love of each other. All their expressions of love shall come from the bottom of their hearts."[18]

In Heaven there will be nothing to clog the exercise and expression of love—no heavy body or lump of flesh or unfit organ or inadequate tongue. We shall have no difficulty expressing our love. Our souls, "life a flame of fire with love, shall not be like a fire pent up but shall be perfectly at liberty, winged with love with no weight tied to the feet to hinder their flight." Nor will there be any wall of separation to prevent the perfect enjoyment of each other's love—neither physical distance, nor want of full acquaintance, nor misunderstanding, nor disunion through difference of temperament or circumstances or opinions or interests. We shall all be united, related to Christ, the Head of the whole society, the spouse, in Edwards's words, of the whole church of saints, which shall be a single family.

As love seeks to have the beloved for its own, so in Heaven all shall have property in one another. The saints shall be God's, preached Edwards, and he theirs. And so with Christ, who bought them with his life and gave himself to them in death. "And the saints shall be one another's." And they shall enjoy each other's love in perfect and undisturbed prosperity, without adversity or pitiful grief of spirit, and shall glory in the possession of all things in common. And Heaven will be a garden of pleasure, a paradise fitted in all respects for an abode of heavenly lovers where they may have sweet society. "The very light which shines in and fills that world is the light of love," said

Edwards. "It is beams of love; for it is the shining of the glory of the Lamb of God, that most wonderful influence of lamblike meekness and love which fills the heavenly Jerusalem with light."

And we will know such perfect love forever, with no fear that such happiness will ever end. "All things," Edwards preached, "shall flourish in an eternal youth. Age will not diminish anyone's beauty or vigor, and there love shall flourish in everyone's breast, as a living spring perpetually springing, or as a flame which never fails. And the holy pleasure shall be as a river which ever runs, and is always clear and full. There shall be no autumn or winter; every plant shall be in perpetual bloom with the same undecaying pleasantness and fragrance, always springing forth, always blossoming, always bearing fruit." He concluded:

> O what tranquility there is in such a word as this! Who can express the sweetness of this peace? What a calm is this, what a heaven of rest is here to arrive at after persons have gone through a world of storms and tempests, a world of pride, and selfishness, and envy, and malice, and scorn, and contempt, and contention, and war? What a Canaan of rest!

Jonathan Edwards did not believe that we could find perfection in this world. If hell is hatred and heaven pure love, this world is a mixture. To find true and perfect love, you have to enter Heaven, which will come only through grace. But he ended this magnificent sermon by telling us that "as heaven is a world of love, so the way to heaven is the way of love. This will prepare you for heaven, and make you ready for an inheritance with the saints in that land of light and love. And if ever you arrive at heaven, faith and love must be the wings that carry you there."

Few biographers consider the Charity sermons. Ola Winslow, Perry Miller, and Patricia Tracy do not mention them at all; Iain Murray gives them three paragraphs, George Marsden a few lines more. One reason may be that they did not appear in print until the nineteenth century; perhaps another, that they were so at odds with Edwards's conventional image. But Paul Ramsey, the editor of the Yale volume that contains *Charity and Its Fruits*, is right to argue that this is a mistake that makes it harder to understand Edwards as a whole.[19] At the very least it shows him employing a positive inducement (heaven and perfect love) to holiness as well as a negative one (hell and eternal agony). There is the pull of love as well as the push of fear to turn one to grace and sanctification. It also adds emotional substance and tangible imagery to the abstract reasoning of other works, for example, *The Nature of True Virtue*. And it draws our attention to a utopian strain of Edwards's thought, a means of resolving the thorny problems of acquisitiveness, lust, and strife, all of which melt together in the collective ownership, complex marriage, and mutual adoration of the heavenly community of the loving

Christ. Human depravity notwithstanding, one can discern here the inspirational seeds not only of Finneyite revivalism but, if more faintly, of that other spiritual blossom of the nineteenth century (which would have distressed Edwards no end), the perfectionism of John Humphrey Noyes.

Lastly, the final sermon in the series, *Heaven Is a World of Love*, gives us a piece easily equal in rhetorical power and brilliance to "Sinners in the Hands of an Angry God." Wilson Kimnach notes this sermon's "Dantean simplicity, scope, and grandeur" and speculates that "Sinners" has stolen the day for the same sensationalist reasons that the "Inferno" has eclipsed the "Paradiso": pain is more riveting than grace.[20]

Which is a pity, for "Heaven" is suffused with light and beauty and charity and love—indispensable attributes of the real Jonathan Edwards. When *Heaven* appears in as many anthologies as *Sinners* we will be closer to grasping what he meant to Northampton and the Connecticut Valley and his time and ours.

A bronze tablet with a bas-relief of Jonathan Edwards hangs on the right wall of the meetinghouse of the First Churches of Northampton on the site of Edwards's original church. Crafted by Herbert Adams and unveiled in 1900, exactly 150 years after Edwards's dismissal from his church for withholding sacraments to unjustified (in his eyes) supplicants, the bas-relief catches much of the conventional wisdom about Edwards—the high forehead of the aloof intellectual, the judging eyes of the fearsome preacher, the lofty, bewigged, unapproachable minister. When the congregation comes into the sanctuary for Sunday service, members drift almost always to the left side, away from the formidable visage on the wall. There are doubtless many reasons why people drift in this direction, not least habit. But it seems likely they are resistant, if only subconsciously, to experiencing the stare of a figure who seems perhaps ready to scold them. As he well might, should he come suddenly to life once more.[21]

But the sculpture is misleading. If you look at the picture by Joseph Badger on which the sculpture is based—the only portrait we have of Edwards—you see an open face and level gaze. There is no smile. The great divines of New England did not smile. (Being liked was not a particular virtue in America until quite recently, and certainly not among these men. God did not put them on the earth to be liked.) Yet the eyes are youthful, almost tender, the face modest, almost vulnerable. It's actually the way the bas-relief is lighted from the bottom and the deep cuts Adams uses to capture the likeness that make the eyes appear dark and glowering and judgmental and the visage stern and lofty. The impression is not exactly wrong. It simply exaggerates certain features at the expense of others, such as the open and inviting right hand at the lower left reaching to touch us. The real Jonathan Edwards, the Edwards of *Heaven Is a World of Love* as well as *Sinners in the Hands of an*

Jonathan Edwards. Herbert Adams. Bronze bas-relief, 1900. *First Churches, Northampton.*

Angry God, is like the wall sculpture. It's the lighting that history has thrown on him that makes him seem so daunting. If you look closely, you see not only the shadowy judging eyes, but also the warm loving hand.

NOTES

1. See the list of publications in Iain H. Murray, *Jonathan Edwards, A New Biography* (Edinburgh, 1987). The first careful historical biography, still serviceable, was Ola Elizabeth Winslow, *Jonathan Edwards, 1703–1758* (New York, 1940).

2. For an assessment of Edwards's influence and popularity, see, e.g., George Marsden, *Jonathan Edwards: A Life* (New Haven, CT, 2003), 8–9, 333, 446, and passim.

3. Perry Miller, *Jonathan Edwards* (New York, 1949); Marsden, *Edwards*, 503–505.

4. William Breitenbach, "Edwards and the New Divinity," in Nathan O. Hatch and Harry S. Stout, eds., *Jonathan Edwards and the American Experience* (New York, 1988), 188; Allen C. Guelzo, "Oberlin Perfectionism and Its Origins," in Stephen J. Stein, ed., *Jonathan Edwards's Writings* (Bloomington, IN, 1996), 160. A useful schematic depiction of the Edwardsian tradition is Mark Noll, "Passing the Torch," *Christian History* 22, issue 77 (2002): 26–28.

5. Joseph Conforti, *Jonathan Edwards, Religious Tradition, and American Culture* (Chapel Hill, 1995), 23, 29–30, 46, 56; Mark A. Noll, "Jonathan Edwards and Nineteenth-Century Theology," in Hatch and Stout, *Edwards*, 260–264. For a contemporary evangelical Calvinist account, see Murray, *Edwards*, 159.

6. Marsden, *Edwards*, 220–224; Winslow, *Edwards*, 193.

7. Patricia J. Tracy, *Jonathan Edwards, Pastor: Religion and Society in Eighteenth-Century Northampton* (New York, 1980), 126–128, 156–163.

8. Marsden, *Edwards*, 67; *The Works of Jonathan Edwards* [hereafter *Works*] (New Haven, 1957–), 19:799–803.

9. *The True Excellency of a Gospel Minister*, in *Works of President Edwards* (Edinburgh, 1847), 10:507; Marsden, *Edwards*, 54–55.

10. Marsden, *Edwards*, 77–78, 99, 157; *True Virtue, Works*, 8:539.

11. *True Virtue, Works*, 8:539; Marsden, *Edwards*, 106, 143–145, 245, 390; *They Sing a New Song, Works*, 22:244; *The Sweet Harmony of Christ, Works*, 19:435.

12. Marsden, *Edwards*, 79, 99, 109; *True Virtue, Works*, 8:539–543, 550, 619, and passim.

13. *Degrees of Charity, Works*, 19:626–627; *Mercy and Not Sacrifice, Works*, 22:118–126; *Mary's Remarkable Act, Works*, 22:379ff.

14. Paul R. Lucas, "The Death of the Prophet Lamented: The Legacy of Solomon Stoddard," in Stein, *Writings*, 83; Marsden, *Edwards*, 189, 259; Gerald R. McDermott, *One Holy and Happy Society: The Public Theology of Jonathan Edwards* (University Park, PA, 1992), 93–116; Miller, *Edwards*, 210.

15. Miller, *Edwards*, 210; McDermott, *One Holy and Happy Society*, 93–116; Marsden, *Edwards*, 260–261, 303–304, 344, 382.

16. Lucas, "The Death of the Prophet Lamented," 83; McDermott, *Holy and Happy Society*, 93–116; *The Excellency of Christ, Works*, 19:567. Every biographer

deals with the famous dismissal, even though it is possible to argue that it constitutes something of a molehill become mountain and that space devoted to its analysis might better be spent on other aspects of Edwards's work. Tracy, *Edwards*, 171–194, and Marsden, *Edwards*, 357–374, cover the episode most thoroughly.

17. The quotations in this and the following four paragraphs are from *Charity and Its Fruits* in *Works*, 8:135–137, 143–148, 166–173, 187–188, 194–200, 241–242, 260–262, 300–301, 357–358, and especially sermon 12, *Christian Graces Concatenated Together*, 326–338 passim.

18. The quotations in this and the following four paragraphs are from *Heaven Is a World of Love*, sermon 15 in the *Charity and Its Fruits* series, in *Works*, 8:366–397 passim.

19. Paul Ramsey, "Editor's Introduction," *Works*, 8:3. Ramsey says, "It is a major fault in any scholar to treat the charity sermons as a surd among Edwards' works." This is if anything an understatement.

20. Kimnach quoted by Ramsey in *Works*, 8:61.

21. The best reproductions of the Adams bas-relief are probably Winslow, *Edwards*, facing 266; and Richard A. Bailey, "Devoted Disciplinarian," *Christian History* 22, issue 77 (2002):16. Neither captures the effect of the bottom lighting. Every biography contains the portrait in black and white. Bailey, *Christian History*, 5, and Murray, *Edwards*, frontispiece, have good color versions.

6

THE religious fervor of the Great Awakening did not, despite Jonathan Edwards, curb the growing demand for consumer goods. But the increasing use of local craftsmen and materials to produce fashionable goods for the gentry helped ensure that these objects would not remain the exclusive possessions of the elite for long. New fashions in architecture and furniture design would become signs of status for prospering farmers and merchants, and the means of advancement for aspiring tradesmen and artisans.

The history of artisanship in early New England has long been represented by male-dominated crafts. The extent to which women contributed to the trades has only recently begun to be explored. The range of crafts plied by women varied, but clothing production was a major, if largely misunderstood, enterprise. In this compelling study, Marla Miller tells the story of Catherine Phelps Parsons, who maintained her Northampton tailoring business as a maker of men's clothing in the last half of the eighteenth century.

The View through the Eye of a Needle

Gender, Artisanry, and Craft Tradition in Early New England *

MARLA R. MILLER

IN 1769, tailor Robert Robinson reproached the gentlemen of Hartford, Connecticut, for allowing their clothing to be made by women. Placing a notice in the advertising columns of the *Connecticut Courant*, he urged readers to "count up the cost / and see how many pounds you've lost / By hiring women to cut your cloaths." Observing that any man of "wit . . . loves to see his coat cut fit," Robinson suggested that employing women in the tailor's trade necessarily meant compromising quality.[1] The disgruntled craftsman would have been no happier upriver. In that year, Catherine Phelps Parsons (1731–1798) was among those thorns in Robinson's side; she had a thriving tailor's trade in the growing commercial center of Northampton, Massachusetts, instructing so many apprentices that many of the town's early nineteenth-century needlewomen would owe their training to her.[2] Parsons's career, obliquely captured in partial transcriptions of Catherine and Simeon Parsons's account book as well as oral histories taken in the early nineteenth century by Northampton antiquarian Sylvester Judd, holds a number of lessons for

* From Marla R. Miller, "Gender, Artisanry, and Craft Tradition in Early New England: The View through the Eye of a Needle," *William and Mary Quarterly* third series, 60, no. 4 (October 2003).

historians interested in gender, artisanry, and craft tradition in eighteenth-century New England. Careful consideration of the artisanal world of this female tailor of men's clothing contributes to a larger effort to unsettle and rethink the categories that have long shaped studies of artisans as well as scholarship on rural economies and women's work. Looking at the careers of Parsons and women like her helps refine further our understanding of the shifting gender divisions of labor in the early modern Atlantic world.[3]

Among historians of women and work, a principal aim over the past twenty years or so has been to comprehend better both change and continuities in gender divisions of labor, generally as part of a larger effort to puzzle out why, despite enormous economic and social change, women on the whole continue to be relegated to the least remunerative, least secure, and least desirable jobs. One of the key insights to emerge from this collective effort is the extraordinary elasticity that the cultural construction of gender divisions of labor exhibits, demonstrating persistence as well as transformation.[4] Within this scholarship, the study of the domestic economy of early American women has flourished and significantly advanced our understanding of the "female economy."[5]

We now understand, with considerable depth and sophistication, how gendered divisions and definitions of labor in housework, in healing occupations, agricultural labor, and other early American employments shaped early American lives vis-à-vis ever-changing economic, social, cultural, and political landscapes. The economy and society of eighteenth-century New England, as elsewhere in the Atlantic world, witnessed constant and dynamic change, including the feminization of some tasks and occupations and the masculinization of others. The acquisition and application of craft skill among early American women has garnered comparatively little attention in this literature, however.[6]

We know much more about women and craft skill, particularly as it pertains to the clothing trades, on the other side of the Atlantic.[7] Women, present from at least the thirteenth century in a wide variety of occupations, were by the fifteenth century and through the sixteenth becoming concentrated in particular craft sectors, mainly those involving textiles—cloth-making and clothing production. Even in those sectors, men, responding to tightening competition, successfully protected their control of key skills.[8]

While gender divisions of labor became increasingly acute, restricting women's formal participation in many occupations, women continued to be "massively involved" in clothing trades as the wives and daughters of craftsmen.[9] In the last quarter of the seventeenth century, however, Europeans witnessed transformations in the clothing trades, particularly following the 1675 creation of exclusively female guilds in Paris and Rouen and the entrance of women into tailors' guilds (with limited privileges) across western and central Europe in the late seventeenth and early eighteenth centuries. Emerging fashion itself played a role, as the mushrooming popularity for women of the mantua (a gown that required far less structure than previous high fashion, was more comfortable to wear, and demanded fewer specialized skills to construct) made it possible for larger numbers of women to work in clothing construction, and larger numbers became necessary to meet escalating demand. Aspiring needlewomen, citing propriety, decency, and economic need and with the support of both the state and the aristocratic women who were their clients, successfully claimed the right to create garments for other women.[10] Over time, the difference between appropriate male and female work in the clothing trades was articulated in new ways; clothing construction, once the province of men, by the nineteenth century had become a "quintessentially feminine occupation."[11]

How those forces played out in Britain's North American colonies is less well understood. Rural New England craftswomen like Catherine Parsons have long eluded historical study, in part because, while historians interested in early American women have directed their considerable energies to work mainly associated with household production, historians of artisanal trades have focused their attention on occupations primarily open to men. The study of artisans in early America, begun with the publication of Carl Bridenbaugh's *The Colonial Craftsman*, has considered precisely that—crafts*men*. Historians have increasingly observed the several ways in which long-standing definitions of artisanry, grounded as much in economic clout and political activity as in craft skill, necessarily emphasize the experience of urban craftsmen at the expense of a larger world of both urban and rural artisans whose access to capital varied widely and whose work was shaped by the size and nature of the markets they were able to serve.[12] Studies that presume artisans to be male, urban, and politically active necessarily overlook the broader contours of early American craftwork, which involved both men and women in a variety of economic, social, familial, geographical, and political settings.

Enlarging our understanding of artisanry along these lines opens up a number of possibilities for historians of early American labor. Assumptions that women's work in early America was unskilled, temporary, and poorly paid in urban settings and homogeneous in rural ones have been especially pernicious when applied to early American needlework, itself a core feature in national mythologies about the colonial past. Laurel Thatcher Ulrich has recently observed that, until at least the mid-1980s, "nearly everybody believed, as the general public still does, that household production [of cloth] was ubiquitous and textiles the universal work of women."[13] Comparable misapprehensions have likewise muddied our understanding of the clothing trades; making clothing (itself routinely conflated with the making of cloth in ways that seldom confuse, say, the milling of wood and the making of furniture) has likewise been viewed as among all women's typical everyday chores. But the ability to cut and construct the many garments required by early Americans was by no means universal, nor were the several occupations comprising the clothing trades themselves undifferentiated or nonhierarchical.[14] Needle skills were not ubiquitous and the clothing trades not simply extensions of women's household labor. Women who worked as gown-makers and tailors in the century before industrialization "did not simply transfer domestic skills to the marketplace"; like their counterparts in crafts more commonly recognized as artisanal, "more often than not, they learned their trades in the workshop, not the home."[15]

The trouble in locating these skilled needlewomen is not a dearth of documentary evidence; manuscript repositories teem with references to women's artisanal work in the clothing trades. Letters and diaries describe trips to the town gown-maker or the arrival of local needlewomen, and financial records document routine transactions in which women offset debts to merchants, artisans, or neighbors by sewing. But important sources have too often been missed or misconstrued. Account books and daybooks have long offered excellent vehicles through which to examine the daily, seasonal, or yearly rhythms of men's craftwork, but it is commonplace to observe that women, at least before about 1810, rarely kept such records. Close examination of account books kept by men, however, reveals that often these ledgers were also the account books of women, though they are not often seen as such. A volume kept in the 1760s by Reuben Champion is cataloged as that of a Connecticut Valley physician. Nowhere does the document's description note the presence of transactions related to needlework, yet more than a third of the individuals listed in the ledger's pages were debited for Lydia Duncan Champion's work making and maintaining apparel.[16] Similar examples are plentiful. Another account book, identified as the ledger of "tailor" Solomon Cooke (a ferryman), records the labors of Cooke's wife, Tryphena Newton Cooke, whose needlework is written down among the transactions of her husband.[17] The Champion and Cooke account books record the labor and skill of both husband and wife as they worked together to support their families; that the former has been defined as Reuben's record and not Lydia's and that the tailoring in the Cooke volume was presumed to be Solomon's, not Tryphena's, are artifacts of the nineteenth and twentieth centuries, not the eighteenth. Evidence recording the trades of Lydia Champion, Tryphena Cooke, and women like them has been there all along, but it is difficult to uncover in records attributed to their husbands or, when found, has been overlooked, misunderstood, and misinterpreted amid assumptions that even historians have had trouble casting aside.

The evidence reclaimed from such sources allows us to see rural clothing production as an artisanal craft that attracted large numbers of women in the century before industrialization. The making of clothing was one of the very few early American crafts in which both men and women participated vigorously, though in different ways that responded very differently to changing circumstances. As such, the clothing trades provide an exceptionally fruitful arena in which male and female experiences can be compared and contrasted. Here, I will examine just one occupation within the clothing trades—tailoring, or the making of men's clothing—though women took on other tasks, including millinery, gown- or mantua-making, staymaking, and plain sewing.[18] Close examination of the working world of Northampton tailor Catherine Parsons suggests new ways to think about not only gender divisions of labor in the American clothing trades on the eve of industrialization, but also the larger world of eighteenth-century craft itself, allowing us to understand more fully the worlds of work for both women and men in early America.

The key to understanding the role of artisanal skill in the production of clothing is the distinction between cutting a garment and sewing it. It was the ability to cut, whether for male or for female clients, that separated artisans from amateurs.[19] In the fall of 1800, for example, Frederick Wardner visited the shop of Windsor, Vermont, merchant Isaac Green, purchasing two and a quarter yards of coating for a surtout (a man's long overcoat), a dozen and half coat buttons, three skeins of thread, linen to line the sleeves and pockets, and a yard of flannel for the interlining. Wardner brought the cloth to a tailor, Thomas Welch, who measured him and cut the pieces for the new overcoat, charging two shillings for his work with the shears. Wardner then carried the several pieces to Windsor tailoress Catherine Deane, who made up the garment. She earned five shillings for the time it took her to assemble the coat, apply the buttons, and press the garment into its final shape.[20]

Like most early American crafts, needle trades fell along a spectrum of training and task difficulty.[21] The making and mending of household linens and work clothes for men, women, and children required basic skills that most women and girls, as well as some boys and men, possessed. Some women turned those skills to profit: open any account book and it becomes clear that, in eighteenth-century New England, tailoresses like Catherine Deane were legion. The garments handled most often by these women were typically those constructed in two dimensions, that is, everyday clothes like shirts, shifts, and skirts, whose construction largely comprised an arrangement of rectangles. Fitting the garment to the body in question was not accomplished through the cut of the material; instead, a loose fit was achieved by adjusting the rectangles with a variety of simple gathering techniques.[22] Although stitching did not require the cultivated expertise that cutting did, neither was the labor altogether unskilled; the ability to sew a strong seam was not necessarily an aptitude possessed by all sewers. Men's shirts, as Jane

Nylander writes, "worn both day and night," had to be durable—they required "firm stitching and careful seam finishing."[23] Other women, like Deane here, assembled garments already cut (and sometimes basted) by someone more skilled with the shears. Women who worked at these aspects of clothing construction offered clients their skill, time, and experience. If this work was not especially physically taxing, it was tedious, difficult, and time consuming.

The large population of tailoresses worked alongside a smaller number of tailors, gown-makers, and staymakers. Just as most New England towns had access to specialists who knew how to make furniture, carve gravestones, or build houses, they also sheltered one or two residents with special expertise in the making of clothing. Most men and women owned at least one set of clothing of better quality, both in materials and in fit.[24]

Even laborers, at the end of their terms of service, typically received two suits of apparel, one suitable for workdays and another for Sunday worship and other more formal occasions.[25] The latter ensemble called for specialists who knew how to cut. Men's coats, for example, were constructed with sufficient shape to manipulate posture, while women's gowns fit tightly around the bodice before releasing into the folds of the skirt. These garments had to be constructed by makers who understood clothing's architectural logic and who could turn the unique qualities of hard-won materials—the gloss of calimanco, the weight of paduasoy, the luster of satin, the stoutness of ducape—to best advantage in terms of economy as well as style. Moreover, men's garments were very different from women's and required different skills to construct. Much like joiners and cabinetmakers, both gown- or mantua-makers and tailors "worked with complex geometry and measurements"; their craft "required advance thinking skills and an understanding of three-dimensional relationships."[26]

Given the high cost of fabric in early America, hiring the skill of a trained artisan generally represented just 5–15 percent of a garment's total cost—well worth the expense when one considers how easily an amateur could ruin yards of expensive material.[27] As one skilled gown-maker warned a novice at the work, "Did you consider that silk does not stick to you like cambric[?] It sets off and needs to be longer than anything else."[28] The younger woman's inexperience nearly caused her to cut her pieces too short; were it not for this timely warning, yards of fabric would have been ruined. Good cutters also knew how to manipulate complex patterns effectively. In the middle decades of the eighteenth century, for example, when large-scaled patterns were popular, special skill was required to assure that the repeating rhythms of vines and flowers were shown to advantage as they stretched across a tightly fitted bodice and cascaded down the bell of the skirt.[29] Given the high risk and serious consequences of error, even laboring women hired trained craftswomen to do the cutting when their best fabrics, whether expensive imported materials or their own wool or linen, were at stake. The eighteenth-century clothing trades, then, encompassed hierarchies of skill and status that turned on the gender of both a garment's maker and its user. Men rarely worked informally in clothing production; after obtaining training in the craft, which involved years spent as apprentices and then journeymen, male tailors generally made apparel for other men, along with a few garments, like riding habits (which were modeled after men's outer coats), for women. Women with advanced training in the creation of women's finer apparel were known as gown-makers (the term favored in rural western Massachusetts) or mantua-makers (the term favored in colonial cities, referring to Mantua, Italy, which supplied the silk most closely associated with the open gown when it became fashionable at the end of the seventeenth century). Women who apprenticed with men and eventually worked at making men's clothing appear to have been called, like their male counterparts, either "tailors" or "man-tailors."[30] Interestingly, the feminine suffix, at least in eighteenth-century western Massachusetts, seems to have denoted one's level of skill, rather than gender; "tailoress" usually referred to women who sewed, but did not possess specialized skills in cutting, while "tailor" applied to either men or women who had the ability to both cut and make men's apparel.

Catherine Parsons was among the few New England women who carved out careers as makers of men's clothes, having carried on a tailoring business for more than forty years in the second half of the eighteenth century. Born in 1731, Parsons was the eldest daughter of gown-maker Catherine King Phelps and bricklayer Nathaniel Phelps. No records survive to document the source of Parsons's own instruction, but she gained sufficient skill to fashion the majority of the vests and breeches worn on town streets in the years prior to the Revolution.[31] For a number of years, Parsons had a monopoly on menswear in Northampton; her daughter Catherine Graves (b. 1755) later recalled that for many years after her mother's 1752 marriage to Simeon Parsons, "there was no man tailor in the place."[32] The political, economic, and social leaders of the community and "a few others" had their finest apparel made in Boston, but they obtained their coats, vests, and breeches from Parsons.[33] Parsons also made and repaired clothing for Northampton residents at the other end of the spectrum; town accounts from the 1770s show debts to Parsons for her work clothing the town's poor.[34]

Women tailors were neither especially common across New England in the second half of the eighteenth century nor especially rare. Of the eleven women who list themselves as makers of clothing in the 1789 Boston directory, only one, Abigail Woodman, a "man tailor" working on Creek Lane, appears to have produced clothing for a primarily male clientele. Of thirty-one women indexed in 1796, again only one, Martha Bowens on Sheaf

Street, called herself a "man tailor," and no woman listed herself as such in 1798.[35] Though no Hartford directories survive from the period, tailor Robert Robinson's 1769 complaint suggests that women tailors were threatening his own livelihood there, and indeed, women in communities throughout the Connecticut River Valley identified themselves as tailors in public documents. In Deerfield, Massachusetts, Susanna Allen was recognized by the courts as a "single woman and taylor."[36] Western Massachusetts women who stated their occupations as tailor before the county Registrar of Deeds included Greenfield's Esther Graves, Hatfield's Martha Nash, Palmer's Mary King, Longmeadow's Jemima Woolworth, and New Salem's Elizabeth Southwick.[37] Moreover, what appear to have been male enterprises were often sustained by investments of female knowledge, skill, labor, and even capital. Husband-and-wife teams worked collaboratively in communities throughout the Connecticut Valley. John and Hannah Sheldon Russell worked together in their Deerfield shop, Hannah continuing to manage the shop's affairs for nearly twenty years after John's death, while similarly, in Glastonbury, Connecticut, Anna Talcott assumed charge of the Talcott tailoring shop after the death of her husband Asa. In Granville, Massachusetts, John and Mary Smith were working tailors in the 1770s.[38] Women and men gravitated toward needle trades for similar reasons, but whereas tailoring offered men one comparatively accessible route to tradesman's status, for women it was among the few avenues to artisanal skill. In other words, the same factors that made tailoring attractive to some men made it feasible for some women. It was among the least costly routes to an artisanal craft, requiring, unlike other occupations, very little capital and equipment to set up shop.[39] The tools of the trade (mostly needles, thimbles, shears, scissors, and pins, as well as an assortment of irons) were small, inexpensive, and easily acquired, and the cost of apprenticeship was usually lower than in other more lucrative trades requiring more expensive tools and more elaborately fitted shops.[40] In many if not most cases, the client, not the artisan, supplied the materials. Most tailors did not maintain an inventory of fabrics or finished goods. Instead, clients secured most of the necessary materials, from cloth to trimmings and sometimes even thread. The artisan supplied only talent and labor, time and skill, and the use of a fairly economical set of tools and supplies. When Parsons's competitor, Deerfield tailor George Herbert, died in 1786, his tailoring tools were valued at a mere twelve shillings, roughly equivalent to just two of the six chairs scattered around his home.[41] How effectively one wielded those tools separated casual producers from specialists, though prosperous needleworkers demanded mastery of other less tangible tools as well. The successful tailor "must be a nice Cutter, and finish his Work with Elegancy."[42] Even more important, adept artisans cultivated a keen eye and quick judgment as to how a suit of clothes might cloak (often literally) flaws in a client's form, posture, and movement and accentuate his or her finer qualities.[43] As the author of the 1747 advice manual *The London Tradesman* phrased it, a true artisan must be able not only "to cut out for the Handsome and Well-shaped, but to bestow a good Shape where Nature has not designed it."[44] The means by which men and women acquired those skills differed in some respects, though both underwent a period of craft training to acquire and cultivate their abilities. Young men apprenticed almost exclusively with other men, while young women who sought training in the tailoring trade learned from either men or women. Women who apprenticed with men are better documented than those who trained with women. Apprenticeships in the needle trades, like apprenticeships more generally, fell into two categories: voluntary agreements arranged by parents and involuntary agreements assigned by selectmen or overseers of the poor. When Wethersfield's Silas and Anna Graham bound their daughter to Glastonbury tailor Asa Talcott, or when Springfield's Clarinda Colton's parents bound her to Deerfield tailor Ithamar Burt, they voluntarily sought to provide their child with training in a craft that they hoped would afford a regular income.[45] The duration of these apprenticeships, even in urban centers, was not necessarily long; in the eighteenth-century Connecticut Valley, one year seems to have been common.[46] In other instances, which account for the larger number of surviving indentures, the apprenticeship was compulsory, as when officials in Middletown, Connecticut, bound seven-year-old Rebeccah Baxter to an apprenticeship in the tailoring trade with Elijah Treadway.

In these cases, the apprentice was generally bound until he or she reached the age of majority; young Rebeccah was obligated to remain in Treadway's household for eleven years, until she reached age eighteen.[47] The apprenticeship system—and specifically the nature of the relationship between masters and apprentices codified in documents like these—has been integral to longstanding conceptions of artisanry.[48] But the traditional model may not reflect the way many artisans actually mastered a given craft. Rather than absorbing primarily the knowledge of one's employer, many aspiring artisans, male and female, acquired their skills through increasing engagement in communities of practice.[49]

Aspiring practitioners began with little or no expertise in a given area and gradually, from their masters or mistresses as well as others more experienced than themselves (whether journeymen in the formal sense or simply others more practiced and adept), accumulated both conceptual and manual abilities that set them apart from the majority of their neighbors. Over time, they became known as specialists, in the neighborhood, in the community, and even the region, prompting others to seek out those special skills, and exchange other goods or skills of value for them. Artisans knew how to make objects that others judged "aesthetically, functionally, and economically acceptable."[50] Craft skill was not merely the mastery of a specific set of manual operations and concepts that could be transferred whole, like the tools of the craft, from experts to novices; rather, skill—among both women and men—is better understood as a relational quality, as abilities cultivated to a lesser or greater degree than others in a given community.[51] Unknown numbers of young women completed periods of training in the clothing trades that, while acknowledged as apprenticeships by the participants, left no paper trail. Scattered references throughout account books, daybooks, and diaries indicate that women took on trainees whom they considered apprentices, whether or not any formal agreement was written or preserved. Hatfield, Massachusetts, gown-maker Rebecca Dickinson recorded the visit of her "former 'printis" Patty Smith in the pages of her diary and recalled fondly another woman with whom she "went to learn the trade of gownmaking."[52] The accounts of Northampton's Sarah Root Clark contained her credit for having made a gown for "Eben Clark's wife's apprentice."[53] Catherine Graves also recalled her mother's several assistants as her "apprentices."[54] For none of these women do documents survive that affirm a formal relationship of the kind traditionally understood as an apprenticeship. The narrower definition, recognizing only those bound by a specific legal instrument, excludes many young women, and perhaps young men too, not because their status as learners of a craft was not recognized in their day, but because these specific legal instruments were reserved for those young men whose economic, civic, and political identities required it. Among the craftswomen of the Connecticut Valley, the apprenticeship relationship was recognized by the artisan, the novice, and the community at large—with or without a written agreement. Whether a contract was created or preserved, would-be tailors embarked on curriculums that were both structured and unstructured. Novices absorbed much of their training through observation rather than instruction, though skills were cultivated through fairly consistent and predictable means. In general, apprentices began by running errands, tending hearths and heating irons, keeping the cutting board and the shop clean and orderly, sorting and organizing threads, buttons, materials, and measurements, keeping tools in good repair, and brushing and delivering the finished garments, all the while gaining exposure to the routines of the trade. As time went on, they learned how to measure clients, noting lengths on strips of parchment that would determine the shapes and sizes of a garment's pieces. The apprentice also assumed other duties, learning the several kinds of stitches required to finish a garment, from basting to buttonholes. Since cutting errors were far costlier than sewing errors, novices did not attempt this work until their conceptual understanding of clothing construction had been well developed by months, or even years, in which they tackled discrete tasks of assembly, stitching, for example, the armscyes (armholes) of a straightbodied coat, or sewing a surtout's long seams. Gradually, the successful completion of these small tasks helped learners cultivate a conceptual understanding of the larger principles of construction and assembly. Only at the end of an apprenticeship, if at all, did aspiring tailors gain access to the art and the mystery of cutting cloth that formed the heart of the trade.

Catherine Graves recalled that her mother "commonly had three or four apprentices, and sometimes more."[55] If her memory was correct, then as many as one hundred young women learned their trade from Catherine Parsons during the four decades that she was in business.[56] Early on, about 1760, Eleanor Strong (b. 1747), daughter of local tanner Caleb and Phoebe Lyman Strong and sister of Caleb Strong, a future governor of Massachusetts, apprenticed alongside Martha Alvord (b. 1747), the eldest of four daughters and a son born to trader Saul Alvord and his wife, Martha Alvord.[57] Some thirty years later, Esther Pomeroy (1777–1857), the only daughter of merchant Heman and Esther Lyman Pomeroy, was among her last. Apprentices who lived at home (as these women surely did) worked one year, while those who lodged with Parsons worked eighteen months, providing the craftswoman with additional labor to offset the expense of their room and board.[58] On arrival, female trainees already possessed at least rudimentary needle skills, learned from their mothers at home. Some of the young women hoping to master the tailor's trade faced an uphill battle before gaining more complex abilities. Tailors occasionally tried to keep apprentices, male or female, insufficiently skilled to become competitors, assigning them routine chores, or otherwise limiting their artisanal education. That trick was even more readily played on young women, since cultural prescription meant that they were more easily asked to perform household duties than were their male counterparts. The correspondence between an early nineteenth-century tailor's apprentice in New Hampshire and her sister reveals the latter's concern that her sibling was being cheated out of crucial information: "You have given him already 14 months time which is more than would be asked for learning to sew & put garmets together a year being the usual time—I suppose you have only learned how to make vests pantaloons & coat trimmings & if he learns you to cut it will be nothing more than he ought to for the time you have staid with him." This young woman constantly struggled "to learn . . . the whole of the trade."[59] Hampshire County tailors were no more generous. A 1791 lawsuit between Deerfield tailor Ithamar Burt and the angry parents of apprentice Clarinda Colton reveals something of apprenticeship practices and pitfalls. In May 1788, Andrew Colton of Springfield had contracted with Burt to place his twenty-four-year-old daughter Clarinda with the craftsman, "to be his apprentice, to learn the art of a tailor . . . and to serve him the said Ithamar, after the manner of an apprentice, the full term of one year."[60] Colton paid half of the fee, thirty-six shillings, to the tailor, with the expectation that he would pay the remaining half when Clarinda completed her service and training. But when the young woman returned home, she had apparently learned almost nothing of cutting clothing. In a scenario repeated throughout New England, she had been more often employed as a domestic servant to Prudence, Burt's wife, than as an apprentice in Burt's shop. As Clarinda herself testified before the courts: "I used generally to take work for the Wife of the said Ithamar and if she had none for me I used to take work out of the Shop but for the most part she found me with work." Apparently Burt permitted Clarinda to "take work out of the shop" only when his wife found nothing better for the young woman to do, which was not often. Instead, Prudence Burt regularly set young Clarinda to cleaning, spinning, and making and mending of the family's own clothes—tasks that employed general housekeeping skills, not those specific to the tailor's trade. What was more, Colton added, her master "never in any instance taught or gave me any instruction, either how to measure any person or to Cut out any garment."[61] Those final phrases were not casually chosen; those two skills—the measure and the cut—were the essence of the craft, and Clarinda had not learned them. Diamond Colton, a Springfield tailor who later wanted to hire Clarinda to work in his shop, testified before the court that he had found her wholly unable to complete even the simplest assignments: "I asked her to measure some Customer that came to the Shop and she told me that she could not do it for she knew nothing about it."[62] Colton made a second attempt, asking her once again "to measure some person that came to have a garment made and to cut her notches on the measure, which she did and after she had done it she did not understand the notches she had made in the measure." Clarinda apparently had observed Burt often enough to mimic his actions, stretching her parchment along the client's sleeve, and notching the paper to note the lengths between shoulder and elbow, elbow and wrist, and so forth, but once she removed her tape, she was utterly at a loss as to what that information represented, or how it might be applied. She had not mastered the conceptual knowledge required to convert her observation of the tailor's actions to a genuine understanding of clothing construction. Apprenticeship suggests knowledge that cannot simply be explained, but must in some way be experienced; Clarinda, who spent more time in the domestic environment of the Burt house than the artisanal environment of the Burt shop, had not spent sufficient time in the company of clothing-makers to penetrate tailoring's "art and mystery." Consequently, Diamond Colton felt justified in cutting her wages to below those "Common to give Girls who had been properly instructed in the Art of Cutting." Fortunately, "before she went from Springfield," Diamond added, "she was a very good Symstress," and after he had provided some remedial instruction, she was finally able to go "out to work at the tailoring business and Cuts the garments mostly that she makes."[63]

Her year of service at Burt's had done nothing to advance her training. For his part, Burt did not feel that he had been remiss: if Clarinda had failed to observe and absorb the necessary information while a member of his household, it was no one's fault but her own. When her father refused to pay the remainder of Burt's fee, Burt sued to recover what he believed to be a just debt.

The Colton-Burt entanglement tells us much about tailoring as a trade for young women in rural Massachusetts. The one-year term of service seems to have been typical in the Connecticut River Valley, and girls who had been "properly instructed" in the art of cutting were commonly employed in the shops of male tailors. The responsibilities of these young women apparently extended to the measuring of clients (suggesting surprisingly intimate physical contact between girls and men) and, once working, these young artisans, still in the employ of masters like Colton, generally made up a client's garments from start to finish. Finally, Diamond Colton was apparently familiar with Clarinda's skills before she embarked on her Deerfield apprenticeship, but for some reason did not supervise her training himself; perhaps it was he who had suggested that Clarinda's father make the arrangement with Ithamar Burt.

Aspiring craftswomen who learned their trade in their families were generally luckier, at least in this regard. Several women in Catherine Parsons's family were noted local clothes-makers. Her mother, Catherine King Phelps (1701–1791), was a well-known gown-maker in Northampton and, during a subsequent marriage, shared her skills with stepdaughter Esther Lyman Wright (1725–1815), who became a busy gown-maker herself at the close of the eighteenth century.[64] Meanwhile, at least one of Catherine Parsons's six daughters took up her mother's trade: Experience Parsons Graves (1767–1856) could be found making surtouts and performing other tailor's tasks in local households before her 1805 marriage to Perez Graves, and likely after.[65] Toward the end of her long and productive life gown maker Catherine Phelps moved in with her daughter Catherine Parsons and granddaughter Experience Graves, bringing three generations of clothes-makers under one roof.[66] Lydia Champion, whose clothes-making accounts—as noted above—for so long went unnoticed, passed her skills on to her daughter, tailor Jemima Woolworth. Women in these families knew the value of skill with a pair of shears. As Edward Cooke observes, for artisanal families, craft skills provided "both a livelihood and a legacy." Knowledge and tools alike became assets "transmitted through the family network." Just as artisanal fathers bequeathed both skills and tools to succeeding generations, so too did artisanal mothers.[67] To understand better Parsons's experience as a female practitioner in a trade dominated by men, it is helpful to examine aspects of the work itself—shops and seasons, products and profits, access to hired help, and circles of clients—in light of those competitors. Deerfield tailor John Russell provides an especially useful point of comparison.

Closely related to the formation and persistence of artisanal identity, as it is usually discussed, is a dedicated work site, that is, a shop space clearly separate from domestic space.[68] Dedicated sites were less necessary for artisans in the clothing trades; both men and women regularly practiced their craft in the homes of employers, their tools were small and portable, and their ongoing projects and materials could be easily folded away. Although early maps of towns in western Massachusetts routinely mark the sites of shops occupied by hatters and cabinetmakers, tailor shops rarely appear, as tailors appropriated spaces in and around homes. They rented shops in commercial buildings, erected small structures on their home lots, or installed shops in ells attached to their houses. Such shops generally consisted of a well-lit room lined with broad tables on which to cut fabric. Russell and his wife Hannah worked out of the ell of her parents' house for six years before they purchased a lot down the street and built a home with a shop space on the ground floor.[69]

Whether Catherine Parsons maintained a traditional shop space is unclear. Judd refers to Parsons's having "opened her shop," but no record of a shop structure associated with Catherine and Simeon Parsons survives. The 1798 direct tax records that the Parsonses' wooden house was two stories high, just over thirteen hundred square feet, and lit by seventeen windows, suggesting that it was a two-over-two-room house typical of the period. No outbuildings are noted.[70] Where Parsons and her "tailor girls" sewed from day to day remains unknown, but wherever they worked, Parsons certainly benefited from the location of her home, one door east of Northampton's Tontine building, a center of artisanal life in that community before the building burned—taking the Parsons house with it—in 1816.[71]

Working largely out of their homes enabled Parsons as well as the Russells to blend family and artisanal life. Catherine Parsons sewed through ten pregnancies, bearing a child every two or three years between 1753 and 1778. Parsons's seven daughters surely contributed to the success of her business, either with needle in hand or by doing the household chores while their mother worked at her trade.[72] John Russell and Hannah Russell had five children between 1761 and 1769. When John died in 1775, all of Hannah's children were still at home, their eldest daughter Hannah, now fourteen, surely stepping in to care for the four boys, who were between ages six and thirteen. Hannah continued to serve the shop's clientele for another eighteen years, until the 1790s. By that time, she may well have had the help of at least one daughter-in-law: Orra Harvey may have been tailoring long before she met and married Elijah Russell, but in any event she came to work at her father-in-law's craft and became a well-known clothes-maker in that community for many years.[73]

Once a shop was established, tailors earned the lion's share of their profits not from producing men's "best" suits but from simple alterations and mending. In this, they conformed to the experience of other artisans of eighteenth-century rural New England, who derived much of their income from farm labor, not craft work, and whose artisanal skills were more often harnessed to everyday maintenance than the production of masterworks.[74] Glastonbury, Connecticut, tailor Asa Talcott, a contemporary of Parsons, spent less than half of his time making new garments. Instead, most of his time was spent cutting and fitting garments that were then sewn and finished in owners' homes, either by members of the household or hired needlewomen, or in "turning" clothing (that is, extending the life of older garments by cutting them apart, reversing the pieces, and rejoining them for several additional years' wear by the present owner or resizing them for a new recipient).[75] Judd's assertion that the leading men of Northampton had their coats made in Boston and their vests and breeches by local tailor Parsons suggests that the bulk of Parsons's business too came from the more mundane work of clothing production and maintenance.[76] The Russells' account books indicate that most days their work involved the creation and repair of men's work clothes. This is not evidence of any lack of skill or training; John Russell was on occasion hired to create silk suits. Rather, it seems that the gentlemen of means who could afford these articles preferred to have them made by comparatively urban tradesmen in Hartford, Boston, or New York.[77]

Few if any Hampshire County tailors received enough work of either kind to support themselves with their shears alone. Demand for artisanal services of all kinds, and an artisan's ability to meet that demand, fluctuated over the course of the agricultural year. Rural women combined farmwifery with clothing trades just as men combined husbandry and craftsmanship. Cabinetmakers, for example, who often had their own fields to tend, produced less furniture during the late spring, summer, and fall, the peak season of the agricultural year.[78] Tailoring was likewise subject to seasonal variation. Clothing was necessarily attended to when time and income permitted. For John Russell, the spring planting seasons and months of harvest were the least active periods for his shop; he produced the bulk of the year's clothing during the late summer, fall, and winter.[79] In Hadley, Josiah Pierce's diary—which contains references not only to Pierce's clothing consumption, but also to the work of his niece, tailoress Esther Pierce—suggests that peak months of clothing production were November and January, when one year's farm work had concluded and the next year's had yet to begin.[80] Their work crowded into pauses in the agricultural calendar, feast could be just as taxing as famine, as needleworkers exchanged slack periods for weeks of chronic overwork.

Craft profits also varied by garment and by artisan, depending largely on the level of skill the tailor had achieved. For plain sewing, commonly paid by the day, women fared poorly in comparison to their male competitors. A study of the 1777 wage ceilings suggested by the Massachusetts General Court and adopted throughout the Commonwealth found that the pay disparity between what female and male tailors could earn—women earning at best roughly 37 percent of what a man could take in—was even greater than the disparity between male and female farm laborers, in which the "*weekly* rates for 'maid's work' equaled the maximum *daily* rates received by male farm laborers," or, approximately 40–42 percent of men's wages, once the additional value of room and board was factored in.[81] In Hampshire County, "women formerly had for a week's work, but little more than a man had in a day, or variously from 1/5 to 1/3 as much as a man [though] sometimes near half as much."[82] The price caps set in South Hadley during the Revolution support these observations: male tailors commanded 2*s*. 8*d*. for a day's work, while women performing the same labor could demand just 1*s*. 2*d*.—less than half the men's rate.[83]

Such gaps close when considering rates paid by the task. In the 1760s and 1770s, Catherine Parsons charged between 6*s*. and 10*s*. to make a coat, between 4*s*. and 6*s*. for breeches, and around 4*s*. for vests.[84] John Russell charged roughly 5*s*. or 6*s*. for breeches, 2*s*.–3*s*. for a vest, as little as 2*s*. or as much as 13*s*. for a coat, and from 17*s*. to 22*s*. for a "sute of clothes."[85] Mending breeches might cost 1*s*. 6*d*., altering a coat, 2*s*. 8*d*., turning a coat, 14*s*., seating breeches, 1*s*. Russell took in 10*s*. for a completed riding habit, but just over 3*s*. if he merely cut it out but did not make it up. Task for task, in other words, Parsons's and Russell's rates were comparable. Men like Russell did not necessarily earn more for the same work than women like Parsons; instead, they were more likely to perform a wider range of services with a wider range of materials and so could command a wider range of fees.

Both men and women artisans employed help during periods of peak demand, though their access to skilled assistants differed. In Deerfield, Russell's relatively small operation nevertheless required occasional temporary employees who worked for several weeks at a time during periods of high demand. Russell records that in early 1768, "Bolton worked for me for 24 days. . . . James Shennan began to work for me Oct 8, 1758." Shennan apparently stayed for just five days and was quickly replaced by Patrick Grimes, who worked for several weeks before moving on in December. Russell never hired more than one journeyman at a time, probably because business did not demand it.[86] In the fall of nearly every year, Russell's Northampton and Hadley counterparts sought "good journeymen tailors" through the pages of the *Hampshire Gazette*. In November 1799, Sylvester Lyman advertised for one or two journeymen "to whom good encouragement will be given." Lyman occasionally needed more than one man at once, and in the fall of 1815 required no fewer than six.[87] As his business expanded, he added more workmen to his seasonal staff: in November of each year he regularly sought journeyman tailors, who could find employment "for a few months, by applying immediately, to Sylvester Lyman." Lyman recognized the financial burden these men's wages would pose, for he followed this notice with another demanding immediate payment for services rendered, along with a warning that "gentlemen are assured that no further notice will be given them except from the attorney."[88] In addition to journeymen, tailors sought the less experienced but also less costly aid of apprentices. Notices seeking "likely," "active" boys about age fourteen, though sometimes as young as twelve or as old as sixteen, were common.[89] Male tailors, like Deerfield's Ithamar Burt, also accepted young women as apprentices, though their advertisements always specified a preference for boys. Unlike journeymen, who were almost always hired in preparation for a busy season, apprentices were wanted the year around, as tailors recognized the need to complete as much training as possible before the winter set in, when demand for their services rose. Journeymen could be taken on as needed, but novices needed more time to learn their work.[90]

While men like Russell and Lyman took on journeymen and apprentices as circumstances demanded, Catherine Parsons employed only the latter.[91] Rather than hiring journeymen, Parsons apparently kept a constant stream of apprentices, or "tailor girls," moving through her shop—three or four, as we have seen, at any given time, suggesting to some extent the size of her enterprise. The two facts are perhaps related: an inability to employ male artisans of advanced skill may have encouraged Parsons to keep a larger and steadier force of less experienced female apprentices on hand to help her meet her demand.

Whereas women were willing and allowed to work with and train under men without comment, men may have been less keen to take positions subordinate to women like Parsons. Also significant here is the role of tramping in artisanal preparation; while moving from place to place proved an essential means by which male journeymen in a variety of trades augmented their training, gaining exposure to new styles and techniques in new communities of practice, such travel was not encouraged among women, limiting the supply of additional needlewomen with comparable levels of experience.[92] Parsons's decision to train at least one daughter in the craft may also reflect her awareness of a regular need for skilled help.

It may be, too, that Parsons's ability to secure the labor of strangers was circumscribed by a reluctance to seek help via the pages of local newspapers; a discrepancy appears when one considers the degree to which men and women in the county's clothing trades used the local press to secure employees and clients. Before the 1786 founding of the *Hampshire Gazette*, both male and female artisans secured clients by referral alone. Most Hampshire County tailors' clients were drawn from the same community as the artisan and thus were known to one another through networks of neighbors and kin. Among John Russell's more than three hundred clients, for example, just ten extended families comprise most of the accounts.[93] After the *Gazette*'s appearance, male tailors regularly advertised in its columns, seeking to attract the business of anyone, stranger or friend, within the paper's circulation. Access to advertising became increasingly important as developments in men's fashion altered relationships between artisans and consumers. Over the course of the eighteenth century, access to quality fabrics widened, prompting elites to find other ways to differentiate themselves. This effort increased the importance of the local tailor: "As gentility became more a matter of manner, society placed less emphasis on material display. . . . The proportions of the coats shrank, requiring less material but better tailoring."[94] As fashionable tailoring became imperative, the stakes for tailors rose; one had to be more savvy and more sophisticated than one's competitors to attract customers. Striking evidence of this can be found in a series of advertisements appearing in the pages of the *Gazette* in the spring of 1798, as Northampton's tailors faced tightening competition. When Sylvester Lyman returned to town that year after having spent some years sharpening his skills in New York and Philadelphia, he flaunted his metropolitan connections. Offering to "all gentlemen who wish" the "most fashionable work," he asserted his "superior advantages, [after] working in the cities of Philadelphia and New York with the most approved workmen in the United States."[95] Lyman boasted that his work was "equal to the best custom work in any seaport in America" and further let it be known that he had "formed a correspondence with the principle tailors in Philadelphia and New York, to receive the fashions as they arrive from London."[96]

Lyman's aggressive advertising raised the ire of at least one fellow tradesman. Aaron Wright, Jr., responded to Lyman's claim by "returning thanks to his friends and old customers, who have resumed the patronage of his business and assures them that, although he does not pretend to boast of any *extraordinary advantages from working in the cities of Philadelphia and New York and forming correspondence with the principle tailors* there[,] . . . he flatters himself he shall always be able to gratify his customers with the newest, and will strive to make his work speak its own eulogy."[97] Wright objected to, and even mocked, Lyman's attempt to tout his urban ties. But not everyone responded with sarcasm. For his part, Hadley tailor Nathan Seymour reminded his own "customers and others that he still carries on the Tailoring business at his shop near the meeting house . . . cloathes made in the newest fashion, from Boston or New York, on the most reasonable terms."[98] At the turn of the nineteenth century, Lyman's hubris irritated his colleagues. But some "eulogy" was in order, for Wright's world of reputation, personal connection, and local patronage was fading fast. Lyman was responding to phenomena that were reverberating throughout the United States and throughout the transatlantic world.

These changes, which introduced more overt competition among Hampshire County's male tailors, eventually expanded opportunities for entrepreneurs like early nineteenth-century Northampton mantua-maker and milliner Sarah Williams, among the first women in that community to harness the power of the press, thus enlarging the prospects of her small shop.[99] But for the first thirty years of the *Gazette*'s existence, neither Catherine Parsons nor any other skilled needlewomen advertised in its pages. Perhaps the 1786 advent of the paper, when Parsons was in her fifties, simply came too late to be of any additional use to the well-established craftswoman. Or possibly the advent of local newspaper advertising reflected one expansion of commerce in the community and the region in which women did not easily participate. Whatever the reason, Hampshire County's female artisans continued to draw clients by word-of-mouth alone for a further thirty years. As male tailors stepped gingerly into a world larger than the local, neighborly network of commercial relations, women stayed, at least for a time, behind.

What is added to our historical vision when we examine closely the routines associated with women's artisanal needlework? Examining female craftwork in eighteenth-century rural Massachusetts suggests a much more faceted world of early American artisanry, restoring to view complex webs of skill and labor present among early American women; at the same time, looking closely at artisanry as it took shape in a trade routinely practiced by women helps trouble the categories of artisanry more generally, calling into question the hallmarks generally associated with artisanal work and revealing how those very conceptions have clouded our understanding of the work of women like Catherine Parsons. Exchanging models of craft knowledge as a package of specialized information transferred from expert to novice for another in which aspiring artisans, by working alongside others more skilled than themselves, cultivate special abilities not widely shared in their communities, and so assume gradually larger roles in communities of practitioners, enables us to enlarge both our conceptions of skill and our understanding of what constitutes artisanal labor. Moving beyond static and hierarchical dichotomies between domestic versus artisanal work makes it easier to recognize both formal and informal learning and to envision a more complex enterprise involving larger worlds of familial and social relations, the latter being especially useful in rural settings where specialization was limited by the nature of local markets.

This more encompassing view more closely describes rural artisanry as it was experienced by men and women in early New England. Many of the core features of craftwork as it has been traditionally understood still obtain. Women who worked as gown-makers and tailors in the century before industrialization did not simply transfer widely held domestic skills to the marketplace. Instead, like others in crafts more commonly recognized as artisanal, more often than not they learned their trades in workshop settings, not domestic ones, and gained those skills during clearly defined periods of training, recognized by themselves and others as their "apprenticeship." Lastly, these women were acknowledged in their communities as craft specialists.[100] These are the core attributes of artisanal labor. Long-standing conceptions of artisanal culture that depend on political action, large shops, and collective artisan identity conflate early American artisanry itself with an artisanal culture experienced by men, and mostly by men in urban settings. While levels of capitalization, the nature of markets, and opportunities for political involvement varied over space and time and across gender, the acquisition and application of craft skill remain the essence of artisanal identity.

Rural needlewomen, whether or not their training was set forth in apprenticeship agreements, whether they worked in shop settings or in homes, considered themselves and each other skilled artisans whose patterns of work, though obviously shaped by gender expectations for their class and race, were in many ways similar to those of other craft specialists in occupations primarily practiced by rural men. Put another way, women's work identities did not necessarily turn on the legal instruments, craft organizations, or political roles that shaped men's occupational lives; instead, many years' experience in a given craft, the patronage of kin, neighbors, and strangers, and the teaching of apprentices also sustained craft identity.[101] Close investigation of women's work in the making of clothing challenges accepted depictions of artisanry as a primarily male preserve, since these women recognized in their craft the same range of tasks, skills, and practitioners found in other early American trades.

Tailoring could prove a worthwhile occupation for those women able to gain the training and means to practice the craft. Women's artisanal work was in many ways similar to men's: both men and women served an apprenticeship through which they learned the "art and mystery" of the craft; both acted as masters who imparted craft tradition to aspiring needleworkers; both asserted an artisanal identity in a variety of arenas, from (most narrowly) the courts to (most broadly) the community. But men and women's experiences also diverged, largely in ways that reflect men and women's differing access to literacy and numeracy skills (which hampered some women's ability to obtain training) and capital (which inhibited one's ability to establish multi-service shops). Prevailing gender divisions of household labor may have brought female apprentices to their trades with greater preparation than men, but may also have caused them to face greater obstacles in obtaining from masters the whole of their training, though some form of apprenticeship was a critical component of female artisanal identity. Dedicated work sites and familial craft legacies, long associated with men's artisanal work, appear to coincide with certain crafts requiring comparatively larger amounts of capital. Tailoring, as it was practiced by both men and women, scores low on both counts, though given the frequency with which women changed surnames, familial legacy may simply be harder to see. Both women and men pursued multiple income-earning strategies during their lives, supplementing their artisanal work with other activities, though in this regard men had greater access to market alternatives for their labors, as well as greater access to commercial spaces and practices and greater flexibility in the hiring of additional laborers. Evidence regarding the comparative income available to men and women is mixed, but suggests that skilled needlework offered women one occupation in which they could compete, task for task, fairly well with their male competitors, while the daily wages assigned semiskilled labor disadvantaged women workers, indicating that the acquisition of special skills was critical if one hoped even to approach a living wage. Catherine Parsons's career, beginning in the middle decades of the eighteenth century, was in some ways a harbinger of things to come. It is possible that she—along with Esther Graves, Martha Nash, and other female tailors in the Connecticut Valley—was among those women who, Gloria Main has argued, entered expanding trades in the middle decades of the century, though women tailors can be found in Northampton records at least as early as the 1710s and 1720s.[102] At present, the evidence is more suggestive than conclusive, but the presence of women tailors like Catherine Parsons affords an opportunity to reflect on how they, as well as Robert Robinson, the Hartford tailor whose complaints open this essay, might fit into the larger picture of evolving gender divisions of labor.

Laurel Ulrich's investigation of a related yet distinct craft—weaving—provides an interesting point of comparison to changes in the clothing trades during these same decades.[103] In the seventeenth century, weaving was a trade for men who possessed special skill; by the turn of the nineteenth century, "cloth-making was not only ubiquitous, it was the foundation of local patterns of barter and exchange" that comprised a "female economy."[104] Sometime in the first half of the eighteenth century, the balance had tipped in favor of female practitioners, and "cloth-making lost its artisan identity."[105] "As weaving passed into the female domain," Ulrich writes, "it disappeared into the household, becoming less rather than more specialized."[106] The reasons for this transformation, she suggests, are not entirely plain but "surely involved both the fragility of artisan weaving as a male occupation and limited opportunities for female employment in an undeveloped colonial economy." By the middle of the eighteenth century, male weavers had been squeezed out, caught between commercial producers across the Atlantic and "women who worked in the anonymity of the household production system" across town. Weaving no longer required any kind of sustained apprenticeship; instead, neighbors exchanged skill, time, and materials within local economies.[107] Clothes-making also saw increased female participation over the course of the eighteenth century, but its artisanal character persisted far longer. In part, this reflects the significant differences between the production of cloth, a two-dimensional product not necessarily associated with its eventual user, and the production of clothing, custom-made until the early nineteenth century, meaning that it had to be fitted to the body in question. Cloth was easily imported: clothing was not. There could be no anonymity while the custom trade and the specialized skills it demanded thrived; comparable transformations did not come until the advent of ready-made clothing—at the turn of the nineteenth century for men's clothing and, for women's, almost a century later. For men like Robert Robinson, increased competition from women like Catherine Parsons clearly became a problem in the years leading up the American Revolution, prompting the anxious craftsman to attempt to cast doubt on the ability of women to master the tailor's craft. But Robinson's claims came too late; they had already lost their resonance in a world that had accepted the success of Parsons and her counterparts throughout the region.

Catherine Phelps Parsons lived until 1798, the same year that tensions erupted among the town's male tailors, each anxious to assert his access to the most fashionable cuts. An alternative reading of those events might suggest that the men were vying for the patronage of Parsons's clientele as the aging craftswoman withdrew from active trade. By the time Sylvester Judd interviewed the tailor's daughter in the second quarter of the nineteenth century, times had greatly changed, but Parsons's influence persisted: as one observer noted, "most of the older female tailors in town are Mrs Parsons apprentices, or those who learned the trade of them."[108] The multigenerational legacy of the tailor's skill was still recognizable. At the same time, however, Parsons's daughters had witnessed the transformation of their mother's trade, as thousands of New England women were drawn into outwork systems, while others learned to make men's clothing via the profusion of trade manuals published in the 1820s and 1830s.[109] Vast impersonal systems were replacing the world of custom production, transformations that prompted the antiquarian to undertake his researches, to capture a world that was vanishing before his very eyes.[110] The desire to remember the artisanal past endures. In Northampton, Longfellow's image of the brawny village blacksmith is strikingly captured in an anvil supposedly carried to America in 1630 and passed down through several generations of blacksmiths in the Pomeroy family. Today contained among the collections of Historic Northampton, the anvil (pictured in chapter 3, above) is a local icon of family identity and craft tradition. The glint of a needle may be nearly impossible to spy in its shadow, but these smaller pieces of metal, too, speak to us of early American artisans whose aprons were linen, not leather, and whose labors were just as skilled, arduous, and valuable to their families and to their communities.

NOTES

1. Robert Robinson, *Connecticut Courant*, January 30, 1769.

2. Interview with Catherine Parsons Graves (b. 1755), Sylvester Judd manuscript, "Northampton," vol. 1:94, 101b, in the collections of the Forbes Library, Northampton.

3. Judd (1789–1860) was the editor of the *Hampshire Gazette* and an avid local historian. Sixty notebooks filled with Judd's historical research on everyday life in colonial New England, including transcriptions of documents that no longer survive and interviews with local residents, can be found at Northampton's Forbes Library. For further discussion of Judd as well as his historical work concerning the eighteenth-century economy, see Christopher Clark, *The Roots of Rural Capitalism: Western Massachusetts, 1780–1860* (Ithaca, 1990), passim, esp. 1–9.

4. The literature here is extensive. Among the most useful recent works are Katrina Honeyman and Jordan Goodman, "Women's Work, Gender Conflict, and Labour Markets in Europe, 1500–1900," *Economic History Review*, N.S., 44 (1991): 608–628, especially 608; Judith M. Bennett, "'History That Stands Still': Women's Work in the European Past," *Feminist Studies* 14 (1988): 269–283, and "Medieval Women, Modern Women: Across the Great Divide," in Ann-Louise Shapiro, ed., *Feminists Revision History* (New Brunswick, NJ, 1994), 47–72; Judith G. Coffin, "Gender and the Guild Order: The Garment Trades in Eighteenth-Century Paris," *Journal of Economic History* 54 (1994): 768–793; Natalie Zemon Davis, "Women in the Crafts in Sixteenth-Century Lyon," in Barbara A. Hanawalt, ed., *Women and Work in Preindustrial Europe* (Bloomington, IN, 1986), 167–197; Pamela Sharpe, *Adapting to Capitalism: Working Women in the English Economy, 1700–1850* (Houndmills, UK, 1996); and Sharpe, ed., *Women's Work: The English Experience, 1650–1914* (London, 1998).

5. The best work on women and the early American household economy includes Laurel Thatcher Ulrich, *The Age of Homespun: Objects and Stories in the Creation of an American Myth* (New York, 2002), "Wheels, Looms, and the Gender Division of Labor in Eighteenth-Century New England," *William and Mary Quarterly*, third series, 55 (1998): 3–38, *A Midwife's Tale: The Life of Martha Ballard, Based on Her Diary, 1785–1812* (New York, 1990), and *Good Wives: Image and Reality in Northern New England, 1650–1750* (New York, 1980); Clark, *Roots of Rural Capitalism*; Gloria L. Main, "Gender, Work, and Wages in Colonial New England," *William and Mary Quarterly*, third series, 51 (1994): 39–66; and Jeanne Boydston, *Home and Work: Housework, Wages, and the Ideology of Labor in the Early Republic* (New York, 1990).

6. An important exception is women's work in textile production, a subject to which this article will return. Significant work here includes Johanna Miller Lewis's

examination of spinning as an artisanal skill in *Artisans in the North Carolina Backcountry* (Lexington, KY, 1995). On women's work in cloth production, see Ulrich, "Wheels, Looms, and the Gender Division of Labor," and Adrienne Hood, "The Organization and Extent of Textile Manufacture in Eighteenth-Century Rural Pennsylvania: A Case Study of Chester County" (Ph.D. diss., University of California at San Diego, 1988). Christine Stansell tracks women's work in the emerging urban clothing industry in *City of Women: Sex and Class in New York, 1789–1860* (New York, 1986).

7. The literature on European women in the crafts, and especially the clothing trades, is far more extensive than the literature on early American craftswomen. Key contributions that are particularly relevant here include Anne Buck, "Mantuamakers and Milliners: Women Making and Selling Clothes in Eighteenth-Century Bedfordshire," *Publications of the Bedfordshire Historical Society* 72 (1993): 142–155; Coffin, "Gender and the Guild Order" and *The Politics of Women's Work: The Paris Garment Trades, 1750–1915* (Princeton, 1996); Clare Haru Crowston, *Fabricating Women: The Seamstresses of Old Regime France, 1675–1791* (Durham, NC, 2001); Madeleine Ginsburg, "The Tailoring and Dressmaking Trades, 1700–1850," *Costume* 6 (1972): 64–71; Gay L. Gullickson, *Spinners and Weavers of Auffay: Rural Industry and the Sexual Division of Labor in a French Village, 1750–1850* (Cambridge, 1986); Beverly Lemire, "Redressing the History of the Clothing Trade in England: Ready-Made Clothing, Guilds, and Women Workers, 1650–1800," *Dress* 21 (1994): 61–74, "'In the Hands of Work Women': English Markets, Cheap Clothing, and Female Labour, 1650–1800," *Costume* 33 (1999): 23–35, and *Dress, Culture, and Commerce: The English Clothing Trade before the Factory, 1660–1800* (New York, 1997); Sharpe, *Adapting to Capitalism*; Sharpe, *Women's Work*; and Merry E. Wiesner, "Spinsters and Seamstresses: Women in Cloth and Clothing Production," in Margaret Ferguson, Maureen Quilligan, and Nancy J. Vickers, eds., *Rewriting the Renaissance: The Discourses of Sexual Difference in Early Modern Europe* (Chicago, 1986), 191–205.

8. Honeyman and Goodman, "Women's Work, Gender Conflict, and Labour Markets in Europe," 611; James R. Farr, *Artisans in Europe, 1300–1914* (Cambridge, 2000), 111–112; K. D. M. Snell, *Annals of the Labouring Poor: Social Change and Agrarian England, 1660–1900* (Cambridge, 1985), esp. 272–276.

9. Snell, *Annals of the Labouring Poor*, 277 (quotation); Crowston, *Fabricating Women*, 96–98, 407.

10. Jean H. Quataert, "The Shaping of Women's Work in Manufacturing: Guilds, Households, and the State in Central Europe, 1648–1870," *American Historical Review* 90 (1985): 1122–1148; Crowston, *Fabricating Women*.

11. Crowston, *Fabricating Women*, 406; Quataert, "Shaping of Women's Work in Manufacturing," 1148.

12. Carl Bridenbaugh, *The Colonial Craftsman* (New York, 1950); Christine Daniels, "'WANTED: A Blacksmith who understands Plantation Work': Artisans in Maryland, 1700–1810," *William and Mary Quarterly*, third series, 50 (1993): 743–767; Edward S. Cooke, Jr., *Making Furniture in Preindustrial America: The Social Economy of Newtown and Woodbury, Connecticut* (Baltimore, 1996), 6–7; Wendy Gamber, *The Female Economy: The Millinery and Dressmaking Trades, 1860–1930*

(Urbana, IL, 1997). For similar observations concerning the study of artisans across the Atlantic, see Gervase Rosser, "Crafts, Guilds, and the Negotiation of Work in the Medieval Town," *Past and Present* 154 (1997): 8–9, and Farr, *Artisans in Europe*, 1–9. On the way that the "meanings of artisanship" are "embedded in a particular reading of the past," see Geoffrey Crossick, "Past Masters: In Search of the Artisan in European History," in Crossick, ed., *The Artisan and the European Town, 1500–1900* (Aldershot, UK, 1997), 1–40. Joy Parr, "Gender History and Historical Practice," *Canadian Historical Review* 76 (1995): 354–376, esp. 367, makes the particularly useful observation that qualities like ambition, competitiveness, entrepreneurship, and other aspects of artisanal ability have been routinely, and ahistorically, considered masculine traits.

13. Ulrich, "Wheels, Looms, and the Gender Division of Labor," 4; Gamber, *Female Economy*, 5. See also Carole Turbin, "Beyond Conventional Wisdom: Women's Wage Work, Household Contribution, and Labor Activism in a Mid-Nineteenth-Century Working-Class Community," in Carol Groeneman and Mary Beth Norton, eds., *To Toil the Livelong Day: America's Women at Work, 1780–1980* (Ithaca, 1987), 47–67.

14. Costume historians like Linda Baumgarten, Claudia B. Kidwell, Nancy Rexford, and Aileen Ribiero are transforming the way historians think about the production and consumption of clothing. See, in particular, Baumgarten, *What Clothes Reveal: The Language of Clothing in Colonial and Federal America* (Williamsburg, VA, 2002), and, with John Watson and Florine Carr, *Costume Close-Up: Clothing Construction and Pattern* (Williamsburg, VA, 1999); Kidwell and Margaret C. Christman, *Suiting Everyone: The Democratization of Clothing in America* (Washington, DC, 1974); and Ribiero, *The Art of Dress: Fashion in England and France, 1750 to 1820* (New Haven, CT, 1995), and *Dress in Eighteenth-Century Europe, 1715–1789*, rev. ed. (London, 2002; orig. pub. 1984).

15. Gamber, *Female Economy*, 5. Crowston, *Fabricating Women*, 186, 297, finds the same to be true of women in eighteenth-century France; while historians there also long emphasized the absence of well-defined occupational training for women, assuming that women obtained their skills largely within their families, the clothing trades "offer a sharp contrast to these conclusions."

16. Champion account book, Special Collections and Archives, University of Massachusetts, Amherst. The volume's in-house description has now been corrected to include references to this needlework.

17. For more on Cooke, see Marla R. Miller, "The Accounts of Tryphena Newton Cooke: Work, Family, and Community in Hadley, Massachusetts, 1780–1805," *Textiles in New England II: Four Centuries of Material Life, Proceedings of the Dublin Seminar for New England Folklife* (Boston, 2001), 161–172. Solomon Cooke was identified as a tailor by compilers of the Great River Archive, Wadsworth Atheneum; see microfilm edition, reel 6.

18. For a more encompassing study of women's work in these several areas of the clothing trades, see the author's larger work, *The Needle's Eye: Women and Work in the Age of Revolution* (Amherst, MA, forthcoming).

19. Crowston, *Fabricating Women*, 2.

20. Isaac Green account book, 1800–1801 (Windsor), Nathan Stone Papers, Vermont Historical Society, Barre.

21. Cooke, *Making Furniture in Preindustrial America*, 13–14; Jeannette Lasansky, *To Draw, Upset, and Weld: The Work of the Pennsylvania Rural Blacksmith, 1742–1935* (Lewisburg, PA, 1980), 16–17.

22. Kidwell, "Short Gowns," *Dress* 4 (1978): 32.

23. Jane C. Nylander, "Textiles, Clothing, and Needlework," in Gerald W. R. Ward and William N. Hosley, Jr., eds., *The Great River: Art and Society of the Connecticut Valley, 1635–1820* (Hartford, 1985), 392. Their work was akin to that done by what we think of today as a "seamstress." Few Hampshire County sources use this term or the older "sempstress," though the latter was in use at the time.

24. On the typical wardrobes of men and women in the Connecticut Valley, see Wendy Kenerson, "Forms, Fashions, and Vanities: 1783–1811: A Study of Men's Clothing in Western Massachusetts through Probate Inventories" (senior thesis, Skidmore College, 1987); Lynne Z. Bassett, "The Sober People of Hadley: A Study of Clothing in the Probate Inventories of Hadley, Massachusetts, 1663–1731" (M. A. thesis, University of Connecticut, 1991); and Alexandra Deutsch, "In Search of the Connecticut River Goddess: Clothing and Status in Eighteenth-Century Hampshire County" (seminar paper, Historic Deerfield, Inc., 1992). Additional insight into patterns of clothing ownership in the Connecticut Valley between 1760 and 1805 is grounded in the Connecticut Valley Clothing File, a database created by this author in the spring and summer of 2001, documenting approximately 12,000 articles of apparel owned by almost 600 decedents (all decedents whose inventories enumerated apparel) in 18 Connecticut Valley towns. I am grateful to the University of Massachusetts Office of Research Affairs for funding this project and for Ned Lazarro's excellent work as a research assistant.

25. See, for example, the 1795 indenture of Northampton's Samuel Breck, Jr., to Thomas Cone of Windsor, VT. At the conclusion of his service, Breck was to receive two full suits of apparel "as is customary to be given to an apprentice at the expiration of his apprenticeship"; Giles Kellogg Papers, Massachusetts Historical Society.

26. J. Ritchie Garrison, "Builders and the Myth of Deskilling: The Case of Calvin and George Stearns" (paper presented at the Eighth Symposium of the George Meany Memorial Archives, "Building History and Labor History: Toward an Interdisciplinary Dialogue," Washington, DC, February 11–12, 1996).

27. For example, in Cambridge, MA, Eleanor Powers's account with Richard and Katharina Champney records that the "cloth for a gound and thread and lining" that Powers purchased from Richard Champney in August 1757 cost more than £5, while Katharina's price for "making a gound" was just 16s, roughly 15 percent of the cost of the fabric. Similarly, in December 1757, "cloth for a gound" cost £1/11/6, while the "making" cost just 4s, or about 13 percent. Likewise, the 9 yd. of pink durant that Hadley's Elizabeth Porter Phelps acquired in 1788 cost 18s, and the cost of cutting and making a gown at that time was typically 2/6, or just under 14 percent. See the Richard Champney account book, 1746–1783, American Antiquarian Society (AAS), Worcester, MA; Porter Phelps Huntington papers, Box 4, folder 20, Amherst College Special Collections and Archives (PPHP); and Judd, "Women's Pay as Makers of Garments," in "Miscellaneous," vol. 9:161–163.

28. Patience Langdon to Sophronia Beebe, undated (c. 1800); Judith Knight's 1995 notes on needlework in the Beebe Family Papers, Old Sturbridge Village, Sturbridge, MA.

29. See Ginsberg, "Tailoring and Dressmaking Trades," 68.

30. See, for example, *The Boston directory: Containing, a list of the merchants, mechanics, traders, and others, of the town of Boston* (Boston, 1789).

31. Judd, "Northampton," vol. 1:101b.

32. Judd, "Northampton," vol. 1:101b. On Catherine Phelps's gown-making see Judd, "Northampton," vol. 2:140, and the Nathaniel Phelps account book, Pocumtuck Valley Memorial Association (PVMA), Deerfield.

33. Judd, "Northampton," vol. 1:101b.

34. Judd, excerpts from "Town Expenses," Judd, "Northampton," vol. 2:106–117.

35. See the Boston city directories published by John Norman in 1789; Manning and Loring in 1796; Rhoads and Laughton in 1798; and John Russell in 1800.

36. Susanna Allen, writ of execution of judgment, 1772, Allen Family Papers, PVMA, box 1, folder 9.

37. Esther Graves, Hampden Country Registry of Deeds, vol. 6:571, 572, Springfield, MA; Martha Nash, Franklin County Registry of Deeds, vol. 6:80, Greenfield, MA.; Mary King, Hampden Country Registry of Deeds, vol. 8:555, 1758; Jemima Woolworth, Hampden Country Registry of Deeds, vol. 30:195, 1788; Elizabeth Southwick II, Hampden Country Registry of Deeds, vol. 22:412.

38. The Russell account book is at PVMA; the Talcotts' accounts are at the Connecticut Historical Society, Hartford. On the Smiths, see Daniel Lombardo, "A Directory of Craftsmen in the Connecticut Valley of Massachusetts to 1850," vol. 3, Memorial Libraries, Deerfield.

39. See Daniels, "From Father to Son: The Economic Roots of Craft Dynasties in Eighteenth-Century Maryland," in Howard B. Rock, Paul A. Gilje, and Robert Asher, eds., *American Artisans: Crafting Social Identity, 1750–1850* (Baltimore, 1995), 3–16.

40. *Book of Trades: or, Library of the Useful Arts*, 3 vols. (Whitehall [Philadelphia] and Richmond, 1807; New York, 1976), 35; Daniels, "From Father to Son."

41. See Daniels, "From Father to Son," 5; George Herbert, 1786 probate inventory, Hampshire County Registry of Probate, vol. 16:7, Northampton.

42. R. Campbell, *The London Tradesman . . .* [1747] (New York, 1969), 192.

43. Richard L. Bushman discusses the importance of posture, movement, and body type in *The Refinement of America: Persons, Houses, Cities* (New York, 1992).

44. Campbell, *London Tradesman*, 192.

45. For Graham, see Connecticut State Library RG 62, Wethersfield, box 3; for Colton, see Burt Family Papers, PVMA.

46. See Judd, "Northampton," vol. 1:101b.

47. Indenture, July 1, 1770, Middlesex County Historical Society, Middletown, CT.

48. See, for example, W. J. Rorabaugh, *The Craft Apprentice: From Franklin to the Machine Age in America* (New York, 1986).

49. My use of the term "communities of practice" is drawn from the anthropology of learning and teaching, a useful survey of which is Catherine Pelissier, "The Anthropology of Teaching and Learning," *Annual Review of Anthropology* 20 (1991): 75–95.

50. Robert Blair St. George, *The Wrought Covenant: Source Material for the Study of Craftsmen and Community in Southeastern New England, 1620–1700* (Brockton, MA, 1979), 16.

51. Farr, *Artisans in Europe*, 42.

52. Rebecca Dickinson diary, October 9, 1788, September 26, 1787, PVMA.

53. Judd, "Miscellaneous," vol. 11:62, and "Northampton," vol. 2:244. Eben Clark's wife was Jerusha Russell Clark.

54. Judd, "Northampton," vol. 1:94.

55. Graves, quoted Judd, "Northampton," vol. 1:101b.

56. Judd, "Northampton," vol. 1:94, 101b.

57. Judd, "Northampton," vol. 1:94; see also James Russell Trumbull, *History of Northampton, Massachusetts, from Its Settlement in 1654*, 2 vols. (Northampton, 1898, 1902), 2:615.

58. Judd, "Northampton," vol. 1:101b.

59. Mary Adams to Thomas Barden, December 18, 1832, and Hannah Adams to Mary Adams, February 11, 1835, both in Jo Anne Preston, "'To Learn Me the Whole of the Trade': Conflict between a Female Apprentice and a Merchant Tailor in Ante-Bellum New England," *Labor History* 24 (1983): 265, 268–269. See also Mary Anne Poutanen, "For the Benefit of the Master: The Montreal Needle Trades during the Transition, 1820–1842" (M.A. thesis, McGill University, 1985), who cites efforts to restrict the use of apprentices as servants via clauses in their indentures.

60. Writ, September 24, 1791, Burt Family Papers, PVMA.

61. Clarinda Colton deposition, Burt Family Papers, PVMA.

62. Diamond and Clarinda were distant cousins; see *Proceedings at the General Celebration of the Incorporation of the Town of Longmeadow* (Longmeadow, 1884). Coltons were also heavily intermarried with Burts, though no direct connection to Ithamar is apparent.

63. Diamond Colton deposition, Burt Family Papers, PVMA.

64. See Trumbull's Northampton genealogies, typescript, Forbes Library. The work of Esther Wright is documented in the account book of Solomon and Esther Wright, Historic Northampton. Solomon was Esther Lyman Wright's son; her daughter Esther Wright (1763–1813) may also have performed gown-making recorded in this volume.

65. Entries for November 27, 1791, December 8, 1793, in Elizabeth Porter Phelps memorandum book (PPHP).

66. Judd, "Northampton," vol. 1:332.

67. Cooke, *Making Furniture in Preindustrial America*, 46.

68. See Daniels, "From Father to Son," passim.

69. Joshua Lane, "Breeches and Rum: An Investigation of Rural Economy through the Account Books of John Russell" (seminar paper, Historic Deerfield, Inc., 1984), 5. The ell at the Sheldon-Hawks house, now part of the museum complex at Historic Deerfield, once housed the tailor shop of John and Hannah Sheldon Russell.

70. See Judd, "Northampton, Land & Dwelling Houses and Various Owners," Forbes Library.

71. Judd, "Northampton," vol. 1:120.

72. Ulrich discusses the relationship between daughters and their mother's trade in *A Midwife's Tale*, 80–81. See also Ulrich, "Martha Ballard and Her Girls: Women's Work in Eighteenth-Century Maine," in Stephen Innes, ed., *Work and Labor in Early America* (Chapel Hill, 1988), 70–105.

73. See George Sheldon, *A History of Deerfield, Massachusetts . . .*, 2 vols. (Deerfield, 1895), 1:623. Orra Harvey Russell eventually shared a shop with shoe-

makers Ebenezer Saxton and Lyman Frink; she lived on this lot for some "thirty or forty years."

74. Scott LaFrance, "Work Habits of Rural Massachusetts Cabinetmakers: A Study of Account Books, 1770–1840" (seminar paper, Historic Deerfield, Inc., 1982).

75. Jane C. Nylander, *Our Own Snug Fireside: Images of the New England Home, 1760–1860* (New York, 1993), 165.

76. Judd, "Northampton," vol. 1:101b.

77. John Russell account books, 1763–1791, PVMA; Lane, "Breeches and Rum," 14.

78. Campbell, *London Tradesman*; LaFrance, "Work Habits of Rural Massachusetts Cabinetmakers," 9.

79. Lane, "Breeches and Rum," 21.

80. Josiah Pierce interleaved almanacs, Hadley (MA) Historical Society.

81. Main, "Gender, Work, and Wages in Colonial New England," 43. Main examined the ceilings imposed by Westboro and Belchertown. I also use data from the ceilings imposed by South Hadley, recorded in Judd, "Miscellaneous," vol. 12:26. Thirty-eight Connecticut Valley towns assembled in convention at Northampton to set uniform prices throughout Hampshire County. Prices were established in proportion to those set for Boston. See Barbara Clark Smith, "The Politics of Price Control in Revolutionary Massachusetts, 1774–1780" (Ph.D. diss., Yale University, 1983), 277–278.

82. Judd, "Miscellaneous," vol. 9:160.

83. Judd, "Miscellaneous," vol. 9:158–160.

84. Judd, "Northampton," vol. 1:101b.

85. John Russell account books, 1763–1791, PVMA.

86. In all, seven men's names appear in Russell's accounts as having been at one time or another short-term employees in his shop. Lane, "Breeches and Rum," 15–16.

87. *Hampshire Gazette*, November 6, 1799; May 28, 1806; November 22, 1815.

88. *Hampshire Gazette*, November 4, 1795; November 6, 1799; May 28, October 29, 1806; November 22, 1815.

89. *Hampshire Gazette*, July 27, 1808. An interesting notice regarding a runaway apprentice appeared in the December 16, 1794, edition: "Ran away from Heman Pomeroy, a boy indentured to the Tailoring business, Thomas Curtis, 17 years old, 5'7," his "complexion rather resembling the American Native, roguish eyes and dark hair." The Native American communities that once flourished in the Connecticut Valley were largely scattered by the end of the eighteenth century, but notices like this one remind us that some remained in the area.

90. It is also possible that tailors sought to hire apprentices in the summer months when, in addition to their work in the shop, they might also be able to assist with summer chores on the farm. I am grateful to Edward Cooke, Jr., for suggesting this possibility.

91. Judd, "Northampton," vol. 1:94, 101b.

92. On tramping as an essential part of craftsmen's training, see Garrison, "Builders and the Myth of Deskilling."

93. Lane, "Breeches and Rum," 20.

94. Karin Calvert, "The Function of Fashion in Eighteenth-Century America," in Cary Carson, Ronald Hoffman, and Peter J. Albert, eds., *Of Consuming Interests: The Style of Life in the Eighteenth Century* (Charlottesville, 1994), esp. 274 (quotation).

95. *Hampshire Gazette*, May 9, 1798.

96. *Hampshire Gazette*, July 17, 1799.

97. *Hampshire Gazette*, August 7, 1799.

98. *Hampshire Gazette*, October 10, 1798.

99. *Hampshire Gazette*, August 14, 1816, October 29, 1817.

100. Gamber, *Female Economy*, 5. By "workshop setting" here, I mean to include workshops proper as well as the spaces and times set aside for remunerative needlework in domestic settings, as opposed to work performed at home for members of the household.

101. See also Carol L. Loats, "Gender, Guilds, and Work Identity: Perspectives from Sixteenth-Century Paris," *French Historical Studies* 20 (1997): 15–30.

102. Main, "Gender, Work, and Wages in Colonial New England"; Judd, "Miscellaneous," vol. 9:161–163.

103. See Ulrich, *Age of Homespun*, and "Wheels, Looms, and the Gender Division of Labor."

104. Ulrich, *Age of Homespun*, 4.

105. Ulrich, *Age of Homespun*, 104.

106. Ulrich, "Wheels, Looms, and the Gender Division of Labor," 12.

107. Ulrich, "Wheels, Looms, and the Gender Division of Labor," 12–13. Interestingly, Catherine Graves's recollection of Northampton, in Judd, "Northampton," vol. 1:98, does not conform to the patterns Ulrich observed. Graves reported that "weaving was most of it performed by men. They followed it as a trade. Women did not weave much."

108. Judd, "Northampton," vol. 1:94, 101b.

109. The first such guide printed in the United States was James Queen and William Lapsley, *The taylors' instructor, or, A comprehensive analysis, of the elements of cutting garments, of every kind . . . Illustrated with eight appropriate engravings* (Philadelphia, 1809), but such literature flooded the market in the 1820s and 1830s. See, for example, Erastus B. Wightman and Joseph Wightman, *The tailor's assistant . . . intended to supersede the necessity of teachers* (New York, 1823); Fielder Clark, *An Easy and Correct Method of Cutting Men's Garments by Geometrical Rules . . .* (Woodstock, VT, 1823); and John Moxley, *Every One His Own Tailor: The Improved Compass Rule, Now Called By The Third, to Cut Garments* (Danville, VT, 1823).

110. The early nineteenth-century transition to industrial production in the clothing industry is described in a number of excellent studies, including Kidwell and Christman, *Suiting Everyone*; Joan M. Jensen and Sue Davidson, eds., *A Needle, a Bobbin, a Strike: Women Needleworkers in America* (Philadelphia, 1984); and Thomas Dublin, *Transforming Women's Work: New England Lives in the Industrial Revolution* (Ithaca, 1994).

7

By mid-century, a growing market-oriented economy in the valley increasingly clashed with the entrenched system of aristocratic preference based on kinship. This contradiction produced deep divisions in Northampton society and in that of the surrounding valley.

The "River Gods," as county magistrates for the royal colonial government, derived their authority from the Crown. During the upheavals of the early 1770s, they had been instrumental in keeping the valley from taking precipitous action against British rule. When Great Britain passed the Coercive Acts in 1774, those in Hampshire County who had quietly supported the Boston patriots now rallied to the cause. The gentry who were colonial officials were the first targets. Angry crowds demanded that the suspected Tories declare their loyalty. If they refused, they were turned out of office and publicly, sometimes violently, humiliated. In Northampton, the Revolution was indeed "The World Turn'd Upside Down" as merchants like Levi Shepherd eclipsed the landholding squirearchy in power and influence.

Gregory Nobles chronicles these events, showing how the regional response to the American Revolution was forged in the crucible of local politics.

Revolution in the Neighborhood*

GREGORY H. NOBLES

THE people of Hampshire County were hardly in the forefront of the Revolutionary movement. For almost a generation they had been too embroiled in their own local affairs—too worried about, for instance, the state of their religion, the boundaries of their towns, the location of their meetinghouses—to pay much attention to the growing crisis in Boston. It was only through the repeated efforts of the urban radicals on the Boston Committee of Correspondence that the majority of people in Hampshire County were awakened to the larger colonial issues. Even so, that awakening came relatively late, generally not until 1774.

But when the westerners did enter the Revolution, their political attitudes were not simply the creation of the Boston Whigs. The parochial disputes that had so engrossed the inhabitants of Hampshire County during the previous thirty years had their own political meaning and importance. On one level many people had gained experience as political actors, organizing and

* From Gregory H. Nobles, *Divisions throughout the Whole: Politics and Society in Hampshire County, Massachusetts, 1740–1775* (Cambridge, MA, 1983).

mobilizing themselves into groups to pursue a particular local issue. Moreover, in defining those issues, many people had gained a clearer and more immediate sense of the fundamental political values, independence and self-government, for instance, that underlay the Revolutionary movement. In that sense local politics helped create the basis for a popular response to the politics of the larger colonial struggle.

At the same time the larger struggle had its effect on local politics. The recent events in the county had begun a political transformation in Hampshire County, giving new groups of people a greater degree of political autonomy and undermining the influence and authority of the traditional county leaders. In the first years of the Revolution many of these people pushed that transformation even further, not just by taking a generally more forceful role in county politics but also by taking the lead in deposing the old county leaders. In that respect the sword of the Revolution cut two ways. Just as the political change in the county helped prepare the way for the Revolution, the Revolution in turn provided an opportunity for emphasizing and accelerating many of those local changes. Put differently, the Revolution both followed and furthered a widespread local revolution in Hampshire County that had been growing for years.

A YEAR or two before the outbreak of the American Revolution, a man with the remarkable name of Silent Wilde began work as an express rider between Boston and the Connecticut Valley. Every two weeks he would ride into Northampton and then on up the river to Deerfield carrying the latest Boston newspapers for his regular customers, each of whom paid him a dollar for six months' service. Wilde's problem was that he had too few customers, only about eight or ten in Northampton, probably no more in Deerfield. As any modern-day news carrier could quickly attest, this was not a terribly profitable route.[1]

Silent Wilde's problem as news carrier was only part of a larger problem that existed in Hampshire County even into the early 1770s: communications between Boston and the west remained sporadic, sparse, and fairly limited. News traveled slowly and was often stale by the time it reached everyone in the far parts of the province. Moreover, Wilde's circulation figures suggest that the demand for such news in western Massachusetts was relatively slight. People did not seem to be clamoring for stacks of newspapers and broadsides; they appeared content to keep to themselves, just as they had done for years.

At the time of the Stamp Act crisis, for instance, the political life of Boston was punctuated regularly by protest and riot, violence and tumult, while Hampshire County remained comparatively quiet on the whole issue. Politics in the city was not confined to the council chambers or House of Representatives but spilled out into the street. The popular anger over the Stamp Act reached a climax as mobs tore through Thomas Hutchinson's house, smashing furniture and household goods, taking vengeance on his belongings when they could not find the man himself. From 1765 on, relations between the people of Boston and the royal government were marked by violence of both word and deed, and the heat of the Stamp Act crisis subsided only temporarily before rising repeatedly during the decade before the Revolution.[2]

In Hampshire County, by comparison, response to the changes in British policy seemed mild and almost nonexistent. Certainly nothing matched the vigor or violence of the Boston crowds. People in the west were aware of the Stamp Act, of course, and there was some scattered reaction. Josiah Pierce, a farmer in Hadley, did record in his diary, "The Repeal of the Burdensome Stamp Act laid upon the American Colonies by the British Parliament . . . was past and assented to by the King 18th March 1766 to take place 2nd May 1766." But then, without any further comment or reflection, Pierce turned his attention to other passing matters and noted in the next entry, "This year Worms prevail in orchards in the Beginning of June."[3] Though radical pamphleteers in Boston might rail against the "parasites" in the British government who seemed to be threatening American liberties, a farmer like Pierce had to be more immediately concerned with the real parasites threatening his fruit crop. Throughout Hampshire County, in fact, the Stamp Act crisis passed without any great burst of protest. A group of men at Westfield, thinking that the unavailability of stamped paper would make it difficult for them to sell land or make bail, banded together to protect each other from debt proceedings. Their minister, John Ballantine, dismissed the matter as a "Jubilee for debtors," since court proceedings were generally rendered ineffective. When Ballantine made further note of the response to the crisis, though, he wrote mostly of the "great tumult in Boston" or even of an ill-fated celebration in Hartford, where a bonfire spread to the local gunpowder supply and exploded. Nothing on the local scene really caught his eye. Indeed, during the 1760s the only serious instance of popular defiance of Crown policies took place in Northampton when a number of men stole over three hundred pine logs marked as royal property under the Pine Laws. Resistance to the Pine Laws, however, was a fairly old and fairly common reaction among New England woodsmen, not necessarily connected to the other problems or protests of the 1760s. In general, people in Hampshire County spent most of the decade before the Revolution still living in a state of relative isolation from Boston, giving only the slightest attention to the wider controversy developing in the east.[4]

Probably the surest sign of Hampshire County's remoteness from the imperial debate was the general failure of county towns to send representatives to the Convention of Towns in 1768. Keeping a man in Boston had never been a common habit, of course, as it was too expensive for most of the small western towns; throughout the 1760s only a few of the larger, wealthier towns of Hampshire County were represented in Boston.[5] But even in this time of crisis the involvement of western towns did not increase; some towns actually drew back from the controversy. Joseph Hawley, for instance, had generally served his town as representative in Boston, and during the 1750s and 1760s he had gradually broken with Israel Williams and the other Hampshire representatives and had risen to some prominence among the radical leadership in the General Court. In 1768 he joined Sam Adams, Thomas Cushing, James Otis, and John Hancock in drafting the Circular Letter in protest of the Townshend Acts. But his radical activity in Boston was essentially a matter of his own doing, not the express wishes of his town. When Governor Bernard dissolved the assembly because of its refusal to rescind the Circular Letter, and when the town of Boston subsequently called for the Convention of Towns in defiance of the governor's action, Hawley's neighbors and constituents at Northampton voted almost unanimously not to send him or anyone else as a representative to the convention.[6]

An even chillier response came from Hatfield, one of Northampton's neighboring towns. There the members of the town meeting, still under the influence of Israel Williams, wrote that "in our opinion the measures the town of Boston are pursuing and proposing unto us and the people of this province to unite in, are unconstitutional, illegal, and wholly unjustifiable, and what will give the enemies of our Constitution the greatest joy, subversive of government and destructive of the peace and good order which is the cement of society."[7]

In the end only three Hampshire County towns—Brimfield, Montague, and Colrain—chose to send delegates to the 1768 convention. Especially for the people of Montague and Colrain, such an act must have been an important undertaking, for both were newer towns that had never sent a representative to Boston before. But other county towns simply failed to send a delegate and let the matter pass without comment; if they, too, worried about possible cracks in the cement of society, they never said so.[8] For Hampshire County as a whole it seems likely that the extraordinary political situation of 1768 failed to alter the political habits of ordinary times: the people of the west made no great effort to participate in shaping either provincial policy or protest.

From 1768 almost until the beginning of the Revolutionary War their reticence continued. While people in Boston denounced the tyranny of each successive British move, their fellow provincials in the west seldom communicated with them or sent their support. Even by late 1772 and early 1773, when the Boston Committee of Correspondence sent out its first pamphlet and circular letter warning each town of the growing danger, there seemed to be little evidence of interest or urgency in Hampshire County. Over half the towns throughout Massachusetts responded, and most offered their hearty support of the efforts of the Boston leaders. In Hampshire County, however, the response was again fairly paltry, as only seven of the forty-one towns and districts bothered to write back.[9]

To be sure, those few that did respond—for the most part smaller, newer towns that had not been active in provincial politics before—were no less supportive than other towns to the east, expressing a sensitivity to the questions of natural rights and British oppression. As the people of Pelham put it in a long and emphatic letter, "We have considered your Circular letter and are Not a little Shoked at the attempts upon the liberty of America." Yet rather than commit themselves to following the possibly precipitous actions of urban radicals, the Pelhamites noted that "we Study to be Quiet and do nothing rashly" in order to avoid the charge of mutiny and sedition. They further urged all others in Massachusetts to "have Patience alonger in our humble Suits for Justice to the British throne." But if patience should prove fruitless, they concluded,

> and our Humble Petitions for our own Natural and Promised Rights Shall be baffled & Refuge on Earth and Hope of Redress Shall fail us we trust We shall be Wanting in nothing in our power . . . to Unite With our Dear Countrymen for our Mutual Good and Shall Venture our Properties & Lives in Executing any Plan Pointed out by the Supreme Ruler and as the innate . . . Principles of Self Preservation & love to our Posterity may oblige us.

Their words of caution gave over to a declaration of resolution, and the Pelham people placed themselves apart from the general isolationism of their neighboring towns; they closed their letter pledging themselves to "Remain united with our breathren in the Common Cause of American Liberty."[10] Such a firm sentiment, though, was exceptional: more often the first appeals of the Boston Committee brought back nothing from Hampshire County towns but the uncertain meaning of silence.

It was not really until the middle of 1774 that most Hampshire towns took it upon themselves to write. In May of that year Parliament, angered specifically by the Boston Tea Party and generally by the rising level of radicalism and resistance in Boston and the surrounding towns, passed what were collectively known as the Coercive Acts, by far the most stringent regulations Boston and the rest of Massachusetts had seen. Almost immediately the political crisis that had hitherto been largely confined to eastern Massachusetts became a much more compelling issue for the province as a whole. With no thought of exaggeration, people throughout Massachusetts—and indeed, throughout the American colonies in general—began to talk seriously of their own enslavement at the hands of the British ministry. Hardly anyone could mistake the harshly punitive effect the Boston Port Act was intended to have on the people of Boston, nor could anyone doubt that such measures might soon be in store for other Americans in other places.[11]

The British officials in London seemed determined to act with a heavy hand; the radical leaders in Boston reacted swiftly by taking pen in hand. Once again the Boston Committee of Correspondence took the initiative in proposing a popular response to such tyranny, and on June 8 it sent out another circular letter to all the towns in the province, this time calling for concrete and concerted action. It drafted a Solemn League and Covenant whereby the towns of Massachusetts would agree to cut off all commercial dealings with the mother country by August 31, 1774, thus establishing a specific timetable for joint action. It was not the kind of demand to be easily ignored, and Hampshire towns could no longer remain aloof from the urgent situation facing Boston and the colonies at large. Throughout the summer of 1774, they responded in numbers far greater than before, and by September half the towns in the county had communicated at some point with the Boston Committee. This upsurge in letter writing created a new and weighty responsibility for Silent Wilde, "our News Carier," who, as the main communications link between Boston and the western region, found himself much more in demand than he had been even a year earlier.[12]

The people of the western Massachusetts countryside, however, did not react just to show their sympathy and support for their fellow provincials in the city. They faced an immediate problem of their own with the Coercive Acts. In order to curtail the growing political activity and unrest that seemed to be emerging in Boston and other towns, the British government had imposed the Massachusetts Government Act, restricting the townspeople to no more than one town meeting a year without special permission from the governor; in addition, to offset further the political independence of all regions of the province, the new regulations placed county judicial officials—judges, sheriffs, and by extension jurors—under direct control of the governor, who alone would have the power of appointment. Much as it had done in the revolutionary times of the early 1690s, in short, the British government sought to consolidate its authority in Massachusetts by increasing its hold on the county political machinery, strengthening it at the expense of the individual towns.[13]

In that respect the Massachusetts Government Act seemed to run counter to the recent movement of events in Hampshire County. For the past quarter-century the history of the county had been marked in large part by the rapid growth of new towns and by the concurrent if somewhat more gradual decline of the county elite. The two trends were by no means unrelated. As the county became more crowded and complex, many people—most notably many of those whose recent arrival had added so greatly to the swell of population—came to seek a kind of smaller-scale simplicity. Rather than try to accommodate themselves to the expansion of the older and larger towns, they struggled to establish their own separate communities, each one an independent entity with its own political institutions and political leaders. In a sense their actions bespoke a fundamentally conservative impulse to recreate for themselves the traditions of localism and communal autonomy that were deeply rooted in the past of early New England. At the same time this parochial conservatism posed a growing challenge to an equally well-rooted (albeit rather more English) form of regional conservatism, the system of county-wide authority defined in Hampshire County by the Williams family's kinship ties and enhanced greatly by the government's generous patronage over the years. That is, as people created new and independent towns, they began to place themselves outside—and in some cases in opposition to—the traditional network of the established county leaders; by the early 1770s the power of Williams and his regional allies had not been destroyed, but it had at least been significantly diluted.

The new Crown regulations seemed clearly destined to reverse that trend. Scarcely had the inhabitants of some of the new towns begun to hold town meetings then they found themselves facing new restrictions on their right to do so. Moreover, as if their own loss of local political authority were not bad enough in itself, they also had to consider the prospect that the authority of the Williams organization would be reinvigorated and reinforced to the point at which it would overshadow the independence of the individual towns and once again stand as a pervasive source of political order for the county as a whole. In short, though the people of Hampshire County did not feel the full weight of repression that fell on Boston in 1774, many of them still had good reason to fear for their own rights in their own neighborhood.

It should hardly be surprising, then, that the people of some of the newer, smaller towns took the lead in communicating with the urban radicals. Indeed, the growing exchange of correspondence seemed to underscore their political emergence. As the Boston Committee recognized even the smallest frontier towns as autonomous, politically independent bodies, the towns had a compelling opportunity to recognize that autonomy and independence for themselves. Faced with framing a collective reply to Boston, the people of these towns necessarily had to assess local feeling and put that feeling clearly into words—in some cases for the first time in the town's history.[14] They might be on the one hand understandably deferential toward the Boston leadership, hesitant about the limits of their own abilities as "infant settlements." It was not for them, as the committee from Williamsburg noted, to "Be so Arrogant as to undertake to direct you as to any Particular conduct in Such an important Critical Day But leave that to your Juditious Judgment together with Those that are better Quallified to give you advice than we."

But even as they drew this self-effacing distinction between themselves and the Boston Whigs, the people of Williamsburg seemed to warm to the task of expressing clearly their own political stance. "The principal aim of our wrighting," they went on, "was to let you know That we are almost unanimously of the opinion by all mean to Resist Great briton in their unconstitutional measures By which they usurp upon our character priveledges even to blood. Also if you (being in the front rank) need our assistance in Aposing them we stand ready to grant it according to the Utmost of our Small capacity." In closing they offered a forceful, almost militant, declaration of their collective will; both their duty and their interest compelled them, they asserted, "and when duty and interest agree We esteem him a poor Souldier indeed that will not exart Himself to his very utmost."[15] For the people of Williamsburg as for people elsewhere, confronting the issues raised by the Boston Committee caused them to confront the reality of their own political identity. The more they wrote to Boston, the more they wrote about themselves.

To some degree, of course, the language of most Hampshire County letters tended to be circumspect, full of both hesitation and resolution, not too different in general tone from that of letters from other towns in Massachusetts. Quite simply, no one wanted to act recklessly or alone. Only a few towns declared themselves to be as militant as Williamsburg or, like the small frontier town of Murrayfield, "Willing and Ready to Assist the Town of Boston together with the Rest of the Province in all prudent and proper measures . . . and likewise . . . ready (if we are called to it) to Defend our Rights and Priviledges even with the point of the Sword." Most other towns were quite a bit more guarded. The overall hope expressed by people throughout Hampshire County—and indeed, throughout the American colonies—was for the "Recovery and Establishment of their just rights and Liberties Civil and Religious and the restoration of that union and harmony between Great Brittan and her Collinies Most Ardently Desired by all good Men." Good Englishmen all, these rural westerners shared the common ability to distinguish between George III as their rightful sovereign and Parliament as a corrupt body whose acts were "callculated to perplex and enslave his Majesty's free and Loyal Province." With absolutely no sense of irony or contradiction they could "Sympathize with their Suffering Brethren of Boston and Charlestown" and yet still see themselves as part of the "Mother Country . . . with Just Rights, Priviledges, and Honour of the English Nation in General." Although British oppression appeared to be real enough, people urged "Prudence, Moderation, and Firmness." To many the exact terms of the Boston proposal, the formal signing of a covenant with a rigid deadline of August 31, seemed "rather Premature and too precipitate." The basic sentiment toward some sort of nonimportation agreement was mostly favorable, and as the people of Granby made clear, they had "generally agreed to enter into the

Measures therein proposed." There was, however, "a Question Arising in the Minds of Some whether the Form of that Covenant should be Literally adopted." Given this almost universal hesitancy, perhaps the radical leaders in Boston had to content themselves with the simple fact of the response itself: more people were writing, and mere communication was an important first step.[16]

Still, some letters went beyond the normal language of response and proved to be especially revealing, providing a fresh look at the parochial political world of Hampshire County. Not surprisingly, these western farmers did not deal simply in abstract political principles or even in terms defined solely by the Boston Committee of Correspondence. They wrote sympathetically about the problems of Boston, but they also took the occasion to discuss a few problems of their own. Many of these letters—again, most notably those from some of the newer towns—clearly drew a connection between the general colonial crisis and the political situation that existed in Hampshire County. However uncertain people might have been about their role in the former, they had emphatic opinions about the latter.

Above all, they made it quite clear that the current situation only heightened their suspicion of the local political elite. As the people of Colrain put it, Hampshire County was a dangerous region where "some of the Great men" were devious enough to spread false rumors and undermine patriotic zeal. From a number of towns came the disturbing message that "It is generally Reported in these parts that Very few Towns fall in with the proposals" of the Boston Whigs, and that

> by false Insinuations, some of our people are led to think the Covenants are a plan laid by the Merchants, in Boston, tye the hands of the people, to vend of the goods they have on hand, and at Extravagant price. We therefore desire, something may be made publick, relative to the affair (which may have a Tendency to open the eyes of a great Number in the County of Hampshire) and if you think best in your wisdom to send to this Town in particular, it will Give Satisfaction to us.[17]

The Boston Committee was quick to counter such rumors and sent back reassuring replies. The "Art of the Tories in your part of the Province" had to be acknowledged, the Committee admitted; someone, it seemed, had been clever enough to take advantage of the backwoods settlers' fears of big city merchants. For that reason the people of the towns had to be especially vigilant and independent, refusing to let themselves be misled by designing men in positions of power.[18]

Some people scarcely had to be warned. At Wilbraham the local Committee of Correspondence noted that anyone not following the lead of the Continental Congress in adopting its "Salutary Measures" could not be a friend to the county, and "We Shall not think our Selves obliged to Show any Special

Regards to them." As the writers added with pointed emphasis, "If they be Judges in Law, or Attorneys at the Bar, we will neglect them as much as possible."[19] For the people of Wilbraham, who counted no judges or attorneys among their neighbors, the specific reference could hardly have been an automatic or unthinking turn of phrase. Their letter reflected a sensitivity to the political loyalties of a whole class of local leaders beyond the bounds of their small town. By no means did they express the toleration of and desire for reconciliation with their errant countrymen that they had declared for their mother country and king. In general, in some of the towns outside the traditional seats of power, people were showing themselves to be increasingly unwilling to take their political cues from the established leaders of Hampshire County. With such "Enemies to American Liberty" in positions of authority, it became important for many towns to communicate directly with Boston; doing so had "opened the eyes of some" and might further "have a Tendency to open the eyes of a great number in the County of Hampshire." Armed with information from the Boston Committee, people could discount the rumors, leaving the perpetrators of falsehood to "tell that to some body else."[20]

Even as the people of Hampshire County embraced the wider provincial and national movement, then, one very important focus of their radicalism remained primarily local. Many westerners may have come to look to Boston for political guidance, but they had to look no further than their own county for political targets. The several unflattering references to the "Great men" of Hampshire County that crop up in the letters to Boston serve as only a small indication of the ill will many people already felt toward the traditional county leadership, a reflection of an antipathy that had been growing for years. That earlier hostility had never been so clearly articulated by so many people at once, of course, but had tended to emerge somewhat sporadically in particular towns over particular grievances. With the heightening of the general colonial crisis, however, the political antagonisms in Hampshire County also became more sharply defined. The established county leaders suddenly seemed not just unpopular but potentially oppressive, their local authority dangerously augmented by a distant and devious group of ministers in the British government. In that sense the actions of the British government focused attention on the position of the county elite and forced people throughout Hampshire to confront the prospects for the future of the county. Unless they were willing to accept a new local political arrangement imposed from outside their neighborhood, they would have to take immediate action within. And for that reason the first burst of revolutionary activity in the county turned out to be an almost entirely local affair. No matter what the people of Wilbraham had said about their desire to ignore their unpatriotic county leaders and "neglect them as much as possible," these leaders quickly became the victims of close and sometimes quite painful attention.

The whole process of local upheaval began on a rather grand scale. On the morning of August 30, 1774, people from towns all over Hampshire County, a mob between one and three or four thousand strong, converged on Springfield, where the county court was scheduled to sit that day. The ringing of the bell across the river in West Springfield provided the signal for the final march, and the crowd moved into the center of Springfield and surrounded the courthouse. There they called out the justices. One by one the members of the court were questioned about loyalty to the Crown and to their country, each one being asked to sign a declaration renouncing all authority derived from royal commissions. Faced with such a menacing throng before them, most of the justices submitted to the will of the crowd quietly if not altogether sincerely. The two most powerful figures, John Worthington and Israel Williams, tried to defend themselves before the mob, but in the end they merely succeeded in increasing the anger and passion of the people. Especially Worthington, who was being humiliated in his hometown by outsiders, attempted to maintain some sense of his authority before the crowd. But according to one witness to the scene,

> The sight of him flashed lightning from their eyes. Their spirits were already raised and the sight of this object gave them additional force. He had not refused his new office of counsellor. For that reason especially he was very obnoxious. But the people kept their tempers. He attempted to harangue them in mittagation of his conduct, but he was soon obliged to desist. The people were not to be dallied with. Nothing would satisfy them but a renunciation.

Likewise, Israel Williams tried to argue that even though he had disagreed with the people before, he would henceforth "join them in the common cause." Few people believed him, of course, and he was forced to renounce his commission along with the rest.[21] His troubles were only beginning.

Such a massive event was something hardly anyone in Hampshire County had ever experienced. To some it offered quite a frightening prospect. As the Reverend Jonathan Judd of Southampton wrote in distress, "Every Body submitted to our Sovereign Lord the Mob—Now we are reduced to a State of Anarchy, have neither Law nor any other Rule except the Law of Nature . . . to go by." Judd's fear of anarchy, however, may have been a bit overblown. As several historians have convincingly argued, one must not assume too readily that mob action—or crowd action, to use a less emotive term—necessarily involved excessive violence, injustice, or anarchy. More often the actions of mobs in preindustrial Europe and America represented a means of defending traditional rights or of dispensing justice when local magistrates seemed unable or unwilling to do so. This European heritage of crowd behavior crossed the Atlantic with the migrants to British North America, and during the colonial period there were recorded numerous instances of mob action throughout the American colonies, even in pre-Revolutionary Hampshire County. Far from being something altogether foreign and fearful, extra-legal activity had its place within the cultural traditions of early American society, and however much some people may have thought it an unwelcome inheritance, others clearly saw it as a legitimate form of political behavior.[22]

Some reports of local mob activity, in fact, emphasized not so much the fear of chaos and disorder as an appreciation of the careful self-restraint of the people involved. At the time of the closing of the Hampshire County court, the Reverend Judd's visions of chaos were countered by a somewhat more sympathetic observation by Joseph Clarke of Northampton, who noted that "the strictest order of justice [was] observed" by the assembled thousands at Springfield. "The people to their honor behaved with the greatest order & regularity, a few individuals excepted, and avoided, as much as possible, confusion." Perhaps nothing could suggest this sense of self-conscious discipline better than the final action of the mob after its work was done for the day. Having come together as a single body to exert mass pressure on the county justices, the people of the various towns ended the day by drawing themselves up into individual town companies and marching around Springfield carrying staves and playing martial music.[23]

The action of the mob at Springfield represented an important break with the political patterns of the past and provided a massive foreshadowing of the changes that were to come over the course of the next few months. The people of the towns, acting together as a coherent group, became a regulating force to challenge and discipline the county's ruling men. Implicit in their final parade was the notion that the large crowd gathered that day was in reality a collection of smaller groups, each one representing a particular town: even in a large collective effort localism still provided a form of order and political identity for the participants. Yet in closing the court the several mobs acted together for a goal of county-wide importance. It became immediately apparent that the established political leaders, especially those whose influence extended into the government of the county, could no longer expect to exercise the power and authority they had long known, nor could they expect to have to deal only with their own townspeople on political matters. People were beginning to express their concerns for the political situation of the county as a whole, and they were therefore beginning to take action on a county level.

In the months following the events at Springfield there erupted a number of other smaller incidents of isolated mob activity in Hampshire County, and in this early period of unrest the crowd actions shared a common pattern that revealed even more clearly the significant changes in the particular political situation of the county. In most cases people of one town moved on another neighboring town to attack the leading citizens there, generally before there had been any real attempt by the local townspeople to take direct action against their own leaders. More to the point, the inhabitants of the newer towns tended to be the first to undertake such actions, just as they had been among the first to respond to the call of the radicals in Boston. Compressed into a fairly brief period in late 1774 and early 1775, these outbreaks of external regulation by outsiders helped bring about a kind of regional revolution within the larger political context of the national revolution. Once the large mob at Springfield had made the first overt challenge to the county leadership, these local mobs pushed that challenge even further.

Some of the older, more comfortable towns quickly became uncomfortable havens for many of their leaders, and as one inhabitant of Deerfield wrote to a friend, "It is a Bisy time with us, mobbing." Just a week or so after the Springfield incident, for instance, a mob from Williamsburg marched on Hatfield to seek out Israel Williams, Oliver Partridge, and some of the other town officials. A crowd from Montague repeatedly threatened to move on Deerfield, and the people of Pelham and Shutesbury were reportedly "ready to act in a mob way" against the suspected Tories in Amherst. In February 1775 a mob from Pelham descended on Hatfield, once again aiming to get Israel Williams. The Pelham people took Williams and his son, carried them to Hadley, and in one of the most locally famous acts of ritual retribution, smoked them overnight in a house with a clogged chimney. Upon their release the next morning both Israel and his son were encouraged to sign yet another confession and declaration of loyalty. The next day the same mob moved on to Northampton to seek out Solomon Stoddard, son of John Stoddard and grandson of the Reverend Solomon Stoddard—certainly one of Northampton's finest pedigrees. Not only was Stoddard generally suspected of being a Tory, but he was also an important creditor for many of the Pelham men and therefore a doubly attractive target. He was in poor health, however, and the Pelhamites spared him the smoking they gave Williams, asking only that he sign a confession and repent. Once again, one of the most succinct observations on the mob's behavior in its dealing with Williams and Stoddard came from Southampton's Reverend Judd, still no friend to extralegal activity. "They act like mad people," he complained, "tho well for a Mob."[24]

Judd was by no means alone in his uneasiness; he could report with grim satisfaction that "People condemn the Mob very freely to Day and I fancy that something will be done by the Committee about it." Even Joseph Hawley, Northampton's leading Whig, reacted with alarm when the Pelhamites came after his kinsman Stoddard, declaring himself opposed to "Such private disturbances and restraining people of yr liberty." Hawley himself had been perhaps too soft on Stoddard, but there were also others in the town who "were engaged . . . to endeavor to stop the Mob from any further abuse to those they have." Throughout Northampton and elsewhere the fear spread among other leading Whigs that people acting on their own accord might too easily go out of control. Indeed, at the very first outbreak of mob activity in the fall of 1774, a group of local leaders meeting in a county convention passed a pointed resolution that "we would heartily recommend to all the inhabitants of this county, not to engage in any riots, or licentious attacks upon the person or property of any one, as being subversive of all order and government." If there was to be a political upheaval in Hampshire County, some men clearly hoped to keep it within certain bounds.[25]

As the local mobs continued their actions, however, others saw them in a much more favorable light and were not so quick to condemn their actions. There may have been people in Northampton, for instance, who "were engaged . . . to endeavor to stop the Mob," but according to the town's historian, the Pelham crowd did its work in Northampton "aided and abetted . . . by men residing here."[26] The point is not that a substantial number of people in Northampton or any of the other county towns actually looked forward to a future of permanent mob rule, but, rather, that extralegal activity represented an extraordinary way of dealing with extraordinary circumstances, and some people accepted mob activity because they appreciated its political possibilities. Outsiders could sometimes do what insiders themselves could not do: they could act without the traditional restraints of neighborliness and local deference and thus take more direct and extreme action against their selected targets. In that sense the outsiders provided a useful service by being the first to disrupt the order within the town, saving the locals from having to take full responsibility later for their own actions or desires.

The most detailed account of one such crowd action in Hampshire County survives in a series of depositions written by members of a mob from the "infant settlement" of Williamsburg. On September 6, 1774, less than two weeks after they had drafted their first reply to the Boston Committee of Correspondence, a crowd of Williamsburg people gathered around the Liberty Pole in the center of their town and made ready to set off for neighboring Hatfield, their parent town and still the home of Israel Williams. From their descriptions of their march we get a sense not only of their own goals and desires, but of the reaction of the Hatfield people as well.[27] On one level, then, the incident serves to reveal something of the changing relationship between the people of the old towns and those of the new and, in even more general terms, to highlight some of the critical issues and tensions underlying the rapidly changing political context of Hampshire County on the eve of the Revolution.

Perhaps buoyed and somewhat emboldened by the force of their own words to the Boston Committee, the Williamsburg people were still uneasy as they milled around the Liberty Pole, and some fell into a nervous discussion about what exactly they were going to do. Fearing resistance in Hatfield, a few men had brought their guns. Most of the members of the crowd seemed unwilling to risk such a potentially dangerous confrontation, and they urged a general agreement that everyone leave his weapon at home. Their hope was that strength lay in numbers, and they sent a representative, James Hunt, to the neighboring village of Cummington to round up a few more people. They also sent another man, Benjamin Read, into Hatfield to get a better idea of the situation there.[28]

When Read arrived at Hatfield he was met by Israel Chapin, one of the Hatfield constables. Chapin asked Read what business the Williamsburg people had in mind, "whether we were comeing to rectifi privet Damages Especly to punish Coll. Williams Reletive to an old Difuculty." As Read later described the incident, the Hatfield constable at first

> Labour'd to Discourage us But after he understood that we had no desire to Rectifi privet Damages he Did not Disapprove of our comeing But incoraged it and said to this purpos that their was a corupt vicious . . . crew in Hatfield and that they ought to be Delt with he said I told Clark Williams last night that he Deserved Stripes he said that the two Colonels Williams and . . . Leut partridg David Biling Obediah Dickenson Asa White Trobridg and Left Biling deserved to be Delt with in Severity.

No doubt startled by such a sudden and vitriolic outburst against Hatfield's leading citizens, Benjamin Read hastened to assure Constable Chapin that "we was comeing in Regular order and that we Do not Desire to damage any person [or] property with whom our Busness might Lead us to have to Do." In response, Chapin assured Read that if the mob acted with the discipline and purpose described, virtually everyone in Hatfield would join them and help take action against "those toryes." Exactly what happened after that remains unclear, lost in conflicting stories and incomplete evidence. There is no record that the Williamsburg people actually found Israel Williams or the other Hatfield leaders that day, or even that they got all the way to Hatfield in one body.[29]

Yet even if the Williamsburg people never did actually lay hands on Israel Williams, the exchange between Benjamin Read and Israel Chapin still had an important meaning of its own. Above all, both men had no trouble agreeing that Williams and his local allies deserved, as Constable Chapin put it, "to be Delt with in Severity." Moreover, both seemed likewise to agree that it was not inappropriate that a mob from outside Hatfield come into town to take action against Williams and the others. Indeed, Constable Chapin seems to have put aside his normal task of maintaining order in Hatfield in favor of giving strong encouragement to the outsiders and in the end even becoming especially vehement in his denunciation of his townsmen. If there was any hesitation or confusion in his mind, it arose only with regard to the actual motives of the people from Williamsburg, a suspicion that somehow they were "comeing to rectifi privet Damages . . . Reletive to an old Difuculty" and not to deal with the Hatfield leaders for being "toryes."

However much Chapin might have been convinced by Read's response, he had raised an important question that defied an easy answer. For insiders as well as outsiders, the issue of motive may have been much more complex than either party was willing to admit. Neither Read nor Chapin said, of course, what private grievances the people of Williamsburg might hold against Israel Williams. Perhaps everyone knew what the problem was, and no one had to say; it may have had to do with the terms of the recent separation of Williamsburg from Hatfield, or it may have stemmed from even earlier problems that may not have been related to or resolved by the separation. Unfortunately, there is nothing in the records of either town to make it possible to identify the issue with any certainty. The point is simply that there apparently was some local grievance recognized fairly readily by people in both towns, and at least one person thought it plausible that the "old Difuculty" might still be the motive for mob action even at a time when newer, more menacing difficulties seemed to be emerging all around. Although Chapin and Read both implicitly agreed that a commingling of past and present complaints should not occur, they both implicitly admitted that it could happen.

Even so, such an admission would not necessarily imply a conscious and cynical attempt by the Williamsburg people to use the broader political context as a convenient cover for pursuing their own parochial ends. In all fairness, one must suspect that they would have been unable to separate one set of issues completely from the other. How could they actually say, for instance, that their animosity toward Williams was simply a product of his stance in the current national crisis and not at least partly related to the position he had held for so long in their community and their county? Certainly Williams was a Tory, and since he had not renounced his allegiance to the Crown he stood as an obvious target. At the same time, however, Williams was a consistent symbol of the conservative social and political order within Hampshire County itself. He was the single most important source of authority in the whole region, and everyone—especially every dissident, whether religious or secular—knew that Williams was not far removed from any issue that affected the towns or people of the county. How could they deny that their desire to take abusive action against him did not indeed grow from a desire to settle old scores? Just as it would be impossible to estimate the variety of private debts people owed him, so would it be impossible to calculate the number of "privet Damages" people held against him. How, in short, could they essentially give Israel Williams a clean slate and then, suddenly in the summer of 1774, start making altogether new marks against him? Try as they might to stress the immediacy of their motives, they could hardly have forgotten all they had known, felt, or feared in the past.

In a somewhat different manner, the past figured equally heavily in the actions of the Hatfield people. If, as Chapin asserted, the townspeople were so hostile toward Williams and the "corupt vicious . . . crew" in Hatfield, why did they not take some action themselves without waiting for the instigation of outsiders? The question had in fact been raised just a few days before the mob appeared. Some Hatfield men had been talking with men from other nearby towns about Israel Williams and some of the other local Tories, and though the Hatfielders expressed the sentiment that someone should deal with Williams and the others, these men declined to take action themselves; explained one Hatfield resident, "It would Brake Neighborhood and therefore would Not Do so well as for . . . Strangers."[30]

It was an important request the Hatfield men made, and an interesting way of expressing it. Their desire for outside action was not simply a sign of cowardice or even hypocrisy among people unwilling to take direct action themselves. It suggested, rather, a conflict between their immediate political desires and their long-term political background. On the one hand, some Hatfielders, like the people of Williamsburg, had their own grudges and grievances from the past. They had challenged Williams and a few other town leaders before, occasionally denying them election to town office in recent years.[31] Now they wanted to go beyond the bounds of normal political procedures, to subject some of their leading townspeople not just to the will of the electorate but to the hands of a mob; implicit in this desire was the notion that mere electoral processes were not strong or forceful enough, and that the designated victims should undergo the personal, visible experience of public humiliation and perhaps even physical harm. On the other hand, though, the traditions of town life had a tempering effect. The inherited standards of communal unity and proper deference toward local leaders made it difficult for the Hatfield men themselves to inflict such exceptional treatment on their fellow townsmen.[32] As they explicitly pointed out to the outsiders, it was a serious matter to "Brake Neighborhood" and be the ones responsible for disrupting the order and integrity of the town. Only if someone from outside could come in and disrupt that order first would Hatfielders feel comfortable about joining in. Their sense of neighborhood, in short, did not keep them from wanting to attack certain neighbors, but it did make them maintain certain appearances.

To some extent, of course, the mob from Williamsburg could likewise have been accused of violating the neighborhood. Until the time of their separation from Hatfield in 1771, the Williamsburg people were themselves part of the Hatfield neighborhood, neighbors also of Williams and the other suspected Tories in the town.[33] Even after they formed their own separate town they could not escape all the old ties. But their political independence ultimately gave them a certain freedom of action their Hatfield neighbors did not have. At the very least they were no longer so directly under Williams's influence and control, no longer expected to deal with him as a fellow townsman or town leader. Despite his unquestioned prominence in the political affairs of the county, Williams could not participate directly in the political affairs of Williamsburg or impose his awesome presence on the town meeting. Indeed, the very fact that the people of Williamsburg had a Liberty Pole around which to gather was a visible indication of their newfound independence from Williams and the other Hatfield leaders. No one had dared raise a Liberty Pole in Hatfield, and as long as Williams and his sympathizers were still powerful in the town, no one was likely to do so. Anyone needing an example had to look no further than Deerfield, where local radicals had raised a Liberty Pole only to have it torn down by the town's strong conservative faction—among them several of Williams's kinsmen.[34]

But the people of Williamsburg did not have to worry about so direct a confrontation, either on the issue of a Liberty Pole or on any other issue. The Williamsburg people acted as an external force somewhat less hindered than Williams's townspeople by the inherited norms of town politics and communal harmony. In a sense they could "Brake Neighborhood" on the county level precisely because they did not have to do so on the town level. It was a subtle and almost artificial distinction, but not an unimportant one. On the eve of a local as well as a national revolution, the old standards of duty, deference, and obligation did not pass easily away. It became the task of outsiders like the Williamsburg mob to help accelerate the change.

In time, of course, the locals became a bit more forthright. After the brief period of mob actions in late 1774 and early 1775, and especially after the outbreak of hostilities at Lexington and Concord in April 1775, there no longer seemed any reason to be overly delicate in dealing with people suspected of political deviance. In towns throughout Hampshire County, 1775 marked the beginning of open attacks by townspeople on their own leaders, both secular and ecclesiastical. In some cases the action taken was relatively gentle; in other cases it was exceedingly harsh. But within the space of about a year important men in a number of towns found themselves humbled, harassed, or even expelled, never again to enjoy power in quite the ways they had known it before. Throughout the county the old figures of authority fell with surprising speed and even more surprising ease. Once the first real challenge had been successfully made at Springfield in August 1774, the pattern of change had begun. It may have been altered in style and intensity in a few instances, but it was never really reversed.

Once again, the case of Israel Williams best suggests the continuities between external and internal regulation. After his vocal encounter with the mob at Springfield, his near encounter with the smaller mob from Williamsburg, and his smoky encounter with the mob from Pelham, he eventually found even more severe trials facing him at the hands of the people of Hatfield. At first with some remnants of deference, but later with a stronger attitude of defiance, his townspeople turned against him and stripped him of his authority and his freedom. He lived the last years of his life among his fellow citizens as an outcast, increasingly a symbol of their rejection of all that he had once stood for.

In May 1775 the town's Committee of Correspondence openly broached the subject of support for the American cause in a letter to Williams and several other suspected Tories in Hatfield, asking that those "whom the Comtee may suspect as being inimical to their Country be requested to sign a declaration" professing their commitment to the defense of American liberties. Even so, the terms of the letter remained temperate if not necessarily deferential. The Hatfield Committee requested that Williams "walk over to Deacon Mortons and Satisfy the Committee of his Readiness to Join his Countrymen." They did nothing to intimidate him, and Williams remained at large, no longer a town leader but not yet a town prisoner. The longer he remained free, though, the more he came to be suspected of actual treason. The Hatfield Committee of Correspondence joined with other committees in the county and with officers of the county militia in writing Williams a blistering letter late in 1775 accusing him of "acting a part & executing a plan perfectly inconsistent with the Sense of this Province and all British America."

> Your Conduct has been from first to last one continued Series of Treason and Rebellion at your County and you have been and are Still an open avowed Enemy to your Country. . . . You with your little Banditti of Sons and Tools made it their Business to collect Names in Order for Prosecutions—your Plans and Designs of betraying and ruining your Country are all laid open . . . you can make no movement to execute your cursed detestable Plans but you are discovered—the People throughout the Province know you and all your Machinations and movements and think Death too mild a Punishment for you.

The letter closed with the suggestion that Williams depart for Boston and stay out of the county until the war should end.[35]

The fear of Williams's sedition was only compounded in late 1776 when some papers addressed from him to Thomas Hutchinson were intercepted. In his letter to Hutchinson Williams allegedly expressed "his certain Hope & expectation that our Enemies would very soon entirely defeat & fully Subdue the Americans," and according to the Hatfield Committee, such sentiments were enough to settle the question.[36] Williams and his son were arrested and locked up despite their protests of innocence.

The concern over so powerful and imposing a man as Israel Williams could hardly be exaggerated in the minds of his fellow citizens. As the Hatfield Committee explained to the Provincial Council after the arrest, "He has been & still is a Man of Considerable Influence with the People, & consequently has perswaded a Considerable number of Persons not only in this Town but we apprehend more or less in every Town in the County to adopt his Sentiments."[37] The charges against him served to indicate the kind of respect his townspeople still accorded him: they no longer recognized him as their own leader, but they still recognized him as a powerful and therefore dangerous man.

Israel Williams remained a prisoner in his own town for over three years, disgraced politically and disdained socially. The church even voted to deny him communion. Throughout the period of his incarceration Williams complained bitterly of "the hard Measures he has met with . . . owing to the People of Hatfield." His former neighbors would not deal with him honestly or openly, he argued, and he called upon them to submit all their accusations to public hearing "That He may vindicate himself if able—For there is no fencing against Daggers and Darts thrown in the dark." In a way, of course, the people of Hatfield may not have been able to express all their true feelings against Williams. Once they had him in jail for what appeared to be legitimate political reasons they could no doubt take some secret satisfaction in punishing him for his pride and power of former years. Those "Daggers and Darts" may have been thrown from the darkness of the past, sharpened long before the distinctions between Whig and Tory ever became clear. When he was finally let out of jail in 1780 and given the relative freedom of staying under house arrest, he remained in Hatfield until his death eight years later, a fallen if not forgotten man.[38] Abused first by the people of his county and then by the people of his own town, he had experienced perhaps more extensively than anyone else the full impact of political change in the region he had long governed. Once the initial break had been made in the neighborhood, he had nowhere to turn for refuge. In the end his own closest neighbors in Hatfield gave him the worst treatment of all.

In other towns local leaders suffered some form of the same treatment, ranging from outright political opposition to imprisonment. Most notably in some of the older towns in the county, where ruling elites had governed for years without any serious disruption in their authority, did the political changes in the early years of the Revolution seem sudden and striking. At Springfield, for instance, the once-powerful John Worthington found himself no longer able to direct the political affairs of his people, but instead was subject to their direction himself. After having to defend himself before the huge crowd of outsiders at the courthouse in August 1774, Worthington had to make a similar declaration of his patriotism before the people of Springfield. His patriotism was already highly suspect, for he had maintained clear allegiance to the Crown throughout the early stirrings of revolt; he had even considered at one point emigrating to Canada to avoid the hostile sentiments of his neighbors. Worthington eventually managed to clear himself in his public declaration and to remain in Springfield, but he was stripped of his power and influence for a few years. He and a number of other Springfield leaders were turned out of office in 1774 and 1775 and replaced with men who had begun to emerge as leaders in the local Revolutionary movement. As a later historian of the town described the political situation of the early Revolutionary period, "The names prominent in the doings at that time were not the best-known Springfield names." Faced with the growing hostility of their fellow townspeople, some of the old leaders decided to leave town for good; others stayed, and some of these, after altering their political views to fit the dominant popular opinion, even made it back into elected office during the middle years of the Revolution. But for a brief period at least, from 1775 until 1778, Springfield was the scene of a minor political upheaval. The old town leaders had been made victims of popular attack and had been deposed according to a new political standard defined by the people of the town.[39]

Similar changes took place in other towns as well, as the first months of the Revolutionary period brought an important break with the politics of the past. Formerly entrenched rulers were finally rooted out and replaced. Israel Williams's kinsmen at Deerfield, for instance, fell at about the same time he did. The Deerfield Williamses and their Ashley cousins had long been dominant both in local and in county offices, variously holding positions as selectman, town clerk, county judge, and justice of the peace; throughout the 1750s the family's power was at its peak. During the next decade that power began to wane somewhat, but even so, the clan continued to play a significant role in the politics of the town: Jonathan Ashley, Esq., repeatedly represented the family on the Board of Selectmen, and Thomas Williams served as town clerk until 1774. Moreover, several members of the family still held on to the appointive offices acquired through the good graces and patronage of their Hatfield relative. In 1774, however, they were cleaned out of office entirely.[40] The Deerfield voters were no longer willing to keep them in positions of power, and Israel Williams was no longer able. Indeed, their connection to Israel Williams, along with their own political attitudes, clearly marked them in the new political context of the county. Whatever degree of indulgence or respect had kept them politically active in the early 1770s vanished. The severe and sharp political distinctions of the Revolution brought on the immediate demise of the family in the town, forcing some into political exile, the others into political limbo. Their only allies were the core of local Loyalists, a sizable but surely suspect lot.

Likewise, in Amherst, the events of the Revolution provided the final setting for resolving internal antagonisms that had been brewing for years. By 1774 the power of newcomers in the town could hardly be taken for granted, and by combining both national and local issues they gained the political impetus to push most of the old leaders out. A few of those leaders made themselves agreeable to the new majority, but a few others wound up in jail. Those latter victims of the political shift in the town complained indignantly of their fall from dignity. From the new jail in Northampton Isaac Chauncy and several other Amherst men incarcerated there wrote bitterly of their fellow citizens, calling their actions "irregular" and "Not Reasonable."[41] Being locked up and exposed to such obvious humiliation was a hard blow for some former leaders, for jail represented the severest form of public expulsion and repudiation. Simply being turned out of office probably seemed mild by comparison. If there remained any consolation for Chauncy and his allies, it might only have been that the walls of the jail offered a gentler form of punishment than the hands of a mob.

It was not only the secular leaders who suffered, but the clergy as well. Ministers, in fact, seemed to be singled out for especially severe abuse and correction by their townspeople, made to declare openly their sentiments toward the Revolutionary struggle and pressured to make those sentiments reflect the will of the community. Townspeople could not well leave their spiritual fates to a man they would not entrust with their political fortunes. Moreover, the symbolic value of the minister's position, more than his actual political function, made this collective pressure necessary and strong, for he was the most visible figure representing the town's communal identity. It was no longer enough that he speak to his parishioners; he also had to speak for them. His role as local leader was far too important for his political opinions to remain his alone.

The nature of the relationship between pastor and people became very clear to Longmeadow's minister, Stephen Williams. Throughout the first months of the Revolutionary crisis he remained torn in his loyalties and unsure of his duty, praying for the safety of the Longmeadow militia company as it went off to fight in 1775, but also praying that God keep him "from doing anything displeasing to His Majesty." His ambivalence apparently became a question among some of his people, for in June 1775 he wrote Eleazar Wheelock that he was disconcerted by

> Reproaches cast upon me because I have prayed that the King might do that which is right in the Eyes of the Lord and not be Led astray by . . . corrupt counsellors (the very expressions I made use of in a public prayer, the very day a warm man reproached me for praying for the King & told me, I ought to have prayed he might have his Head cutt off).

"Such reproaches dont much disquiet me," Williams claimed. "I can & do pray for them, that Abuse me & would represent me as inimical to ye Country."[42] But whatever his disclaimers, such reproaches could hardly leave him unmoved. For almost sixty years he had held his pulpit and led his people, and now in the midst of a confusing political situation some of them were turning on him, threatening to deny the dignity of the office he had maintained for so long. He was, after all, a relative of Israel Williams and somewhat tainted merely by family association. In the end the Reverend Williams's age and long service to the community no doubt tempered the abusive action of the most radical local Whigs, but he had clearly been warned.

So too had the Reverend Jonathan Ashley at Deerfield. Like Stephen Williams, Ashley was part of the kinship network that united most members of the county elite, but unlike Williams, Ashley had no uncertainty about where his loyalty lay. He identified himself clearly with his kinsmen in the Tory faction in Deerfield and in the county at large, and he made no secret of his support for the Crown. As Deerfield became increasingly divided during the early months of the Revolution, Ashley still managed to hold onto his pulpit, just as he had done during the height of the Great Awakening. In the Revolution as in the Awakening, in fact, most of those opposed to Ashley withdrew from the church and left him to his supporters. But he did not escape harsh treatment altogether. Although he was never jailed or removed from office, he was occasionally insulted and treated rudely; throughout the Revolution he also had trouble getting his full pay or allotment of firewood—always a clear sign that people could choose to punish their minister in the town meeting if not in church. By the time of his death in 1780 he had lived with both political and financial uncertainty for over five years. It was with some feeling of bitterness that his heirs brought a substantial claim against the town in 1782 to try to recover some of the money owed the late pastor. By then the harmony between pastor and people had long been broken and was in a state of decay. The posthumous legal action served only as a final indication of just how far the decay had gone.[43]

Some of Ashley's Old Light colleagues suffered even greater personal abuse for their political Loyalism, and their people resorted to much more direct and immediate punishment. Like Ashley, Abraham Hill of Shutesbury tried to douse the inflamed spirits of his people by spreading fear and urging caution. He once warned three would-be volunteers—one of whom was Daniel Shays, soon to be the most famous radical of western Massachusetts—about the danger of enlisting in the colonial army: "I understand you think of taking up arms against your King. The king can send a company of horse through the country and take off every head; and in less than six weeks you will be glad to labor a week for sheep's head and pluck." But Hill's estimation of the Crown's military capabilities proved a little overdone, and he instead found his own head in danger. After a few such incidents of open hostility to the patriot cause, Hill was confined to the town pound and, according to popular accounts, fed only on herring thrown over the wall. After a subsequent confinement under house arrest he was dismissed from his ministerial office in 1778. His thirty-six years of service in the town could not save him from a couple of years of open political disfavor.[44]

Similarly, Jedediah Smith at Granville and Jonathan Leavitt at Charlemont were dismissed during the first years of the Revolution. Smith had been involved in a growing dispute with a group of Separates and eventually with most of the people in his town; his continued support for the Crown after 1775 became the final source of antagonism that sent him on his way to the Mississippi and to death. Leavitt, too, had fallen into disfavor with his people because of his supposed Arminianism and "suspected lukewarmness towards the Revolution." He lost first his salary and eventually his job. David Parsons at Amherst, though never suspected of Arminianism, was suspected of Toryism, and he too had trouble collecting his salary; at one point the people of Amherst even wrote to get help from Northampton "in the important trial of the Rev. Mr. David Parsons upon a Complaint of his being unfriendly to the interests of the Continent." But the people in Northampton had their own minister to think about. Early in the Revolution one of the more vociferous Northampton Whigs felt compelled to offer the Reverend Hooker a pointed reminder that he had better make his opinions about the American cause a little clearer; Hooker understood the suggestion well enough and thereafter added his voice to the cause of liberty. After similar prodding and implied threats, John Hubbard at Northfield and Roger Newton at Greenfield also made themselves more agreeable to the sentiments of their people. At New Salem Samuel Kendal simply despaired of the whole situation and resigned.[45]

IN MANY ways the early days of the Revolution confronted both ministers and secular leaders with many of the problems they had had to face during the Great Awakening. Like the Great Awakening, the Revolution was not just a matter of belief, but also a pattern of behavior. Both the Awakening and the Revolution began as widespread popular movements that swept the American colonies, combining intense emotionalism with sometimes extreme and disruptive activity. The Reverend Stephen Williams, for instance, expressed many of the same fears about the Revolutionary period he had had about the Awakening over thirty years before. Already one of the old ministers in Hampshire County by the time the Awakening reached its peak, Williams had looked out from his Longmeadow parish in the early 1740s and noted his concern at the phenomenon he witnessed. "I find ye country in a tumult," he wrote of the Awakening; "I am in great concern & pray God to help & relieve in this dark day—I fear ye interest of religion is like to Suffer on all hands—& I pray God to Show himself gracious."[46]

By 1774 Williams had still not grown accustomed to displays of violent or extreme behavior among his people. Once again he worried: "I hear uneasiness

& *tumults*—& frettings—in one place & another—some uneasy with civill rules—Some with ministers—oh yt God would have mercy upon us—& Give to thy people to consider—& realize it yt an house divided against it Self *cant Stand*." At other times he complained about "ye mobbish disposition" and the "danger of going to Extreams," and generally he continued to be dismayed and confused by the excess of popular sentiment he saw brewing around him.[47] Williams supported liberty as much as he supported piety. He did not feel happy, however, about the effect those goals seemed to have on his people: a new sense of purpose led a suddenly awakened populace to develop very clear distinctions between good and evil, between right and wrong, and those distinctions were quickly turned on the leaders of society as strict standards of judgment. Especially when he sensed "some uneasy with civill rules—Some with ministers" in the early days of the Revolution, he began to become uneasy himself. He once again saw a danger posed to his society and to his very position.

And yet, however much Williams and others in his situation may have found the sudden intensity of such challenges disturbing, they could hardly have found the general upsurge of local unrest altogether surprising. It must have been obvious to everyone by the summer of 1774 that the recent actions of the Crown represented an immediate crisis that needed an immediate response. Certainly many people in the rural regions of Massachusetts recognized the very real threats inherent in the new imperial policies, and they moved quickly to take action against anyone who seemed in any way sympathetic or even insufficiently hostile to those policies. And in that sense it may have seemed equally obvious that the leading members of the Hampshire elite, like many other local leaders in other parts of the colonies, would be likely targets for attack primarily or even solely because of their apparent continued loyalty to the Crown. Whatever a man's actions or attitudes in the past, his present position—and that alone—would be enough to condemn him.[48]

At the same time, however, such a narrow focus simply on the immediate context of the crisis would tend to obscure the significance of other events, at least for twenty-first-century observers. Taking a somewhat broader view than that available to the Reverend Williams, one must try to appreciate the way the Revolution also represented a moment of historical intensity that reflected a subtler historical transformation that had taken place gradually over the previous decades. That is, the Revolution, like the Great Awakening a generation earlier, provided both the context and the terms, an immediate reason and a new standard, for a sharply articulated critique of the state of society, or at least the state of the county. But that critique had been developing for years, emerging from scattered conflicts over local issues to become a more general spirit of discontent.

Throughout most parts of the American colonies, in fact, expressions of extreme dissatisfaction with local conditions had become commonplace if not altogether constant in the period between the Awakening and the Revolution. Looking eastward from Hampshire County, Stephen Williams could hardly have been unaware of the social turmoil and political turbulence that dominated public life in mid-century Boston. But turning his attention in the other direction, he would find numerous other examples of widespread, even massive, unrest. Across the border in New York, for instance, the Hudson Valley had been scarred by land riots in the 1750s and 1760s, as tenants rose up against the landlords who owned so much land and held so much power over them. Tenants also took violent action in New Jersey, and in Pennsylvania a band of over a thousand western frontiersmen, the "Paxton Boys," marched on Philadelphia in 1764 to protest the government's failure to provide them with adequate protection during Pontiac's Rebellion. Backcountry settlers in the western counties of North Carolina engaged in armed resistance against local officials throughout the 1760s, and the provincial government eventually had to send several thousand armed troops west to defeat the "Regulator" movement in 1771. In many cases the people who undertook these violent uprisings against established authorities were, like the newer settlers on the frontier of Hampshire County, fairly recent migrants to their respective regions, struggling to survive in a world of increasing social dislocation and recurring economic uncertainty. They did not for the most part share some millennial or revolutionary vision of a radically restructured society, nor did they articulate a coherent theory of class conflict. They did, however, attempt to challenge the power of the political and economic elites who governed their regions and, in doing so, to gain a degree of control over their own lives. In the end, of course, their attempts failed; provincial officials usually chose to deal with their protests with arms rather than arguments. Yet however short-lived or unsuccessful, these movements represent the most visible and violent manifestations of a growing tension between authority and autonomy that pervaded much of pre-Revolutionary America and provided part of the context for the Revolution itself.

To be sure, the people of Hampshire County did not engage in huge mass mobilizations in the years before the Revolution. They carried out their struggles at the community level, and in town after town and in church after church the old standards of stability and order—and the men who upheld them—came under frequent attack. The strength of the challenge proved to be cumulative rather than cataclysmic. By the time of the Revolution the established county leaders had suffered a gradual erosion of their power as their domain had come to be populated largely by people who wanted to define their own political and religious standards and who therefore seemed more resentful than respectful of the power those leaders had traditionally held. After some thirty years of recurring unrest in the towns and churches of the county, the Revolutionary crisis of 1774 brought the widespread disorder into a sharper and more immediate focus. For the people of Hampshire County, who were apparently so late in being awakened to the crisis by the Boston radicals, the impending break with the traditions of British authority caused a more rapid and forceful break with the traditions of local authority. Certainly at no other time in the county's past had so many men of high status and position been unseated, punished, and replaced so quickly. With good reason did many of these old leaders feel vulnerable and fearful as they looked out and saw the "tumults" and "danger of going to Extreams" in the people around them. The antagonisms of past and present seemed to merge quite easily, making it much simpler than before for people to oppose their former leaders with proper patriotic zeal, helping them finally to reject men they were no longer willing to follow.

The early months of the Revolutionary period were extreme times for people throughout Massachusetts and the rest of the colonies, but in Hampshire County as elsewhere, the habits of peace had long been disrupted. When the minutemen of Hampshire County marched off to war in April 1775, many of them had already been embattled farmers for quite some time, veterans of significant (if somewhat less violent) engagements within their own neighborhood.

NOTES

1. Sylvester Judd manuscripts, "Northampton," vol. 1:333, and "Miscellaneous," vol. 15:348, Forbes Library, Northampton, MA.

2. The best accounts of the violence and mob activity in Boston are in Edmund S. Morgan and Helen M. Morgan, *The Stamp Act Crisis: Prologue to Revolution* (New York, 1962), chap. 9; and Dirk Hoerder, *Crowd Action in Revolutionary Massachusetts*, 1765–1781 (New York, 1977), chaps. 2 and 3.

3. Josiah Pierce Diary, 1766, n.p., Jones Library, Amherst, MA.

4. Journal of the Reverend John Ballantine, November 11, 1765, Westfield (MA) Athenaeum; Hoerder, *Crowd Action*, 133–135, and Hoerder, "People and Mobs: Crowd Action in Massachusetts during the American Revolution, 1765–1780" (Ph.D. diss., Free University, Berlin, 1971), 128. For the history of the Pine Laws and the resistance to them, see Joseph J. Malone, *Pine Trees and Politics: The Naval Stores and Forest Policy in Colonial New England, 1691–1775* (Seattle, 1964), esp. 62.

5. Between 1760 and 1768, inclusive, only eight Hampshire County towns (Brimfield, Deerfield, Hadley, Hatfield, Northampton, Springfield, Sunderland, and Westfield) consistently sent representatives to the General Court. The new town of Wilbraham, incorporated in 1763, sent its own representative in 1764; after that, however, it joined with Springfield to share the expenses. Other small towns quite often joined with neighboring towns to send a representative (e.g., Southampton with Northampton, Greenfield with Deerfield, South Hadley and Amherst with Hadley);

in those cases, however, the representative almost always came from the older and larger town. See *Journals of the House of Representatives of Massachusetts* (Boston, 1719–1778), esp. vols. 37 and 44. For a summary of the voting records of Hampshire representatives between 1726 and 1765, see William Pencak, *War, Politics, and Revolution in Provincial Massachusetts* (Boston, 1981), 245.

6. James R. Trumbull, *History of Northampton, Massachusetts, from Its Settlement in 1654*, 2 vols. (Northampton, 1898, 1902), 2:324–326; for a general discussion of the Convention of Towns, see Richard D. Brown, "The Massachusetts Convention of Towns, 1768," *William and Mary Quarterly*, third series, 26 (1969): 94–104, and Brown, *Revolutionary Politics in Massachusetts: The Boston Committee of Correspondence and the Towns, 1772–1774* (Cambridge, MA, 1970), 28–31.

7. Daniel White Wells and Reuben Field Wells, *A History of Hatfield, Massachusetts* (Springfield, MA, 1910), 181.

8. For a list of delegates to the Convention see Brown, "Convention of Towns," 103–104.

9. For the period from January 1773 through January 1774—the time when most towns would have responded to the first appeals from the Boston Committee of Correspondence—I have found evidence of correspondence from seven Hampshire towns (Amherst, Brimfield, Colrain, New Salem, Pelham, South Hadley, and Wilbraham), or around 17 percent of the towns in the county. There may be one or two elusive letters from other towns, but it is doubtful that there are many. Brown, in *Revolutionary Politics*, reports that by September 1773, some 22 percent of Hampshire towns had corresponded with Boston. The point here is not to quibble over percentages; whatever the exact figure, it seems clear that Hampshire County lagged behind the eastern half of the province in responding to Boston's first appeals. For Brown's estimates and samples from all Massachusetts counties see 97, 251–253.

10. Pelham Town Records, 1743–1816, 145–147, Forbes Library (microfilm). This letter is also included in C. O. Parmenter, *History of Pelham from 1738 to 1898* (Amherst, 1898), 125–127; the Parmenter version has the virtue of being published but the vice of being inaccurately transcribed.

11. For a discussion of the effect of the British policies in 1774, see David Ammerman, *In the Common Cause: American Response to the Coercive Acts of 1774* (Charlottesville, VA, 1974).

12. Brown, *Revolutionary Politics*, 178–179; see also L. Kinvin Wroth, "Province in Rebellion: An Interpretive Essay," in Wroth, ed., *Province in Rebellion: A Documentary History of the Founding of the Commonwealth of Massachusetts, 1774–1775* (Cambridge, MA, 1975), 36.

As already noted, seven Hampshire towns had written to Boston by January 1774; another thirteen made their first communication with the Committee of Correspondence between June and September 1774; see Wroth, *Province in Rebellion*, "Detailed Table of Contents of Microfiche Texts," 164–166. Brown counts twenty-two towns in Hampshire County that eventually corresponded with Boston; he failed to count West Springfield, which would bring the total to twenty-three. See Brown, *Revolutionary Politics*, endpaper map. There were always the slower towns to be remembered, too. The people of Chesterfield, for instance, never got around to corresponding at all, and it was not until January 1775 that they finally decided "to take into

Consideration Some of ye Resolves of ye Provintial Congress heretofore Neglected." See Chesterfield Town Records, 1762–1815, Forbes Library (microfilm).

The specific references to the role of Silent Wilde are in the letter from Colrain to the Boston Committee and a letter from Montague to Thomas Cushing, in Wroth, *Province in Rebellion*, document 236, 741, and document 270, 801–802. (Hereafter all letters exchanged between towns and the Boston Committee of Correspondence [BCC] will be followed by the microfiche citation for the *Province in Rebellion* collection.)

13. Ammerman, *In the Common Cause*, 7.

14. See Brown, *Revolutionary Politics*, 120–136. The main point here is not simply, as Brown suggests, that "towns met to consider and formulate their basic political beliefs," a process leading to "the elements of a consensus" throughout Massachusetts, a "general agreement about basic political principles" (93–94, 121). It is important to understand the particularism of many of these responses, as the towns expressed general political principles in terms of their own local situations.

15. Williamsburg to BCC, August 25, 1774, document 287, 819.

16. Murrayfield to BCC, July 28, 1774, document 248, 762; Wilbraham to BCC, August 4, 1774, document 256, 780–788; Granville to BCC, July 11, 1774, document 233, 727–738, and August 31, 1774, document 253, 774–776; Granby to BCC, July 11, 1774, document 232, 735–737.

As Richard Brown points out, the town responses to the Boston Committee covered the whole range from "silent repudiation to admiring applause." That variety of opinion "suggests an independence of action which cannot be described as either domination or manipulation by the Boston Committee." The important result of the Boston Committee in the early months was to spur towns into thinking about these issues and thereby to force them to develop a local political response. Again, see Brown, *Revolutionary Politics*, 120–136.

17. Colrain to BCC, July 12, 1774, document 236, 741.

18. BCC to Colrain, July 18, 1774, document 238, 745. Note the quickness of the reply.

19. Wilbraham to BCC, August 4, 1774, document 256, 780–783.

20. Colrain to BCC, August 8, 1774, document 259, 786–787. On the "more particular, confidential relationship between Boston and the towns," see Brown, *Revolutionary Politics*, 136ff.

21. The account is rendered in Trumbull, *History of Northampton*, 2:345–348. There is also a narrative description in Hoerder, "People and Mobs," 497–498.

22. Judd is quoted in Trumbull, *History of Northampton*, 2:346. The literature on crowd action in preindustrial Europe is quite extensive. See especially Natalie Zemon Davis, *Society and Culture in Early Modern France* (Stanford, CA, 1975); George Rudé, *The Crowd in History: A Study of Popular Disturbances in France and England, 1730–1848* (New York, 1964); and E. P. Thompson, "The Moral Economy of the English Crowd in the Eighteenth Century," *Past and Present* 50 (1971): 76–136.

One of the first American historians to focus attention on the comparative history of crowd action was Pauline Maier, whose "Popular Uprisings and Civil Authority in Eighteenth Century America," *William and Mary Quarterly*, third series, 27 (1970): 3–35, provided an important beginning for the recent emphasis on crowd behavior in the Revolutionary era. Maier portrayed pre-Revolutionary mobs as fairly representative of a cross-section of colonial society, more middle-class than their European counterparts. Moreover, she argued that mob action was generally not an attack on established institutions or political and social elites; indeed, she has stressed a kind of harmony between the political goals of colonial leaders and those of colonial mobs. Those leaders, she suggests, were often successful in "focussing popular exuberance" in order to "work with long-established tendencies in the mob toward purposefulness and responsibility" (28).

Though Maier offers a useful analysis of the cultural legitimacy of crowd action in an American context, her discussion of the relationship between crowds and elites gives a rather limited view of the common people themselves, underestimating their autonomy from—and occasional antipathy toward—the established political leaders. For a view giving more emphasis to the distinct political values and goals of pre-Revolutionary crowds, see Hoerder, Crowd Action. Also important are Charles Tilly, "Collective Action in England and America, 1765–1775," and Richard Maxwell Brown, "Back Country Rebellions and the Homestead Ethic in America, 1740–1799," both in Richard Maxwell Brown and Don E. Fehrenbacher, eds., *Tradition, Conflict, and Modernization: Perspectives on the American Revolution* (New York, 1977), 45–99; and Edward Countryman, "'Out of the Bounds of the Law': Northern Land Rioters in the Eighteenth Century," in Alfred F. Young, ed., *The American Revolution: Explorations in the History of American Radicalism* (DeKalb, IL, 1976), 37–70.

23. Trumbull, *History of Northampton,* 2:345–348.

24. George Sheldon, *A History of Deerfield, Massachusetts*, 2 vols. (1896; rpt. ed., Somersworth, NH, 1972), 2:681–700; Judd manuscripts, "Massachusetts," vol. 5:348, and "Revolutionary Matters," 169; Trumbull, *History of Northampton,* 2:373–374.

25. Joseph Hawley to Theodore Sedgwick, May 10, 1775, in Joseph Hawley Papers, II, n.p., New York Public Library, New York City; Trumbull, *History of Northampton,* 2:350–351, 374; Mark Doolittle, *Historical Sketch of the Congregational Church in Belchertown, Massachusetts* (Northampton, 1852), 46.

26. Trumbull, *History of Northampton,* 2:372.

27. The depositions of Benjamin Read, James Hunt and William Read, and Seth Tubbs are in the Israel Williams Papers, II, Massachusetts Historical Society, Boston.

28. "James Hunt & William Read's testimony relating to a mob—September 15, 1775," and "Benj Read to all people, Williamsburgh—September 14, 1774," in Israel Williams Papers, II.

29. Benjamin Read deposition, in Israel Williams Papers, II. Hoerder, in *Crowd Action,* 343, suggests that the Hatfield people "lost interest" in the plans of the Williamsburg mob, apparently because the outsiders seemed too orderly to suit the desires of Williams's Hatfield neighbors.

30. Deposition of Seth Tubbs, in Israel Williams Papers, II.

31. William Lawrence Welch, Jr., "River God: The Public Life of Israel Williams, 1709–1788" (Ph.D. diss., University of Maine, 1975), 150–151.

32. See Edward M. Cook, Jr., *The Fathers of the Towns: Leadership and Community Structure in Eighteenth-Century New England* (Baltimore, 1976), 117.

33. See Nobles, *Divisions throughout the Whole*, chap. 5.

34. Sheldon, *History of Deerfield,* 2:677–678.

35. John Dickinson to Israel Williams, May 23, 1775, and James Easton to Israel Williams, [1775], in Israel Williams Papers, II.

36. House of Representatives, April 15, 1777, order for Israel Williams and son to be jailed, in Israel Williams Papers, II.

37. Hatfield Committee of Correspondence to Provincial Council, March 29, 1777, in Israel Williams Papers, II.

38. Israel Williams to Provincial Council, December 1779, in Israel Williams Papers, II.

39. Mason A. Green, *Springfield, 1636–1886: History of Town and City* (Springfield, 1888), 275–287; see also chapter 14.

40. Bruce G. Merritt, "Loyalism and Social Conflict in Revolutionary Deerfield, Massachusetts," *Journal of American History* 57 (1970): 277–289. Sheldon, *History of Deerfield*, 2:674–676, 680–681.

41. Isaac Chauncy et al. to Northampton Committee, April 28, 1775, in Hawley Papers, II, n.p. See Nobles, *Divisions throughout the Whole*, chapter 5.

42. Clifford K. Shipton, *Sibley's Harvard Graduates: Biographical Sketches of Those Who Attended Harvard College*, 17 vols. (Boston, 1942), 6:32–33.

43. Sheldon, *History of Deerfield*, 2:710–711.

44. Shipton, *Sibley's Harvard Graduates*, 10:199–200.

45. Franklin B. Dexter, *Biographical Sketches of the Graduates of Yale College*, 6 vols. (New York, 1903), 2:119–120, 240–241, 443–454, 543–545, 548–549; Shipton, *Sibley's Harvard Graduates*, 8:614–615, 9:55–57; Judd, "Northampton," vol. 1:334.

46. Stephen Williams Diary, IV, September 11, 1742, Pocumtuck Valley Memorial Association Library, Deerfield, MA.

47. Stephen Williams Diary, VIII, June 20, July 4, August 8, 1774.

48. For a discussion of mob action throughout Massachusetts in the early months of the Revolution, see Hoerder, *Crowd Action*, 271–352; see also Kevin Joseph MacWade, "Worcester County, 1750–1774: A Study of a Provincial Patronage Elite" (Ph.D. diss., Boston University Graduate School, 1974).

8

THOUGH Northampton furnished its own war heroes, like Seth Pomeroy, it was spared the brunt of conflict. In some ways the war was a boon to the region. Surrounded by Whig buffers to the east and west, and owing to its inland position, the valley was safe from the threat of British invasion. Because it was fertile as well as safe, the region became New England's agricultural storehouse. With young men departing to serve in Revolutionary regiments, farm labor was in short supply as every possible acre was pressed into production. Prosperity, long the monopoly of merchants, professionals, and landowners, now trickled down to tenants and farm laborers while the wartime boom lasted. But when the war in the north subsided after 1780, so did the economy.

The economic uncertainty that followed the Revolution prompted creditors to demand cash payments from debtors. To make matters worse, an ill-advised state tax, which had to be paid in cash, was particularly burdensome to valley farmers, who traditionally relied on barter to see them through hard times. Foreclosure and debtors' prison were grim realities for many subsistence farmers. In 1782, a crowd led by Samuel Ely closed a Northampton court to prevent foreclosure procedures. Four years later, the situation had worsened to the degree that armed resistance seemed imminent. On August 29, 1786, 1,500 Hampshire farmers marched on Northampton to close the courts. This was the beginning of what became known as Shays's Rebellion. It took military force to crush the armed insurgents who raided the Springfield arsenal the following winter. But the Rebellion left a lasting impression on the region and the nation.

The valley was bitterly divided. To discontented farmers, the government seemed unresponsive to the needs of the people. To merchants, creditors, and those who depended upon the enforcement of contracts, the government seemed vulnerable to anarchy. Caleb Strong, a prominent Northampton attorney, was part of a group of wealthy townspeople who founded the Hampshire Gazette *to voice opposition to the Shaysites. When Strong went to Philadelphia as a delegate to the Constitutional Convention in 1787, he advocated a federal government with strengthened powers. Northampton was one of the few towns in Hampshire County that backed ratification of the new constitution. Residents of the hill towns, many of which had supported Shays's Rebellion, remained skeptical of the new government.*

Leonard Richards's recent study breaks new ground with his discovery of overlooked archival material documenting aspects of Shays's Rebellion. He shows that the rebels were not simply backcountry anarchists, but property owners and Revolutionary War veterans. The Rebellion's main effect, Richards argues, was to strengthen the movement toward a new United States Constitution.

The Revolution That Failed

*Making Sense of Shays's Rebellion**

LEONARD L. RICHARDS

ON THE last Tuesday of August 1786, well before daybreak, Captain Joel Billings of Amherst led several hundred men toward Northampton, Massachusetts. A thirty-nine-year-old farmer and the father of eight children, Billings was an old hand at leading men. He had commanded troops during the American Revolution and had been a town selectman, the same office his father had held for nearly twenty years. With him were many from east Amherst, including most of the large Dickinson clan. Some carried muskets, swords, or bludgeons. Others were unarmed. Joining them were men from Pelham and Greenwich, who had been on the road for hours, marching west. They were under the command of Captain Joseph Hines, a one-time officer in the Massachusetts Line. As the two contingents proceeded through the center of Amherst and through Hadley, only a few additional men joined them. Upon crossing the Connecticut River, however, they encountered hundreds of others who had converged on Northampton from the opposite direction, from the hilltowns to the northwest and from West Springfield to the south.

After daybreak, the combined forces assembled into military formation and with fifes and drums marched on the courthouse. Several hours later, three justices in full-length black robes and gray wigs, with the sheriff leading their way, tried to get into the courthouse. They were blocked at the door. In a face-saving gesture, they decided to hold court at the house of Captain Samuel Clark, a local innkeeper, and receive a six-man delegation. The delegation, which included Billings and Hines, demanded that the court adjourn without transacting business. The justices quickly decided to "continue all matters pending" until November, "adjourned without delay," packed up, and returned home.[1]

Within weeks mobs ranging from 200 to 1,500 men shut down the courts in five Massachusetts counties. Their actions terrified the nation's elite. George Washington and his colleagues clamored for a stronger national constitution, one that would give the central government more power to maintain order, while Massachusetts Governor James Bowdoin and 153 Boston merchants dipped into their own purses and hired an army of 4,400 men under General Benjamin Lincoln to suppress the uprising.[2] This force marched westward in January. The insurgents, in turn, tried to seize the national arsenal in Springfield. Had they succeeded, they would have had the artillery and arms necessary to

---

* From Leonard L. Richards, *Shays's Rebellion: The American Revolution's Final Battle* (Philadelphia, 2002).

fight Lincoln's army. But they encountered a militia unit under General William Shepard, who let them approach and then turned the arsenal's cannons on them at close range, killing four and wounding others. The insurgents fled, and after that it was only a matter of time before Lincoln's forces gained the upper hand. As it was, it took Lincoln and his army five months to restore "law and order" to western Massachusetts.

The aftermath resulted in seventeen death sentences, two actual hangings, several hundred indictments, and some four thousand confessions of wrongdoing. The latter arose from what was called at the time an oath of allegiance, and later an amnesty, but in many respects was like a modern "plea bargain." In exchange for admitting that they had borne arms against the state and its rulers, and taking an oath of allegiance, the oath takers escaped prosecution and the possibility of being fined, whipped, or hanged for treason.[3] Most were temporarily "disqualified" from bearing arms, holding office, voting, sitting on juries, teaching school, selling liquor, and working in taverns and inns. A few got off scot free.

The oaths, in conjunction with the indictments, provide an unusual opportunity. Usually the participants in uprisings, mobs, riots, and the like remain shadowy figures. A few manage to get their names on the police blotter, but the vast majority get away and disappear from the historical record. In most instances, all that is left for scholars to work with are eye-witness accounts and descriptions provided by the authorities. The former are often contradictory, and the latter are often misleading, written by government officials who had a vested interest in disparaging all those who challenged their authority—and in many instances by officials who hadn't a clue about what actually happened and were simply pretending to be on top of the situation.

Many official reports, to be sure, cite the leaders by name. But that too creates problems. For there is always a temptation to assume that the leaders and the rank and file had much in common. That can be a fatal mistake. Consider again the Northampton incident. The leader of the men who came from West Springfield, the first group to arrive in Northampton, was repeatedly identified.[4] In time he became one of the best-known leaders of Shays's Rebellion. His name was Luke Day.

Forty-three years old at the time of the Northampton incident, Day was a member of one of West Springfield's most prominent families.[5] Scarcely a year passed without one Day or another being elected selectman. In this powerful family, Luke's eminence stemmed largely from his role in the American Revolution. In April 1775, when the first shots of the Revolution were fired, he was a second lieutenant in the local militia. As soon as the Lexington alarm reached West Springfield, Luke and fifty-two other men marched to Boston. They fought bravely, and in May Luke was promoted to first lieutenant. A few months later he joined the expedition to Quebec. In 1777 he was promoted again, this time to captain of the Massachusetts Line, and he held that rank until the end of the war. He was mustered out of the army in June 1783. Overall, he spent a full eight years in the Revolutionary Army.[6]

Toward war's end, Day became a member of the Society of Cincinnati, an exclusive organization that was open to officers like himself and their first-born sons. George Washington was a member; so was Secretary of War Henry Knox; and so was General Lincoln. Day, like other members of the Society, probably hoped that the organization would help him get preferential treatment from either the state or national government after the war. Even before the Society officially organized, their leaders had talked the Continental Congress into granting them half-pay for life, and then when that settlement created a storm of protest into commutating the promised pensions into five years' full pay in government securities bearing 6 percent interest.[7] Getting state support for the commutation settlement, however, proved difficult. In 1784, when the states finally approved the settlement, the notes had depreciated to about one-eighth of their face value.

By this time, Day needed all the financial help he could get. Being an officer in Washington's army had been expensive. Washington had insisted that all his officers dress elegantly, have an enlisted man as a body servant, haul around lots of personal baggage, ride a horse rather than march, and dine in taverns rather than in field messes. Yet Day seldom had been paid—or had been paid in notes that initially had little market value and then quickly depreciated.[8] Meanwhile his farm deteriorated and state taxes increased. To restock the farm and pay taxes, he incurred more and more debt. Within two years of his discharge, his financial affairs were in shambles.[9] Among other obligations he owed some £25 to Nathaniel Lee and Jonathan Tracy of Newburyport and nearly £10 to John Kirkland. In July 1785 both parties had him imprisoned for debt at the Northampton jail.[10] Two months later he was released "by order of law" for the first debt. For the second he "Broke his Bond & made his Escape."

Was Day a typical rebel? In most respects, not in the least. First of all, he was a "gentleman." The authorities sometimes portrayed him as a disreputable dirt farmer, but they knew better. Even the Northampton jailer acknowledged his status as a "gentleman." To the embarrassment of the authorities, he was not the only gentleman who challenged their supremacy. Scores of other gentlemen also took up arms against the government. Yet, as gentlemen, all were atypical. The vast majority of rebels were "yeoman" farmers—and their sons—who, for want of a better term, were usually listed in the records as "laborers."

Day's war record was also atypical. Again, to the embarrassment of the authorities, he was not the only war hero who sided with the rebels. At least thirty officers of the Massachusetts Line took up arms against the government.

Nor was he the only member of the Society of Cincinnati to participate in Shays's Rebellion. At least two other Society men were also involved. But, in reality, only a handful of men in all of Massachusetts could match Day's service record. The typical Massachusetts soldier spent only a few months in arms—and then returned to the farm. Men like Day who spent a full eight years in the Revolutionary Army were exceptional.

Day also had been imprisoned for debt. That was not only unusual for men in Hampshire County but also most unusual for the rebels. In 1785 and 1786 only ninety men in all of Hampshire County were imprisoned for debt, while some 1,800 Hampshire men participated in Shays's Rebellion. Of these, only Day and one other man spent time in the Northampton jail for debt.[11] He too was listed by the jailer as a "gentleman." Of the other 1,800 men, some undoubtedly were like Day in being heavily in debt. Some, even though they hadn't been imprisoned for debt, had been sued for debt. Daniel Shays was the most famous example. But even Shays was atypical. Most of the 1,800 had never been hauled into court for debt. Indeed, for every Shaysite who appeared in court as a debtor, another Shaysite had gone to court as a creditor. Three of Shays's creditors were fellow rebels, and two were subsequently indicted by the state for treason.[12]

In one respect, however, Luke Day had much in common with the oath takers. He came from a town that provided far more than its share of insurgents.

In acknowledging that they had borne arms against the state, the oath takers listed their home towns and sometimes their occupations. From those data emerge a number of curious facts. The one that stands out most prominently is that the western counties as a whole didn't rebel against the state government. Nor did the vast majority of poor farmers. In the five-county area in which courts were shut down, 72 of the 187 towns produced not a single rebel, and 34 others only one to four rebels. Just 45 towns made Shays's Rebellion possible. They provided nearly four-fifths of the rebels. Luke Day's West Springfield was one of the banner towns, yielding 141 rebels, 10 of whom were indicted by the state for treason.[13]

The most rebellious towns were mainly in Hampshire County, which at that time extended from the top of the state to the bottom, from the Vermont and New Hampshire borders to the Connecticut border. Hampshire towns produced nearly half the insurgents, almost as many as the other four counties combined.

Within Hampshire County, however, the turn-out was anything but even. Eight towns produced not a single rebel, five produced over 100. The banner town was Colrain, one of the northernmost towns in the county, lying just a few miles west of the Connecticut River and bordering Vermont. A small town, which had only been founded fifteen years before Shays's Rebellion, Colrain had 234 males 16 years of age and older in 1785. Two-thirds of them bore arms against the state in 1786.[14] In contrast were Heath and Rowe, just a few miles west of Colrain and also bordering Vermont. Incorporated as towns in 1785, just a year before Shays's Rebellion, both were tiny farm communities with a combined population of 144 males 16 or older. Not a single resident took up arms against the state. Also in contrast was Granville, another farm community west of the Connecticut River but at the southern border of the state. Made a town eleven years before the rebellion, Granville had 375 males 16 years of age and older in 1785. Only one man took up arms against the state.

Overall, over half the towns in Hampshire County were like Granville, Heath, and Rowe, providing little or no help at all for Luke Day and other rebel leaders. It was a handful of towns like Colrain that made Shays's Rebellion possible. They provided three-fourths of the county's 1,800 rebels.

Were the authorities aware of this uneven distribution of rebels? In one sense General William Shepard, who sent a report to the governor on the number of insurgents in Hampshire County, was well aware of this fact. In estimating the number of Hampshire men who would march under the direction of Daniel Shays, he knew that West Springfield would provide more men than neighboring Granville, and that Colrain would provide more men than neighboring Heath and Rowe. But he was way off in his numbers. He thought little Colrain would turn out about twenty-five men. And he thought the folks in West Springfield, who lived only a few miles from his farm, would turn out about sixty men. Never did he imagine that the two towns would turn out close to three hundred men.[15]

Shepard was deemed to be the local expert on Hampshire County. Both the governor and General Lincoln depended on his estimates when they put together an army to suppress the rebellion. Shepard, however, underestimated the total by nearly half. That he grossly underestimated the rebelliousness of the people of Colrain is understandable. After all, they lived at the other end of the county. He probably knew next to nothing about them. That he also underestimated the rebelliousness of such towns as Amherst, Pelham, Greenwich, Wendell, and Ware is also understandable. Those folks lived on the other side of the Connecticut River and a long day's journey from his Westfield home. That he underestimated the rebelliousness of West Springfield, however, makes one wonder. They were, after all, his neighbors.

In the long run, not knowing his neighbors proved costly to Shepard. He won the battle at the Springfield arsenal, but the way he won was never forgotten. He later maintained that he acted with restraint, and his biographers have argued that he was a kind and decent man. But men in his own unit heard him order that the cannons be aimed at "waist height." He thus became widely hated as the "murderer of brethren." Within months of his arsenal victory, a band of nine men made their way to his Westfield farm, burned his fences and woodlands "beyond recovery for many years," and cut off the ears and gouged out the eyes of his prize horses. For the rest of his life, he lived as a marked man, harassed by angry neighbors who never stopped seeking revenge. The harassment took its toll. He received honor after honor, was hailed as Westfield's most distinguished citizen, yet died in poverty.[16]

The uneven distribution of rebels undermines the standard explanation of Shays's Rebellion. For many years now we have been told that the rebels were "destitute farmers," "debt-ridden farmers," "hopeless poor farmers," and the like, who were victimized by the postwar Massachusetts economy. At the end of the American Revolution, so the story goes, wholesalers in Boston and other New England port cities imported huge quantities of English goods, thus draining the region of specie and taking on immense debt. The wholesalers then sold the goods on credit to retailers in the interior, in towns such as Springfield and Northampton, who in turn sold them on credit to backcountry farmers. Thus a "chain of debt" was created. For a while it presented only minor problems, but then the British closed their West Indian islands to American shipping. Once that happened, the wholesale merchants suddenly had no way to trade their way out of debt. The wholesalers accordingly sued the backcountry merchants, who in turn sued the farmers. By 1785 and 1786, so the story concludes, nearly one-third of all the men in western Massachusetts had been hauled into court as defendants in debt suits, and it was to prevent those trials that Luke Day and his fellow rebels closed the courts in the summer and fall of 1786.[17]

There are a number of problems with this story. First of all, when it came to private indebtedness, western Massachusetts farmers were hardly unique. Heavy debt was common throughout the backcountry, in the Carolinas as well as in New England. During 1786 Connecticut creditors filed more than six thousand court actions and thus allegedly took 20 percent of the state's taxpayers to court.[18] Why, then, didn't the "chain of debt" lead to a full-scale revolt in Connecticut? Why didn't the whole backcountry explode? Why only western Massachusetts?

Second, the men who sent the Northampton judges packing in August 1786 were hardly doing something new and bold. Members of their families had been doing the same thing, off and on, since 1774. In that year, when British authorities shut down the Massachusetts legislature, a convention in nearby Hadley had split into two camps over whether they should take similar action against the county court. Impatient of debate, some 3,000 men had gathered in Springfield and prevented the court from sitting. In the same summer, further west in Great Barrington, a crowd of 1,500 had shut down the Berkshire County court. These actions had been applauded by patriot leaders as proper responses to British high-handedness. But opposition to the courts continued long after the patriots gained control of the Massachusetts government. Throughout much of the Revolutionary War, state-appointed justices found it impossible to hold court in western Massachusetts, in Hampshire County until 1778 and in Berkshire County until 1781.

The excuse for shutting down the courts during these years was that Massachusetts didn't have a proper constitution. The revolutionary leaders of Massachusetts, so the argument went, were trying to rule the commonwealth without the consent of the governed. Elsewhere, in nearby New Hampshire and far-away South Carolina, revolutionary leaders had appealed directly to the people for guidance in establishing new governments. Why didn't the revolutionary leaders of Massachusetts do the same? Why were they trying instead to build a new government on the rotten and crumbling foundation of the old colonial charter? The old charter, said the "constitutionalists," may have been fit for a people dependent on Great Britain. For a free and independent people, however, it was totally inadequate. Until the state had a proper constitution sanctioned by the people, the "constitutionalists" promised never to allow the state courts to open. At one point they even threatened to secede from Massachusetts and join Vermont, which had constitutional government.[19]

Even when the leaders of Massachusetts wrote a constitution and got it approved in 1780, there was still much hostility to the state courts. The most famous incident occurred in Northampton in the spring of 1782. By this time, about two-thirds of western Massachusetts had concluded that the "Great Men" were taking advantage of them and costing them too much, even more than the king's favorites had in the days of George III. The new constitution, many contended, made a mockery out of the Revolution. Under it the eastern elite had too much power, many good men lacked the right to vote, the Senate was beyond the control of the people, the governor had too much salary, the judges and justices of the peace were not answerable to the people.

Into this discontent stepped the Reverend Samuel Ely, who although educated at Yale had become a spokesman for the downtrodden, first in Connecticut, now in Massachusetts. All the complaints were valid, said Ely at one town meeting after another. The people thus must assert their authority. They must overthrow the new constitution and establish republican government. They must stop the courts, the representatives of this odious constitution, from sitting. He had, so he said, a better constitution in his pocket, one that even the Angel Gabriel could not find fault with.

In April, at Northampton, Ely raised a mob against the court. He called for violence, telling his "brave boys" to "go to the woodpile and get clubs enough to knock their Grey Wiggs off and send them out of the World in an Instant." For this and other offenses he was subsequently arrested and brought to trial in Springfield, where he was convicted and sentenced to jail for six months. In June, hundreds of men, many dressed in military array, broke Ely out of jail. Ely got away but some of his rescuers were run down by the sheriff's posse. They agreed to return Ely to jail, and as surety allowed the sheriff to lock up three of their men, all distinguished Revolutionary War veterans, in the Northampton jail. The governor then ordered that the three prisoners be transferred to Boston. Shortly thereafter, a regiment of men under Captain Reuben Dickinson of Amherst forced the sheriff to release the three prisoners. Nothing was done to bring Dickinson and his men to justice.[20]

There is still another problem with the old story that the fear of debt suits led to the court closings. While it is easy to prove that the number of debt suits skyrocketed in the 1780s, there is no correlation—none whatsoever—between debt and rebel towns. Consider, for example, a table that Van Beck Hall compiled years ago in a fine book entitled *Politics without Parties*. Hall traced the number of "recognizance" cases that made their way to the supreme judicial court. These were cases in which a debtor, in trying to buy time and delay payment of his debt, appealed a lower court decision to the higher court and then failed to follow it up. What this did was force his creditor to file a "recognizance" so that the higher court could affirm the lower court's judgment. Statewide, the number of "recognizances" shot up by about 50 percent between 1782 and 1784. In Worcester County, the number of yearly filings doubled and by 1784 exceeded the state average by over two times. In Berkshire, the annual filings rose from way below the state average in 1782 to equal the state average in 1784. But in Hampshire, the most rebellious county, the annual filings were initially well below the state average and never rose at all, thus dropping to about half the state average by 1784.[21]

It is possible of course to explain away the Hampshire numbers. One could argue, for example, that the rebellious Hampshire towns were over their heads in debt, even worse off than the folks in Worcester County, while the nonrebellious Hampshire towns were debt-free. That, however, was not the way things were. Only two of the most rebellious towns—Belchertown and West Springfield—were among the top ten towns in suits for debt. On the other hand, three of the least rebellious—Granville, Northampton, and Worthington—were also among the top ten.[22]

Then there is a problem with the details. Consider again the "banner town" of Colrain. In 1785 and 1786, the Hampshire courts handled 19 debt suits against Colrain men, which was about "average" for Hampshire County towns. Only 13 men, however, were actually sued.[23] On six occasions the court heard charges against Abner Rockwell, twice against Joshua Hunt, and twice against Josiah Newell, once with his brother Oliver. Rockwell and Oliver Newell subsequently took up arms against the state. So did one other debtor, and two sons of still another debtor. Altogether, then, of the 12 families involved in debt proceedings, four provided men for the rebellion. Yet Colrain supplied 156 men. The leader of those men, singled out by the state and convicted of high treason, was James White, who had spearheaded the assault on the Springfield arsenal. He, too, had been in court, but as one of the two creditors who filed suit against Joshua Hunt.

Or consider again the nonrebellious town of Granville. In 1785 and 1786, Granville residents were hauled into court 42 times as defendants in debt cases. This was an extremely high number, fourth highest in the county. In addition, Granville creditors filed 28 debt suits. Of these 16 were against neighbors. This was even more unusual. In small towns, where nearly everyone was in debt to a neighbor, creditors generally went to great lengths to settle neighborly problems out of court. There were always exceptions, as in the case of James White and Joshua Hunt of Colrain, but generally neighbors didn't sue neighbors. As a result, even though most people never borrowed from anyone outside their own community, only one case out of four was between neighbors. So Granville, in at least two respects, had serious financial troubles. Yet Granville residents never got involved in Shays's Rebellion.

Granville and Colrain illustrate another problem with the chain of debt thesis. Supposedly, Boston merchants were putting pressure on local merchants, who in turn were putting the screws on local farmers. Yet Abner Rockwell, the Colrain farmer who was hauled into court on six different occasions, wasn't being harassed by local merchants. His problem was a New York farmer named Thomas McGee, from whom he had bought land. In fact, no one in Colrain, or the neighboring towns, had been sued by a Boston merchant. In Granville, a family named Tillotson was being hard-pressed by William Phillips, one of Boston's premier merchants and the president of the state's only bank. Yet most of Granville's outside debts were to Connecticut merchants.

This was true not only of Granville, but the entire Connecticut Valley. In a sense Hampshire County was an extension of Connecticut. Most of the towns had been founded by families who came out of Connecticut, by men and women who had followed the Connecticut River north and still had family and business ties with Connecticut residents. The county's storekeepers were no different. They too dealt largely with men who lived further down the river. The court cases clearly reflected this dynamic. In 1785 and 1786, Hartford creditors filed four times as many suits in the Hampshire court as Boston merchants, 160 suits as compared to 38 suits. In terms of money value, the ratio was the same, four to one.

Was there, then, no "chain of debt" running from hard-pressed western farmers back to Boston and beyond? In Boston, merchants were undoubtedly heavily in debt. They had greatly overimported in 1783 and 1784. They had well over £100,000 of unsold goods on their shelves. Every newspaper talked of the need to expand the Boston market. One Danish observer reported that Boston merchants had an "amazing Superfluity of all kinds of European goods." The reason, he said, was because they had "no Back Country to consume their goods."[24] That was clearly an overstatement. Boston merchants were reaching as far west as Worcester. But most of them hadn't reached as far west as Hampshire County. Further west in Berkshire County, trade with Boston was virtually nonexistent.

What, then, triggered Shays's Rebellion? Heavy private debt might account for the behavior of Luke Day, but it hardly explains the behavior of James White and scores of other rebel creditors. What does? The answer is twofold: the new state government—and its attempt to enrich the few at the expense of the many. The men who converged on Northampton and started the uprising saw themselves as Regulators, in the same tradition as men who had risen up elsewhere to chasten the governing elite and restore communal order.[25]

Throughout the backcountry "regulation" had been common for decades. In the 1760s, in both North and South Carolina, men calling themselves "Regulators" had defied the Low Country–dominated court system. They had taken the law into their own hands against local bandits and ne'er-do-wells, terrorized judges whom they deemed obnoxious, and broken their own members out of jail whenever they fell into the hands of the authorities. Similarly New Jersey land rioters had blocked judicial actions that benefited the East Jersey Proprietors, and the Green Mountain Boys in nearby Vermont had thwarted the legal claims of New York aristocrats. In much of the backcountry there was now a tradition that whenever distant authorities got out of hand, or whenever outsiders threatened a bona fide settler's landholdings, the people had an obligation to rise up and restore communal order. This way of thinking, in turn, had been strengthened by the actions and the rhetoric of the American Revolution.[26]

How had the authorities got out of hand? For one thing, the state constitution had increased their authority and their ability to do mischief. It was an "aristocratic" document both by backcountry standards and by the standards of the day. It was even a "reactionary" document given the sequence of events.

Massachusetts had been slow in writing a constitution. By the time the gentry got around to the task, most of the other states had already set examples. The worst example in the eyes of the gentry was that of Pennsylvania, where in the summer of 1776 "democratic" forces had gained control and fashioned a document without any system of "checks and balances." Tom Paine, the leading patriot voice in Pennsylvania, had spoken against any complicated system of government that balanced one social interest against another. In a republic, he had insisted, government should be simple and in the hands of the people. In keeping, the new Pennsylvania constitution established a single, all-powerful legislature, elected annually by all taxpaying males over the age of twenty-one. There were no property qualifications for holding office. Instead of the powerful governor with a veto, there was a plural executive consisting of a president and a council, whose job was to simply carry out the will of the legislature.[27]

A year later Vermont took the Pennsylvania model one step further. In just six days the Green Mountain Boys drafted a constitution that largely copied the Pennsylvania document, except that it also banned slavery and enhanced the power of local governments, even allowing towns to decide such matters as legal fees. In the eyes of many in western Massachusetts, Vermont was an example to be followed. Strengthening town government, enhancing the power of town meetings, was clearly the direction in which to move. In the eyes of the Massachusetts gentry, however, Vermont was an outlaw state and its constitution was an abomination.[28]

The Pennsylvania example also reinforced Rhode Island's decision not to write a new constitution. Rhode Island, which in the eyes of the Massachusetts elite was also a state of ne'er-do-wells, simply deleted all references to the British Crown from its old colonial charter. After the deletions, the charter was much like the Pennsylvania and Vermont constitutions. It also placed power in the hands of an all-powerful legislature, with both the executive and the judiciary being at the mercy of the legislature. It too made it possible for "democratic" forces to gain control of the state by simply winning a majority of the legislative seats.[29]

Horrified by these democratic possibilities, the Massachusetts gentry wanted no part of such constitutions. More to their liking were the recommendations of John Adams, who although born and raised in rural Braintree had gone to Harvard and become a full-fledged member of the professional elite. To Adams, as ardent a patriot as Tom Paine or any other Pennsylvania democrat, it was folly to put all power in the hands of a single chamber legislature. No one could "live" under such a government. It was necessary instead to have "balanced" government, and especially to have an upper legislative chamber that represented the interests of the rich.[30] Maryland came close to satisfying Adams and the Massachusetts gentry, with stiff property requirements for voting, and even stiffer ones for holding office, and longer intervals between elections. So did New York, which created a state senate that essentially represented the rich. Both established strong governorships, whose holders were independent of the legislature rather than servants to it.

Only in Massachusetts, however, did Adams and other supporters of "balanced" political institutions fully get their way. They had two tries at it, submitting one constitution to the voters in 1778, another in 1780. The first constitution was actually more "democratic" and less "aristocratic" than the second. Although it established "balanced" government and excluded from the body politic women, blacks, mulattos, Indians, and white paupers, it allowed all free white male taxpayers to vote for the lower house and those worth £60 to vote for the senate and governor.[31]

The exclusion of blacks, mulattos, and Indians from the electorate irritated some voters. The absence of a bill of rights upset many more. But it was the ratification process itself that virtually guaranteed the defeat of the 1778 constitution. To become law, the document needed the unqualified support of a two-thirds majority. The key word was "unqualified." Objection to details meant rejection of the whole document. Many towns missed that point, and as a rule the people of a town voted as one, all in favor or all against. Several towns clearly supported the overall scheme but thought they still could suggest amendments without killing the entire document. They were wrong. Their objections were counted as "no" votes. The document thus didn't come close to passing and was defeated by a five-to-one margin.[32]

In rejecting the proposed constitution, some towns submitted detailed criticisms. Of these the most influential was the "Essex Result." Written largely by a staunch conservative, a Newburyport lawyer named Theophilus Parsons, it allegedly represented the "considered opinion" of the towns of Essex County. The "Result" essentially attacked the 1778 constitution for lacking a bill of rights and being too democratic. It called for more representation of property, the separation of powers, a veto power for the governor, higher property qualifications for office holders and especially the governor, an independent judiciary, and the indirect election of representatives and senators through county conventions.[33]

How did these proposals sit with westerners? Most western towns never expressed their opinion one way or another. The few that did, however, largely rejected the thinking of the Essex Result. Fourteen towns protested against property qualifications for voting, and twelve insisted that all civil and military officers be elected directly by the people.[34]

The following year the leaders of revolutionary Massachusetts made another concerted attempt to write a constitution. In the fall, 247 towns sent representatives to a state-wide convention. Meeting in Boston, the delegates assigned the hard work of composing a new document to a committee consisting of John Adams, Sam Adams, and James Bowdoin. All three were from eastern Massachusetts. John Adams did most of the writing. Once he finished drafting the document, he left for France on a diplomatic mission. That winter constitutional delegates were supposed to gather again in Boston to approve, disapprove, or modify his handiwork.

Westerners couldn't get there. It was one of the worst winters in Massachusetts's history, worse even than the winter of 1717, and probably as bad as the disastrous winter of 1740. Boston harbor froze solid, and for over a month no vessel left or entered the port. Only one major road was open in the west, the road from Hartford to Boston. Elsewhere travel was possible only by snowshoes. The convention had to wait weeks before there was a quorum, and in the end only forty-seven towns were represented. Nearly all were within ten or fifteen miles of Boston, or near the seacoast. This rump group made the final decisions that became the Constitution of 1780.[35]

The new document was much in keeping with the Essex Result. It included a bill of rights, and overall it enhanced the power of the rich and well-born, more so than the rejected constitution of 1778, and more so than the old colonial charter. It established two legislative chambers, with the upper house based on taxes paid rather than population, and the lower house weighted in favor of the eastern mercantile towns. It also created a strong governor with extensive veto and appointive powers, provided for an independent judiciary that was beyond the control of ordinary people, and raised the property requirements for voting and holding office. No longer could a man worth £500 be elected governor; he now had to have a £1,000 freehold. Nor could a man with a £200 freehold and £400 total wealth still serve in the senate; he now had to have a £300 freehold and £600 total wealth. Gone, too, was the suffrage clause of the rejected 1778 constitution allowing all white male taxpayers to vote for the lower house. Now to vote for any state office a man had to be worth at least £60, which was £20 more than under the old colonial charter. Finally, there was a clause forbidding any amendments to the new constitution for at least fifteen years.[36]

This time the constitution-makers formulated a ratification process that virtually guaranteed approval of their handiwork. Instead of unqualified support being required, this time a town might suggest scores of amendments and still be counted as a "yes" vote. Every town was to vote on the constitution, clause by clause, and state objections to any clause that did not obtain a majority. Then the adjourned constitutional convention was to look at the results and, if there appeared to be a two-thirds majority for each clause, to declare the constitution ratified and, if there did not appear to be a two-thirds majority, to make alterations "in accord with the popular will."

What if there was no popular will? What if sixty towns objected to a provision for one reason, and another sixty for the opposite reason? Such was the case when it came to the relationship of church to state. And what if a town never took a vote on an article it objected to, but rather just suggested an amendment and voted on the amendment? Should the votes for the amendment be counted as votes against the original article? That might seem logical, but that is not what happened. In fact, most towns never took a vote on an article that the majority clearly opposed, just on the substituted amendment, and these votes were not counted as votes against the original article. Often, in one way or another, they were counted as votes in favor of the original article. Similarly, the vote-counters decided other ticklish issues in behalf of their creation. Every article thus passed by a landslide.[37]

Some of the provisions, however, had little support in towns that later became the nucleus of Shays's Rebellion. In one way or another, many of these towns complained that power was being taken out of their hands and given to the Boston elite. They much preferred, it was clear, to be ruled by men who were answerable to them rather than to the governor or the Governor's Council. Rather than endorsing judicial independence, twenty-nine towns wanted Superior Court judges to be either elected or appointed annually, and thirty-one wanted justices of the peace to be elected. Rather than supporting property qualifications for voting, thirty towns insisted that any man who was respected in the community, or who served in the militia and defended the commonwealth, should have the right to vote.[38] Twenty-two towns also censured the new constitution for allowing the house to do business when only sixty members were present. This, they argued, was especially biased in favor of the mercantile elite and the eastern part of the state. It ensured that eastern Massachusetts could pass laws even when delegates from western Massachusetts couldn't get to Boston. Finally, many western towns complained about the fact that this untried constitution could not be amended for fifteen years. What if the new government proved to be unjust? Why was the governing elite afraid of change?[39]

In at least one major respect, these complaints were justified. The constitution of 1780 undoubtedly consolidated power in the hands of mercantile elite and the eastern part of the state. It shifted power from the rural backcountry to Boston, from the poor to the rich, and from town meetings to the state senate and the governor's office.

That, to be sure, might not have mattered if the change in power relations had been only on paper. Before the American Revolution, the royal governor and the Governor's Council also had great power over the backcountry. But for the most part that was only on paper. Apart from the appointment of judges and justices of the peace, decisions made in Boston rarely had much impact on men and women living in Amherst, Colrain, Whately, and other Shaysite communities. What happened in their town meetings mattered. What happened in Boston rarely did. They were largely ruled by men they knew, not by men who lived eighty or a hundred miles away.[40]

That was not the case after 1780. Now what happened in Boston, as never before, came to have a decisive impact on life in towns that had seldom been bothered by distant authorities. That fact was magnified by a number of distressing decisions the legislature made after 1780. Of these the most costly involved the Massachusetts debt.

The Bay State had a heavy war debt, heavier than states that were away from the war zone, but its basic problem was hardly unique. Nearly every battle-tested government faced the same problem: it had issued notes that it couldn't honor, and the question was what to do with the outstanding notes.

One answer was to consolidate the notes and hope to pay them off sometime in the future. But consolidate at what value? What, for example, should be done with the notes Massachusetts issued in April 1778? These notes initially traded at about one-fourth of their face value. By 1781 they had plummeted to about one-fortieth of their face value.[41] Should they be consolidated at their value when issued? Or at their current market value? Or at some other value?

Faced with the same problem, other states generally sank their currency at full depreciation, Virginia as much as a 1,000 to one. So did the central government, at 40 to one.[42] But not Massachusetts. When the mercantile-dominated state legislature took up the matter of consolidation, it ignored what the notes were actually worth and promised to pay what the notes were worth on the day of issue. This decision had enormous consequences. First of all, it was incredibly expensive, obliging the state to pay out at least twice the amount that was necessary for the state to become credit worthy. Of this amount, £1,250,000 was earmarked for the holders of "Consolidated Notes" and £270,000 for the holders of notes originally given to officers and soldiers of the Massachusetts Line in compensation for the depreciation of their wages. The state also owed an equally large sum of money as its share of the continental debt.

The consolidation was a bonanza for speculators. Most of the soldiers had been in no position to hold onto their notes. Their personal affairs generally deteriorated as the war dragged on. Most therefore had long parted with their notes, often for one-eighth or one-tenth of their original value. So too had most people who had received promissory notes or purchased bonds in support of the war effort. Not all of these transactions can be traced, and hence who traded what to whom is often a mystery. But some £600,000 can be traced, and if these transactions are at all typical the overall story is fairly clear: nearly 80 percent of the state debt made its way into the hands of speculators who lived in or near Boston, and nearly 40 percent into the hands of just thirty-five men.

These men claimed that they had come to the government's aid in its time of need. But that was true of only a handful. The vast majority had seldom obtained notes directly from the government—and hence had seldom paid top dollar for their notes. Instead the typical big operator, with £7,500 or more in notes, had acquired 91 percent of his holdings on the open market and often at rock-bottom prices.

All these speculators of course were gambling on the future. Only a few, however, had put themselves in a position where they could lose "everything." Many were market-timers, buying and selling as the volatile securities market dipped one week, rose the next. Some were involved in complicated land speculations whereby they could swap securities for government land. Some bought only from the truly desperate. Jonathan Mason, for example, gradually accumulated nearly £16,500 in traceable notes. All but six shillings was acquired from soldiers and other note holders. Mason also amassed an additional £13,500 in untraceable notes. Most of these, one suspects, also came from soldiers and other note holders. His business partner William Phillips also speculated heavily in notes, obtaining eventually £28,000 worth. So did Mason's son Jonathan, Jr., with over £6,000, and his son-in-law, William Phillips, Jr., with nearly £15,000. Altogether, these four men held about 5 percent of the Massachusetts state debt.[43]

All these men, moreover, had political influence. Mason's partner William Phillips, for example, first became a key figure in Boston politics before the Revolution. On the outbreak of the war, he moved his family to Norwich, Connecticut, and was largely out of Boston politics for as long as the British had possession of the city. Then in 1779, when the war shifted to the South, he was back in Boston and again a major player, serving as a member of the convention that framed the Massachusetts constitution, and then during the 1780s as either a state representative, a state senator, or a member of the Governor's Council.[44]

Similarly, of the thirty-five men who held over 40 percent of the state debt, all of them during the 1780s either served in the state house themselves or had a close relative in the state house. They thus had a big hand in writing law, although never a free hand, as they always needed the acquiescence of other merchants who held few securities and had less interest in paying off speculators. All these men, furthermore, had a vested interest in maintaining the existing government. No other state government had passed laws that were so favorable to public creditors. No other government, in fact, had even come close to passing such laws. Thus, when General Lincoln went looking for money to hire an army, he knew exactly where to go. He went to William Phillips and his associates at the Massachusetts Bank.[45] They provided well over two-thirds of the money he obtained.

Having managed to consolidate the state debt at twice what was necessary, the mercantile-dominated legislature also made several crucial decisions on how to pay the debt. One was to redeem all the "army notes" by 1786, and one-third of the "Consolidated Notes" later in the same year. That meant that Massachusetts somehow had to come up with several hundred thousand pounds in taxes and come up with the money quickly. It also meant that Massachusetts had to increase the tax burden by five or six times. But this wasn't all. The legislature also decided to pay interest on the notes at 6 percent annually in specie. This meant that between July 1782 and October 1786 the state somehow had to come up with £265,000 in hard money. Then there was the question of what to do for the years when the state paid no interest. Here it was decided to compound the amounts due along with the principal, and add another 4 percent as a bounty for not being paid on time. All this was supposed to stop the new notes from depreciating as fast as the old notes.

To retain any creditability at all, the state legislature had to make good on the interest payments that were almost immediately due, and these payments had to be made in hard money. The hard money requirement, by itself, was pernicious. Not everyone dealt in hard money, and this was especially true in the backcountry, where goods, livestock, and labor had usually sufficed in payment of debts. Even well-established rural storekeepers, like Oliver Dickinson in Amherst, dealt in cash transactions only about one-fourth of the time. The rest was in barter. Now, thanks to the state legislature, the demand for hard currency soared.[46] But how was it be acquired? By refusing payment in goods, livestock, and labor—and accepting only hard money? That might work for the short term, but in time every Spanish dollar and every English shilling would be squeezed out of the backcountry. What then?

Initially, the legislature eased some of the tension by turning to import and excise duties. Goods coming into Boston and smaller port cities were to be taxed, and so were wine, tea, rum, brandy, and carriages, with the latter taxes allegedly having the fringe benefit of suppressing "immorality, luxury, and extravagance."[47] All these monies, it was decided, would be used for interest payments on the notes and nothing else. This continued for the next four years, with every year the legislature juggling the figures and toying with the list of items to be taxed. State notes still continued to depreciate, not as quickly as in the past, but to the dismay of speculators.

Just paying the interest, however, was not what the legislature had in mind. It was determined to pay off the entire state debt by the end of the decade—and to pay off the debt in hard money. The army debt was to be paid off in three annual specie payments beginning in 1784, and the consolidated debt was to be redeemed in four annual installments beginning in 1785. That meant heavy taxes, payable in hard money, and the legislature decided to rely on two ways that Massachusetts had raised money in the past. One was a poll tax, a tax on males sixteen years and older; the other was a property tax. Town authorities were told to provide detailed data. How many polls were in each family? Did the family own a house? a barn? any other buildings? How many horses did the family own? Oxen? Milch cows? How many acres did the family have in tillage? in pasture? What was the size of the family's woodlot? unimproved land?[48]

Not only did everyone thus know that the tax-man was coming, everyone also knew that the tax bite was going to be regressive. Only about 10 percent of the taxes were to come from import duties and excises, which fell mainly on people who were most able to pay. The other 90 percent was direct taxes on property, with land bearing a disproportionate share, and on polls. The latter was especially regressive, since it mattered not a whit if a male sixteen years of age or older had any property or not. Rich or poor, he was going to have to pay the same amount, and altogether polls were going to pay at least one-third of all taxes.[49]

Not only was the tax bite going to be heavy, then, it was biased against farm families with grown sons, and the chief beneficiaries were to be Boston speculators. These were inflammable ingredients, but for a while they remained in check because the perennial governor of Massachusetts, John Hancock, had little interest in activating the process.

While still in his twenties, Hancock had inherited the mercantile firm of his uncle, which in turn had made him one of the richest men in Boston. But very early he had deliberately decided to build a public career based on popularity, and he had worked hard to create a following, both among his own employees in Boston and in the countryside, where he provided impoverished churches with free Bibles. When hard times came, Hancock further added to his popularity by giving soldiers top value for their notes and by insisting that indigent debtors pay him in depreciated paper money rather than in silver. His enemies accused him of grandstanding and setting a bad example. They also accused him of not enforcing the tax law. Hancock ignored them. With little of his own money invested in state notes, he had no interest in jeopardizing his great popularity by energizing the cumbersome Massachusetts collection system. Taxes fell in arrears, and by 1786 some £279,000 were delinquent.[50]

In the previous year Hancock declared that he was suffering from an acute attack of gout and would not stand for reelection. In his place was chosen James Bowdoin, who like Hancock had inherited a large estate and added to it. But Bowdoin, although listed as a Boston merchant, spent little time in trade. He was a major landlord and far more interested in land and note speculation. He held at least £3,290 in state notes. More significant were his extensive landholdings in Boston and his huge land claims in Maine. To his dismay squatters on his Maine lands repeatedly challenged his proprietorship and from his perspective caused him serious financial injury. He had a low opinion of them—and of people generally who lived in the backcountry.[51]

Bowdoin's primary supporters were conservative merchants and fellow speculators. In their eyes he was far more trustworthy than Hancock and had long been their mainstay in Massachusetts politics. He had been the president of the convention that drafted the 1780 constitution and chairman of the committee that did the actual writing. Although the document itself was largely the work of John Adams, Bowdoin was given credit for many of its more conservative features. Yet, even though conservatives gave him high marks, electing him was no easy task. Not only did Bowdoin lack Hancock's popularity and Hancock's reputation as an ardent patriot, Bowdoin's only daughter had married a high-level British official who was in line to become a baron. The election was bitter and so close that no one emerged with a majority. Thrown into the legislature, the senate insisted on Bowdoin, and the house at first backed his opponent but eventually gave way to the senate.

Bowdoin, as his backers anticipated, was no Hancock. A public creditor himself, he waxed eloquent in his inaugural address on the state's need to fully honor its debts. The new governor also cared far less about public support and far more about enforcing the state's laws. To his way of thinking, the only support he needed was the backing of the "better sort." Under his prodding, the "better sort" in the legislature enacted new taxes and exerted pressure to collect overdue taxes. The results were disastrous. The combined load of overdue taxes and current taxes was more than many residents could pay in a year, five years, or even a decade. Taxes levied by the state were now much more oppressive—indeed, many times more oppressive—than those that had been levied by the British on the eve of the American Revolution. Even Massachusetts conservatives, men like Rufus King and John Adams, thought the tax bite was now "heavier than the People could bare."[52]

The result was the explosion in the backcountry that came to be known as Shays's Rebellion. But, as we already noted, only one out of three backcountry towns actually participated. What was it about these rebellious towns? Why did 121 men turn out in Amherst and none in neighboring South Hadley? Why did 156 men turn out in Colrain and none in neighboring Heath?

In each instance, the rebellion had the support of prominent families as well as hard-pressed families. In Amherst the key family was the Dickinsons. Nineteen Dickinson men took up arms against the government. So too did seven men who were married to Dickinson women, two who were sons of Dickinson women, and two who were courting Dickinson daughters. All told, one-fourth of all the Amherst rebels were connected in one way or another with the Dickinson family.[53] The Dickinsons were anything but down-and-outers. They were one of the town's premier families. They held far more than their share of town offices. They dominated the Second Congregational Church. They were also the town's leading patriot family, providing far more than their share of soldiers during the American Revolution.[54] In contrast, of the thirteen Amherst men who supported the state during the rebellion, over half had been Tories during the American Revolution.

In the nearby town of Pelham, the key family was the Grays.[55] Of the 110 Pelham men who marched behind Daniel Shays, twenty in one way or another were members of the Gray family. Among their number was Daniel Gray, the richest man in town, who also was a deacon of the church and frequently was elected selectman and town moderator. Also participating was the leader of the clan, Deacon Ebenezer Gray, who served as town treasurer for over twenty-five years. These men carried much weight in town, far more than Daniel Shays, who although highly respected was a relative newcomer to Pelham with few family connections.

In West Springfield, three families were central. Of the 141 men who bore arms against the state, 26 were connected by blood or marriage with the Day family, 24 with the Leonards, and 15 with the Elys.[56] The most prominent of these men was Colonel Benjamin Ely, a wealthy landowner and easily the most popular man in town. Elected selectman 7 times, town moderator 6 times, state representative 5 times, he was indicted for treason and barred from holding office in 1787. The next year the town folk elected him to represent them in the state legislature and at the state convention called to ratify the United States Constitution. Also indicted for treason was Reuben Leonard, Jr. Thirteen years younger than Ely, he was just reaching his prime in town affairs at the time of Shays's Rebellion. The son of a deacon and prominent selectman, he was elected selectman in 1788 and held that office until 1797.

In Colrain no single family matched the Leonards, the Grays, or the Dickinsons in providing rebel soldiers. Instead, a half-dozen families contributed far more than their share. These families undoubtedly had clout. Of the 156 men from Colrain who took up arms against the state, 32 either served as selectmen at one time or another or were the sons of selectmen.[57] Also on the list were several men who were elected to the state legislature and several deacons of the local church. Given this formidable group, it is no surprise that two-thirds of the men in the town took up arms against the state.

Both Colrain and Pelham were Scotch-Irish towns. Even though they were more than thirty miles apart, and getting from one to the other was a long day's journey even in good weather, they were close socially. At one point the two towns had even shared the same minister, and for years young men in one town had gone to the other in search of potential brides. Like many Scotch-Irish towns throughout the backcountry, they had a reputation for being extremely clannish and for standing up for their "own." Having come out of a culture in which the "family" encompassed all kin within four generations, and in which all family members were expected to band together whenever danger threatened, these people could be formidable. They had proved it time and again during the Revolution. For them, assembling a company of warriors was relatively easy.[58]

But it also seems to have been relatively easy for tight-knit communities that came out of the New England Puritan tradition. What is striking about most of the rebels is that they came out of unified cultures. Class divisions are almost impossible to find. Towns that supported the rebellion were not divided rich versus poor, creditor versus debtor. People either moved as one, or didn't participate.

John Brooke, in his study of Worcester County, makes much of religious strife and the lack of ministerial authority.[59] Yet even in towns that were riven over religious matters, there was unity in subcultures. In Amherst, for example, members of the Second Church were virtually "at war" with the Tory pastor of the First Church and his supporters. Included in the Second Church were some of the richest families in town and also some of the poorest. Yet members of the Second Church overwhelmingly supported the rebellion. Only one member, a government appointee, sided with the state. All the rest either took up arms against the state or supported their friends in arms. The government appointee, Ebenezer Mattoon, felt so uncomfortable in this situation, or so threatened, that he temporarily moved his family out of town. Later, when peace returned, Mattoon went out of way to get back in the good graces of his one-time friends, writing letters in their behalf, and in one instance even flat-out lying to save a man in neighboring Pelham from the gallows.[60]

Without such community loyalties, Shays's Rebellion would never have become a reality. The "poor and desperate" did not come out of every nook and cranny in western Massachusetts to do battle against the state and its "grasping" elite. Nor did the vast majority of debtors who found themselves in court or in debtors' prison. More "hard-pressed debtors" lived in Hadley than in Amherst or Pelham. And more lived in Granville than in West Springfield or Colrain. Yet these men never took up arms against the state. Only in tight-knit communities where men and women acted as one were rebel leaders like Reuben Dickinson, James White, and Luke Day able to raise hundreds of men to join the "regulation" and try to restore "communal order."

NOTES

1. *Hampshire Herald*, September 5, 1786; *Massachusetts Gazette*, 8, September 26, 1786; Massachusetts Archives (hereafter MA) 189:5; 318:4, 6.

2. List of Subscribers, MA 189:66, 217–218; Receipts on Loan to Suppress the Rebellion, 1787, MA; "To the Forty Thousand Pound Loan established by the Act of the General Court, passed the 6th February 1787," Treasurer's Office, Journal B, 1786–1787, 477–478, MA.

3. "Report of the Commissioners, April 27, 1787," MA 190:277–281. The oaths are in MA 190:67–225. They have to be used with care, as some men took the oath more than once.

4. *Hampshire Herald*, September 5, 1786; *Massachusetts Gazette*, 8, September 26, 1786; MA 189:5; 318:4, 6.

5. Biographical information for Day was gleaned from George Edward Day, *A Genealogical Register of the Descendants in the Male Line of Robert Day*, 2nd ed. (Northampton, MA, 1848), 17, 23, along with town histories, town records, and

court records. Bernie Lally, the town historian of West Springfield, provided me with a wealth of information and documents about Day and his neighbors.

6. "West Springfield's Minuteman Company," in Esther M. Swift, *West Springfield, Massachusetts: A Town History* (Springfield, 1969), 321; *Massachusetts Soldiers and Sailors of the Revolutionary War* (Boston, 1898), 579–580; Francis B. Heitman, *Historical Register of Officers of the Continental Army Units* (Harrisburg, PA, 1972), 68, 73, 149; Kenneth Roberts, ed., *March to Quebec: Journals of Members of Arnold's Expedition* (New York, 1938); John Richard Alden, ed., *The War of the Revolution* (New York, 1952), vol. 1, chap. 13; Willard M. Wallace, *Traitorous Hero: Life and Fortunes of Benedict Arnold* (Freeport, NY, 1954), 55–93.

7. Wallace Evans Davies, "The Society of the Cincinnati in New England, 1783–1800," *William and Mary Quarterly* (hereafter *WMQ*) 5 (January 1948): 3–25; Henry Knox to John Adams, August 21, 1776, Massachusetts Historical Society (hereafter MHS); Louis Clinton Hatch, *The Administration of the American Revolutionary Army* (New York, 1904), 82; Sidney Kaplan, "Veteran Officers and Politics in Massachusetts, 1783–1787," *WMQ* 9 (January 1952): 34–40; Sidney Kaplan, "Pay, Pension, and Power: Economic Grievances of the Massachusetts Officers of the Revolution," *Boston Public Library Quarterly* 3 (January and April 1951): 15–34, 127–141; Charles Royster, *A Revolutionary People at War: The Continental Army and American Character, 1775–1783* (Chapel Hill, 1979), 353–354.

8. Sidney Kaplan, "Rank and Status among Massachusetts Continental Officers," *American Historical Review* 56 (January 1951): 318–326; Kaplan, "Pay, Pension, and Power," 15–34, 127–141; Jackson Turner Main, *The Social Structure of Revolutionary America* (Princeton, 1965), 213–215; Gerhard Kollmann, "Reflections on the Army of the American Revolution," in Erich Angermann et al., eds., *New Wine in Old Skins: A Comparative View of Socio-Political Structures and Values Affecting the American Revolution* (Stuttgart, 1976), 153–176.

9. Computed from data: West Springfield Tax List, 1775, and West Springfield Assessment, June 26, 1786, Connecticut Valley Historical Museum, Springfield, MA.

10. *Two-in-One Book: Hampshire County House of Correction, 1784–1830*, Forbes Library, Northampton.

11. Computed from data: *Two-in-One Book*, and oaths of allegiance, MA 190:67–225.

12. Mary Ann Nicholson, ed., *The Family of Daniel Shays* (Boston, 1987), 12; petition of Timothy Hinds, May 1787, MA 189:367; bills of indictment, Robert Treat Paine Papers, MHS; "Names of the Persons Before Supreme Judicial Court, Northampton, April 1787," Suffolk County Court, File 159008.

13. Computed from data in the oaths of allegiance, MA 190:67–225.

14. Lois McClellan Patrie, *History of Colrain, Massachusetts, with Genealogies of Early Families* (Troy, NY, 1974), lists only eighty-eight rebels, mainly those who took the oath before Justices of the Peace Hugh McClellan of Colrain and Hugh Maxwell of neighboring Heath. Missing from her list are sixty-eight Colrain men. Most of these men took the oath before other justices of the peace; a few were under indictment or in jail; a few were simply left off her list. For a complete list, see the oaths of allegiance in the MA 190:90–91, 118–119, 138, 146, 173; Black List County of Hampshire, Robert Treat Paine Papers, MHS; "A Return of Prisoners now confined in Gaol in Northampton . . . 9 April 1787," Robert Treat Paine Papers, MHS;

"Names of the Persons Before Supreme Judicial Court, Northampton, April 1787," Suffolk County Court, File 159008; and "Number & Names of the People in Colrain that have Taken Arms Against Government in the year 1786 & 1787," Colrain Town Records, Pocumtuck Valley Memorial Association Library, Old Deerfield. The last document lists the participants by their military rank.

15. "Maj. Shepard's Estimate of the No. of Insurgents in Hampshire, Dec 14, 1786," *The Bowdoin and Temple Papers, Collections of the Massachusetts Historical Society* (Boston, 1907), 66:116–117.

16. David P. Szatmary, *Shays' Rebellion* (Amherst, 1980), 113; Mason Green, *Springfield, 1636–1886* (Springfield, 1888), 330; *Hampshire Gazette*, April 11, 1787; Benjamin Lincoln to Colonel Murray, April 16, 1787, Robert Treat Pain Papers, MHS.

17. See especially Szatmary, *Shays' Rebellion*, chaps. 2 and 3. See also Robert J. Taylor, *Western Massachusetts in the Revolution* (Providence, 1954), chaps. 6 and 7; and Marion L. Starkey, *A Little Rebellion* (New York, 1955).

18. *New Haven Gazette*, December 14, 1786. For states other than Connecticut, see E. P. Walton ed., *Records of the Governor and Council of the State of Vermont*, 8 vols. (Montpelier, 1873–1880) 3:360; Laurel Thatcher Ulrich, *A Midwife's Tale: The Life of Martha Ballard Based on Her Diary, 1785–1812* (New York, 1990), 86–87; Jere R. Daniell, *Experiment in Republicanism: New Hampshire Politics and the American Revolution, 1741–1794* (Cambridge, MA, 1970), 183–205; Rachel N. Klein, *Unification of the Slave State: The Rise of the Planter Class in the South Carolina Backcountry, 1760–1808* (Chapel Hill, 1990), 126–134; Jean B. Lee, *The Price of Nationhood: The American Revolution in Charles County* (New York, 1994), 228–258; Main, *Social Structure of Revolutionary America*, 159–160; and Terry Bouton, "A Road Closed: Rural Insurgency in Post-Independence Pennsylvania," *Journal of American History* 87 (December 2000): 858–862.

19. Taylor, *Western Massachusetts in the Revolution*, 78–87, 99–102; Theodore M. Hammett, "Revolutionary Ideology in Massachusetts: Thomas Allen's 'Vindication' of the Berkshire Constitutionalists," *WMQ* 33 (October 1976): 514–527.

20. Robert E. Moody, "Samuel Ely: Forerunner of Shays," *New England Quarterly* 5 (January 1932): 105–108; Franklin Bowditch Dexter, *Biographical Sketches of the Graduates of Yale College*, 5 vols. (New York, 1903), 3:67–69; Samuel Ely, "Two Sermons Preached at Somers, March 18, 1770, when the Church and People Were Under Peculiar Trials" (Hartford, 1771); Samuel Ely, *The Deformity of a Hideous Monster, Discovered in the Province of Maine* (Boston, 1797); diary of Jonathan Judd, February 14, April 12, May 6, 17, 1782, Forbes Library; Joseph Hawley to Caleb Strong, June 24, 1782, Hawley Papers, Box 1, New York Public Library; John Hancock, message, June 17, 1782, in E. M. Bacon, ed., *Supplement to Acts and Laws of Massachusetts* (Boston, 1896), 141; John H. Lockwood, *Western Massachusetts: A History, 1636–1925*, 2 vols. (New York, 1926), 1:115–118; Stephen A. Marini, "The Religious World of Daniel Shays," in Robert A. Gross, ed., *In Debt to Shays: The Bicentennial of an Agrarian Rebellion* (Charlottesville, VA, 1993), 267–269; Alan Taylor, *Liberty Men and Great Proprietors: The Revolutionary Settlement on the Maine Frontier, 1760–1820* (Chapel Hill, 1990), 105–108.

21. Van Beck Hall, *Politics without Parties: Massachusetts, 1780–1791* (Pittsburgh, 1972), 192, 195. For similar interpretation, see Forrest McDonald and Ellen

Shapiro McDonald, *Requiem: Variations on Eighteenth Century Themes* (Lawrence, KS, 1988), 65–66.

22. Calculated from two databases: participants in Shays's Rebellion and parties in debt suits. The latter database was constructed from the records of the Court of Common Pleas, Hampshire County, vol. 18, MA, microfilm no. 00886429.

23. Szatmary, *Shays' Rebellion*, 29, claims that 31.4 percent of Hampshire men sixteen years of age or older were involved in debt suits. That number, although very specific, is way too high. In most Hampshire towns, as in Colrain, a handful of men were sued repeatedly, and that drove up the number of lawsuits.

24. Colonel Christian Febiger to J. Sobotken, September 27, 1784, in "Extracts from a Merchant's Letters, 1784–1786," *Magazine of American History* 8 (1882): 352. See also Samuel Otis to Joseph Otis, February 6, 1785, Otis Papers, Columbia University; Martin Gay to Benjamin Holmes, October 7, 1785, Gray-Otis Collection, Columbia University; Stephen Higginson to John Adams, December 30, 1785, "Letters of Stephen Higginson," in *Annual Report of the American History Association* (Washington, DC, 1896), 1:732; David P. Szatmary, "Shays' Rebellion in Springfield," in Martin Kaufman, ed., *Shays' Rebellion: Selected Essays* (Westfield, MA, 1987), 3–4; Robert Haas, "The Forgotten Courtship of David and Marcy Spear," *Old-Time New England* 7 (January 1962): 67; William B. Weeden, *Economic and Social History of New England, 1620–1789*, 2 vols. (New York, 1963), 2:819; McDonald and McDonald, *Requiem*, 61–62.

25. MA 189:429; C. O. Parmenter, *History of Pelham* (Amherst, 1898), 373; Edward W. Carpenter and Charles F. Morehouse, *The History of the Town of Amherst, Massachusetts* (Amherst, 1896), 126; *Hampshire Gazette*, October 4, 1786.

26. John S. Bassett, "The Regulators of North Carolina, 1765–1771," in *American Historical Association Annual Report for the Year 1894* (Washington, DC, 1895), 141–212; Marvin L. Michael Kay, "The North Carolina Regulation, 1766–1776: A Class Conflict," in Alfred F. Young, ed., *The American Revolution* (De Kalb, IL, 1976), 71–124; James P. Whittenburg, "Planters, Merchants, and Lawyers: Social Change and the Origins of the North Carolina Regulation," *WMQ* 34 (1977): 215–238; Paul David Nelson, *William Tyron and the Course of Empire: A Life in British Imperial Service* (Chapel Hill, 1990), 70–89; Arthur Palmer Hudson, "Songs of the North Carolina Regulators," *WMQ* 4 (October 1947): 470–485. For this and other backcountry uprisings, see also Richard Maxwell Brown, "Back Country Rebellions and the Homestead Ethic in America, 1740–1799," in Richard Maxwell Brown and Don E. Fehrenbacher, eds., *Tradition, Conflict, and Modernization: Perspectives on the American Revolution* (New York, 1977), 83–85.

27. Because of its treatment of Tories and pacifists, historians are at odds over just how "democratic" the Pennsylvania constitution was. Cf. Elisha P. Douglass, *Rebels and Democrats: The Struggle for Equal Rights and Majority Rule during the American Revolution* (Chapel Hill, 1955), chap. 14; Eric Foner, *Tom Paine and Revolutionary America* (New York, 1976), chap. 4; Anne M Ousterhout, "Controlling the Opposition in Pennsylvania during the American Revolution," *Pennsylvania Magazine of History and Biography* 105 (January 1981): 3–34; Owen S. Ireland, *Religious, Ethnicity, and Politics: Ratifying the Constitution in Pennsylvania* (University Park, PA, 1995); and Francis Jennings, *The Creation of America: Through Revolution to Empire* (New York, 2000), chap. 28.

28. Michael A. Bellesiles, *Revolutionary Outlaws: Ethan Allen and the Struggle for Independence on the Vermont Frontier* (Charlottesville, VA, 1993), 136–140; Jackson Turner Main, *The Sovereign States, 1775–1783* (New York, 1973), 176–177; Chilton Williamson, *Vermont in a Quandary* (Montpelier, 1949); Nathaniel Hendricks, "A New Look at the Ratification of the Vermont Constitution of 1777," *Vermont History* 34 (1966): 136–140; Gary A. Aichelle, "Making the Vermont Constitution: 1777–1824," *Vermont History* 56 (summer 1988): 166–190; Taylor, *Western Massachusetts in the Revolution,* 78–79.

29. Irwin H. Polishook, *Rhode Island and the Union, 1774–1795* (Evanston, IL, 1969), 41–42; John P. Kaminski, "Democracy Run Rampant: Rhode Island in the Confederation," in James Kirby Martin, ed., *The Human Dimensions of Nation Making: Essays on Colonial and Revolutionary America* (Madison, WI, 1976), 244.

30. John Adams, "Thoughts on Government" (1776) in Charles Francis Adams, ed., *Works of John Adams,* 10 vols. (Boston, 1850–1856), 4:185–203.

31. Oscar Handlin and Mary Handlin, eds., *The Popular Sources of Political Authority: Documents on the Massachusetts Constitution of 1780* (Cambridge, MA, 1966), 192–193; Main, *The Sovereign States,* 179.

32. Michael Zuckerman, *Peaceable Kingdom: New England Towns in the Eighteenth Century* (New York, 1970), 94–95, 105–106, 272–273.

33. Theophilus Parsons, *Memoir of Theophilus Parsons* (Boston, 1859), 359–363, 384–389; Handlin and Handlin, *Massachusetts Constitution of 1780,* 324–365.

34. See the responses of Greenwich, Hardwick, Charlemont, Belchertown, Rochester, Chesterfield, Williamstown, Sutton, New Salem, Lenox, Upton, Mendon, Blandford, Shelburne, Spencer, and Pelham, in Handlin and Handlin, *Massachusetts Constitution of 1780,* 212–213, 215–221, 226–228, 230–238, 244, 253–258, 262–264, 266–268, 281–282, 285–286, 301–303, 321–322.

35. Samuel Eliot Morison, "The Struggle over the Adoption of the Constitution of Massachusetts, 1780," *Proceedings of the Massachusetts Historical Society* 50 (May 1917): 356–358; *Journal of the Convention for Framing a Constitution for the State of Massachusetts Bay, September 1, 1779, to June 16, 1780* (Boston, 1832).

36. Handlin and Handlin, *Massachusetts Constitution of 1780,* 334–335, 441–472; Main, *The Sovereign States,* 181–183.

37. Morison, "Struggle over the Adoption of the Constitution," 360–363, 396–400; Douglass, *Rebels and Democrats,* 209–210; Handlin and Handlin, *Massachusetts Constitution of 1780,* 693–700; MA 276:59; *Manual for the Constitutional Convention of 1917* (Boston, 1917), 22–23.

38. Handlin and Handlin, *Massachusetts Constitution of 1780,* 475–506, 533–626, 807–901. See also "A Lover of American Independence," in *Massachusetts Gazette* (Springfield), October 15, 1782.

39. Handlin and Handlin, *Massachusetts Constitution of 1780,* 475–506, 533–626, 807–901.

40. Zuckerman, *Peaceable Kingdom,* 10–45; J. R. Pole, *Political Representation in England and the Origins of the American Republic* (New York, 1966), 38–75; Samuel Eliot Morison, *The Maritime History of Massachusetts, 1783–1860* (Boston, 1921), 28–29; Samuel Eliot Morison, "Comments on Ralph V. Harlow, 'Economic Conditions in Massachusetts, 1775–1783,'" in *Colonial Society of Massachusetts, Publications* 20 (1920): 192–193.

41. Whitney K. Bates, "The State Finances of Massachusetts, 1780–1789" (M.A. thesis, University of Wisconsin, 1948), 166; E. James Ferguson, *The Power of the Purse* (Chapel Hill, 1961), 245.

42. Bates, "Finances of Massachusetts," 91; Ferguson, *The Power of the Purse*, 245.

43. Ferguson, *The Power of the Purse*, 237–275. For information about individual creditors, two sources are especially valuable: William H. Dumont, "A Short Census of Massachusetts—1779," *National Genealogical Society Quarterly* 49–50 (1966–1967), and the Subscription Register, Loan of 1790, Massachusetts, National Archives, University of Maryland branch. In recent years, the National Archives has been unable to locate the key document from these "Old Loan" records that lists the state creditors in 1790, their holdings, and how they obtained their holdings. I was able to obtain a microfilm copy, thanks to George Kennedy of Amherst, from the Church of Jesus Christ of Latter Day Saints. Some of these documents list holdings in pounds, others in dollars. To minimize confusion, I have converted the dollar figures to pounds, which was the Massachusetts currency at the time.

44. Hamilton Andrews Hill, "William Phillips and William Phillips, Father and Son, 1722–1837," *New England Historical and Genealogical Register* 39 (April 1885): 109–117; N. S. B. Gras, *The Massachusetts First National Bank of Boston, 1784–1934* (Cambridge, MA, 1937), 17–18.

45. Benjamin Lincoln to George Washington, December 4, 1786 to March 4, 1787, in W. W. Abbot et al., *The Papers of George Washington: Confederation Series*, 6 vols. (Charlottesville, VA, 1995), 4:422.

46. Oliver Dickinson's account book, 1783–1793, Jones Library, Special Collections, Amherst.

47. Hall, *Politics without Parties*, 111.

48. Massachusetts Tax Evaluation List, 1785, MA. The town assessors of every Massachusetts town filled out one of these documents. So the information demanded by the state, as well as a town's response to it, can also be found in many town archives.

49. Bates, "Finances of Massachusetts," 96, 99; Harold Hitchings Burbank, "The General Property Tax in Massachusetts, 1775 to 1792" (Ph.D. diss., Harvard University, 1915), 96–98; Franklin Russell Mullaly, "The Massachusetts Insurrection of 1786–1787" (M.A. thesis, Smith College, 1947), 10–11; Charles J. Bullock, *Historical Sketch of the Finances and Financial Policy of Massachusetts from 1780 to 1905* (New York, 1907), 5f.

50. F. E. Oliver, ed., *The Diary of William Pynchon of Salem* (Boston, 1890), 54; Herbert S. Allan, *John Hancock: Patriot in Purple* (New York, 1948), 310; William M. Fowler, Jr., *The Baron of Beacon Hill* (Boston, 1980), 213–216, 259; Hall, *Politics without Parties*, 133–136.

51. For Governor Bowdoin, a controversial figure, I have drawn together material from the following sources: Gordon E. Kershaw, *James Bowdoin II: Patriot and Man of the Enlightenment* (New York, 1991), chap. 3 and passim; Robert L. Volz, *Governor Bowdoin and His Family* (Brunswick, ME, 1969); Hall, *Politics without Parties*, 118–120; Forrest McDonald, *We the People* (Chicago, 1958), 200; Gras, *First National Bank of Boston*, 530; *Boston Directory*, 1787; Tingba Apidta, *The Hidden History of Massachusetts: A Guide for Black Folks* (Roxbury, MA, 1995), 22–23;

Gordon E. Kershaw, *The Kennebec Proprietors* (Somerworth, NH, 1975); Taylor, *Liberty Men and Great Proprietors*, chaps. 1–3.

52. Rufus King to John Adams, October 3, 1786, in Charles R. King, ed., *The Life and Correspondence of Rufus King*, 6 vols. (New York, 1804), 1:190; John Adams to Thomas Jefferson, November 30, 1786, in Lester J. Cappon, ed., *The Adams-Jefferson Letters*, 2 vols. (Chapel Hill, 1959), 1:156.

53. Computed from data on rebel families and Amherst Town List, August 1786, Jones Library, Special Collections, Amherst.

54. On military service, a handy guide is "Hampshire County Soldiers and Sailors in the War of the Revolution," Forbes Library (1939), an index to *Massachusetts Soldiers and Sailors of the Revolutionary War*, 17 vols. (Boston, 1896–1908). I have repeatedly relied on both sources. For officers and men of the Massachusetts Line, some additional information can be gleaned from Francis B. Heitman, *Historical Register of Officers of the Continental Army* (Washington, DC, 1914), and Fred Anderson Berg, *Encyclopedia of Continental Army Units* (Harrisburg, PA, 1972).

55. For information on the Grays and other Pelhamites, I have relied primarily on Parmenter, *History of Pelham;* Daniel W. Shelton, "'Elementary Feelings': Pelham, Massachusetts, in Rebellion" (honors thesis, Amherst College, 1891); the New England Genealogical Society's *Vital Records of Pelham to 1850*; Gregory H. Nobles, "Shays's Neighbors: The Context of Rebellion in Pelham, Massachusetts," in Gross, *In Debt to Shays*, 185–203; and the genealogical collection assembled by Robert Lord Keyes of the Pelham Historical Society. Subsequent to my using Keyes's collection, he published "Who Were the Pelham Shaysites?" *Historical Journal of Massachusetts* (Winter 2000): 23–55. His emphasis differs from mine. So do some of his findings. The main difference is that I began with a longer list of rebels, relying on jail records and indictments as well as the published list of oath takers in Parmenter's town history.

56. For information on the Days, Leonards, Elys, and other West Springfield families, I have relied on the New England Genealogical Society's *Vital Records of West Springfield to 1850* as well as on a wide assortment of town histories and town records. On the Leonard family, I obtained much from John Adams Vinton, *The Giles Memorial* (Boston, 1864), which traces not only the male line but also the female line. My most helpful source, however, was the town historian of West Springfield, Bernie Lally, who had collected a wealth of information which he was happy to share.

57. For Colrain, I have relied primarily on the New England Genealogical Society's *Vital Records of Colrain to 1850* and Patrie's *History of Colrain*. In a few cases, I have also acquired information from gravestones in Colrain.

58. Of the many fine studies of the Scotch-Irish and their cultural outlook, I have relied mainly on James G. Leyburn, *The Scotch-Irish: A Social History* (Chapel Hill, 1962); David Hackett Fisher, *Albion's Seed: Four British Folkways in America* (New York, 1989), 605ff; and Carlton Jackson, *A Social History of the Scotch Irish* (New York, 1993), chap. 6.

59. John L. Brooke, "A Deacon's Orthodoxy: Religion, Class, and the Moral Economy of Shays's Rebellion," in Gross, *In Debt to Shays*, 207; John L. Brooke, *The Heart of the Commonwealth: Society and Political Culture in Worcester County, Massachusetts, 1713–1861* (New York, 1989), 214–221; Stephen A. Marini, "The Religious World of Daniel Shays," in Gross, *In Debt to Shays*, 249–277; Harold

Field Worthley, *An Inventory of the Records of the Particular (Congregational) Churches of Massachusetts Gathered 1620–1805* (Cambridge, MA, 1970), passim.

60. Mattoon to Thomas Cutler, May 6, 1787, MA 189:300–301. In this letter, Mattoon essentially argued that Henry McCulloch, the man facing the gallows, was just a dumb youth who had been misled by the leaders of Pelham. In fact, McCulloch was thirty-six years old and Mattoon's senior by four years. For further details about McCulloch and his pardon, see Gregory H. Nobles, "The Politics of Patriarchy in Shays's Rebellion: The Case of Henry McCulloch," *Annual Proceedings* of the *Dublin Seminar for New England Folklife* (1985): 37–47.

9

THE return of economic prosperity in the 1790s softened the political divisions of the previous decade. Like most of New England, Hampshire County rallied around the Federalist candidate for president, John Adams, in 1796 and 1800. The power of the River Gods was gone forever. In their place were those whose economic ties were linked to the destiny of the new nation. Men like Caleb Strong, future governor of Massachusetts, invested heavily in internal improvements to facilitate trade and communication. They built the turnpikes and canal locks on the Connecticut River that connected Northampton to a wider world.

Merchants and artisans from outside the region were drawn by Northampton's growth as a commercial center. Silversmith Nathan Storrs and clockmaker Isaac Gere were joined by a host of furniture- and cabinetmakers such as Ansel Goodrich and David Judd. Replacing local craft traditions, the tastes of New York, Philadelphia, and Boston now set the standard. Printers like Jonathan Wright made Northampton a publishing center. The American Musical Miscellany, *published in Northampton in 1798, was the first anthology of nonsacred American popular music, reflecting the growing secular tastes of American audiences. Northampton and the surrounding region were becoming more and more part of the regional culture of the Northeast.*

By 1800, Northampton, like the rest of the young Republic, was no longer isolated but was increasingly linked to a growing network of commerce and communication. This new national economy profoundly altered local relationships. In pre-Revolutionary Northampton, a more localized economy was based on trade and barter where debt and credit were face-to-face transactions. As communication and transportation opened distant markets, credit came to be based less on reputation and more upon assets.

Enterprising shop owners and merchants, who had accumulated capital in trade, now began to invest in local manufactures. In 1788, Levi Shepherd, an apothecary, opened a canvas and rope factory. In 1809, his sons established the Shepherd Woolen Manufacturing Company. With a capitalization of $100,000 and 118 employees, it was one of the earliest and largest industrial concerns in New England. America's Industrial Revolution began, in fact, long before Boston investors established textile mills in Lowell. Local merchants like the Shepherds, concerned with diversifying their business activities, provided capital to set up full-fledged factories, financing expansion and improvement with their own profits.

In his prize-winning study of this transition period in western Massachusetts, Christopher Clark chronicles the process whereby independent rural households, once self-sufficient centers of economic production in the eighteenth century, slowly became enmeshed in an increasingly cash-based economy.

The Roots of Rural Capitalism*

CHRISTOPHER CLARK

Distant Trade and Local Exchange

SINCE the beginnings of white settlement, trade had been conducted into and out of the Northampton region, overland to Boston or by river to Hartford and the Connecticut coast. Economic historians have estimated that in parts of the rural Northeast by 1800, households spent as much as 25 percent of their disposable incomes on goods obtained outside their localities; households in the Connecticut Valley may have spent as much. But these purchases were either of necessities unobtainable locally, or of "luxuries" and "decencies" such as liquor, tea, sugar, and dry goods, which formed a substantial proportion of imports. Even in a prosperous rural region, households satisfied three-quarters of their demand, including most of their basic needs, by their own production or by local exchange. Some of these needs were foodstuffs that would largely have been unobtainable from stores or traders and available only from other households. Because the Connecticut Valley lacked a staple export crop in the late eighteenth century, the sale of produce from the region to purchase imported goods took second place to the provision of basic needs at home. The economy was primarily a "subsistence-surplus" one; that is, most of the products exported beyond the valley were necessities extra to the requirements of local households or by-products of their production.[1]

Trade on the Connecticut River reflected this economic pattern. The accounts of a shipper who carried goods in the 1750s from Middletown, Hartford, and other Connecticut points to customers in Springfield, Northampton, Hatfield, and Deerfield show that upstream traffic was in goods unavailable locally, while return cargoes consisted of the kinds of goods also used by the households producing them. In 1754 he brought up grindstones, tools and implements, pots and pans, nails, glass, turpentine, codfish, sugar, molasses, rum, and large amounts of salt. He returned with peas, flaxseed, and wooden products such as laths and boards, none of which was produced solely for market sale. From year to year the pattern varied slightly. The volume of dry goods and of luxury items for the valley's elite increased in the 1760s and 1770s. Potash and pearl ashes, produced by farmers who burned felled lumber to make "black salts" and lye for processing and shipment, were an important export item until the 1790s. But these were by-products of settlement

---

* From Christopher Clark, *The Roots of Rural Capitalism: Western Massachusetts, 1780–1860* (Ithaca, 1990).

and land clearance; in time the potash trade would decline. Trade at the century's end was essentially little different. The accounts of a Williamsburg teamster show that during the 1790s he carried pork, beef, butter, leather, and tallow out of the region and returned from Boston or the downriver towns with dry goods, earthenware, rum, sugar, salt, glass, paper, and gin. In 1802 a Deerfield boatman carried barrel staves down to Hartford and brought back brandy, sugar, tea, and salt. The Hadley merchant William Porter sent and received similar shipments in 1810.[2]

The lack of a staple export and the subsistence-surplus character of the economy meant that the valley's traders had to work hard and use far-flung networks of connections to bring together consignments to pay for imported goods. The diffuse, diverse, and irregular pattern of local supplies kept the mercantile sector small and relatively centralized. The most prominent merchants were based in old towns like Northampton and Hadley, whose position on the river helped them control the flow of goods in and out. From there, they relied on contacts and partnerships scattered throughout the region. When the Northampton merchant Levi Shepard dissolved his partnership with Ebenezer Hunt in 1784, his share of the proceeds included promissory notes from 175 customers scattered between Ludlow, Massachusetts, and southern New Hampshire. Toward the end of the century some traders organized branch stores in partnership with settlers of newly expanding hill towns. But the number of traders was small. Northampton appears to have had no more than nine merchants at any one time before 1800, Hadley no more than four.[3] Their influence was spread thinly throughout the valley.

By contrast, local exchange among neighbors and kin was frequent, often involved essential goods, and was part of the cooperation and division of labor vital to the household economy. Relatively few families in the late eighteenth century owned all the necessary means of earning a livelihood. Reciprocal exchanges enabled them to borrow what they did not own. In Amherst in 1795, for instance, about seven out of ten landholders owned cows, but only four out of ten owned draft oxen for plowing or carting. Those who did not relied on hiring teams to get their work done, paying for this with food or other goods, or by providing labor in exchange. Local exchanges of work and goods supported the craft occupations of blacksmiths, shoemakers, house carpenters, weavers, and tailors, whose trades households could not or chose not to provide for themselves.[4]

Exchanging work also provided essential extra labor during haying or harvest, or for special tasks such as framing and raising buildings whose demands exceeded families' own supply of labor. As many account books show, members of poorer households worked more frequently for their wealthier neighbors than the other way around and often took their pay in food or other essential items. But only the largest farmers did not swap some work with their neighbors, and there was an essential assumption of reciprocity in the informal rituals and obligations that governed this exchange. It did not simply correct imbalances of resources, for example. Two Amherst farmers, Elisha Smith and James Hendrick, who both owned yokes of oxen, combined efforts in September 1788 to complete fall plowing, each putting in two days' work with his team on the other's farm.[5]

Kinship and neighborhood both created obligations to cooperate in exchanging work and goods. Not only did farm families—whether in old or in new towns—live comparatively close to one another, but they were frequently related as well. In 1798, Northampton's 400 taxpayers shared only 133 family names. The fact that 129 were placed on the (nonalphabetical) list next to another taxpayer of the same name suggests that neighbors were often kin as well. President Timothy Dwight of Yale praised the Connecticut Valley towns for their "general harmony and good neighborhood, . . . sober industry and frugality, . . . hospitality and charity," characteristics he attributed to their distance from commercial markets. Local exchange was part of a set of reciprocal practices deeply embedded in the cultural fabric of the countryside, whose significance was not just instrumental.[6]

Long-distance "trade" and local "exchange" were distinct from one another, served different purposes, and conformed to separate patterns. Although they often involved the same goods, the significance of these goods differed. Local products traded locally were often essentials. Sold to traders, they were surplus to requirements. Superficially, local and long-distance dealings often seemed to follow similar methods and practices. But, involving trade over differing geographical distance, they operated in different social contexts and so followed contrasting, sometimes conflicting, moral standards. Indeed, it is possible to talk of an "ethic" of local exchange quite distinct from that governing long-distance trade.[7] We can see the distinction if we compare the correspondence of a prominent trading firm of the 1770s and 1780s with the account books that recorded the transactions of farmers and others exchanging goods locally.

Shepard and Hunt's Northampton firm traded not only throughout western Massachusetts but with the port towns of the lower Connecticut River, with Boston, and even with London. Their business, like that of all long-distance merchants, rested on a paradox: they had to establish bonds of trust amounting to friendship with men whom they would not normally meet. They conducted business by letter, using the accounts, receipts, notes, and bills of exchange that were the machinery of trade. They relied on recommendations and connections to assess the men they were trading with and closely observed each other's conduct of business. To reduce the risks of trading over long distances with strangers, merchants expected transactions to be conducted according to certain standards, violation of which could result in loss of reputation and credit. Above all, they required regular payment for goods consigned, within the terms set by any extension of credit. If they could have got it, merchants would always have liked immediate payment in cash. In practice, they had to grant credit and accept payment in whatever goods or paper the state of trade made available. But they charged for these deviations. Prices offered for remittances in goods were bargained over, bills were often discounted, and late payments charged interest on the grounds that they represented an opportunity cost to the creditor. Jonathan Brown, of the London firm of Thomas Corbyn and Company, writing to Shepard and Hunt early in 1771, noted that he had not yet received a remittance for a previous consignment and would in future charge interest on balances for which cash was not received within twelve months of shipping. Six months later, Brown had still not received payment, despite several letters to Northampton warning that Corbyn's might have to withhold the next shipment of goods. Corbyn himself wrote in August that "we can't be easy to send your present order." The goods were sent, but by the next year Corbyn was advancing them only on six months' credit.[8]

Delays required explanations. Not only were Shepard and Hunt writing to London and elsewhere explaining the difficulties they faced collecting the means for repayment, but they also received excuses and pleas for understanding from their own contacts in the countryside. Two physicians in Williamstown described in 1774 how a smallpox outbreak was preventing them from sending a remittance for drugs supplied by the Northampton firm: "our Patients at Present in Inoculation are in No upwards of 20 and in a Very Scatter'd situation, and altho' upwards of 100 have safely Pass'd the Operation . . . we have not Collected more than about 30 dollers Cash." The merchants' response to this is not recorded. Three decades later a West Springfield firm asked to delay payment for goods shipped them by a Hartford merchant and got a sharp lecture in return: "such disappointments are of evil tendency in Society, but the reverse, viz, slow to promis, prompt to fulfill enables us not only to command our own [respect?] but our neighbours."[9]

Failure to repay would eventually lead to a lawsuit. The mechanisms of long-distance trade, the correspondence, circulating paper, systematic accounts, fixed-term credit, and interest charges were all calculated to permit pressure to be exerted for payment and, if necessary, to provide the sound evidence of the existence of a debt that would be essential to sustain a debt action in court. Long-distance trade had an insistent rhythm and strict expectations. Promptness and system were essential to commercial morality.

The rules of local exchange were different. Dealings were over short distances, often face-to-face, and frequently between relatives or neighbors. From 1796 onward the Westhampton farmer Solomon Bartlett kept regular accounts with sixteen other people. Seven of them were neighbors who lived

Levi Shepard (1744–1805). Winthrop Chandler (1747–1790). Oil on canvas, 29 in. x 26 in. *Historic Northampton.*

Levi Shepard was an enterprising Northampton merchant and manufacturer, representing the new elite that replaced the River Gods after the Revolution. His father, a successful merchant in Hartford, moved to Northampton in 1764, opening a shop there and one in Worcester. Levi, who served an apprenticeship to an apothecary in Hartford, also moved to Northampton and began trading there in 1765. By 1768, he had a thriving business that was patronized by customers from a wide region. After the Revolution, Shepard was the leading merchant in town. Several years later, he expanded his business interests by opening a rope and duck cloth manufacture. With his sons, he established one of the earliest woolen mills in New England. Merchant-entrepreneurs like Shepard sparked the Industrial Revolution that was to sweep New England a generation later.

within two miles of Bartlett's farm in the southern part of town. Another six were relatives—three brothers and two nephews, who were also neighbors, and his niece's husband, who lived in the adjacent town of Norwich. Only three of Bartlett's sixteen contacts are not identifiable as near neighbors or relatives. Like those of thousands of rural people his dealings centered on people he knew.[10]

Moreover, as the French traveler Brissot de Warville observed, these dealings rarely involved cash:

> Instead of money incessantly going backwards and forwards into the same hands, they supply their needs reciprocally in the countryside by direct exchanges. The tailor and the bootmaker go and do the work of their calling at the house of the farmer who requires it and who, most often, provides the raw material for it and pays for the work in goods. These sorts of exchanges cover many objects; they write down what they give and receive on both sides and at the end of the year they settle, with a very small amount of coin, a large variety of exchanges which would not be done in Europe other than with a considerable quantity of money.[11]

Cash payment connotes immediacy and a certain anonymity between dealers. Once a debt is paid off, obligation ceases. A debt paid off in cash implies abstraction—a social distance between buyer and seller—because the form of payment can be turned to any use. We shall see later that in the countryside of the late eighteenth and early nineteenth centuries cash did, indeed, have specific social uses and meanings distinct from other forms of payment. Non-cash payment and extended indebtedness entailed a different kind of relationship. Forms of payment had always to be negotiated, with due recognition of particular households' needs and abilities. Delays to payment resulted in perpetual, complex webs of credit and debt throughout the countryside that linked households to one another. Local exchange created networks of obligation alongside those already created by kinship or neighborhood. These obligations should not be sentimentalized. Frequently enough they gave rise to conflicts. But they were real, and they embodied the distinctive moral demands made by rural people on each other when they exchanged goods, labor, and other services.[12]

In practice the accounting process was less tidy and orderly than Brissot's description implied. Many farmers may not have kept written accounts at all. Those who did were often unsystematic or careless. A memorandum book presented as evidence in an 1806 court case contained "the items of said account filed, which were entered therein intermixed with various charges, notes, receipts and memorandums, related to . . . dealings with other persons, alike irregular, in whatever blank spaces [the owner] happened to find, without any regard to order of dates or pages." From the 1790s onward almanac writers urged farmers to keep clear accounts and settle them regularly, but many ignored this advice. As a newspaper editor scathingly remarked in 1830, "it matters not how much business a man does if he be not regular in keeping his accounts. Mechanics and farmers are proverbial for their neglect in this particular. Many keep no account book at all; a piece of chalk and a pine board constitute their only materials of record."[13]

Credits and debits accumulated over considerable periods. Settlements were infrequent and irregular. Almanacs repeatedly suggested that accounts be settled each winter when there was little work to do. But over three-fifths of the accounts kept by the Amherst farmer William Boltwood between 1800 and 1805 show no sign of having been finally closed, while repayment times on outstanding debts to him ranged from four months to thirteen and a half years.[14] Boltwood's accounts were kept in a well-ordered and systematic manner; the delays reflected not carelessness, but the distinctive rhythms and demands of local exchange.

Some local dealings were literally barters, direct swaps of work or goods considered to be of equivalent value. Their extent is hard to measure, because many probably went unrecorded. Book accounts occasionally contained adjustments for uneven trades, such as the charge of two shillings and sixpence set down by Solomon Bartlett against his neighbor Chester Strong "in swoping sise for ½ bu[shel] of be[a]ns." But most recorded transactions were running tallies of credits and debts incurred in a continuous process of bargaining and exchange. Goods, labor, or services were given out in the expectation that a return for them would be made in due course. Farmers provided food to poorer neighbors on the promise of future work in their fields. Men worked for others on the expectation of repayment in kind at a future date. Even the language of local exchange differed from that of long-distance trade. People did not speak of "buying" or "selling" things. They "took" or "gave" them.[15]

The spirit of "give and take" helps explain the complex tangle of unsettled debts that crisscrossed the countryside. Many accounts were closed only when administrators sorted out the estates of the dead, if then. People "gave" when they had the means to. After balancing accounts with a servant in 1790, Joseph Clarke of Northampton noted that "there is now due to her seven dollars which I am to pay her as soon as I conveniently can." In this instance, and in many others, the poorer woman had to wait upon the convenience of the richer man for her pay. But it worked both ways. Whereas in long-distance trade creditors assumed the right to press for repayment and sue when debts were not settled, the local exchange ethic emphasized restraint, caution, and consideration of debtors' means to pay.[16]

Securing repayment required tact and subtlety. The means existed, of course—they were the same as in long-distance trade—but they had to be used carefully. Interest was rarely charged on book accounts. Indeed, even to calculate it required drawing a balance, and that was often difficult enough to arrange. Robert B. Thomas's almanac reminded farmers that in order "to preserve a good understanding and continue in friendship with friends and neighbors," they should each December "call upon all those you have had any dealing with the preceding year, and make a complete settlement."[17] But pressing for settlement could cause offense by implying lack of trust, or could be seen as an attempt to take advantage.

Especially when resources were scarce, the ideal time to settle accounts was when they were close to balancing, so that little payment would have to change hands. But in the uneven tempo of rural life and work, these occasions did not occur regularly. Although some farmers, including William Boltwood, kept ledger accounts of both credits and debits—what was "given" to him and what he "gave" to others—the majority whose books have survived kept complete records only of debits—goods they had given or work they had done. An English description of rural accounting suggested that neighbors resented men who kept both credit and debit accounts because it enabled them to calculate balances and call for settlement when these were in their favor. Possibly many New England farmers also regarded keeping both sides of the ledger an affront to neighborhood and were content to see the whole picture only when they met with other men and their books to make a reckoning.[18]

"Reckonings" could involve bargaining over the goods and work to be counted and the values to be assigned them. Disagreement was quite possible. "Noah Thompson [was] here," wrote the Reverend Justus Forward of Belchertown in his diary in 1786; "we did agree to settle Accounts by his letting me have a calfskin on his Account which I had of Capt Watson last fall." But Thompson was still dissatisfied: "he did not chuse to sign my Book, pretended he had paid me a Dollar the forepart of August '83." The minister evidently felt that *he* was being taken advantage of. Even the agreement that he almost came to had not involved any repayment, merely an adjustment involving a transaction that had already occurred between Forward and a third man. Although this would have brought Forward's account with Thompson into alignment, both Forward and Thompson would have needed to square things with Watson as well. The debt was thus transferred, not expunged. Bargaining such as this enabled householders to eke out their resources to the utmost and helped create the complex tangle of rural debts and credits.[19]

Striking a balance often led only to the continuation of a debt. Even Robert B. Thomas, advocate of the regular settlement, saw that payment would not necessarily follow. "Pay them off," he advised, "if the balance be in their favour," and "if convenient." If the balance is "in yours and they find it not convenient to pay, put it to the new account and pass receipts."[20] Account books reveal that this often happened. Balances were simply carried forward into another period of "give" and "take." Thomas's advice assumed that "convenience" rested on having means available at that moment to pay off the outstanding balance. The frequency with which this was avoided, or efforts made to square accounts somehow, suggests that this view of "convenience" was widely accepted. Two comments from as late as 1830 throw light on common attitudes. An editor criticized those "too indolent to dun others" and the "false delicacy which prevents them," urging that "fear of giving offence by asking payment of honest dues, should never be indulged." But an almanac writer was more acerbic: "If you wish to make friends, trust and never demand your pay; if enemies, demand it."[21] At this point the contrast between the ethics of local exchange and long-distance trade was at its clearest.

"Putting a balance to the new account" usually meant that no interest would be charged on the debt. Neighbors rarely charged interest on small amounts. Where larger sums were involved, however, or if the creditor did not know or distrusted the debtor, he might demand security in the form of a note, sometimes with the endorsement of a third party. Usually payable on demand, in theory permitting peremptory calling-in, these notes were often used in the countryside to avoid specifying a particular date for payment. Merchants, preferring specified payment dates, sometimes accepted them reluctantly, as one put it, to "benefit . . . country People."[22] Interest was payable if it was specified, usually after at least one year had elapsed. It was also due on mortgages and other loans to acquire land, houses, or livestock, where wealthier men were usually granting credit to their poorer neighbors. The instruments of negotiable paper and of debt enforcement were therefore part of local exchange in circumstances of inequality, where the reciprocal assumptions of "give" and "take" did not apply. However, to go to law to seek repayment of these debts was still regarded as a violation of "neighborhood" well into the nineteenth century. In many towns lawsuits for debt were brought by one townsman against another only infrequently. Most debt actions were between strangers who lived at a distance from each other.[23]

Rural households' sense of "independence" therefore rested on circumstances that held them distinct from, but interdependent with, their neighbors and held their neighborhoods at arm's length from the pressures of the commercial world beyond their part of the valley. Cooperation and division of labor within households was based on the unequal assumptions and realities of patriarchal authority. The desire to secure livelihoods for the present was complicated by the need to make provisions for the future of parents and children. The aspiration for household "independence" relied on the necessity of exchanging goods and labor with neighbors and kin. The assumptions of reciprocity and equality in local exchange were, on the one hand, undermined by the realities of bargaining and negotiation between individuals who were not always equal, and, on the other, sustained by the restraints of "neighborhood." Both the household itself and the wider terrain of rural society were arenas of conflict and negotiation. No one knew this better than the ministers, merchants, and larger landowners who formed the valley's social and political elite, for whom the ideal of the patriarchal household remained the model for wider social authority. In the last quarter of the eighteenth century their assumptions of power were widely challenged by household producers for whom the model of the local exchange system, with its notions of reciprocity, had much appeal.

Households and Elites

Family labor and household production had evolved in seventeenth-century New England as assumptions brought by English settlers were adapted to conditions of widespread landownership and relative equality. Daniel Vickers has pointed out that, as in some other freehold farming regions, use of family labor was rural New England's response to the labor shortages faced by all early American colonies. Whereas the staple-crop regions of the South came to rely on slaves, and indentured servants filled many households' demands for labor in the middle colonies, most New England households relied on their own family members to work for them. Rural slavery was rare; taxes on "servants for life" were levied on only 4 taxpayers out of 132 in Hadley and 2 out of 134 in Amherst in 1771, for example. Servants were more common, but only wealthy families constantly employed them; Timothy Dwight noted that there were fewer servants in the New England interior than in commercial towns on the coast. Many were, as one woman put it, young men and women "lent" by their families to neighbors and relatives.[24] But the household system we have observed at the end of the eighteenth century was not simply "traditional." It had come about in the context of important changes in rural society, despite the fact that much of the original labor shortage came to an end.

The household system had dissolved other types of social organization in the countryside by the early 1700s. Springfield, for example, the first white settlement in the valley in Massachusetts, had been strongly controlled by its proprietors, the Pyncheons, during the seventeenth century; many inhabitants had been obliged to rent land or provide labor for them in order to make a living.[25] But after 1700 the Pyncheons' authority broke down; Springfield became like other valley towns, where property had from the start been more widely distributed and where wealthier families could exert less of the same influence over their independent neighbors. The defeat of Indian resistance to white settlement during the first half of the eighteenth century made possible an expansion into the hills surrounding the valley proper. Especially after 1720, migrants to the region joined the offspring of local families to carve out new farms and townships.

Beyond the bounds of the original town grants, migrants purchased land individually or in groups from proprietors and speculators who had held large acreages in the hope that settlement would expand. In the 1740s, for instance, a group of Scotch-Irish Presbyterians purchased what would become the town of Pelham, in the hills to the east of the valley. In the center of the valley, though, the outlying lands of older towns were divided off from them, to create new towns or districts often settled by children of the old towns' residents. Hadley's Third Division became a separate parish in 1739 and the district of Amherst in 1759. In 1771 Hatfield contributed its northern section to the formation of Whately, and its hilly northwestern extremities to the new district of Williamsburg. Northampton split four ways. Early settlement in the broad valley west of Mount Tom led to the incorporation of Southampton in 1753 and later the district of Easthampton in 1785, while movement into the hills west of the original town gave rise to Westhampton, set off in 1778. The availability of land at the edges of the valley ensured that labor remained scarce during the first half of the eighteenth century. Wages for farm labor doubled between the 1680s and about 1750. Farm families used their own labor as much as they could and bargained with their neighbors for what they could not provide themselves.[26]

But as towns were settled and population grew, the labor shortage began to end. Wage rates flattened out, remaining approximately even for the rest of the century. Between 1720 and the 1760s most of the newly available land was purchased and divided up. From 1763 to 1774 alone seventeen new towns were established in Hampshire County. Population growth, fed by high fertility rates, low mortality, and in-migration, was rapid. Between 1765 and 1790, population in what later became "new" Hampshire County rose by an average of 7.7 percent a year; from then to 1810 it continued to grow at an average rate of 1.5 percent. The area had 6,500 inhabitants in 1765. By 1810 there were 24,553. Population density trebled, and was especially high around the better farmland, in towns such as Amherst and in valleys and meadowlands in the hill towns. The conditions that had given rise to the household system had largely ceased to exist.[27]

Yet the system essentially survived. There was no return to the kinds of social and economic control exercised by the Pyncheons in seventeenth-century Springfield. Neither did the systematic use of wage labor supplant family-based labor in this period. The number of poor, transient people had increased by the 1760s, and there was more hiring and servanthood than there had been before.[28] But these increases took place largely within the framework of the household system and according to its terms. They did not threaten the independence of most rural households. Why was this so?

Foremost among the reasons was the absence of a rural elite powerful enough to create and control a dependent labor system. The wealthy families

Sack-back Armchair. Ansel Goodrich (c. 1773–1803). Northampton. 1795–1803. Maple, basswood, and hickory. H: 37 ¾ in.; W: 24 ⅞ in.; D: 14 ½ in. *Historic Northampton.*

The Tontine building in Northampton was daily proof of an urban concentration of craftsmen after the doors were opened to the public in 1786. The wooden frame building at the corner of Bridge and Hawley Streets was three stories high and included eight shops, which craftsmen could buy or lease. The third floor was an assembly hall. The building separated craft activity from the home sites of the men who labored there and professionalized the working patterns of specialized tradesmen independently from the agricultural year. Among the craftsmen who competed for the consumers' dollars with the furniture-makers and others in the Tontine building was the Windsor chair specialist Ansel Goodrich, who worked on nearby King Street. The sack-back chair here is typical of Goodrich's work, even though the designs of the chairs vary. The seats are exceptionally thin with sharp edges. The baluster and cylinder shape of the turned legs are intersected by a compressed unit composed of a spool above a flattened ball. Although the origins of Ansel Goodrich are unclear, his training equipped him to compete effectively in the urban economy of this market town "a few rods north of the court house, Northampton."

that did live in the valley faced problems of their own after the 1750s. Their situation was such that they could negotiate to secure various kinds of peripheral influence over middling and poorer households in some towns, but not so strong that they could alter these households' essentially independent status by controlling their labor.

Rapid population growth not only enhanced Hampshire County's overall political significance in Massachusetts but brought a number of families in the older towns to social preeminence. At the apex of these families was the small group, including Stoddards, Williamses, Worthingtons, and Hawleys, who came to be referred to as the "River Gods." As well as having significant landholdings and positions in trade or as lenders of credit, these families had by the middle of the century succeeded in dominating county institutions—the courts, the militia, and the ministerial association at the core of ecclesiastical politics. Most judges, senior officers, and pastors were members of the leading families or had met their approval. Less wealthy families with local influence, such as the Strongs and Lymans of Northampton and the Porters of Hadley, had business or kinship ties with them. Israel Williams of Hatfield maintained such influence in the 1750s and 1760s, including connections with the colonial government in Boston, that he became known as the "monarch of Hampshire." Williams and the others distinguished themselves from the majority of their neighbors by assuming the characteristics of a rural gentry. Their houses were larger, and sometimes more elaborately and finely finished. They purchased imported wines and household goods and wore distinctive styles of dress. They were also more substantial employers of labor. They hired craftsmen to make, furnish, and decorate their houses; retained house and field servants, including some slaves; and hired extra hands at busy times of year. Charles Phelps, who married into the Porter family in 1770 and, with 600 acres, became Hadley's largest landowner, "kept," according to his grandson, "quite a retinue of laborers and at times . . . made considerable levies on the working force" of the village. After the Revolution he employed a former soldier who was reputed to be the only gardener in the valley.[29]

But these families never came close to matching the power and position, say, of the Virginia gentry in the same period. Indeed their weakness became increasingly evident after mid-century, and explains why their modes of living and organizing work did not become more common as labor supply increased. Large landowners were weakened economically by the decline of the one local crop—wheat—which has historically been a staple export and which had formed the basis of the Pyncheons' earlier prominence in Springfield. Just when world demand for wheat was increasing, stimulating increased production in the middle colonies and the upper South, New England's wheat crops were stricken by soil exhaustion and disease. "Rust," "blast," and the so-called Hessian fly discouraged wheat production, and it declined rapidly, especially in older towns. Even in newer areas such as Amherst, where fresher soil encouraged one farmer in ten to raise wheat at the end of the century, it was grown only in small quantities. By 1801, wheat accounted for only 3.4 percent of Hampshire County's grain output, and almanacs were suggesting that it be sowed along with rye "to have it free from smut." The lack of a marketable staple crop made elite control of land and labor difficult, indeed pointless, even though the labor now potentially existed to be hired. The effect was to restrain the elite's accumulation of wealth. Some of the large houses built in the middle of the century were never finished to

Sideboard. Possibly David Judd (d. 1828). Probably Northampton, c. 1810. Mahogany, pine, and birch. H: 41 ⅛ in.; W: 73 in.; D: 26 ⅞ in. *Historic Northampton.*

In spite of its position as the commercial, political, and geographic center of Hampshire County, few examples of high-style cabinetwork of Northampton origin have been identified. This is surprising, because Northampton was a major center of professional cabinetmaking where tradesmen and hardware merchants flourished by developing extensive local and regional markets. By 1810, there were half a dozen professional cabinetmakers working in Northampton, not including numerous looking-glass makers, chair-makers, and unspecialized carpenters and joiners who also made furniture there. Among the most active of them was David Judd, who probably operated Northampton's largest cabinetmaking shop. Between 1799 and 1820, he advertised more frequently than his competitors.

This sideboard was made for or shortly after the marriage of Ezra Clark (1788–1870) and Laura Hunt (1789–1862) of Northampton in 1809. They were the son and daughter of Lieutenant Jonas Clark and George Hunt, two influential Northampton residents who are notable for having served in the military regiment that suppressed Shays's Rebellion in 1787. The sideboard was one of the most expensive and complex forms of the period, and this example, with its sash-cornered top and delicately inlaid and veneered surfaces, epitomizes the neoclassical taste which such sideboards convey so vigorously.

the intended standard. A few were merely imposing facades, masking commonplace household interiors.[30]

The elite's political prominence turned out to be something of a facade too. Counties, the level of government that the elite controlled, were not as powerful or important in New England as they had become farther south. Relatively autonomous towns counterweighed the influence of county officers. Elite influence was greatest in old towns and in those, such as Westhampton, which had been settled by the descendants of old valley families, but inevitably its sway was reduced as settlement spread and new towns were created on the edges of the valley. In any case, it faced popular opposition. Numerous disputes during the middle of the century, especially over religion and the splitting off of new towns and parishes, revealed the fragility of the gentry's position in a rapidly expanding region.[31]

In 1774 this opposition surfaced decisively in resistance to British rule. Whereas the Stamp Act crisis and other disputes in the 1760s had produced only muted protest from the valley, this time the organizing work of the Boston Committee of Correspondence after 1772 and widespread outrage at the Coercive Acts' assaults on local Massachusetts institutions ensured that things would be different. Determined, as the people of Williamsburg expressed it, "to Resist Great briton in their unconstitutional measures," committees visited the prominent men appointed as mandamus councillors or judges under the Massachusetts Government Act, and urged them to resign their royal commissions. Armed crowds confronted those suspected of refusing, surrounded courthouses, and extracted resignations. Clergymen sympathetic to the Crown were also subjected to "regulation." Within a few months in 1774 and 1775, many members of the valley elite found their power broken. Israel Williams and his son, confined to a smokehouse in Hadley one night by a crowd, returned home, left office for good, and remained suspected of pro-British activities. Others, like the Stoddards of Northampton, also left public life for a period. Tories faced being disarmed and removed from office. Men like the Southampton merchant Jonathan Judd, Jr. expressed concern about "mob rule" in private but were careful not to question the authority of revolutionary committees too openly. His colleague Samuel Colton of Longmeadow, accused of profiteering, had goods seized from his store by a town committee. Refusing the payment he was offered for them at the legal price, he ended his life in a bitter and fruitless quest for compensation. Even Joseph Hawley of Northampton, the most prominent River God to support the patriot cause, withdrew from politics into insanity during the Revolution.[32]

The decline of wheat and the absence of a staple export crop encouraged many of the wealthier men in the valley to enter trade or the land market, rather than to attempt to hire labor directly for production. The political reverses the elite suffered in the Revolution led them to negotiate for influence over their neighbors rather than assume it, and no new leaders attained the county-wide prominence that the River Gods had held. Economically and politically, therefore, conditions favored the preeminence of the household system. There was no power base within Hampshire County with the means or the wish to challenge it.

Shays's Rebellion

When crisis arose in the 1780s, it centered not on rural households' control of labor, which remained untouched, but on their participation in exchange and the terms on which farmers handled their connections with long-distance trade. Shays's Rebellion, rural Massachusetts' most serious political crisis, touched on a complex series of issues whose implications continue to be explored by historians.[33] Important among these issues, and the two most pertinent to this discussion, were a clash between the ethics of local exchange and long-distance trade, and the ability of the elite in some valley towns to establish their claim to political authority on certain terms.

Shays's Rebellion was the ultimate result of mounting rural indebtedness and pressure to pay it off, which brought the relaxed, informal practices of local exchange and the insistence of long-distance trade into sharp conflict. Debts of three kinds combined to create a formidable debt crisis throughout much of the Massachusetts interior by the mid-1780s. Many households had suffered material or financial losses during the Revolutionary War and sought to recover their depleted resources. The state government, meanwhile, strongly influenced by coastal mercantile interests in the General Court, tried to reduce its own public debt by raising taxes, doing so by laying particular emphasis on poll taxes, which fell disproportionately on rural households and their labor. In addition, peace with Britain in 1783 unleashed both a flood of new imported goods, payment for which became pressing in 1784 and 1785, and the revival of lawsuits by British creditors for debts incurred before the war. The combination of depleted resources, tax demands, and new debts placed heavy burdens on country people. They, in turn, found their attempts to negotiate repayment of debts hampered by the General Court's refusal to grant debtor relief and its insistence on the use of specie or other limited items of tender for the repayment of public debts. The trade depression of 1784–1785 also reflected the difficulty of procuring goods from the interior for settlement of trade debts.[34]

The existence of these burdens, added to the already complex patterns of local indebtedness which, as we saw, were a normal part of rural life, prompted widespread attempts by creditors to secure repayment. In Hampshire County alone, just under 3,000 debt suits were brought before the court of common pleas between August 1784 and August 1786. Household goods, land, and other property put up for sale at sheriffs' auctions were often knocked down at ruinous prices to satisfy executions for debt. The jails began to fill with able-bodied men who had no property to be attached. Petitions to the General Court for relief, such as that drawn up by a convention at Paxton in Worcester County in September 1786, emphasized that rural resources were being overwhelmed by the speed with which repayment of debts was sought:

> The produce of the present year and the remainder of our cattle even were we to sell the whole, are totally inadequate to the present demands for money—such has been our situation for a long time past—an amazing flood of law suits have taken place—many industrious members of [the] community have been confined in gaol—and many more are liable to the same calamity—in a word, without relief we have nothing before us but distress and ruin.[35]

Rural people who normally frowned upon insistent dunning of debtors, and who believed that when pressure was exerted it should take regard of debtors' means, were overwhelmed by an avalanche of lawsuits demanding repayment at an impossible rate.

Pressure to settle debts came from three directions. Importers and other coastal creditors with remittances to pay overseas pressed for payment from their own inland customers. Where these inland traders had good connections, payment was often forthcoming, but Boston and Connecticut merchants complained of the great difficulty they faced collecting debts during what one called "the Troubles in Hampshire."[36] Local traders sought, in turn, to collect remittances from their own debtors. Finally, the general pressure of debt, including demands from traders and other local creditors, caused people who had not necessarily been involved in trade to seek repayments either to cover the demands being made on them or to secure themselves in the general collapse of credit. "I need the Ballance of your Note," wrote Abraham Burbank of West Springfield to Captain Lemuel Pomeroy of Northampton in April 1785: "I wish you may be disposed to pay it without a Suit." No single cause could therefore be ascribed for the crisis. The pattern of debt suits did not reveal a single line of pressure from coast to interior, for example. As the historian George R. Minot wrote in his account of Shays's Rebellion in 1788, crisis had been precipitated by "a relaxation of manners, and a free use of foreign luxuries; a decay of trade and manufactures, with a prevailing scarcity of money; and, above all, individuals involved in debt to each other." The pressures of debt were so widespread, a local newspaper had commented during the crisis, that "the most prudent people were deeply embarrassed."[37]

These circumstances led individuals to collect debts owed them by people relatively nearby, including their own neighbors. Of fifty-three debt actions brought by or against residents of Pelham between 1783 and 1786, over a quarter involved plaintiffs and defendants who both lived in the town; in

1784 the figure reached 36 percent. Violation of the usual standards of neighborhood dealing caused much of the resentment that led to Shays's Rebellion. The sense of disgust created is illustrated by evidence that among the Pelham men who joined the insurrection were former plaintiffs, as well as defendants, in these suits. Legislation of 1786 compelling courts to proceed with suits and to execute judgments further inflamed opinion against laws that systematically conflicted with rural economic morality.[38]

Rural outrage had accumulated over several years. Sporadic riots in early 1782 to break up sheriffs' sales of the property of poor families coalesced with Samuel Ely's armed march to close the Northampton courts in April that year. By 1783 demands for modifying the debt process were being voiced more widely. A county convention held in Hadley called for court fees to be reduced and for the upper value of cases that could be heard in local justices' courts to be raised from forty shillings to twenty pounds. When this plea failed, some petitioners sought the division of the county itself, so that the courts would be more localized.[39] By 1785 and 1786 condemnations of the debt process were numerous, and many towns based petitions for relief on principles central to the local exchange ethic: that debts would be paid as means were available and that legal action circumvented the normal processes of negotiation and accommodation that should occur between creditor and debtor.

Many of these pleas made it clear that it was not the debts themselves that were seen as unjust, but the peremptory demands for their repayment. "We are sencable . . . that a great debt is justly brought upon us by the war," declared the town of Greenwich in January 1786, "and are as willing to pay our shares towards itt as we are to injoy our shars in independancy and constatutional priviledges in the Commonwealth." If only "prudant mesuers were taken and a moderate quantety of medium to circulate so that our property might sel for the real value," the petition concluded, "we mite in proper time pay said debt." Armed men gathered and marched to close courthouses, not to avoid paying debts in the long run, but to suspend a collection process that seemed unjustly swift and indiscriminate. As conflict between rebels and state militia lay immediately in prospect in January 1787, John Billings, chairman of a county convention held at Hatfield, called for restraint. "Our matters may all be compromised," he argued, urging "that we may be in a way to convince each other of our error, and cultivate that unity which is necessary in a community."[40] His language—"compromise," "unity," "community"—was that of local assumptions about how to settle debts.

The affront to rural economic morality did not send all the men sued for debt to take up arms. In Pelham, although some plaintiffs and defendants in debt cases joined the insurrection, they were more likely to have supported petitions for relief. Young, poor, or transient men for whom the crisis had spelled poor employment and dismal future prospects made up more of the rebels' armed support from the town.[41] Action was taken by such people who lived in the towns most pressed by the crisis. As John Brooke has found, these were often places where elite authority was weak. Many insurrectionists, for example, were Congregationalists from towns or parishes without settled ministers.[42] Conversely, where the elite was strongest, support for the insurrection was weak. Daniel Shays exaggerated when he claimed that the rebellion was supported by all Hampshire, except for fifty or so men in Northampton and Hadley.[43] But he correctly identified the centers of support for the government. Had he literally been correct, he and his fellow rebels might have won their argument. But the valley elite, centered in those two towns, had resources of their own to call on.

Not only were Northampton, Hadley, and Hatfield prosperous compared with the hill towns that supported the rebellion, but they had strong ties with the towns around them, especially with families descended from former residents who had settled in Westhampton, Williamsburg, Amherst, and elsewhere. Prosperity and kinship provided important channels of influence for the river towns' leading families. Northampton merchants and landowners helped found the weekly *Hampshire Gazette* in September 1786 as an organ of support for the government. Ministers with whom they were connected, such as Joseph Lyman of Hatfield and Enoch Hale of Westhampton, preached against the rebels.

Above all, it was easier in towns where wealthy men lived or had connections for the debt burden to be eased by informal means. Court cases were still brought, but neighborly assistance or indulgence was more likely to be forthcoming than in poorer towns. Elite patronage also played a role. Probate records of the unpaid debts of men who died in the 1780s suggest that obligations to prominent supporters of the government were quite common. Twenty years later, John Miller, a small farmer in Northampton, related how after being "reduced to misfortune" and owing more than he was worth, he had applied to Caleb Strong for assistance and been given it on several occasions. Though Miller owed Strong "a considerable sum, and more than I owed every body else, he never asked me for the money, but told me to pay him as fast as I could conveniently, and no faster."[44] But such assistance was overwhelmingly confined to the oldest valley towns and those adjacent to them. Of twenty-one such debts that can be traced in the probate records, only two were owed by men in the hill towns. Obligations of kinship and neighborhood helped inflame passions against the government in outlying towns; similar obligations helped maintain support for government where the elite had connections or where means of relief were available. In Amherst, for example, support for the rebellion was stronger in the town's east parish than in the older west parish, where descendants of older county families and the county sheriff, Ebenezer Mattoon, lived. In Westhampton, opponents of the Shaysites included not only the Reverend Hale but many of the town's farmers, who had close kinship ties with old Northampton families.[45]

Yet government's defeat of the Shays rebels did little to alter the real balance of rural economic power. This still rested firmly with household producers and with the local exchange ethic they subscribed to. Merchants trying to collect rural debts during and after the insurrection found attitudes unchanged. The Granby physician Daniel Coit ordered a new supply of drugs from Levi Shepard in Northampton early in January 1787, while making it clear that he could not yet pay for the last consignment. "Well may you think I mean to take advantage of the *Times*," he wrote, but "Disappointments are the sertain Concomitents of human nature therefore he who expects to pass the sceans of life without them, will shurely meet with the greatest." If Shepard had not already grasped what was coming, Coit quickly reached the point: "I cannot possibly get the grain for you at present which I thought I was as sertain of as tho' I had it by me." He offered some fox and sable skins instead, which he thought he would be able to obtain if Shepard offered a good price.[46] In May 1787, when the Boston merchant Jonathan Amory sought to collect debts in Hampshire and Worcester Counties, his agent reported a familiar litany of responses. One man "would do nothing concerning the debt"; another "refused to give any further security . . . he says that by the Fall he can pay you if you incline . . . in neat stock." A woman "cant pay you at present she will send you something in one or two months." One man explained that, although "it would give him pleasure to discharge the debt," he would have to treat Amory "as the Laws enable others to treat him."[47] Merchants must have been frustrated by the sense of self-righteousness these letters conveyed, but they would have been wrong to regard it as humbug. From the local perspective, refusal to pay a debt could be justified if means were unavailable or if other obligations had to be met. These people were not avoiding payment but proposing ways to make it in the future.

Although the military defeat of the rebels led to the reopening of county courts and the resumption of the debt process, widespread sympathy was evident for the Shaysites and the economic morality they had defended. The spring elections of 1787, Minot wrote, "seemed to indicate a revolution in the publick mind." Having proposed amnesty for the rebels, John Hancock defeated the incumbent governor James Bowdoin by a three-to-one margin. Three-quarters of the representatives and two-thirds of the senators in the General Court were replaced. The new representative from the town of Chesterfield was instructed "that the whole weight of your influence may be for the encouragement of the labouring part of the community," and, specifically, that he vote to reduce taxes on polls and estates and increase those on luxuries.[48] The General Court did reduce taxes. It also passed exemption laws, permitting delays to debt suits, and reduced the scale of court fees. Jonathan Judd remained anxious during the summer of 1787 that military success would turn to political defeat. Writing to his brother about selling cattle, he noted, "I am much at a loss what to do but think it better to wait . . . until I know whether the General Court are so infatuated as to make Paper Money."[49]

The legislature did not make paper money. Demand for paper ebbed as the crisis eased and debtors found other ways of settling or compromising with creditors. But the issue of the timing and pressure of calls to settle debts did not go away. In the longer term, according to the historian Peter J. Coleman, Massachusetts governments learned lessons from Shays's Rebellion and began to build into the law some of the lenience that petitioners had sought and that was embedded in the ethics of local exchange. A 1794 statute exempted certain household goods and other property from attachment and permitted the taking of a poor debtor's oath to obtain discharge from obligations. Legal changes well into the nineteenth century continued this move toward leniency.[50]

Tensions between local exchange and long-distance trade remained after the rebellion as before. Traders often had to take what households were prepared to grant them, on terms dictated by local needs and concerns. For several decades to come, the ethics of local, rather than long-distance exchange, would dominate rural economic life. And although they were never again so serious, the kinds of conflicts over debt that had been behind Shays's Rebellion remained endemic.

A Marginal Elite

The defeat of Shays helped restore the political morale of the valley elite. Order and deference had been restored. The Reverend Joseph Lyman of Hatfield remarked in an election sermon in 1787 that "communities constitute certain of their brethren to rule over them: and, thus constituted, they are the *ordinance* of the Supreme Ruler."[51] The dangers of Shays's Rebellion and its example of disorder were frequently reiterated by the builders of western Massachusetts federalism, as they obtained formidable political support in Northampton and environs during the 1790s, using the *Hampshire Gazette* as a mouthpiece. By 1800, with Caleb Strong's election as governor, they had created the semblance of a unified, deferential politics. In several towns between 1800 and 1803, Strong consistently received 75 percent or more of the votes cast in elections, and support for him remained high after that.[52] Consistency and deference often marked town politics as well. Amherst selectmen chosen between 1800 and 1810 served an average of 3.5 years. Hatfield selectmen averaged 4.5 years, and all were from among the top 40 percent of the town's taxpayers.[53] Serious religious divisions were rare. Orthodox Congregationalism was stable and dominant. Most towns had only one organized church. Ministers served long careers, in several cases up to fifty years or more, in the same town.[54] Although tensions lay beneath the surface, political and religious leaders could claim some of the authority once associated with the River Gods. Merchants such as Jonathan Judd in Southampton and his brother Sylvester Judd, Sr., in Westhampton, with close ties to church and bench, retained preeminence in local affairs, including some power over appointments. "Tell Ensn. King," wrote Jonathan to Sylvester, after they had organized a shipment of military supplies, "by his loading the Teams he will be fit for a Deacon by and by." When another man sought appointment as justice of the peace in Westhampton, nineteen neighbors supported Sylvester Judd, Sr.'s petition opposing it.[55]

Deference relied partly on the use of patriarchal rhetoric. Town leaders and ministers claimed the authority that fathers claimed in their own households. Like those of fathers, who were having increasing difficulty maintaining their control of families, these claims were sometimes resisted, but the use of familial metaphor to bolster political authority seems to have succeeded in the valley, at least for a time. Federalist rhetoric emphasized respect for age. When young men gathered to vote for the first time in Northampton in 1811, reported the *Hampshire Gazette*, they were led to the polls by one of the town's oldest citizens and all cast their votes for the Federalist candidate. Patronage, the ability of men with means to provide the kind of indulgence and flexibility that the local exchange ethic stressed, reinforced this order. The Northampton farmer John Miller explained in 1806 what the assistance of Caleb Strong had meant for him. Without it, he declared, "I should probably now have been poor and destitute." He continued: "I am lame and have seldom gone to town for five or six years, except on the first Monday of April, when I have attended, every year, to give my vote for Mr. Strong as Governor. Though I don't pretend to meddle in politics; yet as long as I can ride five miles, and he is a candidate, I will attend to vote for him. I don't know as he desires to be chosen, but I wish to shew that there is one man who is not ungrateful." The historian James M. Banner located rural support for federalism among farmers concerned to maintain a distance from the market. But these men were also drawn to a vision of patriarchal order that conformed with their hopes for their own households and their position in local exchange.[56]

While they sought to construct political order in the context of a powerful household system, members of the valley elite knew that their economic power was relatively slight. They could not directly control land or labor for production. There were limits to the amount of land that could effectively be worked as one unit and no staple crop that could be raised for export on the large farms that did exist. The absence of a staple, and the diffusion, irregularity, and variety of produce available for shipment out of the region made trade uneven and perplexing. Consequently, men with wealth to invest were impelled to support risky schemes, seemingly marginal to the economy's operation. Family labor and household production pushed capital to the edge of the rural economy.

Several Northampton men, with associates in other towns, turned in the 1780s and 1790s to speculating in "western" land and sponsoring internal improvements. They included members of old elite families, like the Stoddards; substantial local merchants, like Levi Shepard and Ebenezer Hunt; and smaller traders, like Benjamin Tappan. Through both types of venture they sought to profit indirectly from a rural economic structure direct control of which was closed to them. Buying land in regions beyond the margins of settlement, they hoped to profit from rising prices, as land-pressed New England farmers or their children migrated north or west. In the 1790s they were particularly interested in western New York State and the Connecticut Reserve lands in Ohio, but valley speculators had dealings elsewhere too. Closer to home, they hoped that by building river improvements to circumvent obstacles to navigation on the Connecticut and by establishing bridges and turnpike roads, they could stimulate trade and then charge carriers for the use of their facilities. River improvements in particular would benefit from increasing traffic from the upper Connecticut Valley as settlement proceeded in New Hampshire and Vermont. Receipts from land sales and tolls from road, bridge, and canal traffic were the lowest common denominators for seekers of profit from an economy that gave little scope for other kinds of investment.

A close-knit group of local merchants and lawyers dominated most public improvement schemes chartered in the Northampton region between 1791 and 1806. Eleven Northampton men led the founding of nine canal, bridge, turnpike, banking, and insurance companies. Several of them, including Levi Shepard and Ebenezer Hunt, were involved in four or more projects each, using their connections to draw in outside capital, including some from Europe. Most of these schemes shared common local sponsors with others. The principal exception, the Hatfield Bridge Company, which completed the first bridge across the Connecticut River in 1807, was also the shortest-lived. The better-backed Northampton Bridge opened at a more convenient site the following year. The Hatfield bridge gradually fell into disuse before it finally collapsed about 1820.[57]

But few of the schemes were wholly successful or fulfilled the early hopes of their founders. With the high costs of upkeep, and tolls that could be evaded, turnpike companies made profits slowly. The Third Massachusetts Turnpike, from Northampton to Pittsfield, averaged a net return of only $600 a year between 1801 and 1814 and had barely repaid the capital invested in it when it was made a free road in 1829. Canal companies also faced difficulties. The South Hadley Canal provoked vigorous criticism from farmers and fishing interests upstream and, after 1800, accusations that by swamping lands and restricting drainage its dam was causing disease in Northampton and elsewhere. The company finally agreed in 1805 to rebuild its works and pay compensation for damages. Timothy Dwight, though noting that traffic on the river increased, summed up the early canal ventures as "a serious misfortune to the proprietors, and a source of not a little regret to the community." River traffic was, in any case, restrained by the continued need to transship goods at the falls in Enfield, Connecticut, which were not bypassed by locks until 1829.[58]

Land speculation also brought misfortunes. Some local figures, such as Jonathan H. Lyman of Northampton and Oliver Smith of Hatfield, were eventually to make money successfully from land in New York, Pennsylvania, and Ohio. The Northampton merchant Benjamin Tappan also had holdings in and around Cleveland that promised substantial profits by the early nineteenth century. But others were unlucky. John Stoddard of Northampton wrote to John Worthington in Springfield in 1798, lamenting the latter's loss of $400 in a purchase Stoddard had advised him to make. With a gambler's optimism, he urged Worthington to part with more cash to "make good that loss [and make?] something handsome to yourself." William Edwards, who had been Worthington's partner in the venture, later claimed to have lost several thousand dollars by it. Even Benjamin Tappan's good fortune became apparent only over time. For many years, his son Lewis was later to write, his speculation in Western Reserve lands "was a subject of anxiety and embarrassment to him," from which he was relieved only by the assistance of one or more of his sons.[59]

Internal improvements and investments in land were, at best, long-term solutions to the weak position of merchants and other investors in a household-centered economy. Over several decades such ventures provided part of the basis for more concentrated and successful capital investment. But for the most part, the late-eighteenth- and early-nineteenth-century rural economy kept power diffused, in the hands of the farmers, craftsmen, and other household producers who dominated the social structure. These men and women, despite the upheavals of the revolutionary period and its aftermath, had succeeded in retaining effective control of rural production and the patterns of exchange.

Households and Conflict

Most rural households were able to maintain the independence that they valued well into the nineteenth century. By then, commentators extolling the virtues of family life gave the image of the rural household a roseate tinge that has surrounded it ever since. In 1834, for example, the Reverend James Flint wrote an article, "Picture of a New England Family," nauseating in its sentimentality. "Ambition has infused no storm into their tranquil bosoms," he wrote of an imaginary husband, wife, and children seated round the fireplace. "Behold the scene! It is the sole-surviving trace of paradise on earth, unspoiled by the perverted tastes and distempered cravings of artificial life, or the costly inventions of pride and luxury."[60] Late-eighteenth-century people would have found this description ludicrous. The world of households they inhabited was often hard, cramped, and fraught with conflict.

Farmers' and artisans' houses were crowded, busy places. Few could advertise, as did Noah Webster when he prepared to leave Amherst in 1822, a house with "eight large rooms, exclusive of the kitchen, which contains two rooms." Evidence on house sizes, collected for the federal direct tax of 1798, has not survived for the towns of Northampton, Hatfield, Amherst, Hadley, Williamsburg, or Westhampton, but returns for the surrounding area suggest the probable pattern. Large two-story houses were most common in old settlements near the river. Toward the hills and in newer towns, smaller dwellings predominated. Everywhere, though, in poorer households and in many young ones where children were being brought up, space was at a premium. In 1805 a young Hadley farmer, Jonathan Warner, was given an old schoolhouse to live in, which probably contained only one or two rooms.[61] Working, eating, and sleeping places became more crowded during the winter, when rooms were closed off and fires kept in kitchens for warmth. Except in some new settlements, such as Westhampton, a number of dwellings housed more than one family, usually parents together with a married child and the child's spouse and own children. Between 1790 and 1830 roughly 11 percent of Amherst and Hadley families shared houses in this way. As Mary Graham of Buckland learned when her widowed mother was courting a second husband, privacy was hard to find in a small house. "It reminds me of a few years ago when you got out of the window so many times," she wrote to her sister; "I have not exactly done that but sat on the stairs till I was tired." Going into the room once in time to hear "the old man" say "he could not tell until he tried it," she "did not dare stay longer, did not know what would come next."[62] Family life may have been warm, but it was not easy.

Sharing out work, reconciling the uneven burdens of men's and women's tasks, providing for daily needs and for the future livelihoods of children were constant sources of friction. To the catalog of difficulties caused by illness, death, separation, and migration may be added those resulting from the need to operate in a constrained economic environment. Rebecca Dickinson of Hatfield, though saddened at being single, consoled herself in 1787 that "family blessings" were double-edged: "the gifts of time alwais bring sorrow along with them[;] a numerous family and a great Estate bring a great concern upon the minds of the owners more than a ballance for all the comfort that they bring."[63]

The pursuit of independence by families hedged in by material constraints did engender local cooperation of the kind we examined earlier, but it also led to attempts to exclude from consideration people unable to provide reciprocal goods or work, and those otherwise regarded as "outsiders" or subordinates. John Miller explained that he had originally applied to Caleb Strong for assistance with his debts when his neighbors had ceased to help him; "although I believe [they] all thought me honest, they were not generally fond of trusting a man who had no estate."[64] As Douglas L. Jones has shown, one of the consequences of eighteenth-century population growth was an increase in the numbers of poor, landless, often transient people forced to live at the margins of rural society. To avoid supporting outsiders who became destitute, older towns continued to "warn out" newcomers until new laws of the 1790s provided for state assistance to paupers without legal residence. In 1791, for example, 119 families or individuals totaling well over 200 people were formally "warned out" of Northampton; Hadley dealt similarly with another 29. This happened again, on a smaller scale, in 1794 and 1796. Some of the people named remained in town and settled. Nathan Storrs, one of Northampton's jewelers in the early nineteenth century, had been named in the warning-out warrant of 1791. But others were less fortunate. Caesar Prutt, a black man warned out of Hadley in 1796, was being supported as a pauper in Amherst in 1800.[65] Many others just moved on.

After 1800 perhaps several hundred people a year were passing through the valley, sick or seeking employment: here a man who "supported himself by day labor"; there an Irish-born journeyman hatter who "has of late years been to[o] feeble to labor and has led a wandering life"; here a woman unable to find work, and "such have been her habits of life, that she has never earned any property."[66] Even after the law provided support for "state paupers," endless wrangles over residency occurred, as towns tried to pass costs back to places paupers had previously lived in. Independent farmers, gathered in town meetings each spring, watched the poor rolls closely and bargained hard to reduce the cost of relief as much as possible. In 1801 the Amherst town meeting voted that Caesar Prutt "be Set up at vendue, to the Lowest bidder For Victualling and Beding," and he was then "Struck of[f]" to a farmer for a dollar a week. The next year the town got the weekly price down to eighty-five cents. What sparked the town's indignation was a successful attempt in 1803 by Daniel Kellogg, one of Amherst's most prosperous farmers, to have his insane brother supported by the town. While the town meeting, on legal advice, reluctantly voted to provide the money, it had a strong condemnation of Kellogg placed on its records, "as a rare instance of the want of brotherly affection." "Devoid of all the natural and social feelings of humanity; wrapt up in the barbrous garb of self-interest," Kellogg stood as "a deplorable monument of human depravity."[67]

Kellogg's public rebuke by his neighbors reflected the fine tensions inherent in farm families' intent, on the one hand, to "keep a good neighborhood" and, on the other, to provide for their own and their children's livelihoods. "Neighborhood" implied a recognition of needs and abilities that, although it obliged the town to support Kellogg's "wretched and distressed" brother, more strongly implied that Kellogg himself could afford to do this better than his neighbors. "Livelihood" impelled someone in Kellogg's position to put his own interests first, but it also provoked the resentment of neighbors forced to assume the burdens he had avoided. This tension, together with the other conflicts in the household system, drove the rural economy into the nineteenth century. The ways in which rural households acted in their diffuse social structure, pursuing independence but demanding interdependence, powerfully influenced the shape the economy would take.

NOTES

1. Carole Shammas, "How Self-Sufficient Was Early America?" *Journal of Interdisciplinary History* 13 (1982–1983): 247–272; Bettye Hobbs Pruitt, "Self-Sufficiency and the Agricultural Economy of Eighteenth-Century Massachusetts," *William and Mary Quarterly* 41 (July 1984): 333–364; Sarah F. McMahon, "A Comfortable Subsistence: The Changing Composition of Diet in Rural New England, 1620–1840," *William and Mary Quarterly* 42 (January 1985): 26–65. On subsistence-surplus economies, see James A. Henretta, "Families and Farms: *Mentalité* in Pre-Industrial America," *William and Mary Quarterly* 35 (January 1978): 20, and Steven Hahn, *The Roots of Southern Populism: Yeoman Farmers and the Transformation of the Georgia Upcountry, 1850–1890* (New York, 1983), 29–40. For a critique, see David F. Weiman, "Farmers and the Market in Antebellum America: A View from the Georgia Upcountry," *Journal of Economic History* 47 (1987): 627–648. Gavin Wright, *The Political Economy of the Cotton South: Households, Markets, and Wealth in the Nineteenth Century* (New York, 1978), chap. 3, provides a useful discussion of the distinctions between production for use and production for market.

2. Evidence for the 1750s is in an anonymous Account Book, 1753–1756, Boltwood Collection, Special Collections Room, Jones Library, Amherst, MA; the Williamsburg teamster: Jesse Wild, Account Book, Bodman Family Papers, Box 1, Sophia Smith Collection, Smith College; Deerfield boatman: deposition in the case of Arms v. Loomis, Hampshire County Court of Common Pleas, Files, May 1802, no. 286, Massachusetts State Archives, Boston; Porter's accounts are in William Porter Papers, Box C, folder 1810, Research Library, Old Sturbridge Village, Sturbridge, MA.

3. "A List of Notes and Book Accts due at this Time to the Late Compy of Shephard and Hunt and this day set of[f] to Levi Shephard," Northampton, July 12, 1784, Shepard Papers, Manuscripts Collection, Trustees' Room, Forbes Library, Northampton, Box 31. (Members of the Shepard family spelled their name several different ways. Except in quotations, I have adopted one spelling throughout.) Estimates of

the number of traders are based on advertisements in *Hampshire Gazette* (Northampton), 1790–1800; see also Margaret E. Martin, "Merchants and Trade of the Connecticut River Valley, 1750–1820," *Smith College Studies in History* 24 (1938–1939).

4. Amherst, Tax Valuation List, 1795.

5. Elisha Smith, Account Book, Amherst, 1784–1822, Boltwood Collection.

6. Northampton, Tax Assessment List, 1798; proximity of kin was a notable aspect of New England society in this period: see Daniel Scott Smith, "'All in Some Degree Related to Each Other': A Demographic and Comparative Resolution of the Anomaly of New England Kinship," *American Historical Review* 94 (February 1989): 44–79. Timothy Dwight, *Travels in New England and New York*, ed. Barbara M. Solomon, 4 vols. (Cambridge, MA, 1969): 1:240 and 2:230, commented on neighborliness in the older valley towns; Barbara Karsky, "Sociability in Rural New England," *Travail et loisir dans les sociétés pre-industrielles* (Nancy, forthcoming), provides a wider view. Kinship and neighborhood did not, however, imply absence of conflict, as the following discussions make clear.

7. I owe this suggestion to discussion with Michael Merrill and to his "Gifts, Barter, and Commerce in Early America: An Ethnography of Exchange" (paper presented to the 78th Annual Meeting of the Organization of American Historians, Minneapolis, April 1985).

8. Thomas Corbyn and Co. to Shepard and Hunt, London, February 28, August 17, 20, 1771, Shepard Papers. On the importance of short-term credit to a commercial economy, see Jeanne Chase, "Credit à court terme et croissance d'une capitale commerciale: New York, 1786–1820," *Géographie du capitale marchand aux Amériques, 1760–1860*, ed. Jeanne Chase (Paris, 1987), 79–108.

9. Fay and Mack to Shepard and Hunt, Williamstown, February 21, 1774, Shepard Papers; Ebenezer Barnard to Hanford and Ely, Hartford, November 18, 1806, Barnard Family Papers, Library of Congress.

10. William and Solomon Bartlett, Account Books, 2 vols., Westhampton, 1704–1857, Manuscripts and Archives Department, Baker Library, Harvard University Graduate School of Business Administration, Boston.

11. Etienne Clavière and J. P. Brissot de Warville, *De la France et des Etats-Unis, ou de l'importance de la révolution de l'Amérique pour le bonheur de la France* (London, 1787), 24; the authors remarked that "it is most astonishing that of all the travelers who have gone through the United States not one has given a detail of the manner of exchanging the various necessities and comforts of life."

12. This discussion accords with Bruce H. Mann, *Neighbors and Strangers: Law and Community in Early Connecticut* (Chapel Hill, 1987), although the intention of his argument may differ from mine. Mann notes the differing character and social implications of book accounts and written instruments (39) and the different treatment accorded neighbors and strangers (19), though he stresses (19, 66) the potential for conflict among neighbors.

13. The case was Cogswell, exx. v. Dolliver, 2 Mass. Reports (1 Tyng) 217–218. Robert B. Thomas, *The Farmer's Almanack for the Year 1798* (Boston, [1797]); *Hampshire Sentinel* (Belchertown), November 24, 1830. Useful unpublished work on local exchange, in addition to that already referred to, includes Michael Bellesiles, "The World of the Account Book: The Frontier Economy of the Upper Connecticut River Valley, 1760–1800" (paper presented to the 79th Annual Meeting of the Organization of American Historians, April 1986), and Mick Reed, "Neighbourhood

Exchange in Nineteenth-Century Rural England" (paper presented to History Workshop 22, Brighton, November 1988). I am grateful to both authors for sharing their findings with me. Jack Larkin's "Accounting for Change: Exchange and Debt in the New England Rural Economy" (paper presented to the 10th Annual Meeting of the Society for Historians of the Early American Republic, July 1988) is an excellent discussion of the subject.

14. William Boltwood, Account Book, Amherst, 1789–1830, Boltwood Collection.

15. Solomon Bartlett, Account Book, vol. 2, entry for 1819.

16. Joseph Clarke, Account Book, Northampton, 1786–1794, Historic Northampton, A.A.17.5. The *Anti-Monarchist* (Northampton), January 17, 1810, condemned the well-off who neglected to pay poorer creditors but noted, nevertheless, that "there is but one valid apology for not paying money when it is due, and that is, not having it to pay.

17. Thomas, *Farmer's Almanack for 1798*. William J. Gilmore, "Elementary Literacy on the Eve of the Industrial Revolution: Trends in Rural New England, 1760–1830," *Proceedings of the American Antiquarian Society* 92 (April 1982): 150, notes that the ritual of signing accounts formed part of a network of community trust.

18. Walter Rose, *Good Neighbours: Some Recollections of an English Village and Its People* (Cambridge, UK, 1942); the description appears in a chapter called "Gnawing It Out." I am grateful to Mick Reed for this reference. Of a sample of sixteen from among the Connecticut Valley ledgers I examined, only two contained complete entries on both the debit and credit sides. The remainder had room for debit and credit entries on facing pages but were incomplete on the credit side. Harris Beckwith (Northampton) gave the goods and services he provided on the debit pages of his ledger, but often recorded credits only *after* settlements, with entries such as "by his account," or "by his account and note to balance" (Harris Beckwith, Account Book, 1803–1807, Manuscripts Collection, Trustees' Room, Forbes Library). In other words, he did not record payments as they were made to him. A small proportion of surviving ledgers contain debit pages only.

19. Justus Forward, Diary, August 26, 1786, MS Collection, American Antiquarian Society, Worcester, MA.

20. Thomas, *Farmer's Almanack for 1798*.

21. *Hampshire Sentinel*, November 24, 1830; Nathan Wild, *The Farmer's, Mechanic's, and Gentleman's Almanack for 1831* (Amherst, 1830).

22. The quotation is from Jno. Brown to Shepard and Hunt, London, February 28, 1771, Shepard Papers; Brown noted that he was "troubled by taking notes on demand," but felt obliged to do so.

23. This conclusion is based on an analysis of debt suits in Hampshire County Court of Common Pleas, Records, vols. 7–8 (1804–1809), Hampshire County Courthouse, Northampton. Similar findings have been made for southern Vermont: see Bellesiles, "The World of the Account Book."

24. Tax data are from Bettye Hobbs Pruitt, ed., *The Massachusetts Tax Valuations of 1771* (Boston, 1978); Dwight, *Travels*, 2:184, referred to servants; on "lending" kin and neighbors: [Arethusa Hall], "Sathurea: The Story of a Life," 1864, Judd Papers, 55M–1, Box 2, Houghton Library, Harvard University, 37; on the blurred line between living with kin and hiring out as "help," see Faye E. Dudden, *Serving Women: Household Service in 19th-Century America* (Middletown, CT, 1983), 20.

25. Stephen Innes, *Labor in a New Land: Economy and Society in Seventeenth-Century Springfield* (Princeton, 1983).

26. The daily wage rate for general farm labor, quoted at two shillings in Springfield in the 1680s (Innes, *Labor in a New Land*, 170), was usually four shillings in mid-eighteenth-century account books.

27. Land settlement and division in the mid-eighteenth century is discussed in Gregory H. Nobles, *Divisions throughout the Whole: Politics and Society in Hampshire County, Massachusetts, 1740–1775* (Cambridge, UK, 1983). On population growth, see Jesse Chickering, *A Statistical View of the Population of Massachusetts, 1765–1840* (Boston, 1846).

28. Douglas Lamar Jones, "The Strolling Poor: Transiency in 18th Century Massachusetts," *Journal of Social History* (spring 1975). Daniel Vickers, "Working the Fields in a Developing Economy: Essex County, Massachusetts, 1630–1675," in Stephen Innes, ed., *Work and Labor in Early America* (Chapel Hill, 1988), esp. 55–56, documents the low rates of servanthood in earlier New England agricultural communities.

29. Kevin M. Sweeney, "River Gods in the Making: The Williamses of Western Massachusetts," in Peter Benes, ed., *The Bay and the River, 1600–1900* (Boston, 1982), 101–116; see also Kevin M. Sweeney, "From Wilderness to Arcadian Vale: Material Life in the Connecticut River Valley, 1635–1760," in Gerald W. R. Ward and William N. Hosley, Jr., eds., *The Great River: Art and Society of the Connecticut Valley, 1635–1820* (Hartford, 1985). Phelps is mentioned in T. G. Huntington, "Sketches by Theodore G. Huntington of the family and life in Hadley, written in letters to H. F. Quincy," n.d., Porter-Phelps-Huntington House, Hadley, MA (typescript).

30. On the decline of wheat: Dwight, *Travels* 1:31; Sylvester Judd, *History of Hadley, including the early history of Hatfield, South Hadley, Amherst, and Granby, Mass.* (Northampton, 1863), 362–363; Percy W. Bidwell and John I. Falconer, *History of Agriculture in the Northern United States, 1620–1860* (Washington, DC, 1925), 90; on the elite and their houses: Kevin M. Sweeney, "Mansion People: Kinship, Class, and Architecture in Western Massachusetts in the Mid-Eighteenth Century," *Winterthur Portfolio* 19 (winter 1984): 231–255.

31. Political conflict is discussed in Nobles, *Divisions throughout the Whole*, chap. 6; the weakness and eventual decline of the regional elite, in Robert Blair St. George, "Artifacts of Regional Consciousness in the Connecticut River Valley, 1700–1780," in *The Great River*, 29–40.

32. Robert J. Taylor's *Western Massachusetts in the Revolution* (Providence, 1955), chap. 4, is the standard account. Nobles, *Divisions throughout the Whole*, chap. 7, details several episodes in the unseating of Hampshire County leaders, and quotes the Williamsburg letter on p. 163. Jonathan Judd, Jr., Diary, August 31, September 3, 7,13, 20, 1774; February 18, 19, April 1, 12, 22, 1776, Forbes Library. Barbara Clark Smith, *After the Revolution: The Smithsonian History of Everyday Life in the Eighteenth Century* (Washington, DC, 1986), 3–7, 30–42, recounts Colton's fate.

33. Taylor, *Western Massachusetts in the Revolution;* Barbara Karsky, "Agrarian Radicalism in the Late Revolutionary Period, 1780–1795," in Erich Angermann, Marie-Luise Frings, and Hermann Wellenreuther, eds., *New Wine in Old Skins: A Comparative View of the American Revolution* (Stuttgart, 1976); David Szatmary, *Shays' Rebellion: The Making of an Agrarian Insurrection* (Amherst, 1980). I have

also benefited from reading the essays in Robert A. Gross, ed., *In Debt to Shays: The Bicentennial of an Agrarian Insurrection* (Charlottesville, VA, 1990), and am grateful to Robert Gross for the opportunity to see these papers before publication.

34. See George R. Minot, *The History of the Insurrections in Massachusetts, in the Year MDCCLXXXVI, and the Rebellion Consequent Thereon* (Worcester, 1788); Robert A. Gross, *The Minutemen and Their World* (New York, 1976), 178–179, traces the effects of British debt collection on one family in Concord, MA.

35. Petition, September 28, 1786, Shays's Rebellion Collection, folder 1, American Antiquarian Society, Worcester. Szatmary, *Shays' Rebellion*, 29, calculates that the 2,977 debt cases brought before the Hampshire County Court of Common Pleas between August 1784 and August 1786 involved 31.4 percent of all males in the county aged sixteen or over.

36. Matthew Talcott to Jonathan Amory, Middletown, CT, March 27, 1787, Amory Papers, Box 3, Library of Congress.

37. Abraham Burbank to Lemuel Pomeroy, West Springfield, April 18, 1785, Pomeroy Family Papers, Manuscripts Collection, Trustees' Room, Forbes Library, Box 30; Minot, *History of the Insurrections*, 28–29; *Hampshire Herald*, September 7, 1784, quoted in Taylor, *Western Massachusetts in the Revolution*, 125.

38. Daniel Shelton, "'Elementary Feelings': Pelham, Massachusetts, in Rebellion" (Honors thesis, Amherst College, 1981), table following 119.

39. John L. Brooke, "Towns, Courts, Conventions, and Regulators: Revolutionary Settlements and the Crisis of the Economy in Massachusetts, 1786–1787," in Gross, *In Debt to Shays*.

40. Town of Greenwich, Petition, January 16, 1786, Shays's Rebellion Collection, folder 1, American Antiquarian Society; "An Address from the Convention at Hatfield," *Massachusetts Centinel*, January 17, 1787 (copy provided me by Robert Gross).

41. Shelton, "'Elementary Feelings,'" 114–122. Alan Taylor has suggested to me that some young men joined the insurrection because their families assigned them the task of taking up arms for them, as in previous wars; this would imply that participants' motives must be sought in social values and neighborhood rifts and alliances, as well as in the grievances of individuals. See Gregory H. Nobles, "Shays's Neighbors: The Context of Rebellion in Pelham, Massachusetts," in Gross, *In Debt to Shays*.

42. John L. Brooke, "A Deacon's Orthodoxy: The Religious Context of Shays's Rebellion" (paper presented at a conference at the Colonial Society of Massachusetts, Boston, October 1986).

43. Quoted in a purported interview, *Massachusetts Centinel*, January 20, 1787.

44. Miller's story was printed in the *Hampshire Gazette*, March 26, 1806.

45. Data drawn from inventories and administrators' accounts, Hampshire County, Probate Records, vol. 15 (1784–1789), Connecticut Valley Historical Museum, Springfield, MA (microfilm).

46. Daniel Coit to Levi Shepard, Granby, January 2, 1787, Shepard Papers.

47. "R.G." to Jonathan Amory, Springfield, May 31, 1787, Amory Papers, Box 3.

48. Minot, *History of the Insurrections*, 175–177; the Chesterfield instructions were printed in the *Hampshire Gazette*, October 24, 1787.

49. Jonathan Judd to Sylvester Judd, Sr., Southampton, June 2, 1787, Judd Papers, Manuscripts Collection, Trustees' Room, Forbes Library, Oversize Files.

50. Peter J. Coleman, *Debtors and Creditors in America: Insolvency, Imprisonment for Debt, and Bankruptcy, 1607–1900* (Madison, WI, 1974), 34–52.

51. Joseph Lyman, *A Sermon Preached before His Excellency James Bowdoin, esq., Governour . . . of the Commonwealth of Massachusetts, May 30, 1787, being the Day of General Election* (Boston, [1787]), 13.

52. Election returns reported in the *Hampshire Gazette*, April 9, 1800; April 8, 1801; April 7, 1802; April 6, 1803; April 4, 1804; April 3, 1805; April 9, 1806; April 8, 1807. The number of votes cast in Northampton in the gubernatorial election of 1800, for example, was 108 percent higher than in the election of 1790, though the town's population had grown by only 35 percent: *Hampshire Gazette*, April 7, 1790; April 9, 1800.

53. Town Meeting Records for Amherst reprinted in Edward W. Carpenter and Charles F. Morehouse, *The History of the Town of Amherst, Massachusetts* (Amherst, 1896); Bernard R. Kubiak, "Social Changes in a New England Agricultural Community: Hatfield, Massachusetts, 1800–1850" (University of Massachusetts, Amherst, 1972), 24, tab. 8.

54. Lists of ministers in *Creed, Covenant and Rules, and List of Members of the First Congregational Church in Amherst, Mass.* (Amherst, 1859); Daniel W. Wells and Reuben F. Wells, *History of Hatfield, Mass., 1660–1910* (Springfield, 1910), 343; Northampton First Church, *Meetinghouses and Ministers from 1653 to 1878* (Northampton, [1878]).

55. Jonathan Judd to Sylvester Judd, Sr., Boston, November 6, 1780, Manuscripts Collection, Trustees' Room, Forbes Library, Box 18; the petition against Joseph Kingsley is in Judd Papers, Manuscripts Collection, Trustees' Room, Forbes Library, Oversize Files.

56. James M. Banner, *To the Hartford Convention: The Federalists and the Origins of Party Politics in Massachusetts, 1789–1815* (New York, 1969); Miller's story: *Hampshire Gazette*, March 26, 1806; the account of polling day: *Hampshire Gazette*, April 10, 1811.

57. On bridges, see Samuel Willard, *A Sermon Preached at Northampton, October 27, 1808, at the Opening of Northampton Bridge* (Northampton, 1808); Wells, *History of Hatfield*, 214–216. On canals, see *Private and Special Statutes of the Commonwealth of Massachusetts*, 7 vols. (Boston, 1805–1837), 1:329. On turnpikes, see *Private and Special Statutes* 2:78–81, 130–134, 140–144, 295–299, 327–331. See also Martin, "Merchants and Trade," 200–202.

58. Harry A. Wright, *The Story of Western Massachusetts*, 4 vols. (New York, 1949), 2:485–486; Dwight, *Travels*, 1:236; W. DeLoss Love, "The Navigation of the Connecticut River," *Proceedings of the American Antiquarian Society*, n.s. 15 (April 1903): 385–441.

59. John Stoddard to John Worthington, Northampton, March 1, 1798, Historic Northampton, A.S.L.17.2; William Edwards, *Memoirs of Col. William Edwards* (Washington, DC, 1897); on the Tappans' holdings, see the *Republican Spy* (Northampton). July [?], 1806, and Lewis Tappan, "Autobiographical Sketch," Lewis Tappan Papers, Container 14, Library of Congress (microfilm, reel 7). See also Martin, "Merchants and Trade," 176–183.

60. James Flint, "Picture of a New England Family," *Hampshire Gazette*, February 26, 1834.

61. Webster advertisement, *Hampshire Gazette*, April 10, 1822. There was a higher proportion of small houses in upland towns than in the bottomlands; in 1798, 70 percent of houses in Pelham and 54 percent in Belchertown had only one story, compared with 35 percent in Westfield and 21 percent in Easthampton (Massachusetts, Direct Tax Censuses, 1798, 17:78–83 and 19:789–802, 816–820, New England Historic Genealogical Society, Boston [microfilm]). None of the relevant schedules for the six towns has survived. Warner is mentioned in Elizabeth Phelps, Diary, November 3, 1805, Porter-Phelps-Huntington House, Hadley, MA.

62. Mary Graham to Lewis Edwards, Buckland, August 5, 1842, Edwards Family Correspondence, Manuscripts Collection, Trustees' Room, Forbes Library.

63. Rebecca Dickinson, Diary, August 2, 1787, Pocumtuck Valley Memorial Association Library, Deerfield, MA; Jan Lewis, *The Pursuit of Happiness: Family and Values in Jefferson's Virginia* (Cambridge, UK, 1983), discusses the difficulties of family life.

64. *Hampshire Gazette*, March 26, 1806.

65. Jones, "The Strolling Poor," passim; Warning-Out Warrant, Northampton, November 24, 1791, Boltwood Collection; Hadley warrants copied in Judd MS, "Hadley," 3:355, 361; Storrs is mentioned in Philip Zea, "Clockmaking and Society at the River and the Bay: Jedidiah and Jabez Baldwin, 1790–1820," in Benes, *The Bay and the River*, 44; for Prutt, see Amherst, Town Meeting Records, reprinted in Carpenter and Morehouse, *History of the Town of Amherst*, 187, 189.

66. Northampton, Overseers of the Poor, Case Histories, Town Papers Collection, 5.14, Forbes Library.

67. The town's proceedings in the Kellogg case are reprinted in Carpenter and Morehouse, *History of the Town of Amherst*, 192–193.

10

"THE villages of New England are all more or less beautiful," wrote English author Harriet Martineau, "and the most beautiful of them all is Northampton." Travelogues like Martineau's Retrospect of Western Travel, *published in 1838, made Northampton a frequent destination for a new class with the means and the leisure to travel for pleasure. Swedish singer Jenny Lind, perhaps the nineteenth century's most popular entertainer, performed in Northampton, but returned in 1852 for her honeymoon. "Northampton," she proclaimed, "is the paradise of America."*

Ease of travel also brought an increasing stream of visitors who sought out Northampton as a refuge from the growing pressures of urban life in America. The view from Mount Holyoke began appearing in European and American travel guides in the 1820s. In 1836, Thomas Cole immortalized the scene in his monumental painting of the Oxbow. "The imagination," Cole remarked, "can scarcely conceive Arcadian vales more lovely or more peaceful than the valley of the Connecticut—its villages are rural places where trees overspread every dwelling and the fields upon its margin have the richest verdure."

In the following essay, Martha Hoppin shows us how artists like Cole came to portray the environs of Northampton as the epitome of the "picturesque"—the ideal middle landscape between civilization and wild nature.

Arcadian Vales

*The Connecticut Valley in Art**

MARTHA J. HOPPIN

DESCRIBING the Connecticut Valley in the late 1790s, Yale University President Timothy Dwight was full of superlatives. The meadows near Hartford, Connecticut, were "superior to any in the state," the main street of Hadley, Massachusetts, was "the handsomest" in New England, and the prospect from Mount Holyoke, Massachusetts, was the "richest" in New England.[1] For Dwight, as for later travelers, the valley represented the New England ideal of "sobriety, industry," and "good order."[2] On his two journeys up the Connecticut, Dwight noted in particular the neat and orderly character of the valley, both visually, in terms of its fields and architecture, and spiritually, in terms of its social organization and values. He found the inhabitants refined

*This essay is an edited excerpt drawn from Martha J. Hoppin, ed., *Arcadian Vales: Views of the Connecticut River Valley* (Springfield, MA, 1981).

and softened by their practice of clustering in villages. In contrast to the Hudson River settlements, where Dwight observed that commerce determined the manner of development, patterns of settlement along the Connecticut derived from a stronger, superior sense of community. Connecticut Valley inhabitants, he concluded, had a "common character," which linked them to each other more strongly than to residents in their respective states.[3]

Called "the beautiful river," the "queen of New England rivers," and "the Nile of New England," the Connecticut River was, and still is, distinguished principally by its rich, extensive meadow lands, or "intervals."[4] These have been cultivated since Indian times. According to Dwight, "Each interval appears, not as artificially fruitful, but as a field of nature, spontaneously producing all its vegetation, and originally furnished by the hand of the Creator with all its bounties."[5] He estimated that the valley encompassed some 60,000 acres of interval land, most concentrated in Connecticut in the Hartford area, in Massachusetts from Springfield to Northfield, in Vermont near Windsor, Newbury, Lunenburgh, and Guildhall, and in New Hampshire in Charlestown, Haverhill, and Lancaster.[6]

Both the meadowlands and the orderly, prosperous towns of the Connecticut Valley attracted artists early in the nineteenth century. They almost invariably portrayed the region as a pastoral haven, an ideal combination of nature and man, beautiful because of its balance of the two forces. In his "Essay on American Scenery" of 1835, Thomas Cole characterized the Connecticut River as "gentle" and the valley as "Arcadian."[7] This image of the Connecticut Valley as Arcadia prevailed throughout the nineteenth century despite growing industrialization along the river's course. Rarely did the railroad appear in painted views of the valley. Such idyllic images of the domesticated landscape expressed a desire for social order and settled community equal in importance to the uniqueness of American nature expressed through the images of wilderness identified with the Hudson River School. The Connecticut Valley was, above all, the epitome of the settled landscape.[8]

In 1827 the young Thomas Cole came to Hartford, thus beginning an association with the valley that culminated in 1836 with his famous painting of the Oxbow of the Connecticut River at Northampton, Massachusetts (Metropolitan Museum of Art). Cole's trip to Hartford was recorded in a sketch, *View of Hartford* (Detroit Institute of Arts), which was possibly the basis of an unlocated oil painting.[9] An engraving of the same view was published in London in 1832 in John H. Hinton's *History and Topography of the United States*. Cole also visited Daniel Wadsworth, who that December commissioned a painting of Monte Video.[10] The work was completed in 1828 and shown in the National Academy that year. *View of Monte Video, the Seat of Daniel Wadsworth, Esq.* (Wadsworth Atheneum), taken from a position near Wadsworth's tower atop Talcott Mountain, looks out toward the valley of the Farmington River, a tributary of the Connecticut. Wadsworth's house appears surrounded by cleared land and forest beyond. The idyllic setting is underscored by a solitary figure musing in the foreground, by the lush, rounded trees and generally rounded contours of the land, and by the peaceful prospect of the panorama. Cole's personal symbolic motif, a blasted tree trunk, is balanced by an opposing mass of foliage to frame the scene.

After visiting Wadsworth in July, 1827, Cole continued on to the White Mountains via Boston. His route had been mapped by Wadsworth, who advised returning through the Connecticut Valley:

> Haverhill-Hanover-Windsor to Mount Aschutna-Charlestown & 8 miles *Bellows Falls*-Brattle Borough-Greenfield-Northampton *with Mount Holyoak* [*sic*]—are all handsome & worth passing—There are many other pleasant Villages & Towns on the way—Especially Springfield in Massachusetts . . . 27 Miles from Hartford.[11]

This trip was presumably Cole's first exposure to the valley, which he later described in his 1835 lecture on American scenery. Only two rivers, the Hudson and the Connecticut, were singled out for discussion in Cole's account.

> In the Connecticut we behold a river that differs widely from the Hudson. Its sources are amid the wild mountains of New Hampshire; but it soon breaks into a luxuriant valley, and flows for more than a hundred miles, sometimes beneath the shadow of wooded hills, and sometimes glancing through the green expanse of elm-besprinkled meadows. Whether we see it at Haverhill, Northampton, or Hartford, it still possesses that gentle aspect; and the imagination can scarcely conceive Arcadian vales more lovely or more peaceful than the valley of the Connecticut—its villages are rural places where trees overspread every dwelling, and the fields upon its margin have the richest verdure.[12]

That Cole very early took a special interest in the Oxbow is documented by his tracing (Detroit Institute of Arts) of an etching after Basil Hall's drawing of the same subject. An Englishman, Hall toured the United States in 1827 and 1828, publishing his sketches in 1829 in Edinburgh and London as *Forty Etchings from Sketches Made with the Camera Lucida in North America in 1827 and 1828*. Cole spent the years 1829 to 1831 in England, where his own designs were engraved for Hinton's *History and Topography of the United States*. Probably he copied Hall's drawing during this time.

Cole next visited the Connecticut Valley in 1833, following his return from Europe in November 1832. En route from Catskill, New York, to Boston, he sketched the view from Mount Holyoke looking toward the Oxbow.[13] A detailed rendering of the river, the drawing bears notations on color, distance, and specific details. In the lower margin Cole noted that rows of corn could be distinguished in the fields, and that the trees were mostly elms.

In March 1836, Cole wrote to Luman Reed, "Fancy pictures seldom sell, and they generally take more time than views, so I have determined to paint one of the latter—I have already commenced a view from Mount Holyoke; it is about the finest scene I have in my sketchbook and is well known—it will be novel and I think effective."[14] The final result, known today as *The Oxbow*, dated 1836, was exhibited at the National Academy of Design that year as *View from Mt. Holyoke, Northampton, Massachusetts, after a Thunder Storm*, a much more specific title identifying it expressly as a view. Cole painted his landscapes in the studio, basing them on drawings made during summer sketching trips, and small oil studies executed in the studio.[15] A surviving oil study of the Mount Holyoke view, painted about 1835–1836, rounds out the full sequence of images tracing Cole's development of the theme.

When Cole wrote that the scene was well known, he was referring to both literary and artistic precedents. Beginning in the 1820s the site was specifically admired in travel accounts by English visitors, such as Basil Hall, and by Americans like Theodore Dwight, whose guidebook, *The Northern Traveller*, 1825, published probably the first view of the Oxbow. Amherst College president and noted geologist Edward Hitchcock compiled a *Report on the Geology, Mineralogy, Botany, and Zoology of Massachusetts* in 1833, which illustrated the Oxbow as drawn by his wife, Orra White Hitchcock, and lithographed by Pendleton's in Boston. General public interest in the prospect had already brought thousands of visitors by the 1820s. The site's general familiarity attracted Cole, who felt his view would have added appeal.

Compared to these previous images, Cole's treatment of the theme was on a wholly different plane. Its scale and medium alone set it apart. A particularly large landscape (51 ½ x 76"), *The Oxbow* may reflect the monumental scale of Cole's *Course of Empire* series, completed in 1836; but he wrote that he had only a large canvas available, and that because it would be his only entry in the Academy exhibition that year, he wished to make it especially impressive.[16] Cole's intention was also different from that of previous illustrators. Dwight's *Northern Traveller* presented the river's unusual formation rather than its surroundings. By raising the entire Oxbow up a bit, the artist made the far curve more visible. Orra Hitchcock concentrated on the length of the river, the Oxbow forming only a portion of its course. Basil Hall's rendering, and Cole's tracing after it, were correct topographically, since Hall copied the image provided by his camera lucida. Cole's on-the-spot sketch also recorded the view accurately, but his viewpoint was slightly different from Hall's scene. In this drawing Cole had already begun the adjustment of perspective which eliminated most of the near shore line and with it the small village of Hockanum in the final painting. The curve of the Oxbow is more pronounced and visible in Cole's sketch as well. He concentrated detail on the particular configuration of the river and the layout of fields along it, but especially on the trees. Their position and shape are carefully recorded.

The foreground is only barely suggested, the angle of the foreground slope as it meets the water being most important.

Cole's small oil sketch contains the basic features of the final painting. The dark foreground triangle of the hill is contrasted to the light river; a rough tree form is suggested at the left, storm clouds now appear, and an artist sketches in the right corner. Compared to the sketchbook drawing, the upward slant of the Oxbow is more pronounced. Combining the general composition and light patterns of the oil sketch with the detail of the on-the-spot drawing, Cole made what still seems like a remarkable leap to the final painting, so filled is it with authentic-seeming detail. The Oxbow assumes a nearly perfect circular shape in harmony with the regular, neatly outlined fields surrounding it. These clear signs of settlement contrast with the irregularity and wildness of the foreground, as the dramatic thunderstorm contrasts with the clear sky over the land.[17] The strong diagonal of the hill bisects the painting, dividing the realms of wilderness and civilization bridged by the figure of the artist at work in the foreground. Cole made this juxtaposition of the wild and the settled more forceful and elemental by bringing the river closer to the viewer and silhouetting the hillside against it, an angle that would be impossible in reality but which conveys Cole's meaning. The painting celebrates the fertility of the region, while stressing the role of nature in creating it. Cole's view also became a historical record just four years later. In the spring of 1840 the Connecticut River cut through the narrow neck of the Oxbow, forever altering the paddle shape and creating instead a circular Oxbow lake.

Further proof that the view from Mount Holyoke had become a familiar site was the arrival in 1836 or 1837 of English artist William Henry Bartlett. Sent by his London publisher to illustrate a travel volume on America, Bartlett toured important sites in the Northeast. His drawings were engraved in England, issued with text in portfolio form beginning in 1837, and in 1840 gathered in one volume titled *American Scenery*, which had extensive circulation in Europe and America. Four of the volume's 119 plates were Connecticut Valley scenes; two of these depict the view from Mount Holyoke, one a view of Mount Tom from the river, and one the streets of downtown Northampton. However, the book's author, American Nathaniel Parker Willis, did little more than repeat Timothy Dwight's words for his descriptions of the Connecticut Valley.

Bartlett's rendering of the Oxbow belongs to the English topographical tradition, and in its accuracy resembles Basil Hall's earlier work. Instead of Cole's dramatic skies and decaying trees, Bartlett included an idyllic picnic scene at the top of the mountain. The peaceful village of Hockanum is pictured below, and a corner of the rudimentary mountain house appears at the left to frame the scene.[18] Bartlett's emphasis is on the beauty of the domesticated

View from Mt. Holyoke. W. H. Bartlett. Engraving, c. 1837–1838. 5 ¾ in. x 8 in. Published in Nathaniel P. Willis, *American Scenery* (London: George Virtue, 1840). *Historic Northampton.*

In 1836, the London publisher George Virtue dispatched William Henry Bartlett to the United States to record its scenery for a travel book aimed at the popular market. This view from Mount Holyoke, already a popular tourist destination, was made just after Thomas Cole completed his famous painting of the Oxbow.

landscape. The text likewise extolled the land's fertility. Echoing Dwight, Willis pronounced the scene, "Probably the richest view in America, in point of cultivation and fertile beauty. . . ."[19]

Almost all later views of the Oxbow derive from the Bartlett print, rather than from Thomas Cole's masterpiece or from nature. *American Scenery* was widely accessible; Cole's painting was privately owned and apparently never engraved, although it was shown in New York in 1836, 1838, 1848, and 1862. Using Bartlett as guide, the copyists never had to set foot on the mountain. Most views of the Oxbow, therefore, were by painters who never saw it. The most extreme example is French artist Victor de Grailly, who never crossed the Atlantic but painted numerous views from Mount Holyoke in the 1840s.

As significant as Bartlett's view of the Oxbow was his choice of a companion view looking northwest toward the town of Hadley. This scene had been represented once before in Theodore Dwight's *Sketches of Scenery and Manners in the United States* (1829), but after Bartlett, it became equally popular with copyists. Cole probably chose to paint the Oxbow instead of the view toward Hadley because it was better known, more dramatic, and less obviously

View from Mt Holyoke. Attributed to Victor de Grailly. c. 1845. Oil on canvas. 19 1/16 in. x 23 7/16 in. *Historic Northampton.*

Although he never visited the United States, French artist Victor de Grailly became one of its most prolific portraitists by using William Henry Bartlett's engravings for his inspiration. De Grailly made numerous copies of this particular view for the popular market in Europe and America.

inhabited, while many ordinary artists were attracted to the Hadley scene for the opposite reasons. The view toward Hadley offered not only cultivated fields, but also more evidence of settlement. In the engraving after Bartlett, church spires and wisps of smoke dot the landscape, while the great loop of the river encircles the town of Hadley, recognizable by the two parallel straight streets running from one bend in the river to the next. This view appealed for its image of progress and harmony, but also because it fit the popular conception of the picturesque mode. By mid-century the picturesque view included as standard elements a rough, irregular foreground, winding river in middle distance, and mountains beyond.[20]

During the Civil War at least two artists worked in the Connecticut Valley between Hartford and Northampton. Edward Nichols, a little-known New York City landscapist in the Hudson River School tradition, painted two scenes of the meadows around Mount Holyoke in 1864. *Northampton Meadows* (Historic Northampton), probably the *Mount Tom* exhibited at the Academy in 1864, is typical of his work in its broad, panoramic view, strongly horizontal composition, and diminutive trees which convey vastness of space. The painting is similar in composition to an 1864 view by Nichols taken from below the mountain looking north across the Oxbow. This is probably the work exhibited at the Brooklyn Art Association in 1865 as *Mt. Holyoke*. Both paintings view the bucolic meadow expanse from a slightly elevated, bowl-shaped stage, probably a compositional formula used on other occasions by Nichols. These paintings, as well as a third work, *View in the Connecticut River Valley* (Mattatuck Historical Society, Waterbury, Connecticut), stress peace and tranquility in an Arcadian setting. Nichols also painted at least one scene further north, for he exhibited *Fairlee Lake* (in Vermont near Orford, New Hampshire) at the Brooklyn Art Association in 1863; his *Valley of the Deerfield* was also shown there in 1870. For the rest of his career, Nichols regularly painted sites in the Hudson Valley and White Mountains.

In the summer of 1865 Thomas Charles Farrer spent several months in Northampton and painted a number of landscapes of the region.[21] Farrer came to this country from England about 1858, having studied at Workingmen's College in London. He brought the tight, meticulous technique, fidelity to nature, and careful rendering of detail typical of a Ruskin disciple. In New York in 1863 he helped found the Society for the Advancement of Truth in Art to further Ruskinian ideals. Farrer may have been drawn to Northampton partly because another Ruskin follower, Charles Eliot Norton, was summering in nearby Ashfield. While in Northampton Farrer must have been visited by his colleague John William Hill, for the *Northampton Free Press* of August 29, 1865, announced, "Mr. Hill, also a New York artist of celebrity, arrived in town last evening, having just returned home from a European tour."

Northampton Meadows. Edward W. Nichols (1819–1871). 1864. Oil on canvas, 22 1/8 in. x 36 1/16 in. *Historic Northampton*.

Edward Nichols's *Northampton Meadows* was painted in 1864 and exhibited at the National Academy of Design. It is reminiscent of the Hudson River School in the panoramic view and spreading agricultural meadow scene which focuses on Mount Tom in the center background.

Before leaving Northampton in the fall, Farrer held an exhibition of his local landscapes; only three of these are known today. *View of Northampton from the Dome of the Hospital* (Smith College Museum of Art) adopts an unconventional viewpoint for a panoramic view of the meadowlands. In the foreground is the Mill River, while in the distance the Connecticut snakes through the fields, and Mount Holyoke rises at the far right. The flatness and vastness of the meadows are emphasized in a composition of repeated horizontal and curved lines. Trees play an important role in the picture; lush and dense, they surround the buildings, while in the distance they help pace the progression into space. Other artists, including Cole and Nichols, had also focused on the shape and pattern of the trees in these meadows.

Farrer's *View of Northampton* summarizes not only the beauty and fertility of the land, but also the prosperity and order of a New England town. By contrast, a second work, *Mount Tom* (private collection), expresses the peaceful solitude and quiet beauty of nature. Painted with the same clarity and precision, this work captures the vivid intensity of fall color on the mountain, which Farrer viewed from almost the same spot as Bartlett had some thirty years earlier. In a third painting, *Mount Holyoke* (Mount Holyoke College Art Museum), Farrer chose an unusual vantage point deep within the Oxbow. Looking across the water he included a tiny train in the middle ground below the looming mountain.

Contemporary accounts of Farrer's Northampton exhibition mention also a view of "Paradise," described as representing "the road curving and winding under the arching of green that overhangs it," and admired for its "rays of sunlight gleaming through the dark.[22] Except for a scene near Farmington, Connecticut, most landscapes exhibited were of local scenery. Along with *Mount Tom*, Farrer exhibited *Sunset on Mill, Northampton*, at the Brooklyn Art Association in 1867. Unfortunately, the subjects of his other Northampton paintings are not known.

The meadow theme so popular in the 1860s received its final distinctive interpretation in Martin Johnson Heade's *Spring Shower, Connecticut Valley* (Museum of Fine Arts, Boston), painted in 1868. Heade departed from his usual marsh and coast scenes to restate Cole's theme in *The Oxbow*, but without Cole's overtones of the sublime. Heade celebrates the fertility of cultivated fields and productive orchards in a thoroughly pastoral image. The shower and the season both symbolize regeneration. The extended horizontal composition, here not as flat as usual for Heade, further conveys the vast scale of the meadows.

Prints of the 1870s maintained the image of the garden, but also gave some indication of the changing landscape. *Picturesque America*, a lavish, two-volume publication of 1874, included a chapter describing Connecticut Valley scenery and prosperous farms and towns. Despite actual changes in

View of Northampton from the Dome of the Hospital. Thomas Charles Farrer. 1865. Oil on canvas, 28 ⅛ in. x 36 in. *Smith College Museum of Art.*

Thomas Charles Farrer, a student of John Ruskin, painted this landscape in scrupulous detail. The *Hampshire Gazette* observed: "The whole broad valley, the town in embowered green, the far-off mountains bordering the horizon, with the river curving and gleaming at intervals through the openings in the foliage are most admirably rendered and true to nature." (See jacket illustration.)

the region's appearance brought about by the arrival of the railroad about 1850 and by the growth of industry along the river (most notably the planned industrial city of Holyoke), only a few illustrations in *Picturesque America* were devoted to these aspects. The great majority presented an idealized view of familiar scenery, stressing the rural character of the area. The author, W. C. Richards, regarded industry as a sign of progress, but at the same time paid little attention to it.[23]

Connecticut Valley town views, especially bird's-eye lithographs, of the 1870s and earlier, manifested pride in the achievements of industry. They typically gave a prominent place to the railroad. The works most expressive of the popular ideal were the lithographs by P. F. Goist which served as frontispieces for the two-volume *History of the Connecticut Valley in Massachusetts* published in Philadelphia in 1879. Panoramic views from the Poet's Seat in Greenfield and from Mount Nonotuck in the Mount Tom range, they totally embody mid-nineteenth-century travelers' descriptions of the beautiful, fertile valley. In the midst of Arcadia appears that symbol of progress, the train, following an unobtrusive course across the meadows.

By contrast, painted views of the Connecticut Valley from the 1870s do not document industrial growth. This reflected the change in landscape painting that was taking place at the time with the decline of the Hudson River School. The influence of French art, particularly of the Barbizon School, contributed to a sketchier technique, a focus on narrower segments of nature, and a generalized treatment of form and detail. Landscape painting moved gradually away from the grand visions, panoramic compositions, and particular detail of the Hudson River School. Artists continued to enshrine the meadowlands of the Connecticut, but their visions were more personal and less specific.[24]

The Connecticut Valley landscape represents almost two centuries of continuous artistic activity in the region, beginning in the 1820s. Its greatest popularity came in the mid-nineteenth century, coinciding with the success of the Hudson River School of landscape painting. In general artists moved up the Connecticut River, working first in the lower valley around Hartford in the 1820s through the 1840s.[25] At mid-century the valley in Massachusetts particularly appealed to artists, while after about 1850, the upper valley, including the segment bordering the White Mountains, increased in importance. Connecticut Valley views from the first half of the nineteenth century also frequently reflect the topographical landscape tradition, establishing high vantage points for prospects incorporating vast spaces. Later landscapes focus more closely on the fertile meadowlands. Despite this evolution, the homogeneous nature of Connecticut Valley images is most significant. In the Connecticut Valley landscape, artists created an idealized image of the fertile valley and sustained this vision of rural peace and simplicity for over one hundred years. Only in popular art—the many lithographs, illustrations, and especially town views—did discrepancies between the Arcadian dream and the conflicts and tensions of reality begin to surface.

NOTES

1. Timothy Dwight, *Travels in New-England and New-York* (London, 1823), 1:201, 315, 318.
2. Dwight, *Travels*, 1:201.
3. Dwight, *Travels*, 2:315–317.

4. Dwight, *Travels*, 2:319; William C. Bryant, ed., *Picturesque America*, 2 vols. (New York, 1874), 2:61; *History of the Connecticut Valley in Massachusetts* (Philadelphia, 1879), 1:14.

5. Dwight, *Travels*, 2:314.

6. Dwight, *Travels*, 2:314.

7. Thomas Cole, "Essay on American Scenery," *American Monthly Magazine*, n.s. 1 (January 1836): 1–12, as cited in John W. McCoubrey, *American Art, 1700–1960* (Englewood Cliffs, NJ, 1965), 106.

8. For a discussion of the importance of the settled landscape see Roger Stein, *Susquehanna: Images of the Settled Landscape*, Roberson Center for the Arts and Sciences (Binghamton, NY, 1981), 12–14.

9. *Thomas Cole 1801–1848, One Hundred Years Later*, Wadsworth Atheneum (Hartford, 1949), no. 72.

10. Richard Saunders, *Daniel Wadsworth, Patron of the Arts*, Wadsworth Atheneum (Hartford, 1981), 29.

11. Thomas Cole Papers, New York State Library, Albany, Box 2, folder 1, Letters to Cole, 1821–1829, as cited in Saunders, *Daniel Wadsworth*, 27.

12. Cole, "Essay on American Scenery," as cited in McCoubrey, *American Art*, 106.

13. Sketchbook no. 8, Detroit Institute of Arts, 66–67. The book is inscribed, "Naples, May 17, 1832," and contains Italian and American scenery. Among the American subjects is a view (87) inscribed, "Sunset after a Showery Day, Catskill, June 14, 1833."

14. Letter to Luman Reed, March 2, 1836, Thomas Cole Papers, New York State Library, Albany, microfilm, Archives of American Art, reel ALC 1.

15. Howard S. Merrit, *Thomas Cole*, Memorial Art Gallery of the University of Rochester (Rochester, NY, 1969), 30.

16. Letter to Luman Reed, March 2, 1836.

17. Matthew Baigell and Allen Kaufman ("Thomas Cole's 'The Oxbow': A Critique of American Civilization," *Arts Magazine* 55 [January 1981]: 136–139) argue that Cole no longer believed in the harmony of man and nature he presented in the Oxbow. They also detect the Hebrew words "Shaddai" and "Noah" written upside down on the large hill on the horizon.

18. Bartlett made Hockanum into a small town, which it was not, by adding buildings. In later copies after Bartlett, Hockanum grew even larger in size.

19. Nathaniel P. Willis, *American Scenery*, Imprint Society (Barre, MA, 1971), 14.

20. Lisa F. Andrus, "Design and Measurement in Luminist Art," in John Wilmerding, ed., with Lisa F. Andrus, *American Light: The Luminist Movement, 1850–1875*, National Gallery of Art (Washington, DC, 1980), 32, 35.

21. It is through the research of Betsy Jones, Associate Director, Smith College Museum of Art, that Farrer's activity in this region became known. She also informed me of John W. Hill's presence in the area.

22. *Northampton Gazette*, September 26, 1865; *Northampton Free Press*, October 13, 1865.

23. Bryant, *Picturesque America*, 2:74–87.

24. In addition to those mentioned, other artists who showed Connecticut Valley landscapes in the 1860s and 1870s include William Hart (*On the Connecticut*),

Horace W. Robbins (*On the Connecticut*), William Louis Sonntag (*View on the Connecticut, Near Lancaster, N. H.*, and *A View Near Amherst, Mass.*), S. A. Noble (*View on Connecticut River*), Frank S. Shapleigh (*Mt. Ascutney*), John Williamson (*On the Connecticut, Afternoon* and *A Passing Shower, Valley of the Connecticut*), E. L. Custer (*View on the River*), Nelson Moore (*Sunset on the Agawam*), J. C. Wiggins (*Summer in the Northampton Meadows*), Joseph Ropes (*Valley of the Connecticut, New Hampshire*), Richard Hubbard (*Along the Connecticut* and *Mt. Lafayette from Newbury, Vt.*), and Aaron D. Shattuck (Scenes in Simsbury, Granby, and Avon, CT). See Clark S. Marlor, *A History of the Brooklyn Art Association with an Index of Exhibitions* (New York, 1970); and Maria Naylor, *National Academy of Design Exhibition Record, 1860–1900*, 2 vols. (New York, 1967).

25. The presence of Alvan Fisher, Thomas Cole, Thomas Doughty, Robert Havell, and Frederic Church in Hartford during this period has already been documented; in addition, George Loring Brown, better known for his Italian landscapes, exhibited a *View Near Hartford* at the National Academy of Design in 1837, and Edwin Whitefield, an English topographical artist like Havell, included a *View of Hartford, Ct.*, 1849, among the major cities he lithographed.

11

The Look of Paradise

The Built Landscape of Nineteenth-Century Northampton

ALMOST no visual images of seventeenth- and eighteenth-century Northampton exist, except for hand-drawn maps with little detail. From these, we do know that present-day streets follow, essentially, the same paths that were laid out in the original settlement. We begin to have a glimpse of Northampton in the early nineteenth century, when, nestled among the elms, could be seen the Greek Revival and Classical style public buildings and private homes so characteristic of the proud young Republic. At the center of town was the Warner House—an inn and coffeehouse at the midpoint of the Boston and Albany stage route. With the blast of a trumpet, the stage would announce its arrival, then all would be bustle until a cloud of dust as it departed signaled a return to tranquility. It was here that grateful citizens received the Marquis de Lafayette.

The 1840s was a decade of profound change, bringing the railroad and the telegraph. By the eve of the Civil War, the peaceful village was still serene, but its commercial center had connections to a wider world. Following the war, Northampton became a manufacturing town. Its center became a business district, with offices for the new professionals who serviced the financial and legal needs of manufacturers, and with shops that catered to the growing ranks of wage earners who worked in the mills.

Chronicling these transformations were artists, illustrators, and, later, photographers who captured fleeting glimpses of a landscape now lost.

Northampton, Massachusetts. W. H. Bartlett. Engraving, c. 1837–1838, 5 ¾ in. x 8 in. Published in Nathaniel P. Willis, *American Scenery* (London: George Virtue, 1840). *Historic Northampton.*

William Henry Bartlett's idyllic view of Northampton was very popular and widely reproduced. From the porch of Warner's Coffeehouse and Tavern, the view of Main Street framed by Isaac Damon's 1812 church and Merchants Row testifies to the town's prosperity.

This 1839 woodcut (above) from Barber's *Massachusetts Historical Collections* depicts Main Street from the direction opposite to Bartlett's view. The 1864 composite photograph (below) shows the street largely unchanged. The three buildings depicted (from left, Old Church, 1812; Courthouse, 1813; City Hall, 1814) were built by Isaac Damon, a student of Asher Benjamin. *Historic Northampton.*

Eastern View of Round Hill, Northampton. John Warner Barber (1798–1885). Wood engraving. From John Warner Barber, *Massachusetts Historical Collections, Being a General Collection of Interesting Facts, Traditions, Biographical Sketches, Anecdotes, &c., Relating to the History and Antiquities of Every Town in Massachusetts* (Worcester, 1839). *Historic Northampton.*

A number of elegant residences were built on Round Hill starting in 1806 with a brick house erected by Thomas Shepard (1778–1846), seen here at the center of the hilltop. The next house was built by his brother Levi Shepard, and the third by a cousin who later sold the house to another of the brothers, Charles. The Shepard brothers were sons of Levi Shepard, a prominent and affluent Northampton merchant. Thomas, a merchant and landowner, was involved in several business ventures with his brothers, but is reported to have lost his entire estate when he contracted to build the northern end of the Farmington Canal stretching eighty-two miles from New Haven to Northampton, which proved to be a financial disaster.

(*Facing page*) *Residence of Joseph Bowers, Northampton, Massachusetts, 1830.* Alexander J. Davis (1803–1892). Engraved and printed by Fenner, Sears & Company. *Historic Northampton.*

The Bowers House, overlooking Northampton on Round Hill, was a landmark example of Greek Revival architecture, the popular style in America from 1820 to 1850. Inspired by classical Greek buildings, designs like this temple-front mansion with its two-story columned porch, were spread by carpenter's guides, pattern books, and meticulously drawn house views like the one seen here. The Bowers House, built in 1826, was designed by the distinguished architect Ithiel Town of New Haven and New York, who was instrumental in popularizing the style. In 1829, Town had taken as his partner the young "architectural composer" A. J. Davis, who became famous for his accurate delineations of buildings. Town & Davis became a very fashionable firm, and their designs were sought by many important and distinguished citizens. The Bowers House is also visible in the far right of Barber's *Eastern View of Round Hill, Northampton.*

View of the Town Hall, Northampton, Massachusetts. Wood engraving, 1854. From *Gleason's Pictorial Drawing Room Companion. Historic Northampton.*

By mid-century, the simple elegance of Northampton's buildings began to give way to the tastes and fashions of a new era of commercialism. William Fenno Pratt, who designed many of the Victorian buildings on Northampton's Main Street, conceived of the City Hall as a novelty. Completed in 1850, it combines elements of the then "new" revival styles of Gothic, Tudor, and the trademark Norman towers replete with arrow slits. Its appearance jarred many residents who were used to public buildings designed with restraint. One of its most powerful detractors dubbed it a building with "flip-flops and flap-doodles."

Round Hill Water-Cure Hotel. Wood engraving. From H. Halsted, Round Hill Water-Cure Hotel and Motorpathic Institute at Northampton, Mass., promotional pamphlet, c. 1860. *Historic Northampton.*

The urban pressures of an industrializing America made Northampton an ideal location for spas that promised tranquility and health. The Round Hill Hotel was built on the site of George Bancroft's Round Hill School. In the years before the Civil War it also drew southern families accompanied by their slaves, producing deep divisions between the town's commercial sector and abolitionist groups.

VIEW OF THE INSANE ASYLUM, NOW BUILDING AT NORTHAMPTON, MASSACHUSETTS.

View of the Insane Asylum at Northampton, Massachusetts. Wood engraving. Ballou's Pictorial Drawing-Room Companion, 1858. *Historic Northampton.*

Dorothea Dix's movement for mental health reform led to the establishment of the Northampton State Hospital in 1858. Institutions like this were designed to create an orderly environment that would shape the behavior of the mentally ill through a predictable daily regimen. The sites for these sprawling structures were often bucolic rural settings like Northampton, where serenity and natural beauty would counteract the unsettling effects of urban life. Like the penitentiary, the asylum was designed to restore the individual to productive life. Only later did that mission succumb to a less sanguine view of human nature.

"Shop Row" on Main Street, Northampton, about the time of the Civil War. Jenny Lind shopped at Mrs. R. B. Dickinson's millinery shop, at far right. A tailor, a dry goods store, a jeweler and watchmaker, and the largest book and publishing house in western Massachusetts made Northampton a regional emporium that catered to the tastes of a growing middle class. *Historic Northampton.*

The Old Church. Charles C. Burleigh, Jr. Lithograph, 6 ½ in. x 10 ¾ in. *Historic Northampton.*

Charles C. Burleigh, Jr., a promising Northampton artist, sketched this view of Isaac Damon's Federalist era church shortly before it was destroyed by fire in 1876. The old Warner House, a rambling inn from the stagecoach era, had been replaced by the Draper Hotel, at left, to accommodate the steady stream of travelers who arrived on the railroad. The four-story brick structure loomed impressively over the more modest buildings lining Main Street.

Untitled. Charles C. Burleigh, Jr. Sepia wash, 6 in. x 10 in. *Historic Northampton, Burleigh Collection.*

Founded in 1871, Smith College erected its first building on a hill overlooking the town below. In this carefully composed study, Charles Burleigh noted the contrast between the imposing gothic structure and the colonial-era farmstead in the foreground.

Untitled. Charles C. Burleigh, Jr. Sepia wash, 3 in. x 4 ½ in. *Historic Northampton, Burleigh Collection.*

Another Burleigh sketch depicts the site of the Northampton–New Haven Canal. Begun in 1822 and completed in 1835, the project was ill fated from the start. Although the canal was in service until 1847, it could not compete with the technological revolution of the railroad, which came to Northampton in 1845. The canal ran along what is now State Street. This 1870s view looks toward Main Street. The church at center, now vanished, is on the site of the Edwards church, a splinter congregation from the founding church at the center of town.

By 1885, when this photograph was taken, only the 1813 courthouse remained of Isaac Damon's white-clad, leafy village. Northampton had become the brick-and-mortar Victorian town that we recognize today. *Historic Northampton.*

12

THE romantic American scenery around Northampton inspired writers like Washington Irving, William Cullen Bryant, and James Fenimore Cooper, furnishing settings for their poems and novels. "All the broad meadows . . . through which the Connecticut winds," wrote Ralph Waldo Emerson, "make a beautiful picture seldom rivaled." It was in Northampton that a young Henry James first began to take himself seriously as a writer. Living there made a lasting mark on his work, as it has for many others who began to find their voices in this place.

Jill Hodnicki takes us on a journey through American literature showing that it was not just the beauty of the landscape that inspired nineteenth-century writers but also the experiences of those whose lives were bounded by it.

The Literary Landscape: A Delightful Excursion*

JILL A. HODNICKI

"I HAVE had a most delightful excursion," wrote Washington Irving in a letter of August 1, 1832, "along the enchanting Valley of the Connecticut—of which I dare not speak at present—for it is just now the topic which I am a little mad upon. It is a perfect stream for a poet."[1] Although not the spectacular scenery of Irving's native New York, the Connecticut Valley offered delightful views of low rolling hills and broad, fertile flood plains through which the placid river pursued its winding course. The fertility of the meadowlands was the dominant image of the valley from the beginning, when American travelers first recorded their impressions of the region in private and published journals in the late eighteenth century. To the artist, novelist, poet, or traveler, the Connecticut River Valley was the embodiment of the pastoral landscape.

Before 1850

The most important early description of the valley was set down by Timothy Dwight in his travel journals of 1796 and 1797 (which were revised in 1810 and published in 1821). Dwight, who was at that time president of Yale College, devoted his vacations to a regular course of traveling with the aim of

* From Martha J. Hoppin, ed., *Arcadian Vales: Views of the Connecticut River Valley* (Springfield, MA, 1981), 11–24.

recording for posterity the appearance of the countryside in his time. In letters written during his two journeys along the banks of the Connecticut from source to mouth, Dwight did more than relate his observations of the landscape. His *Travels in New-England and New-York* (New Haven, 1821) established a tradition for the description of the valley.

Dwight summarized contemporary thought by referring to the valley as a garden. For Dwight, as for the many travelers who made this same journey through the nineteenth century, the most inviting section along the whole of the river's course was the region between Springfield and Hadley. There the vast expanse of meadowlands, with river, forests, and surrounding hills was most like a garden. Dwight twice remarked in his *Travels* that in this region the "extended margin of beautiful intervals" was formed like "terraced gardens."

Earlier appraisals of the valley had already focused on the valuable farmland. In one of the first published evaluations, *Summary, Historical and Political of the . . . Present State of the British Settlements in North America* (Boston, 1749), William Douglas wrote that the lower valley was good country valuable for grain and pasture. The first traveler to describe the prospect from Mount Holyoke, the Reverend Paul Coffin of Maine, actually compared the cultivated land to a garden. On July 29, 1760, Coffin wrote in his journal, "The View here far exceeds all I ever had before. Hundreds of Acres of Wheat, Rye, Peas, Flax, Oats, Corn, &c., look like a beautiful garden, variously yet elegantly laid out."

Those who would be concerned with the formation of a new political system in the former colonies saw the lands along the Connecticut as a valuable asset. During a tour of his native New England on June 8, 1771, John Adams rode along the river from Hartford to Wethersfield and noted in his journal that he wished the Connecticut River flowed through Braintree, since "Nothing can exceed the Beauty, and Fertility of the Country."[2] When President George Washington passed through the same area in October 1789, on his way to examine the Continental stores at Springfield, he noted in his diary, "Country hereabouts is beautiful and the Lands good."[3] Other early visitors also recognized the potential of the rich meadowlands and compared the Connecticut to great foreign rivers. An Englishman, Henry Wansey, remarked in his journal of 1794 that the Connecticut was a "charming river, winding, like the Thames, through a very fruitful valley."[4] In the 1804 edition of the *American Gazetteer*, the geographer Jedediah Morse compared the Connecticut to the Nile, since it fertilized the land through which it ran.[5]

Another important account was *Remarks Made on a Short Tour Between Hartford and Quebec in the Autumn of 1819* (New Haven, 1820), by Benjamin Silliman, the only other traveler besides Dwight whose journals of this route were published in the early decades of the century. Silliman was enchanted by the valley above Hartford and dedicated an entire chapter to praise of "this lovely scene, which appears a perfect garden." On the other hand, Silliman only mentioned the bold scenery of Mounts Holyoke and Tom, noting that they "have often been described, and can hardly be exaggerated." By 1825, Theodore Dwight, who was Timothy's nephew, reported in his *Northern Traveller* (New York, 1825) that the fertility of the meadows along the Connecticut River was almost proverbial.

The image of the garden dignified a harmonious landscape characterized by peace and prosperity. For many, all of America represented a garden, and in the introduction to *American Scenery* (London, 1840), Nathaniel Parker Willis contended that in comparison to the old countries of Europe, "the vegitation is so wonderously lavish, the outlines and minor features struck out with so bold a freshness and the lakes and rivers so even in their fulness [*sic*] and flow, yet so vast and powerful, that he may well imagine it an Eden newly sprung from the ocean." The Connecticut River Valley, as much as any other region, represented a place where Paradise could be regained.[6]

With the garden image, Dwight also established in his description of the meadowlands around Mount Holyoke the use of the word *beautiful* as a specific, yet all-encompassing description of the whole valley. Dwight's use of the term *beautiful* reflects late-eighteenth-century aesthetic theory which categorized the experience of nature as beautiful, sublime, or picturesque. In reflecting on scenes in the English landscape, theorists like Edmund Burke and William Gilpin discovered natural elements that had positive effects on the mind. Depending on the different aspects of the landscape, nature revealed either its benevolence or its complete indifference to human destiny. Like the paintings of Salvator Rosa, the wilderness suggested the sublime indifference of nature as an environment where man had no dominion. Like the paintings of Claude Lorraine, meadows and orchards suggested the beautiful benevolence of nature as an ideal environment where man was promised peace and prosperity.

While the term *beautiful* described the pastoral landscape of meadows and rolling hills, interspersed with forests, orchards, and cultivated land, and touched with church spires that marked the locations of towns, the Connecticut River as a whole was also frequently mentioned as affording scenes which were picturesque—a term largely used to describe the variety of rocky and wooded banks mingling with patches of cultivated ground. Trees along its course, especially the grand old elms that flourished on its shores, were also considered picturesque. However, the prospect from Mount Holyoke overlooking the valley was referred to in literature exclusively as beautiful.

Timothy Dwight perceived the Connecticut River Valley around Northampton as beautiful because the scene retained nature in an unaltered state and still revealed the work of man. It was this contrast of nature and man that

Dwight remarked on when he emerged from what he called an "almost absolute wilderness" below Springfield to a "very romantic prospect" of "Long Meadow" and the river, and again further up the river at South Hadley, where the falls and canal lay physically and ideally in apposition. "A cataract," contended Dwight, was naturally beautiful and was "of course a romantic and delightful object, particularly in a great river. This spot is uncommonly interesting and beautiful." The man-made canal removed the inconvenience of getting around the falls, where the water was thrown "into all the fine forms of fantastical beauty, excessive force, and wild majesty." Later in his journey Dwight was to note these contrasts in his view of the valley from the summit of Mount Holyoke.

Ascending a prominence to get a better look at things was always a natural inclination. When Timothy Dwight's nephew Theodore described a climb to the summit of Mount Holyoke in his *Sketches of the Scenery and Manners in the United States* (New York, 1829), he noted that the eminence "presents to the traveller an advantage which it is natural for him to desire: an opportunity to view from an elevated position the most charming scene in the compass of his tour," for "fine as the region is, without this eminence half its beauty would have been lost." The significance of the prospect view—the panorama of land seen from an eminence—in the nineteenth century was that it gave man not only a vantage point, but a vision as well. In art and literature, the prospect view was a device used to convey the vastness of space and nature, and a symbol of the relative insignificance of man in the landscape. The works of nature (sky, mountains, trees, and river) in such a vast space were large and looming, and the works of man (habitations and cultivated fields) were superficial. The subject of the prospect view, therefore, was not only the physical locations, but an intellectual theme which included ideas about man in space and time.[7]

Certainly, what Timothy Dwight associated with the view from the summit of Mount Holyoke was the transcendence of the creator as revealed by a scene of highest perfection. "When the eye traces this majestic stream," remarked Dwight, "meandering with a singular course through these delightful fields . . . when it explores the lofty forests, wildly contrasted with the rich scene of cultivation . . . it will be difficult not to say, that with these exquisite varieties of beauty and grandeur the relish for landscape is filled; neither a wish for higher perfection, nor an idea of what it is, remaining in the mind." This perfection, though, was revealed by the juxtaposition of lofty forest wilderness and rich cultivation, both aspects of the beautiful in nature.

Another kind of contrast was afforded by the tragic history of the valley which now seemed so peaceful. While discussing the variety in the landscape around Mount Holyoke, Timothy Dwight observed that a small hamlet at its base, called "Hoccanum" had been destroyed by the savages. Few writers after Dwight failed to mention that early valley settlements were plagued by Indian attacks. These accounts provided not only historical associations but a striking contrast to the scene of pastoral calm. In his chapter "Connecticut Valley, from Mount Holyoke" for *American Scenery* (1840), Nathaniel Parker Willis noted, for example, that the broad open lands along the river "contain some of the most sunny and fertile pictures of cultivation to be found in our continent," but that the history of these towns "presents some of the bloodiest traits marked on the early settlements of New England." Recalling especially the Indian massacres at Bloody Brook and Deerfield a century before, John Eden in his *Mount Holyoke Hand-Book* of 1851 looked down on a landscape that now reflected the "most perfect rural peace and happiness that can be imagined."

Timothy Dwight was not the first and certainly not the last to recognize the unique beauty of the prospect from Mount Holyoke, although few described the scene with such eloquence. In the following decades, Dwight's observations were repeated again and again as writers, artists, poets, philosophers, and travelers climbed the eminence to observe the surrounding country, for no other view in America more closely resembled a perfect description of the beautiful prospect.

Dwight's *Travels* greatly influenced the production of literary works about the valley. His descriptions encouraged acquaintances and readers to journey along the Connecticut and later became the source for other writers who echoed Dwight's ideas and phrases in their descriptions. Theodore Dwight studied with his uncle at Yale until 1814 and after a European trip became editor and author of a series of travel books. Among these works were the *Northern Traveller*, which was successfully published through a sixth edition in 1841, the *Sketches of Scenery and Manners in the United States* (New York, 1829), and *Things As They Are, or Notes of a Tour Through Some of the Middle and Northern States* (New York, 1834), all of which contained references not only to the Connecticut River but to Mount Holyoke as well.

While president at Yale, Dwight brought in his former student Benjamin Silliman to head a new department of chemistry. Although known primarily for his geological surveys, Silliman also wrote *Remarks Made on Short Tour Between Hartford and Quebec in the Autumn of 1819*, in which he described his journey through the Connecticut Valley. Benjamin Silliman's brother, Augustus Ely Silliman, published his own travel book, *The Gallop Among American Scenery* (New York, 1843), in which he gave a lengthy description of the valley and a climb to the summit of Mount Holyoke. As a professor of chemistry and geology, Benjamin Silliman influenced a generation of scientists, including Edward Hitchcock, who later became the first professor of chemistry and natural history at Amherst College and its third president. As state geologist for Massachusetts, Hitchcock wrote extensively on the formation of the valley in his *Report on the Geology, Minerology, Botany and Zoology of Massachusetts* (Amherst, 1833) and on its sceneographical importance in his *Sketch of the Scenery of Massachusetts* (Northampton, 1842). Benjamin Silliman was also a congenial host and welcomed a number of English travelers into his home, including Captain Basil Hall.[8]

Tours of the Valley

In the early nineteenth century, at the time that visitors started touring the Connecticut River Valley, the upper regions beyond Hartford were removed from the main travel routes. Transportation on the river was by sloop until about 1810, when steamboats opened the lower course to Springfield and provided a quicker and more dependable means. Early travelers beyond Springfield frequently went on walking tours, but for the first three decades of the nineteenth century the most popular means of travel was by stagecoach. Regular coach routes were in operation through the valley, connecting larger towns with centers on the eastern seaboard. One of the more popular stops was Northampton, which not only was situated among beautiful meadowlands, but was also near Mount Holyoke.

In order to accommodate the numbers of visitors to Mount Holyoke, the residents of Northampton cut through a carriage road and path to its summit and in 1821 constructed a simple house where visitors could find shelter and refreshments. The site increased in popularity, hosting hundreds of visitors each year. In 1832, the Englishman Thomas Coke wrote in his *Subaltern's Furlough: Descriptive of Scenes in the Various Parts of the United States* (New York, 1832) that Mount Holyoke was a favorite resort for travelers and "parties of pleasure." While resting at Northampton, which he considered "the most delightful and enviable place" he had ever seen, Coke set out to climb Mount Holyoke and encountered seven carriages filled primarily with ladies who had arrived for an outing there.

In 1851, the original house was replaced by a small hotel with a dining room and six sleeping apartments, which allowed visitors a place to stay to observe the setting and rising of the sun. This hotel was surmounted by an observatory equipped with a telescope. By 1854, an inclined railway was constructed from the carriage road to the Prospect House, allowing visitors the choice of walking or riding up and down. The total number of visitors during a single year in the peak decades of the 1830s and 1850s was about 3,000, and between the building of the railway in 1854 and its remodeling in 1866, there were 125,000 passengers.[9]

During the first half of the nineteenth century a number of English visitors made tours of the former colonies to see the cities and enjoy the natural beauty of the landscape. Although these visitors were mostly interested in economic, political, and social conditions, they also left important descriptions of the scenery. Since America was a popular topic in England, many of those who came in the early decades soon published their journals. During the height of English travel in America, between 1830 and 1840, twenty-five accounts appeared in five years—all of them enthusiastically received in England.[10] The accounts met with much less enthusiasm in the United States, since the foreigners' views were usually quite narrow-minded and critical. However, the reception was still good, perhaps because the observations of the scenery may have prompted Americans to look more closely at their own surroundings.

The route which these Englishmen followed began at the major ports of Boston or New York and covered all of the sights required for a proper "Grand Tour" of America. Because of limited transportation facilities, few travelers strayed from the main routes, which brought them through major centers. New England was always at the beginning of the tour, since it was the longest settled region, and consequently had more and better roads than any other part of the country. The shortest route consisted of a circular loop around the northeast states and included stops in Boston, New York, Niagara Falls, and Washington. A longer tour also included the Ohio Valley and the Great Lakes, while the longest included a trip down the eastern seaboard to New Orleans and up the Mississippi, which was then considered the absolute limit of civilization. For any visitor with the perseverance, it was possible to make side trips, but it seems that most were content with the beaten paths.[11]

The main route in the Northeast generally ran straight from Boston to New York by way of Springfield, Hartford, and New Haven, which gave the traveler an opportunity to view the Connecticut River Valley. At New York, then, the visitor would board a sloop and ascend the Hudson River to Lake George, followed by a trip to see Niagara Falls. From Niagara, the visitor could return to New York City or continue on to Montreal and then down through the Connecticut River Valley to Springfield. Although at first quite unusual, this last route became more popular as the years went by and transportation facilities improved. In the 1830s the railroad was laid in sections between Boston and New York along the stagecoach routes, and in December 1845, the Connecticut Valley Railroad made Springfield the crossroads of New England.

Several Englishmen on the Grand Tour took a side trip along the Connecticut River to Northampton and beyond to the White Mountains and Canada. Like the earlier American visitors, they noticed the contrast of rural villages and cultivated land with the natural beauty of the river and its meadows. Charles Joseph Latrobe wrote in the *Rambler in North America: 1832–1833* (London, 1833) that the valley of the Connecticut River was one of the loveliest he had ever beheld. "Many are the beauties with which nature has decked the verdant, fertile, and park-like shores of that pastoral stream in its lower course. . . . The whole style of scenery about Springfield and Northampton is lovely in the extreme." Although the great majority of travelers saw New England in warmer weather, Captain Thomas Hamilton gave a rare winter view of Springfield. Hamilton wrote in *Men and Manners in America* (London, 1833) that the morning after his arrival there in December 1831, he took a ramble in the village "which is by far the gayest I had yet seen in the course of my tour" but which he found too new for a landscape painter. The freshness and regularity of the houses needed time, he noted, in order to diminish the "unpleasant contrast which is here so obtrusively apparent between the works of man and those of nature." On July 25, 1832, Edward Thomas Coke packed his pencils and sketch-pad and climbed Mount Holyoke. He reported in his travel log, *A Subaltern's Furlough*, that he was so awestruck by the panorama formed by the fantastic winding river, and the high and rocky mountains contrasted with the smiling valleys, that he could not even presume to take his pencil from his pocket. Later, while standing at the top of Mount Washington, Coke noted the extensive view but added, "It did not, I must confess, altogether answer my expectations, nor, to my taste was it equal to that from Mount Holyoke, where all was richness and life."

The most important Englishman to make a Grand Tour of America at this time was Captain Basil Hall, a retired officer of the Royal Navy famous for his travel books. In April 1827, Hall sailed from Liverpool with his wife, child, and servants, and arrived at New York after a four-week voyage ready to see things with his own eyes, "in order to ascertain by personal inspection, how far the sentiments prevalent in England with respect to that country were correct or otherwise." Hall's personal narrative of his tour, *Travels in North America in the Years 1827 to 1828* (London, 1829) was published the following year in three volumes and was remarkably popular in England and America.[12] Although primarily noted for their social commentary, Hall's volumes contained important descriptions of the landscape, especially the view from Mount Holyoke. Hall was greatly impressed by the beauty of the land which lay at his feet on the fourth of October, 1827, and wrote that the view "is really splendid and is otherwise most satisfactory for travellers, from bringing under their eyes a great extent of country."

The feature which Hall found particularly pleasing about the prospect was the degree of cultivation. He noted that since many of the hills and dales had been long cleared of woods, "the eye was not offended by that ragged appearance, so comfortless and hopeless-looking in most newly settled countries." The scenery prompted Hall not only to write but to draw as well, and a view from Mount Holyoke looking toward the Oxbow was published in a companion volume to his *Travels*. In *Forty Etchings from Sketches Made with the Camera Lucida in North America in 1827 and 1828* (London,

1829), this particular scene, which Hall described as one of the most beautiful in America, appeared on the same page with an etching of the Erie Canal. Like Timothy Dwight, who had compared the canal with the cataract at South Hadley Falls, Hall sought to reveal the beauty of the river scenery by contrasting "a scene entirely artificial and one where nature is left to her own course."

The view and the settled landscape no less impressed Hall's wife, Margaret Hunter Hall, whose letters were finally published in 1931 under the title *The Aristocratic Journey*. "I am looking down upon one of the most beautiful prospects I ever saw," wrote Mrs. Hall to her sister. "The country at our feet is rich. . . . In the Northampton plains, or meadows I believe they call them, there are not ugly, wooden fences dividing the fields, and very picturesque trees are scattered over them, at the same time there is not a stump nor a girdled tree to be seen." In fact, she noted that the country "has the appearance of having been much longer settled than any part of the State of New York that we have seen."

The towns along the valley of the Connecticut also impressed the Halls, because their domesticated appearance was so familiar to inhabitants of the English countryside. The day before their ascent of Mount Holyoke, the Halls left Stockbridge and proceeded across the countryside to Northampton, "another of those beautiful New England villages, which is impossible to over-praise." Hall was not much impressed with his tour of New York State, as the greater part of the country "always, of course, excepting the beautiful Lake George, and delightful Hudson—consisted either of ploughed fields, or impenetrable forests, or it was spotted over with new villages, as raw and unpicturesque as if they had just stepped out of a saw-pit." On the other hand, the towns of Massachusetts "were embellished with ornamental trees and flower gardens." In the Northampton meadows, the Halls found that beautiful landscape and town which represented an ideal environment.

Those aspects of the Connecticut Valley landscape which most appealed to the Halls in 1827 inspired other Englishmen to travel there. One of the most fascinating accounts of travel through the Connecticut River Valley was written by English novelist Charles Dickens after a tour in 1842. *American Notes* (London and New York, 1842) included Dickens's journey from Boston to Springfield by rail and from there to Hartford by steamboat down the Connecticut River.[13] When he arrived in Springfield on February 6, Dickens found that the roads at that time of the year were so bad that the journey to Hartford would have taken ten or twelve hours. "Fortunately," he wrote, "the winter having been unusually mild, the Connecticut River was 'open,' or in other words, not frozen," so that he could take advantage of the first steamboat trip of the season. The voyage, which lasted less than three hours, was not without its hazards, and Dickens remarked that although the river was full of floating blocks of ice and it "rained all day as I once thought it never did rain anywhere, but in the Highlands of Scotland," he was able to enjoy the journey. "The Connecticut River," Dickens added, "is a fine stream; and the banks in summertime are, I have no doubt, beautiful." At Hartford on February 7, 1842, Dickens celebrated his thirtieth birthday and then spent four days in touring the city.

Basil Hall's *Travels* also inspired some Americans to travel to the Connecticut Valley in the next few years. In fact, the *Forty Etchings* from Basil Hall's *Travels* can be directly connected with the visit of the artist Thomas Cole. While in England between 1829 and 1831, Cole traced Hall's view from Mount Holyoke on a sheet of paper which he put in his sketchbook.[14] Although it is not certain when Cole first visited the site, he traveled along some parts of the Connecticut River Valley before his "Essay on American Scenery" was presented as a lecture in 1835. "In the Connecticut, behold a river that differs widely from the Hudson. . . . Whether we see it at Haverhill, Northampton, or Hartford," remarked Cole, "it still possesses that gentle aspect; and the imagination can scarcely conceive Arcadian vales more lovely or more peaceful than the valley of the Connecticut—its villages are rural places where trees over-spread every dwelling, and the fields upon its margin have the richest verdure."

Cole finally painted these Arcadian vales in 1836, and like Timothy Dwight and Basil Hall, he selected for his subject the Oxbow of the Connecticut as seen from Mount Holyoke. An ideal combination of the wild and domestic, the painting is divided diagonally so that the wilderness, represented by Mount Holyoke and a storm, is on the left, and the cultivated pastoral Connecticut Valley is on the right.[15]

This contrast of nature and man was not necessarily a painterly or literary device, since the elements were part of the actual landscape. In fact, Basil Hall and his company observed both the beauty of autumn and the sublimity of a storm during their excursion on Mount Holyoke. "The beauty of the prospect from the summit of this noble hill," wrote Hall in his *Travels*, "by completely arresting our attention, had rendered us careless about sundry threatening squalls of rain, which stalked slowly over the landscape, like enormous giants with their heads thrust into the clouds, and adding much to the grandeur of the scenery, both by their own majestic and half mysterious appearance, and by the long belts of shadow which trailed behind them for many a league." Storm clouds "took possession of the high ground, so as to shut us completely out from the wide world we had been admiring." Like the artists of their time, the Halls interpreted natural events in the aesthetic terms of the eighteenth century.

Literary Travelers

In the first half of the nineteenth century, many literary and political figures could be counted among the visitors to the valley and to Mount Holyoke, and a number of these left records of their visits in their personal writings. During a walking tour on August 29, 1823, Ralph Waldo Emerson climbed Mount Holyoke with two of his cousins. In his journal Emerson noted that "the prospect repays the ascent and although the day was hot and hazy so as to preclude a distant prospect, yet all the broad meadows in the immediate vicinity of the mountain through which the Connecticut winds make a beautiful picture seldom rivaled." In the summer of his junior year at Harvard, the future senator Charles Sumner set out with some companions on a walking tour to Lake Champlain. Sumner wrote in his journal for July 18, 1829, that they were determined to visit Mount Holyoke and set out upon an old path which made their climb quite hazardous. At the summit they spent considerable time looking at the surrounding country. "The prospect was most beautiful," wrote Sumner, "embracing a view of the Connecticut, winding its way through the most delightful fields, without a fence on the road or in the fields; but all presenting the appearance of one extensive field."

Washington Irving traveled through the valley in August 1832 on his return from an extended tour of Europe, and Nathaniel Hawthorne rode through the area on a night coach in 1838. Hawthorne found at dawn that they were driving through quite romantic country with a stream on one side and mountains all around. In July of the same year, Emerson returned and wrote to a friend that he had had a very good journey seeing the Connecticut River, "in its lovely intervales ridged in by guardian mountains a joyful, plenteous, tranquil picture."

Other American writers who visited the Connecticut Valley in these decades recorded their impressions in novels. James Fenimore Cooper used the Connecticut River Valley as the setting for his *Wept of Wish-ton-Wish* (New York and London, 1829). In a slightly earlier work, *Notions of the Americans* (London, 1828), Cooper appeared as an imagined foreign visitor writing to his friend in England about his travels. Like his novels, *Notions* was intended to explain the nation's history, manners, and customs, and to delineate the ideal of American scenery. In describing the ideal prospect, Cooper chose a pastoral, beautiful scene which in certain aspects is similar to descriptions of the view from Mount Holyoke: "Fancy yourself on some elevation that will command the view of the horizon that embraces a dozen miles. . . . The country within this boundary must be undulating, rising in bold swells . . . counterbalanced by broad and rich swales of land, that frequently spread out into lovely little vallies. . . . Here and there, a spire, or often two, may be seen pointing toward the skies from the centre of a cluster of roofs. Perhaps a line of blue mountains is to be traced in the distance, or the course of a river is to be followed by a long succession of fertile meadows. . . . In the midst of this picture must man be placed, quiet, orderly and industrious."

The Wept of Wish-ton-Wish, a novel of pioneer life, chronicles the transformation of a frontier settlement into a peaceful and tranquil valley town. *The Wept* opens on a setting of great natural beauty in the valley, where there is a proper distribution of land, water, woods, and man.[16] The settlement established by Captain Mark Heathcote and his Puritan followers is a "picture of prosperity and peace." From an eminence overlooking the valley, Heathcote describes the scene as the image of the pastoral landscape: "The fertile flats that extended on each of its banks for more than a mile had been early stripped of their burden of forest, and they now lay in placid meadows, or in fields from which the grain of the season had lately disappeared." Near the base of the hill, an orchard "put this smiling valley in such strong and pleasing contrast to the endless and nearly untenanted woods by which it was environed." In *The Wept of Wish-ton-Wish*, Cooper uses the valley to represent the pastoral landscape, and through the novel chronicles the change which civilization brought to the rural haven in the wilderness. As in the whole country, the valley and the dream of creating a rural haven in the wilderness were ruined by the avarice of its inhabitants.[17]

Throughout the nineteenth century, fictional literature set in popular locations that the general reading public would recognize was also intended to endow the American landscape with some historical associations. Between the first and last quarter of the century, the Connecticut River Valley provided the setting for several romantic novels which embroidered on local legend or created fictional characters to bring together the lives of various historical figures. In 1827, Catherine Marie Sedgewick published a remarkably popular romantic tale of historical and fictional characters on an excursion about the whole of New England and New York. In one chapter of *Hope Leslie, or Early Times in the Massachusetts* (New York, 1827), the heroine and a companion engage an Indian guide in Northampton to conduct them to the summit of a mountain, "which rises precipitously from the meadows and overlooks an ocean of forest," so that they might have an extensive view of the surrounding country. At the summit, Hope Leslie views the scene with an undeniably nineteenth-century reverence for nature. "We looked down upon a scene that made me clap my hands, and my pious companions raise their eyes in silent devotion." Hope's companion is none other than Elizur Holioke [*sic*] himself, and on the day of their visit, the summit is named in his honor by the heroine.

Another interesting work from the 1820s was *Mount Holyoke, or The Travels of Henry and Maria* (Amherst, 1828), published by J. S. and C. Adams and S. C. Carter for Sabbath School Libraries. For his tenth birthday Henry and his younger sister Maria are treated to an excursion to the summit of Mount

Holyoke, where the two young children reveal some extraordinarily mature ideas about their vision of the scene before them. After a long climb along the path, where the branches of trees seem to form a perfect arch over their heads, Henry and Maria arrive at the summit. Upon raising their eyes, both utter an exclamation of astonishment, for below them flows the beautiful and majestic Connecticut River. Echoing the observations of the Halls, who came the same year, Henry notes that the "extensive forms, in the cultivation of which farmers spent their toilsome lives, were but as the flower bed of a garden."

Guidebooks to the Connecticut Valley

In addition to journals, foreign accounts, and historical novels, guidebooks were an important category of literature about the valley. For the traveler on the Grand Tour, there were a number of guidebooks containing valuable information on routes, transportation, accommodations, and descriptions of the scenery. One of the earliest guides to the Northeast, *The Northern Traveller; Containing the Routes to Niagara, Quebec and the Springs* (New York, 1825), published anonymously by Theodore Dwight, advised the traveler in New England to take the route up the Connecticut—the most fertile, wealthy, and beautiful tract of the country. For the journey north from Hartford the traveler was informed that the whole valley was thickly populated, the accommodations generally very comfortable, the scenery ever new and varying, the places rich in history, and the coaches scheduled three times a week.

The most beautiful town along the route was Northampton, surrounded by charming country—one of the richest, most extensive, and beautiful plains on the river. Of the eight landscapes illustrated in the volume, one depicted the view of the Oxbow from Mount Holyoke. The ascent of this mountain, the author claimed, had lately become as fashionable as any similar enterprise in the country. The view north toward Hadley was also described for the visitor in terms similar to earlier accounts. "You look up the charming valley of the Connecticut, bordered by distant ranges of hills and mountains . . . covered with the richest coat of vegetation, and scattered with villages and innumerable farm houses . . . The whole peninsula is rich and fertile . . . and is the richest sight upon the river."

In 1829, Theodore Dwight published *Sketches of Scenery and Manners in the United States*, which contained an entire chapter on the Connecticut River. Of all the spots in the valley, Dwight chose the summit of Mount Holyoke as the ideal site for a general view of the river. "If there be any thing beautiful in the bank of the Connecticut, those beauties may well be descanted upon here; for in the vicinity are they presented in greater variety, and in a larger extent, than in any other part of its course; and if any eminence may claim particular attention for being extensively known and greatly admired, surely it must be the one on which we have taken our station." In delineating the "View from the Summit" toward Hadley, the only scene chosen for illustration, Dwight wrote that it would be a hopeless task for an artist to attempt "the representation of all the beauties which are here presented in one view to the eye."

The most celebrated of these publications was a travel book written by the American author Nathaniel Parker Willis, who was known for his books and columns on the scenic American routes, and illustrated by the British artist William Henry Bartlett. *American Scenery* (London, 1840), which supplanted all previous guides in popularity and attractiveness, was composed of descriptions and illustrations of the various popular views along the Grand Tour route and provided the readers with some legends or anecdotes.

Since the 119 engravings in *American Scenery* were intended to delineate the most fashionable scenes on the tour, the greater number were of the Hudson-Erie route and the Catskills, but the four illustrations of Northampton, Mount Tom, and the views from Mount Holyoke, along with the lavish praise of the scenery, attest to the popularity of the Connecticut River Valley. In his description of the prospect, Willis wrote that in its degree of cultivation and fertile beauty, the view from Mount Holyoke was probably the richest in America. "The view below presents a singular phase of the scenery of the river, which seems here to possess a soul for beauty, and loiters, enamored and unwilling to flow on, in the bosom of the meadow which has no parallel in New England for loveliness and fertility."

Poetry about the Valley

Some mention should be made of the poetry inspired by river and valley even though its development did not follow any chronology connected with the creation of novels, journals, or guidebooks. Although she never mentioned the Connecticut River Valley by name, Emily Dickinson drew on the landscape for her poetry. Many others also devoted verses to town and river from Vermont to Connecticut. Despite their varied origins and subjects, these poems paid tribute not only to the beauty of the setting, but also to the calm and peaceful appearance of the valley. Probably the earliest was an "Ode to Connecticut River" written by a Dartmouth alumnus who lived along the river, Josias Lyndon Arnold, and published in a collection of his verses in 1797. "On thy lov'd banks, sweet river, free/From worldly care and vanity,/I could my every hour confine,/And think true happiness was mine." Certainly the most notable poem was that written by the very young William Cullen Bryant in May 1808 and privately published in the second edition of *Embargo* in 1809. Written when the poet was thirteen, Bryant's "Ode to Connecticut River" was a celebration of the charms of the river and a plea for it to remain a place for peace to dwell. "On thy green banks let flowers

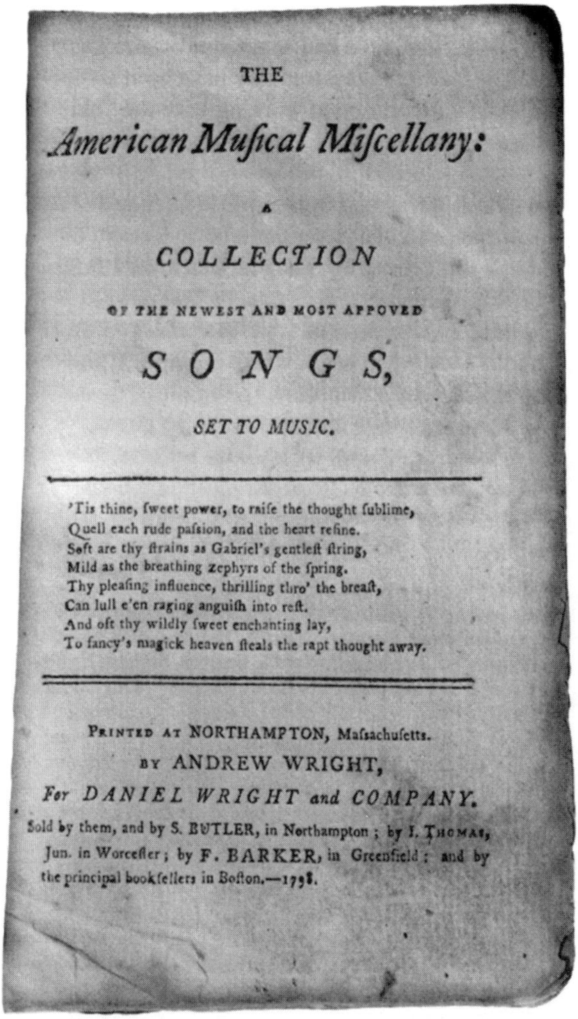

THE

American Muſical Miſcellany:

A

COLLECTION

OF THE NEWEST AND MOST APPROVED

SONGS,

SET TO MUSIC.

'Tis thine, ſweet power, to raiſe the thought ſublime,
Quell each rude paſsion, and the heart refine.
Soft are thy ſtrains as Gabriel's gentleſt ſtring,
Mild as the breathing zephyrs of the ſpring.
Thy pleaſing influence, thrilling thro' the breaſt,
Can lull e'en raging anguiſh into reſt.
And oft thy wildly ſweet enchanting lay,
To fancy's magick heaven ſteals the rapt thought away.

PRINTED AT NORTHAMPTON, Maſsachuſetts.
BY ANDREW WRIGHT,
For DANIEL WRIGHT and COMPANY.
Sold by them, and by S. BUTLER, in Northampton; by I. THOMAS, Jun. in Worceſter; by F. BARKER, in Greenfield; and by the principal bookſellers in Boſton.—1798.

The American Musical Miscellany: A Collection of the Newest and Most Approved Songs, Set to Music. Printed by Andrew Wright, for Daniel Wright and Company (Northampton, Massachusetts, 1798). Ink on paper. H: 6 ¾ in.; W: 4 7/16 in. *Historic Northampton.*

Although Northampton inspired visiting writers and poets, it was a publishing center in its own right by the late eighteenth century. Sermons and religious tracts dominated the early output, but one genre reflected growing secular tastes. Religious music was dominant in colonial America, but the secular song became increasingly important with the flowering of cultural life in the period after the Revolution. The songster, a pocket-sized book containing the words but usually not the music for well-known songs, was issued in growing numbers. In the 1790s, the popularity of theater songs, particularly those of the London stage, led to the publication on a wide scale of new popular songs in the sheet music format, which included both music and words. *The American Musical Miscellany* is unusual in having the characteristics of both the songster and sheet music. As its subtitle implies, it includes new popular songs as well as old favorites, all provided with music. *The American Musical Miscellany* is an important book. It is the first anthology of popular songs with music printed in the United States and contains many songs not preserved elsewhere. Moreover, it is an early and major example of American secular music printed from type.

perennial bloom,/And forests shade thee with a grateful gloom;/Bright towns descending flourish on thy shore,/And cultur'd gardens spread their balmy/shade."

In her *Illustrated Poems* of 1849, the prolific Hartford author Lydia Howard Huntly Sigourney included "Connecticut River," in which she celebrated the "Fair River, not unknown to classic song,/Which still in varying beauty roll'st along." The beauty of the valley was also remembered by visitors such as Henry Theodore Tuckerman, author of poetry, travel literature, biographies, essays, and critical publications on the arts, including the *Book of the Artists* and *America and Her Commentators*. Among the works collected in his *Poems* (Boston, 1851) was a verse to "Northampton." "Ere from thy calm seclusion parted,/O fairest village of the plain,/ The thoughts that here to life have started,/Draw me to Nature's heart again."

After 1850

The most notable study of the scenery along the Connecticut River published after mid-century appeared as an article in *Harper's New Monthly Magazine* in August 1856. Written and illustrated by T. Addison Richards, "The Valley of the Connecticut" was an illustrated chronicle of the walking tour which Richards made with some companions. He signed the Prospect House register on Thursday, July 7, 1853, directly above the name of his traveling companion, S. R. Gifford (presumably Sanford Robinson Gifford).[18] The text and illustrations of Richards's article reveal an enthusiastic response to the natural scenery of the valley. Northampton, wrote Richards, must be seen at loving leisure, for "it is the frontispiece of the book of beauty which nature opens in the Valley of the Connecticut, and one of the most winsome pictures in the volume." Of the extraordinary panorama from Mount Holyoke, he wrote that the Connecticut turned to the east and west "threading its silver tide through the tender verdure as capriciously as a vein in the neck of beauty."

In another article, which appeared in the *Atlantic Monthly* in August 1858, Oliver Wendell Holmes mentioned the Connecticut River in reference to the grand old elm trees that lined its banks. Holmes, who had a "most intense, passionate fondness for trees," wrote in the tenth article in the series *The Autocrat of the Breakfast Table* that one of these first-class elms was found in Springfield and another in the Northampton meadows. In describing their setting, Holmes offered a romantic vision of the course of the river "where it comes loitering down from its mountain fastnesses like a great lord, swallowing up the small proprietary rivulets very quietly as it goes, until it gets proud and swollen and wantons in huge luxurious oxbows about the fair Northampton meadows, and at last overflows the oldest inhabitant's memory in profligate freshets at Hartford and all along its lower shores."

In the same period, several historical novels by local authors were set in locations along the Connecticut River. In 1857 Josiah G. Holland, editor of the *Springfield Republican*, published his first fictional work, *Bay-Path; A Tale of New-England Colonial Life* (New York, 1857), which recounted the story of the first settlement at Springfield. In one incident of this tale of adventure and romance, William Pynchon's daughter Mary is given credit for naming the mountains to the north—Holyoke, for her fiancé Elizur Holyoke, and Tom, for her dog. As a resident of Springfield, Holland wrote several works about the valley. His early *Verses Read at the Hadley Centennial* on June 9, 1859, described the river as the "Heart of Hadley, slowly beating. . . ." After giving up his career in journalism, Holland went on in 1870 to found *Scribner's Magazine*, to which he contributed a number of poems. Among the poems collected for a separate publication in 1876 was the "Mountain Christening," which recounts the romantic tale of the naming of the mountains by Elizur Holyoke and Rowland Thomas. "Up the rough ledges they clambered amain,/Holyoke and Thomas on either hand,/Till high in mid-passage they paused, and then/They tearfully gazed on the lovely land."

After the Civil War Northampton served as the setting for two novels by important American authors. In the introductory paragraph of *Norwood; or Village Life in New England* (New York, 1867), noted minister and orator Henry Ward Beecher turned his readers' attention toward the town, which "looks over upon that transcendent valley from under its beautiful shade trees." Northampton was also the setting for the opening chapters of Henry James's first full-length novel. In *Roderick Hudson* (Boston, 1875), James, who had vacationed in Northampton some years before, used the town to symbolize representative features of life in a small American town.[19] Before they left for Europe, Roderick Hudson and his companion walked down to the river and, as they sat, "watched the shadows on Mount Holyoke, listened to the gurgle of the river, and sniffed the balsam of the pines." As he looked away at the "far-spreading view," it seemed "beautiful, and suddenly a strange feeling of prospective regret took possession of him. Something seemed to tell him that later, in a foreign land, he should remember it with longing and regret." *Roderick Hudson* was the last nineteenth-century novel by an important author set in the Connecticut River Valley, and after 1875 literary references to the valley were confined to guidebooks.

The greatest change in references to the Connecticut River Valley came with the railroad. By mid-century railroads provided transportation to travelers between the major cities and along the Grand Tour route. Travel became quicker, cheaper, more comfortable, and more available to a wider range of persons. Travelers endeavored to see as much as possible in as little time as could be arranged. Consequently, guidebooks designed for the railroad passenger provided a window-seat tour concentrating less on the scenery than on the sites. In 1849, tour books like J. Calvin Smith's *Illustrated Hand-book, A New Guide for Travellers Through the United States of America* (New York, 1849) published a complete list of timetables and fares for the railroad, stage, and steamboat routes. Springfield, one of the crossroads of New England by this time, was reported to have railroad connections with the Boston, Albany, and New York railroads, which arrived twice daily, and the Connecticut Valley Railroad (opened 1845), which arrived several times daily.

In September 1851, with the opening of the new Prospect House on its summit, John Eden published the *Mount Holyoke Hand-book and Tourist's Guide for Northampton and Vicinity* (Northampton, 1851). Eden's general survey of the country that could be seen from the summit was interspersed with quotations from poetical works. The prospect, he claimed, "presents to the vision of the beholder one uninterrupted and magnificent amphitheatre of landscape" where the "grand and beautiful are united." With the new observatory atop the summit house, Eden was able to describe the prospect as it extended in every direction. In addition to the new town of Holyoke, which was laying the foundations for an industrial site, Eden also described the appearance of another new object visible on the landscape, which stood in odd contrast to the scene of natural beauty. "Mount Holyoke commands also a view of the Connecticut River Rail Road for many miles," wrote Eden, "and it is a novel and interesting sight to witness the Iron Horse suddenly emerging from the Willimantic bridge; and pursuing its impetuous and resistless course along the picturesque bank of the stream and through the beautiful meadows below us." Certainly, there were some ambiguous feelings toward the appearance of the Iron Horse, for although it heralded a new era in travel, it also marked an irreversible path through the landscape.

For the next decade, the Iron Horse brought thousands of visitors along the Connecticut River. Scenery was still a very popular attraction, and books like *A Pictorial Description of the United States* (New York, 1852) by Robert Sears and *American Scenery Illustrated* (New York, 1854) by T. Addison Richards continued to praise the beauties of the landscapes and prospects. What distinguished these guidebooks from their predecessors was the wide use of illustrations. These publications, with pages of land and city scapes for the benefit of the armchair tourist, were in the tradition of the British illustrated guides like the Willis/Bartlett publication of 1840.

Illustrated tour books published after mid-century were popular, but they did not display the same quality of materials as before and were frequently reduced to copying either text or scenes from earlier works. Some books, like Thirsty McQuill's *The Connecticut by Daylight from New York to the White Mountains* (New York, 1874), and *Appleton's Illustrated Hand-book of American Travel* (New York, 1857), by T. Addison Richards, were directed toward railroad travelers. *Appleton's Hand-book* even offered an outline of "skeleton tours" for its readers. The itinerary for the tour of two weeks in the Valley of the Connecticut included the train ride from New York to Springfield, dinner and a visit to the Armory on Monday, on Tuesday the ride to Northampton, on Wednesday the visit to Mount Holyoke, on Thursday the ride to Greenfield and walk to the Poet's Seat, on Friday the journey to Brattleboro, etc. In the text, which was nothing more than a copy of Eden's *Hand-book*, Richards revealed that the valley was a popular tour because it was speedily and pleasantly accessible from every point, and because it could be traversed en route to most of the principal summer resorts. In addition to its beautiful scenery, Northampton offered the visitor distinguished water-cure establishments, admirable hotels, pleasant people, social enjoyments, and much-sought-after summer residences.

Burt's Illustrated Guide of the Connecticut Valley (Northampton, 1867) aimed to increase interest in what was described as New England's fairest and liveliest regions, and to assist the seeker after pleasure to obtain a more perfect knowledge of the grandeur and beauty of Connecticut Valley scenery. The book was designed for the railroad passenger, since the "extension of more rapid and comfortable modes of travel has opened the doors to the elysian fields, and thousands come with the recurring period of foliage and flowers to worship at the shrine of beauty found in the lofty mountains, broad meadows and a majestic view." A complete list of timetables and passenger fares was provided, as well as a description of every site on the railroad tour.

It was inevitable that the Valley of the Connecticut could not forever remain the beautiful garden of America. The railroad was the harbinger of change—a symbol of progress at the expense of the pastoral ideal. In 1851, John Eden had viewed the Iron Horse in the landscape with interest and consternation, but by 1855, Josiah Gilbert Holland recognized that the railroads would irrevocably intrude upon nature, and wrote in his *History of Western Massachusetts* (Springfield, 1855) that the reader who loved nature should visit the mountains. Regretfully, Holland added that "a few such places, however, are only left now in all Massachusetts, for the demands of railroads and iron furnaces and the growing prosperity of the commonwealth are, to the lover of nature, making sad havoc upon the wild forest trees, and, in one case at least, expect to assail the vitals of the everlasting hills themselves."

Although the railroads brought increasing numbers of visitors through the Connecticut River Valley, the convenience and location of the stations dictated the popularity of the resort areas. Since the Connecticut Valley Railroad was built across the river from Mount Holyoke, the summit house became isolated from the main course of travel. In 1854, soon after the new hotel was built at the summit, the proprietor, J. W. French, constructed an inclined railroad from the carriage road to facilitate the ascent. In order to convey passengers from the railway junction at Mount Tom, French purchased a side-wheel steamer which he ran twice daily for the convenience of guests beginning in 1866. Even after French was forced to discontinue transporting visitors by steamboat because of the log drives down the river, he was able to attract visitors, so that Mount Holyoke remained a favorite resort. In 1894 a new addition was added to the Prospect House. In that same decade a hotel was opened on Mount Tom, which also attracted a large number of visitors.[20]

The prospect of Mount Tom was deemed considerably more extensive than that from Mount Holyoke, but as Holland noted in his *History of Western Massachusetts*, it was "by no means so beautiful." The summit house at Mount Tom was destroyed by fire in 1901 and again in 1929, never to be rebuilt, but in the peak years, Mount Tom hosted hundreds of visitors. In the first decade of the twentieth century, Gerald Stanley Lee edited a magazine published in Northampton called *Mount Tom*, which was advertised as an all-outdoors magazine devoted to rest and worship. Lee's monthly column "The Look-Off" indicated that Mount Tom was considered more as a retreat and less as an eminence from which to get a view of civilization.

Part of the attraction of the prospect from Mount Holyoke had always been the combination of civilization and wilderness. As early as 1796, Timothy Dwight noted the contrast of the cataract and canal in South Hadley. For Dwight, the Connecticut River Valley was the embodiment of the beautiful, where man and nature exhibited a balanced and harmonious existence. For travelers, writers, poets, and artists throughout the nineteenth century, the Connecticut River Valley was the pastoral middle landscape which could only be described as beautiful. The railroad, first noted by John Eden in his *Mount Holyoke Hand-book* of 1851, appeared to be in permanent opposition to the natural aspects of the scenery in the valley. As a symbol of the advance of civilization, the railroad threatened the continued existence of the middle landscape and the beautiful. By 1855 Josiah Gilbert Holland recognized that growing prosperity and the railroad would irrevocably intrude upon the landscape and assail even the mountains. Fortunately, Mount Holyoke and Mount Tom were both preserved as state parks, but the Oxbow was crossed by an interstate highway. Although the prospect of the Connecticut River Valley now includes obtrusive reminders of progress, it still retains elements of the pastoral ideal, and its Arcadian vales are preserved in various literary and artistic works from the nineteenth century. In considering these works, perhaps it is again possible to contend, as Daniel Webster did in a speech of 1847, that "throughout the whole United States, I do not know of a richer or more beautiful valley, as a whole, than that of the Connecticut River."[21]

Less than a decade after his first tour book of the valley, Henry M. Burt published *Guide through the Connecticut Valley to the White Mountains and the River Saguenay* (Springfield, 1872), in which he still gave ample attention to Mounts Holyoke and Tom as favorite places of resort. Although he included four wood engravings of the prospect from Mount Holyoke, Burt explained that nothing could surpass the actual view, which "diversified by the different crops under cultivation, resembles a magnificent carpet, the beauty and richness of coloring transcending anything produced by art."

That same year, a more elaborate picture of the valley was published in the second volume of *Picturesque America* (New York, 1874), edited by William Cullen Bryant. The chapter "Valley of the Connecticut" contained 32 wood engravings by J. D. Woodward depicting scenes from Saybrook, Connecticut, to Barnet, Vermont, and including several views around Northampton. Along with the traditional views from Mount Holyoke was a single steel engraving depicting the prospect from Mount Tom looking north beyond the Oxbow to Hadley. Mount Tom, the author explained, although not as much visited as its twin across the river, was "well-worth climbing, and not disappointing the highly-raised anticipations of the tourist."

As the nineteenth century moved into its last few decades, many changes occurred in the Connecticut River Valley. Where towns along the lower course of the river in Connecticut and Massachusetts had first been outposts of civilization and then cultivated havens for visitors, the valley became the domain of factories and train stations. The meandering Connecticut was bridged and dammed, its waters harnessed for civilized pursuits. Only in its upper regions did the river retain aspects of the wilderness that once surrounded its whole length, so that tourists were drawn farther and farther north in order to obtain a view of the beautiful in nature.

In Henry M. Burt's 1874 guide through the valley to the resort areas of the White Mountains and Saguenay River there was still some space devoted to the fair Northampton meadows and the panorama from Mount Holyoke. By 1887, the *Connecticut River Guide Book of the Most Direct Route from New York to the White Mountains* (New York, 1887) could make no new contributions to the praise of years past. John W. Chadwick, writing on "Western Massachusetts" for *Harper's New Monthly Magazine* in November 1880, stated the situation most clearly when he wrote of his ascent of Mount Holyoke. At the summit overlooking the valley which had awed and inspired so many to such lavish praise, Chadwick did not even mention the prospect. Instead he looked north to the hills beyond, where he would vacation—to the Berkshires and the White Mountains.

NOTES

1. Washington Irving, *Letters,* ed. Ralph M. Aderman, Herbert L. Kleinfield, and Jennifer S. Banks (Boston, 1979), 712. Irving continued, "In short I recommend you, if ever you have the power, make the tour that I have done, and you will have made one of the most beautiful, for natural scenery, in the world."

The following sources provide some references to either authors or specific works: Katherine M. Abbott, *Old Paths and Legends of the New England Border* (New York, 1909), 194–216; Edwin M. Bacon, *The Connecticut River and the Valley of the Connecticut* (New York, 1907), 418–421; Edwin M. Bacon, *Literary Pilgrimages in New England* (Boston, 1902), 424–463; Frederick H. Hitchcock, ed., *The Handbook of Amherst, Massachusetts* (Amherst, 1891), 16–35; Clifton Johnson, ed., *Historic Hadley Quarter Millennial Souvenir, 1659–1909* (Northampton, 1909), 32–36; *Meadow City's Quarter Millennial Book: A Memorial of the Celebration of the Two-Hundredth and Fiftieth Anniversary of the Settlement of the Town of Northampton, Massachusetts* (Northampton, 1904).

2. L. H. Butterfield, ed., *Diary and Autobiography of John Adams* (Cambridge, 1961), 2:28–29. After his journey through Connecticut, Adams noted that he had "spent this Morning in Riding thro Paradise." In fact, Adams noted that the air was very clear and dry and if he were to plan another journey for his health, he would go to No. 4 (now Charlestown, New Hampshire) and "thence down to N. Hampton, Deerfield, Hadley, Springfield, then to Enfield, and along down to Seabrook."

3. John C. Fitzpatrick, ed., *The Diaries of George Washington* (Boston, 1925), 27.

4. David John Jeremy, ed., *Henry Wansey and His American Journals* (Philadelphia, 1970), 65.

5. Jedediah Morse (1761–1826), the father of Samuel F. B. Morse, was a clergyman with an interest in the study of geography. In 1784, he published *Geography Made Easy*, the first textbook of its kind in the country, and later published both *American Geography* and *American Gazetteer* in 1789. An interesting note may be added here about his son Samuel, for his name and those of B. H. and B. T. Morse appeared in the Register from the Prospect House on Mount Holyoke for May 28, 1824.

6. For discussion of the concept of America as a Paradise to be regained see Leo Marx, *The Machine in the Garden: Technology and the Pastoral Ideal in America* (New York, 1967), 36–46 and 73–144; Roderick Nash, *Wilderness and the American Mind* (New Haven, 1967); Barbara Novak, *Nature and Culture: American Landscape and Painting, 1825–1875* (New York, 1980); and Henry Nash Smith, *The Virgin Land: the American West as Symbol and Myth* (Cambridge, 1951), 123–132.

7. It was significant that the prospect presented was to the west. Beyond the cultivated intervales representing civilization was a wilderness of forest and mountains like that which lay in the west of the whole American continent. The river winding through this scene was significant also in that it represented the passage of time—the eternal cycle of nature and man. In his unpublished lecture on *Prospects* given at the University of Michigan and Smith College, David Smith contended that the new interest in prospects in the eighteenth century in England was the culmination of a revolutionary shift in the understanding of perspective, and therefore of space—"to move outward into the world, to observe, to travel, and, as it were, to prospect." As for time, the prospect provided a way of being involved with the past, but since America had no past the prospect was "employed in exclusively optimistic visions of the glorious American republic." The prospect from Mount Holyoke was not only a landscape view but a view of America.

8. In a letter some years after his 1828 tour along the Connecticut River, Hall remembered Silliman's hospitality and noted that although he and his family had since been great wanderers, they would always look back to America with the warmest feelings, not only for friends, but for the country generally. See George P. Fisher, *Life of Benjamin Silliman* (New York, 1866), 407. As a renowned scientist, Edward Hitchcock also received a number of visitors to his home. Among these was an Englishman, James F. Johnson, who wrote in his *Notes on North America: Agricultural, Economical and Social* (London, 1851), 2:49, that he spent a pleasant evening with President Hitchcock and his amiable family. Johnson observed a charm in the valley and ranges of hills which made him regret that "a chilling winter wind froze up external nature" instead of inviting "a more detailed examination of the numerous striking points of landscape."

9. The list of notable visitors to the summit of Mount Holyoke is extensive. Jenny Lind, who was there in 1851 after a concert in Northampton, reportedly called the area the "Paradise of America." According to a pamphlet published for the Mount Holyoke Summit House, Charles Sumner noted, as he stood there on August 12, 1847, that "I have been all over New-England, have travelled through the Highlands of Scotland, have passed up and down the Rhine, have ascended Mount Blanc and stood on the campagna in Rome but have never seen anything so surpassingly lovely as this."

For a further discussion of the early history of the summit house see Clifton Johnson, *Mount Holyoke and Vicinity, Historical and Descriptive* (Northampton, 1887), 10–12; and Johnson, *Historic Hampshire in the Connecticut Valley* (Springfield, 1932), 120–121; and John Eden, *The Mount Holyoke Hand-book and Tourist's Guide for Northampton and Its Vicinity* (Northampton, 1851). For later history see William Henry Wright, "Historic Spot, Rich in Associations of 119 Years, Lured Thousands to Enjoy Entrancing View," *Holyoke Transcript Telegram*, July 7, 1940; and the clippings file on Mount Holyoke, Historic Northampton.

10. Robert E. Spiller in his introduction to James Fenimore Cooper, *Notions of the Americans* (London, 1828; rpt. New York, 1963), vii. Max Berger in *The British Traveler in North America 1836–1860* (New York, 1843), 14, contended that the tourist trade was fairly large, and of the hundreds of English visitors approximately 230 published accounts of their travels. The two most notable accounts were written by Harriet Martineau and Alexis de Tocqueville. Harriet Martineau was a professional author and commentator who was encouraged to publish her impressions of America from a visit in 1834 and 1835. In *Society in America* 3 vols. (New York, 1837), 2:200, Martineau mentioned that from Mount Holyoke she saw the village of Hadley seated in the meadow below. In his various accounts of travels in America, including his *Journey to America*, Alexis de Tocqueville did not mention any part of the Connecticut River Valley.

11. Discussion of early tourists in America can be found in Berger, *The British Traveler*; Jane Louise Mesick, *The English Traveller in America, 1785–1835* (Westport, CT, 1970); and Allan Nevins, *America through British Eyes* (New York, 1948).

12. According to Nevins in *America through British Eyes* (103), Hall's *Travels in North America* "had a remarkable popularity in Great Britain, reaching the third edition in 1830, and were reprinted in the United States and read with even greater avidity." Nevins also noted that Hall's book exasperated the American public, since

the author was "a bluff, honest, clear-headed, practical-minded mariner, whose High-Tory prejudices were inimical to the crude democratic society he found in America, who had little tact with which to smooth his way and who candidly sets down his displeasure with all that he disliked." Mrs. Hall's letters were not available until 1931, when they were collected as Una Pope-Hennessey, ed., *The Aristocratic Journey* (New York, 1931).

13. Dickens's *American Notes* sold well in both England and America. According to Nevins in *America through British Eyes* (90), the whole tour made by Dickens was chronicled by the press. "When it was known that the novelist was to write a book on his experiences, expectation was on tiptoe. Nineteen hours after a copy had reached New York it had been reprinted and was on sale. Within two days, the New York publishers had sold 50,000 copies, and the 3,000 copies first consigned to Philadelphia were exhausted in half an hour."

14. Cole's tracing of Hall's camera lucida sketch in *Forty Etchings* was probably done while he was in England between 1829 and 1832.

15. For a discussion of space in American literature see Norman Foerster, *Nature in American Literature* (New York, 1923); Edward Halsey Foster, *The Civilized Wilderness; Backgrounds to American Romantic Literature, 1817–1860* (New York, 1975); Blake Nevins, *Cooper's Landscapes: An Essay on the Picturesque Vision* (Los Angeles, 1976); and Donald A. Ringe, *The Pictorial Mode: Space and Time in the Art of Bryant, Irving, and Cooper* (Lexington, KY, 1971).

16. In the first chapter of *The Wept of Wish-ton-Wish*, Cooper introduced the characters who had journeyed from Massachusetts Bay to ascend the Connecticut River to the English fort at Hartford. After an exploring expedition, Capt. Heathcote decided on an "estate that should be valuable, rather from its quality and beauty, than from its extent," that was located near the northern boundary of Hartford. The name of the settlement of Wish-ton-Wish was taken from the call of the whip-poor-wills. In 1889, the Northampton Canoe Club, with its clubhouse at Hockanum Village on the Oxbow, changed its name to the Wish-ton-Wish Club. As F. N. Kneeland noted in *Northampton, the Meadow City* (Northampton, 1894), 69, "The name is singularly appropriate, as in this same little village many of the important events of Cooper's 'Wept of the Wish-ton-Wish' took place."

17. According to Donald Ringe, in *Pictorial Mode* (163), the theme of *The Wept* was the land, which was changed with the encroachment of man; and the people, who show a moral loss with their material gain. For Cooper, Ringe believed, this theme had far-reaching implications that went beyond the Connecticut River Valley to embrace his concept of nineteenth-century America. In fact, the Valley of the Connecticut could be considered a "microcosm in which the development of America is enacted in small—its original faith tarnished by the change and development that transforms it, despite its material prosperity, into something less than the original dream."

18. The registers for the summit house on Mount Holyoke are in the collection of Historic Northampton. Ila Weiss in *Sanford Robinson Gifford, 1823–1880* (New York, 1977) makes no mention of any sketchbook that survived from 1853.

19. According to Dean Flower in *Henry James in Northampton* (Northampton, 1971), 16, James used Northampton, which he had visited in 1864, "to represent the innocence, charm, quietness and dullness of the artist-hero's background," but did

not intend to mock the place as his narrator did. Flower noted that when James revised the novel in 1907 and wrote a preface, he explained that he chose the site because it was the "only small American ville de province of which one had happened to lay up long before, a pleased vision."

20. Mount Tom seemed to attract much less commentary than its companion across the river, possibly because its summit house was built so many years later. President William McKinley, who visited the summit in June 1899, was supposed to have said that this "was the most beautiful mountain outlook in the whole world."

21. Daniel Webster, *Works*, 6 vols. (Boston, 1858), 2:417.

13

DESPITE its evident charm and tranquility, Northampton itself was transformed during this period. Shop Row, along Main Street, became the region's emporium. Wealthy merchants and entrepreneurs built mansions on Round Hill. Household furnishings and clothing once considered luxury goods came within reach of the average family.

There were those in Northampton who did not always welcome change. Turnpike and canal building had attracted laborers foreign to Yankee ways. In 1806, a crowd of fifteen thousand assembled to witness the hanging of two itinerant Irishmen accused (falsely it turned out) of murder. Although the Irish, like later ethnic immigrant groups, assimilated into the mainstream, tensions and conflicts around that process persisted.

Others saw the growing commercialism as a threat to moral order. The revivals of the Second Great Awakening, which swept over New England in the early nineteenth century, sought to stem the tide of encroaching materialism and the moral laxity it nurtured. Their religious fervor inspired secular reform movements designed to improve and perfect the human condition on earth. In Northampton, Sylvester Graham preached dietary reform and sexual discipline as the pathway to better health and moral fitness. Dorothea Dix's movement for mental health reform led to the establishment of the Northampton State Hospital as a bucolic asylum for the mentally ill—a place where behavior could literally be re-formed in this pastoral setting far away from the stress of urban life. Hundreds flocked to the several water-cure facilities in Northampton that promised to cure the body through hydropathic medicine.

Stephen Nissenbaum looks at Sylvester Graham's theories on diet, temperance, and sexuality as part of the "ferment of reform" that intoxicated many during a period of profound change in American society.

Sylvester Graham and Health Reform

*The Physiology of Subsistence**

STEPHEN NISSENBAUM

RALPH Waldo Emerson called Sylvester Graham "the prophet of bran bread and pumpkins." In his own day he was widely regarded as a wild-eyed fanatic and a crank, and even many of his own supporters viewed him with a curious

* From Stephen Nissenbaum, *Sex, Diet, and Debility in Jacksonian America: Sylvester Graham and Health Reform* (Chicago, 1980).

mixture of idolatry and exasperation. Like the radical abolitionist William Lloyd Garrison, he became the target of mob violence during the 1830s. Like Garrison, too, he looked for posterity to redeem his reputation. But posterity failed to do so. Sylvester Graham wished to purge the souls of his generation by cleansing their debauched bodies. In his view, the source of the nation's woes lay not in slavery but in diet. In retrospect, his crusade came to appear more trivial than dangerous, and it may be difficult to understand the intensity of his commitment as anything more than the expression of personal gullibility or neurosis. No statue in his memory is to be found alongside that of Garrison on the Boston Common—or anywhere else. His house in Northampton, Massachusetts, which he predicted would become a national shrine, still stands, unmarked and unrecognized, for many years the site of a local tavern. His name is memorialized, devoid of personal associations, only in his one enduring legacy: Graham crackers.[1]

Sylvester Graham may be remembered in that single phrase, but the commercial product to which it refers bears only the most distant and ironic connection to a man who spent most of his adult life in a crusade against just such products. Graham began his career as a temperance worker in the early days of the organized temperance movement. As a result of his work, he became the first important American exponent of vegetarianism and diet reform. His vegetarian ideas were first clearly articulated in a controversial lecture he delivered about the dangers of masturbation and marital excess—the first important expression of a new fear of human sexuality that would become one of the trademarks of the later nineteenth century. Graham himself may have been largely forgotten, but his ideas on these subjects came to find widespread acceptance among middle-class Americans. They were adopted, directly and virtually intact, by the Seventh-Day Adventists; and on a more secular level, they ultimately led to the rise of the modern American breakfast cereal industry. They reemerged at the turn of the twentieth century in surprising quarters: among a diverse group of spiritualists, British socialists (including George Bernard Shaw and H. G. Wells), and Indian pacifists including Mahatma Gandhi—all of whom associated abstinence from animal food with sexual continence.

For Graham himself, the need for vegetable diet and controlled sexuality was based on a coherent and complicated theory of human physiology, a theory that emphasized the lethal dangers of physical stimulation, and hypothesized the existence of a complex network of physiological interconnections that made the human body an exceedingly fragile and vulnerable organism exposed to constant assaults from the outside world.

In retrospect, it was clearly no accident that this theory first emerged in the 1830s. As historians have come to see, these were years of profound change in the way many Americans were living and working. Above all, the

Jacksonian period was a time when the marketplace was beginning to replace the household and the community as the major locus of economic activity and social relationships. Set off by the widespread dispersal of the population after 1800 and the subsequent development of new modes of transport, the emergence of a marketplace economy broke up families at the same time it linked distant communities into a single interdependent network. More people were starting to buy rather than to make what they used, and to sell rather than use what they made. These transactions were taking place within an increasingly impersonal setting—a system in which even the most basic products (furniture, clothing, and food) might be produced by people who lived hundreds of miles from the homes in which they were finally used.

As late as 1800, 85 percent of America's manufactured goods was produced in the household, and the bulk of these goods was consumed either by the family that made them or by a neighboring household in the same community. But by the 1830s, this figure had been reduced dramatically. For many people, within a single generation, the household had ceased to be the basic unit of production.

It was to these people that Graham spoke. Nor was it fortuitous that many of them came to associate him almost exclusively with a single point in his general message: the proper preparation of bread. Through the ages, bread had been the basic stuff of human existence—the "staff of life." For ages, too, breadmaking had played a central role in the system of household production—baked on the domestic hearth, from home-grown grain. Yet during these very years, bread itself was becoming just another commercial commodity. The staff of life was removed gradually from household production and came to be manufactured, marketed, and consumed in the new depersonalized marketplace. By focusing on this change—for all the ridicule it evoked from Emerson and other skeptics—Graham touched a resonant note in the experience of Americans. From this perspective "Graham bread" was a serious, if symbolic, attempt to come to terms with life in a marketplace society; and, if only because this bread has so completely defined Sylvester Graham's place in history, it is a good place to begin an exploration of his ideas.

"IN CITIES and large towns," Graham wrote in 1837, "most people depend on public bakers for their bread." The evidence bears out his statement. In Boston alone, the 1846 city directory listed forty-eight commercial bakeries. Moreover, the bread sold by those bakers was generally manufactured from wheat grown in the distant Ohio Valley. This wheat was less expensive than the New England product because of the greater fertility of midwestern soil and the existence of a network of recently constructed canals that greatly reduced the cost of transportation over long distances. Even in the more fertile agricultural districts of New England such as the Connecticut River Valley, where Sylvester Graham had been born and where he lived after 1838, many people (including farmers) were buying cheaper western flour by the 1830s. Throughout the Northeast, in fact, people were making or purchasing their bread from market flour, raised in distant regions by commercial farmers who remained forever faceless and anonymous to them.[2]

The commercialization of grain agriculture was not simply an abstract development. It had palpable effects on the final product—and Sylvester Graham and his followers may be forgiven if they exaggerated the impact of those effects. Raising wheat for sale in a highly competitive market, commercial farmers were understandably interested in maximizing their production. As Graham noted, such farmers were eager to "extort" from their acreage "the greatest amount of produce, with the least expense of tillage, and with little or no regard to the quality of that produce." In order to "extort" as much as they could from the soil, for example, many commercial farmers by the 1820s were coming to abandon a long-standing reluctance to fertilize their land with animal manures. Graham worried that fertilization, which he considered "unnatural," destroyed the "virgin purity" of "undepraved soil," and that manured soil was "exhausted by [constant] tillage, and debauched by the means which man uses to enrich and stimulate it."[3] The idea that the earth itself could be "debauched" and "exhausted," and that such a process was the result of artificial "stimulation," had its origin in the complex theory of physiology that Graham had developed by the 1830s. The language itself, with its conscious sexual connotations, was characteristic of Graham (as it was of other Jacksonian reformers).

The farmers who cultivated the grain were not the only people responsible for the poor state of store-bought bread. Even more serious offenders were the commercial bakers who prepared and sold it. These men, too, were interested simply in their profit. "Public bakers," Graham wrote, "like other men who serve the public more for the sake of securing their own emolument than for the public good," will inevitably be tempted to resort to whatever "expedients" may promise "to increase the lucrativeness of their business." As Graham pointed out, the quality and price of commercial flour was "very unstable," since it fluctuated wildly in response to changing domestic and foreign markets. For this reason, and in order "to make the most profitable use of such flour as the market affords them," commercial bakers were only too willing to adulterate their already inferior flour with a variety of artificial "chemical agents." These additives, Graham claimed, were known to include "alum, sulphate of zinc, sub-carbonate of magnesia, [and] sulphate of copper." To make matters even worse, many bakers had been able to "disguise their adulterations" by adding such materials as "chalk, pipe clay and plaster of Paris," which served to "increase the weight and whiteness of their bread" without risk of "being detected by the consumers."[4]

But even when commercial bakers refrained from engaging in such shady practices, the bread they sold was still an inferior product. Frequently, it was leavened with the same commercial brewer's yeast that was used in the manufacture of alcoholic beverages. Furthermore (and this is the point to which the name of Sylvester Graham would become irretrievably linked), such bread was baked from "superfine flour"—bolted flour from which the husks of the grain had been removed, and which had been ground up or "refined" to the point where its natural granular texture had been "torture[d]" into an unnatural state of "concentration." In other words, public bakers were vending an early variety of *white bread*, bread with a thin crust and a soft interior that could be prepared more efficiently than the traditional crusty whole wheat product. What soon came to be termed "Graham bread" was in fact nothing more than traditional homegrown and homemade whole wheat bread with a few added twists in preparation and an aggressively ideological rationale.[5]

In his *Treatise on Bread and Bread-Making*, Graham was explicit about this point. Even the most honest of commercial bakers, he insisted, ended up with a product that was invariably inferior to the bread made from "what is called good 'family flour.'" The best bread was always that produced "within the precincts of our own thresholds." There was a "natural sweetness and richness" in such bread that made it "always desirable." It was this, and this only, that could truly be regarded as the staff of life, and Graham wrote almost ecstatically about the few households in which he had stayed during his travels where it had been served to him. But he ruefully acknowledged that such households were few and far between, and that the very possibility of being able to prepare this delicious and wholesome bread had become slim. In an implicit concession to the fact that he was addressing a public that no longer had the means to grow its own flour, Graham urged his audience to purchase the best flour they could find, to grind it themselves with "a modern patent hand-mill," and, of course, to bake it in their own ovens.[6] If Graham bread was a version of traditional bread, it was a version that had come to at least minimal terms with the realities of a marketplace society. Its appeal to tradition was, on a practical level, more symbolic than real. It represented the moral equivalent of vanishing economic self-sufficiency.

Perhaps for this very reason, Graham's analysis of the decline of traditional bread-making conveyed a moral urgency that transcended the physiological and scientific terms in which it was couched. To Graham, the technological changes that accompanied the transformation of domestic bread into a cheap and potentially lethal article of commerce were a single manifestation of the basic social change that comprised the larger transformation of America in the first third of the nineteenth century.

The ultimate problem with commercial bread was not technological but spiritual. Even though it was extremely helpful to follow carefully all the "correct rules" of making bread (and there are eighteen pages devoted to these rules in his *Treatise on Bread-Making*), Graham went out of his way to argue that the finished product would always be inferior when it was a commercial baker who followed those rules. Precisely because he was a man of commerce, the public baker necessarily lacked the one crucial element that made for really healthful bread: not technical know-how, but a "moral sensibility" that comprehends "the importance of the quality of bread, in relation to the happiness and welfare of those who consume it." Such a moral sensibility, Graham insisted, was not to be found in commercial bakers.[7] These men baked their bread in the impersonal ovens of the marketplace and not on the warm hearth of the domestic circle. For them, the only effective leaven was cash.

Where was the requisite sensibility to be found? "Who then shall make our bread?" Graham asked. The answer was obvious:

> It is the wife, the mother only—she who loves her husband and her children as woman ought to love, and who rightly perceives the relation between the dietetic habits and physical and moral conditions of her loved ones, and justly appreciates the importance of good bread to their physical and moral welfare—she alone it is, who will be ever inspired by that cordial and unremitting affection and solicitude which will excite the vigilance, secure the attention, and prompt the action requisite to success, and essential to the attainment of that maturity of judgment and skillfulness of operation, which are the indispensable attributes of a perfect breadmaker.[8]

It was thus an essentially social vision that was evoked in Graham's mind by the image of well-baked bread: the vision of a domestic idyll, of a mother nursing her family with bread and affection. It was a historical vision as well—the sentimentalized memory of a precapitalist order in which the household functioned simultaneously as a productive unit and a protective one, where people did not have to rely on the unfeeling exchanges of the marketplace for either their physical or their emotional sustenance. Graham recognized and lamented the fact that such a world had all but disappeared. In a highly significant and uncharacteristically lyrical passage, the ordinarily strident reformer explicitly associated the twilight of that world with the time of his own childhood and the childhood of his generation at the turn of the nineteenth century:

> Who that can look back 30 or 40 years to those blessed days of New England's prosperity and happiness, when our good mothers used to make the family bread, but can well remember how long and how patiently those excellent matrons stood over their bread troughs, kneading and molding their dough? And who with such recollections cannot also well remember the delicious bread that those mothers used invariably to set before them? There was a natural sweetness and richness in it which made it always desirable; and which we

> cannot now vividly recollect, without feeling a strong desire to partake again of such bread as our mothers used to make for us in the days of our childhood.[9]

Graham himself had good reason to sentimentalize this nurturing social environment, and to shun the impersonal and menacing capitalist marketplace that had replaced it. His own family had once been a prominent and stable part of its community—for fifty years his father had served as its minister—but in the course of his childhood Graham was the witness and victim of his family's total disintegration as a coherent institutional unit. The "blessed days of New England's prosperity and happiness" had come to a rude end with the death of his father, the emotional collapse of his mother, and the failure of anyone else effectively to replace them.

Sylvester Graham's paternal grandfather, the Reverend John Graham, was a Scotsman—a minister and a 1714 graduate of the University of Glasgow—who had emigrated to the New World four years after his graduation. He occupied several pulpits in the western part of New England, and it was there that his first son and Sylvester's father, John Graham, Jr., was born in 1722. The younger John Graham was graduated from Yale College in 1740 and licensed to preach the following year, just as the first important religious revival in America, the Great Awakening, was sweeping through New England. Both father and son were fervent supporters of the awakening. In 1746, twenty-four-year-old John Graham, Jr. was ordained as pastor of a new congregation (spawned by a combination of religious upheaval and population growth) in West Suffield, a small town in the Connecticut River Valley just south of the Massachusetts border. He retained this pulpit, and the prominent position in his community that went with it, for exactly half a century until his death in 1796, at the age of seventy-four. During these years he married twice, and his two wives bore him a total of seventeen children, all of whom survived their father. Sylvester Graham was the last of these seventeen children. When he was born, in 1794, his father was seventy-two years old and had less than two years to live.[10]

Ruth Graham, the minister's second wife and Sylvester's mother, was only forty-one when her elderly husband died. It was her job to rear the seven children she had borne, all of whom were still young enough to be living at home. But, since John Graham had died without leaving a will, she was left without any clear holdings in his £1,000 estate. (John Graham's ten children by his first wife had all moved away by this time, and most of them apparently had received property settlements while he was still alive.) It was not until 1800—four years after his death—that a distribution of the estate finally was made. But by that time other difficulties had emerged within the Graham family. Ruth Graham failed to remarry, and she seems to have become emotionally unable to care adequately for her children. As Sylvester Graham later said,

"My mother's health sunk under her complicated trials, the family was broken up, and . . . I fell into the hands of strangers." When Sylvester was three years old, he was sent to live with neighbors—a fairly common practice in late-eighteenth-century rural communities. Two years later he was lodged with a local tavern keeper, but after falling seriously ill, he moved into the household of one of his married half sisters. In 1801, when he was six, in a sad contrast to his later recollection of the times "when our good mothers used to make the family bread," the county probate court decreed that Ruth Graham was "in a deranged state of mind," and the selectmen of West Suffield appointed a local farmer to be his legal guardian.[11]

This arrangement lasted for five years, during which young Sylvester worked as a "farmer's boy." When he was eleven, one of his older brothers sent him to school in distant New York City, but the unfamiliar life there made him unhappy, and at his own request he soon returned to West Suffield. For a time during his mid-teens Sylvester again lived with his mother, finding employment where he was able. At one point he worked briefly in a local paper mill, but after a month he quit and moved in with still another local farmer. Ever dissatisfied, he left the farm and worked at different times as assistant to a traveling horse dealer and as a clerk in various shops in the area. Falling ill at age sixteen, he was sent to live with one of his sisters in Middlebury, Vermont. At nineteen, in an effort to become a schoolteacher, he spent some four months studying with a private tutor, but after teaching in several small towns for a short time, he was forced by exhaustion and illness to abandon this occupation. In a state of intense depression he moved to Albany to stay with another of his sisters, and then in 1817, at age twenty-three, to Newark, New Jersey, the home of still another sibling.[12]

It was sometime during these years that Graham for the first time began to emerge from his long miasma. As a teenager, he had been ardently fond of attending social gatherings—especially parties and balls. While he never drank the hard liquor served at these affairs, his abstinence stemmed from physical distaste rather than any principled objection. Nevertheless, as he later recalled, the pressure of his peers and his concern for their good opinion of him had exposed him to "many temptations" along these lines—temptations that were especially intense because, as he pointedly recalled, "I had no particular employment, and was left almost entirely to follow my own will." On one of these occasions, though, he finally discovered the true direction and force of his will, and in the process the vocation that had so long eluded him.[13]

The crucial event was what Graham later referred to as "one of those peculiar trials which young men too seldom have the courage to endure." A group of friends had invited him to a party at a local tavern. Graham agreed to attend, but because it embarrassed him to be the only nondrinker in the group, he proposed that no alcohol be served at the affair. His stipulation was ostensibly accepted all around, and the party got under way in pleasant fashion. But Graham unwittingly had been set up by his friends. Late in the evening one of them called for a glass of "rum-sling." Immediately a hush fell over the group, and "all eyes were turned" on Graham to see how he would react to the challenge. He protested, but his protests were rebuffed. When the glass, by now emptied and refilled several times, was finally handed to Graham, he tried to pass it along without raising it to his lips. That was what the assembly had been waiting for, and they taunted him: "'He is too stingy to call for his glass and that is the reason he won't drink!'" It was, as Graham later acknowledged, "a most trying moment." The idea of being thought stingy by his friends was "almost intolerable." But while Graham "felt the reproach keenly," he was "determined not to yield." He pretended to ignore the barrage of taunts, until finally, when the humiliation seemed complete, the young man sitting next to Graham drank the glass of rum.

It was at this point that Graham acted to prove he was not stingy, to regain his dignity—and to assume control of the situation. As soon as his glass had been drained, Graham dramatically ordered the tavern keeper to bring another glass of rum *for him*. When the fresh drink arrived, Graham "planted it with firmness in the middle of the table," rose out of his chair, and with a "stern voice" announced to the rest of the party, "gentlemen, good night." Now it was his friends' turn to feel embarrassed. They attempted to detain Graham, but, ignoring their pleas just as they had previously ignored his protests, Graham calmly picked up his hat and walked out of the tavern. The spirit had gone out of the joke, and the group soon dispersed. In retrospect, Graham felt this was a moment of profound significance for him. Not only had he saved his friends from a probable "debauch," but—of even greater importance—the incident "gave a direction to the whole course of my life."

Despite Graham's retrospective comment that few young men would have had the "courage to endure" such a "trial," the episode was similar in form to the experience of many directionless young men who came of age in the Jacksonian years, involving as it did Graham's loss of shame and dependence and his simultaneous discovery of a new sense of personal autonomy and power. In characteristically Jacksonian fashion, too, the incident at the tavern moved Graham away from his purely personal and somewhat abashed reluctance to drink and into what he called an "open and frequent" effort to persuade others to believe and act as he did. Graham began to "contend" passionately with his fellow farmhands about the evils of drink. Then, early in 1823, he delivered his first public lecture on the subject to a debating society near his hometown of West Suffield, Connecticut, and shortly afterwards he organized an informal temperance club there.

Later the same year, at the age of twenty-nine, Graham entered Amherst Academy (a preparatory school associated with the fledgling Amherst College) in order to prepare for the evangelical ministry. But he was unable to adjust to the academic routine. After a short stay at the academy he fell into a state of "mental despondency and wretchedness," and before the end of his first semester, he was dismissed from the institution, apparently on a trumped-up charge of assault. His dismissal, coming on top of his already depressed state, soon led to an acute physical and emotional collapse. In this condition, he made his way (for reasons that remain obscure) to the Rhode Island coastal town of Little Compton. There he was slowly nursed back to health by the two daughters of a sea captain at whose house he was staying. In September 1824, Graham was married to the older of these two women.[14]

With his health restored, and a wife to support, Graham now resumed his preparation for the ministry. Probably because his attempt to gain a more formal education had failed, he resorted to the increasingly dated practice of studying privately with the local parish minister—in this case the very man who had officiated at his wedding in Little Compton. In 1826 Graham was licensed to preach; and after his ordination as an evangelist two years later, he moved back to the Newark area where his mother, confined to an institution, was still living.[15] At the age of thirty-four, Sylvester Graham finally seemed embarked on a career—the same ministerial career as his father and grandfather before him.

But, unlike his clerical forebears, Graham never managed to settle down with a parish of his own, and within two years he had abandoned the ministry altogether. He served for a while as guest preacher in the New Jersey community of Belvedere, and for more than a year during 1829 and 1830, he served as acting minister to a small congregation in the nearby town of Bound Brook. (There, as an account book reveals, his wife baked bread from locally grown flour.) But a large part of Graham's new congregation turned against him when he delivered a series of sermons against intemperance. Even though his admonitions resulted in the closing of a nearby distillery and the formation of a local temperance society, Graham's position in the Bound Brook community had become tenuous. Under the circumstances, he was quick to accept the next job that was offered. In June 1830, Sylvester Graham became an agent of the Pennsylvania Temperance Society.[16]

Graham immediately moved to Philadelphia, and in his new capacity as temperance reformer he traveled around eastern Pennsylvania, lecturing in churches and factories and helping to form new local and county temperance societies. In this capacity Graham seems to have been notably successful—his lively and impassioned style of extemporaneous speaking began to attract large audiences—and by early 1831, he was asked to deliver a series of lectures on the subject in New York City. He did so that summer and again the ensuing autumn (at which time he was prevailed on to repeat his entire series several times). At this point Graham had come to consider himself not simply a temperance reformer, but a lecturer on a far more inclusive subject that he called "The Science of Human Life," and over the next few years he would come to expand his repertoire to cover the cholera epidemic (which ravaged the United States in 1832), the importance of sexual chastity and vegetarian diet, and, of course, the virtues of bran bread. For the rest of the decade he delivered these lectures throughout the Atlantic states and New England, and eventually he traveled as far afield as upstate New York. His lectures on cholera, sexuality, and bread-making were published between 1832 and 1837 (each of them going through a number of editions), and in 1839 he published his magnum opus, *Lectures on the Science of Human Life*, in two volumes of more than 1,200 pages.[17]

But the growing celebrity of his ideas, along with his contentious and abrasive manner, made Graham a controversial figure. As one of his supporters later recalled in an obituary notice, Graham was a gifted orator, but his temperament was marred by "combativeness, extreme cautiousness, excessive ideality, and more than full self-esteem."[18] He was publicly mobbed at least three times, once in Portland, Maine, in 1834 and twice in Boston during the winter of 1837. The first time an angry crowd prevented him from delivering his lecture on chastity to an all-female audience, and the second time he was attacked by a group of commercial butchers and bakers who feared his ideas were bad for their business.

Graham's eventual eclipse may have been hastened by the fact that he came to be dismissed as a charlatan by several respectable medical publications (notably the *Boston Medical and Surgical Journal*) which had initially welcomed his work as a serious contribution to the field of personal health.[19] Furthermore, like William Lloyd Garrison (who had likewise been mobbed in Boston during the mid-1830s, and who had similarly been dismissed as a fanatic by the more moderate members of his own party), Graham often personally alienated even those followers who were ideologically close to him. He also remained aloof from the very people who paid him the homage he craved. He never stayed in any of the "Graham boardinghouses" opened by his disciples in Boston and New York during the mid-1830s in an attempt to institutionalize healthy diet and regimen. He maintained only minimal contact with the American Physiological Society, a Boston group he helped to found in 1837. He took no part in editing the *Graham Journal of Health and Longevity*, published from 1837 to 1839 by his disciple, David Cambell, who also managed the Graham boardinghouse in Boston. (Graham once acknowledged privately that he tended to act with "gall and vinegar" toward the very people for whom he most deeply cared.)

In the last decade of his life, Sylvester Graham was effectively cut off from the intellectual and institutional currents he had helped set in motion. After 1839 he gave up his itinerant lecturing and settled down into semi-retirement with his wife and two children in Northampton, just twenty-five miles upriver from the town in which he had been born. There he spent the last dozen years of his life, something of a crotchety local character, writing self-pitying poetry, letters to the editor of the local newspaper, and a lengthy defense of vegetarian diet on biblical grounds. He died in 1851, after violating his own strictures by taking liquor and meat in a last desperate attempt to recover his health.[20]

IT WOULD be naive to attribute Sylvester Graham's chronic career problems simply to the disruptions he experienced in his early life. After all, the years in which Graham was coming of age was a time when such newly emerging careers as those of professional lecturer and writer were not yet able to provide a reliable source of income. Nevertheless, the failure of Graham's family to ease his way into adulthood certainly played an important role in determining the difficult course of his later life. In any case, this particular failure mirrored the larger transformation of American rural society in the early years of the nineteenth century.

The disintegration of traditional kinship ties in this period is dramatically revealed in the contrast between the two different "families" that Sylvester Graham's father sired and reared over his long career: the ten children of his first marriage, born between 1749 and 1768, and the seven children of his second marriage, born between 1780 and 1792. Of the six sons and four daughters born to John Graham's first wife, each of the four daughters married, and married well; and five of the six sons attained some degree of prosperity.

John Graham's eldest son was sent, like his father before him, to Yale College. By graduation he had become interested in medicine, and went directly from Yale to earn a medical degree from King's College (Columbia) in New York City. He established his practice with the professional assistance of one of his father's brothers, a prominent physician who lived outside New York City in suburban White Plains. Largely because of these advantages, all of them derived from the concern and connections of his family, the eldest son was able to establish an extremely successful practice of his own. It was only appropriate, and no doubt entirely expected of him, that some twenty years later he trained and supported one of *his* younger brothers—the last son born of John Graham's first marriage—and helped him to complete his medical studies in London and Edinburgh. A third son, who as a young man received his start in the form of a generous gift of real estate from his father, became a well-to-do land speculator and merchant in western New York after the Revolutionary War. Another son became a prosperous if somewhat shady merchant in the Boston area; and the last a wealthy land speculator in South Carolina.[21]

It is significant that the children whom John Graham fathered by his first marriage were all established in their careers well before their father died.

(They ranged in age from twenty-eight to forty-seven at the time of his death.) Because a dozen years elapsed between the birth of the last child of his first marriage and the first child of his second, the oldest of the seven children of this second marriage was only sixteen when the father died, and the youngest—Sylvester—was not quite two. All the children of the first marriage, moreover, had left the West Suffield area by this time, and it appears that the two "families" did not have any contact after the father's death. Since Sylvester Graham's mother herself never remarried—indeed, since she was declared insane after seven years of widowhood—it is clear that what remained of the Graham family in West Suffield after 1796 had no other role in the community than as its wards.

There is an obvious difference between the careers of the seven children of John Graham's second marriage and the ten children of his first. Two of the four girls born of this second union never married, and a third remained single until she was nearly forty. The most stable of the seven children, both economically and (from what can be inferred) emotionally, were the two oldest, both boys. (They were also the only ones to have reached adolescence at the time of their father's death.) Even these two children enjoyed only modest success. One of them, Isaac King Graham, remained in West Suffield almost until his death; all that is known of him is that he was quiet and attended church regularly. The other, Charles Graham, began his career as an accountant in New York City. He later moved to Newark, where he made a good marriage and ended his days in comfortable circumstances as a cashier in a banking house.

It was Charles Graham who tried to keep what Sylvester would later term the "little remnant" of the Graham family together. When Charles moved to Newark in 1817 he was followed by his mother, three of his four sisters, and his twenty-three-year-old brother Sylvester. Whatever aid Charles Graham did provide, however, was too little and too late to guide his sisters into marriage or his younger brother into a career. All he was able to offer was a modicum of respite from the burden of living in a community where the name of Graham had once carried an assurance of stability, prosperity, and respect.

Sylvester Graham came to maturity, then, without much effective help or guidance from his family or his community. When at length he discovered his vocation, he did so substantially on his own—and then only when he was in his mid-thirties, after a long series of false starts accompanied by chronic bouts of debilitating illness and depression. The career in which he finally achieved some measure of success was one that represented the essence of the emerging world of the capitalist marketplace. Like his better remembered cohort, Ralph Waldo Emerson (and at almost exactly the same time), Graham first entered the established ministry but soon abandoned it in order to become a professional writer and traveling lecturer, forced to deal with an ever-changing array of impersonal and undependable audiences.

It is, therefore, a revealing irony that Sylvester Graham tried to romanticize the secure family life he had never known. As he grew older he developed an interest in his genealogy, especially in what he insisted were the Graham clan's royal origins in Scotland. In his last years he openly lamented the way the family had disintegrated over the years. In two poignant letters written late in life to his brother Isaac, who was still living in West Suffield, and whom he had apparently not seen in some time—"I trust you are living, for if you were not the newspapers at least would inform me of your death"—Sylvester Graham pleaded for "a measure of cordial love and harmony between the little remnant of our father's family." Referring to the two of his sisters who were still alive, he admitted that "Jerusha's alienation from me I fear will never be overcome—and now Harriet is also torn from me I fear by the demoniacal infatuation of one of her children." He added desperately, addressing his brother in biblical language, "'Wilt thou also go away?'" He reminded Isaac that "when I was a little, unprotected fatherless boy, you were not only a brother but in a father's stead to me"; and speaking of the father he could scarcely have remembered, he asked, "Could our venerated Sire return to earth . . . would he not say to us—'My little children love one another'?"[22]

It is characteristic of both his personal and his professional life, that what Graham seems to have craved most of all was the feeling of being remembered and cared for, and that what he most feared was the possibility of being forgotten or ignored. He exhibited no desire that his family be knit together by any bonds other than those of mutual concern. All he wanted was for his family to be a community of feeling. He did not expect it to provide any services other than emotional ones. Within this emotional community he saw his own role as wholly passive—much like that of the children he remembered, feeding on "the delicious bread [their] mothers used unvariably to set before them," watching their mothers stand "long and patiently . . . over their bread troughs, kneading and molding their dough" in a manner appropriate to those who love their families "as woman ought to love." (The loveliness of this scene, as Graham described it, lay both in the security, love, and nourishment the mother lavished on her family, and in the passivity, the absence of reciprocal responsibility, with which they received it. There may be some significance in the fact that Graham married a woman who literally was his nurse.)

Graham's sentimentalization of a protective family life he had never known finds its direct parallel in the way he extolled the superiority of a personalized, self-sufficient society even as he traveled around the lecture circuit addressing faceless urban audiences he rarely encountered more than a few times. Each of these paradoxical stances expressed perfectly the complex dynamics of Jacksonian social change: they provided a means by which both

Graham and his disciples were able to begin making the difficult psychological transition into a capitalist society. Graham was not the only member of his generation to idealize the remembered past at the very point when that past had ceased to wield significant force in the life of the present. All over Western society, both in America and in Europe, nineteenth-century reformers, writers, and painters were creating nostalgic pictures of yeomen with their hoes, shepherds attending to their flocks, and patient women at their spinning wheels (or, in Graham's case, at their ovens). The toil and monotony of these tasks were forgotten as they were transformed by the light of nostalgia into scenes of beauty and harmony. By the very act of looking back, the emergent bourgeoisie was able to come to terms with the future.

When Sylvester Graham romanticized the life of the traditional household, he unknowingly helped prepare women to find a new role as the guardians of domestic virtue, just as he helped prepare men—himself included—to adjust to the demands of the capitalist marketplace. The passive security Graham associated with the image of protective mothers preparing bread for their beloved children was as much a vestige of the past as was wholesome family flour. The present-day order had no room either for domestic bread or for the trusting security it symbolized. The world of Jacksonian America was everywhere fraught with menace. Commercial bakers, with their undetectably adulterated flour and their dismaying lack of "Moral sensibility," were only the tip of the iceberg. In every area of modern life people were faced with similar situations—distant farmers who could not be trusted because they could not be known, or unscrupulous merchants who could not be trusted because they were more concerned with turning a profit than with securing the well-being of those who were forced to depend on them. American society, Graham worried, was being consumed by its "untiring pursuit of wealth." At each turn, people were besieged "every luxury . . . that the market can supply."[23]

Commercially baked bread was only a metaphor of the Jacksonian marketplace itself—a place of fevered chaos, laden with products manufactured by invisible men and corrupted with invisible poisons. Anonymity encouraged conspiracy; consumers were beset at every point by forces that threatened their well-being and even their survival. In the face of such a minatory situation, old-fashioned passivity and trust were a potentially lethal indulgence. It was necessary to be wary and alert, on constant guard.

Sylvester Graham shared this phobic vision of Jacksonian society with many other Americans of his day. Anti-Masons focused on the Masonic order as the source of the threat, nativists attributed it to the increasing influx of immigrants, and abolitionists blamed the slave conspiracy. Andrew Jackson himself pointed the finger of guilt at the "monster" Bank of the United States. In Sylvester Graham's particular version, the threat was primarily physiological in nature—directed against the individual human organism rather than against the body politic. Inverting the process by which traditional political theorists had used "organic" language to describe the social order, Graham applied the rhetoric of late-eighteenth-century republican social philosophy to the individual human organism. The human body, he claimed, had its own proper form of "government," based on a natural "constitution" which in turn provided for "constitutionally established laws." This physiological government was "endowed" with certain specific "powers," and when these powers were misused or undermined, the inevitable consequence was a state of "anarchical depravity" or "despotism."[24]

Graham was able to describe in detail the precise nature of the physiological "constitution" and its extraordinary vulnerability to the hostile elements constantly threatening its annihilation—disease, diet, and sexuality. Graham had prepared himself to deal with these subjects in purely scientific terms. He prided himself on the depth of his technical competence. He allowed himself to be addressed as "Dr. Graham" even though he had received no medical training. He had, however, read in limited areas of recent physiological theory. It was from some key ideas he gained in his reading, along with several predispositions he picked up from his work in the temperance movement, that Graham developed the complex and coherent body of principles he proudly dubbed, as early as 1830,"The Science of Human Life."

GRAHAM derived two of his key ideas from the work of a pair of French medical theorists, Xavier Bichat (1771–1802) and François Broussais (1772–1838). Bichat had proposed that all living organisms were engaged in a continuous struggle for survival against the inorganic forces that surrounded them: life itself was a constant battle between the principles of vitality and those of physics and chemistry, and death was simply the victory of the latter over the former. Broussais had proposed that food and drink, upon which living organisms depended for their survival but which literally invaded them from without, constituted the single greatest threat to vitality. From Broussais, then, Graham picked up the idea that it was the digestive system that formed the crucial battleground in the struggle between organic and inorganic forces.

A third important principle that Graham derived from his reading involved the connection between two bodily conditions: *stimulation* and *debility*. Until the end of the eighteenth century, these two states were universally conceived to be opposite and mutually exclusive. Debility (that is, weakness or lack of vital energy) was generally regarded as the more dangerous of the two states—and artificial stimulation was its obvious antidote. (For this reason, people who were exhausted from illness or from hard work generally took stimulants such as alcohol or meat in order to restore their health and strength.) But late in the eighteenth century, the Philadelphia physician and statesman Benjamin Rush proposed that artificial stimulation, far from being a cure for debility, was actually its most common cause. Alcohol and similar stimulants, in Rush's view, served only to further weaken a person who was in a debilitated state. Rush's ideas gained widespread acceptance in his native Philadelphia; indeed, they placed an important role in causing that city to become a major center of the emerging temperance movement in the late 1820s.

Graham probably encountered Rush's work, along with that of Bichat and Broussais, about the time he moved to Philadelphia in 1830 to become an agent of the Pennsylvania Temperance Society. By the end of that year, he had begun to integrate these ideas, and others, into the system he called "The Science of Human Life." To the end of his career, Graham tried to convey the impression that the principles he was expounding in his books and lectures were his own personal discoveries, perhaps confirmed but never influenced by his readings in medical literature. This impression was an integral part of his own self-image as a kind of romantic "natural" who was able to perceive the true nature of things precisely because he had not been corrupted by the artifices of modern civilization—artifices that might include formal book-learning.[25]

In a sense Graham was right. In a very real way, he invented these ideas for himself even though he had read them elsewhere, and he did so in a serious and original effort to come to terms with his own experience and that of his generation. If Xavier Bichat defined life as a desperate struggle between organic and inorganic principles, for Graham that definition became a symbol of the struggle of the localized rural world into which he had been born to fend off the powerful incursions of a depersonalized marketplace society. Similarly, if Benjamin Rush postulated that "artificial" stimulation led only to exhaustion and debility, Graham used that idea as a powerful way of portraying the fevered quality of Jacksonian life—and its deleterious effects on those who experienced it.

Graham urged his audience to adopt a mode of living premised on minimal consumption and the systematic effort to achieve inner serenity. "The Science of Human Life" was ultimately Graham's personal attempt, and in its own way a pathetically eloquent one, to provide what might be termed a physiology of subsistence, a practical strategy by which he and his countrymen might survive in alien, unsettling social terrain.

NOTES

1. [Editor's Note] Graham's home is now a restaurant named "Sylvester's." His grave is marked by a tall brownstone shaft in Northampton's Bridge Street Cemetery—a site that he believed would be visited by generations of pilgrims.

2. Sylvester Graham, *Lectures on the Science of Human Life*, 2 vols. (Boston, 1839), 2:423; Boston Directory for 1846 (Boston, 1847). The *New England Inquirer* [Amherst, MA], April 3, 1828, contains an advertisement for "85 bbls. Rochester Superfine Flour" (reference courtesy of Christopher Clark). A fine discussion of eco-

nomic and social change in the area where Graham was reared, but with wider geographical implications, is Christopher Clark, "The Household Economy, Market Exchange, and the Rise of Capitalism in the Connecticut Valley, 1800–1860," *Journal of Social History* 13 (1979): 169–189.

3. Graham, *Science*, 2:418–419. See also Sylvester Graham, *A Treatise on Bread, and Bread-Making* (Boston, 1837), 33–34. (The *Treatise on Bread* was incorporated almost verbatim into the *Lectures on the Science of Human Life.*) Clarence Danboff, *Change in Agriculture: The Northern United States, 1820–1870* (Cambridge, 1969), 257–262, discusses the increasing use of manures in this period. Graham argued that the odor of manure could be detected in flour milled from wheat grown on fertilized land.

4. Graham, *Science*, 2:424.

5. Graham, *Science*, 2:423. Graham maintained (428–430) that "a due proportion of innutritious matter in our food is as essential to the health and functional integrity of our alimentary organs, as a due proportion of nutritious matter is to the sustenance of our bodies"; in addition, bran was "one of the most soothing substances in nature." Whatever the merits of Graham's argument, the fact is that bread had been prepared from unbolted grain for centuries as a matter of course. "White bread" did not become common in either America or England until the nineteenth century—and even then it was to be found mostly in urban commercial bakeries. See John Burnett, *Plenty and Want: A Social History of Diet in England from 1815 to the Present Day* (London, 1966), 56, 83; J. C. Drummond and Anne Wilbraham, *The Englishman's Food: A History of Five Centuries of English Diet*, rev. ed. (London, 1958), 186–190, 295–299; and Siegfried Giedon, *Mechanization Takes Command: A Contribution to Anonymous History* (New York, 1948), 169–208. In any case, Graham was not even the first American to stress the healthful properties of bran bread. Edward Hitchcock, an Amherst College professor, had recommended much the same recipe in his 1829 book, *Dyspepsy Forestalled* (Northampton, 1831), and a Philadelphia newspaper carried an advertisement for "dyspepsia bread," baked from unbolted wheat flour, at the very time Graham was beginning to lecture on temperance in that city (*Poulson's American Daily Advertiser*, July 20, 1830).

6. Graham, *Science*, 2:425; *Treatise on Bread*, 39, 49, 131; Giedon, *Mechanization Takes Command*, 205.

7. Graham, *Science*, 2:455.

8. Graham, *Science*, 2:455–456. See also *Treatise on Bread*, 43–49, 105.

9. Graham, *Science*, 2:448–449.

10. Helen Graham Carpenter, *The Rev. John Graham of Woodbury, Connecticut and His Descendents* (Chicago, 1942), 6–90. The length of John Graham's tenure, the large number of children he sired, and the fact that all of the children survived him, were unusual.

11. Carpenter, *Rev. John Graham*, 6–90. The autobiographical quotation appeared in William Goodell's magazine, *Genius of Temperance*, May 5, 1831. The inheritance Graham finally received in 1801 amounted to $50.

12. Biographical information from Edith Cole, "Sylvester Graham, Lecturer on the Science of Human Life: The Rhetoric of a Dietary Reformer" (Ph.D. diss., Indiana University, 1975), 9–12; Mildred Naylor, "Sylvester Graham, 1794–1851," *Annals of Medical History*, series 3, 4 (1941): 236–240; Carpenter, *Rev. John Graham*, 184; and the *Genius of Temperance*, May 5. 1831.

13. Graham recalled this episode in a letter to the *Genius of Temperance*, May 5, 1831.

14. Cole, "Sylvester Graham," 16; *Northampton Courier*, July 15, 1840; Naylor, "Sylvester Graham," 236–237.

15. Carpenter, *Rev. John Graham*, 184; Naylor, "Sylvester Graham," 237.

16. *Genius of Temperance*, May 25, 1831; Cole, "Sylvester Graham," 15–18; Naylor, "Sylvester Graham," 236–240. The manuscript records of the Bound Brook Presbyterian Church do not mention Graham's association with that church, nor does the manuscript of an address (on deposit with the church records) delivered by Graham's successor on the twenty-fifth anniversary of his pastorate. Graham is, however, discussed in a published history of the church: Joseph H. Kler, M.D., *God's Happy Cluster: 1688–1963, History of the Bound Brook Presbyterian Church* (n.p., 1963), 64, 73. The only reference to Graham's ordination in 1826 is in the Reverend Mortimer Blake, *Centennial History of the Mendon Association of Congregational Ministers* (Boston, 1853), 78, 309.

17. *Genius of Temperance*, March 30, April 6, and June 1, 1831; Pennsylvania Temperance Society, *Annual Report of the Managers of the Pennsylvania Society for Discouraging the Use of Ardent Spirits* (Philadelphia, 1831), 22; Othniel A. Pendleton, Jr., "The Influence of the Evangelical Churches upon Humanitarian Reform: A Case Study Giving Particular Attention to Philadelphia, 1790–1840," *Journal of the Presbyterian Historical Society* 25 (1947): 22; Cole, "Sylvester Graham," 20–22, 65–69.

18. Russell T. Trall, "Biographical Sketch of Sylvester Graham," *Water-Cure Journal* 12 (1851): 110. (Trall's terminology is phrenological—the relationship among Grahamism, phrenology, and the water cure, and Trall's association with these movements, is discussed in Nissenbaum, *Sex, Diet, and Debility*, 149–151.) Another interesting reference to Graham's abrasive temperament can be found in Theodore Dwight Weld's notation on a letter he received from Graham, in Gilbert H. Barnes and Dwight L. Dumond, eds., *Letters of Theodore Dwight Weld, Angelina Grimke Weld, and Sarah Grimke, 1822–1844*, 2 vols. (New York, 1934), 2:755.

19. Compare, for instance, the favorable review of Graham's *Lecture on Chastity* that appeared in the *Boston Medical and Surgical Journal* in 1835 with the disdainful materials printed in the same periodical through much of the following year.

20. Trall, "Biographical Sketch," 111.

21. This and the following material are gleaned from Carpenter, *Rev. John Graham*, 123–190.

22. Sylvester Graham to Isaac King Graham, Carpenter, *Rev. John Graham*, 188–189. Another letter written three years later to the same brother consists almost entirely of queries about the whereabouts and condition of various forgotten members of the family: Carpenter, *Rev. John Graham*, 189. Graham's interest in the family's genealogy is revealed in Carpenter, *Rev. John Graham*, 55–56.

23. Graham, *Science*, 2:401.

24. Sylvester Graham, *A Lecture to Young Men, on Chastity, intended also for the serious consideration of parents and guardians* (Providence, 1834), 63, 165–169. This inversion of republican political rhetoric is the origin of such modern usages as referring to walking for one's health as taking a "constitutional."

25. See, for example, *Science*, 1: v–ix. In cultivating this image, Graham was by no means unique: a number of writers who flourished during the Jacksonian period seemed to believe they could enhance their credibility by asserting that they had never read a single book in the area of their competence.

14

THE reform movement that produced Graham also produced those who believed that only a radical reordering of society itself could redeem the evils its institutions fostered. In 1842, members of the Northampton Association of Education and Industry established a utopian community organized around a communally owned and operated silk mill. Those who were drawn to this community sought to challenge the prevailing social attitudes of their day by creating a society in which "the rights of all are equal without distinction of sex, color or condition, sect or religion." They were especially united around the issue of the abolition of slavery. Most were followers of William Lloyd Garrison. Sojourner Truth was a member of the community, and visitors like Frederick Douglass were regular lecturers. "The place and the people," Douglass later recalled, "struck me as the most democratic I had ever met. It was a place to extinguish all aristocratic pretensions. There was no high, no low, no masters, no servants, no white, no black. I, however, felt myself in very high society."

Christopher Clark looks at the Northampton Association within the wider context of the antebellum reform era when utopian communities challenged the limits of conventional social organization.

The Communitarian Moment

*Founders, Origins, and Contexts**

CHRISTOPHER CLARK

ON APRIL 8, 1842, seven men met at a little settlement known as Broughton's Meadow, two-and-a-half miles west of the center of Northampton in the Connecticut River Valley of Massachusetts, to incorporate their new community, the Northampton Association of Education and Industry. Present were the abolitionists George W. Benson, Erasmus Darwin Hudson, and William Adam; two silk manufacturers, Joseph Conant and Earl Dwight Swift; Theodore Scarborough, a farmer; and Hiram Wells, a mechanic. They gathered at the property purchased for the community, much of which had belonged to a bankrupt silk manufacturing firm, the Northampton Silk

*From Christopher Clark, *The Communitarian Moment: The Radical Challenge of the Northampton Association* (Ithaca, 1995). Clark is co-editor, with Kerry W. Buckley, of *Letters from an American Utopia: The Stetson Family and the Northampton Association, 1843–47* (Amherst, 2003), which documents the lives of a remarkable family who lived at the association for four years. *The Communitarian Moment*, has been reissued in paperback by the University of Massachusetts Press.

Company. The place included about 470 acres of land, a four-story brick factory, a dam and water-power site on the Mill River, a sawmill, several houses, and some small workshops and outbuildings. The meeting concluded several months of preparation and marked the start of a communitarian venture that would last until November 1846. The seven men discussed the community's principles and regulations, which they set down in a printed document for circulation in reform circles, and elected officers from among themselves and their associates to undertake the tasks necessary to start the community. Among these officers were four men not present at the meeting who were nevertheless expected to play a leading role in the association: three more abolitionists, Samuel L. Hill, Hall Judd, and David Mack, and Samuel Brooks, a farmer. The eleven men present or mentioned at the April 8, 1842, meeting can fairly be regarded as the "founders" of the Northampton community.[1]

The meeting elected by ballot a president, a treasurer, and a secretary, who would head the association's officers and also act under its constitution as trustees, with legal title to its property and authority to represent it in the wider world. The seven present chose from among their number Joseph Conant as president and William Adam as secretary. Adam, in his new capacity, started recording the community's proceedings in a large journal acquired for the purpose. As treasurer they elected Samuel L. Hill, absent that day but eventually to become most closely identified with the community and its local influence. Four men were elected to serve as directors of the association's stock company; they would represent those members who invested in the community and would also, for a time at least, be responsible for most business and financial decisions. Of these, George W. Benson, Theodore Scarborough, and Earl Dwight Swift were present at the meeting, and David Mack would soon be coming to Northampton from Cambridge, Massachusetts, with his family. The meeting also created two bodies to take practical steps in building the community: a board for admitting new members, and a committee to allocate accommodations for them. To the former they elected Benson and Hiram Wells from among their number and added Hall Judd and Samuel Brooks from among those expected to arrive shortly. On the latter committee, Benson and Wells were joined by Conant. Of the seven men present on April 8, only Erasmus Darwin Hudson kept aloof from the responsibilities of office.

Over the next few days and weeks further meetings would draw in new figures and press on with the tasks of shaping community life and recruiting people to share in it. Though during the next four years some 240 men, women, and children would join the group, by the time the association disbanded in 1846 only one (Hiram Wells) of those actually present on April 8, 1842—and only three (Wells, Samuel L. Hill, and Hall Judd) of the eleven founders—would still be members.

But that all lay in the future. First, we need to understand why the founders and their families came to be setting up a community at all. To do so we must examine the overlapping interests and commitments that brought these eleven men to Northampton, the broader contexts in which they were acting, and the issues and principles that led them, by the early 1840s, to seek a communitarian solution to the problems they perceived. What brought them to meet that April day in 1842 so hopeful that they could change American society for the better?

Founders of a Community

The Northampton Association would assemble men and women with a variety of material, ideological, and spiritual concerns that although often complementary, would at times jostle for priority. Prominent among the interests of the eleven founders were radical abolitionism, nonresistance, temperance, manufacturing, and education, themes significant in the early shaping—even the naming—of the community. Dividing the eleven men into groups allows us to capture the varied importance of these and other influences. That they can be divided into four pairs—each with a dominant and minor member—and three individuals, none of whom can easily be grouped with any of the others, incidentally tells us something about the internal dynamics of the nascent community.

The dominant figure in the first pair was George W. Benson, the minor player his neighbor from Brooklyn, Connecticut, Theodore Scarborough. Of all the Northampton community's leaders Benson would become the most prominently associated with it in reform circles, in part because of his impeccable abolitionist credentials and connections. He was, first of all, linked to the old antislavery movement of the early republic. His father, George Benson (1752–1836), had been a Providence merchant and a founding member, and later secretary, of the Providence Society for Promoting the Abolition of Slavery. During the 1790s Benson senior abandoned his Baptist faith for Quaker sympathies, which much of the family shared. Persuaded by his son to retire to a farm in Brooklyn in eastern Connecticut in 1824, he had devoted the last part of his life to the two reforms, peace and abolitionism, that would play an important part in the lives of his son and his son's associates. He was active in the Rhode Island Peace Society, a founder and vice-president of the Windham Peace Society in 1826, and in 1834 third president of the New England Anti-Slavery Society, the region's crucial early proponent of immediate abolitionism.

Before his father's death, George W. Benson had earned abolitionist laurels in his own right. With his younger brother, Henry Egbert (1814–1837), George formed friendships early in the abolitionist campaign with William

Lloyd Garrison and other leading advocates of immediatism. In 1833–1834 he worked closely with Brooklyn's Unitarian minister, Samuel J. May, to defend Prudence Crandall and her school for black girls in the neighboring town of Canterbury. On visits to the Benson household during the Crandall affair Garrison had courted George's sister Helen, and their marriage in 1834 cemented the Bensons' position close to the heart of New England's abolitionist leadership. Partner in a Providence wholesale wool and leather firm after 1831, George W. Benson gave that up to take overall charge of the farm in Brooklyn at his father's death five years later and devoted an increasing amount of time to abolitionist activities. He was a local agent for the *Liberator*, became prominent in the Windham County Anti-Slavery Society, and from 1837, served as Connecticut agent for the American Anti-Slavery Society. The Benson house, which Prudence Crandall apparently called "the asylum of the oppressed," was an important stop for abolitionist lecturers touring the state or traveling between New York and Boston. In the late 1830s, under Benson's sisters, it was the effective headquarters of the Brooklyn Female Anti-Slavery Society. After the Crandall affair and a split in the town's Unitarian church it served to focus a network of sympathetic neighbors and supporters that would, in time, provide many members of the Northampton Association.

The Bensons' seventy-five-acre farm was supposed to support George's mother and sisters and his own growing family of small children. By 1840, he later wrote, it was evident that it could not. Why this was so is unclear: possibly the rolling upland soil was not very productive; more likely Benson's other activities left him insufficient time to devote to farming. At all events he sold it in the spring of 1841 and moved his family to Northampton. He persuaded one of his neighbors, another abolitionist farmer, Theodore Scarborough, to move his family too. At first, they even brought the Unitarian minister, May's successor William Coe, with them, but Coe withdrew from the group as the Northampton community was forming. It seems that Benson moved to Northampton intending to invest the proceeds of his farm in the property of the Northampton Silk Company, and that during 1841 he was gathering partners together to go in with him in silk manufacturing. Over the course of the year, as prospective partners were assembling, the manufacturing project turned into a wider effort to promote social change by creating a community of reformers, if not at Benson's instigation, then certainly with his support.[2]

Close counterparts to Benson and Scarborough were Samuel L. Hill and his friend Hiram Wells, though they were artisans, not merchants and landowners. Hill, seventh child of a Quaker farmer and carpenter in Rhode Island, had broken with the Society of Friends when he married outside it, had himself trained as a carpenter, and then tried unsuccessfully to be a trader before becoming a mill overseer in the growing factory town of Willimantic, Connecticut, in the late 1820s. Here, while he advanced in the management of successive cotton mills, he had become a pillar of the Baptist church, but broke with it in the mid-1830s as he developed his sympathy with Garrisonian abolitionism, and never joined a church again. He gained some local prominence as an abolitionist leader, helped found a male antislavery society in 1836 in emulation of the Female Anti-Slavery Society of Willimantic, set up the previous year, and became well known to abolitionists across eastern Connecticut as he took part in their meetings or offered hospitality to traveling lecturers. Wells was a blacksmith who had grown up in the nearby town of Lebanon and later moved to Mansfield to work as a machinist. He also had reform sympathies and, though less active in the movement, had, with Hill, become acquainted with the circle of Windham County abolitionists based in Brooklyn. In 1841 Hill purchased a farm at Broughton's Meadow and found Benson, Coe, and others already negotiating for the Northampton Silk Company property that lay adjacent to it. Consolidating the two properties, Hill and Wells joined what turned into the community, bringing with them a sort of businesslike determination and skepticism that may explain why they stayed in the association for the duration of its existence, and would take a leading part in its later transformation. As with the Bensons, though to a lesser extent, their abolitionist, work, and neighborhood contacts in the Willimantic area enabled them to recruit members.[3]

Kinship, proximity, and industry, as much as reform or abolition, linked these men to the third pair of founders, Joseph Conant and Earl Dwight Swift, to whom Hill was related by marriage and whom Wells would have known and perhaps worked with. As New England's household-based rural economy evolved in the early nineteenth century, northeastern Connecticut became engaged in silk raising and manufacturing. The scattered hamlets and rapidly flowing streams of the town of Mansfield emerged as the single most significant center of silk production. Beginning in about 1810, local merchants and mechanics had introduced machinery to process locally raised raw silk, and by the 1830s some small mills were established at water-power sites in the town. Always uncertain and unstable businesses, these silk mills were run by a few families, occasionally reinforced by skilled silk workers from England and elsewhere. Joseph Conant, born in Mansfield in 1792, became involved in 1829 in a venture that would grow into the Mansfield Silk Company, the town's first substantial joint-stock firm in the silk business. Though the company went bankrupt in the mid-1830s it drew others into silk manufacture permanently. Among Conant's assistants was Orwell S. Chaffee, who had grown up on a farm in Mansfield, married Conant's daughter Lucina in 1834, and worked with his father-in-law until he tried to set up his own mill four years later. Conant also employed Earl Dwight

Swift, who also came from a trading and silk-manufacturing family and would marry another of Conant's daughters, Olive, in 1839. The economic conditions of the late 1830s, however, played havoc with the prospects for silk production in Connecticut. When the Northampton Silk Company in Massachusetts, already bankrupt, sought an experienced man to supervise its mill in 1839, Conant took the job and moved north. Olive Conant Swift and her new husband went with him, and were also employed by the Silk Company. In 1840 Joseph Conant took a three-year lease on the Northampton mill from the company's assignees for $1,000 a year and operated it on his own account. In 1841 Benson arrived, probably intending to join him in the business, but as Hill and Coe also became involved during the year, the idea of forming a community began to take hold.

Little evidence survives of Conant's opinions or his stand on abolition, though a claim made much later that he had been involved in the Underground Railroad in Mansfield suggests that he was sympathetic to the cause. The memoir of a Northampton community member indicated that Conant and Swift were happy to go along with the change from silk company to association because they were amenable both to its principles and to its potential as a profitable investment. Conant's experience in silk manufacture and his ability to invest in the association made his presence valuable to Benson and the others, and they honored this by choosing him as their first president. From Conant's viewpoint Benson's interest in investing in the mill probably seemed the best chance of surviving in the silk industry at a time of great uncertainty. The formation of the community enabled him to keep his family and its skills together, because he brought into it both of his sons-in-law and their families. Swift brought $1,000 in capital to invest. Chaffee had evidently had difficulty establishing his own firm in Mansfield and probably found coming to Northampton an attractive way of staying in what was becoming a precarious industry.[4]

The business anxieties of Conant and his extended family had little connection with the concerns of the fourth "pair" of community founders, Hall Judd and Samuel Brooks. These men may have had little in common, except in two respects: both were among the few members of the association who came from the immediate vicinity of Northampton, and both lived very simply. We know little about Brooks, but he seems to have been poor. He had owned a very small farm in the nearby town of Hadley, had a mortgage on it, and sold this land in 1842 for no more than he had paid for it. He also had a large family, whom he brought with him into the Northampton community soon after it was founded. Evidently the Brooks family was seeking something the group could not provide, for later in 1842 they left Northampton for the Shaker community at Enfield, Connecticut, where a number of them were still living in 1850.[5] Judd came from a background that rejected extravagance and embraced evangelical religion, temperance, abolition, and nonresistance. He preferred an ascetic life. His father, Sylvester Judd, a Northampton editor and historian, retained a firm republican suspicion of fashion or display of any kind; his brother Sylvester, Jr. was a Unitarian minister whose minor transcendentalist writings also evoked the simplicity of a vanishing way of life.[6]

Hall Judd turned these ideas into a set of precepts about diet, dress, and worldly comforts so rigid that even his family teased him about it. A brother told of visiting the family home while Hall was away and sleeping in his bed, "if bed it might be called . . . 'The soft side of a *Plank*' would be *Down* compared to it." On another occasion his mother brought pies to the dinner table, and Hall "as usual, denounced all *living* except on Faith and Saw Dust." Hall had worked as a clerk and as a farm laborer in Connecticut and western Massachusetts. His views on slavery and religion got him excommunicated from churches in Hartford and Northampton, but his movements and connections with radical abolitionists had led him to a Connecticut woman, Frances Birge, of principles similar to his. She could, wrote Hall's mother, "turn her hand to any kind of work, she is a good sewer, is economical, is healthy, a thorough Grahamite, her views of dress, and of fashions, and of things which belong to the world perfectly agree with Hall's." Over several months in early 1842, Hall Judd spent time in Northampton discussing reform principles with Benson and his colleagues; and though he was apparently not at the initial meeting, he was clearly regarded as a potential community member. Shortly after its founding, Hall Judd and Frances Birge married and formally joined the association. They were to remain in it to the end.[7]

Though arbitrary in part, this "pairing" of some of the men who started the Northampton community allows us to identify common strands of interest and commitment that led members to join. To differing degrees, abolition, nonresistance, and manufacturing were interwoven in the lives of them all, and for some a commitment to asceticism was a further draw toward community. Their backgrounds and acquaintanceships also overlapped and helped bring them together. Even Conant and his sons-in-law acted together, they joined the association early in its life and would leave together later in 1842 to set up again as silk manufacturers on their own.

Though they also had overlapping interests—in abolition, nonresistance, and education—the three remaining figures among the founders are less easy to group with others. David Mack, Erasmus Darwin Hudson, and William Adam were all strongly committed to social reform, but came from quite distinct backgrounds and traditions. All would make a mark on the life of the community, but their dealings there with one another would be tense, at times even hostile. Their work together would be the result of coalition rather than personal loyalty. Not only would this affect the character of the community's development but it would help explain why all three men and their families withdrew between 1843 and 1845.

Of Northampton's "founders" David Mack was probably the most enthusiastic about the prospects for communities as instruments of social change. Born in Middlefield, a hill town west of Northampton, son of a merchant who later settled in nearby Amherst, Mack had studied at Yale and then started to train as a lawyer, but abandoned that for a teaching career, and in 1831 became preceptor of a Quaker school in New Bedford. In 1836 he joined the New Bedford Young Men's Anti-Slavery Society. By then he had married another teacher, Maria Brastow, and they later moved to Cambridge to set up their own school for girls. Intellectual interests and reform sympathies brought the Macks to the edges of both the transcendentalist circle and Garrison's abolitionist clique.

In 1841 David and Maria observed with interest the formation of the Brook Farm community. In fact, both signed Brook Farm's articles of association in February 1842 with the intention of joining. By early March, however, they had changed their minds and planned instead to move to Northampton in May. The reasons for the switch are unclear, but a letter sent to Mack from Brook Farm the previous summer by Nathaniel Hawthorne hints at some of Mack's anxieties. Hawthorne was evidently keen to assure Mack of the untruth of rumors then circulating that Brook Farm's founder George Ripley exercised undue power over the members: "We have never looked upon him as a master, or an employer, but as a fellow laborer on the same terms as ourselves, with no more right to bid us perform any one act of labor, than we have to bid him." Mack evidently overcame any misgivings sufficiently to sign up at Brook Farm, but must have learned almost immediately of the proposal to create a new community at Northampton. Possibly the prospect of joining a group where there was no single leader, but a set of elected officers, caused him to change his family's plans. In time Mack would himself serve in several capacities at Northampton, as president after Joseph Conant left, and then as secretary and director of education, in place of William Adam. He may even have persuaded Hawthorne to consider joining the Northampton community with him; the author at any rate thought it necessary to write to Mack in late May 1842 to explain that he was not coming after all.[8]

Erasmus Darwin Hudson was drawn to Northampton by his abolitionism and by the connections he had made with Benson, Hill, and Judd, but his career had been different from any of theirs. Brought up and married in the town of Torringford in western Connecticut, he had trained as a physician—indeed, still practiced on occasion—and then become successively a schoolteacher, amateur geologist, and avid temperance reformer. A Congregationalist, his orthodox religious views were unshaken until he became involved in the abolitionist movement in the mid-1830s, first in Litchfield County, then as a founder of the Connecticut Anti-Slavery Society. Increasingly sympathetic with the radical wing of immediate abolitionism, he became a tireless itinerant agent for both the Connecticut and American Anti-Slavery Societies, using his lecture tours and his contributions to the Connecticut society's newspaper, the Hartford *Charter Oak*, to advocate the Garrisonian cause in a state largely hostile to it.

Hudson had lectured with Benson, valued Benson's home in Brooklyn as a base and a haven, spoken at meetings organized by Hill, and found himself in strong sympathy with Hall Judd. On a lecture tour in 1839–1840 Hudson carried a pocket-sized memorandum book to compile comments, for future reference, on the men and women he encountered. All three men came in for praise: Benson as a hospitable "whole soul reformer," Hill as "a good Christian philanthropist," and Judd as a man of principle with whom he felt particular affinity. Hudson's move to Northampton followed from Benson and Hill's decision to set up a community. Indeed, he may, like Judd, have been involved in discussions about it during the early spring of 1842. But Hudson seems to have regarded the community more as a home for his family and a base for his work as an abolitionist lecturer than as something to engage his own wholehearted commitment; at any rate he had clear notions about the terms on which he could be content with community life. Much more than Conant or Swift that day in April 1842 Hudson held himself back from participating too directly in its business.[9]

Of these ten men, seven were from Connecticut and three from Massachusetts. In both a geographical and a cultural sense the eleventh founder, William Adam, and his family, had traveled much further than the others to be present at the start of the Northampton community. Adam's extraordinary story suggests that he was a man of considerable talent, resourcefulness, and courage who, nevertheless, never quite succeeded at what he set out to do. Born in Scotland in 1796, educated there and in England in the classics, theology, and Asian languages, he had sailed to India in 1817 to join the Baptist mission at Serampore, just outside Calcutta. Two years later he married Phebe Grant, daughter of another missionary, at Calcutta's Anglican church. Despite his early efforts as a missionary, in 1821 he was himself converted to Unitarianism by a prominent Hindu reformer, Ram Mohun Roy. Scandalized missionaries spoke of him as "the second fallen Adam." At times supporting himself as a mercantile clerk, he spent the next seventeen years working against long odds to influence the British East India Company's rule in Bengal.

He assisted in the running of an Anglo-Indian school, but angrily resigned after a disagreement. Having become a Unitarian minister after his conversion, he tried and failed during the 1820s to convince Ram Mohun Roy to accept Christian monotheism. He established a church in Calcutta, with some support from British and American Unitarians, only to see his Bengali brahmin

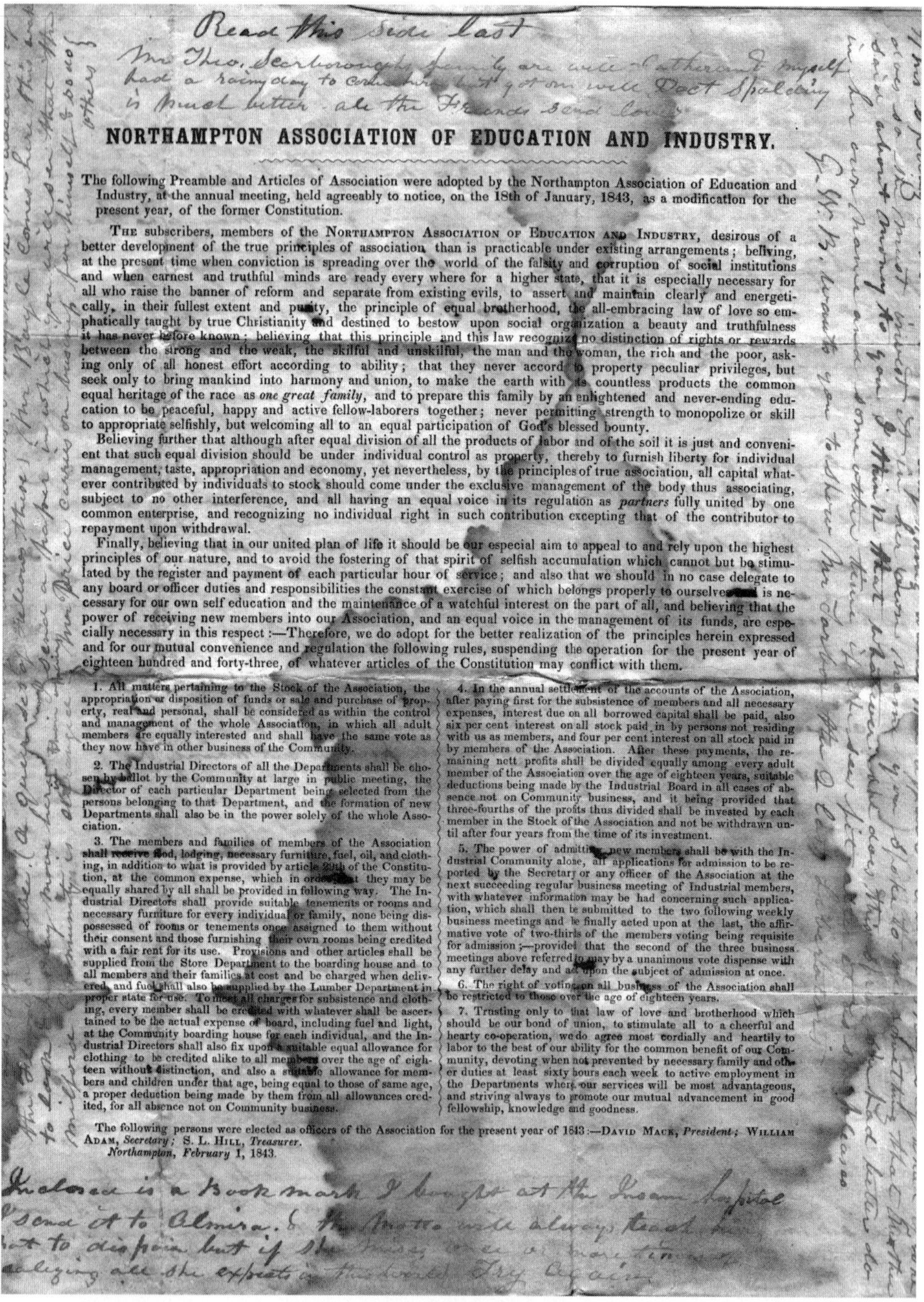

Read this side last

NORTHAMPTON ASSOCIATION OF EDUCATION AND INDUSTRY.

The following Preamble and Articles of Association were adopted by the Northampton Association of Education and Industry, at the annual meeting, held agreeably to notice, on the 18th of January, 1843, as a modification for the present year, of the former Constitution.

THE subscribers, members of the NORTHAMPTON ASSOCIATION OF EDUCATION AND INDUSTRY, desirous of a better development of the true principles of association than is practicable under existing arrangements; beliving, at the present time when conviction is spreading over the world of the falsity and corruption of social institutions and when earnest and truthful minds are ready every where for a higher state, that it is especially necessary for all who raise the banner of reform and separate from existing evils, to assert and maintain clearly and energetically, in their fullest extent and purity, the principle of equal brotherhood, the all-embracing law of love so emphatically taught by true Christianity and destined to bestow upon social organization a beauty and truthfulness it has never before known; believing that this principle and this law recognize no distinction of rights or rewards between the strong and the weak, the skilful and unskilful, the man and the woman, the rich and the poor, asking only of all honest effort according to ability; that they never accord to property peculiar privileges, but seek only to bring mankind into harmony and union, to make the earth with its countless products the common equal heritage of the race as *one great family*, and to prepare this family by an enlightened and never-ending education to be peaceful, happy and active fellow-laborers together; never permitting strength to monopolize or skill to appropriate selfishly, but welcoming all to an equal participation of God's blessed bounty.

Believing further that although after equal division of all the products of labor and of the soil it is just and convenient that such equal division should be under individual control as property, thereby to furnish liberty for individual management, taste, appropriation and economy, yet nevertheless, by the principles of true association, all capital whatever contributed by individuals to stock should come under the exclusive management of the body thus associating, subject to no other interference, and all having an equal voice in its regulation as *partners* fully united by one common enterprise, and recognizing no individual right in such contribution excepting that of the contributor to repayment upon withdrawal.

Finally, believing that in our united plan of life it should be our especial aim to appeal to and rely upon the highest principles of our nature, and to avoid the fostering of that spirit of selfish accumulation which cannot but be stimulated by the register and payment of each particular hour of service; and also that we should in no case delegate to any board or officer duties and responsibilities the constant exercise of which belongs properly to ourselves [illegible] is necessary for our own self education and the maintenance of a watchful interest on the part of all, and believing that the power of receiving new members into our Association, and an equal voice in the management of its funds, are especially necessary in this respect:—Therefore, we do adopt for the better realization of the principles herein expressed and for our mutual convenience and regulation the following rules, suspending the operation for the present year of eighteen hundred and forty-three, of whatever articles of the Constitution may conflict with them.

1. All matters pertaining to the Stock of the Association, the appropriation or disposition of funds or sale and purchase of property, real and personal, shall be considered as within the control and management of the whole Association, in which all adult members are equally interested and shall have the same vote as they now have in other business of the Community.

2. The Industrial Directors of all the Departments shall be chosen by ballot by the Community at large in public meeting, the Director of each particular Department being selected from the persons belonging to that Department, and the formation of new Departments shall also be in the power solely of the whole Association.

3. The members and families of members of the Association shall receive food, lodging, necessary furniture, fuel, oil, and clothing, in addition to what is provided by article 29th of the Constitution, at the common expense, which in order that they may be equally shared by all shall be provided in following way. The Industrial Directors shall provide suitable tenements or rooms and necessary furniture for every individual or family, none being dispossessed of rooms or tenements once assigned to them without their consent and those furnishing their own rooms being credited with a fair rent for its use. Provisions and other articles shall be supplied from the Store Department to the boarding house and to all members and their families at cost and be charged when delivered, and fuel shall also be supplied by the Lumber Department in proper state for use. To meet all charges for subsistence and clothing, every member shall be credited with whatever shall be ascertained to be the actual expense of board, including fuel and light, at the Community boarding house for each individual, and the Industrial Directors shall also fix upon a suitable equal allowance for clothing to be credited alike to all members over the age of eighteen without distinction, and also a suitable allowance for members and children under that age, being equal to those of same age, a proper deduction being made by them from all allowances credited, for all absence not on Community business.

4. In the annual settlement of the accounts of the Association, after paying first for the subsistence of members and all necessary expenses, interest due on all borrowed capital shall be paid, also six per cent interest on all stock paid in by persons not residing with us as members, and four per cent interest on all stock paid in by members of the Association. After these payments, the remaining nett profits shall be divided equally among every adult member of the Association over the age of eighteen years, suitable deductions being made by the Industrial Board in all cases of absence not on Community business, and it being provided that three-fourths of the profits thus divided shall be invested by each member in the Stock of the Association and not be withdrawn until after four years from the time of its investment.

5. The power of admitting new members shall be with the Industrial Community alone, all applications for admission to be reported by the Secretary or any officer of the Association at the next succeeding regular business meeting of Industrial members, with whatever information may be had concerning such application, which shall then be submitted to the two following weekly business meetings and be finally acted upon at the last, the affirmative vote of two-thirds of the members voting being requisite for admission;—provided that the second of the three business meetings above referred to may by a unanimous vote dispense with any further delay and act upon the subject of admission at once.

6. The right of voting on all business of the Association shall be restricted to those over the age of eighteen years.

7. Trusting only to that law of love and brotherhood which should be our bond of union, to stimulate all to a cheerful and hearty co-operation, we do agree most cordially and heartily to labor to the best of our ability for the common benefit of our Community, devoting when not prevented by necessary family and other duties at least sixty hours each week to active employment in the Departments where our services will be most advantageous, and striving always to promote our mutual advancement in good fellowship, knowledge and goodness.

The following persons were elected as officers of the Association for the present year of 1843:—DAVID MACK, *President*; WILLIAM ADAM, *Secretary*; S. L. HILL, *Treasurer*.

Northampton, February 1, 1843.

Constitution of the Northampton Association of Education and Industry, revised version adopted January 18, 1843, with letter by James Stetson. *Historic Northampton.*

When James Stetson wrote his wife, Dolly Witter Stetson, on Februrary 20, 1843, he penned his remarks in the margins and on the reverse of this copy of the association's constitution. "I think you will find congenial spiritts here," he wrote, "with whome you will be happy and in whose projects you can hartily unite. . . ."

congregation depart for Ram Mohun Roy's new religious society, the Brahmo Sabha, in 1828. Abandoning the ministry, Adam then edited a succession of Calcutta newspapers. Objecting to East India Company policies, he was obliged to move from one paper to another as the government suppressed them. Against the background of a fierce debate about the future of education in British India, he was commissioned in the mid-1830s to study schooling in Bengal and neighboring Bihar. Knowing, even as he set out, that the government had determined to support education conducted in English, Adam spent three years of travel and systematic research preparing reports that firmly advocated the contrary policy of sponsoring education in vernacular languages. As he left India in 1838, it was evident that his recommendations would be ignored. William Adam had apparently failed again.

Yet his years in India gave him connections and ideas that would indirectly pave the way to involvement with the Northampton community. Adam's effort to establish Unitarianism in Calcutta gave him contacts with leading churchmen in Massachusetts. His mercantile work introduced him to Boston shipowners and merchants in the East Indies trade, including members of the Dixwell family, who would provide hospitality and financial assistance to the Adams when they came to the United States. His friendship with Ram Mohun Roy, though often strained (and ended by the latter's death during a visit to England in 1833), introduced Adam to concepts of religious toleration not very different from those later adopted at Northampton. With hindsight, Adam would come to see Ram Mohun Roy's involvement in a successful campaign to obtain a law against *sati* (widow-burning) in 1829 as his own introduction to women's rights. Adam's journalistic campaigns for reform made him critical of governmental power. The work for his reports on schooling gave him a detailed, sympathetic understanding of Asian rural society matched by few, if any, contemporary westerners. Though Adam's background and experience would lead to important differences with New Englanders, his views on equality and religion were close enough to theirs for him to make common cause with other founders of the community. He was the only member of the Northampton community who had considered in some depth how a whole society might be reformed by education. At the same time, he recognized that change through education was gradual, and that radical reform demanded other social changes as well.[10]

William's precarious income and the Dixwells' patronage led Phebe Adam to leave Calcutta for Boston with her children in 1834. He followed four years later with the intention of taking them on to London. Probably because Phebe refused to move, William instead visited England briefly by himself, then accepted a post created for him at Harvard as professor of Oriental Literature and returned to take it up. He disliked Cambridge and his job, but made contacts among Garrison's circle of abolitionists. They completed his conversion to radical abolitionism; he, in turn, captivated them with the prospect that land reform in Bengal, for which he was starting to campaign, could strike a blow against American slavery by producing cheap cotton for European markets. When Adam sailed for England again in 1840—this time with his family—it was as a Massachusetts Anti-Slavery Society delegate to the World's Anti-Slavery Convention held in London that June. There he cemented his alliance with the Garrisonians by supporting their demand that the convention seat the women delegates who attended. When the demand was refused, it was Adam who drafted the radicals' formal protest.[11]

At this point he resigned from Harvard and stayed on in London to become secretary of the British India Society, a group with close abolitionist and free trade connections formed to press the British government for reforms in India. He also edited its newspaper, the *British Indian Advocate*. Adam's knowledge and experience excellently qualified him for this work, but he was restless and discontented in England and soon thought of emigrating again. Now, he decided, he would become a farmer. His family was anxious to return to America, but Adam wavered, and even paid a deposit on some land in Australia before acceding to their wish. They set out in the late summer of 1841 with the intention of buying a farm in Pennsylvania, but Adam had also read articles in the transcendentalist journal, the *Dial*, lent him by Wendell Phillips, and this may have given him the idea of joining one of the new communitarian experiments instead. Still undecided, he made inquiries about Brook Farm, but late in the year ended up in Northampton. Having first looked around for land to buy, he decided instead to join Benson and the others in setting up the Northampton community. With the strong endorsement of William Lloyd Garrison, he came highly recommended to the new group. This, his unusual experience, and his status as a "professor" gave him considerable influence. He became an early investor in the scheme and almost certainly played a major part in the discussions over the winter of 1841–1842 that preceded the community's founding. His credentials would both help and hinder his acceptance of community life. His cultural distance from some of the American reformers he had joined would lead to mutual awkwardness that ultimately contributed to his departure.[12]

The Communitarian Context

The "founders" of the Northampton community were not "typical" members. The absence of women at the opening meeting signaled an assumption of superiority by men that though challenged, was never fully overturned. Still, the stories we have just outlined, of William Adam and the other ten founders, suggest both the common factors and the diversity of experience that they brought with them. An examination of these stories in the wider context of the kinds of influence—material, intellectual, and ideological—

that led them to construct a new type of social organization; an examination of the economy and ideas about business and industry, of abolitionism and nonresistance, and of the effects of those movements on religious experience, will help explain why such diverse groups of men and women as the members of the Northampton Association should have sought to found communities, and why they did so in the early 1840s.

Two sets of circumstances created the immediate context for the interest in communities among radical reformers: the financial panic of 1837 and subsequent depression, and the disputes in the abolition movement that caused it to splinter in 1839 and 1840 into two or three antagonistic fragments. In addition to these general conditions, though, there were particular ideological influences that crystallized efforts to start communities and helped determine the makeup of the group that created the Northampton Association.

The economic crisis in New England both created the opportunity for founding communities and spurred certain men and women to seek to take advantage of it. As they moved to Northampton, George W. Benson and Samuel L. Hill were among thousands responding to the long depression that began in the financial panic of 1837. Trouble began with the collapse of banks and prominent mercantile firms and spread as credit was tightened and other institutions were dragged down. Anne Talbot, sister of a Northampton capitalist, wrote in March 1837 that one of the town's two banks had closed and noted, too complacently, that that left "one here, which I should think was as much as such a place required." Among the activities hit hard by the depression, manufacturing of various kinds was prominent. In the Connecticut Valley region carriage-building, toolmaking, hat-making, and broom-making, along with parts of the textile industry, were forced to shut down or severely to reduce their scale of operation and would recover, if at all, only after several years of weakness and uncertainty. In Willimantic, Connecticut, Samuel L. Hill survived these early years of financial panic, but not untouched; the textile firm he managed was shaken by the failure of one of its backers in 1837, and Hill apparently changed jobs at around this time. Other future members of the community also faced the prospect of ruin as the depression spread.[13]

Newspapers began to fill with articles and editorials advocating farming as a superior, stable livelihood. Many men in uncertain businesses with enough capital to buy land of their own contemplated becoming farmers. Samuel L. Hill moved to Northampton in 1841 for this purpose. When William Adam arrived in town that October, he was still pursuing the plan he had conceived before leaving England: "He is resolved on purchasing a farm," wrote a Boston friend; "he is to work on it himself and be aided by his family." Hall Judd too, tired of clerkships and laboring jobs, had been planning to become a farmer, and had gone to Connecticut in October 1841 to look for a suitable place near Bloomfield. It was already commonplace among reformers to connect the wish to take up farming with a wider desire to influence society by setting up communities. The link had been made most prominently by George Ripley, as he led the movement to turn transcendentalism from philosophy to social action and set up the Brook Farm community. If the plans for Brook Farm had not worked out, Ripley would have taken up farming anyway.[14] When Hill, Adam, and Judd turned from their plans to farm to the effort to form a community, they were following a path already taken by the founders of Brook Farm.

The Northampton community, however, was not primarily the result of a drive "back to the land" from cities and industry. All kinds of activity—rural, urban, and industrial—had been disrupted by the depression. Many members would be drawn from rural backgrounds. Few, if any, shared William Adam's expectation that he could take up farming for the first time at the age of forty-five and make a living at it. The economic crisis had strongly affected rural areas, and it was characteristic of the confusion it had produced that Hill and others "returning" to the land encountered George W. Benson and others trying to leave it. Among Benson's Brooklyn neighbors who would join the community were the members of the Scarborough family, which was heavily in debt by the late 1830s, and the mechanics Enos L. Preston and James A. Stetson, who had both been obliged to sell property to pay debts.[15] Interest in setting up communities reflected not a flight from one sphere to another, but the hope of establishing a better society capable of providing stable livelihoods.

The coalescence of the Northampton community around a silk company did not result simply from chance or opportunism. Silk production embodied the vision that farming and manufacturing in balance with each other could provide the basis for a healthy, successful form of society. Cultivating mulberry trees would provide food for silkworms, whose silk would be the raw material for the manufacture of thread and other goods. Industries that were inherently unstable even at the best of times suffered disproportionately in the depression, and silk production in Connecticut and Massachusetts was particularly vulnerable. But, ironically, as the crisis had deepened in the late 1830s, farmers and manufacturers placed increasing hope in silk as an activity that could rescue them from financial difficulty. After interruptions and business reorganizations before and during the 1837 panic, investors began to speculate in mulberry trees.

Throughout northern Connecticut and western Massachusetts mulberry cultivation expanded, and in centers such as Mansfield and Northampton silk manufacturers tried to survive the contraction of credit. The collapse of the Mansfield Silk Company in 1836 had prompted men such as Joseph Conant and Orwell S. Chaffee to try and restart production on their own on a smaller scale. Meanwhile, the Northampton Silk Company, set up in 1835–1836 with an unusually large stockholders' investment of almost $100,000, found itself in trouble as the crisis spread and struggled to rearrange its business in order to continue in the straitened circumstances of the late 1830s.[16] When the bubble of mulberry speculation finally burst in 1839, farmers and manufacturers alike were thrown into further difficulty. A desperate effort to keep the Northampton silk mills going led to Joseph Conant's appointment as superintendent late that year, and to the migration of manufacturers from Mansfield to Northampton to try their luck in this new silk region. The failure of these efforts and the stockholders' decision in 1841 to seek a buyer for the Northampton Silk Company's property prepared the ground for the formation of the Northampton community. In some ways, the Northampton Association's hope of building a community around silk seemed to perpetuate the inflated visions of the late 1830s. But the intention was to realize the balance and benefits of silk production while avoiding the evils of speculation and competition that had apparently destroyed the business in 1839.

For the depression did not lead merely to instrumental efforts to recoup losses or earn livelihoods. It also concentrated minds on a wider critique of the economic practices that led to social injustice. Hill and Benson, among other members of the community, had had painful experience of trade, its uncertainties, and the wage system and what they saw as its elements of unfairness. As former manufacturers and traders, they sought not to overthrow the existing economic system, but to organize it on more stable and equitable principles. To them, an association of people living and working together would have a chance to establish a harmonious balance between the organizational advantages of a joint-stock enterprise and the social benefits of a community of equals. It would banish the uncertainties of speculation and competitiveness. Hill commented, later in his life, on the motivations of the early members of the Northampton community: "We expected to work out an improved state of society, and make ourselves and friends happier—to get rid of the competition so omnipresent and oppressive."[17]

If they wanted an example of the things they wished to avoid in a competitive economy, they needed to look no further than the story of the property they were buying in the winter of 1841–1842. The Northampton Silk Company was built on the optimism and plausibility of Samuel Whitmarsh, a New York merchant who had settled in Northampton and bought an extensive property there at the end of the 1820s. Whitmarsh became one of a number of promoters convinced that the United States was destined to be a major silk-producing nation. Like other enthusiasts he planted mulberry trees, built a cocoonery to feed silkworms, and publicized his methods. He looked around for investors in a factory that could process raw silk into finished goods and secured backing from New York merchants led by the Talbot family, China traders who also owned a house in Northampton. The Northampton Silk Company was conceived on a large scale, but hopes for its success were dashed even before the buildings were complete. The Talbots and others were threatened by the 1837 panic, and the company was only kept going over the next two years to promote interest in silk and so fuel mulberry speculation. Whitmarsh himself faced failure, resorted to dubious tactics to stave off ruin, and was suspected of misstating the value of property and materials. When at length the company went bankrupt and Whitmarsh was forced out, a local writer recalled that he "had neither cash nor credit to buy a barrel of flour"; at least four creditors sued him. He sought to retrieve his losses in a visionary scheme to establish a silk factory in Jamaica, for which he managed to obtain substantial English backing. With him went his brother Thomas—later briefly a member of the Northampton community—and several young men from Northampton, including the son of one of his creditors, who were to help build the establishment. But this scheme also failed when, owing to carelessness or ignorance, its shipment of imported silkworms died.[18]

Different people drew different lessons from the tale of Whitmarsh and the Northampton Silk Company. At the height of his troubles in 1837, Charles Nicholl Talbot received a letter from his father advising him—with pointed reference to Whitmarsh's overconfidence—that "at your time of life a pull back will serve to give you caution and enable you to avoid engaging with those who however honest, have no doubts." It would be best for Talbot, he continued, "to commence on Mr Girard's rigid plan, 'keep my plans to myself' . . . : study your own interest, consult your own judgment, . . . however friendly you may be to others." That way, the writer concluded, "I seldom went wrong, but the moment I suffered others to influence me, I never succeeded well and often not at all."[19] Such advice led in the direction of single proprietorships, commercial independence, and individualism. Appropriate as this might be for many mercantile activities, it was hardly feasible for manufacturing efforts of much size. The Northampton Association, eventual successors to the Northampton Silk Company, sought instead to promote cooperative ownership and communal social arrangements. These, it was hoped, would permit the concentration of investment that a large factory demanded, but avoid the uncertainties and immoralities of speculative, overconfident business practice.

Abolitionists Divided

Economic depression and business crises formed part of the web of connections that brought the Northampton community together. Another was the crisis that faced the abolition movement. It was this crisis much more than economic concerns alone that had thrown crucial leaders and members of the community together in the first place and had helped define their place in the wider reform movement.

Historians of abolitionism have devoted much attention to the schisms that nearly destroyed the movement at the end of the 1830s; it is necessary here only to provide a broad outline of the issues before looking more carefully at their influence on the founders of the Northampton community. The campaign for the immediate abolition of United States slavery expanded rapidly in the early 1830s. To its early supporters among the black community were added the considerable weight of white abolitionists inspired by the evangelical revivals and the urge for social action they created. The insistence that slavery was not merely an institution to be reformed, but a "sin" to be expunged, was both the core of their campaign for immediate abolition and the entry point for the argument that northerners as well as southerners were implicated in its evils. During the mid-1830s antislavery societies were founded across New England and other parts of the North, sustained not only by indignation at chattel slavery itself but also by the political success of the South and its sympathizers in banning the distribution of abolitionist tracts and curbing debate in Congress and other public forums. Their early organizational success had several consequences for abolitionists. It provoked popular, often violent opposition in the North; it raised questions about the denial of equality to northern blacks; and it attracted strong support from women as well, whose concerted action in local and national antislavery societies itself started to bring into question widespread assumptions about the gendered bounds of public behavior. In addition, Garrisonian abolitionists in particular, critical of the political system's complicity in the crimes of slavery and increasingly suspicious that the United States Constitution was protecting slaveholders, became wary of political action as a means to effect abolition. Moral suasion and renunciation of all contact with those seen as complicit with slavery became the heart of their strategy. Their disputes with colleagues who held other views were to shatter the movement.

Gender and politics were the rocks on which the united immediate-abolitionist campaign of the 1830s broke apart. Evangelicals, led by Lewis Tappan of New York and supported by many clerical members, brought part of the split about by walking out of the 1840 annual meeting of the American Anti-Slavery Society in protest at its policy of permitting women to speak on public platforms and the appointment of Abby Kelley to its executive committee. At the same time the Garrisonian champions of women's participation were also challenged by groups seeking to form a separate antislavery political party. This would, in their view, entail a compromise with the Constitution and so signal complicity with slavery; it would also exclude women, because they could not vote.

Together these two splits left the radicals in an embattled state. They retained control of their national organization, the American Anti-Slavery Society, and of the state societies in Massachusetts, New Hampshire, and Ohio where they were particularly strong. From these bases they proclaimed their adherence to what they called "old organization" abolitionism. But they faced opposition from "new organization" abolitionism at the national and state levels, from Tappan's new American and Foreign Anti-Slavery Society, which curbed women's public participation, and from the advocates of independent political action, who formed the Liberty Party in 1840. Abolitionist publications and correspondence from 1839 to 1842 provide ample evidence that these splits and the often subtle differences of opinion and alignment that they entailed occupied an increasing proportion of reformers' time and attention. The "old organization" abolitionists (loyal to Garrison) took particular pains to distinguish themselves from both Tappanite evangelicals and political abolitionists, whom they regarded as tainted with "new organization" and "third partyism." Contemporaries and historians alike have often asked what these disputes had to do with the movement's ostensible purpose, to free slaves.[20]

Historical interpretations of these disputes have tended, until recently, to consider their role in the movement's own strategies or their more general impact on antebellum history. Aileen S. Kraditor, for example, argued that Garrisonian policies and tactics did further the movement's overall purpose of ending slavery. A more skeptical school of thought dismisses the abolitionists' splits as petty sectarian wranglings among a small group of men and women whose influence was insignificant. A third type of argument, succinctly expressed by Ronald G. Walters in his study *The Antislavery Appeal*, suggests that the abolitionists' divisions should not be overemphasized because they merely masked the more fundamental patterns of agreement between radicals, evangelicals, and Liberty Party advocates that were ultimately to draw the various factions closer together again in the 1850s.[21]

But for our purposes the wider implications of these disputes are less important than their effects on the men and women who took part in them. There is little doubt that they took them very seriously indeed; otherwise they would not have filled newspaper columns and countless letters writing about them. Both the radicals and their opponents were convinced that the debates over women and politics, and the other issues that followed from these, presaged fundamental social change. As an unsympathetic minister had written at the prospect of the Grimké sisters' appearance to lecture at Fourth of July celebrations in Newburyport in 1837, "A man . . . might as well attempt to stem the current of some mighty river or the fury of a hurrican[e] as to oppose the Abolition torrent which is now sweeping over the northern portions of our land and threatening to destroy and prostrate whatever it cannot carry along with it," and he expressed himself opposed to "everything which is ultra and wrong."[22] The splits in the abolition movement were highly significant in creating the radical "moment" of the early 1840s, and in several ways they helped shape the context in which communitarianism grew up.

Recent studies of the abolitionist movement that emphasize personalities and group culture have implied that the splits of the late 1830s and 1840s can be attributed to a built-in proclivity for instability and dispute. Undoubtedly there were psychological and structural conditions that fostered fragmentation among these reformers;[23] nevertheless, there is an impersonality about such interpretations that overlooks two important aspects of events. First, abolitionists disputed with one another and broke apart their organizations not just because their personalities disposed them to it, but because they were fighting for what they recognized as real issues of principle—principles, moreover, that were as deeply held on the conservative or evangelical side of the split as they were on the radical side. Second, the splits over women's rights and politics caused considerable pain to men and women who found ranged against them friends and colleagues with whom they had once shared hard campaigns. Horace Cowles, who had been active in western Connecticut, wrote to George W. Benson early in 1841 expressing regret at the break in the antislavery movement and the silence of more than a year that this had caused between them; however, he also ended his letter with a condemnation of Garrison and his followers' positions on women's rights and third-partyism, which, given that it was addressed to Garrison's own brother-in-law, was presumably not an effort to strike a compromise. At the same time Benson was criticizing attacks made on Garrison by Reverend Nathaniel Colver and his "new organization" allies: "No stone will be left unturned . . . to destroy his [Garrison's] reputation. Judgeing them by their conduct I should think they more earnestly desired [that] than the emancipation of the slaves."[24] Many among the abolitionists who came to the Northampton community were deeply embroiled in the movement's rifts and were preoccupied by them between 1839 and 1841.

Connecticut was the scene of particularly bitter conflict. With local exceptions, such as in the Bensons' own Windham County, immediatist abolitionism had been slow to take root, and there was no separate state antislavery society until 1838, five years after the founding of the Massachusetts society. No sooner did the movement gain ground than it split apart, and Garrisonians largely lost control of the state's main antislavery societies and newspapers to their opponents. Adherents to "new organization" captured the Connecticut Anti-Slavery Society and its organ the *Charter Oak* and cast off Erasmus Darwin Hudson, Benson, and others who remained loyal to Garrison. Hudson revealed his disappointment at the rift when, shortly after being removed from his post, he recorded a visit to Hartford in his diary: "Called at my former home the Anti Slavery Depository!—It is now a gloomy place! The anti slavery spirit . . . has fled—a bitter Sectarian, anti woman, anti Garrison-time serving, *popularity seeking* spirit has taken full possession!" The only thing that cheered him up was meeting his "good warm hearted brother" Hall Judd.[25] Even Windham County, where considerable support for Garrison remained, proved uncertain and divided. Local societies, including the Brooklyn Female Anti-Slavery Society, supported by the Bensons and their neighbors, ceased to function. In February 1841 Garrisonians had called an eastern Connecticut antislavery convention to meet the following month in Willimantic, and Benson claimed that "in this section of the country the cause never looked more promising, the people are almost wholly united in the life giving principles of old organization." But the convention proved his optimism misplaced, showing support for plans to organize a third party and condemning Abby Kelley's participation in the American Anti-Slavery Society's executive committee. When the Connecticut Anti-Slavery Society met in Hartford in May, and Kelley rose to speak, she was denied the right to do so on the grounds that the meeting's invitation to "all persons" did not include women. Garrison supporters were losing ground rapidly in the state as a whole, to which Kelley would refer in a letter to Benson as "your inhospitable region."[26]

Against such a background of dissension and defeat these abolitionists, their families, and some of their friends decided to search for somewhere else to move to, a search that would lead them to set up the Northampton community. Four founders of the community, Benson, Hudson, Samuel L. Hill, and William Coe, had been prominent at the Willimantic convention; six men and women who would later join it were among the signers of a protest against the Connecticut Anti-Slavery Society's silencing of Kelley. One of them, Susan Byrne, treasurer of the Willimantic Female Anti-Slavery Society (Working), also wrote to Garrison to criticize the "disorderly conduct" of Kelley's opponents. She linked the campaign for women's rights to demands for radical social change: "We have not forgotten the taxes which caused revolutionary war, [nor] . . . the aristocratic feeling that keeps the laboring people destitute of knowledge." But the pain of the abolitionist split was an inducement to members of the many small groups of Garrisonians across Connecticut to gather together for mutual support. When Samuel L. Hill said that the Northampton community was intended to "make ourselves and friends happier—to get rid of the competition so omnipresent and oppressive," he was referring not just to wider economic and social conditions, but also to the strife he and his abolitionist colleagues faced at the beginning of the 1840s.[27]

So a mixture of material and ideological circumstances led reformers to Northampton. But to understand more fully why they chose to form a community and sought to construct a new way of life we must look further at their beliefs and at the practical issues those beliefs had posed for their position in the abolition movement in the late 1830s. For some abolitionists the split between old and new organization was much more than a debate over the tactics and strategy of achieving reform; it was a cultural struggle that engaged them in a fundamental reevaluation of society at large.

Nonresistants

For none was this more true than for the groups of men and women, many of them supporters of Garrison, who by the late 1830s had identified themselves as "nonresistants" and were ready to extend antislavery reform into a full critique of existing society, government, and institutions. Following Christ's injunction to "resist not evil," they rejected any recourse to the use of force, and relied on the power of moral suasion to carry their arguments. There was, of course, a lengthy tradition of Christian nonviolence evident in America from the seventeenth century on among Quakers and other sects. Quakers had contributed to the growth of peace societies in the 1820s, and in time this involvement led some of them to embrace abolitionism. Two factors helped strengthen the abolitionist peace movement and turn it toward nonresistance. First, popular opposition to abolition, which grew as it did in the 1830s, demonstrated the realities of a society many of whose citizens were intent either on using violence themselves, or on acquiescing in its use, to defend the sin of slaveholding. Second, as they refined the theoretical underpinnings of their attacks on slavery, some immediatists—including Garrison—came to see that slavery was only one manifestation of "the ancient and universal recognition, contrary to Christian teaching, of the right of coercion by some men in regard to others, . . . that the only irrefutable argument against slavery is a denial of any man's right over the liberty of another under any conditions whatsoever."[28] To work against the authority of any institution backed by force or the threat of it therefore became both a realistic practical action and a logical principle. The formation of the New England Non-Resistance Society in 1838 marked the merging of abolitionist and peace principles and a radicalization of the two movements. Nonresistance was a crucial strand, both in the splits in the antislavery movement and the subsequent creation of utopian communities.

As the historian Lewis Perry has shown, radical abolitionists of the late 1830s adopted a particular form of nonresistance. They did not follow its conservative version, which counseled passive submission to authority. Nor, though it was fundamental to their principles, did they limit themselves to the practice of nonviolence. They went further, condemning all institutions based on force and rejecting the legitimacy of existing governments, churches, and other organizations in any way implicated in the coercion of other human beings. To abolitionist nonresistants several sets of convictions came to fit together. Not only should war, capital punishment, and other forms of governmental coercion be rejected, but participation in government at any level should be avoided.[29] Not only should Christian fellowship with slaveholders be avoided, but efforts should be made to reform existing churches to bring this about, and connections broken with churches that refused to banish them. Not only should "all persons," men and women, be free to speak out against sin, but organizations that curbed that freedom should be spurned. As nonresistance grew among New England immediatist abolitionists in 1838 and 1839, it played a powerful and logically consistent role in the radicals' rejection of evangelical and political antislavery. The splits in abolitionism over women's rights and plans for a new political party were underpinned by nonresistance principles.

Their opponents termed the nonresistants "no-governmentists," claiming that they were willing to attack all existing institutions in any way implicated in the use of force. Many abolitionists condemned nonresistants, as they condemned other advocates of women's rights, for bringing "extraneous" issues into the antislavery movement and diverting it from its true purposes. One logical outgrowth of nonresistance was, obviously, a form of radical individualism or anarchism that rejected all kinds of organization whatsoever and placed individual men and women in atomized relationships with one another and in direct, unmediated relationship with God. Those who called them "no-governmentists" or "no-organizationists" feared the social disorder and lack of control that might flow from this position. But, as Perry has pointed out, Garrison and his nonresistant allies rejected these labels. Though they attacked existing "human government," they sought to establish the "government of God" and social institutions that could embody it. Their arguments contained a strong streak of perfectionism, inspiring action to build a better way of life. Nonresistance in this form led not to a rejection of institutions as such but to a search for new social organizations uncorrupted by existing evils.[30]

Many of the founders and early members of the Northampton community were connected with nonresistance. At least twenty, including Benson, Hill, Hudson, Judd, Mack, and Scarborough, had attended nonresistance meetings, contributed to the Non-Resistance Society, or actively advocated its principles; others, such as William Adam, were sympathetic. It may be significant that William Coe, the Unitarian minister who at first joined Benson, Conant, and Hill to purchase the silk company property in 1841 and then relinquished his place to Adam, had expressed reservations about nonresistance and never embraced it. Meanwhile, it was as nonresistants that residents of Northampton who observed the group's preparations identified them. After meeting William Adam in December 1841, Hall Judd's father noted in his diary that "he and some other nonresistants have purchased lands in and about Broughton's Meadow" and wrote a few weeks later of Hall that "a few of his nonresistant brethren have planted themselves . . . near the Silk Factory."[31] These men and women were among numbers of nonresistants for whom community appeared a sensible outgrowth of their criticisms of existing institutions. Various strands in their reform and religious experience led them to set up a new social structure with particular ways of realizing the ideal of perfect government on earth.

The nonresistance principles of key founders and members of the Northampton community were not just abstractions. They had been forged and reinforced by harsh practical experience, and were all the more powerfully held for that. Their view that northern society rested on violence was rooted not just in political theory, but in the treatment they often saw meted out to free blacks and escaped slaves, and in the hostility they met in their own work as abolitionists. Benson had become acquainted with mob violence, some of it officially sanctioned, during the Prudence Crandall affair and had subsequently faced down threatening crowds on more than one occasion. In 1835 Samuel L. Hill had confronted a mob led by a fellow deacon in his own church, an incident that led him to leave the church and adopt nonresistance.[32] Itinerant lecturers like Erasmus Darwin Hudson frequently faced disruption, threats, and actual violence. At Harwinton, Connecticut, in August 1838 rioters released a herd of pigs onto the meeting ground while Hudson was speaking. More seriously, having spoken at a Baptist meetinghouse in Georgetown that November, Hudson awoke the next morning to find that his horse had been attacked: "My *old grey* had been in *bad hands* during the night and was badly sheared—her tail was all cut off." Word then arrived that the meetinghouse had been blown up. He did not believe this at first, but went and "found it too true." Someone had put twenty-five pounds of gunpowder under the pulpit he had lectured from and set it off. Three years later (the "old grey" evidently having gone to greener pastures), another of Hudson's horses suffered for his actions. After an argument with some Universalists at Clinton, Connecticut, Hudson found the animal's mane cut off, its tail trimmed, and two-thirds of one of its ears missing. Having spent some time cheering "Old Dick" up, Hudson and five others sewed back together the remnants of his buffalo robe, which the attackers had also shredded. At Newtown a week later the traces to his wagon were cut. Hudson wrote of these events as trials heroically overcome, but they both reinforced an emergent critique of society and the need to rely on the minority of stout souls who would assist the cause. The people who gave Hudson shelter, helped repair his torn robe, or "[did] not flinch or grumble" when their meetinghouse exploded were scattered members of an abolitionist community some of whom might be gathered in a single place to further the cause. Evil and its agents would be countered by the moral power of men and women gathered to "uphold the right."[33]

"Come-Outers"

Many evangelical and other conservative abolitionists also strongly opposed nonresistants' condemnation of existing churches and the ministry for alleged implication in the sin of slavery. As radical abolitionists sought to make their churches free of the taint of slaveholding, and to use churches to propagate the antislavery campaign, they often confronted popular and institutional objections to their efforts, and by the late 1830s an increasing number were following the biblical injunction to "come out" from among sinners and break their links with the churches, or set up new ones. As one radical editor asked, how could men and women work for social reform "while we cling to those systems and arrangements, the influence of which is destructive to the peace and happiness of our fellow beings?"[34] Upholders of denominational orthodoxy condemned what they saw as "infidelity" to the word and authority of God. Nonresistants and "come-outers," for their part, attacked what they saw as a "priesthood" intent on retaining its own power over the minds and actions of its followers. As three members of the Northampton community argued in 1843, "the highest and purest form of worship is that which gives to every man the utmost liberty of speech, consistent with the exercise of a spirit of love and brotherhood"; therefore no gathering that reserved the right to speak to "a distinct body or order of men" like the clergy could be truly Christian.[35]

To these nonresistant abolitionists nothing was of greater concern than their argument with the churches. Because it was widespread and constant, ecclesiastical hostility seemed to them more pernicious even than political opposition; the Massachusetts Anti-Slavery Society reflected this view in 1844 when it attacked the Liberty Party for diverting attention "from a corrupt church and clergy to the less guilty state." If abolition was to be brought about by moral suasion, obstruction by politicians who were inherently likely to bow to expediency mattered less than opposition from clergymen who should have been leading the fight against sin. But this was more than a view that the churches should supply moral leadership; it conveyed, too, a conception of society that emphasized the importance of local communities, in which religious gatherings were a more immediate and regular source of moral influence than politics or other public activities. Protesting and withdrawing from churches that opposed abolition appeared to be an effective tactic for ordinary people committed to the cause.[36]

"Come-outerism" took two forms, only one of which concerns us here. Some of the men and women who withdrew from the churches over slavery formed themselves into smaller groups, continued to worship together and sometimes turned these groups into new church organizations. These "come-outer sects" contributed to the endless fragmentation of American Protestantism that some commentators have seen as its perpetual institutional condition.[37] But other "come-outers," perhaps because of their wider acquaintanceships in the abolitionist and nonresistance movements, saw withdrawal from the churches as the first step away from sectarianism in general, as the start of a movement that might unite all Christian reformers in a nondenominational fellowship and abandon the authority of churches and ministers altogether.

Nonsectarian "come-outerism" was an important source of inspiration (and members) for the Northampton community. It united people from several religious traditions, Quaker, Baptist, Congregationalist, Unitarian, and others. The founders of the Northampton community carved different spiritual paths to the same point. Samuel L. Hill had become an active member of the Baptist church in Willimantic, Connecticut, soon after his arrival there at the end of the 1820s, when it was the only formally organized church in the new factory village. He served as the church's clerk and then its treasurer, but in 1835 broke with it: not only had he become a nonresistant, opposed to the bearing of arms, but he had also become convinced that water baptism, the use of visible bread and wine at communion, and the payment of regular salaries to ministers were unscriptural.[38] Erasmus Darwin Hudson underwent a less radical, but still profound change in the second half of the 1830s, from orthodox Congregationalist to doctrinal liberal. In his diary for 1835 Hudson described the last illness of Samuel Woodward, a physician who was an unbeliever, with the mixture of awe and smugness of the righteous regarding the death of an infidel. Woodward "could not think that there would be an eternal punishment," wrote Hudson the day before the older man died. "Oh God! will he not be fearfully surprised?" By 1840, Hudson had added marginal comments to this diary to mark the repudiation of his old beliefs. "What a change of my own mind," he wrote. "Much [was] written in this book under the influence of *educated bigotry*—contrary to the natural spirit of the writer—Evangelical heresy." Hudson's "natural spirit" had turned him into an eloquent critic of slavery and an implacable opponent of the sectarianism, "priestcraft," and doctrinal tyranny of the conventional churches. Although Hudson and his wife did not formally break their connection with the Congregational church in Torringford until the end of the 1840s, their expressed criticisms of the churches were indistinguishable from those of many who had "come out."[39]

Some individuals moved from sectarian to nonsectarian "come-outerism." In Bloomfield, Connecticut, which was Hudson's home in the late 1830s and early 1840s, several nonresistants had withdrawn from the local church to worship together, and were excommunicated for their pains. Hall Judd worshiped with this group when he was in the area. In 1842 and 1843 several of its members left for Northampton, turning their allegiance to a small, sheltered group into commitment to a larger, more embracing, nondenominational community.[40] Hudson, Hill, and others were also in touch with a further group, in the small town of Chaplin, Connecticut, that fought a long battle over abolitionism and women's rights within their Congregational church before being forced to give up. Chaplin's antislavery movement, active and close-knit, had cooperated closely with the church until the abolitionist split of 1840 set Garrisonians and Tappanites—including the minister—at odds. According to Joseph C. Martin, one of the radicals, the minister acted to stop revival meetings at which women could speak and in March 1841 preached what Martin called the "Frog Sermon," in which he compared the Garrisonians to the three unclean spirits ("like frogs") in the book of Revelation. They were a "disorganizing" influence, refusing to follow the "old way"; their arguments against civil government represented "infidelity concealed under the mask of philanthropy and religion"; and their criticisms of churches and ministers were the work of "the man of sin." For two more years Martin and his friends fought the minister and sought to get the church to condemn slavery. Failing at this, they "came out" from it in 1843 and were then formally excommunicated. A few months later, Martin and several others moved to the Northampton community.[41]

These "come-outers" turned the charge that they were sectarians back on their clerical accusers by proclaiming their tolerance for the beliefs of others. Rather, it was the churches, they countered, with their resistance to the opposers of sin and their restrictions on "free speech" and women's rights that were guilty of sectarianism. This argument embraced a general attack on practices, such as observing the Sabbath, that nonresistants associated with the arbitrary exercise of clerical power. Their meetings, such as the convention "to discuss the origin and authority of the ministry," held at the Chardon Street chapel in Boston in November 1840, drew furious criticism from evangelicals and others who labeled it an "anti-sabbath convention," and correctly perceived in it a root-and-branch assault on existing organized churches. Among the participants were George Ripley, who had left the Unitarian ministry and was about to found Brook Farm, and at least five future members of the Northampton community, including David Mack.[42] Opposition from churches and their ministers to radical abolitionist principles lay at the core of many men's and women's experience of the splits of the late 1830s and early 1840s. To George W. Benson it was one of the main reasons for giving up his Brooklyn farm and his family's dedication to Windham County abolitionism. Though "fully persuaded on the whole, that the principles we love and have advocated, are beginning to make some impression on the public mind, sectarianism is the hindrance to this peoples advancement in Truth and holiness," he wrote early in 1841.

At first sight Benson's solution appeared to be a straightforward rejection of institutions: "Man cannot be free while laboring to build up a sect or party, he must be left untrameled to follow truth withersoever it may lead, before he can attain to a perfect man in Christ Jesus."[43] There were indeed nonresistants who drew this conclusion. But Benson's own abolitionist experience had helped leave the way open to a different conclusion, that institutions consistent with true Christian principles were possible and should be supported. As his own Windham County Anti-Slavery Society had resolved in 1840, while corrupt organizations were not worthy to be preserved, "we cannot . . . be hostile to any institution which is not inherently corrupt." Abolitionism itself provided a model of uncorrupted organization. William Adam, writing about the American Anti-Slavery Society in 1840, noted that "the principle on which this Society has based its operations is that all the members of civil society irrespective of religious and political distinctions may harmoniously cooperate" in pursuit of abolition. Adam's references to nondenominational, harmonious cooperation directly prefigured the efforts he, Benson, and others were soon to join in as they created a community at Northampton.[44]

The divisions in the abolitionist movement of the late 1830s and early 1840s therefore went much deeper than disputes over tactics. They reflected fundamental disagreements about the makeup and conduct of society itself. The four themes we have identified—economics, abolition, nonresistance, and nonsectarian "come-outerism"—helped shape the lives of not only its founders, but many of the other men and women who would join the Northampton community over the next few years. Few were unaffected by any of them. In many cases several themes overlapped, or were joined by and reinforced further concerns with moral reform, temperance, diet, and health. Of the eleven "founders," for instance, at least five—Hudson, Judd, Benson, Hill, and Mack—are known to have campaigned for or expressed sympathy with temperance principles, and others may have done so in ways that went unrecorded.

The Logic of Community

By 1840 reformers in general were becoming gripped by debates over communal organizations. Late that autumn Margaret Fuller wrote that "one thing seems sure, that many persons will soon . . . throw off a part, at least, of these terrible weights of the social contract, and see if they cannot lie more at ease in the lap of Nature."[45] Reform journals of all kinds published a constant stream of material about plans for communities and discussed their advantages and disadvantages. Abolitionists and nonresistants shared this interest fully. It was from these discussions that the idea of forming a community at Northampton would arise, and through them that the abolitionist critique of slavery would turn into a wider critique of American society in general.

There were several parallel developments. Albert Brisbane's works on the ideas of the French utopian Charles Fourier were starting to circulate in intellectual, radical, and labor circles. Even as they were promoting direct imitation by American devotees of the rapidly growing Fourierist movement, they also inspired critical debate among moral reformers attracted by the community idea but who rejected the secular and materialist bases of Fourier's program. Discussions in the transcendentalist circle, coupled with a growing sense of the need for social action, prompted George Ripley and others to set up the Brook Farm community at West Roxbury, outside Boston, in 1841.[46] Meanwhile, the Universalist abolitionist and nonresistant Adin Ballou had published plans for a "Practical Christian" community that would not only put basic Christian principles into operation but could satisfy the demand of many New England reformers that such ventures be founded on moral, not materialist grounds; by 1841 these plans were evolving into the Hopedale community at Milford, Massachusetts.[47]

Talk of communities became widespread among radical abolitionists. In 1839, Erasmus Darwin Hudson defended the principle of "associated action" as a means of achieving social change. Two years later he was praising an article on phrenology by a member of Ballou's Universalist church, pondering the Old and New Testament promises of "the coming of the Kingdom of Christ," and predicting that God was "testing the religion of the day and bringing out the pure gold from the dross." Even a hesitant communitarian such as Hudson drew inspiration from a variety of the influences that were to shape the movement. "What say you to a little social community among ourselves?" wrote William Lloyd Garrison to George W. Benson early in 1841: "I think we must be pretty bad folks if we cannot live together amicably within gunshot of each other." He noted that Benson's former business partner in Providence was proposing to set up a small farm community. Later in the year the Lynn abolitionist James N. Buffum wrote that the nonresistant campaign for change in the churches was bringing forward concepts of tolerance, duty, and common interest that led logically to associations to bring about widespread reform.[48]

The Bostonian abolitionist and nonresistant Edmund Quincy went further, writing that "cooperative associations" were "one of the marked tendencies of this age" and "a most encouraging sign of an earnest purpose to search after and to remedy the cause of the evils which prevail in this disjointed world." To the "co-operative principle," Quincy wrote, we owe "whatever is best in our social and domestic institutions," and he expressed optimism that communities would succeed in furthering "the advancement of the highest individual and social interests of man." As he was writing, Brook Farm, Hopedale, and other communities of various kinds were being established or mooted, but Quincy was not put off by the existence of simultaneous efforts in different places, made "without concert" or coordination. Rather, he saw that as a sign that history was on the side of the communities, "that there is an inexorable need that thus urges men to forsake the institutions which their fathers had builded for them, and go forth in search of new homes." The only matter for debate, he felt, was the overall influence of community ventures. Were they, as their critics suggested, merely efforts to withdraw "from danger to congeniality," which would leave the lights of reform hidden under a bushel, or were they "the concentration of the hosts of light to do more effectual battle with the armies of the aliens"?[49]

Some comparisons with the other main nonresistant community, at Hopedale, suggest that from its inception the Northampton community was intended to fulfill the second of Quincy's purposes, "the concentration of the hosts of light to do more effectual battle." Hopedale, like Northampton, grew out of abolitionist and nonresistant principles, but its origins were in a particular religious group, six or so restorationist Universalist ministers led by Hopedale's founder, Adin Ballou. These men resolved in 1838 to live in a way that would be "perfect in all possible respects" and attempted to carry out their resolve in the Hopedale community three years later. Membership was open only to those subscribing to a religious test. Men and women prepared to accept and follow its precepts could join Hopedale and seek to live as perfectly as possible, to make the community "an outward manifestation" of the kingdom of God eventually to be realized within all individuals. Hopedale was intended to be the first of many such communities to which, as Lewis Perry put it, the regenerate would withdraw, leaving the unregenerate under the government of worldly tyranny. Ballou's restorationist beliefs (that all would be saved, but only after a period of punishment for their sins) embodied a conservative fear of social chaos. The Hopedale community would offer a bulwark against this, and an example of social order. The community was regulated by a series of rules, many of them highly specific, which Ballou modified from time to time in an effort to achieve a workable ordered society. These principles and the rules to be followed marked Hopedale out quite specifically as a place separate from the world. Though it maintained constant links with reform movements and other communities, its religious separation was also to keep it distinct from Brook Farm and Fourierist groups with whom cooperation and even mergers were periodically contemplated.[50]

Northampton's approach, also strongly influenced by nonresistance, was different. There was no single leader, never any individual with as strong a role as Ballou in defining and influencing the community's shape and development.

The former silk factory that became the community boardinghouse of the Northampton Association. Early twentieth-century snapshot. The building no longer stands. *Historic Northampton.*

Though Northampton had rules and regulations, they had more to do with the framework within which decisions would be made, and less with prescribing what those decisions would be. Northampton's founders were not only a diverse group of individuals, but less pessimistic than Ballou about the ability of human beings to live together in harmony. Above all, they desired no religious test for membership, and never prescribed one. Instead they pursued the radical abolitionist ideal of a society in which people of all religious views could associate in a nonsectarian organization. In this sense, therefore, Northampton was conceived more as a "concentration of . . . light" than a withdrawal of the perfect from the world.

"This Desert Where No Water Is"

Even the community's location underscored this hope. As we have seen, it had strong roots in Connecticut—seven of its eleven founders, including four of the seven abolitionists among them, were from there—and Connecticut had just proved a desperate disappointment to the Garrisonians. But Benson, Hill, Hudson, and their friends were hardly "withdrawing" to a more hospitable region when they moved to western Massachusetts. Rather, they were setting up an outpost of Garrisonian abolition and nonresistance in an area strongly disposed to disapprove of them. Samuel L. Hill's son would later comment that radical abolitionists like his father were in "decided conflict with the respectability of the northern towns and cities." Nowhere was this more true than in Northampton, Massachusetts.[51]

Northampton, originally settled in 1654, was one of the oldest towns in western New England, and tended to pride itself on its political and religious conservatism. Old families traced their colonial forebears and maintained their connections among a regional elite based on business, land, law, and the Congregational church. The town still had many farmers who tilled the rich meadowlands of the Connecticut River Valley, but it was also a commercial center, with merchants and small manufacturers in a variety of trades; by 1840 less than half its population of 3,750 primarily supported themselves by agriculture. It was the Hampshire County seat and a base for the lawyers, judges, and minor functionaries who congregated around its courts. It was also starting to become a tourist center, its three hotels catering to visitors who came to enjoy the romantic scenery of the mountains that rise close by. In addition to north-south road and river connections, and good east-west roads, there was the new (though short-lived) canal to New Haven. In the mid-1840s the railroad would reach the town from Springfield. The population had risen only slowly during the 1830s, but over the next decade Northampton would experience more rapid growth, based on manufacturing, transportation, and immigration. The place still recalled its former position as one of the bastions of New England Federalism, and by 1840 the Whig Party was firmly entrenched. There was also a vocal Democratic minority, and a new pattern, derived from the Antimasonic and Workingmen's politics of the late 1820s and early 1830s, of political challenges to the major parties that would prove valuable to the Free-Soil movement of the late 1840s.[52]

The radical reformers who came to take over the former silk company property out at Broughton's Meadow found little welcome in Northampton. There were strong veins of anti-abolitionist feeling and of racism betrayed in lack of sympathy, or worse, for the plight of slaves and free blacks. There was support for the American Colonization Society, which asserted that blacks were inferior and should be denied citizenship. Like many towns, Northampton listed black residents separately at the end of its annual tax lists. When reformers started an antislavery society at the end of 1835, at least one of the town's two newspapers expressed violent opposition to the movement, and meetings were periodically disrupted. After David Lee Child moved onto a farm in the town in 1837 to grow sugar beets in an experiment to promote reduced dependence on slave-grown sugar, he helped promote abolitionist activities. A copy of a handbill he had issued in 1838, calling citizens to celebrate the anniversary of the August 1 emancipation of slaves in the British Empire, was nailed to his door with the word "persons" crossed out and "NIGGERS" inserted. Northampton also had significant southern connections. Members of several of its leading families had married southerners or moved to the South to live. Southern visitors came to its hotels, and a sprinkling of wealthy families from the South had settled there, all of whom found abolition repellent. Tradesmen and hoteliers, watchful for their businesses, also found it offensive. Few Whigs or Democrats among the town's political leaders were inclined to disagree.[53]

Though Northampton had its antislavery society, which grew rapidly and was quite active in the mid-1830s, its members, like most of the abolitionists in the surrounding region, attached themselves to "new organization" or political abolitionism in the splits at the end of the decade.

The few remaining Garrisonians were isolated or, like the master carpenter Moses Breck, obliged to adapt their views in order to be able to work with evangelical abolitionists.[54] Northampton was strongly attached to orthodox evangelicalism. It had been Jonathan Edwards's town; one of its two Congregational churches was named after him. The Tappan brothers were born and had grown up there, and though they had left, there were still connections with them; one of Northampton's leading abolitionists was their nephew, who, like several of his colleagues, was a prominent local merchant and pillar of one of the evangelical churches. Hostility to a public role for women was strong. The traditional view had just been restated in a forthright pamphlet by the minister in neighboring Westhampton, who argued that women were bound to keep silent whenever their pastor or any of their brethren were present.[55] The character of local religion and abolitionism made Northampton peculiarly unreceptive to the founders of the new community in its midst; as Garrisonian abolitionists, as nonresistants, as advocates of women's rights, and as nonsectarians they stood opposed to the town's more conservative traditions. The orthodox took a narrow view of the community; one woman, asked to describe it in 1843, simply wrote "they call themselves 'community people' or 'come outers'. They are some thing like Quakers—do not believe in keeping the Sabbath."[56]

We can get a good idea of what Northampton was like for a radical abolitionist from the letters of Lydia Maria Child, who lived there intermittently between 1838 and 1841 as she and David Child struggled with the sugar-beet farm. For a short time after she arrived in town she was optimistic. Two-thirds of the people, it was claimed, were sympathetic to abolition, and there was polite interest in the sugar-beet experiment. But she quickly came to feel that this sympathy was formal, not strongly felt, and that "Orthodoxy has clothed most of the community in her strait-laced garments." Child's attempts to raise abolition issues in conversation quickly led to her ostracism by leading families, whose conservatism she gauged when she heard a Springfield minister denounced for his extreme abolitionist views, and then discovered that the man was a colonizationist.

Child privately criticized Northampton abolitionists who regarded peace in their churches as more important than agitation to end slavery. Roxana Starkweather, for example, was "just such an abolitionist. . . . The supposition that the Presbyterian church would have ten less members . . . would at any time have rendered the emancipation of the slaves a doubtful measure in her eyes." She attributed their weakness in part to the influence of a former merchant with southern connections, Thomas Napier, a church deacon whom Child portrayed as a "rich slave-auctioneer" and pious hypocrite. Napier, their next-door neighbor for a while, "prays much louder than he talks, for the sake of being heard better, either by God or his neighbors." David Child would play his accordion to muffle the sound of the man's voice and its "tone . . . of whining expostulation." More important, Napier was said to contribute $250 a year to the salary of his minister, who "in return preaches against all reforms, and puts as many obstructions in the way of reformers as possible." There were, she added, "many abolitionists belonging to that church; but they never open their lips—so highly do they value 'the peace of the church.'"

Child saw religion and materialism at the heart of the radicals' weakness. "Calvinism sits here enthroned," she wrote, "with high ears, blue nose, thin lips and griping fist." Though she and David worked hard to obtain signatures on petitions to Congress, she quickly became despondent: "I have never been so discouraged about abolition as since we came into this iron-bound Valley of the Connecticut." Her chief solace lay in the support of Northampton's Unitarian minister John S. Dwight, at whose ordination in 1840 George Ripley had advocated "the kingdom of God on earth." But Dwight was soon to leave the town, to follow Ripley out of the ministry and into the Brook Farm community. In 1841, as Child herself was about to leave for New York to edit the *National Anti-Slavery Standard*, she could write, "I wish George Ripley had stated his plan [for Brook Farm] before we came here, to this Desert where no water is."[57] Shortly afterward Benson and his colleagues started to prepare their own community in a climate that would be no more hospitable than it had been for her.

Preparing for Community

Because the Northampton Association did not keep records until its first formal meeting there is little precise documentation of the preparations made before April 8, 1842. We know that there were discussions over several months among some of the founders, but letters, deeds, and memoirs provide only glimpses of their plans. During 1841 the economic and ideological context we have been discussing, and the widely canvassed prospect that communities might be effective instruments of moral and social reform induced the founders of the association to turn their private endeavors into a cooperative venture.

George W. Benson moved his family from Brooklyn, Connecticut, in the spring of 1841, probably to the house at Broughton's Meadow they were to occupy for almost a decade, near the Northampton Silk Company property. One of his daughters recalled that after the sociability of Brooklyn, the Bensons were relatively isolated for the first few months, and the child lived a "lonely life" until the community got going. Samuel L. Hill and his family also arrived sometime that year, intending to settle on a fifty-acre farm just to the west of the silk company estate. But before he could complete his arrangements for farming, Hill later recalled, Benson and others "brought forward the idea of forming the Community Association," and Hill added his land to the community's property. This switch from planning business partnerships to forming a community cannot be dated exactly, but it was almost certainly before October 1841. That month Benson and Hill, together with Joseph Conant and William Coe, purchased the silk mill and estate from the silk company trustees.[58]

By the end of October the Adam family had also arrived. They made arrangements to have a house at Broughton's Meadow fitted up for them—work that would take until December. As he reached Northampton, William Adam still had plans to farm, but within two or three weeks he had been convinced to act on the idea that had been planted in his mind earlier in the year and join the effort to form a community. Boston friends who visited in mid-November reported that Adam had invested "with four others" in "the great silk farm," and that although Phebe and her daughters were "desponding" at the prospect, William was going around "in a perpetual excitement." Either then or later, Adam bought out William Coe's share in the venture for about $2,000, though the deed formalizing this arrangement was not executed until February 1842. Meanwhile, Adam read Vattel on natural law, with its discussion of community property, and its argument that the poor had inherent rights to subsistence. He and Conant also took legal advice, probably on the group's plans to draw up articles of association.[59]

Adam was one of the authors of a "Preliminary Circular" issued in February 1842, announcing the new community and opening the recruitment of members. This was one of the final stages in the preparations that would lead to the April 8 meeting. Shortly after it was issued, David and Maria Mack, who had just signed the Brook Farm articles of association, changed their plans and opted instead to move to Northampton. Hall Judd also became involved about this time, and Erasmus Darwin Hudson must have been drawn in too, though precisely how and when is not clear. The April meeting, in addition to instituting the community, marked the completion of its legal arrangements. Once they had been elected to office, Adam, Conant, and Hill formally sold their portions in the silk company estate to Benson, and so consolidated the property once again. Immediately Benson sold it back to them, this time not as individuals, but as the trustees of the Northampton Association of Education and Industry. They were now embarked on their effort to change the world.[60]

A patchwork of sources has enabled us to retrace some of the steps that led to the April 1842 meeting. But to interpret these steps and to understand the community's progress once it was under way, we need a broader overall view of what the founders were doing. Were they following some kind of blueprint for an ideal society, already formed in their minds and agreed between them? Or were they proceeding in an ad hoc manner, to see where each step would lead them? The answers to these questions will not only help us locate the Northampton Association in the wider history of "utopian" communities, but will help explain the developments that were to take place within it over the next four years.

Only one of the founders gave his own view of the matter. Samuel L. Hill left two brief memoirs of the community, one of which appeared in 1867, twenty-five years after the founding, and the other in 1908, just over twenty-five years after his death in December 1882. Both stress the community's ad hoc character. Hill notes that he, Benson, and others had originally come to Northampton for their own private purposes and only adopted the community idea as their plans developed in 1841. Even as the community was starting, he remembered, they were improvising, not following a preconceived plan. This is what he meant by his remark that "we expected to *work out* an improved state of society."[61]

There are reasons for doubting this claim. By the time he made it, Hill was a successful manufacturer who might have wished to disassociate himself from organized socialist or Fourierist theories that had become discredited. He did not deny the abolitionist and religious influences on the group, but by the end of Hill's life abolition was respectable and toleration more tolerable. Hill's memoirs dwelt neither on the reasons that might have led them to a community venture nor on the previous connections between members of the group. Perhaps the community was more thoroughly planned and less accidental than Hill implied?

The evidence does suggest a more complicated picture than Hill's version of events. But his claim for spontaneity is significant, because it fits with the abolitionist, nonresistant, and "come-outer" origins that would help shape the community's character and development. The founders would provide a framework for community, but not the precise rules under which it must be conducted. They would leave details to be drawn in by members, a challenge that was taken up repeatedly in the next few years. Following their consciences and the principles they had learned in their struggles over slavery, women's rights, and the churches, they would work toward a new form of society. By doing this, Hill wrote, and by educating their children in the new community they were forging, they would "ultimately revolutionize the old system."[62]

NOTES

1. Minutes of the meeting are in Record of Proceedings, 1842–1848, Northampton Association of Education and Industry Records, American Antiquarian Society, Worcester, MA, 3–5.

2. Information on the Benson family in the preceding paragraphs is drawn from [Wendell Phillips Garrison], *The Benson Family of Newport, Rhode Island, together with an Appendix concerning the Benson Families in America of English Descent* (New York, 1872), 38–44, 51–54. Samuel J. May, *Some Recollections of our Antislavery Conflict* (Boston, 1869), 42–43, 53–56, describes Benson's role in the Prudence Crandall affair; Crandall's epithet for the Benson house was reported by Helen E. Benson to William Lloyd Garrison, Providence, February, 11, 1834, Houghton Library, Harvard University, bMS Am 1906(13); Benson's abolitionist activities are recorded in Windham County A[nti]-S[lavery] Society, Record, 1837–47, Connecticut State Library, Hartford, and George W. Benson to Samuel J. May, Boston, December 30, 1837, Boston Public Library MS A.1.1.2.74; his plan to move from Brooklyn, in Benson to May, Brooklyn, CT, February 8, 1841, Boston Public Library MS A.1.2.11.59. See also Brooklyn Female Anti-Slavery Society, Records, 1834–40, Connecticut State Library, Hartford.

3. Biographical material on Hill is in *Hampshire Gazette* (Northampton), April 21, 1866, April 2, 1867, December 19, 1882; Charles A. Sheffeld, ed., *The History of Florence, Massachusetts, Including a Complete Account of the Northampton Association of Education and Industry* (Florence, 1895), 205–211; and William Sanford Hills, comp., *The Hills Family in America*, ed. Thomas Hills (New York, 1906), 331, 398. Evidence of his role in Willimantic abolitionism is in Samuel L. Hill to Amos A. Phelps, Willimantic, January 13, 1836, Boston Public Library MS A.21.6(4), and February 24, 1836, Boston Public Library MS A.21.6(17).

4. Information on Conant, Swift, and Chaffee is in William H. Chaffee, *The Chaffee Genealogy* (New York, 1909), 412; *Commemorative Biographical Record of Tolland and Windham Counties, Connecticut* (Chicago, 1903), 595; L. P. Brockett, *The Silk Industry in America: A History Prepared for the Centennial Exposition* ([New York], 1876), 57–58; Ruth V. Munsell, "Early Years of the Silk Industry in Mansfield" (Mansfield Historical Society, Mansfield, CT), and other notes collected by Mrs. Munsell that she kindly allowed me to see; and J. R. Cole, *History of Tolland County, Connecticut* (New York, 1888), 259–264 (which contains many inaccuracies). Accounts of Joseph Conant, Earl Dwight Swift, and Olive Conant Swift with the Northampton Silk Company are in Northampton Silk Company, Account book, Northampton Association of Education and Industry Records, American Antiquarian Society. On Conant's reform sympathies, see Wilbur H. Siebert, *The Underground Railroad from Slavery to Freedom* (1898; rpt. ed., New York, 1968), 403, and Frances P. Judd, memoir dated 1853, in A. J. Macdonald Collection, 67–70, Beinecke

Rare Book and Manuscript Library, Yale University (misattributed by Macdonald to "Mrs. Judson").

5. Samuel Brooks's property transactions are recorded in Deeds, 90:320 and 96:30. U.S. Seventh Census, Population Schedules, Connecticut, 1850, National Archives, Washington, DC (microfilm 432, reel 39, 41–42), lists three of his children, Joshua, Lorenzo, and Lucinda Brooks, among the Church Family of Shakers at Enfield.

6. On Hall Judd's father and his views, see Christopher Clark, *The Roots of Rural Capitalism: Western Massachusetts, 1780–1860* (Ithaca, 1990), 3–7. Sylvester Judd, Jr.'s best-known work was the novel *Margaret: A Tale of the Real and Ideal, Blight and Bloom, Including Sketches of a Place Not Before Described, Called Mons Christi* (Boston, 1845); the biography of him by Richard J. Hathaway, *Sylvester Judd's New England* (University Park, PA, 1981), also contains material about the Judd family.

7. Quotations are from Hophni Judd to Chauncey Parkman Judd, Windsor, October 19, 1841 (emphasis in original), and Apphia Judd to Arethusa Hall, Northampton, May 1, 1842, both in Judd Papers, *55M–1 Box 2, Houghton Library, Harvard University.

8. Nathaniel Hawthorne to David Mack, Boston, July 18, 1841, MS Am1067(4), and May 25, 1842, MS Am 1067(5), both in Boston Public Library. Biographical information on Mack is in *Obituary Record of Graduates of Yale College deceased during the Academical Year ending in June 1879* (n.p., n.d.), 337, and Isabella Mack Hinckley, "Recollections of Some Interesting People I Have Known and Met" (typescript, n.d.), 18–20, Belmont Historical Society Collection, Belmont Memorial Library, Belmont, MA; these memoirs of Mack's daughter stress that it was her father who was eager to move to a community. There is an advertisement for the Macks' school in Cambridge in *Liberator*, December 25, 1840.

9. Hudson's biography is outlined in Samuel Orcutt, *History of Torrington, Connecticut, from its First Settlement in 1737, with Biographies and Genealogies* (Albany, NY, 1878), 146, 177, 209, 218, 463, 498–512; see also *Charter Oak* (Hartford, CT), March 1838–April 1840. His assessments of the others were in his copy of T. H. Gallaudet, *The Philanthropist's Remembrancer* (Hartford, 1835), in Hudson Family Papers, Box 1, folder 9, Manuscripts and Archives Department, University of Massachusetts Library, Amherst.

10. William Adam, "Reminiscences," *The Liberty Bell: By Friends of Freedom*, [ed. Maria Weston Chapman] (Boston, 1844), 74–88, was his own account of his early career. Other details are from *Second Memoir Respecting the Unitarian Mission in Bengal* (Calcutta, 1828); Sophia Dobson Collet, *Life and Letters of Raja Rammohun Roy*, ed. Hem Chandra Sarkar ([Calcutta, 1913]), 65–74, 117–128; William Adam, *A Lecture on the Life and Labours of Rammohun Roy*, ed. Rakhal-Das Haldar (1879; rpt. ed., rev. Dilip Kumar Biswas, Calcutta, 1977), esp. 23–25; S. C. Sanial, "The Rev. William Adam," *Bengal Past and Present* 8 (1914): 251–272; see also William Adam, *Third Report on Vernacular Education in Bengal* (Calcutta, 1838). Other background is from Joseph Di Bona, ed., *One Teacher, One School: The Adam Reports on Indigenous Education in Nineteenth-Century India* (New Delhi, 1983); Kenneth W. Jones, *The New Cambridge History of India*, vol. 3, part 1, *Socio-Religious Reform Movements in Modern India* (Cambridge, 1989), 30–39; David Kopf, *The*

Brahmo Samaj and the Shaping of the Modern Indian Mind (Princeton, 1979); and Spencer Lavan, *Unitarians and India: A Study in Encounter and Response* ([Boston], 1977). The Brahmo Sabha was the forerunner of the better-known Brahmo Samaj.

11. Phebe Adam's arrival in Boston and her contacts there are noted in Epes Sargent Dixwell, Diary Extracts, Wigglesworth Family Papers, Box 17, Massachusetts Historical Society, Boston. William Adam's academic appointment is detailed in Harvard University, Overseers' Records, vol. 8, 322 and 325, and Corporation Records, vol. 8, 87 and 122, both in Harvard University Archives; and his antislavery activity in *Proceedings of the General Anti-Slavery Convention, Called by the Committee of the British and Foreign Anti-Slavery Society and Held in London, from Friday, June 12th, to Tuesday, June 23rd, 1840* (London, 1840), esp. 573–584; see also William Adam, *The Law and Practice of Slavery in British India, in a Series of Letters to Thomas Fowell Buxton, Esq.* (London, 1840).

12. *British Indian Advocate* (London), 1841–1842. In William Adam to Wendell Phillips, London, June 29, 1841, Houghton Library, Harvard University, bMS Am 1953(187), Adam asked for information about settlements and praised the *Dial*'s "pure generous and free spirit which I love and admire"; William Coe's transfer to Adam of his interest in the former Northampton Silk Company property is in Deeds, 95:16; William Lloyd Garrison to George W. Benson, Boston, March 3, 1843, in Walter M. Merrill and Louis Ruchames, eds., *The Letters of William Lloyd Garrison*, (Cambridge, MA, 1971–1981), 3:137, praised Adam as "a man who would be constantly rising in my estimation, if that were possible; for I have long regarded him as one of the noblest specimens of manhood to be found among our race."

13. Anne Talbot to Charlotte Richmond Talbot, Northampton, March 16, 1837, Charles N. Talbot Papers, folder 3, Rhode Island Historical Society, Providence. On the depression in western Massachusetts, see Clark, *Roots of Rural Capitalism*, 201–203, 243–246. S. N. Richmond to Charles N. Talbot, Providence, April 17, 1837, Charles N. Talbot Papers, folder 3, reported the failure of a partner of Crawford Allen, a Rhode Island manufacturer who had employed Hill in Willimantic.

14. Hill recalled his plans to farm in *Hampshire Gazette*, April 2, 1867; Adam's plans were mentioned in Esther Dixwell to George B. Dixwell, Boston, October 30, 1841, Wigglesworth Family Papers, Box 3, and Hall Judd's in Hophni Judd to C. Parkman Judd, October 19, 1841. On Ripley's preparations for Brook Farm, see Anne C. Rose, *Transcendentalism as a Social Movement, 1830–1850* (New Haven, CT, 1981), 104–106; his intention to farm instead is mentioned in Sophia Ripley to Anna Alvord, Boston, October 30 [1840], Society for the Preservation of New England Antiquities (microfilm).

15. Brooklyn, Assessment List Abstracts, 1837–1841, Town Clerk's Office, Brooklyn, CT.

16. A certificate in Deeds, 84:221, shows that the Northampton Silk Company had paid-up capital of $94,450 by March 1839.

17. Samuel L. Hill, undated memoir, quoted in William A. Hinds, *American Communities and Cooperative Colonies*, 3rd ed. (Chicago, 1908), 279.

18. The story of the Northampton Silk Company is outlined in Alice Eaton McBee, *From Utopia to Florence: The Story of a Transcendentalist Community in Northampton, Mass., 1830–1852* (Northampton: Smith College Studies in History, vol. 32, 1947), chap. 1. *Hampshire Gazette*, June 8, 1836, advertised the company

and listed its officers. The Talbots' difficulties with the company and with Whitmarsh are noted in G. W. Talbot to Charles N. Talbot, Northampton, July 26 and September 21, 1837, Charles N. Talbot Papers, folder 3, and John Taylor to Charles N. Talbot, Northampton, January 1[6?] and May 5, 1838, Charles N. Talbot Papers, folder 4, Rhode Island Historical Society, Providence. Lawsuits against Whitmarsh are noted in Charles E. Forbes Papers, folder 24, Forbes Library, Northampton. Accounts of the Jamaican silk scheme are in *National Anti-Slavery Standard* (New York; hereafter *NASS*), March 11, 1841, and Levi Pratt to Thomas Pratt, Ocha Rios, Jam., March 12, 1841, Historic Northampton A.L.18.97b.3a.

19. G. W. Talbot to Charles N. Talbot, September 21, 1837.

20. The preceding paragraphs are based on *The Letters of William Lloyd Garrison*, vols. 2 and 3; Aileen S. Kraditor, *Means and Ends in American Abolitionism: Garrison and His Critics on Strategy and Tactics, 1834–1850* (New York, 1967), chaps. 3–7; Bertram Wyatt-Brown, *Lewis Tappan and the Evangelical War against Slavery* (New York, 1969), chap. 10; James Brewer Stewart, *Holy Warriors: The Abolitionists and American Slavery* (New York, 1976), 88–116; Ronald G. Walters, *The Antislavery Appeal: American Abolitionism after 1830* (Baltimore, 1976); Blanche Glassman Hersh, *The Slavery of Sex: Feminist-Abolitionists in America* (Urbana, IL, 1978); and Dorothy Sterling, *Ahead of Her Time: Abby Kelley and the Politics of Antislavery* (New York, 1991).

21. Kraditor, *Means and Ends*; the second view derives in part from David H. Donald, "Towards a Reconsideration of the Abolitionists," in *Lincoln Reconsidered* (New York, 1961); Walters, *Antislavery Appeal.*

22. John C. March to Eben Hale, Newbury, July 3, 1837, March Family Papers, Box 1, folder 4, James Duncan Phillips Library, Peabody and Essex Institute, Salem, MA.

23. On this approach, see Richard Ellis and Aaron Wildavsky, "A Cultural Analysis of the Role of Abolitionists in the Coming of the Civil War," *Comparative Studies in Society and History* 32 (January 1990): 89–116.

24. Horace Cowles to George W. Benson, Farmington, January 19, 1841, printed in *NASS*, March 18, 1841; the letter was also something of a valedictory statement, for Cowles was shortly to die, and his obituary appeared in the same issue of the *NASS*. George W. Benson to Samuel J. May, February 8, 1841.

25. A report on the founding convention of the Connecticut Anti-Slavery Society, held in Hartford on February 28, 1838, appeared in *Charter Oak*, March 1838; those present included Benson, Hill, and Hudson, together with Joseph C. Martin of Chaplin, a future member and president of the Northampton community and the father of two other future members. Erasmus Darwin Hudson, Diary, 1840, Historic Northampton A.m.d.18.51, entry for June 5, 1840 (emphasis in original); Hudson's engagement as agent for the Connecticut Anti-Slavery Society had expired on June 1.

26. Brooklyn Female Anti-Slavery Society, Records, Connecticut State Library, Hartford; George W. Benson to Samuel J. May, February 8, 1841; *NASS*, March 18, 1841, reported the Willimantic convention; *NASS*, June 3 and June 10, 1841, the Hartford meeting and the protest. Abby Kelley to George W. Benson, Pawtucket, September 13, 1841, Boston Public Library MS A.1.2.12, part 1.107.

27. Susan Byrne to William Lloyd Garrison, Willimantic, June [22?], 1841, Boston Public Library MS A.1.2.12:1,47; Hill quoted in Hinds, *American Communities*, 279.

28. Leo Tolstoy, quoted in Lewis Perry, *Radical Abolitionism: Anarchy and the Government of God in Antislavery Thought* (Ithaca, 1973), 5. Perry's work remains crucial to an understanding of nonresistance, and I have relied heavily on it for the discussion that follows. On the relationships between peace, nonviolence, and abolitionism, see also Valarie Ziegler, *The Advocates of Peace in Antebellum America* (Bloomington, IN, 1992); Carleton Mabee, *Black Freedom: The Nonviolent Abolitionists from 1830 through the Civil War* (New York, 1970); and Margaret Hope Bacon, "By Moral Force Alone: The Antislavery Women and Nonresistance," in Jean Fagan Yellin and John C. Van Horne, eds., *The Abolitionist Sisterhood: Women's Political Culture in Antebellum America* (Ithaca, 1994), 275–297.

29. Perry, *Radical Abolitionism*, 56–57. See also Louis P. Masur, *Rites of Execution: Capital Punishment and the Transformation of American Culture, 1776–1865* (New York, 1989).

30. Perry, *Radical Abolitionism*, 57.

31. Nonresistants were identified from notices, reports, and subscription lists in *Liberator*, *Non-Resistant* (Boston), *Practical Christian* (Milford, MA), and *Reformer* (Worcester); Northampton attitudes are reflected in Sylvester Judd, "Notebook," vol. 2, Judd MS, Forbes Library, entry for December 27, 1841; Sylvester Judd to Arethusa Hall, Northampton, January 13, 1842, Judd Papers, Box 2, Houghton Library, Harvard University.

32. Benson's encounters are referred to in *Liberator*, July 13, 1838, and *Non-Resistant*, January 22, 1840. On anti-abolitionist violence generally, see Leonard L. Richards, *"Gentlemen of Property and Standing": Anti-Abolition Mobs in Jacksonian America* (New York, 1970); and Michael Feldberg, *The Turbulent Era: Riot and Disorder in Jacksonian America* (New York, 1980), esp. 44–53.

33. The Harwinton incident was recorded in *Charter Oak*, September 1838, the others in Erasmus Darwin Hudson, Journal 1838–39, Historic Northampton A.m.d.18.50, entry for November 29, 1838; idem, Diary 1841, Historic Northampton A.m.d.18.52, entries for April 3 and April 10, 1841.

34. *Union Herald* (Cazenovia, NY), June 17, 1841.

35. David Mack, William Larned, and Enos L. Preston to William Lloyd Garrison, in *Liberator*, January 27, 1843.

36. *Twelfth Annual Report, Presented to the Massachusetts Anti-Slavery Society, by the Board of Managers, Jan. 24, 1844* (Boston, 1844), 55.

37. See John R. McKivigan, "The Antislavery 'Come-Outer' Sects: A Neglected Dimension of the Abolitionist Movement," *Civil War History* 26 (June 1980): 142–160; idem, *The War against Pro-Slavery Religion: Abolitionism and the Northern Churches, 1830–1865* (Ithaca, 1984).

38. Willimantic First Baptist Church, Records, vol. 1, 4, 68, 88, First Baptist Church, Willimantic, CT (copies kindly provided me by Mrs. Earl W. McSweeney).

39. Erasmus Darwin Hudson, Case and Sketch Book, 1834–37 and 1840, Shaw-Hudson Letters, Box 7, Folder 1, Historic Northampton, A.m.d.18.51, entries for January 25 and 26, 1835 (emphasis in original).

40. The Bloomfield group, which included the Bumstead family and Roxcy A. Brown, is described in Erasmus Darwin Hudson, Diary, February–May 1841, Historic Northampton, A.m.d.18.52., entry for April 24, 1841; Judd's involvement is mentioned in Hudson, Journal, October 1840–February 1841, Hudson Family Papers,

Box 1, folder 12, Manuscripts and Archives Department, University of Massachusetts Library, Amherst, entry for December 14, 1840.

41. Joseph C. Martin to William Lloyd Garrison, Chaplin, December 17, 1843, published in *Liberator*, January 5, 1844, contained his account of the conflict with the minister over the previous three years; manuscript annotations in the Connecticut State Library's copy of *A Brief Historical Sketch of the Church of Christ in Chaplin, Connecticut, including the Confession of Faith and Covenants adopted by said Church* (Hartford, 1840) show that this letter was written shortly after Martin and several others were excommunicated from the church on December 6, 1843. Martin had been a church officer: Chaplin Ecclesiastical Society, Records, 1809–1906, Connecticut State Library, Hartford (microfilm), 80, show his appointment as collector in 1840.

42. The report of the Chardon Street Church, Ministry and Sabbath Convention printed in *Liberator*, November 27, 1840, listed among the participants David Mack, Sidney Southworth, William Bassett, Joseph S. Wall, and Herbert Scarborough, all of whom would join the Northampton community between 1842 and 1844.

43. George W. Benson to Samuel J. May, February 8, 1841.

44. George W. Benson, report of the annual meeting of the Windham County Anti-Slavery Society, March 1840, in *Charter Oak*, April 1840. William Adam, draft of a letter of introduction for John A. Collins and Charles L. Remond as delegates of the American Anti-Slavery Society to raise funds in Great Britain, London, November 27, 1840, Boston Public Library MS A.1.2.10.57.

45. Margaret Fuller to [William H. Channing?], about October 31, 1840, in Robert N. Hudspeth, ed., *The Letters of Margaret Fuller* (Ithaca, 1983–1988), 2:180.

46. Carl J. Guarneri, *The Utopian Alternative: Fourierism in Nineteenth-Century America* (Ithaca, 1991), 44–51; Rose, *Transcendentalism as a Social Movement*, 93–108.

47. Perry, *Radical Abolitionism*, 136–137; Edward K. Spann, *Hopedale: From Commune to Company Town, 1840–1920* (Columbus, OH, 1992).

48. Erasmus Darwin Hudson, Diary, February–May 1841, Historic Northampton A.m.d.18.52, entries for March 12, 14, 15, 1841. William Lloyd Garrison to George W. Benson, Boston, January 7, 1841, *Letters of William Lloyd Garrison*, 3:9; reference to William M. Chace's interest in a community is made here and on 38n. Buffum's remarks appeared in *NASS*, October 14, 1841.

49. *Non-Resistant*, October 13, 1841.

50. Perry, *Radical Abolitionism*, 131 and chap. 5; Spann, *Hopedale*.

51. Arthur G. Hill, "Antislavery Days in Florence" (typescript), Florence Civic and Business Association, Florence.

52. Henry S. Gere, *Reminiscences of Old Northampton: Sketches of the Town as it Appeared from 1840 to 1850* (n.p., 1902); Robert Doherty, *Society and Power: Five New England Towns, 1800–1860* (Amherst, 1977); Clark, *The Roots of Rural Capitalism.*

53. Northampton, Tax Assessors, Assessment on the Inhabitants of Taxable Property in Northampton, 1843, Town Papers Collection 5.88, Forbes Library; David Lee Child's handbill is in Slavery and Abolition file, Historic Northampton; the *Liberator*, January 31, 1835, referred to the editor of the *Northampton Courier* as "a very decided and active opposer of Abolition doctrines." Lydia Maria Child cataloged the

town's southern connections in a letter to Theodore Dwight Weld, Northampton, December 18, 1838, in Milton Meltzer and Patricia G. Holland, eds., *The Collected Correspondence of Lydia Maria Child, 1817–1880* (Millwood, NY, 1980), no. 156.

54. Northampton Anti-Slavery Society, Record Book, Forbes Library; Lydia Maria Child to Caroline Weston, Northampton, March 7, 1839, Meltzer and Holland, *The Collected Correspondence of Lydia Maria Child*, no. 172, remarked: "I do not know of one Garrison abolitionist here. Moses Breck . . . is so, when left to his own good sense and spontaneous feeling; but he is very easily influenced by the members of the church." The *Ninth Annual Report of the Board of Managers of the Massachusetts Anti-Slavery Society* (Boston, 1841), 59–64, noted that the adjacent town of Hatfield had raised $86 for the "new organized" Massachusetts Abolition Society.

55. Horace B. Chapin, *Women Forbidden to Speak in the Church* (Northampton, [1837]).

56. Eliza Strong to Sidney Strong, Northampton, July 18, 1843, MS Collection, Box 34, Forbes Library.

57. Quotations of Lydia Maria Child in this and the previous two paragraphs are from letters written in Northampton, all in Meltzer and Holland, *The Collected Correspondence of Lydia Maria Child*: to Louisa Loring, June 3, 1838, no. 135; to Ellis Gray Loring and Louisa Loring, July 10, 1838, no. 137; to Caroline Weston, July 27, 1838, no. 141, and August 13, 1838, no. 143; to Abby Kelley, October 1, 1838, no. 149; to Henrietta Sargent, November 18, 1838, no. 151; and to Louisa Loring, Northampton, February 17, 1841, no. 226. George Ripley, *The Claims of the Age on the Work of the Evangelist: A Sermon Preached at the Ordination of Mr. John Sullivan Dwight, as Pastor of the Second Congregational Church in Northampton, May 20, 1840* (Boston, 1840), 20; see Rose, *Transcendentalism as a Social Movement*, 103–104.

58. [Anna Benson Percy?], "When I Was a Girl," in Sheffeld, *History of Florence*, 123. Hill's recollections were published in *Hampshire Gazette*, April 2, 1867. The purchase of the silk company property, dated October 21, 1841, was recorded in Deeds, 92:270.

59. The Adams' first two months in Northampton are documented in Esther Dixwell to George B. Dixwell, Boston, October 30 and November 11, 1841, and in Henrietta Sargent to George B. Dixwell, Boston, November 14 and December 22, 1841, all in Wigglesworth Family Papers, Box 3. Adam's purchase from Coe is recorded in Deeds, 95:16, dated February 26, 1842. He borrowed a copy of Emmerich de Vattel, *The Law of Nations*, from the lawyer Charles E. Forbes in December 1841 for one month; he and Conant also took legal advice from Forbes. See entries in Forbes, Account Book (marked "Income"), Charles E. Forbes Papers, Forbes Library.

60. The property transactions of April 8, 1842, are recorded in Deeds, 95:230, 232.

61. *Hampshire Gazette*, April 2, 1867; Hinds, *American Communities*, 279 (emphasis added).

62. Hinds, *American Communities*, 279.

15

THE Northampton Association was but one manifestation of a much larger movement. The 1840s witnessed a flowering of utopian communities in Europe and America. The most well known in New England were the Trancendentalists' Brook Farm and Bronson Alcott's Fruitlands. These were based upon the notion that a return to nature and an agrarian way of life would counter the advance of industrialization. The Northampton community, however, embraced the factory but sought to humanize it through communal ownership and enlightened purpose. Sharing the division of labor freed women from domestic chores and permitted their involvement in the full range of community life. "I have now tried another day in my new home," wrote Dolly Witter Stetson, mother of six, "and am sure for the present I shall like it very much after almost seventeen years of more or less care of housekeeping concerns—it is a great change to have no responsibility about what we shall eat and what we shall drink—it seems as if I were visiting, only that I cannot make out whose guest I am!" It was here that Sojourner Truth composed her narrative of an ex-slave. "No other place," she wrote, offered her the same "equality of feeling, liberty of thought and speech and largeness of soul."

Sojourner Truth is both a historical figure and a cultural icon. In her acclaimed biography of Truth, from which the following is taken, Nell Irvin Painter seeks to unravel the layers of myth that surround the reality of Truth's experience, while pondering the underlying forces that gave rise to the need for these symbolic truths in her own time, and in ours.

Sojourner Truth

A Life, a Symbol *

NELL IRVIN PAINTER

MILLERITE second adventists knew enough about the world they saw ending to steer Sojourner Truth to the utopian Northampton Association for Education and Industry. The people in the Northampton Association were not second adventists; they were counting on the world to last long enough for them to cure its savagery and injustice.[1] They were starting on a small scale, with the manufacture of silk under enlightened principles. Surely this would ultimately reform the global political economy.

In mid-1843, the commune consisted of thirty men, twenty-six women, and forty-six children, plus six townswomen hired to work in the silk room.

* From Nell Irvin Painter, *Sojourner Truth: A Life, a Symbol* (New York, 1996).

Intellectual exchange was its greatest pride, based in a library, reading room, and more or less formal lectures from illustrious visitors. Lecturers included the most prominent of American reformers: William Lloyd Garrison, president of the American Anti-Slavery Society and editor of the Boston *Liberator*; Frederick Douglass, who in the Northampton years was just starting a long and illustrious career as a journalist and statesman; Wendell Phillips, Boston Brahmin pillar of antislavery and labor reform before and after the Civil War; as well as the health evangelist Sylvester Graham, who lived in Northampton.

Intellectual enrichment was one thing, physical comfort another. Northampton Association residents took their baths in the river. Even sympathizers saw the community's living conditions as rough and tactfully praised its "simplicity."[2]

When Truth first saw the huge stone building that doubled as factory and dormitory, she "did not fall in love at first sight." The place looked so primitive that she agreed only reluctantly to stay even one night.

But meeting the leaders of the Northampton Association gave Truth pause; the sight, she said, of "accomplished, literary and refined persons" living so simply and enduring such privation suspended her negative judgment, and led her to remain. Over time she became so attached to the place and its way that the community, which she thought consisted of "some of the 'choicest spirits of the age,'" became her professed home. No other place, she concluded, would have offered her the same "equality of feeling," "liberty of thought and speech," and "largeness of soul."[3]

THE Northampton Association of Education and Industry began during the nineteenth century's greatest utopian moment; one-fifth of the 270 utopian communities founded in the United States between 1787 and 1919 were begun between 1842 and 1848.[4] During this period the proto-socialist thought of Henri Saint-Simon, Charles Fourier, and Robert Owen inspired intentional communities (what we now call communes) meant to improve the future of mankind. Little utopias sprang up in Russia (where Fyodor Dostoyevsky joined a socialist commune in 1846), Romania, France, and England, as well as in the United States. Ralph Waldo Emerson remarked that in those days, there was "hardly a reading man but carried a draft of a new community in his waistcoat pocket."[5] Massachusetts produced several utopian communities in the 1840s, the best known of which were Hopedale and Brook Farm.

The Northampton project grew from a strong center, out of William Lloyd Garrison's conversations with his brother-in-law, George W. Benson. Benson, a lawyer-turned-businessman from Brooklyn, Connecticut, belonged to an abolitionist family. His father had been a founder of the Providence, Rhode Island, anti-slavery society, and his sister Helen had married Garrison in 1834. Benson was in the thick of an incident that in 1833 exposed the racial intolerance of supporters of colonization, who often passed themselves off as moderate abolitionists. This was the Prudence Crandall affair.

Prudence Crandall, a Quaker teacher, opened a school for girls in Canterbury, Connecticut, six miles from Brooklyn, in 1831. The following year, Crandall admitted a well-known tri-racial girl, so light-skinned that she could pass for white, whose father was a prosperous Canterbury farmer. This seemingly innocuous act provoked deep outrage among the parents of the other students. As the parents threatened to withdraw their daughters, Crandall

Sojourner Truth. Woodcut illustration from the 1853 edition of the *Narrative of Sojourner Truth. Historic Northampton.*

decided to expel them and open a school that would serve only black girls. At the prospect of a school for blacks, a local colonizationist mobilized even greater opposition, which intensified after the passage in May 1833 of a "black law" that prohibited blacks from coming into Connecticut.

Crandall endured two trials in Brooklyn, the county seat, and was finally freed on a technicality. Her school and her twenty well-mannered black scholars were so constantly terrorized that the harassment forced her to close down in 1834. The ordeal marked a watershed in the evolution of the antislavery movement. Moderate opposition to slavery had meant support for the removal—"colonization"—of American blacks to Africa. But Crandall's attackers, self-professed stalwarts of the American Colonization Society, now revealed themselves as extreme negrophobes.

After the Prudence Crandall affair, colonization looked more like racism than forbearance in opposition to slavery. The affair also increased the prestige of radicals like Garrison, who had supported Crandall throughout her persecution by official Connecticut. It sealed the antiracist sentiments of her supporters around Canterbury and Brooklyn, including George Benson.[6] Benson soon moved to Northampton, where he and his family spent the 1840s.

In 1841, after the silk boom of the mid-1830s and bust of the late 1830s, Benson, Samuel L. Hill (a Quaker-turned-Baptist also from Brooklyn, Connecticut), and two others bought the bankrupt Northampton Silk Company along Mill River in what became Florence, Massachusetts, two and a half miles from Northampton. The property included a fully outfitted large brick factory building that was four stories high and measured 120 by 40 feet, plus several other industrial outbuildings and six dwelling houses on 420 acres of land, situated on the 27-foot falls of the Mill River.[7]

The lofty principles of the Northampton Association began with a rejection of the current state of the American political economy that was reminiscent of Fourier's criticism of civilization.[8] According to the organizers of the association,

> Life is with some a mere round of frivolous occupations or vicious enjoyments, with most a hard struggle for the bare means of subsistence. The former are exempted from productive labour while they enjoy its fruits: upon the latter it is imposed as a task with unreasonable severity and with inadequate compensation. The one class is tempted to self-indulgence, pride, and oppressions: The other is debased by ignorance and crime, by the conflict of passions and interests, by moral pollution, and by positive want and starvation.[9]

This conflict appeared in much of the literature of economic reform throughout the balance of the nineteenth century, in the writing of the Enlightenment-inspired utopians Karl Marx and Friedrich Engels, and of the late nineteenth-century American visionary Henry George. The Northampton community, proposing itself as an object lesson of remedy, took as its first principle of incorporation that all people have the duty to perform productive work and the right to the fruits of their labor. Competition was deemed an evil; cooperation, in the interest of women's rights, freedom of expression, liberal education, and the abolition of slavery, a good.[10]

Although animated by many of Fourier's ideals, such as harmonizing social and economic relations—in Fourier's words, "harmonism" and "harmonic utopia"—the Northampton Association was not a Fourierist community. It did not hold property in common or attempt to supplant existing family arrangements. According to Garrison, it was organized "by religious men, upon anti-slavery ground."[11] The need to heal the class conflicts of the larger society, the worst of which was slavery, was one of the Northampton Association's basic tenets. Its prevailing religious sentiment was tolerant and of a decidedly antislavery bent; members were critical of orthodox religion, and, like Sojourner Truth, condemned a paid ministry. Appropriate to such unorthodox religious sentiments, the Northampton Association generated a nondenominational free meeting that later became the Florence Free Congregational Society, where Truth was an invited speaker.[12] But religion was only a small part of the association's ideology, for the many abolitionists in the community took women's equality as a given and supported temperance, vegetarianism, and peace.

The association's unusual intellectual and ideological attractions brought in so many people that housing quickly ran short. While a few of the community's leading families (including the Bensons) lived in houses of their own, most were put on the top floor of the factory, which served as a cramped boarding house. One former member recalled that the "quarters were rude and plain, and the fact that the members were willing to submit to the many inconveniences, and to forego all luxuries and many of the comforts to which they had been accustomed, showed how dear to their hearts was the cause they had espoused."[13]

At its peak in 1844–1845, the association had some 210 members from eight states (98 from Massachusetts, 88 from Connecticut) and two foreign countries.[14] Able-bodied adults worked ten hours a day; children also worked, but fewer hours, according to age and strength. All adult workers received 6 cents per hour, and they paid 50 cents a week for board and lodging.[15] The association operated a highly regarded school that accepted black children (one, from New Bedford, was the grandson of the prominent black Bostonian sea captain Paul Cuffee) and children who were nonresidents for $100 per year.[16]

The association's refreshingly good-natured egalitarianism gratified members and guests. Frederick Douglass visited in 1843, on the edge of his career as a leading abolitionist and the foremost black man of the nineteenth century. He recalled that the "place and the people struck me as the most democratic

I had ever met. It was a place to extinguish all aristocratic pretensions. There was no high, no low, no masters, no servants, no white, no black. I, however, felt myself in very high society." Douglass, like Truth, was enthralled by the lack of class and racial stratification. He listed the upper-class people he met there who were "yet fraternizing with the humblest members of the association." (Douglass was evidently not aware that the association had voted to pay a woman $1.50 per week to do housework.)[17]

The community held two main goals: to create a noncompetitive, open-minded, intellectually stimulating place in which to live and work; and to realize a profit from the manufacture of silk. The former goal quickly overshadowed the latter, and members interested in financial well-being started to peel off as early as 1842. A January 1843 amendment to the constitution that gave all members, whether or not they owned stock, equal say in the debt-ridden enterprise fatally undermined its finances. Another innovation, "mutual criticism," encouraged more forthright critique than the society could manage amicably. Samuel L. Hill, one of the founders who stuck to the community to the bitter end, nonetheless resented the "*taunts* & unkind *insinuations*" and "unjust accusations of my fellows."[18] Chronic debt and the eventual withdrawal of nearly all the founders led to the dissolution of the community in November 1846.[19]

DURING the Northampton Association's days as a commune, Sojourner Truth seems to have fit in easily. Here there was no hanky-panky as in the Kingdom of Matthias, no elevating of "Father" and "Mother" out of the ranks of labor. Truth worked in the laundry and complained when others gave her too many clothes to wash or items that were too dirty. She was one of the more memorable characters—at least in retrospect—and former associates memorialized her with varying amounts of imagination. George R. Stetson, George Benson's nephew, who had joined the association with his family in 1843 when he was six years old, recalled Truth many years later and in the light of her subsequent fame.

Stetson remembered her as an African of possibly royal stock who bore tribal markings, "a conspicuous figure during the anti-slavery controversy," who was "accustomed to speak and sometimes to sing." He quoted Truth as having once remarked that "three thirds of the people are wrong." When someone noted that that accounted for everyone, she replied, "I am sorry, as I had hoped there were a few left." When a boy fell off the dam into the river, he was lucky enough to fall into a small but deep pool, the only place he could escape serious injury. Truth said, "If the Devil made him fall the Lord had a fixed place for him to light in." Singing, working, or speaking, Truth commanded attention, having "a tall imposing figure, a strong voice, and a ready wit."[20]

The Northampton Association provided Truth's opening to the reformers of antislavery feminism. One of these was James Boyle, another was Giles Stebbins. Boyle was a Methodist minister about Truth's age who had been born Catholic in Ontario. He had been a New Haven perfectionist with John Humphrey Noyes in the mid-1830s, had broken with Noyes, become a manual worker in Newark, New Jersey, then, in the early 1840s, took up antislavery socialism, which brought him to Northampton.[21] Stebbins, from central Massachusetts, was twenty years younger than Truth and did not enroll as a member. He came only to study, and stayed for a year. Truth, Boyle, and Stebbins would share their belief in abolitionism, woman suffrage, and spiritualism in the decades to come.[22]

There were other black residents, including David Ruggles, formerly of New York City, and Basil Dorsey, a young fugitive who arrived in 1844.[23] Dorsey has fallen out of history, but three of the black people who were at the Northampton Association became historical figures: Truth; Ruggles; and the occasional visitor, Douglass, who left the fullest direct testimony.

Douglass, Ruggles, and Family

Sojourner Truth had something in common with each of the other prominent black people associated with the Northampton Association: with David Ruggles, it was New York City; with Frederick Douglass, slavery and, to a certain extent, Methodism. In the late 1820s and early 1830s, both Douglass and Truth had become Methodists, but Methodists of very different persuasions. Douglass encountered Methodism in Baltimore, where he attended an African Methodist Episcopal (AME) church and Sabbath school. This experience reinforced his allegiance both to the written word and to urban, preacher-centered orthodoxy.

Douglass was licensed to preach in the AME church in about 1840 in New Bedford, and had he not turned his gift as a speaker toward the struggle against slavery, he might well have enjoyed a career in the ministry. Truth, on the other hand, was an itinerant preacher who, as a woman, could never have become an AME minister, even had her religion been more conventional. Conventional it was not, and twenty-first-century people who are unfamiliar with pentecostalism are tempted to see her reliance on the power of the Holy Spirit as a manifestation of her African, rather than her perfectionist heritage. But Douglass, though also African American, had little in common with Truth beyond their race.

Frederick Douglass's first meeting with Truth occurred at Northampton, as Douglass was charting a course into freedom divergent from hers. Like many other fugitive slaves, Douglass associated illiteracy with enslavement, and strove to complete his emancipation through the acquisition of fluency—

Sojourner Truth, c. 1867. Charles C. Burleigh, Jr. Pencil drawing, 6 ¾ in. x 4 ½ in. *Historic Northampton.*

elegance, in his case—in reading and writing. He saw himself as a statesman-in-the-making and modeled his comportment on the well-educated antislavery leaders with whom he worked.

Though some twenty years younger than Truth, Douglass patronized her industry and amiability, calling her one of the community's most useful members "in its day of small things." What most galled Douglass was Truth's lack of sympathy with his own means of personal rebirth. While Douglass was schooling himself to "speak and act like a person of cultivation and refinement," Truth, he said, "seemed to feel it her duty to trip me up in my speeches and to ridicule my efforts." Douglass saw Truth as "a genuine specimen of the uncultured [N]egro," who "cared very little for elegance of speech or refinement of manners."

For all his condescension, Douglass grasped the key to Truth's impending success among white reformers, the qualities that made her memorable and were so widely described in print. Truth, Douglass said, was a "strange compound of wit and wisdom, of wild enthusiasm and flint-like common sense," who "seemed to please herself and others best when she put her ideas in the oddest forms." "Her quaint speeches," he noted, "easily gave her an audience."[24] Testimonials from the decades that followed corroborate his insight. Truth's persona, her seeming utter differentness, proved irresistibly entertaining to white reformers. Over the years after 1850 they usually tried to show her otherness through the use of what they thought was Negro dialect, and they dwelled at length on descriptions of her body.

Douglass was more respectful toward the other black New Yorker at Northampton. Five years earlier, as one of New York's leading abolitionists and head of the Vigilance Society, David Ruggles had arranged the New York–New Bedford stage of Douglass's flight from slavery. Douglass found Ruggles at Northampton a figure of "sterling sense and worth."

Ruggles had arrived in Massachusetts in 1842, blind, ill, and destitute, but had subsequently cured himself of his unspecified illness, though not of his blindness. In the process he learned the theory and practice of water cure and set up Northampton's first water-cure establishment.

Water cure, or hydropathy, was one of many interrelated reforms that flourished in the mid-nineteenth century, although the benefits of clean water had been recognized earlier. John Wesley's eighteenth-century *Primitive Physic* advocated cold water as a cure for disease, and in the 1830s Sylvester Graham had included it in the list of practices he recommended to remedy disease and foster health: temperance, a vegetarian diet, regular exercise, fresh air, nonrestricting clothing, sexual moderation, and frequent bathing. In the United States, water cure was most closely associated with temperance, which meant abstinence not merely from alcohol but also from coffee, tea, and tobacco. The people who frequented water-cure establishments tended to embrace other reforms, notably women's rights. Water-cure spas, like the one in Dansville, New York, sometimes functioned as feminist refuges from the ravages of activism.

In 1840, the first American water-cure establishment appeared in New York City, modeled on Vincenz Priessnitz's Grafenberg spa in the mountains of Silesia. Employing a series of cold water baths, drips, and wraps, and the drinking of lots of water, water cure eschewed drugs but offered a comprehensive system of prevention and healing that appealed to reformers as natural and gentle. Water cure could be practiced at home, provided one had access to abundant clean water—not to be taken for granted at a time when indoor plumbing and pure city water were not commonly available. More often patients journeyed to water-cure establishments, such as the one David Ruggles set up in Northampton in 1846.[25]

Ruggles's own Northampton Water Cure was the first in its vicinity, and it succeeded even though he screened his clients: Everyone had to apply in writing, allowing him to discourage those he could not help. Hopeless cases may have been few, for he recommended water cure as appropriate for the treatment of a wide variety of ailments: "headache, tendency of the blood to the head, cold extremities, general and nervous debility, bronchitis, pulmonary affection, liver complaint, jaundice, acute or chronic inflammation of the bowels, piles, dyspepsia, general debility, nervous and spinal affectations, inflammatory and chronic rheumatism, neuralgia, sciatica, lame limbs, paralysis, fevers, salt rheum, scrofulous and erysipelas humors." Stays at Ruggles's establishment, where patients had to supply their own blankets and linen, cost $5.50–$8.50 per week, at the low end of the price range. At the time, one visit to a regular (allopathic) physician usually cost at least $5.00.[26]

From January 1846 to December 1849, Ruggles operated the Northampton Water Cure in the "old mill house" in Northampton. He had outfitted it through purchases at the Northampton Association store of graham flour, sugar, yards and yards of cotton cloth, nails, saws, frames, one door latch, butts and screws, linseed oil, carpet binding, soap, bed ticking, and lamp wicking and oil, among other supplies.[27]

A fugitive notation in the store ledger raises intriguing romantic possibilities: "1 shawl for Elizabeth Gedney," $2.50, and $1.25 for "½ dozen tumblers."[28] Elizabeth Gedney was Sojourner Truth's twenty-one-year-old daughter (named for Truth's mother), one of three who were with her in Northampton during 1843–1845. But if David Ruggles planned to marry Truth's daughter Elizabeth, nothing came of it, not in 1846 or later.[29] His business fortunes, too, declined after his modest establishment faced fancier competition in the late 1840s. Had he not died on the day after Christmas 1849, he would have gone bankrupt in 1850.

The listing of Sojourner Truth's daughters—if daughters they all were—in the Northampton Association store ledger is full of mystery. Elizabeth and Sophia definitely were daughters, born in about 1825 and 1826. But the name "Jane" appears nowhere else in the sources surrounding Truth; she may have been Truth's elusive second child, or she may have been a granddaughter or niece. For lack of guidance, I will speak of her as a daughter, acknowledging that the sole clue to her identity consists of a single notation of her name in a store ledger.

Truth appears in the ledger as "Sojourner"—the only patron at the community store mentioned with only one name—as well as "Isabel" and "Isabella," "Van Wagner" and "Van Wagnen," and, once, as "Mrs. Sojourner."[30] Her daughters also appear under several titles. Elizabeth, Sophia, and Jane are each mentioned as "Van Wagner," "Van Wagnen," and "Gedney." The names "Van Wagner" and "Van Wagnen" establish the relationship between Truth and her daughters; but "Gedney," the name of the family of Truth's Ulster County, mistress, Sally Dumont, implies a deeper, longer-standing, and more complicated attachment between the two families.

To the thorny employer-employee relationship that Truth mentions in the story of the illegal sale of her son to Alabama and her children's indentures (only vaguely cited) must now be added a voluntary identification. The keeper of the store ledger at the Northampton Association, after all, had no independent source for the daughters' identification. Sojourner Truth's daughters must have decided on their own to perpetuate the link with the Gedneys, who appear in the *Narrative of Sojourner Truth* as little more than spoiled, rich white people.

Just as the sources do not permit any further understanding of David Ruggles's purchase of an expensive shawl for Sojourner Truth's daughter Elizabeth, so they are silent on the tangled feelings that Truth and her daughters harbored about each other and toward the Gedneys. The *Narrative of Sojourner Truth* was written while Truth was at Northampton, but it gives no sign of the presence of Elizabeth, Sophia, and Jane, and says nothing about their sense of self as expressed in their names. The daughters inexplicably remain shrouded in the *Narrative*, and the section on Northampton is no exception.

Peter is the only one of Truth's children whose history and character are visible in the *Narrative*. This may be because he was the source of his mother's greatest anguish, or because he was male and by that token his experiences seemed to merit recording. Twin conventions of biography—according to which the family of the protagonist does not appear and the black American acts against a backdrop of white racism—may also be reinforcing each other. Or the daughters may have been figures whom Truth thought best to leave beyond the autobiography's ken. Silence was the easiest means of avoiding misgivings about how little she had been able to do for her daughters, and Truth says nothing; speaking in circumlocution, Olive Gilbert, to whom Truth dictated her autobiography, impugns both the daughters' morals and the mother's care.

Gilbert tells Truth's readers that Truth's children have not benefited from the salutary atmosphere of a proper home, in which she could "instill into the opening minds of her children those principles of virtue, and that love of purity, truth and benevolence, which must ever form the foundation of a life of usefulness and happiness." Gilbert recognizes that part of the blame lies at the door of slavery and indenture. Isabella was unable to make her children a home while she was enslaved or immediately after her emancipation, when her wages were too small to afford a home together.

After their own emancipation, the daughters were still indentured to various members of the Dumont-Gedney-Waring family. During this time, Gilbert says, Truth's children were "scattered, and eminently exposed to the temptations of the adversary, with few, if any, fixed principles to sustain them." But lack of freedom is only part of the explanation that Gilbert sees for the daughters' corruption.

Gilbert also blames Truth herself for neglecting, even in difficult circumstances, to inculcate strong moral values in her children. Bringing them up properly was "far beyond [Truth's] power or means, in more senses than one," states Gilbert, who, while recognizing the challenge of child-rearing in slavery, does not wish to "shield any one [i.e., Truth] from merited rebuke!" Gilbert judges Truth a failed parent and the shortcomings of her children the product of parental disregard. She describes Truth's children as disreputable, but in the late 1840s they were adults, and Gilbert thought them old enough to take responsibility for their own failings. "If they now suffer themselves to be drawn by temptation into the paths of the destroyer," that is their own sin, for which they will ultimately pay.[31]

For Gilbert, and perhaps also for Truth, the lack of a home, with all its Victorian connotations of shelter from a cruel and heartless world—a haven of femininity in a sea of masculine predation—explained much of the weakness in Truth's family life. From a farther vantage point, however, the absence of Truth's daughters from her life story can be recognized as the familiar shroud of silence around black women who, for lack of protection, become sexual prey. Unwilling to focus on women who had not been shielded from predatory men or who were possibly unchaste, Gilbert and Truth made a commonplace erasure of the most vulnerable and least visible people in American history.[32]

The Narrative of Sojourner Truth

The Northampton Association dissolved in late 1846, having uplifted only a tiny part of its world. Truth stayed on, first trying to make her own way, then lodging with the Bensons, who had withdrawn from the association in 1845 and bought a nearby cotton mill. Although she was with people who cared for her, Truth was impatient with her situation and longed, once again, for her own home. The success of Frederick Douglass's 1845 autobiography, the *Narrative of the Life of Frederick Douglass, An American Slave*, which sold 4,500 copies in less than six months, doubtless suggested a means of affording a house of her own.[33] A year after Douglass published, Truth began dictating her autobiography to Olive Gilbert.

Of Gilbert, I know little: She was born in 1801 and died in 1884. Well educated and well read, she belonged to the Northampton Association in 1845–1846, and after the Civil War she was still living in the Northampton environs. Gilbert's original connection to the association came through the Bensons, her neighbors in Connecticut, more exactly through George and Helen's spinster sister Sarah. Sarah lived with the Bensons in Northampton and, like Olive Gilbert, never married. Gilbert was also friendly with Helen and her husband William Lloyd Garrison, and spent time with them in Boston.[34] Although the sources are virtually silent about Prudence Crandall's female supporters, Gilbert undoubtedly was involved in her Connecticut neighbor's defense, which closely engaged the Benson family.

Between the commencement of Truth's narrative and its completion three years later, Gilbert spent more than two years in Daviess County in northwestern Kentucky, probably as a governess.[35] Otherwise, the outline of Olive Gilbert's life is unclear. The joint project provides nearly all the extant information about her, some of which can be glimpsed only between the lines.

Like Truth, Gilbert may have been attracted to Millerism in 1843–1844, for the *Narrative* contains a great deal of material, sympathetically presented, on Truth's experiences with the Millerites. Instead of a description of Truth's stay in the Northampton Association, for instance, the section on 1843–1849 concerns Truth's encounter with hostile young men at a Millerite camp meeting in the spring of 1844. As one of the rare depictions of Truth's preaching by someone who had often heard her preach and sing, Gilbert's report of this episode deserves a closer look.

During 1844, Millerite meetings were frequently subject to ridicule and disruption, as was the case at a nighttime camp meeting near Northampton.[36] A mob of rowdy young men burst into the services, terrifying the worshipers and threatening to burn down the tents. Truth's first impulse was to hide behind a trunk, thinking, "I am the only colored person here, and on me, probably, their wicked mischief will fall first, and perhaps fatally."

But as the ruffians were shaking the tent, she had a little talk with herself in biblical terms:

> Shall I run away and hide from the Devil? Me, a servant of the living God? Have I not faith enough to go out and quell that mob, when I know it is written—"One shall chase a thousand, and two put ten thousand to flight"? I know there are not a thousand here; and I know I am a servant of the living God. I'll go to the rescue, and the Lord shall go with and protect me.[37]

As when she defied the rich and powerful of Ulster County over the sale of her son, Truth's religious faith gave her strength: "I felt as if I had *three hearts!* and that they were so large, my body could hardly hold them!" Thus emboldened, she urged other Millerites to help her face down the attackers. They declined, and she left the tent alone, walked to a high place, and began singing in what Gilbert terms "her most fervid manner, with all the strength of her most powerful voice, the hymn on the resurrection of Christ":

> It was early in the morning—it was early in the morning,
> Just at the break of day—
> When he rose—when he rose—when he rose,
> And went to heaven on a cloud.[38]

This was one of Truth's favorites, and Gilbert remarks, "All who have ever heard her sing this hymn will probably remember it as long as they remember her. The hymn, the tune, the style, are each too closely associated with to be easily separated from herself, and when sung in one of her most animated moods, in the open air, with the utmost strength of her most powerful voice, must have been truly thrilling." Truth would sing the same hymn on her deathbed, forty years later.

Fulfilling a requirement of spiritual autobiography, Truth pacified the unbelievers; she preached and sang to them for the better part of an hour.[39] Her sermon began with a metaphor of the second advent's Judgment Day: "Well, there are two congregations on this ground. It is written that there shall be a separation, and the sheep shall be separated from the goats. The other preachers have the sheep, *I* have the goats. And I have a few sheep among my goats, but they are *very* ragged." The crowd laughed and settled in to be entertained.

Truth grew weary, wanted to stop preaching, but her audience would not let her go. She addressed them as "children," as she had the fanatical Connecticut Millerites: "I have talked and sung to you, as you asked me; and now I have a request to make of you: will you grant it?" She would sing one more song if they would leave in peace afterwards; she had to ask them three times. Long after the demise of Millerite camp meetings, Truth would repeat her song:

I bless the Lord I've got my seal—to-day and to-day—
To slay Goliath in the field—to-day and to-day—
The good old way is a righteous way,
I mean to take the kingdom in the good old way.

Running back to the main road, the roughnecks frightened the other Millerites but created no further trouble. Truth had assuaged their angry spirits and saved the meeting.[40]

The Sojourner Truth memorial statue. Thomas J. Warren. Bronze.
The statue, dedicated in 2002, stands on a hill overlooking the site of the Northampton Association of Education and Industry.

The twenty pages of the *Narrative of Sojourner Truth* dedicated to her time with the Millerites contain none of the internal strains of other parts of the story. Elsewhere, Gilbert the abolitionist is often at odds with Truth the autobiographer. The abolitionist presses Truth to provide examples of the iniquities of slavery, which Truth delivers and Gilbert amplifies, but which must be tacked on to Truth's own, more enigmatic story.[41] And toward the end of the book, Gilbert addresses Truth rather than the reader, admonishing her to revise her harsh judgment of the Bensons.

Gilbert comes close to calling Truth paranoid, and, returning her address to the reader, builds a case for the purchase of the *Narrative* based on Truth's and her daughters' own deficiencies. The daughters are too sinful and foolish to care for their mother in the old age that is now upon her, and the mother has wasted her money on the likes of the Prophet Matthias.[42]

Whether or not Gilbert shared Truth's second adventism, together they produced a narrative that is strikingly spiritual. This emphasis on the evolution of Truth's faith and her religious experiences—including the long episode in which she pacifies rowdies at the camp meeting—has made the *Narrative of Sojourner Truth* difficult for readers to fit into the more familiar southern drama of slavery, with its contest between virtuous slave and cruel master.

To this day, the *Narrative of Sojourner Truth* remains outside the canon of ex-slave narratives. It ends not with indictment, but with the Christian forgiveness of a slaveholder, on the occasion of Truth's 1849 visit to her oldest daughter, Diana, who had remained with John Dumont in Dutchess County, New York. These last two pages of the *Narrative* are about Dumont, not hardworking Diana, and they convey Truth's satisfaction that he had come to see that slavery was wrong. She closes with exultation: "A slave-holding master turned to a brother! Poor old man, may the Lord bless him, and all slaveholders partake of his spirit!" Phrases too tender for an antislavery message in the decade of discord before the Civil War![43]

The *Narrative of Sojourner Truth* marks a turning point in the biography of Sojourner Truth—her first step into deliberate representation of self. In her interviews with Gilbert Vale in 1835, Isabella had sought only to vindicate herself as a vulnerable member of a suspect community. The *Narrative* makes her a person worth reading about in her own right.

HAVING furnished a writer, Truth's Northampton connections also found her a printer. The most illustrious of Northampton's visitors, William Lloyd Garrison, was editor of the Boston *Liberator* and president of the American Anti-Slavery Society, which had already published Frederick Douglass's narrative. Garrison put Truth in touch with his own printer, George Brown Yerrinton.

Truth had met Garrison in the fall of 1843, when the Garrison family paid an extended visit to the Bensons, and she probably saw him again in July 1848, when Garrison accepted David Ruggles's offer of free treatment at his Northampton Water Cure.[44] Yerrinton, originally from Providence, was a Free Thinker (like Gilbert Vale) whose ties to progressive causes and publications dated back to the 1820s.[45] He printed Truth's *Narrative* on credit, and the debt weighed heavily on Truth until she was able to repay it fully in the early 1850s. Having paid for the printing, Truth, rather than Yerrinton, is the publisher of her book. It is unclear why the plates remained for the time being in the possession of one of Truth's Northampton Association colleagues turned spiritualist-physician in New York, James Boyle, but he later gave them to her and made possible the editions of the 1850s, 1870s, and 1880s.[46]

In 1850, Truth's publishing herself was not unusual, for the line between publisher and printer was only then becoming established, and the functions of printing, distributing, and selling books were not always distinct. Acting as her own distributor and bookseller, Truth was well within the bounds of ordinary practice. More unusual, though, was the cheapness of her book: 25 cents per copy for a 128-page, 7 ¾-by-5-inch, soft-covered edition. She kept the price low, perhaps to encourage purchase, for sales of the *Narrative* were to be her means of paying off the mortgage on her new house. An advertisement for Truth's *Narrative* appeared in the *Liberator* in May 1850 with a blurb from Garrison: "This is a most interesting Narrative of a most remarkable and highly meritorious woman, the sale of which is to be for her exclusive benefit. We commend it to all the friends of the colored people."[47] Once the *Narrative* was printed, Truth had the means to fulfill her dream. For the first time in her life, she acquired a home of her own.

We cannot know what went wrong between Truth and the Bensons, but her preference in 1843 for wintering in an intentional community over prolonging her stay in a private home makes a statement: When she had a choice, she preferred being one among many to one among a few. She resisted situations in which she was "just like one of the family" and dependent strictly on her hosts. In the event, Truth had no choice but to find new lodging. George Benson's cotton mill failed, and the family moved to Long Island.[48] Meanwhile, Northampton Association stalwart Samuel Hill and his brother-in-law acquired the property that had belonged to the association and were selling it to various former members. Truth took out a $300 mortgage from Hill, bought a house on Park Street, across from the cemetery, and made it her home until the mid-1850s.

The world did not yet know her exclusively as "Sojourner Truth," for her 1850 deed names her as "Isabella Vanwagner . . . sometimes called 'Sojourner Truth'"; the 1854 deed omits "Truth" entirely. Although her identity wavered

Sojourner Truth house, Park Street, Northampton.

With financial backing from Samuel L. Hill, Sojourner Truth purchased this house with the proceeds of the sale of her *Narrative*. She lived in the house from 1847 to 1857. Though much altered since Truth's time, the structure is still supported by the original timber frame.

between that of working-class New Yorker and itinerant preacher, one thing was clear. In 1854, she discharged the mortgage and, at last, owned her own house free and clear.[49] She was about fifty-seven years old.

IN LATE middle age, Sojourner Truth emerges from her *Narrative* as a complex individual, a mixture of brightness and shadow. She is a woman of "native enthusiasm," with the "energy of a naturally powerful mind—the fearlessness and child-like simplicity of one untrammeled by education or conventional customs." Her character is pure, her adherence to principle unflinching. She is a singing evangelist whose religion is joyous, optimistic, and "at times ecstatic. Her trust is in God, and from him she looks for good, and not evil. She feels that 'perfect love casteth out fear.'" But her faith consorts with foreboding.

Apparently facing the twilight of her years, Truth has "set suspicion to guard the door of her heart," allowing it "to be aroused by too slight causes." She magnifies the "phantoms of her fears into gigantic proportions." Olive

Gilbert presents a figure of fervor and enthusiasm, but also one of apprehension and distrust.[50] Fervor and enthusiasm were what her audiences would see as she became famous as an abolitionist.

NOTES

1. Millennialism (including second adventism) and utopianism shared a fundamental common assumption: that this world needed to be and would be changed radically. Many Millerites in the leadership and the rank and file had been active in moral reform, tightening the connection between Millerite millennialism and utopianism.

2. David Mack to A. J. Taylor, April 23, 1843, Letters of the Northampton Association of Education and Industry, vol. 4, Northampton Association of Education and Industry Papers, American Antiquarian Society, Worcester, MA; Alice Eaton McBee, *From Utopia to Florence: The Story of a Transcendentalist Community in Northampton, Mass., 1830–1852* (Northampton: Smith College Studies in History, vol. 32, 1947), 49. See also Christopher Clark, *The Communitarian Moment: The Radical Challenge of the Northampton Association* (Ithaca, 1995).

3. [Olive Gilbert and Frances Titus], *Narrative of Sojourner Truth; A Bondswoman of Olden Time, Emancipated by the New York Legislature in the Early Part of the Present Century; with a History of her Labors and Correspondence Drawn from her "Book of Life"* (1878; reprint Salem, NH, 1990), 120.

4. Michael Barkun, *Crucible of the Millennium: The Burned-Over District of New York in the 1840s* (Syracuse, 1986), 82.

5. Emerson quoted in Hope Hale Davis, "The Northampton Association of Education and Industry," in *The Northampton Book: Chapters from 300 Years in the Life of a New England Town, 1654–1954* (Northampton, 1954), 114.

6. Susan Strane, *A Whole-Souled Woman: Prudence Crandall and the Education of Black Women* (New York, 1990), x, 19, 24, 189, 191, 200, 220, 227; Donald Yacovone, *Samuel Joseph May and the Dilemmas of the Liberal Persuasion, 1797–1871* (Philadelphia, 1991), 43–55. Crandall became what she called a "Unitarian spiritualist" in the 1850s and settled in Kansas in 1876. In 1886, the state of Connecticut apologized to Crandall and awarded her a $400 per annum pension for the rest of her life. She died in 1890.

7. McBee, *From Utopia to Florence*, 8–13; Davis, "The Northampton Association," 110.

8. Frank E. Manuel and Fritzie P. Manuel, *Utopian Thought in the Western World* (Cambridge, MA, 1979), 653.

9. Record of Proceedings of the Northampton Association of Education and Industry, April 8, 1842, vol. 2, Northampton Association of Education and Industry Papers, American Antiquarian Society.

10. [John Metcalf], *Social Reform: or An Appeal in Behalf of Association, Based Upon the Principles of a Pure Christianity* (Northampton, 1844), 18–19.

11. Garrison quoted in Arthur E. Beston, Jr., "Fourierism in Northampton: A Critical Note," *New England Quarterly* 13, no. 1 (March 1940): 110; Barbara Goodwin, *Social Science and Utopia: Nineteenth-Century Models of Social Harmony* (Hassocks, UK, 1978), 38–39.

12. Alice Manning, "When Freedom Flourished in Cosmian Hall," *Daily Hampshire Gazette* (Northampton), August 7, 1976; Esther Terry, "Sojourner Truth: The Person behind the Libyan Sibyl, with a memoir by Frederick Douglass, What I Found at the Northampton Association," *Massachusetts Review* 26, nos. 2 and 3 (1985) (no page numbers).

13. Frances P. Judd, "Reminiscences," in Charles A. Sheffeld, ed., *History of Florence, Massachusetts. Including a Complete Account of the Northampton Association of Education and Industry* (Florence, 1895), 116.

14. Sheffeld, *History of Florence*, 105.

15. Davis, "The Northampton Association," 111. Prevailing adult wages in Northampton were 10 cents an hour for adults, and a week's room and board cost 75 cents.

16. David Mack to John Bailey, June 8, 1844, Letters of the Northampton Association of Education and Industry, vol. 4, Northampton Association of Education and Industry Papers.

17. Douglass, "What I Found at the Northampton Association," in Sheffeld, *History of Florence*, 130; Record of Proceedings of the Northampton Association of Education and Industry, May 16, 1842, vol. 2, Northampton Association of Education and Industry Papers.

18. Samuel L. Hill to David Mack, June 30, 1846. Northampton Association of Education and Industry Letter Book, Northampton Association of Education and Industry Papers.

19. Sheffeld, *History of Florence*, 101–102.

20. George R. Stetson, "When I Was a Boy," in Sheffeld, *History of Florence*, 121. Stetson's family was also from Brooklyn, Connecticut.

21. Whitney R. Cross, *The Burned-Over District: The Social and Intellectual History of Enthusiastic Religion in Western New York, 1800–1850* (1950; New York, 1965), 189–190, 240; George Wallingford Noyes, ed., *Religious Experience of John Humphrey Noyes, Founder of the Oneida Community* (New York, 1923), 59, 209–210, 253; Robert Allerton Parker, *A Yankee Saint: John Humphrey Noyes arid the Oneida Community* (New York, 1935), 22, 35–39; and Northampton Association of Education and Industry Papers, vol. 2: 95, 96.

22. Frederick Douglass, "What I Found at the Northampton Association," in Sheffeld, *History of Florence*, 130; Giles B. Stebbins, *Upward Steps of Seventy Years. Autobiographic, Biographic, Historic* (New York, 1890), 55–57.

23. On the black people at the Northampton Association see Clark, *The Communitarian Moment*, 71–75.

24. Douglass, "What I Found at the Northampton Association," in Sheffeld, *History of Florence*, 131–132. Douglass did not mention the third black adult in the Northampton Association, Basil Dorsey, a fugitive slave who arrived in 1844, after Douglass's visit. Dorsey was a good worker with a pleasing but evidently not very memorable personality, who stayed on as a cotton mill worker in Florence after the dissolution of the Northampton Association. In 1850, the people of Northampton took up a collection that Dorsey added to his own personal savings and used to purchase his freedom. McBee, *From Utopia to Florence*, 69.

25. Susan E. Cayleff, *Wash and Be Healed: The Water-Cure Movement and Women's Health* (Philadelphia, 1987), 2–15, 20–29; Dorothy B. Porter with Edwin C. Rozwenc, "The Water Cures," in *The Northampton Book*, 123.

26. Porter with Rozwenc, "The Water Cures," 123; Cayleff, *Wash and Be Healed*, 80, 86; McBee, *From Utopia to Florence*, 71.

27. Porter with Rozwenc, "The Water Cures," 123. Store Department of the Northampton Association of Education and Industry, Day Book No. 4, April 1, 1846, vol. 1: 194–197, 205, 217, 226–228, 237, 250, 258, 270, 343–350, 355–357, and 365. Northampton Association of Education and Industry Papers.

28. Store Department of the Northampton Association, Day Book No. 4, April 1, 1846, vol. 1: 352, Northampton Association of Education and Industry Papers.

29. Elizabeth married a man named Banks and gave birth to Samuel Banks in Connecticut in 1850. In about 1860, she married again in Battle Creek, Michigan. Berenice Lowe, "The Family of Sojourner Truth," *Michigan Heritage* (summer 1962): 182, 184.

30. Accounts, April 1844, Northampton Association of Education and Industry Papers, vol. 5: 235.

31. *Narrative of Sojourner Truth*, 71–73.

32. Darlene Clark Hine, "Rape and the Inner Lives of Black Women in the Middle West: Preliminary Thoughts on the Culture of Dissemblance," *Signs* 14, no. 4 (1989): 912–920.

33. William L. Andrews, *To Tell a Free Story: The First Century of Afro-American Autobiography, 1760–1865* (Urbana, IL, 1986), 97, 138. Douglass's narrative was reprinted six times in four years.

34. *International Genealogical Index, 1988 Edition*; Family History Library, Church of Jesus Christ of Latter Day Saints, Salt Lake City; *Narrative of Sojourner Truth*, 276–278; Walter M. Merrill, ed., *The Letters of William Lloyd Garrison*, vol. 3, *No Union with Slaveholders, 1841–1849* (Cambridge, MA, 1973), 165, 203, 499; Louis Ruchames, ed., *The Letters of William Lloyd Garrison*, vol. 4, *From Disunionism to the Brink of War, 1850–1860* (Cambridge, MA, 1975), 40, 60–61; Northampton Association of Education and Industry Papers, vol. 3: 229; vol. 7: 304–327.

35. *Narrative of Sojourner Truth*, 36, 84–85.

36. Jonathan M. Butler, "The Making of a New Order: Millerism and the Origins of Seventh-Day Adventism," in Ronald L. Numbers and Jonathan M. Butler, eds., *The Disappointed: Millerism and Millenarianism in the Nineteenth Century*, 2nd ed. (Knoxville, TN, 1993), 197.

37. *Narrative of Sojourner Truth*, 115–116. Truth was paraphrasing several biblical verses: Numbers 32:6; Judges 15:16; Luke 3:14; Revelation 19:11–15.

38. *Narrative of Sojourner Truth*, 115–116. Emphasis in the original.

39. *Narrative*, 116–118.

40. *Narrative*, 119–120.

41. See *Narrative*, 82–85.

42. *Narrative*, 72, 122–123.

43. *Narrative*, 124.

44. *William Lloyd Garrison, 1805–1879: The Story of His Life Told by His Children* (Boston, 1885), 3:228–231.

45. Printer's file, American Antiquarian Society.

46. *Narrative of Sojourner Truth*, 263, 264; Sojourner Truth to William Lloyd Garrison, Salem, Ohio, August 28, 1851, *Black Abolitionist Papers* (New York: Microfilming Corporation of America, 1981), reel 7, 79; Sojourner Truth to William

Lloyd Garrison, Detroit, April 11, 1864, *Black Abolitionist Papers*, reel 15, 261; McBee, *From Utopia to Florence*, 53; Cross, *The Burned-Over District,* 189–191, 196, 240–246, 276, 343.

47. Boston *Liberator*, May 24, 1850. The book had been published in April.

48. According to Alice McBee, Benson's cotton mill failed, and he and his family moved to Wakarusa (now Lawrence), Kansas, where he continued to be active in the peace, temperance, and antislavery movements. However, letters between Truth and Garrison and between the Garrisons show that after leaving Northampton, the Bensons spent the early 1850s living on Long Island, New York, where James Boyle boarded with them while his wife was visiting in Ohio. McBee, *From Utopia to Florence*, 70. See also Sojourner Truth to William Lloyd Garrison, Salem, Ohio, August 28, 1851, *Black Abolitionist Papers*, reel 7, 79; William Lloyd Garrison to Helen E. Garrison, New York, May 12, 1858, Ruchames, *The Letters of William Lloyd Garrison*, 4:528.

49. McBee, *From Utopia to Florence*, 67–70. Hampshire County, Massachusetts, Registry of Deeds, Book 133, 106–107, 124–125, Northampton.

50. *Narrative of Sojourner Truth*, 121–122.

16

ALTHOUGH most in Northampton opposed slavery, few espoused the egalitarian notions of the Garrisonians. True, the underground railroad numbered several stations in the area, but abolitionist Lydia Maria Child wrote in despair of the indifference of "this iron-clad valley of the Connecticut." Indeed, Northampton was a popular summer destination for wealthy southern planters and their families. Its water-cure facilities were highly regarded by the man who was to become known as "Stonewall" Jackson. These contradictions reflected the tensions and deep divisions of the country as a whole on the eve of the Civil War.

When war came, Northampton raised four companies of volunteers. Charles Harvey Brewster enlisted in Company C of the Tenth Massachusetts Volunteers in April 1861. Over the next three and a half years, he saw action in every major campaign in the eastern theater. In July 1863, he wrote from the battlefield of Gettysburg:

> *I thought I had seen the horror of war before, but the like of this battle is seldom seen. Men, Horses, Canon, Caissons, and all the implements of war piled up in almost inextricable confusion. Men with heads shot off, limbs shot off, Men shot in two, and men shot in pieces, and little fragments so as hardly to be recognizable as any part of a man. We passed yesterday 9 dead Rebels in one heap in the road probably killed by one shell, and dead Rebels were scattered everywhere and yet the ground was dotted with single graves and pits full of them."*

The Civil War was America's first "total war" in the modern sense. A larger proportion of the American population died in the Civil War than of the British population in World War I. When the Tenth Massachusetts finally returned from the war, only 220 of the 1,000 originally enlisted remained in the ranks.

*The Civil War letters of Charles Harvey Brewster, now preserved in the Historic Northampton archives, have been edited by David W. Blight and published by the University of Massachusetts Press (*When This Cruel War Is Over, *1992). In his introduction to the letters, Blight shows how the Brewster letters reflect the great events of the Civil War as experienced by the individual soldier and reveal Brewster's personal struggle to come to terms with his own reasons for fighting.*

When This Cruel War Is Over*

DAVID W. BLIGHT

The soil of peace is thickly sown with the seeds of war.

AMBROSE BIERCE

WITH the First World War as his model, Paul Fussell wrote that "every war is ironic because every war is worse than expected." As national calamity and as individual experience, certainly this was the case with the American Civil War. That slavery could be abolished only by such wholesale slaughter, that new definitions of freedom could be affirmed only in the world's first total war, and that national unity could be preserved only through such fratricidal conflict provide some of the most tragic ironies of American history. Epic destruction of life and treasure led to epic possibilities in a new and redefined American republic in the 1860s. The freedom of the slaves and the liberties of the free were achieved or preserved at horrifying costs. The Civil War was ironic because it both violated and affirmed the nineteenth-century doctrine of progress; it would become the source of America's shame as well as its pride; and it would haunt as well as inspire the national imagination. For many Americans, the whole affair would become humankind's madness somehow converted to God's purposes. On a grand scale, such ironies are easily summarized, but as Fussell observes, all "great" wars consist of thousands of "smaller constituent" stories, which are themselves full of "ironic actions."[1] The thousands of individuals, North and South, who brought the values and aspirations of their communities to so many campgrounds, battlefields, and hospitals provide the constituent stories of this American epic.

One of those stories is recorded in the remarkable Civil War letters of Charles Harvey Brewster of Northampton, Massachusetts. When viewed through the lens of social history, letters like Brewster's reveal the experience of an ordinary American man caught up not only in the sweeping events of the Civil War, but also in the values of his age and the struggle of his own self-development.

In a 1989 article historian Maris Vinovskis asserted that American "social historians have lost sight of the centrality of the Civil War." In recent years, responding to this and other challenges, a new social history of the Civil War era has begun to emerge, and nowhere is this more apparent than in new studies of the common soldier's experience. The questions, assumptions, and subjects of social historians have tended to make them deemphasize, if not

---

* From David W. Blight, *When This Cruel War Is Over: The Civil War Letters of Charles Harvey Brewster* (Amherst, 1992).

ignore, major political, military, or diplomatic *events*. Social historians are typically concerned with the values and life cycles of ordinary people, with social structures, community dynamics, demography, family patterns, and change as *process*. Conversely, too many Civil War historians have treated the war as almost exclusively an affair of presidents and generals, of leadership in unprecedented crises. But there is now good reason to believe that these two approaches to the Civil War era can find common ground. The magnitude of casualties suffered in the war, the social and psychological dislocation experienced by so many soldiers, women, and children, the economic growth or stagnation caused by unprecedented war production and destruction, and the emancipation of more than four million slaves demonstrate that the Civil War was an event in which profound social changes occurred. More than three million Americans, including 189,000 blacks in the Union forces, served in the armies and navies. At the end of the war, one of every six white males and one of every five blacks who served were dead. A larger proportion of the American population died in the Civil War than the British population in the First World War. Many towns and farming communities sent large percentages of their male citizenry to the war to have them replaced only by monuments on their town greens and commons in years to come. White northern widows would ultimately benefit from a pension system, but white southern widows and African American widows in both sections would make do on their own. Some social historians now consider broad social structure, the lives of ordinary people, racial, gender, and class values, and the impact of such transforming events as the Civil War on an equal footing. That major *events* may be returning to the agenda of social historians is, indeed, a welcome occurrence.[2]

A close reading of the Brewster letters affords an intriguing window into most of the categories of inquiry mentioned above. The letters will be of interest to military historians and readers; they are an excellent source for the study of men experiencing war. But as Bell Wiley first observed in the 1940s and 1950s, the letters of Civil War soldiers are an extraordinary source for the social history of nineteenth-century America, and Brewster's letters from the front are an especially illuminating example of this phenomenon.[3] The emotions and ideas represented in these letters range from naïveté to mature realism, from romantic idealism to sheer terror, and from self-pity to enduring devotion. Most of all, Brewster seems honest with his correspondents; there are very few simple pieties in his writing and he was boldly descriptive about the immense tragedy he witnessed. His homesickness and despair, as well as his ambition and sense of accomplishment, are quite palpable.

Born and raised in Northampton, Brewster was a relatively unsuccessful, twenty-seven-year-old store clerk and a member of the local militia when he enlisted in Company C of the Tenth Massachusetts Volunteers in April 1861.

Companies of the Tenth Massachusetts were formed from towns all over the western section of the state: Springfield, Holyoke, Great Barrington, Westfield, Pittsfield, Shelburne Falls, Greenfield, and Northampton. The citizens of Northampton were infected by the war fever that swept the land in the spring and summer of 1861 On April 18, only three days after the surrender of Fort Sumter, the first meeting of the Company C militia (an old unit chartered in 1801) turned into a large public rally where forty new men enlisted. By April 24, seventy-five Northampton women rallied and committed their labor to sew the uniforms of the local company. As the cloth arrived, some women worked at home and others sewed in the town hall. Local poets came to the armory to recite patriotic verses to the drilling, would-be soldiers. Yesterday farmers, clerks, and mechanics; today they were the local heroes who would "whip secesh." On May 9, Company C marched some seven miles to an overnight encampment in Haydenville, passing through the towns of Florence and Leeds on the way. In each village, a brass band, an outdoor feast, and a large crowd cheered them. War was still a local festival in this first spring of the conflict. By June 10, the seventy or so members of the company attended a farewell ball, and four days later they strode down Main Street through a throng so large that a corridor could hardly be formed. Flags waved everywhere, several brass bands competed, and Brewster and his comrades joined two other companies of the Tenth on a train for Springfield. En route, the soldiers continued the joyous fervor of the day by singing "patriotic airs" to the accompaniment of a lone accordion.[4] Like most of his comrades; Brewster had enlisted for three years, never believing the war would last that long.

After a three-week encampment in Springfield, the Tenth Massachusetts again departed by train and with great ceremony. In Springfield, as in so many other American communities that summer, the "ladies" of the town formally presented the regimental colors to the commander of the regiment, in this case Colonel Henry S. Briggs. It was a time, said the women's announcement, for "reverence" to flags, and they urged the men to "defend them to the death." The spokeswoman, Mrs. James Barnes, assured these young warriors that "the heart of many a wife and mother and child and sister, will beat anxiously for your *safety*, but remember, no less anxiously for your *honor*." In Palmer, on the way to Boston, several hundred women, some with bouquets of flowers, gathered at the station to bid the troops goodbye. The regiment would camp ten more days in Medford, next to Charlestown, on the banks of the Mystic River. Before boarding transports for the voyage to Washington, D.C., the Tenth stood for one more ceremony, this time addressed by the former Massachusetts governor George N. Briggs, father of the commander. In a message fathers have passed to their sons for centuries, but rarely so explicitly, Briggs called upon farm boys and clerks to show themselves "to be *men* and *New England men*." He urged them to be gallant and fierce, but always kind to their wounded or captured enemy. He then concluded with a flourish: "When the army of an ancient republic were going forth to battle a mother of one of the soldiers said to him: 'My son, return home *with* your shield or *on* your shield.' Adopting the sentiment of the

Members of Company C, Tenth Massachusetts Volunteers. *Historic Northampton.*

Seated, left to right: Will Bishop, George Bliss, Edward Nally. Standing, left to right: Will Kingsley, Alvin Rust, Fred Clark. The cloth hats worn by Bliss and Nally were probably knitted by Charles Brewster's sisters, Martha and Mary.

noble mother, let me say . . . bring back those beautiful and rich colors presented you by the ladies of Springfield, the emblems of your country's power and glory, waving over your heads, unstained, or return wrapped in their gory folds."[5] One can never know how closely soldiers listened to such rhetoric in that romantic summer of 1861. The fathers' and mothers' call to war and manliness in the war their sons were soon to fight would indeed become for some men an exhilarating and ennobling challenge; others grew disillusioned by the fight that became unbearable. Brewster was to experience (and record) both the exhilaration and the disillusionment.

The Tenth Massachusetts spent the rest of 1861 and the winter of 1862 in Camp Brightwood, on the edge of the District of Columbia. There they joined the Seventh Massachusetts, the Thirty-sixth New York, and the Second Rhode Island as part of "Couch's Brigade." For three years, Brewster shared the same brigade and battle experiences as Second Rhode Island Private (ultimately Colonel) Elisha Hunt Rhodes, whose diary became famous as part of a 1990 PBS television documentary on the Civil War.[6] The Tenth participated in almost every major battle fought by the Army of the Potomac, beginning with the Peninsula campaign through Antietam and Fredericksburg in 1862, Chancellorsville, Gettysburg, Bristow Station, and Rappahannock Station in 1863, and the Wilderness, Spotsylvania, and Cold Harbor in 1864. When the survivors of the Tenth were mustered out at the end of their three-year enlistment and returned to Springfield in June 1864, only 220 of the nearly one thousand in the original regiment were still on active duty. They had witnessed their summer outing transform into the bloodiest war in history, seen thousands die of disease, practiced war upon civilians and the southern landscape, loyally served the cause as variously defined, and tried their best to fulfill their communities' expectations. They returned, in the words of their last commander, Colonel Joseph B. Parsons, a "shattered remnant" of "mourners."[7] Brewster would probably have agreed with Parsons's characterization of the survivors; as the adjutant of the regiment he had had the duty to record that shattering constantly in casualty reports and death notices. But Brewster's letters to the women in his family record not only the ugliness and futility of war—and there is plenty of that—but also the myriad social attitudes, values, and self-perceptions of a relatively ordinary and reflective mid-nineteenth-century white American male. Brewster's father, Harvey Brewster, a seventh-generation *Mayflower* descendant, died in 1839 when Charles was only five years old, leaving Martha Russell Brewster a widow with three small children, including two daughters, four-year-old Martha and two-month-old Mary. Brewster's wartime letters, virtually all of which were written to his mother and two sisters, exhibit deep affection and clearly reflect a family background of financial distress. His wartime adventures and sufferings exacerbated Brewster's estimation of himself as a frustrated, if not failed, provider in his capacity as the sole male member of his family. Nevertheless, for Brewster, as has been sadly true for men throughout the ages, war gave an ordinary man the opportunity to escape from the ordinary.[8]

Brewster would come to loathe war itself; after imagined and romantic warfare gave way to real battle in 1862, he would describe it in honest and realistic terms. He came to understand that in war, perhaps even more than in civilian life, fate was often indifferent to individual virtue. Educated in the Northampton public schools, sensitive and remarkably literate, Brewster was no natural warrior. He aspired to leadership and craved recognition, but in 210 surviving letters, the only time Brewster ever mentions discharging his own weapon is in describing target practice. He was under fire countless times, experienced some of the worst battles of the Virginia campaigns, frequently wished his enemies dead, and participated in the mass killing that was the Civil War. Yet, consistent with the behavior of most soldiers, nowhere does he describe his own actual killing of a Confederate soldier. This silence probably reflects an emotional distancing and a soldier's natural sense of duty, as well as some consideration of his women correspondents. But the army and his incessant desire for status within its ranks became for Brewster the source of community and even vocation that he had not known before. It is tragic but true that Charles Harvey Brewster found existential meaning only when he went to war and became an officer in the cause of preserving the Union and freeing the slaves.

Brewster survived more than three years of battle, hardship, sickness, and boredom by a combination of devotion, a recognition of diminished alternatives, self-righteous ambition, and a sense of irony. He wrote letters from all kinds of places and postures, and on all kinds of stationery. As with literate soldiers in all ages, or with anyone undergoing loneliness and stress, letters became for Brewster both monologues of self-discovery and dialogues with home. Letters were a humanizing element in a dehumanizing environment, evidence that however foreign civilian life might come to appear, something called "home" still existed. Lying in a rifle pit in June 1862, having experienced his first major battle at Fair Oaks during the Peninsula campaign, Brewster scolded his mother for not writing more often: "It is the little common place incidents of everyday life at home which we like to read," Brewster declared. "It is nothing to the inhabitants of Northampton that the beans are up in the old garden at home, or that Mary has moved her Verbena bed into the garden, but to me, way off here in the swamps, and woods, frying in the sun, or soaking in the rain, it is a very important thing indeed. You do not realize how everything that savors of home, relishes with us."[9] This is only one of many times that Brewster would contrast the pursuits of peace with the pursuits of war, partly out of self-pity and partly to remind himself that he was alive. In a letter full of volatile emotions, in which he wrote matter-of-factly about the prospect of his own death, he informed his mother that her letters were like "Angels visits." But when one was sleeping in the mud, even letters were sometimes inadequate to the task of sustaining hope and self-respect. "I think it is too bad," said Brewster from the Peninsula, "when letters are the only thing that makes existence tolerable in this God forsaken country."[10]

Letters were a soldier's means of expressing and understanding the absurdity of war, as well as a way of reaffirming commitment to the enterprise. But nothing threw this paradox into greater relief than letters to and from dead men. There are two examples of this in Brewster's letters. In the immediate aftermath of the battle of Gettysburg, Brewster lifted three letters from "a dead Rebels cartridge box, written to his mother and sisters." He sent them to his sister Mary as a souvenir. "Poor fellow," Brewster remarked, "he lay upon the field with his entrails scattered all about by a cannon shot, I cannot help pity him although as you see he expresses no very kindly intentions towards poor us." Backhandedly, Brewster expressed a sense of kinship with his dead enemy. "The mother & sisters will look in vain in the far off Florida for his return," wrote the New Englander, "or even his grave among the green hills of Penn. where his body probably lies in a pit with lots of his comrades." Brewster maintained a certain emotional distance from his unnamed foe in an unmarked grave. But the symbol of the confiscated letters to "mother & sisters" could only have made him and his family back home wonder in what "pit" beneath which "green hills" Brewster might soon find oblivion. Moreover, during the worst of the Wilderness-Spotsylvania campaign of 1864 he expressed the great "joy" with which the regiment received two large grain bags of mail. Brewster saw to the sorting of the letters, "but alas," he declared, "there was terrible sorrow connected with it which was the many letters for our dead and wounded comrades. I think I found as many as a dozen letters for poor Lt Bartlett who was killed only the day before."[11] Letters represented the continuity of life, even when they were to or from the dead.

One of the principal themes of Brewster's letters was his quest for and pride in a commission. Readers will find very little abstract discussion of patriotism here, but a great deal about Brewster's desire for a "chance" to "better" himself, for the respect of his fellow soldiers, for the symbols and authority of rank, and for increased wages so that he could send money back home. To a significant degree Brewster's war was one man's lonely effort to compensate for prior failure and to imagine a new career within the rigid and unpredictable strictures of the army. Brewster was disappointed that he had to enter the service as a noncommissioned first sergeant, and he spent the first summer and autumn of the war pining for the status a commission would bring. Put simply, Brewster had a chip on his shoulder about the hand that life had dealt him. He frequently referred to a prewar pattern of bad luck as he gossiped about those who got promotions, resented perceived slights, desperately relished compliments about his performance, and moaned to his mother that it was "hope deferred that maketh the heart sick."[12] Brewster constantly measured himself against his fellow soldiers and calculated his chances of promotion against their character and health. He could not hide his increased hope in November 1861 when he reported that the "Adjutant is very sick and to day the Doctors report that he cannot live." "Consequently," Brewster concluded, "they will have to promote a 1st Lieutenant to his place, so I am quite certain that I shall have a chance." But his desires are noteworthy for their commonality, not their venality; his relations with his comrades were a typical combination of male bonding and competition. Brewster also had a workingman's sense of practical self-interest. "A fellow can sleep very warm even in the woods," he told his mother in December 1861 "with a commission in his pocket."[13]

Brewster received his much-coveted commission and promotion to second lieutenant in December 1861. In one of the most revealing letters in the collection, he sent a detailed description of the sword, sash, belt, and cap which were purchased for him as gifts at considerable cost by members of his company. The letter reads like a description of an impending graduation or a wedding night. "My heart is full to overflowing tonight," Brewster informed his sister. All pettiness and resentment vanished as he realized the "evidence of my standing in the affections of the men." His comrades pooled more than fifty dollars to buy the officer's accoutrements, and Brewster confessed to feeling "wicked" over his good fortune while his comrades in the ranks honored him. The army in winter quarters had become a society of men living together, developing their own rituals and conventions of domestic relations. On the eve of a ceremony that would recognize his new rank, Brewster prepared for a rite of passage and new living arrangements. "I am writing in *my* tent," he told his sister. "I have not slept in it yet but am going to tonight. Lieut. Weatherill and myself have been arranging things all day." There were "new bunks" in his "future home," and he informed Mary that he would be ready to entertain her when she visited. Brewster made the most of this milestone in his life, and a certain tenderness crept into his language as he marveled at the "spontaneous outbreak of feeling" among the men.[14]

Brewster learned what war has often taught us: that men frequently find love and respect for each other more readily in warlike activities than in civilian pursuits. After first wearing his "new uniform," Brewster declared that he felt "quite like a free man once more, now that I am a commissioned Officer. it is wonderful what a difference two little straps on the shoulders make." Once again, he recognized his own aims as practical and personal. "Before I had lots of work and very little pay," he wrote, "and now I have

Second Lieutenant Charles Harvey Brewster. *Historic Northampton.*

This photograph was taken soon after Brewster received his commission in December 1861. Reflecting local bonds of Civil War units, soldiers in his company donated fifty dollars toward the purchase of his uniform, including his sword and sash.

very little work and lots of pay."[15] In other words, to Brewster promotion meant increased wages, status, and independence in controlling his own labor. But Brewster's new status also represented some ideals in the relations among men that only the army seemed to provide: loyalty, respect, and the opportunity to experience the burdens and joys of leadership. Brewster would have been deeply heartened by a September 1861 letter written by Henry W. Parsons, a twenty-two-year-old private in his company. "In reguard to Charley Brewster," Parsons wrote to his aunt, "he improves every day he is the best officer in the company that we have had with us yet you will find a large heart beneth his coat." Within a month of writing this tribute to his favorite officer, Parsons would die of disease at Camp Brightwood, but not before informing his aunt that Brewster was "a gentleman to all and will do all for the men that lays in his power—his friends may feel proud of him . . . let me tell you Aunt that this is the place to find out mens disposition one can soon tell a man from a knave or coward." Deeply affected by the loss of such a friend so early in their service, Brewster told his mother that he could not "get over Henry Parsons' death. it came so sudden and he was a particular friend of mine, and he and myself had many a confidential talk together."[16] The quest for status, the love and respect of friends, and the sheer struggle for physical survival all became part of a young officer's daily existence.

As soldiers like Brewster developed their military identities, their letters revealed what historian Reid Mitchell has called the "immense distance that grew up between the worlds of civilian and soldier." Soldiers who find themselves in a "community of the front," as Eric Leed has aptly described it, or those who experience extreme alienation because of the violence and degradation of soldiering, become acutely aware of how different they are from civilians.[17] Frequent letter writers like Brewster were readily reminded of the radical disjuncture between their precarious existence and that of the community left behind. "How I wish some of the stay at homes could enjoy one winter campaign with us," Brewster complained in 1862, "I fancy we should hear less of 'onward to Richmond.'" Once a soldier was fully initiated to war and to its psychological shocks, his misery found expression in his contempt for civilians. "People at the north do not realize at all what a soldier's life is . . ." Brewster wrote in 1863; "a soldier has more misery in one day than occurs in a lifetime of a civilian ordinarily and their greatest comforts would be miseries to people at home." Brewster left a veteran volunteer's classic statement of the increasing estrangement of soldiers from civilians in a prolonged war. "It is the general feeling among the old regiments, the real *Volunteers*," he said, "that the generality of the citizens loathe and hate them." Well into his third year of campaigning, the end of the war nowhere in sight, and about to face another winter at the front, Brewster retreated to personal and unit pride—to comradeship and fatalism—in order to give meaning to his experience.[18]

By 1864 Brewster felt estranged from his hometown and homesick at the same time. Conscription laws exacerbated such ambivalence, creating greater distance between the original volunteers—who by 1863–1864 had constructed a self-image as suffering victims—and the draftees from their hometowns. As Northampton strained to fill a draft quota in February 1864, Brewster declared that he did not "believe in drafted patriotism." "I do not love the people of that delightful village as a whole," he informed his sister Martha, "and as I owe them ooo I would not lift my little finger to get a man for them." The otherness of his military experience also made him genuinely fearful of his chance of making a living in the civilian world and would prompt him, eventually, to reenlist. War defined a man's future as well as his days, and Brewster worried about what would become of him once his war was over. "This Military is a hard worrying and at the same time lazy miserable business," he wrote in April 1864, "but it pays better than anything else so I think I had better stick to it as long as I can." In words representative of Everyman's lament, Brewster declared that he had done his "share of campaigning but somebody must campaign and somebody else must have all the easy money making places and as the harder lot was always mine in civil life I suppose I must expect the same in Military."[19]

Brewster's sentiments toward civilians, as well as his fears about making a living after the war, will remind many readers of dilemmas faced by veterans of other American wars. "I don't know what I am to do for a living when I come home," Brewster wrote in his last letter from the front in June 1864. "As the end of my service grows near," he said, "I cannot but feel rather bad to leave it for all its hardships and horrors & dangers it is a fascinating kind of life, and much freer from slander jealousy & unkindness than civil life which I almost dread to come back to." Brewster groped to explain why the joy of going home should be so tarnished by fear about civilian livelihood. Suddenly, the army seemed an island of clarity, honesty, and genuineness in a laissez-faire sea of treachery. "The Veterans," he said, "wear rather long faces." He spoke for the veterans in warning that "those who will welcome them with such apparent joy," will be "ready to do them any injury for the sake of a dollar." Brewster had learned much about the terrible irony of war, about its capacity to pervert values and make organized violence seem like an ordered and strangely attractive alternative to the disorder of society.[20] Even while still in the trenches of Virginia with one week remaining in his term of service, Brewster had begun to think like a veteran of a bygone war. His fears of civilian life and nostalgia for the comradeship of the army already made him a candidate for the cycles of selective memory that would both plague and inspire Civil War veterans. Brewster's wartime letters presaged what historian Gerald Linderman has called the "militarization of thought and the purification of memory" in postwar American society.[21]

Brewster, like most men of his generation, was deeply imbued with the Victorian American values of "manhood" and "courage." He perceived war as the test of his courage, and he constantly sought reassurance that he could meet the challenge. He aspired to the individualized and exemplary conception of bravery by which officers especially had to exhibit their courage to the rank and file. "Courage was the cement of armies," writes Linderman, in the best study of this concept among Civil War soldiers.[22] Especially in the early stages of the war, there is no question that fear of personal dishonor, so rooted in social constructions of masculinity and in American culture, provided the motivation and much of the discipline of Civil War armies.

But the social expectations of manliness in the face of modern war and the degradation of disease almost overwhelmed Brewster, though he only guardedly admitted it. He was both a victim and a perpetrator of these values. His letters are full of observations about the endless struggle between courage and cowardice, his own and that of his comrades. Like most young men who went to war in the nineteenth century (and in our own more violent century as well), Brewster followed a destructive quest for manhood, fashioned a heroic self-image at every opportunity, and marveled at the capacity of war to subdue the environment. He also wrote of camp life and war itself as places strictly separating men from women, all the while imagining their scenes and horrors for his female correspondents. Such sentiments, of course, are not merely stored away in the nineteenth century to be unpackaged for modern boyhood fantasies or for the mythic uses of the vast Civil War literature. Readers of great memoirs from recent wars, like William Manchester's *Goodbye Darkness: A Memoir of the Pacific War*, may find certain echoes in Brewster's letters. When Manchester, the son and grandson of soldiers, writes of his withdrawal from Massachusetts State College and enlistment in the marines in 1942, "guided by the compass that had been built into me," he represents a male tradition deeply ingrained in American society—one that common and less literary men like Brewster had helped to cultivate.[23] Brewster's own manly compass sent him irresistibly off to war, however unprepared or ill equipped for what it would do to his body or his imagination.

In May 1862, just before the battle of Fair Oaks, Brewster wrote almost daily for a week. His letters are dramatic accounts of the impending battle, but even more they are chronicles of his desperate struggle with dysentery and "terrible exposure" while sleeping nightly in the mud. At one point he declares himself so sick that he will have to resign and go home, but to fall back then to some makeshift hospital, he believed, would surely mean a hideous and ignoble death. He declared himself eager for battle, because it represented movement, and compared to sickness and exposure it meant a welcome "chance to live." Courage in this instance, Brewster learned, merely meant endurance and a few strokes of good luck. He could "give up" and seek a furlough, he reasoned, but he feared that the "brave ones that staid at home would call me a coward and all that so I must stay here until after the fight at any rate." In a despairing letter two months later Brewster described "burying comrads who die of disease" as the "saddest thing in the service." Wondering what he would write to a dead comrade's parents, he took heart at how well the man had performed in battle: "thank the lord I can tell them he was brave."[24]

Unable to walk and humiliated by his chronic diarrhea, Brewster spent the battle of Fredericksburg (December 1862), five miles behind the lines where he could only hear that desperate engagement. "I never felt so mean in my life . . ." he wrote. "I lie here like a skulking coward and hear the din of battle but cannot get there it is too bad." The situation is reminiscent of the scene in Stephen Crane's *The Red Badge of Courage*, where Henry Fleming, tormented by the sounds of battle—"the crackling shots which were to him like voices"—feels "frustrated by hateful circumstances." Henry and Brewster had different burdens to bear; the latter had not run from battle. But in a letter a week later Brewster demonstrated his ambivalence about the vexing concept of courage. He hoped that the sickness would not seize him again "when there is a battle in prospect, for it lays me open to the imputation of cowardice, which I do not relish at all, although I don't claim to be very brave."[25] This final touch of honesty is an interesting contrast with all the times Brewster complained about "cowards" in his letters. In the boredom, frustration, and danger of three years at the front, sometimes Brewster could manage to assert his own manhood only by attacking that of others. But with time he became a realist about the meaning of courage. On the eve of the Wilderness campaign in April 1864, he hoped that his corps would be held in reserve in the impending fight. "I suppose you will call that a cowardly wish," he told Mary, "but although we see a great many in print, we see very few in reality, of such desperate heroes that they had rather go into the heat of battle than not, when they can do their duty just as well by staying out." A veteran's hard-won sense of self-preservation prevailed over these sentiments, and it may help explain why Brewster survived what his regiment was about to endure. Having just lived through the worst combat of the war in late May 1864, he could write about courage without pretension. "You are mistaken about their being nothing cowardly about me," Brewster informed Martha. "I am scared most to death every battle we have, but I don't think you need be afraid of my sneaking away unhurt."[26] When introspection overtook the need for camaraderie and bravado, as it frequently did in the last months of his service, Brewster found the moral courage to speak honestly about physical courage.

On the experience of battle Brewster's letters are often dramatic and revealing. Readers will find much of interest in his accounts of the Peninsula campaign of 1862, the Chancellorsville and Gettysburg campaigns of 1863, and the Wilderness-Spotsylvania-Cold Harbor battles of 1864. In these letters one can follow a young man's romantic anticipation of battle through to his experience of pitilessly realistic warfare. After landing on the Virginia

Captain James H. Weatherell (left), Lieutenant Colonel Joseph B. Parsons (center), Captain Flavel Shurtleff (right) of the Tenth Massachusetts. *Historic Northampton.*

This photograph was probably taken at the regiment's camp in Warrenton, Virginia, in 1863. A year later, on May 12, 1864, Wetherell was fatally wounded in the battle of Spotsylvania. Parsons commanded the regiment from July 1862 until June 1864, when the Tenth completed its term of service.

peninsula in April 1862, active now in the great mobilization of McClellan's army and describing his first image of the "horrible" destruction of a town (Hampton, Virginia), Brewster contrasted the "sounds of drums," the "neighing of horses," and the "hum of voices" among the multitude of troops with the quietude of a "Mass fast day" back home. Torturing his mother's emotions, he concluded the letter with the story that he had been awakened from a dream the night before by a "tremendous Thunder shower" that he mistook for the "firing of cannon."[27]

Brewster kept his women correspondents informed but probably full of tension as he encountered real war. Upon seeing the aftermath of a battlefield for the first time at Williamsburg, he described it as a "fearful, fearful sight." "The ground was strew [strewn] with dead men in every direction . . ." he told his mother. "But language fails me and I cannot attempt to describe the scene, if ever I come home I can perhaps tell you but I cannot write it." Brewster would see much worse yet, and he would continue to write it into and out of his memory. But he was caught in that dilemma of literate soldiers in all modern wars: the gruesomeness of battlefields seemed, as Fussell put it, "an all-but-incommunicable reality" to the folks back home. Brewster's letters seem to have anticipated what Alexander Aitken wrote about his own rendering of the battle of the Somme in 1916: "I leave it to the sensitive imagination; I once wrote it all down, only to discover that horror, truthfully described, weakens to the merely clinical."[28] Brewster had a sensitive imagination, and he did try to write it all down; one wonders, though, if after the war, looking back at his letters, he might not have felt the same way Aitken did. In its own historical moment the obscenity of war, it seems, begs description; whereas, in retrospect, it often must be repressed in memory as people confront the tasks of living.

During Brewster's first major battle campaign (the Peninsula and the Seven Days, April–July 1862), he wrote a stunning series of letters where he expressed virtually every reaction or emotion that battle could evoke. At the battle of Fair Oaks, Brewster's regiment lost one of every four men engaged (killed, wounded, or missing) and, with good reason, the young officer wondered why he was still alive. He tried to describe the sounds and the stench of the battlefield, and the excitement and pulse of the fighting. He also began to demonize the enemy at every turn. In surviving such madness Brewster felt both manly exhilaration and dehumanization. The "life" the soldiers sustained, he said, "would kill wild beasts"; and the farmers of Northampton, he maintained, "would call it cruelty to animals to keep their hogs in as bad a place as we have to live and sleep." Most of all Brewster coped with fear and loaded up on opium to command his bowels. Anticipating the great battle for Richmond, he said he could only "dread it," as he had already "seen all I want to of battle and blood."[29] But he had two more years of this to endure; his demeanor and his language would both harden and expand with the experience.

While squatting in a field or brooding in a trench, Brewster sketched battle and its aftermath from a soldier's interior perspective, rather than from the sanitized vantage point of headquarters. References to generals and grand strategy are relatively scarce in these letters; they provide an example, as John Keegan put it, of how very different the "face of battle" is from the "face of war."[30] Although he had no serious literary pretensions, Brewster's horror-struck depictions of battle scenes will remind some readers of the agonizing ironies and relentless realism of Ambrose Bierce's short stories. After Gettysburg Brewster described the countless corpses of dead men and horses as if they were macabre monuments. At Spotsylvania in 1864 the "terrors" he witnessed had become so common that he sometimes worried about his own lack of "feeling," and other times just lost himself in grim details. Describing one trench with dead and wounded Confederates piled "3 or 4 deep," he saw "one completely trodded in the mud so as to look like part of it and yet he was breathing and gasping." In the next letter came the vision of "the most terrible sight I ever saw, a breastwork fought over for twenty-four hours with the dead "piled in heaps upon heaps." As Brewster gazed over the parapet at dawn, "there was one Rebel sat up praying at the top of his voice and others were gibbering in insanity others were groaning and whining at the greatest rate." Steeling his nerves, preparing himself to continue this "terrible business," and ever the partisan, Brewster took an awkward solace that he had not, he claimed, heard any wounded Union soldiers "make any fuss."[31]

As he increasingly and self-consciously became part of a machine of total war, Brewster justified the pillaging of southern civilians, supported the execution of deserters, and in his harshest moments advocated the killing of Confederate prisoners. Yet, through nature's diversions and a healthy sense of irony, he preserved his humane sensibilities in these letters. Brewster nurtured a life-long interest in flowers, gardening, and the natural landscape. He was an astute observer of the beauty and the strangeness of the Virginia countryside. The Virginia Blue Ridge would sometimes remind the New Englander of the Berkshires or even of Vermont. Other times, especially when he was in the coastal region, he blamed slavery and a lack of proper husbandry for the misuse of land and human labor in the South. But he never ceased to describe beauty when he found it. A moonlit camp during the autumn of 1861 made him brood that "it seems strange to see anything so beautiful and peaceful connected with 'grim visaged war."' Ever on the watch for the contrast of peace with war, many a "beautiful morning" in Brewster's letters provided a pastoral backdrop for the dullness of camp or the terror of battle. "I wish you could see what a splendid morning this is," he said to his mother while seated on an oak log on Chickahominy Creek in the spring of 1862. "The trees are in full foliage and the Birds are singing in the trees and the water ripples and sparkles at my feet with the sun shining gloriously over all, and if it were not for the Regt I see before me each with his deadly Enfield rifle on his shoulder I could hardly imagine that there was war in the land." Brewster savored opportunities to tell his womenfolk about wild roses and a host of other flower species he observed on the march. In a field near Cold Harbor in May 1864, "magnolias in full bloom" made him reverently grateful, for "their perfume is very refreshing," he said, "after the continual stench of the dead bodies of men and horses which we have endured for the last 19 days." Brewster confessed to some hesitation about digging a breastwork "through a farmers garden and close to his back door through peas in blossom and radishes & tomatoes." Every war brings us these contrasts of ugliness and beauty, images of life next to death, a single poppy blooming in no-man's-land, visions of nature that somehow survive the worst of human nature. Sentimentalized blossoms so often outlast and even replace the stench of the dead and the vileness of war. Brewster's expressions about beauty often came when he knew he teetered on the precarious edge of life and death. It is also worth noting that after the war Brewster would become the first successful professional florist in the upper Connecticut River Valley. One can only imagine how much the old soldier reflected on his deep memories of life and death in the fields of Virginia as he nurtured the perennials in his greenhouses during the 1880s.[32]

Perhaps the most striking irony, as well as one of the most intriguing themes, in Brewster's letters is his attitudes and actions regarding race and slavery. Brewster had voted for Abraham Lincoln in 1860, and he embraced the Republican Party's free labor and antislavery ideology. He had lived all his life in reform-minded Northampton and believed from the first giddy days of the war that he was fighting to save the Union and free the slaves. But Brewster was no radical abolitionist (their ranks were very small in the Union army), and he enjoyed mocking the piety and earnestness of reformers. His racial views were those of a sardonic white workingman who believed that blacks were a backward if not an inferior race. As historians Bell Wiley and Joseph Glatthaar have shown, such terms as "nigger" and "darkie" were very common in the letters of Union soldiers. Brewster's language was typical rather than exceptional in this regard.[33] But at the same time Brewster believed that slavery was evil, that the South was a repressive society, that a war against secession was inherently a war against racial bondage, and that out of the bloodshed a different society would emerge. Moreover, he seemed to have held these views earlier than most Union troops. Although his estimations of black character did not change as much as one might wish, wartime experience forced an interesting evolution in Brewster's attitude toward blacks.

During the autumn and winter of 1861–1862 the status of slaves who escaped into Union lines remained ambiguous. Lincoln had countermanded the order of General John C. Frémont in August 1861 that would have emancipated all slaves in Missouri. Sensitive to the disposition of the four border states that remained delicately in the Union and mindful of northern racism, the president steadfastly resisted converting the war into an abolition crusade. His commanding general in the east, George B. McClellan, obliged Lincoln on this particular issue, insisting that all fugitive slaves be returned to their lawful masters. But very early in the war, at Fortress Monroe, Virginia, General Benjamin F. Butler declared that slaves who entered his lines would be considered "contraband of war" and be treated as confiscated enemy property. The idea caught on, and in early August, striking a balance between legality and military necessity, Congress passed the First Confiscation Act, which allowed for seizure of all Confederate property used to aid the southern war effort. Although not technically freed by this law, the slaves of rebel masters came under its purview, and thus a process toward black freedom began. But in November, General Henry W. Halleck, commanding in the west at St. Louis, issued a general order contradicting the contraband policy and requiring all Union commanders to accept no new fugitives and to eject all those currently within their lines. This contradictory policy toward fugitive slaves caused considerable controversy in the Union ranks during 1861–1862, and Brewster's regiment was affected by it.[34]

All major wars tend to chart their own course of social transformation, and Halleck's exclusionary edict and Lincoln's pragmatic ambiguity were both rendered unworkable with time. Indeed, the slaves themselves were forcing a clearer settlement of this issue by their own courage and resolve. The Civil War was a conflict of such scale that its greatest lessons, collectively and individually, were being learned on the ground, where abstractions must be converted daily into pragmatic decisions. From Camp Brightwood on the outskirts of Washington, D.C., Brewster learned firsthand that many slaves were freeing themselves and converting the war's purpose. Slaves took "leg bail," Brewster wrote approvingly in November 1861; and in language that might have been fitting at a small-town, wartime abolitionist rally, he declared that "this war is playing the Dickens with slavery and if it lasts much longer will clear our Countrys name of the vile stain and enable us to live in peace hereafter."[35] In such passages Brewster represented an attitude among white Northerners that, driven by the exigencies of war against the South, prompted Lincoln to eventually commit the nation to the reality of emancipation.

By December 1861, the Lincoln administration's policy toward blacks remained limited and conflicted. The president's annual message offered little hope to friends of the "contrabands"; he proposed only a plan to colonize escaped slaves and free blacks outside the country. From winter quarters,

Brewster offered his own crude antislavery assessment of the situation. "We have got the Presidents message," he told his mother, "but I don't think it amounts to much he don't talk nigger enough, but its no use mincing the matter. Nigger has got to be talked, and thoroughly talked to and I think niggers will come out of this scrape free."[36] Written in the common coin of

"Contrabands." *Historic Northampton.*

Runaway slaves flocked to the Union banner, but early in the war their status was ambiguous. Until the Emancipation Proclamation in 1863, some Union generals considered escaped slaves to be "contraband of war," or confiscated enemy property, in order to avoid returning them to their masters. Some "contrabands" became personal servants to officers like Charles Harvey Brewster.

camp and, apparently, of Northampton as well, Brewster's letters provide an example of the way in which racist language and antislavery ideology combined in the hearts and minds of Yankee soldiers. Brewster lacked eloquence, to say the least, when it came to the question of race; but in language that great ironist in the White House would have fully understood, he argued unequivocally that the war should be prosecuted more vigorously against slavery.

Brewster spent his first winter at war intensely interested in the "contraband" issue. In January 1862, frustrated by how "slow" the war progressed, he complained "it seems to be a war for the preservation of slavery more than anything else." Shortly after receiving his commission and setting up his new domestic quarters, Brewster took a seventeen-year-old runaway slave named David as his personal servant. Proud and possessive, he treated his "contraband" with a gushing paternalism. Young David's former master had whipped him, according to Brewster, and forced him to run away. The young lieutenant took pride in relieving the Confederacy of this lone asset. "He was the only slave his master had," said Brewster, "and his master never will have him again if I can help it."[37]

During the long, dull winter months, the clandestine protection of his contraband from the former master's clutches became for Brewster the only war he had. He described at least two successful episodes of deception while protecting David from his pursuing master. But the contraband issue bitterly divided the Tenth Massachusetts, causing by March 1862 what Brewster called nearly "a state of mutiny" in the regiment. Brewster and his antislavery cohort (six contrabands were harbored in Company C alone) would lose this dispute to the proslavery officers in the regiment who were determined to enforce a Halleck-like policy of exclusion. Some fugitives were tearfully returned to their waiting owners; others were spirited away toward Pennsylvania to an ambiguous fate. Brewster himself believed at one point that he would be charged and court-martialed for his resistance, and at another juncture claimed he was prepared to "resign." "I should hate to have to leave now just as the Regiment is going into active service," he wrote in March, "but I will never be instrumental in returning a slave to his master in any way shape or manner, I'll die first."[38] As Brewster describes this three-month-long dispute at Camp Brightwood it has the quality of both tragic farce and high seriousness. This little war within a war reveals in microcosm the much larger social revolution American society was about to undergo, whether it was prepared to confront it or not.

Describing himself as a "free man" because he had received his commission, the recognition-starved Brewster now saw himself as a liberator of his fellow man. As a soldier he was well trained in tactical maneuvers and eager for a taste of battle. As a man he had a yearning to belong to some kind of community. In his contraband Brewster may also have found an outlet for his need to give and a form of companionship he could truly control. One can only speculate, but the letters suggest that Brewster and his contraband may have gained a mutual sense of freedom during their short relationship. The same letter that begins with Brewster appearing in his "new uniform" for the first time ends with him asking his mother to help him outfit his servant. "I wish I could get some of my old clothes to put on him," Brewster wrote, "especially my old overcoat. I do not suppose you will have any chance to send them, but if you should I wish you would . . . make a bundle of coat Pants O Coat and vest . . . send them along, and then I could rig him up so his master would hardly know him." Rejoicing in his acquisition of the contraband in another letter, Brewster described David as "quite smart for a nigger though he is quite slow." But he "is willing," Brewster continued, "and I think has improved a good deal since I got him. I have not heard anything of his master, and if I do I shan't give him up without a struggle." Out of sheer self-interest as well as moral concern, Brewster objectified and coddled his contraband. One is reminded here of the relationship between Huck and Jim in *The Adventures of Huckleberry Finn*. Like Huck, Brewster ultimately had a "sound heart" when it came to the right of a slave to his freedom, and he too decided to "go to hell" rather than return fugitive slaves to bondage. "Without the presence of blacks," Ralph Ellison aptly wrote, Mark Twain's classic "could never have been written." Without Jim, Huck's commitment to freedom could never have developed into the "moral center" of that novel. On a simpler and hidden level, without his "*right smart nigger,*" Brewster might never have developed or even understood his own commitment to freedom. Brewster's struggle to free his "contraband" has the same ironic pattern as Huck's: acts of conscience mixed with adventure, and moral revolt interrupting a life on a raft moving south. Brewster never matched Huck's revelation that "you can't pray a lie," but Brewster's experience forced him to clarify his beliefs and to understand much of what the war was about. In his own crude way, Brewster would grasp the meaning of Lincoln's haunting claim, made at the end of 1862, that "in *giving* freedom to the slave, we *assure* freedom to the free."[39] Although much of his prejudice would remain intact, the former store clerk from Northampton learned something valuable from his "contraband."

The dramatic tension that often grips Brewster's 1864 letters stems not only from the bloody Virginia campaign, but also from the calendar itself as the regiment's term of enlistment drew to a close. Many regiments in the Army of the Potomac were reaching the end of three-year enlistments that summer, and as they did so, they were sometimes slowly disengaged from the front lines during their final weeks. The brigade that included the Tenth Massachusetts, however, remained under steady fire for the final thirty-six hours of their life at the front. What remained of the Tenth departed from City Point, on the James River, on June 21, for the return to Springfield and Northampton. But before leaving Virginia, on June 20, Sergeant Major George F. Polley, who was originally in Brewster's company and had just reenlisted, carved his name and the inscription "Killed June—, 1864" on a piece of board torn from a cracker box. After participating in the "goodbye" rituals with his comrades and sharing an awkward amusement with them about his carving, Polley was struck flush by an artillery shell and killed. In his diary, brigade member Elisha Hunt Rhodes recorded this incident in his matter-of-fact style. Polley "showed me a board on which he had carved his name, date of birth and had left a place for the date of his death," reported Rhodes. "I asked him if he expected to be killed and he said no, and that he had made his head board only for fun. To day he was killed by a shell from a Rebel Battery." The last act of the Tenth before boarding the mailboat for Washington, D.C., was to bury Polley.[40] Adjutant Brewster had one last death to include in a morning report.

After the Tenth returned home, Brewster, anxious about civilian life, reenlisted under the auspices of the state of Massachusetts to be a recruiter of black troops in Norfolk Virginia. From late July to early November he worked as a recruiter, and during this final stage of his service, he wrote some of his most interesting letters. Away from the front, living in a boardinghouse, Brewster could observe the war and society from a new perspective. He was merely one among a horde of recruiters who descended upon eastern Virginia and other parts of the upper South in 1864. Brewster quipped in frustration that "there are two agents to every man who will enlist." He frequently denigrated the very blacks he sought to recruit, commenting on their alleged propensity to "lie and steal" and their "shiftless" attitude toward work. But he seemed delighted at the presence of a black cavalry regiment that made the local "secesh" furious, and, after holding back judgment, he finally praised the black troops who had "fought nobly" and filled the local hospitals with "their wounded and mangled bodies."[41] For Brewster, as for most white Americans, a full recognition of the manhood of blacks only came with their battlefield sacrifices.

Unhappy and shiftless in his own way, feeling as though he were "living among strangers," and deeply ambivalent about what to do with the rest of his life, Brewster went about his business with an element of greed and very little zeal.[42] He continually took stock of himself as well as of the ironies and absurdities of war that surrounded him. He boarded with a southern woman named Mrs. Mitchell, who had just taken the oath of allegiance to the Union. Her husband and one brother were in the Confederate army, while a second brother served in the Union navy. All the servants at the house, of course, were black and now "free." When Brewster, the Yankee conqueror and occupying officer, was not trying to find and spirit black men into the army, he spent time playing with Mrs. Mitchell's three small children, or going to the market with his landlady's mother and a "darky girl." Such bizarre domestic tranquility in the midst of this catastrophic civil war makes an unforgettable image. Moreover, images of death and maiming frequently appear in Brewster's last letters from the war. He writes compassionately of the family of a dead New Hampshire soldier who had lived at the boardinghouse, of a former sergeant in the Tenth Massachusetts who returned from the hospital hobbling on a cane and insisting that he wanted reappointment at the front rather than in the Invalid Corps, and of street "murders" committed in Norfolk, which he contrasts with the killing in war. His only use of the concept of "courage" in these final letters was applied either to black troops or to the surgeons who volunteered to go fight a "raging" yellow fever epidemic in North Carolina.[43] Living among a subdued enemy, and quietly observing the revolution that Confederate defeat and black emancipation might bring, Brewster sat in a recruiting office reading and writing "love letters" for black women to and from their husbands at the front. This is what remained of his job and his war, and it was a remarkable vantage point. Still patronizing toward the freedpeople, he nevertheless acknowledged their humanity and their influence. "We have to read their letters from and write letters to their husbands and friends at the front daily," Brewster observed, "so that I expect I shall be adept in writing love letters, when I have occasion to do so on my own account, they invariably commence (the married ones) with 'my dear loving husband,' and end with 'your ever loving wife until death.'" If we can imagine Brewster sitting at a table with a lonely freedwoman, swallowing his prejudices toward blacks and women, and repeatedly writing or reciting the phrases "give my love to . . ." and "you Husband untall Death" we can glimpse in this tiny corner of the war the enormous potential of the human transformations at work in 1864. Thousands of such quiet ironies—the Northampton store clerk turned soldier, recruiter, and clerical conduit for the abiding love among black folks that slavery could not destroy—helped produce what Lincoln referred to in his Second Inaugural Address as "the result so fundamental and astounding."[44]

Brewster left the war for good in November 1864, and for a while he returned to working in a store. By 1868, he must have written some love letters of his own, for he married Anna P. Williams, the sister of one of his friends in the Tenth, Sidney Williams. Charles and Anna would eventually have six children, some of whom achieved local prominence in western Massachusetts. By the mid-1870s Brewster had reversed his prewar failures and was the owner of a steady sash, door, and paint business. By 1880, he had bought one of the most prominent houses in Northampton, built three greenhouses, and opened a successful year-round florist business. Local friends remembered him as a man "of great independence of character"; he remained an active Republican until the election of 1884 when, for reasons unknown, he supported the Democrat Grover Cleveland rather than James G. Blaine. Brewster became a financially successful, Gilded Age businessman and a prominent citizen. The disdainful, insecure, ambitious soldier of the war letters became the old veteran and family man who grew flowers, speculated in land and other property, made a comfortable living, and actively participated in the G.A.R. (the Grand Army of the Republic, the Union veterans organization). The soldier of 1864 who so feared civilian life had married well and prospered after all. His sister Mary remembered that she had always looked upon her garden for signs of Charlie's "interest in and love for us."[45] Brewster's story seems prosaically American, chronicling as it does the ups and downs of a white middle-class life and generational mobility, and that of an entrepreneur who, through pluck and luck, seems to have beaten the boom-and-bust cycles of the Gilded Age.

But the war, and those remarkable letters, became part of Brewster family lore. By the 1880s, like most veterans, Brewster was ready for reconciliation with Confederate veterans and willing to suspend competitive prospecting in favor of a misty retrospection. He seemed to love regimental reunions and other G.A.R. activities. In October 1886 he attended Blue-Gray reunions at Gettysburg and Fredericksburg, writing to his children that "papa has had the grandest time he ever had in his life." Of the Confederate veterans, he could only marvel at how they "seem as glad to see us as though we were brothers or cousins at least." The landscape of Virginia, like Brewster's own memory, was still scarred from the war. The veteran wrote that the tour of the Gettysburg battlefield "brings the fearful old days so fresh." He was reminded of all the "old miseries," but was also full of a survivor's awe and pride. The visit to the slopes where he had endured the battle of Chancellorsville was the "most glorious time," he reported, marred only by the regret that he did not get to see the "old long breastwork" at Spotsylvania. Partly as tourists, partly as icons of a refurbished martial ideal, partly just as old men searching for their more active and noble youth, and partly as "symbols of changelessness" in a rapidly industrializing age, veterans like Brewster discovered a heroic nostalgia in these reunions.[46] The former soldier who had so fervently sought a sense of community and status in the army could now truly belong in a society building monuments and rapidly forgetting the reality of combat and the deep racial and ideological roots of the war.

Brewster died in October 1893 aboard the clipper ship *Great Admiral* in New York Harbor. He had sailed from Boston down to New York to accompany his twenty-two-year-old daughter, Mary Katherine, on the initial leg of her around-the-world voyage to Australia. Brewster was the guest of the ship's captain, James Rowell, himself a Civil War veteran. During the brief journey Brewster and Rowell reminisced day and night about their war experiences. Father and daughter walked all over lower Manhattan and took care of some "Wall St. business." On the day before the ship's departure and his planned return to Northampton, Brewster was stricken with severe head pains and died within hours. His coffin was ferried to Staten Island shortly before the ship's departure for sea. The grief-stricken daughter decided to stay on the voyage as planned. Secure in her possession and prominent in her plans for work at sea were her father's original War letters, which she intended to transcribe for publication. Mary Kate Brewster was a bright young woman with literary ambitions and considerable skill. She wrote articles for local Massachusetts newspapers while at sea, and later in life became a local author and theater critic. She cherished her father's letters which, of course, had all been written to her grandmother and aunts. To the end Brewster had an adoring female audience for his letters and his "war stories." At sea, Mary Kate and Captain Rowell spent evenings reading the letters aloud to each other. After hearing the details of Brewster's funeral, the daughter rejoiced that surviving members of the Tenth Regiment had served as pallbearers. "That pleased the capt.," she reported, "for we both have 'lived' as you might say with that regiment the past months, spending hour after hour reading those letters."[47] She transcribed most of the letters, often cleaning up her father's grammar, erasing some passages, and probably embellishing the stories with her own literary flair. Fortunately, most of the originals survived this year-long journey around the world.

As we imagine Mary Kate Brewster aboard ship somewhere in the Indian Ocean on her way to Australia, vicariously reliving her father's war experiences, reading his many reflections on life and death, war and peace, physical and emotional anguish, courage and cowardice, we can also imagine American society distancing itself from and sentimentalizing the horror and the causes of the Civil War. By the 1890s, the next generation of daughters and sons were following their parents' lead in constructing an idealized national memory of the war, rooted in a celebration of veterans' valor that rarely included Brewster's horrifying image of the screaming soldier in the trench at Spotsylvania, and instead preferred his descriptions of moonlit campgrounds and sun-drenched mornings on the march. Mary Kate was probably too young and too consumed with life to have understood fully the telling paradoxes and ironies of Charles Harvey's letters: the way he cursed and embraced war, hated and worshiped violence, condemned slavery and practiced racism. Brewster's interior struggle with his own values and with war itself, recorded in these letters, was not the one best fitted to the emerging social memory of the Civil War, nor to the imagination of a young Victorian woman. But over time the letters have been lovingly preserved and today they serve as another reminder of the recurring power of war to attract and destroy individuals and to draw and repel the human imagination.

NOTES

1. Paul Fussell, *The Great War in Modern Memory* (New York, 1975), 6.

2. Maris A. Vinovskis, "Have Social Historians Lost the Civil War?: Some Preliminary Demographic Speculations," *Journal of American History* 76 (June 1989): 57. For the new social history of the common soldier, also see Maris A. Vinovskis, ed., *Toward a Social History of the American Civil War* (New York, 1990); Joseph T. Glatthaar, *The March to the Sea and Beyond: Sherman's Troops in the Savannah and Carolinas Campaigns* (New York, 1985); Joseph T. Glatthaar, *Forged in Battle: The Civil War Alliance of Black Soldiers and White Officers* (New York, 1990); Reid Mitchell, *Civil War Soldiers: Their Expectations and Their Experiences* (New York, 1988); Phillip Shaw Paludan, *A People's Contest: The Union and Civil War, 1861–65* (New York, 1988), 316–338; Randall C. Jimerson, *The Private Civil War: Popular Thought during the Sectional Conflict* (Baton Rouge, 1988); James I. Robertson, Jr., *Soldiers Blue and Gray* (Columbia, SC, 1988); Michael Fellman, *Inside War: The Guerrilla Conflict in Missouri during the American Civil War* (New York, 1989); Warren Wilkinson, *Mother, May You Never See the Sights I Have Seen: The Fifty-seventh Massachusetts Veteran Volunteers in the Army of the Potomac, 1864–65* (New York, 1990); Michael Barton, *Goodmen: The Character of Civil War Soldiers* (University Park, PA, 1981); Earl J. Hess, *Liberty, Virtue, and Progress: Northerners and Their War for the Union* (New York, 1988); and Marvin R. Cain, "A 'Face of Battle' Needed: An Assessment of Motives and Men in Civil War Historiography," *Civil War History* 28 (March 1982): 5–27.

3. Bell I. Wiley, *The Life of Billy Yank: The Common Soldier of the Union* (Baton Rouge, 1952), 15; Bell I. Wiley, *The Life of Johnny Reb: The Common Soldier of the Confederacy* (Baton Rouge, 1943).

4. *Hampshire Gazette and Courier* (Northampton, MA), April 23, 30; May 7, 14; June 11, 1861, Forbes Library; Northampton; Alfred S. Roe, *The Tenth Regiment Massachusetts Volunteer Infantry, 1861–64* (Springfield, MA, 1909), 378–384.

5. Roe, *Tenth Regiment*, 18–28.

6. Robert Hunt Rhodes, ed., *All for the Union: The Civil War Diary and Letters of Elisha Hunt Rhodes* (New York, 1991); Geoffrey C. Ward, with Ric Burns and Ken Burns, *The Civil War: An Illustrated History* (New York, 1990). For the creation of the brigade in which the Tenth served, see Frank J. Welcher, *The Union Army, 1861–1865: Organization and Operations*, vol. 1, *The Eastern Theater* (Bloomington, IN, 1989), 8. On March 13, 1862, Brewster's brigade became part of the Fourth Corps of the Army of the Potomac, and from September 1862 until the end of its service in June 1864, it was part of the Sixth Corps (Roe, *Tenth Regiment*, 318–319).

7. Roe, *Tenth Regiment*, 295.

8. Emma C. Brewster Jones, comp., *The Brewster Genealogy, 1566–1907: A Record of the Descendants of William Brewster of the Mayflower, Ruling Elder of the Pilgrim Church Which Founded Plymouth Colony in 1620*, vol. 2(New York,

1908), 868–869. On the ordinary soldier escaping from ordinary life, see Philip Caputo, *A Rumor of War* (New York, 1977).

9. Brewster letter, June 15, 1862, Historic Northampton (all letters published in Blight's book are hereafter cited simply as "letter"). On the importance of letters and connections to "home," see Reid Mitchell, "The Northern Soldier and His Community" in Vinovskis, *Toward a Social History*, 78–92.

10. Letters, July 12; June 21, 1862.

11. Letters, July 9, 1863; May 23, 1864. Brewster refers to the death of Edwin B. Bartlett, who was killed at Spotsylvania on May 18 (Roe, *Tenth Regiment*, 271).

12. Letter, November 24, 1861.

13. Letters, November 10; September 22; November 6, 10, 17, 24; December 14, 1861. Also see letter, November 21, 1863, where he describes himself as "cursed with ill luck all my life."

14. Letter, January 9, 1862. Brewster was subsequently promoted to first lieutenant, September 29, 1862, and as adjutant of the regiment, December 1862. He was technically a staff officer and not a field officer.

15. Letter, January 15, 1862.

16. Henry W. Parsons to Aunt Julia, September 1861, Parsons Family Papers, Historic Northampton. Both Parsons's quotations come from a single letter.

17. Mitchell, "The Northern Soldier," 89; Eric J. Leed, *No Man's Land: Combat and Identity in World War I* (New York, 1979), 213.

18. Letters, November 25, 1862; February 23, November 21, 1863.

19. Letters, February 3; April 3, 1864.

20. Letter, June 15, 1864. See Leed, *No Man's Land*, 12–33.

21. Gerald F. Linderman, *Embattled Courage: The Experience of Combat in the Civil War* (New York, 1987), 284, 266–297.

22. Linderman, *Embattled Courage*, 7–110; quotation is from 34.

23. William Manchester, *Goodbye Darkness: A Memoir of the Pacific War* (New York, 1979), 46–47. A growing literature exists on the questions of manhood, male tradition, and war making. Helpful to me have been Linderman, *Embattled Courage*; Kim Townsend, "Francis Parkman and the Male Tradition," *American Quarterly* 38 (spring 1986): 97–112; Peter G. Filene, *Him/Herself: Sex Roles in Modern America* (New York, 1975), 69–112; and Edward O. Wilson, *On Human Nature* (Cambridge, 1978), 99–120. An important critique of Fussell's *Great War in Modern Memory*, which is useful to understanding what maybe peculiarly male about the experience of war, is Lynne Hanley, *Writing War: Fiction, Gender, and Memory* (Amherst, 1991), 18–37.

24. Letters, May 24, 25, 27, 28, 29, 31; July 27, 1862.

25. Stephen Crane, *The Red Badge of Courage*, Avon Edition (New York, 1979), 39–40; Letters, December 15, 23, 1862.

26. Letters, April 30; May 26, 1864. From May 5 to May 12, the Army of the Potomac suffered 32,000 casualties: killed, wounded, or missing. During the first seven weeks of Grant's campaign against Lee in Virginia, northern casualties reached the appalling figure of 65,000, a daily cost in life and limb that Brewster's letters help document. These seven weeks also constitute almost exactly the final days of the enlistment of the Tenth Massachusetts, which was mustered out on June 22. These casualty figures were horrifying to northerners because of the devastation they represented for

so many families in towns like Northampton, but also because in spite of them, there was no clear sign of an end to the war; Lee's lines in Virginia had not been broken as the siege of Petersburg began, though his casualties had been proportionately as high as Grant's. See James McPherson, *The Battle Cry of Freedom* (New York, 1988), 732, 741–742.

27. Letter, April 3, 1862. This very date was actually a "fast day" in Massachusetts. See also letters, February 21; March 16, 1862. Brewster missed the battle of Antietam while on furlough. Some of Brewster's letters were printed in the *Daily Hampshire Gazette*, though he protested about their publication to his mother and others. See letter, July 13, 1862.

28. Letter, May 7, 1862; Aitken is quoted in Fussell, *Great War in Modern Memory*, 174.

29. Letters, June 2, 5, 12, 15, 21; May 10, 1862.

30. John Keegan, *The Face of Battle: A Study of Agincourt, Waterloo, and the Somme* (New York, 1976), 35–45, 320–343.

31. Letters, July 30, 1863; May 11, 13, 15, 1864. Many of Bierce's stories would serve as comparisons, but see for example "A Horseman in the Sky" and "The Mocking-Bird," in *The Civil War Short Stories of Ambrose Bierce*, compiled by Ernest J. Hopkins (Lincoln, NE, 1970), 97–108.

32. Letters, October 23; September 25, 1861; May 21, 1862; May 23, 26, 1864. "The Death of Charles H. Brewster" (obituary), *Daily Hampshire Gazette*, October 9, 1893.

33. See Wiley, *Life of Billy Yank*, 109–115; Glatthaar, *Forged in Battle*, 11–12.

34. See Dudley T. Cornish, *The Sable Arm: Black Troops in the Union Army, 1861–65* (Lawrence, KS, 1956), 24–25; Ira Berlin et al., eds., *Freedom: A Documentary History of Emancipation, 1861–67*, ser. 2, *The Black Military Experience* (New York, 1982), 1–7.

35. Letters, November 24, 17, 1861.

36. Letters, December 4, 1861.

37. Letters, January 2, 15, 1862.

38. Letters, March 5, 8, 12, 4, 1862.

39. Letters, January 15, 23; February 9, 1862. Ralph Ellison, "What America Would Be Like without Blacks," in *Going to the Territory* (New York, 1986), 109; Mark Twain, *The Adventures of Huckleberry Finn (*1884; New York, 1966), 282–283; "Annual Message to Congress," December 1, 1862, in Roy P. Basler, ed., *The Collected Works of Abraham Lincoln* (New Brunswick, NJ, 1953), 5:537.

40. Roe, *Tenth Regiment*, 291, 342; Rhodes, *All for the Union*, 164.

41. Letters, August 20; October 12, 1864. On recruiting black troops, see Glatthaar, *Forged in Battle*, 61–80; Berlin, *Freedom*, 6–15. Brewster's appointment as a recruiter, signed by Governor John A. Andrew, July 23, 1864, is in Brewster Family Papers, Sophia Smith Collection, Smith College. Brewster was appointed assistant adjutant general on the staff of Colonel J. B. Parsons.

42. Letters, August 30; September 16, 1864.

43. Letters, August 4; October 5, 12, 1864. One of the murders Brewster describes is that of a "colored barber," who, while jailed with three white sailors, was thrown to his death from a third-story window. A year earlier, in July 1863, as a newly organized company of the United States Colored Troops (USCT) marched through the

streets of Norfolk, led by their lieutenant, Anson L. Sanborn, Sanborn was publicly assassinated by a prominent physician and secessionist. The physician was later executed, but the incident and others like it diminished recruiting efforts in the area for many months to come. On this incident, see Glatthaar, *Forged in Battle*, 69. As Brewster described these "occasional murders" that few paid any attention to, he concluded that "it is just the difference between a state of war and a state of peace" (letter, October 12, 1864).

44. Letter, October 27, 1864. The two examples from a freedman's letters that I quote here were not written by Brewster, but they were sent from the Norfolk recruiting area in 1864. See letters by black soldier Rufus Wright, February 2, May 25, 1864, in Berlin, *Freedom*, 661–663. Wright uses the phase "give my love to" eight times in these two short letters, forming the very kind of example that Brewster found so memorable and educative.

45. "The Death of Charles H. Brewster" (obituary), *Daily Hampshire Gazette*, October 9, 1893; letter, Aunt Mary to Mary Kate Brewster, November 9, 1893, Brewster Family Papers. Brewster's real and personal estate was valued at approximately $15,000 at his death in 1893. Administrator's Estate Inventory, filed October 26, 1893, Probate Court, Hampshire County, Northampton. Brewster's more than twenty land transactions are recorded in Register of Deeds, Hampshire County, Northampton.

46. Brewster to "My Dear Children," October 7, 10, 11, 1886, Historic Northampton. Linderman, *Embattled Courage*, 297. On the G.A.R. also see Stuart McConnell, "Who Joined the Grand Army? Three Case Studies in the Construction of Union Veteranhood, 1866–1900," in Vinovskis, *Toward a Social History*, 139–170.

47. Mary Kate Brewster, "Log Book" (diary 1893–1894), 3–7 19, 21, 26–27; letter, Mary Kate Brewster to Gertrude, January 9, 1894, Sydney, Australia, Brewster Family Papers; "The Death of Charles H. Brewster," *Daily Hampshire Gazette*, October 9, 1893; Mary K. Brewster obituary, *Gazette*, January 7, 1951.

17

THE Civil War burned out the passions that had fired the conflict. Somehow the lofty ideals and assumptions of antebellum America seemed naive, complacent, and obsolete to a younger generation. Chauncey Wright, a product of Northampton's first families, joined William James in an informal circle of thinkers that styled themselves, with tongue in cheek, "the Metaphysical Club." Instead of "truths" they sought systematic, hard-headed, pragmatic solutions to real-world problems.

This practical realism was reinforced by the way the war had transformed the home front. Northampton mills and factories provided a steady stream of supplies to fuel the Union army. Local manufacturers of farm implements and cutlery literally transformed plowshares and pruning hooks into swords and bayonets. The war stimulated industrial production in the region. After the war, expansion continued until the end of the century. Northampton produced consumer goods for a national mass market made possible by the expansion of America's railroads. Silk, bicycles, cutlery, tools, stoves, sewing machines, and toothbrushes all bore Northampton trademarks. Retail shops and services multiplied. Leisure pursuits reflected national pastimes. The Victorian architectural character that defines Northampton today took shape during this period. Residential neighborhoods expanded to house workers, managers, and mill owners. The Norman Rockwell of his generation, John F. Rogers, Jr., mass-produced uplifting, plaster-cast scenes of everyday life. Rogers grew up in Northampton and drew on his childhood memories for inspiration. Every American family aspiring to middle-class refinement in the last quarter of the nineteenth century had a "Rogers Group" displayed on the parlor table. The view from Mount Holyoke that enraptured painters like Thomas Cole had become an icon on souvenirs carried away by tourists who swarmed up the mountain by steam rail.

It was this Northampton that Henry James characterized in his first novel, Roderick Hudson. *James describes his heroine as having three misfortunes: "first, she had lost her husband; second, she had lost her money, . . . and third, she lived at Northampton, Massachusetts." Years later, James took pains to explain his meaning. Northampton, for James, was a metaphor for all of American society and culture—a "humane" community, as he put it, but a "vivid antithesis to a state of civilization providing for 'art.'"*

In the following essay, Dean Flower suggests that James's characterizations of Northampton over the years reflect the deep ambivalence he felt about his native land.

The View from Prospect House*

DEAN FLOWER

WHEN Thomas Cole painted "The Ox-Bow at Northampton" in 1836, he placed an artist unobtrusively at work in the foreground, looking down from the crest of the Holyoke Range upon well-tilled fields, the meandering Connecticut River, and the play of light and shade on the distant hills. A rain shower has just passed, as if to cleanse and refresh the sight. Scaled down by distance, the town blends into the land as if the two could never be at odds. This is Cole at his most benign, offering an American pastoral, a vision of peace and plenty on a golden summer day.

Henry James saw the same scene from different angles in the fall of 1864, and the prospect was grim. From the windows of his hotel on Round Hill Road, the Northampton view was rainy, leafless, gray, black, and boring—"a true suicidal day," James wrote to a friend. He found the place "so stupid that I swear a mighty oath that I will pack off the next day." James had come to take the waters (he was, as they used to say, "costive"), put some distance between himself and home, send unsolicited book reviews to the *North American Review*, and make a start on his own career as a writer of fiction. He also went to inspect the view Thomas Cole had made famous:

> I went up Mount Holyoke t'other day for the 2nd time. Of all the concentrated vulgarities it is the greatest. You ascend halfway in carriages. Then you get into a little car, like that of a balloon and are hauled up the remainder on perpendicular grooves. On reaching the top, you find your self on a level with the floor of the elegant Prospect House where a lot of women are playing on the piano and curling their hair in the looking glass. It must be owned that the view is fine as such things go.

No doubt the scene was vulgar to James because he had already lived in Paris and London, already seen castles on the Rhine and the Coliseum by moonlight. Perhaps too he felt, at the age of twenty-one, that none of the music and hair-curling at Prospect House was meant for him. In any case, he saw no reasons for pastoral celebrations. The landscape was "fine as such things go," but—he would make this criticism of America throughout his career—the society was wanting. Nevertheless James chose to remain in this distinctly provincial place from August to December 1864, writing and rewriting his first tentative sketches and tales. He had, queerly enough, found it a good place to set up his easel.

---

* From Dean Flower, "The View from Prospect House," *Massachusetts Review* (summer–autumn 1985): 217–232.

Ten years later James drew upon his memories of Northampton for the opening chapters of *Roderick Hudson* (1875), his first full-length novel. Its well-traveled narrator, Rowland Mallet, goes to visit a female cousin whose "misfortunes were three in number: first, she had lost her husband; second, she had lost her money, or the greater part of it; and third, she lived at Northampton, Massachusetts." The novel goes on to make sardonic fun of the place: "If beauty's the wrong thing, as people think at Northampton," says the sculptor-hero Roderick of a woman, "she's the incarnation of evil." Although it seemed that in Jamesian parlance "Northampton" stood for America as a social and cultural desert, the novel offered another view. Having just chosen in 1874 to live and write abroad, James had by no means forgotten the arguments for remaining in America. He sends his characters on a walk to the edge of town where they stop to gaze across "the generous Connecticut," and take in "the shadows on Mt. Holyoke," the "elm-dotted river-meadows," and the "smell of the mown grass!" Cole's pastoral suddenly becomes possible here: "the far spreading view . . . affected [Rowland] as melting for them both into such vast continuities and possibilities of possession." He even feels a "prospective regret," in what must be James's most autobiographical note of all, that later, in a foreign land, he should be haunted by it, should remember it all with longing and regret. James seemed fully aware that his whole conception of himself as an exile, a writer at odds with his own country, was a fabrication: "It's a wretched business, [Rowland says] this virtual quarrel of ours with our own country this everlasting impatience that so many of us feel to get out of it. Can there be no battle then, and is one's only safety in flight? This is an American day, an American landscape, an American Atmosphere."

Over the next few years James gradually dismissed these sanguine possibilities; he had chosen expatriation. After a year in Paris he settled into a London literary life. American *villes de province* might be rendered sympathetically by William Dean Howells or Sarah Orne Jewett, but James would not. In *Hawthorne* (1878) he conjured up more ironic visions of provincial America: "lonely frigidity" he writes, "characterized most attempts at social recreation in the New England world some forty years ago. . . . The initiated mind . . . has a vision of a little unadorned parlor; with the snow-drifts of a Massachusetts winter piled up about its windows, and a group of pensive and serious people, modest votaries of opportunity, fixing their eyes upon a bookful of Flaxman's attenuated outlines."

James recalled "no great things to look out at (save forests and rivers)" and a society where "introspection, thanks to the want of other entertainment, played almost the part of a social resource." Scenarios for "Four Meetings," "Europe," and *The Europeans* are all hinted here. The whole of *Hawthorne* may be read, in fact, as a study of American provincialism, with James using his rather sketchy knowledge of New England village life to construct his argument. Here for example is his version of the Transcendentalists as archetypal provincials: "They appeared unstained by the world, unfamiliar with worldly desires and standards, and with those various forms of human depravity which flourish in some high places of civilization; inclined to simple and democratic ways, destitute of pretensions and affectations, of jealousies, of cynicism, of snobbishness." Clearly the destitution was, for James, worse than the "depravity." To be thus unstained was to be abysmally dull.

James returned to his native land in 1882, but his image of the bleak New England village remained unchanged. For *The Bostonians* (1886) he imagined a place somewhere near Buzzards Bay, called Marmion. It had an "unfriendly inn, which suggested dreadfully . . . an early bedtime" and, "seemed to have no relation to anything, not even itself." Some of these details might have been drawn from James's memories of Round Hill Road in Northampton: a flyblown register, a haughty waitress, "horsehair rocking chairs in the little public parlor," a dim assemblage of "lady boarders wrapped in shawls," village-philosophers ready to chat, a dining room kept locked at all but sacramental hours, a single elusive servant, and a management virtually "invisible." For all the ironic comedy, James's criticism went deep. These were places from which he had to run for his life.

Yet in the fall of 1904 James returned to America, reawakened like Rip Van Winkle to a new sense of the New England landscape. As *The American Scene* would testify in 1907, it was something of a revelation. James himself had changed, and so had the world; now for example, he viewed the hills and valleys of the Berkshires from the vantage point of Edith Wharton's chauffeured touring car. She whisked him from Lenox to Ashfield, or to Albany or Farmington, in what James liked to call her "chariot of fire." In a rhapsodic letter to his brother William he marveled at "the potent way" the automobile allowed him "to rope in, in big free hauls, a huge netful of impressions at once." He had come to visit relatives and see old friends, to explore regions new to him (the South, the vast Midwest, the exotic Pacific Coast), and to write a book of his travel impressions. He financed his tour in the classic way—by lecturing. It was, he knew, a very uncharacteristic "public developement." He told Edmund Gosse, "I repeated the horrid act at Chicago, Indianapolis, St. Louis, San Francisco. . . . In fine I have waked up *conferencier* and find, to my stupefaction, that I can do it." James was more pleased than he cared to admit. Whatever his quarrels with America were, he had come home to be lionized.

Toward the end of his long and exhausting national tour—on May 6, 1905, to be exact—James came to repeat "the horrid act" in Northampton. Whether he even hinted of any personal recollections of the place to his audience at the Smith College Assembly Hall that evening is unknown. He did write in the 1907 preface to *Roderick Hudson* that Northampton was "almost the only small American *ville de province* of which [he] happened to lay up, long before, a pleased vision." That evening in May, however, James delivered his lecture—"The Lesson of Balzac"—for perhaps the thirtieth time. It is unlikely that he enjoyed himself. A month earlier he spoke of giving "my (now loathly) lecture to a female culture club of 900 members (whom I make pay me through the nose)." Another letter mentions "spouting" the lecture at Bryn Mawr; and in St. Louis he "spouted my stuff' to an audience of "300 plain gapers." So the Northampton reading could not have been a great success. A student editorialist in the *Smith College Monthly* observed, no doubt rightly, "How nice it would have been to have heard James on James instead of James on Balzac!" By that time James was fully aware of such disappointment. In an injured, defensive letter to William he said, "my lecture is too special and too literary—too critical—for these primitive promiscuities"; and in the lecture itself he apologized to his audience for speaking as if "you all, without exception, were novelists."

Not least of the "primitive promiscuities" of lecturing were its attendant social events. The *Daily Hampshire Gazette* ignored the lessons of Balzac and reported that James was "entertained at dinner" by Charles Downer Hazen, a professor of history and his wife. (One hopes they did not have to discuss Flaxman's drawings.) On the next evening George Washington Cable and Ida Tarbell ("Miss lda M. Tarbell of New Jersey the well-known writer;" said the *Gazette*) made a more cosmopolitan company for James. Still, he had already dined with hundreds of famous and nearly famous people across the country, including President Theodore Roosevelt (and a hundred others) at the White House, and James was weary of endless "presentations." In St. Louis he had endured "a long preliminary dinner" and "150 'presentations,' well nigh undoing me." Perhaps the smaller scale of events in Northampton made them less trying. In any case the *Gazette* noted that "Mr. James left the city Sunday evening" (May 7), and one can see why. "The mixture of the social effort and exposure with the lecturing," he wrote to William, "is, for *my* powers, really too upsetting."

Surely the happiest event in James's return to Northampton was his visit to 44 State Street, the studio of Katherine McClellan, the Smith College photographer. She took twelve pictures of him seated near her large north window, enabling us to see him now in a way that no single image of this much-photographed, sketched, and painted figure can rival. The McClellan sequence recreates the physical and mental presence of James in that room, caught from moment –to moment in a variety of angles and shifting moods. Individually, some of these pictures are as fine as the best portraits that have been made of James—from the Mathew Brady photograph of the boy with his father to the John Singer Sargent painting of the seventy-year-old man.

Henry James, Northampton, Massachusetts, 1905. Katherine Elizabeth McClellan. *Smith College Archives.*

But it is the sequence that fascinates, for single images of James fail to convey as much of his personal complexity.

In New York one month earlier James had been photographed by Alice Boughton. She left a written record of the sitting, helping us to conjecture something of what happened in Northampton. Boughton said James "terrified" her with his courtly manners and imperious bearing, and she found his eyes so disconcerting that she asked him to read a book while she readied the camera. Other observers had similar experiences. Theodora Bosanquet, James's typist-amanuensis after 1907, was impressed by his physical massiveness, "that sensitive mobile mouth," and his "keen gray eyes." Ford Madox Ford noted, "his eyes were singularly penetrating, dark and a little prominent" and quoted approvingly a servant's remark: James's "eyes seem to look you through to the very backbone." Edmund Gosse, who knew the private James better than these, acknowledged "the intolerable scrutiny of the eyes." Elizabeth Jordan, the American novelist and editor, wrote "the strange power of Henry James's eyes [could] read me to the soul." Perhaps the best observation of all was made by Ella Hepworth Dixon, who said that James's "eyes were not only age-old and world-weary; as are those of cultured Jews, but they had vision—and one did not like to think of what they saw." Katherine McClellan seems to have understood much of this gravity and intensity in James, but she saw as well his humor, relaxed moments, and quiet contemplation. He is less romanticized by her lens, and more human.

When James returned from his "long dusty adventure" in America, he had already chosen to begin *The American Scene* with a chapter on the landscape of western New England. Drawing upon his visits to Chocorua and North Conway, New Hampshire, to Stockbridge, Pittsfield, and Lenox, Massachusetts, and to Salisbury and Farmington, Connecticut, James found much to praise. He had expected "New England scenery" to fit his preconceptions of the 1870s: "hard and dry and thin, scrubby and meagre and 'plain.'" He admitted that view was now thoroughly "routed." What he saw really for the first time, was a "great autumnal harmony, . . . [a] fusion of earth and air and water, of light and shade and color." It was all "a gorgeous blur" and he was in awe of nature's "almost shameless tolerance . . . for the poor human experiment." In many of these villages and towns the "goodly elms" and fine old houses freshly painted white could suggest—as Farmington did to James—something "fastidious and exceptional" perhaps, even, "a note of the aristocratic."

Yet the "restless analyst" of *The American Scene* cannot help looking deeper and listening more critically in such places to "the discreet voice of the air." He wonders about "the inscrutability of the village street in general, for instance, in any relation but its relation to its elms." He notices in all these places an "outward blankness," a "quantity of absence," a certain "monotony of acquiescence." While the natural landscape seems to James richly nourishing, the social landscape was queerly neutral. The picturesque villages did not "bristle with the truth" of the human history, but remained maddeningly out of reach, complacent, and "common," as if impervious to moral drama. If these saintly villages were "whited sepulchres," James decided, nobody seemed in a position to know it. He concludes his chapter by describing the Shaker settlement at Hancock, Massachusetts, "sounding the heart of New England beyond its depth." He saw the settlement, "savagely clean" and "economically impersonal," as a nightmare reflection of the virtuous old New England Community: "It wore, the whole settlement, as seen from without, the strangest air of active, operative death; as if the state of extinction were somehow obscurely, administered and applied—the final hush of passions, desires, dangers, converted into a sort of huge stiff brush for sweeping away rubbish, or still more, perhaps, into a monstrous comb for raking in profit."

If that was what the religious impulse or the pastoral dream had come to in America, the picture was grim indeed. James saw the generous autumnal landscape about to be indifferently used and squandered in the name merely of money. Perhaps worse, he saw too the internal destitution in America as he never had before, in its dearth of passionate life. If this was in part what those keen gray eyes were meditating in the McClellan photographs, "one did not like to think of what they saw."

But the picture was not all dark. James remembered Northampton, after all, with "a pleased vision," and connected it with the time of his own self-discovery and first ambitions. Writing in his *Notebooks* on March 29, 1905, James recalled "the far-off unspeakable past years" when he was just beginning his career. He associated the end of the Civil War in the "epoch-making weeks of the spring of 1865" with "that pathetic heroic little personal prime of my own," with its "unforgettable gropings and findings and sufferings and strivings and play of sensibility and of inward passion." In the course of his pilgrimage to America, James had come to terms with the fact that much of his identity was rooted—for better or for worse—in New England. We can go up to Prospect House today and see something of what he saw. Time has washed away the crudity and inelegance.

> The paint-peeled
> Hundred-year-old hotel sustains its ramshackle
> Four-way verandah, view-keeping above
> The fallen timbers of its once remarkable
> Funicular railway, witness to gone
> Time, and to graces gone with the time.

So wrote Sylvia Plath in 1959.

18

THE new wealth fostered by the war and distained by James also formed the basis for Northampton's golden age of philanthropy. Samuel Hill, one of the founders of the Northampton Association and later independent silk producer, built Cosmian Hall in Florence and America's first free kindergarten. Judge Charles Edward Forbes willed his estate to found Forbes Library. Edward Lyman built the Academy of Music to house America's first municipally owned theater company. In 1867, John Clarke established and endowed the Clarke School for the Deaf. In 1870, Sophia Smith signed a will that left her estate to "furnish for my own sex means and facilities for education equal to those which are afforded now in our colleges for young men." The next year Smith College became the first women's college to be chartered in New England. From the beginning, the college saw itself not as a finishing school, but as the home of the feminine scholar. It offered no preparatory department like other women's colleges but accepted only those who could meet the entrance requirements of a regular liberal arts college. Challenging contemporary notions of women's nature, Smith produced thinkers and leaders that set about to disprove those assumptions.

Helen Lefkowitz Horowitz argues that the very architecture of the Smith campus reflected the college's unique mission and embodied changing conceptions of what education meant for women.

Smith College and Changing Conceptions of Educated Women*

HELEN LEFKOWITZ HOROWITZ

WHEN Smith College opened in 1875, its campus and buildings expressed a clear conception of educated womanhood.[1] As the college grew and changed, differing visions shaped its development on the land. Always, however, Smith faced a hurdle not shared by colleges for men: to offer the liberal arts to women posed a threat to the culture. Educating women beyond traditional ways has been perceived as a dangerous experiment challenging basic notions of women's nature and threatening the social order.

In the twenty-first century, we need to remind ourselves of the opposition to women's higher education if we are to understand the history of women's colleges. Smith and other women's colleges were designed to confront this opposition. The campus is a text upon which we can read this intention.

* From Ronald Story, ed., *Five Colleges: Five Histories* (Amherst, 1992).

It is not a simple text, however, for over time different ruling images have come into play. Between its founding and the late 1930s, Smith College countered the opposition to women's higher education with four different positive conceptions of the college woman, and each shaped a portion of the campus. At the outset, the college imagined itself as the home of the feminine scholar. College students reframed the image as they promoted the all-round girl. In the early twentieth century, a new administration saw its student as a university coed, who just happened to come to Smith. And under William Allan Neilson and Ada Louise Comstock, the college reshaped itself to promote what they saw as the modem view of the Smith undergraduate, the democratic—and dating—college girl.

THE initial design of Smith College—its application of the cottage system for a women's college—was intended as a means to preserve the femininity of women subjected to the danger of the liberal arts. Its dominant conception of the educated woman was that of the feminine scholar.

To explain how this is so, I must explore the distinctive building tradition in women's higher education. The one thing that neither Smith nor other women's colleges did until the very end of the century was to follow the plan of colleges for men. By the early nineteenth century, men's colleges, whether formed piecemeal as at Yale or as a comprehensive plan as at the University of Virginia, were "academical villages." Men recited, studied, prayed, slept, and ate in a variety of structures. The buildings we would call dormitories, represented on the Yale campus by Connecticut Hall, were generally three- or four-story stretches of rooms, reached through four entries, two on a side.

Women's colleges drew on another institution, with its own distinctive history, the women's seminary, which reached its greatest influence at Mount Holyoke under Mary Lyon. In the years following the American Revolution, a new form of schooling for young men and women emerged—the academy or seminary. For female students, it offered the first hint of higher education, not a full college course, but one that in our terms straddled secondary school and college. In the early nineteenth century, the best female seminaries were those designed to train teachers. They offered training in mathematics and science, English usage, and Latin. In founding her seminary, Mary Lyon hoped both to give young women the highest education available to their sex and to change their consciousness. She sought to encourage them to bring order into their lives and to move outside the private claims of the family circle. As she put it, she would take the "daughters of fairest promise" and draw forth their talents "to give them a new direction, and to enlist them permanently in the cause of benevolence," i.e., missionary work and teaching.[2] In creating her seminary, she worked with key Amherst College professors; but never considered planning it on the pattern of Amherst or

College Hall, Smith College, 1880s. *Historic Northampton.*

any other male college. Instead she drew on the ideas and the building tradition of the asylum.

Nineteenth-century reformers believed that if one separated those who were disordered in their minds and placed them in a structure of external order, they would internalize the rules to create an inner psychic order. This is just what Mary Lyon wanted to do. She knew the asylum well and adapted its system to a school for women. The system of Mount Holyoke Seminary thus followed the system of the asylum. The rules were strict: between the bell that awakened students at five and the one that required their lights to be off at nine, students followed a prescribed schedule of recitations, study, prayer, and housework in which they changed direction every fifteen minutes. They lived along a corridor with their teachers, and each week at "section meeting" they monitored their own behavior in a required public confessional to a specific teacher, in which they testified to how they had abided by or broken the rules.

The seminary building, erected in 1837, both expressed and enforced these rules. Everything happened in a single building, designed as an enormous house for over one hundred students and teachers. With its central entrance and stairwell, its hierarchical organization, its complete provision for living, learning, and working, Mount Holyoke had adapted the asylum to women's higher education.

In Mount Holyoke alumnae records, there is firm evidence that through the seminary system and through the power of bonding between teachers and students, Mary Lyon did change the consciousness of her pupils. To a striking degree they entered public life as teachers and missionaries. They also became internal missionaries for education, bringing the seminary system to countless other academies and to the female departments of the pioneer coeducational colleges. What happened inside the consciousness of students, however, was not necessarily observable on the outside. To most eyes, the seminary looked safe. Its rules and building protected the purity of the young women in its charge. Thus conventional daughters were sent there. The form was copied in countless schools across the country.

When, in 1861, Matthew Vassar, a Poughkeepsie brewer, followed the advice of Milo Jewett, the former head of the Judson Female Seminary, and decided to create the first real college for women, "to be to them, what Harvard and Yale are to young men," he hedged his bets by taking away with one hand what he was giving with the other.[3] He founded the first real college for women, with an undiluted liberal arts course and a full college faculty; but he linked to it the plan of governance and building form of the female seminary, a quite different institution. As a result women went to college in buildings altogether different from their brothers at Yale, under supervision that their brothers would never have tolerated.

Thus, when Vassar College took form in brick and mortar, it was as an immense seminary building, designed by one of America's foremost asylum architects, James Renwick. In keeping with the newest approaches of asylum planners, Vassar College was placed on a picturesque site in the country. In a building four and five stories high and one-fifth of a mile long, the largest building in America when it was built, Renwick essentially copied the plan of Mount Holyoke Female Seminary, now for four hundred students and faculty. The central pavilion functioned as Mount Holyoke's principal floor, housing all the public spaces. One entered through ceremonial steps to find reception hall, parlor, dining room, chapel, museums for science and art, library, president's quarters, and classrooms. The male college faculty lived with their families in apartments in the end pavilions. Along the corridor, students lived with their teachers, the young female assistants of the professors. These women supervised their charges under the direction of a Lady Principal, who had the responsibility for creating and maintaining the seminary system, which attempted to control students as firmly as Mount Holyoke.

Both Vassar and Mount Holyoke were firmly established in fact and in consciousness when Hatfield, Massachusetts, resident Sophia Smith found herself late in her life, alone and with a considerable fortune, and turned to her minister, Amherst alumnus John Morton Greene, for guidance. Greene tried to interest her in his alma mater and that of his wife, Mount Holyoke

Female Seminary, but she refused to visit either institution or consider leaving her money there. Greene presented her with the option of a school for the deaf or a women's college; she initially chose the former, but when another philanthropist in western Massachusetts beat her to it, she decided to endow a women's college. Greene enlisted the aid of powerful Amherst professors, and together they convinced Sophia Smith to leave the bulk of her estate for a women's college and to entrust decisions to a small group of Amherst professors and alumni.

From the outset of his conversations with Sophia Smith, John Greene was clear that Smith College should differ from Vassar and Mount Holyoke in several critical ways. Smith would not put its students into one large building, but rather build several "cottages." And instead of the isolated village or rural site, Smith would be located in the town of Northampton. Together these two features would mean that students would remain in touch with the social life of the town and would remain, as Greene put it, "free from the affected, unsocial, visionary notions which fill the minds of some who graduate at our girls' schools."[4]

When the trustees met in 1871, after Sophia Smith's death, to plan for the new college, they ratified this vision and decided that the president of Smith ought to be a man. In 1873 L. Clark Seelye agreed to be that president, confirming Amherst's influence: he was an Amherst professor and the brother of Smith trustee Julius Seelye, soon to be Amherst's president. He gave a clear articulation to the conception of Smith College and with his Amherst colleagues developed it into a plan.

At the time of Smith College's founding, reformers responsible for hospitals and asylums were questioning the proper form of institutional care. The large setting, or "congregate" system, came under attack as dangerous to the physical and mental health of its inmates. Samuel Gridley Howe, the chairman of the Board of State Charities of Massachusetts, began to understand the culture of the asylum, where inmates learned not inner order, but how to become patients. The solution that Howe found in Gheel, Belgium, was to break up the large "congregate" building and to place patients in "cottages" which simulated the family home.

Essentially, what the Amherst shapers of Smith College did was to apply this same principle to the women' s college. The problem was that the women's college was breeding new dangers. The issue for Smith was less the fear of promiscuity than the fear that college women would become manly. The all-female world did not serve to protect women and conventional femininity. Instead it fostered intense female friendship and generated strong-minded women. President L. Clark Seelye had quite strong feelings on the subject of professional women, in whom "the gentle-woman is lost in the strong-minded." Quite frankly he despised them. "Is it mere prejudice," he asked, "which causes so general a feeling of aversion to some women whose energy, heroism, and ability we cannot but admire? Has not their training repressed their amiable qualities, made them bigoted, what the English would call bumptious?"[5] The solution President Seelye and his coworkers found to strong-minded women was quite wonderful in its simplicity: Educate women in college but keep them symbolically at home. Erect a central college building for instruction and surround it with cottages where the students live in familial settings. Keep them in daily contact with men as president and faculty. Build no chapel or library to encourage them to enter into the life of the town. Place students under family government as members of the town and prevent the great harm of the seminary—the creation of a separate women's culture with its dangerous emotional attachments, its visionary schemes, and its strong-minded stance toward the world.

In September 1875, when Smith College opened, it presented a bold front to the world. College Hall testified to Smith's shapers' fundamental belief in the liberal arts for women. The trustees hired a talented young Boston firm, Peabody and Stearns, to design Smith's first buildings. They planned College Hall in the design tradition of the "Old Main," the primary building of male and coeducational colleges. Accordingly they placed it on a hill, giving it a dominant place. The Victorian Gothic building that arose boldly asserted its power over the setting. It is a nervous, vital building, an assertion of muscular Christianity. Smith offered to women the liberal arts as taught at Amherst. The building for instruction therefore betrays no suggestion that it is designed for women.

Dewey House, the first student residence, stands in sharp contrast to the main building. Its associations came not from the power of Christian learning, but from the life of Northampton through the adaptation of the handsome home of one of its most prominent early-nineteenth-century families. Designed in 1827 for Charles A. Dewey, its four Ionic columns adorned a solid two-story box to which a three-story ell was added in the back. Dewey House contained all the components of a family residence: porch, hall, parlors, dining hall, bedrooms. Nearby stood the ample house of the college president. Upon its opening the Smith College campus had every element important to the new vision: the dignified setting for intellectual life; the domestic dwelling house; the male patriarchal presence; placement on a central street; and no library or chapel.

Smith decided to start small. It accepted only those who could meet the entrance requirements of a liberal arts college, creating no preparatory department, as had Vassar and Wellesley. Its initial student body of fourteen entered in September 1875. They were greeted by the president, a small faculty, and a director of social culture to shape their manners and morals. In contrast to Vassar, only one rule governed their lives, the ten o'clock rule, setting the

Smith College houses, 1880s. *Historic Northampton.*

Smith's first student residence, Dewey House (foreground), was adapted from the dwelling designed for Charles A. Dewey in 1827. In the background is Washburn House, one of the early residences designed and built for the college. This photograph is part of a series taken in the 1880s.

bedtime hour of students. The daily schedule and the students' sense of decorum established order. Students were treated as "sensible, honorable" adults and were allowed to entertain visitors, come and go freely, and accept invitations from friends in town. Social freedom was part of Smith's experimental design to protect students' femininity by keeping them within the heterosocial culture of village life: to ensure that it was creating feminine scholars.

THE scholars, however, came to have different ideas. Students at Smith College, and at other nondenominational women's colleges outside the South, effectively subverted all schemes designed to keep them within the bonds of nineteenth-century notions of feminine behavior. It did not really matter whether you put four hundred of them in large congregate structures separate from the world or dispersed them in cottages integrated into a town. Either way they continued to develop and embellish their communal world of peers, what they came to call "The Life."

The college culture that students created at Smith and at other women's colleges that I have studied led a fair number of them to have notions as "affected, unsocial, [and] visionary" as that of any Mount Holyoke student; but it did so by a different, albeit related process. At Mount Holyoke, it was

"The Life" at Smith College. Residence hall, mid-1890s. *Historic Northampton.*

the influence of the female teacher on the student within the structure of rules which reshaped her consciousness in 1837. But as early as the first years at Vassar in the late 1860s, faculty retreated to the background to become shadowy presences. There is much that one can say about this world of young women—its social divisions, inclusions, and exclusions—but for our purposes here, the most intriguing element is the way, in the bifurcated world of the late nineteenth and early twentieth centuries, that these girls taught each other to be boys. The college life that they created gave highest prestige to social roles and behaviors that the culture identified as masculine.

At issue here is not sexuality—though it may have been a contributing factor—but rather social roles, learned in the college setting. College life at Smith had the usual panoply of college organizations: newspaper, yearbook, athletic teams, drama groups, student government, honorary societies. It also contained the informal organization of student cliques, parties, and dances. The central distinction of college life in these women's colleges is that in their organizations, women compose all the officers, play all the parts. The type of student that others most admired was the one they called the "all-round girl." She was the leader—the captain of the basketball team, the president of the class, the male lead in the senior play. She had learned to wield power and to act collectively; to play as a team member and to win; to wear men' s clothing and to play male dramatic roles. In a society in which gender differences attributed aggression, strength, and directness to men, the "all-round girl" of the women's college learned how to act as a man.

In the all-female dances, upperclass women took the male parts, escorting the underclass women, who had the female roles. Rather rigid rules marked upperclass students, especially seniors, off from freshmen, preserving the social distance coupled with respect. As one was initiated into the college community and moved up the hierarchy of classes, one shifted from female to male roles as one grew in power and prestige.

At the turn of the century, it was still possible for young college women to develop without embarrassment highly sentimental relationships with each other that included a strong erotic component. One finds this in letters, fiction, and college poetry, some published under official college auspices. Students begin to condemn college "crushes" in the student publications; but letters and short stories suggest that female collegians accepted them as a part of the college experience. The "crush"—which is distinctive because it links to erotic feeling a power relationship—seems in fact merely an exaggeration of the basic dynamic of college life in the women's colleges of the turn of the century. The freshman admires the prestigious senior and seeks to win her through imitation. Nothing is new about this discovery—except that in the women's college it is the way that women become socialized to play male roles.

Students re-created the social roles of men and women with their hierarchical relationships. But women took both parts, assuming masculine prerogatives as upperclass students. This encouraged the development of the forcefulness and direct stance of men rather than the tilts and smiles that marked female subordination. Designed to contain the threat to femininity posed by the liberal arts, Smith became a setting for the dramas of college life, a place where women learned to act as men.

This is partially visible on the land. When Smith alumnae became established enough to begin to add to college buildings, they gave Alumnae Gymnasium, now the fitting home of the College Archives and the Sophia Smith Collection. Designed by Hartford architect William C. Brocklesby, who ultimately planned nine buildings on the Smith campus, its red brick trimmed in brownstone and its steep roofs, gables, dormers, and cupola relate it well to its companion buildings. It was here, in 1892, that women first played their own version of basketball, devised by Senda Berenson. Its vast expanse of polished floor presented space adaptable for dramatics and dances. For college-wide occasions, students transformed the gymnasium into festive settings with their private possessions.

Undergraduates began a campaign for a special building to house college life, raising the money for the Students' Building, erected in 1903. In Smith's one red brick nod to Tudor motifs, students had club rooms, a large smooth floor for dancing, and a makeshift stage for theatricals. The round-arched loggia

The gymnasium at Smith College, 1896. *Historic Northampton.*

which adorned its facade gave the proper setting for strolls during the all-female dances and the annual Promenade, the big event that brought college men onto campus. Following the universal custom in the women's colleges, Smith students took up step-singing, locating it at the entry to the Students' Building.

As intriguing as are Alumnae Gymnasium and Students', they hardly measure the impact of college life on the landscape. College life did not confine itself to particular buildings. Rather students subverted the entire campus into a great stage setting for "the life." Chapel became a place for the demonstration of status, campus politicking, or the celebration of victors. The dining hall added class cheering to meals or became the scene of banquets and promenades. Students not only reshaped the spaces contained in buildings, they claimed the places in between as favorite haunts and retreats for important conversations or self-examination. College rituals which gave form to communal life cast a special aura over the landscape. Through them students claimed the college buildings as their own. On Ivy Day at Smith each class left a mark upon the land. As the settings of rituals, archways, hills, and lakes assumed a sacred quality. Thus the college campus that began as Amherst alumni's scheme for preserving femininity became transformed both in fact and in consciousness. Whatever the intentions of founders and builders, in the minds of students the buildings and landscapes of the women's colleges became the material embodiment of college life. And thus Smith, constructed so carefully to create feminine scholars, became the college of the all-round girl, and as a result created a fair share of those "strong-minded," "bumptious" women that Seelye so abhorred.

SMITH College started out as the smallest among the women's colleges; by President Seelye's retirement in 1910, it was the largest, with almost two thousand students. All the elements that Seelye had once forsworn stood on campus: large residential halls; a library; an assembly hall for chapel. They did not come by any conscious plan, but rather as a result of Seelye's growing ambition, business sense, and ability to charm philanthropists.

Smith had begun so small because it had made its entrance requirements equal to those of Amherst, limiting itself to candidates—few among women at the time—who passed the classical secondary course. Vassar and Wellesley, by contrast, had established preparatory departments to train their own students. Seelye never considered opening a preparatory school, but in 1880 he found a way to bring in more students. He created a School of Music and a School of Art. He did not integrate them into the rest of the college, but rather created largely autonomous schools with their own programs and their own diminished entrance requirements. A student needed only the equivalent of a standard high school course to qualify.

Quite unexpectedly, Winthrop Hillyer, a Northampton resident, gave $25,000 for a building for the School of Art. In 1882, the Hillyer Art Gallery opened, designed by Peabody and Stearns. When no donor appeared for a companion building for a School of Music, the college erected Music Hall to the southwest of College Hall where, as Pierce Hall, it still stands. Another variation by Peabody and Stearns on the theme of the Gothic Revival, Pierce is a solid, calm building. Only at the roofline is there any drama—a high-pitched roof, gables, smokestacks, and finials, all of which relate Pierce to its more richly decorated neighbor, College Hall.

Buttressed by the Schools of Art and Music, Smith grew quickly. Increasing numbers of students meant a need for classrooms and laboratories. In 1886, the college put Lilly Hall of Science next to the School of Music. In the twentieth century, Smith added large functional buildings for classrooms, laboratories, and communal gatherings. The early academic buildings formed an external perimeter, fronting the street. In 1900, Seelye Hall started a second tier of buildings, which filled in the center of the campus, destroying internal vistas and introducing a discordant architectural note.

With increasing numbers of students, the college erected cottage after cottage, and they grew larger and larger. The first cottages after the Dewey House—Hatfield, Washburn, and Hubbard—although of increasing size, resembled family houses in their irregular interiors and exteriors, marked by porches. So did Brocklesby's series of four cottages of the 1890s—Morris, Lawrence, Dickinson, and Tyler. Despite their size, their public rooms remain warm and domestic; and the student rooms, doubles and triples and upstairs parlors, vary in size and shape.

The original plan that Smith students use the town library grew increasingly impractical in time. Depending upon the Forbes Library, the college installed a small library within Seelye Hall. But as conflict developed between the Forbes and Smith, in 1909 Smith erected its own library, financed by Andrew Carnegie and alumnae contributions. Designed by Lord and Hewlett, the library took a classical form, a serene and calm element on an otherwise visually complicated campus. John M. Greene Hall met a need that size mandated for a place for communal gatherings and morning chapel.

When Seelye retired in 1910, the college that he turned over to his successor bore little relation to its original scheme. It had simply outgrown it. But in the years that followed, conscious planning replaced rampant growth.

From 1910 to 1917, Smith College thought "Big." At a critical moment, it harbored a midwesterner who looked at the college through the lens of a Big Ten university. In 1910 Marion LeRoy Burton came to Smith to remain until 1917, when he became president of the University of Minnesota. He brought to Smith the principles of modern college administration. He launched a successful endowment drive to increase faculty salaries. He encouraged faculty efforts to revamp the curriculum. He overturned existing admissions procedures to open Smith up to students from high schools. As Burton conceived of the college's student, he imagined her as a university coed, who just happened to come to Smith.

Essentially Burton devised a plan to turn Smith into a university. The existing Smith campus would become one unit of a larger institution composed of colleges either of social science, art, music, and drama or of a nonspecialized nature, following the English model. To enable this he sought to expand the campus by acquiring more land. And he hired landscape architect and city planner John Nolan to evaluate the existing campus and devise a scheme. When Burton returned to the Midwest, his university plan went with him. He had set in motion, however, the processes of land acquisition and planning that would be turned to quite different purposes.

IN 1912 Burton had brought Ada Louise Comstock, a Smith alumna, as his dean. She had been dean of women at the University of Minnesota since 1907. As she surveyed the campus, she found herself disturbed by what had happened at Smith: increasing divisions had emerged between students, divisions that were intensified by the growth of off-campus housing. The college had admitted more students than there were college rooms. By the turn of

Ivy Day at Smith College, 1896. *Historic Northampton.*

the century one-half of Smith's student body, including the upper classes, lived in rooming houses.

While the college regulated these off-campus boardinghouses, the conditions they offered varied considerably. For the poorest students, they could be less expensive than the dormitory. For richer, they became a way of confirming social prestige and living in luxury. One joined some of them through a network of friends. When a group of students set up their own house, renting it and hiring a matron, they created an "invitation house" which chose the next year's occupants through a formal vote. While never receiving the name "sorority," White Lodge and Delta Sigma linked residence and social selection in much the same manner as did the Greek societies on coeducational campuses. Smith had gotten something of a Gold Coast as well. De Witt Smith, a speculative builder from New York and a Yale man, erected the Plymouth, a handsome Richardsonian-Romanesque apartment house adjacent to the campus. With its grand marble-encased public rooms, expensive suites for sixty-four students, gymnasium and swimming pool, and dining room equipped with a stage, the Plymouth created a new level of extravagance and exclusion among college women. Unwittingly Smith's residence policy had allowed students to sort themselves out economically and socially: cliques embedded themselves in residential groups, giving spatial form to distinctions within the student body.

This was disturbing to Comstock. She believed strongly in the ideal of Smith democracy. "Of all the disguises which the human spirit assumes none is so complete as that embodied in circumstances of living." Inhibitions springing from economic differences existed in the outside world, but "in college . . . we have our chance to see what the human spirit can do when unhampered either by deprivation or by excess."[6] In her campaign to democratize Smith College, Comstock was joined by William Allan Neilson, who followed Burton as president. Neilson's primary concern was with intellectual quality, not with campus expansion; and he only accepted the presidency once the trustees tabled plans for a women's university. He came with the hopes of remaining a scholar: he quickly became a master fund-raiser. His Scottish commitment to the principles of equality required him to seek funds to build residential halls. After major campaigns, in 1934 he announced that Smith at last could house its students.

While the college received the bequest of the Capen School and purchased private dormitories, to house over a thousand additional students it had to undertake major building. The result for Smith was dramatic: the Quadrangles on Allen Field, ten residential halls designed by the Boston architect John W. Ames and his collaborators Edwin Sherrill Dodge and Karl S. Putnam. Each dormitory was named in honor of a distinguished member of the Smith community, including Ellen Emerson, Martha Wilson, Laura Scales, Franklin King, and Comstock.

With the Quadrangles, Smith entered the mainstream of collegiate architecture—in its red brick Georgian variant. In many ways Smith's complex of residential halls looks like the new Harvard houses which rose in the same period on the Charles River. Initially, Ames's scheme seemed to the trustees too like industrial buildings. As a result, Ames enlivened the regularity and symmetry of the four-story structures by generous use of white trim for windows, stringcourses, and cupolas, by dormer windows and tall red brick chimneys, by round-arched loggias and white service buildings. In their associations, the Quadrangles assert the dignity of college life.

Yet in their interiors, the Quadrangles quietly continued the separate building tradition of women's dormitories. At Harvard the houses had suites of connecting undergraduate rooms, each sharing bathroom and living room, designed to foster male friendship and camaraderie. In the 1920s and 1930s, Smith and other women's colleges became fearful of female intimacy. The dormitories reflect this fear. They lost the informal, irregular space of the cottages, with their doubles, triples, and suites. Instead they put students in single identical Spartan cubicles on both sides of a long corridor. Such interiors were intended to discourage socializing upstairs away from adult eyes. Downstairs, elegant public rooms, designed by alumnae who were professional interior decorators, allowed gatherings that could be monitored and provided luxurious spaces in which male guests could be received.

The building group allowed Smith to create a planned, regular space in keeping with Beaux Arts principles then governing campus design. The other side of this is that the Quadrangles created a world different from that of the rest of the campus and of the town. Brick walls front the street; courtyards create an inner enclosed space. The cottages and boardinghouses had interspersed students both on campus and in the town. With the Quadrangles, Smith set half of its students off in their own residential quarter and away from Northampton. Their construction signaled the supplanting of Smith's original vision of the feminine collegian by Neilson and Comstock's hope for a democratic, heterosexual college girl.

THE campus of Smith College is a text that dramatizes significant episodes in the college's past. Even in its outlines, the narrative of college building at Smith, from its founding until the late 1930s, is richly complex. Differing conceptions of educated womanhood offered alternative patterns for building. Four visions of the ideal Smith student are embedded in bricks and mortar: the feminine scholar; the all-round girl; the university coed, who just happened to come to Smith; and the democratic and dating college girl. Implicit is a dialectical understanding. Each vision is posed in part as an answer to a question grounded in the opposition to women's higher education.

Buildings always have unintended consequences. Moreover, the history of Smith's building intentions is not the whole history of Smith. Looking at Smith's structures, however, affords a window for looking into Smith's design that tells us much about the hopes and fears that offering women the liberal arts has evoked.

Today, the design of the college, with all its tensions and contradictions, does not determine the present. It does, however, establish part of the ground of dialogue, debate, and choice. As the decisions that will shape future campus plans are posed, there are echoes of the past, as well as new conceptions of educated womanhood that the past could not begin to envision.

NOTES

1. This article abridges sections of my *Alma Mater: Design and Experience in the Women's Colleges from Their Nineteenth-Century Beginnings to the 1930s* (New York, 1984), especially 69–82, 147–179, and 213–217, where full documentation can be found. Here I have cited only direct quotations.

2. M[ary]L[yon], *Mount Holyoke Female Seminary*, South Hadley, Sept. 1835, 2. Copy in the Huntington Library, San Marino, CA.

3. Quoted in Milo P. Jewett, "Origin of Vassar College," March 1879, typed copy, 6, Vassar College Library.

4. John M. Greene to Sophia Smith, April 28, 1869, quoted in Elizabeth Deering Hanscom and Helen French Green, *Sophia Smith and the Beginnings of Smith College* (Northampton, 1926).

5. L. Clark Seelye, "The Need of a Collegiate Education for Women," paper presented at the American Institute of Instruction, July 28, 1874 (n.p.: American Institute of Instruction, 1874), 14.

6. Ada Comstock, "Why Smith College Should House Its Students," *Smith Alumnae Quarterly* 11 (November 1919): 17.

19

AUTHOR George Washington Cable, whose novels challenged American racial stereotypes, lived in Northampton as a virtual exile from his native New Orleans, where his relatively tolerant views were not welcome. But his views on race and ethnicity had their limits. Cable, like many Americans, was alarmed by the welter of immigrants flocking to America in the late nineteenth century. With the backing of Andrew Carnegie, he founded the Home Culture Clubs in Northampton to "Americanize" and uplift working girls unaccustomed to New England ways. The Home Culture Club movement caught on around the country as cities and towns struggled with the problems of assimilating large numbers of ethnic groups into the American mainstream.

Yet if minorities were not always fully accepted, racial and ethnic boundaries were fluid in Northampton. Wrapped in a black silk stocking, letters recently discovered beneath the floorboards of an old house reveal a long lost passion between Alice Hanley, an Irish Catholic coachman's daughter, and Channing Lewis, an African American who migrated north from South Carolina after the end of Reconstruction. "O' how I do wish you were here . . ." wrote Alice, "I hope the day will come when we can always be together . . . but oh my how lonesome . . . I am all alone." Though tolerated, such a relationship was hardly encouraged. It was precisely at this time that the color line was being sharply drawn across the country. In 1901, after speaking in Northampton, Booker T. Washington was denied accommodation in three Springfield hotels, just fifteen miles away.

The Alice Hanley letters themselves are not articulate, but bear a kind of eloquence akin to the blues. Kathy Peiss, has drawn upon her knowledge and insight to sift through the layers of meaning beneath the surface of the historical record. Peiss not only draws a sensitive portrait of Alice Hanley, but connects her life and that of her family with the matrix of social relationships that characterized day-to-day life in turn-of-the-century Northampton.

Love across the Color Line*

KATHY PEISS

ONLY a gravestone testifies in public to Alice Hanley's life. Born into an Irish immigrant family, Hanley lived her forty-five years in obscurity. When she died in 1920, she was interred at St. Mary's cemetery in Northampton, Massachusetts, in the plot where her mother already lay buried. Over the years, her

* From Helen Lefkowitz and Kathy Peiss, eds., *Love across the Color Line: The Letters of Alice Hanley to Channing Lewis* (Amherst, 1996).

father, her siblings, and their spouses would be entombed there. Death returned Alice to her family, but at a cost; the secrets of her life were buried under her married name, Brennan.

Sometime before she died, Alice Hanley wrapped a bundle of letters in a black lace stocking and hid them in the attic of her family house.[1] If cold granite marked her civil role as daughter and wife, the lace stocking summoned Alice's passion as a single woman. The fragile net and fancy design, made by women much like herself, delighted the eye and hand with their elegant refinement and sensuous intimacy. Within the stocking were letters of the heart, dispatched to a lover twenty miles away. Alice Hanley wrote these letters in 1907 and 1908 to Channing Lewis of Springfield, Massachusetts. When their love affair ended, she probably asked Channing to return her correspondence, as was customary. None of his letters survives: Alice either returned or destroyed them to prevent their discovery. Although she married another man in 1916, she had preserved and concealed the memory of her earlier romance.

These love letters register the commonplace. Alice expressed her longing for Channing's kisses, her desire for good clothes, her need for money. She recorded her work cleaning Channing's apartment, her travel on streetcars, her struggles with illness, and, probably, a pregnancy. She described an often stormy, occasionally violent relationship, with Alice tacking from desperation to transcendent happiness and back to despair. It is the social identities of the two lovers that foremost catch our attention: at the time she wrote the letters, Alice Hanley was thirty-two years old, a single woman who lived with her Irish American working-class family and had no regular employment; her lover, Channing Lewis, was an African American man in his early forties, working as a cook and separated from his Irish American wife.

Alice Hanley's letters are a singular record of a consensual relationship between a black working-class man and a white woman. We know very little about such relationships: social segregation, virulent racial prejudice, and family shame made the need to dissemble acute. The very uniqueness of the letters, their specificity and ambiguities, makes it hard to find any sure ground for historical generalization. The aims of this essay are modest: to explore how one woman negotiated "forbidden desires" in the early twentieth century, how she grasped the ethics of sexuality and race as a working-class woman. Yet Hanley's letters challenge us more broadly to understand gender, race, and class not simply as conceptual abstractions, as they are all too often invoked, but as dimensions of lived experience in all its complexity and contradiction.

RECORDS documenting the history of sexuality across the color line are fragmentary at best. For several decades, attention has been focused on the history of racial oppression in the United States, and it has been difficult to perceive how racism and intimacy might live side by side. Nevertheless, historians and other scholars have begun to shed light on a subject that has been both controversial and suppressed. Their work challenges us to understand these relationships as emerging from specific historical and ideological circumstances. That is, relationships become "interracial" in circumstances where social groups are classified and behave as "races" (based on phenotype or kinship), and these circumstances change over time. Because they are considered taboo, such relationships also powerfully affect the way a society organizes and perceives gender and sexuality in general.[2]

The term "interracial" obscures the precise character of social and sexual relationships that might have existed, not only between Americans of European and African descent, but for those of Asian, Spanish and Latin American, and American Indian backgrounds as well. At the turn of the century, white men's sexual access to black women, once integral to their authority over slaves, continued to be tacitly condoned politically and ideologically. In direct contrast, the pairing of white women and African American men was proscribed. White Americans' justifications for lynching obscured a truth they could not readily entertain, as Ida B. Wells-Barnett astutely observed: their defamation of African American men as uncontrollable and criminal, desiring and raping innocent white women, concealed the fact that a number of black men and white women had entered into consensual relationships.[3]

Concern about interracial sex and marriage intensified in the late nineteenth and early twentieth centuries, manifest particularly in the South and West, but articulated as well in some northern states. This coincided with the reconsolidation of southern white men's control over African Americans after 1877; the rise of scientific racism, particularly as manifested in eugenics; and the growing anxiety over "new" immigrants and urban subcultures, perceived as agents of disorder. Prohibited relationships were embedded in overlapping systems of sexual regulation and racial control. That these systems were under severe strain may be seen in the very visible drama surrounding the black prize-fighter Jack Johnson and his relationships with two white women in 1912 and 1913; Johnson was charged under the Mann Act with criminally transporting a white woman across state lines for sexual purposes. The act had been designed to control "white slavery" and prostitution, yet it is clear that much of what reformers perceived to be sex trafficking was, rather, voluntary encounters and sexual experiments of young women and men.

The Johnson affair brought out with particular force how sexually charged public perceptions of these relationships were, with newspaper reports and legislative hearings offering up a rich brew of desire and denial, fascination and revulsion. The case led to renewed calls for so-called antimiscegenation legislation, even in Massachusetts, which had earlier repealed such laws. The words of a Georgia representative epitomize the viciousness and frenzy unleashed by the Johnson affair: railing against the "slavery of white women to black beasts," he called upon Congress to "uproot and exterminate now this debasing, ultra-demoralizing, un-American and inhuman leprosy."[4]

One of the striking paradoxes of the history of interracial relationships is that a highly elaborated legal and extralegal apparatus emerged to prevent consensual liaisons, particularly marriages, which occurred relatively infrequently in the first place. Marriage rates between Americans of African and European descent were low, but they varied by region and locality. In the early twentieth century, only about 1 percent of African Americans in New York and Philadelphia had white spouses. In Boston, however, the figure rose to 10 to 13 percent, with most of the marriages between black men and white women. Relationships between black and white Americans outside of legal marriage, whether heterosexual or homosexual, are extremely difficult to document and impossible to quantify for this historical period.[5]

Although laws and lynching frequently enforced the prohibition on these relationships, undoubtedly most effective in the North were social codes and reflexive understandings forbidding "race mixing." Still, we know relatively little about the place of such informal rules in the daily lives of working people. The public concern swirling around Jack Johnson may have mounted in part because sites for sociability and sexual encounters between black and white Americans had become more visible around the turn of the century. But these encounters had been going on quietly for decades among poor and working-class Americans. The history of Irish Americans' animosity and racism toward African Americans in the nineteenth century is amply documented; less well known is evidence of a small but significant number of intimate relationships between urban Irish and black Americans in the mid-nineteenth century. Servants and laborers, these people were thrown together by poverty, lived side by side, and performed menial work in a job market that discriminated against both groups. Vulnerability and proximity could spark hatred, but it could also beget cooperation and love.[6]

Alice Hanley's letters do not reveal whether her experience was typical or representative, but they do offer a rare inside look at one such romance. Yet here there is an enigma: the letters offer us a firsthand account of an intimate relationship between a white woman and a black man, but they have little explicit to say about racial differences or racial prejudice. Historians are increasingly mindful of what lies unspoken in a text, but silence remains difficult to interpret. Faint traces in the letters point to the discrimination Channing faced in the job market and the conflicts Alice had with her parents; they suggest how the burden of racial difference exacerbated the difficulties they had. But these really are traces: Why was race, in a sense, "unspeakable"? Was it part of the air Alice and Channing breathed, a "metalanguage," as historian Evelyn Brooks Higginbotham calls it, whose grammar needed no acknowledgment yet structured every locution? Was it simply too dangerous, indeed tabooed?[7]

Or perhaps Alice had other things on her mind. She was, after all, poor, unemployed, likely pregnant, and in conflict with her parents. For present-day readers, it is the interracial dimension of Alice and Channing's story that commands our notice and marks these documents as rare and significant sources. But the story is also, less obviously, about other kinds of experiences and differences. Alice was a practicing Catholic, while Channing had ties to the black Baptist church. Alice's "whiteness" was ethnically specific, that is, she was the American-born daughter of Irish immigrants; Channing's African American identity, as a migrant from Virginia in the aftermath of the Civil War, was inflected with a particular regional and generational experience.

Most notably, differences constructed around and through gender and sexuality structured the language in which Alice spoke of her behavior and Channing's. After all, in breaking the taboo against interracial relationships she had also violated the prohibition against nonmarital sexual behavior. Indeed, throughout the letters Alice was most agitated over the ethics and consequences of nonmarital heterosexuality. These were undoubtedly complicated by racial difference, but were not necessarily determined by them.

The letters capture Alice's sensibility and concerns for little more than a year. They are at times maddeningly opaque, referring to people and events now impossible to trace. We hear Channing Lewis only through Alice's voice, and it is difficult to take the full measure of their relationship. There is much we cannot know about the couple, but the letters nonetheless allow us to glimpse a turn-of-the-century world otherwise hidden from view.

BIRTH certificates, census schedules, and deeds—a handful of official records—disclose a fragmentary picture of Alice Hanley's life before she met Channing Lewis. Her family struggled in the harsh economic and social climate Irish immigrants encountered in the nineteenth century. As Alice grew into adolescence, her family was scrambling out of poverty toward a life of some stability and even comfort. Given the paucity of evidence, it is difficult to know exactly how the rush of feelings she expressed, the psychic pleasures and costs of being with Channing Lewis, were embedded in her experiences as a daughter of the immigrant generation. Yet the family chronicle provides a context that helps explain the historically specific ways Alice Hanley experienced dependency and loneliness, desired refinement and security, and wanted belonging and love.

Alice's father, James Hanley, was about sixteen years of age when he journeyed from Ireland to the United States around 1870. He may have traveled with his older brother John or joined John shortly after landing. According to Hanley family lore, the brothers first sought work in New Haven, but by 1870 or 1871 they had arrived in Pittsfield, Massachusetts, having cast their lot with a young Irish worker, Thomas Ryan, and his relatives. The men worked as laborers on the Hoosac Tunnel, a massive railroad project in the Berkshire hills of western Massachusetts. Initiated before the Civil War, the project to link Boston and upstate New York had cost millions of dollars, employed hundreds of Irish immigrant workers, and consumed many lives. The final push to completion had begun in 1869, just as James Hanley arrived in the United States.[8]

Off the job, James Hanley courted Alice Ryan, whose father, according to a family story, was a contractor on the tunnel project and had hired James. The match may have served both parties well. Alice Ryan was in her mid to late twenties by the time she married; although Irish immigrant women tended to marry later than American-born women, she was older than all those who appeared on the Pittsfield marriage register near her name. James was young—as much as eight years younger than Alice Ryan—uneducated, and poor, and the marriage gave him an extended family and a footing in America only a year or two after his arrival. They married in 1871 and boarded for a few years. In 1873 they moved to 46 Clough Street, on a block that was an enclave of Ryans and Hanleys: Thomas Ryan lived in the house, as had James's brother John before he shipped to Australia, and a "Mrs. Ryan" and a "J. Ryan" lived there as well.[9]

In 1875, James and Alice Ryan Hanley's first child, Alice, was born. Two years later, the family moved to Weston, at the time a largely rural area, not far from Boston. The Hanleys lived with a small group of Irish immigrants working as servants and laborers amidst large landowners and farmers. In Weston, James became a coachman and Alice Ryan Hanley bore two more children, Katharine in 1877 and John in 1880. Little more is known about the family until they moved to Northampton in 1892.[10]

NORTHAMPTON at the turn of the century was a small city of 18,000, set in the rich farmlands of the Connecticut River Valley. It had gained a reputation as a center of social reform and women's higher education. From the standpoint of its working classes, however, Northampton offered a diverse and vigorous manufacturing base and commercial hub for the surrounding agricultural area. Its entrepreneurs built large factories along the Mill River, and industrial plants sprang up in the outlying villages of Florence and Leeds. Silk cloth, hosiery, brushes, and cutlery dominated the local economy, but there was a wide range of employment opportunities for working women and men. A number of small shops employed skilled workers, while Smith College, the Northampton State Hospital, and other institutions provided many service jobs as well.[11]

Immigrants and their American-born children performed the bulk of the manual labor in Northampton's expanding economy. Building the railroad north from Springfield, Irish laborers had begun to settle in Northampton before the Civil War, clustering around the railroad tracks and mill yards. In the 1870s and 1880s, many Irish immigrants, as well as growing numbers of French Canadians, gained manufacturing jobs.[12] By 1895, as the Hanleys settled into life in Northampton, foreign-born women and men accounted for one-quarter of the city's population: four in ten immigrants were Irish; a growing number of inhabitants were French Canadian; Italians, Poles, Russian Jews, and others were beginning to arrive in small numbers. Most telling, only 40 percent of Northampton's residents had parents who were born in the United States. From the Civil War to 1900, the population of Northampton had doubled, and what had once been a fairly homogeneous Protestant town was now a small city where religious differences, ethnic diversity, and the extremes of wealth and poverty were visible to all. Northampton's citizens could see elements of the social problems endemic to the nation's metropolises, although hardly on the same scale. Tenement houses sprang up among the single-family dwellings. Arrests for drunken and rowdy behavior dominated the annual police report. The school committee wrestled with the problem of educating laboring children and non-Anglophone adults. And the town's established leaders initiated reform efforts to socialize and uplift the immigrant working classes.[13]

Many Yankees held an image of Northampton as a tolerant city, but nativism took hold there as it did throughout the country. One local observer noted pointedly that members of the Congregational church closed their blinds on Sundays to avoid seeing Catholics walking to Mass. Nor were immigrants welcomed into Masonic or other fraternal orders that opened employment and social opportunities for Protestant men. In 1880, nearly all the Irishmen in the town were mill laborers or farm workers and remained cut off from most avenues of occupational mobility during their lives; opportunities widened by the turn of the century, but mainly for the American-born second generation. Fearing that the numbers of immigrants would soon overwhelm the Yankee population, political leaders chartered Northampton as a city in 1883, dividing it into wards that diluted Irish and French Canadian voting strength. Despite these efforts, the first Irish mayor, John B. O'Donnell, was elected in 1891—by three votes in a three-way race.[14]

In this climate, the Catholic parish, composed mainly of foreign-born congregants, sought both to make the church visible and influential and to integrate the immigrants into Northampton's life. The Reverend Michael Barry sat on the public school board and chose not to wear the Roman collar about town. At the same time, he built an imposing and strategically placed structure for the parish, St. Mary's of the Assumption—high on the hill near Smith College, overlooking the downtown shopping district, visible to all. When St. Mary's was consecrated in 1885, there were 1,700 church members, the majority of whom were Irish and French Canadian. In these years, Catholic temperance and mutual benefit societies began to spread an institutional web of aid and uplift throughout the immigrant community. In 1891, the church opened a parochial school, St. Michael's, located on a large property called Shady Lawn, which over the years had housed different private schools and institutions.[15]

Unlike many immigrant families that settled in Northampton, the Hanleys did not take up residence near the factories or in the new tenements springing up in the city. Rather, they moved into the rear of a house on parochial school property. The parish priest at the time, John Kenney, was known as a "friend of the poor" and was especially kind to the students at St. Michael's. Perhaps in offering housing to James Hanley he was helping one of the church's needy. It is more likely, however, that the move reflected connections James Hanley had made within and outside the church: as his obituary in 1931 put it, "he had many friends both in Northampton and surrounding towns."[16]

Simply by living on parish property, the Hanleys came into the social and educational orbit of the Catholic church. Although not an officer, James Hanley had close ties to at least one Catholic lay organization. Christopher Adams, a carpenter by trade, had boarded with the Hanley family on St. Michael's property from 1894 to 1896. Adams was also an officer in the local "court" of the Ancient Order of Foresters, a Catholic fraternal and mutual benefit society. The organization, composed of working-class Irishmen—masons, barbers, city workers, bartenders—met twice a month, provided assistance in the event of sickness and death, sponsored social events, and enabled Catholic men to forge useful social and business connections. Within a few years, Adams had become a contractor and builder, successful enough to take out an advertisement in the city directory. Whatever official affiliation James Hanley had with the Foresters, he maintained a close friendship with Adams who, thirty-five years after they had boarded together, was a pallbearer at James's funeral.[17]

Living at St. Michael's also meant that the Hanley children received religious instruction and at least a grammar school education. Although James Hanley and probably his wife could not read or write, they valued learning. Their daughters Alice and "Katie," ages nineteen and seventeen respectively, attended the parochial school in the 1894–1895 school year; they were among 113 girls ranging in age from twelve to twenty. The next year, their son John, age sixteen, appeared on the school register. It was unusual for children of immigrants to attend school for so long; the state required attendance only until age fourteen, and most left school for the workplace. Northampton's superintendent of schools complained that immigrant parents were only interested in "the dollars received from their [children's] labor and in the education they can get in a shop or factory."[18]

St. Michael's was not divided into classes at this time, so we cannot know much about the educational attainments of the Hanley children. Alice probably did not matriculate into high school, which required rigorous diocesan entrance exams and offered only a college-preparation curriculum. More likely, she was an older student at the upper level of grammar school. Judging from the style and content of her letters, Alice Hanley could read fairly advanced texts, but wrote relatively unsophisticated compositions. What is perhaps most striking about her learning is her elegant script and the care she took with handwriting. Penmanship was generally considered a mark of gentility and artistic sensibility in the nineteenth century, and St. Michael's taught the well-known Palmer method of writing.[19]

THE Hanleys may have benefited from the religious and social network of resources and support available to working-class immigrants, but they also found a patron among the town's elite. When James arrived in Northampton, he quickly secured a job as coachman to Benjamin Colman Blodgett, known as a member of "Northampton's First Circles." Blodgett had taught music in Pittsfield at the Maplewood Institute, a private school for girls, from 1865 to 1878, when he opened his own school of music. In 1881, he moved the music school to Northampton, where it became affiliated with Smith College. Blodgett's presence was immediately felt in the cultural life of Northampton. He led the orchestra at civic events; he helped found the Home Culture Clubs, an educational and reform organization; he saw his daughter, who was active in local reform for "the advancement of the young women of the city," married to a "son of Old Amherst" in "the most important social event of the season." Befitting his status, Blodgett purchased the Bright estate in 1881, a large piece of property located near the Smith campus. On the grounds were two stables or sheds, which in 1892 became James Hanley's domain for more than a decade.[20]

This was not the first time the two men had met. When he was a young man laboring on the Hoosac Tunnel, James Hanley had boarded at Benjamin Blodgett's spacious home on Circular Avenue in Pittsfield. James Hanley and Alice Ryan were married not far from Blodgett's house; the priest who officiated was a musician of local note and undoubtedly knew the music professor. No record exists to tell us whether or how Blodgett helped the Hanley family before 1892. We do not know why the Hanleys moved to Weston in 1877 and for whom James worked there as a coachman. Benjamin Blodgett's brother, a wealthy carpet merchant, lived quite nearby, in Newton, but there is no evidence to link the two men. Still, the suspicion lingers that some ongoing tie between Blodgett and Hanley motivated James to move to Northampton. In any event, the two men, whose paths had crossed twenty years earlier, found their lives strangely intertwined.[21]

In Northampton, Benjamin Blodgett became a benefactor of sorts for the Hanleys. He not only provided James with steady employment for about a decade, but he also apparently eased the family's way. Such clientage relationships between working people and their social "betters" may have become increasingly anachronistic in large industrial cities by the late nineteenth century. But even though Northampton grew more diverse and stratified, social relationships still retained a semblance of intimacy and familiarity, especially for those who worked directly for the wealthier families in service jobs. Indeed, despite the social changes that had occurred there, local leaders imagined a place where the qualities of noblesse oblige, patronage, and deference could still be maintained.[22]

In 1897, five years after arriving in Northampton, the Hanleys moved to a house at 15 Bright Avenue, the house where Alice eventually hid her letters to Channing Lewis. Down the hill from Benjamin Blodgett's mansion and stables, this part of the Bright estate had been sold and developed in the late 1880s as a short side street with five houses. James Hanley purchased the house from Minnie Mason, wife of the proprietor of the Connecticut Valley Kennel. To do so, he took out a $1,400 mortgage from the Northampton Co-operative Bank, a lender that served the working-class population. The two-story frame dwelling, with a shingle roof and "piazza," as Alice grandly called the porch, was modest, but its purchase indicated that the Hanleys had achieved some measure of working-class success and respectability.[23]

Although James Hanley had steady employment, the mortgage payments, more than fifteen dollars a month, may have been too much to bear without the contribution his children made to the family economy. James purchased the house a year after his daughter Katharine, not yet twenty, had found work as a stenographer. John followed Kate into the labor force in 1899, first selling paint and wallpaper, then taking a position as a clerk at Kelton and Company, a "public market" selling fish and meat, in 1902. Estimating wages is a difficult exercise: in Boston in 1907, grocery clerks earned about nine dollars a week, and female stenographers averaged about seven dollars. Even if wages were lower in western Massachusetts, Kate and John together probably earned more money than their father. As was the case in many working-class families, the children's wages, contributed while they boarded at home, enabled the Hanleys to improve their standard of living substantially.[24]

It is significant that the two siblings sought out work in the growing retail and office sector of the economy. John went to the Northampton Commercial College, newly opened in 1896; it had drawn a number of Catholic students from St. Michael's, which offered no vocational training. He suffered from migraine headaches that made it impossible for him to work in an office, and he turned to retail sales.[25]

Kate's position carried the cachet of white-collar work. Two years after she appeared on the roster of St. Michael's School, she had become one of a handful of stenographers in Northampton, skilled work just opening to women. She possibly learned stenography from a tutor or attended the commercial college's earliest classes. Kate's first job, one she held for at least fifteen years, was highly coveted: private stenographer and, later, bookkeeper to banker and manufacturer A. Lyman Williston, working out of his Round Hill mansion. One suspects the hand of Benjamin Blodgett in this. Blodgett and Williston lived nearby, traveled in the same civic and cultural circles, and had worked together establishing the Home Culture Clubs. By recommending a capable stenographer from a reliable family, Blodgett may have done his friend a favor and at the same time, done his coachman another good turn.[26]

Alice Hanley, in contrast to her younger siblings, had no discernible source of regular employment or income in these years.[27] It was not for want of opportunities. In 1895, more than one-quarter of the women living in Northampton worked for wages. Of these, almost all who were foreign born labored as domestic servants or in manufacturing jobs. Many of those born in the United States turned away from domestic work, with more than 50 percent working as factory operatives in the silk mills, hosiery shop, and brush factory. They were mainly daughters of Irish and French Canadian immigrants. Although James Hanley no doubt would have resisted his daughter's becoming a "factory girl," there were other positions available to young women in these years. With her education, she might have become a clerical worker like Katharine. She knew how to sew and might have apprenticed to one of the many dressmakers in Northampton. Some women worked in the boardinghouses catering to Smith students.[28]

Poor health or a physical disability may have kept Alice from wage work: she certainly complained of illnesses and "lameness" in her letters to Channing Lewis. A more likely reason is that Alice's mother wanted her first-born child, her namesake, by her side. Alice never spoke fondly of her father but her love for "mamma" was deep and abiding. In one letter, Alice suggests their close emotional bond by likening her feelings for Channing to her love for her mother: "outside of mamma you are my dearest friend on earth & the only two I ever look to for any thing." She did housework for her mother, who rewarded her with hats, corset covers, and stockings. Her mother apparently cooked on special occasions at Smith College, and Alice helped out: "I cleaned the parlor yesterday & I served until 10.30 last night." Alice knew how to make laundry white, iron drapery and "shams," and grow flowers in the garden. If Kate and John contributed financially to the household's welfare, Alice enhanced through domesticity the "lace-curtain" respectability the family so dearly coveted.[29]

What Alice Hanley actually did and thought as a young woman, before she fell in love with Channing Lewis, remains a mystery.

We do not know how or when Alice Hanley met Channing Lewis. Born in Virginia during the Civil War, Lewis had arrived in western Massachusetts by 1880, following his brother Edward and other relatives in a chain migration begun during Reconstruction. In his early years in Springfield, Channing worked at a paper and cloth factory, married an African American woman, Amelia Peters, and had two children. Tragedy struck the family in 1884 when Amelia died at age twenty-two. Channing married again in 1890, this time to an Irish woman, Josephine Murphy, who had arrived in the United States three years earlier. By now Channing had become a cook, changing restaurant jobs every few years. Although usually based in Springfield, for a period between 1896 and 1898 he lived in Northampton and worked at Daniel and Kellogg's restaurant, bakery, and grocery.[30] Perhaps Alice somehow met Channing in this period, at Daniel and Kellogg's or on the streets of Northampton. More likely, they became involved with each other after 1903, the year Channing and his wife Josephine separated.[31]

Before this time, Alice had cared enough for a Holyoke saloon keeper, Mike Manning, to preserve three of his letters, written in 1902. In them we catch a glimpse of Alice at twenty-seven, leading an active social life. On several occasions she invited Mike out for the afternoon; she enjoyed a Saturday night in Holyoke with her crowd; she relished company and entertainment. Addressing her as "friend," Manning was a somewhat reluctant beau. He assured Alice that "if I could meet you we [would] have a pleasant time" but, overworked and ill, "I have not much time for pleasure." Alice did not, at this time, object to drinking. When he wrote to explain his absence, Manning observed, "if I had seen you I would give you a hot one something to cheer you up, as it was a very cold day."[32]

Although she was not employed, Alice's social world revolved around markets, saloons, restaurants, and railway depots. She likely shopped for provisions for the family, knew the local groceries and stores well, and, through her brother John, was probably acquainted with clerks, shippers, butchers, and others in his trade. Northampton had a vibrant commercial culture, readily accessible from Alice's house on Bright Avenue. The city boasted a main street known as "Shop Row," with an array of department stores and small retailers, a municipal theater, and, by 1908, a movie house. Although the temperance movement was strong in Northampton, there were a number of saloons and restaurants, some free standing, some located in hotels, where people socialized.[33]

Whatever her duties at home, Alice was not homebound. She traveled frequently on the railroads and streetcars that connected Northampton with the nearby cities of Springfield, Holyoke, and Westfield. The continuous stream of traffic, with people moving about to earn money and to spend it, is one of the most striking aspects of life in the largely rural Connecticut River Valley in this period. The Northampton Street Railway began operation in 1873 and went electric in 1893. The first run of the day was at 5:00 a.m.; the last, fifteen minutes after midnight. Streetcars ran daily, including Sundays when pleasure seekers headed to Pequot Park and Mount Tom. Fraternal orders and large businesses hired special cars for working-class excursions and picnics; extra trolleys would be put on for civic celebrations, church dedications, and important funerals. The trolley's frequent schedule made it easy for Alice to come and go, and the five-cent fare was her ticket to freedom.[34]

Alice and Channing probably did not encounter each other in their leisure time, at a music hall, or on an excursion. They likely met in a working-class milieu where work and leisure intertwined: the provisioning and sale of food and drink gave rise to sociability that flowed through the commercial nexus. These were not places specifically for social contact among Americans of African and European descent, the "black and tan" saloons and interracial music halls that could be found in large cities.[35] In western Massachusetts, Alice's and Channing's paths probably crossed through connections made in the world of work, by workers on the job.

Irish Americans had established themselves firmly in the restaurant and saloon trade as owners and as skilled craft workers, for example, as meat cutters and bartenders. The racial hierarchy of the trade meant that African Americans typically found work bussing tables and washing dishes, yet the position of cook—which Channing held—could be a fairly prestigious one. In this setting, Irish Americans and African Americans came into contact. Given that these workplaces were also places of leisure and sociability, their interactions might produce a kind of camaraderie and even friendship.

Alice most likely met Channing Lewis through her brother John, a grocery clerk and meat cutter, or her sister's fiancé David Hoar, a bartender. All three men traveled frequently in their trades or in search of new employment, and they developed a wide range of contacts. John Hanley probably encountered Channing Lewis in the ordinary round of business, selling meat, fish, and other provisions to the restaurant trade. He knew the African American cook well enough to pay his respects with a present of premium Hennessey cigars—called in one local advertisement "as good a ten cent smoke as can be found."[36]

There is no direct testimony that David Hoar knew Channing Lewis, but circumstantial evidence—the proximity of their jobs—raises that possibility. From 1898 to 1899, when Channing Lewis was a cook at the Haynes House, "centrally located" in downtown Springfield, Hoar tended bar at P. H. Dunbar's saloon and poolroom several blocks away. After a sojourn in Chicago in

1903, Hoar returned to Springfield in 1905, working downtown at the City Hotel, then moved to Northampton to work at the Hampshire House, opposite the railroad station and a short distance from John Hanley's workplace, Kelton's market. City directories do not reveal all of Lewis's places of employment in these years, but for a time he worked at the Springfield depot restaurant. In 1907, Hoar returned to the City Hotel, although he probably visited Northampton frequently to court Kate Hanley. In November 1907, Alice asked if Channing was "still at the Nelson," a theater, hotel, and restaurant complex on Main Street, where, presumably, he was employed. The Nelson was directly across the street from the City Hotel.

Hoar circulated among local political and business leaders as president of the Northampton bartenders' union. Lewis also had influential connections, or so, as Alice reminded him, he claimed: "You told me also you know so many people & would see I could meet some of them & get some money." If David Hoar introduced Channing to Alice, it would probably have been in 1906 or 1907.[37]

IN THE first extant letter, from August 1907, Alice states tersely, "I will call for my things Sunday evening." The letter indicates her affair with Channing had been ongoing and intimate enough so that Alice would leave her belongings at his apartment, but not so long-lived and committed that Channing had entrusted her with a key: "if you are not there put them in the hall so I can get them."[38] She lived at home in Northampton, but took the streetcar often to see him, stayed overnight on numerous occasions, and at times, wrote almost daily.

This relationship between a black man and white woman was not a secret, but it did require discretion and dissemblance. Alice did not want the affair trumpeted in Northampton, and Channing did not visit her there. At one point she instructed him to ring a neighbor, Mary Ryan, a canvasser who had a telephone. "She will call me but don't tell her who you are even if she ask," Alice warned. "I will know[.]"[39]

The racial attitudes of white residents in Northampton were little different from those in other parts of New England, although the local history of abolitionism and reform may have moderated them somewhat. The *Hampshire Gazette*'s coverage of race relations generally opposed racial prejudice and supported black citizens' advancement, but apparently drew the line at "close social relations between white and colored." An editorial commented favorably on a meeting of black and white reformers in New York but noted approvingly there was no attempt "to defend or urge intermarriage." At the same time, the *Gazette* reported crimes and scandals involving interracial couples in a salacious and sensational manner. And whatever the local tradition of tolerance, *The Clansman* played at the Academy of Music on its "first

New England Tour" in 1909. Northampton's actual population of African Americans was very small in 1900: six-tenths of 1 percent. The city itself, while growing, was intimate enough that Alice and Channing would likely have been seen by family or friends.[40]

Although in Springfield the couple might have met with disapproval from both African American and white residents, their situation was perhaps less charged. Channing lived on the Hill, a neighborhood with a mix of ethnic and racial groups, not far from downtown. Springfield's relatively large black community may have tolerated this interracial relationship if not approved of it. There were other interracial couples and, after all, Channing did have an Irish wife, from whom he was separated. Indeed, his adultery with Alice might have elicited more comment than the fact that she was white. In one instance, Alice even masqueraded as Channing's wife Josephine. She had gone on an errand for Channing to Hubbard's restaurant, where he had once worked, and she spoke to the cook there: "He asked me if I was Mrs. L & I told him yes & he said he guess he met me once before so I laughed to myself." It is also possible that Alice might have been perceived as an African American woman with a very light complexion.[41]

The letters offer only faint clues of the familial opposition Alice faced as she pursued her romance with an African American man. For James Hanley, the affair must have been a bitter pill to swallow: his eldest daughter defied his authority and threatened his respectability, at a moment when James himself had become vulnerable. The fragile security the Hanleys had achieved received a blow in 1903 when Benjamin Blodgett "removed to Seattle" and left James Hanley without a job. In 1905 he mortgaged the Bright Avenue house to his son John and, although he continued to be listed in the Northampton directory, James moved back east to Newton, Massachusetts, where he worked for a widow as a coachman and lived in her boardinghouse. By 1909, as the automobile made his occupation increasingly anachronistic, James became a gardener. Until the mid-1910s, James spent much of his time physically apart from the family, returning mainly for visits. In this period, he seems to have suffered some kind of mental lapse that may have diminished his authority: Alice wrote that Kate went "to see pa twice one time he didn't know her or Maggie & the day she came home he seemed quite bright."[42]

Despite his absences, James Hanley tried to police the boundaries of acceptable sexual behavior and race relations. When he returned to Northampton, Alice was in some danger. Her father or both parents—her mother's role is unclear—intercepted Channing's letter when she "was too sick to be up & watch for it." On another occasion, she asked Channing to "write me a long letter *as I will get it myself*. You can put the money in the letter" [emphasis added]. When he was away, Alice was fearful that her father would hear about her from one of Channing's many acquaintances. "Papa is not in Brighton," she wrote. "He works in Newton but I don't want you [to] mention my name to any of them people out there because you know how easy news travels."[43]

James Hanley's anger and humiliation, barely visible in these private letters, are etched in the public records of property and probate. Several years after Alice and Channing broke off their relationship, James determined to provide homes for his children John and Katharine. After a series of transactions between father and son—taking out loans from each other and transferring deeds back and forth—John finally took permanent possession of the family home in 1919. That same year, James Hanley purchased a nearby property for Katharine and her husband, David Hoar, who together took out a mortgage from James for $1,900.[44] Alice, by then married and "respectable," received nothing from her father.

James's last will and testament similarly declares the split between father and daughter. Written five years after Alice's death, it divided his estate (worth over $7,000 in 1931) between his only living child, John, and his grandchildren, with one notable exception. After her relationship with Channing had ended, Alice married an Irish American man and soon thereafter adopted a son. James Hanley willed this grandson a token amount of five dollars, recognizing his legal existence but refusing to embrace him as a legitimate heir. Perhaps he could not view an adopted child as a "blood" relation, but that belief would likely have mixed with his ongoing fury over Alice's betrayal of the family's honor.[45]

James's frequent absences undoubtedly cleared the way for Alice to see Channing without harm to herself. It is striking that other family members knew about Alice's African American lover and apparently turned a blind eye on Alice's sexual transgressions. Alice's mother cooperated with her husband's efforts to intercept Channing's letters but otherwise indulged Alice. Alice's siblings did not shun her, nor did her aunt Mary, who may even have provided cover for her in Springfield. Alice at times impudently flaunted the affair: on Christmas, a day of religious observance and domestic celebration, Alice took samples of the family's turkey and cranberries to Channing.[46]

JUST as her letters screen out paternal opposition to their affair, Alice dodged matters of race when she wrote Channing. She said nothing about Channing being a black man or about her own racial identity. It may be that racial discourses of the time, particularly those that represented black male sexuality, were so powerfully rooted in the imagination that they needed no articulation. Yet a closer look at Alice's letters suggests it was the particulars of her life as a working-class woman that induced her to comprehend Channing as a lover and a man in ways that played down, even obscured, matters of race.

Alice used a language of endearment, not sexual pleasure, when writing to Channing. "When I hear you say 'dear' & 'sweet' you dont know what a feeling I have," she wrote. "It seems so good to be dear to some one." Addressing him as "dear friend," she closed letters conventionally, only once deviating from the formula "with love & lots of kisses" by noting, "only I wish they were the real ones." She described her love for Channing not as a sexual desire but as a transcendent friendship on which she could lean for aid and counsel: "outside of mamma you are my dearest friend on earth." The letters represent the couple's physical intimacy only obliquely, implied in terse comments, "I will call for my things Sunday evening" and "I will be over to see you as soon as your bed is fixed."[47]

At times she wrote of troubles besetting their relationship, but never named their source or content. Her letter of April 29, for example, reveals that Alice had done something grave and harmful. "I cant tell you how bad I feel about it but hereafter will do the right thing and then either of us wont have to worry." What this harm was, however, can only be imagined: a consequence of their sexual relations, a danger brought about by racist attitudes toward the interracial couple? About this, Alice was silent.

On only one occasion might Alice have addressed the interracial dimension of their relationship—when she discovered that she had become pregnant. When she reported her parents' interception of Channing's letters, she wrote: "And what harm if I was O.K. now but I know I am caught & the Dr. tells me so too." In this somewhat ambiguous passage, she suggests that interracial intimacy per se did not cost too high a social and psychological price, except for its possible reproductive consequences.[48] The comment raises a question about her parents' motives for the surveillance: Was the central issue Channing's racial identity? Alice's nonmarital sexuality? Or specifically the visible result of Alice's sexual behavior? Alice, at least, answered the question for herself: No "harm" if Alice was "O.K."; much if she was carrying a mixed-race, "illegitimate" baby.

Anguished, Alice told Channing, "I want to see you & see what I can do." She likely sought an abortion or hoped that Channing would divorce his wife and make her "respectable." If this was a pregnancy, what happened remains unclear. There is no official record in Massachusetts of Alice Hanley bearing a child. It is possible that Alice was attended by a midwife who did not file the paperwork; doctors were expensive and the local hospital did not admit people "suffering the results of a vicious life." More likely, she had an abortion or miscarriage, or the baby was stillborn.[49]

Hanley family lore tells that Alice had a baby who was "so dark everyone thought it was Italian." The comment has the ring of truth: for kin and friends in Alice's circle, sexual relationships between an African American man and an Irish American woman would have been so unimaginable that a "dark" baby could only be safely thought of as "Italian." We do not know when the birth occurred, whether the baby died or was given up for adoption. Still, it seems unlikely that this child resulted from the pregnancy reported in the letters. In the spring of 1908, a suit and dressmaker's fittings preoccupied Alice, an implausible concern if she were pregnant.[50]

Alice's worries about her health were ongoing and became a frame through which she viewed her attachment to and need for Channing. It is difficult to establish what ailed her. She may have been pregnant again in late July 1908: "I am going to see the Dr. about 2 oclock & I do hope he will help me," she wrote. "It is awful to be the way I am & no one cares & the only one in the world I am asking help from is you." She referred often to being "sick," a term used to describe any number of problems, including irregular menstrual periods, pregnancy-related difficulties, venereal disease, or conditions that were unrelated to gynecology at all.[51]

On a few occasions, being "sick" may have denoted the effects of Channing's verbal abuse or physical violence. On April 29 and again on May 4, she wrote about feeling sick—"you know what I mean"—and attributed it to "too much shaking up." In these letters, she chastised herself for causing them "worry," assured Channing "it will never happen again," and implied a dire threat: "You may think I was fooling but you certainly shook me up awfully." Alice Hanley described a wide range of physical problems, including a "very sore eye" and being "so lame I can hardly stir my arms." Like many Americans at this time, but especially poor women, she felt vulnerable to pregnancy and disease, to her body's disabilities, to her indigence and dependency: "to think just when sickness did come with all other troubles it is hard to think that is the time you have no one to turn to for help or even a dollar."[52]

Yet Alice Hanley was not "all worked up," as she put it, solely out of concern for her physical well-being. The discovery that she was "caught" brought her face to face with the morality of her behavior. If Alice spoke little of her transgression of socially defined racial codes, she repeatedly voiced her apprehension about sexual propriety and ethics. She pressed Channing to honor his commitment to her: "You always promised to stand by me if any thing happened & I guess it has so I hope to God you wont leave me now for I have no one to help me out of it only you for I went with no [one] else." She underscored Channing's obligation in moral and religious terms, observing that "there is a just God. & you have a conscience of your own."[53] Alice feared that Channing would leave her, a theme that runs throughout the letters. He frequently failed to appear when Alice expected him to, largely because of his work, but also, perhaps, because he felt conflicted about the relationship.

While holding Channing responsible for his obligations as a man and as an individual moral agent, Alice pondered her own sexual ethics. To be a "tramp" or to be "decent": these terms defined Alice's moral universe, a universe that encompassed most obviously gender identities, sexual behavior, and economic roles, but must also have resonated with the challenges racial difference brought to her relationship with Channing. Her sexual activity, she sensed acutely, was displayed in her appearance for all to see. In the letter about being "caught," she pointedly observed: "I look like a tramp too."[54]

WHAT social codes of morality and respectability shaped Alice Hanley's sexual ethics? How was female "decency" articulated and reinforced in a small rural city like Northampton? Alice's sibling Katharine offers an instructive counterpoint to the older sister who so violated social and sexual norms. Kate had followed one of the paths of economic mobility open to working-class Irish American women by going into office work. With weekly wages likely above seven dollars in 1908, she had money to spend on fashionable attire, the "new Copenhagen blue suit & hat" Alice so dearly coveted. Kate probably met her fiancé David Hoar at the tavern in the Hampshire House, where he tended bar. They married in 1909 and had a child the next year. Through her white-collar work, marriage, and well-bred appearance, Kate marked herself as a "decent," respectable woman.[55]

Northampton had an unusual way of acknowledging working-class women's virtue, rewarding it with a marriage gift. Smith Charities, established in 1848 to provide apprenticeships to indigent boys and girls and aid to widows, also awarded dowries of fifty dollars to respectable women "in indigent or moderate circumstances" upon marriage, for the purchase of furnishings for their new households. The organization required that applicants "sustain a good moral character" and that their fiancés be men "of sober and industrious habits." "The most popular benefit" of the charity, bridal gifts were awarded to 147 women in 1909, including, according to family legend, Katharine Hanley.[56]

It is tempting indeed to draw a distinct line between the two sisters, respectable Kate and sinful Alice. Certainly American society sharply etched these lines in its scrutiny of working-class women. At the local level, Northampton's press, schools, churches, and reform organizations magnified the divide between sexual virtue and vice, even when their aims were ostensibly focused elsewhere.

In the 1890s, when Alice and Kate were coming of age, wealthy and middle-class citizens of Northampton founded a variety of organizations to inoculate working-class youth against the temptations of public disorder and private immorality. The Young Men's Christian Association and Women's Christian Temperance Union sought self-control through exercise and abstinence. The White Cross Society, "recognizing the face of the sexual temptation upon every young man," urged men to stay pure, shun indecent language, and show respect for women.[57]

One of the most popular local institutions was the Home Culture Clubs. With its motto "the private home is the public hope," the organization embedded notions of proper sexual and social conduct in its wide range of activities. As devised by novelist and Northampton resident George Washington Cable in 1887, these were initially reading clubs in private dwellings. As the working-class population of Northampton swelled, it turned to settlement-house social work and eventually changed its name to the People's Institute. The organization involved many of the town's business and cultural leaders, including all of the Hanleys' employers in the 1890s.[58]

In the clubs, foreign-born adults learned English, math, and other subjects from Smith College students. Women took a range of classes in domestic science, dressmaking, shorthand, and physical culture. In 1897 a new clubhouse was built to compete with "objectionable dances," commercial amusements, and the attractions of the streets. At Saturday night "receptions," with as many as three hundred in attendance, "drinking, swearing, undue familiarity are not allowed." Hundreds of wage earners in factories, mills, and domestic service took advantage of these programs; two-thirds of the patrons were Catholic, and women greatly outnumbered men.[59]

For employers, fraternal organizations, and parish societies, wholesome recreation was both a symbol of young men and women's respectability and a means of safeguarding it until marriage. The Florence mill owners served up a fare of lectures, concerts, and chaperoned dances to their young factory operatives. The Father Mathew Society offered Catholic men a bowling alley and pool table as wholesome substitutes for the saloon, and opened a separate women's social room as well. Other Catholic lay organizations sponsored frequent lawn parties, church suppers, and outings: St. Joseph's Society hired special streetcars to take members to Marshall's Grove for a picnic, for instance, and St. Mary's Temperance, Abstinence, and Benevolent Association held a "watch social" one New Year's Eve. Whatever their nominal purposes, all of these activities socialized young men and women into behavior deemed moral and appropriate. According to historian Hasia Diner, despite an increase in mixed-sex activities, Irish Americans were "still committed to both gender boundaries and sexual prudery."[60]

Working-class women in Northampton had a complex relationship to these institutions. We know most about the "Florence girls" who worked in the brush factory and silk mills on the outskirts of Northampton and were akin to young working women throughout the United States. Before 1909, they toiled fifty-six to fifty-eight hours a week and earned on average seven or eight dollars for their labor. At night, said one, "our rooms or homes . . . must be cared for, our washing, ironing, and mending done." They relished the camaraderie of the mills, the pleasure of walking to work together, the "surreptitious lunches and forbidden chats with the girl across the table" when the foreman was not looking.[61]

Some identified strongly with the institutions of respectability, making time for self-improvement and church work. A Florence operative observed that the local "churches, the King's Daughters, and the temperance societies, all number among their best workers girls who, in common parlance, 'earn their own living.'" The working women at the Nonotuck Silk Mill even formed a club to read Shakespeare in their boardinghouse.[62]

Other Florence working women bore the directives and enticements toward "decency" with some skepticism. Many embraced the boisterous public behavior visible among working women in the nation's urban centers. They liked to stay out late at night, flirt with men, and spend money on clothes and a good time. The *Hampshire Gazette* occasionally reported stories of "our reckless young girls." In one account, two Florence women, standing on the brush shop bridge with their escorts late at night, called out to a passing carriage for a ride; the driver turned out to be their pastor, who delivered a sermon the following Sunday on the "night-strolling habit" of young girls. The *Gazette* delineated the popular local image of the Florence girls as clothes-crazy and gold-digging. "Their meditations have not been revealed," admitted the article, yet proceeded to imagine their musings about "what kind of a hat they should want for winter, or of the one whom they should eventually select to pay for the same."[63]

In their search for pleasure, working-class women apparently even duped the reformers at the Home Culture Clubs who were so intent on providing wholesome recreation. As a letter to the *Gazette* charged, they had discovered that club meetings "make an excellent excuse for the young misses to be away from home in company with boy friends until a late hour." The clubs had unwittingly become places "for meeting associates that they would not dare invite to their homes."[64]

Young working women negotiated standards of public deportment and sexual morality among their peers and families at a time when Americans in general were increasingly concerned and divided about what those standards should be. Popular culture promoted mixed messages about sexual and social mores. For weeks the *Gazette* closely followed the notorious upstate New York sex-and-murder trial upon which Theodore Dreiser based his novel *An American Tragedy*: Chester Gillette had been dating a young woman, Grace Brown, while courting a "society girl"; when Brown became pregnant and pleaded with him to "stand by her in her trouble," Gillette drowned her. The coverage warned upright readers against sexual immorality, but simultaneously offered a titillating tableau of desire, sensuality, and violence to those who scanned the newspaper's pages.[65]

Still, Northampton's residents affirmed and rewarded an ethics of propriety for "decent" unmarried working women, whereby they would be chaste, earn wages in a factory, home, or shop, and present themselves as virtuous through proper appearance and conduct. Northampton's institutions reinforced the sanctity of marriage and home life through domestic instruction, sermons, wholesome recreation, and bridal dowries. The press celebrated Protestant and Catholic weddings alike with detailed coverage of sumptuous receptions, exquisite bridal gowns, and "beautiful and substantial" gifts.[66]

At first glance, the picture of Katharine Hanley closely resembles the cultural model of the virtuous working woman. But she did not quite fit the image, so firmly fixed in middle-class culture, of the young bride given away by her father to her husband. Kate was already thirty-two, older than most working women who married; David Hoar was Kate's senior by fifteen years and although steadily employed, was a bartender who moved about frequently in his work. Despite church law and custom that marriages be held in the parish of the bride's family, Kate and David were married by a priest in New York City. The reason is a mystery: this might have been a romantic adventure or reflect a degree of parental opposition. For several years after they married, Kate continued to work and live in her family home in Northampton while her husband worked and boarded in Springfield.[67]

Unlike Smith College students or Northampton clubwomen who were secure in their respectability,[68] working-class women felt the question of their decency hovering around them. The margin of virtue between the Hanley sisters might have been little more than an accident of fate. Being born second of three children, having a gift for stenography, getting a good job from the first: this may have been all that was necessary for Kate to make of herself a "decent" woman. Alice Hanley could not apply for a bridal gift because, living in Springfield when she married in 1916, she did not reside in the counties covered by Smith Charities' mandate. We cannot know how she might have presented herself to the philanthropy's trustees as a respectable woman, marrying at the advanced age of forty. Had she lived in Northampton, her sexual reputation would likely have disqualified her.

Being pregnant outside marriage was, according to conventional notions of women's virtue, reason enough for Alice to castigate herself as a "tramp." In her letters, however, she suggests that female decency was not a permanent or inherent condition, but could be achieved, lost, and regained. Promising to reimburse Channing for all he had spent on her, she wrote, "never mind I wont always be one [a tramp] I hope." The term referred specifically in Alice's letters to the prostitute who, selling sex to make a living, represented the bottom reaches of dependency and degradation. Alice was more deeply humiliated by her lack of money than by her sexual behavior. On one occasion she "borrowed [her] fare from a little boy next door," only able to repay him when Channing sent her some money. She felt acute shame over her old and unfashionable clothing, piteously telling Channing, "perhaps you may think I dont feel it when I cant dress even half decent but indeed I do." Disgrace lay in the possibility that she had become and would be seen as a woman without any resources but her body.[69]

Thus Hanley voiced her relationship with Lewis simultaneously in the language of romantic love and in the currency of exchange. Tokens of affection were goods—in both senses of the word—that, in the face of economic and sexual vulnerability, allowed Alice to maintain a fragile sense of dignity in her own eyes and in the eyes of others. Without a job or financial resources of her own, she depended upon a married man for her well-being, but she could not transform dependency into respectability as Channing's legal wife. Whether wheedling money from Channing or demanding it, she simultaneously effaced the sexual-monetary exchange embedded in their relationship. An African American in a discriminatory labor market, Channing himself was vulnerable as a provider. At various times he lashed out at Alice, calling her a prostitute when she asked for too much. In response Alice held onto a notion of moral economy. "When you had plenty money you know what you gave me," she wrote. "How many times did I even pay my own fare?"[70]

In the face of behavior that defied social custom and religious teachings, Alice sought to render the illicit relationship normal, even sacred. Gift-giving bore the heavy burden of creating the binding covenant that could not be made through marriage.

ALICE thought she could achieve the respectability she coveted by clothing herself in it. She craved fashion with a passion seemingly equal to her feelings for Channing Lewis. Significantly, one of the few objects she preserved with her letters to Channing was an itemized list of clothing and accessories. Alice envied her sister Kate's attire, however she disingenuously skirted the issue: "it makes me feel bad not to look as good as she does for I know it pleases her."[71] The felt need to look "decent" and fashionable animated Alice in her relationship with Channing and brought her great joy and sorrow.

Over a number of weeks, the "drama of the suit" consumed Alice. As spring approached, the newspapers were filled with advertisements for the latest "Prince Chap" and "Panama Cutaway" suits, "fashionable large sailors," and smaller "so-called practical hats." She ordered a suit and hat in "Copenhagen blue" (in fashion that season), had an endless series of fittings, fretted over her accessories, and in letter after letter badgered Channing for the payments. The suit cost twelve dollars, a relatively low price in 1908. The more prestigious department stores in Springfield, like Forbes and Wallace, advertised ladies' suits with prices starting at fifteen dollars and rising to sixty. Still the garment must have cost Channing Lewis at least a week's wages.[72]

Advertisements for Easter suits, spring, 1908. *Daily Hampshire Gazette.*

Alice ordered the suit from a store in downtown Springfield, where twenty-seven establishments sold "ladies' cloaks and suits." She may have bought it at The Washington, a cheaper shop that advertised Easter suit "specials" ranging from $12.75 to $19.59. Alice often passed by the store, located on the corner of Main and State; Channing went to a dentist in the building; and she bought or pawned a watch from a jeweler-pawnbroker across the street.[73]

Department stores offered fashionable patterns, fabrics, and tailoring but were cheaper than going to a modiste. The dressmakers' trade had begun its decline as ready-to-wear fashions—with their looser styles and lower costs—began to compete for women's dollars. Alice insisted upon a well-tailored suit, returning several times to have it fitted. For women of her generation, "fit" was a subtle but legible sign of affluence and taste that ready-made could not convey. In an 1891 article, Northampton dressmakers stressed the importance of fit. "To my perfect fitting I owe my success and popularity," observed Madam Lloyd. "You cannot make a $5 suit and have it fit," warned Miss L. C. Knapp. "People who know a good fit know that they have to pay for it."[74] Alice was well aware of this principle.

As Easter approached, Alice worried that she still wore her winter hat. The hat was a particularly sensitive index of respectability and style. "Hats of enormous size," their large brims trimmed with ribbons, plumes, and birds' wings, were the rage in 1908. They certainly created quite an impression—and some commotion—in public. "Big hats in church hide the few men," announced one writer in the *Hampshire Gazette*, while another complained about "dodging under and over hat brims" while "travelling in crowded cars." This was precisely the kind of hat Alice coveted: "I think you are going to like . . . my hat as it is quite large & I think it is very stylish."[75]

Alice had a finely honed sense of the semiotics of style. At one point she complained, "I have my suit & like it real well but I have no gloves yet so cant wear it." The well-fitted, tailored suit, embellished with hat, stockings, pocketbook, and watch, conveyed a woman's "decency" and right to social participation, to friends and strangers alike.[76]

When finally dressed in the full ensemble, Alice had a transcendent moment: "If you knew what a different feeling I have when I am dressed like every one else. Really my heart raises & to night I was proud as a peacock going into Mary's & Louis." She reported her friends' comments: "Mary said 'My but your man keeps you dressed slick.[')] Charlie was there & he said Yes her man is O.K."[77] The suit bespoke Alice's respectability; ironically she wanted to be "dressed like everyone else," but she knew well that style distinguished her from the poor, from immigrants, from "tramps." The suit also registered Channing's masculine success as a breadwinner, which may have been particularly meaningful given the discrimination African American men faced in the labor market. His willingness—however grudging—to make good on the promised suit also made clear his commitment to her.

Yet Alice's attire was a flash point in their relationship. Ironically, the very clothes she desired for the decency they conveyed focused questions in Channing's mind about Alice's morality. He watched as Alice shopped for a hat, ordered a suit, and bought a timepiece on credit at breakneck speed. In less than a month, she had run up bills totaling more than thirty dollars. With millinery silks, toiletries, hose, and jewelry beckoning in the shops and advertisements, Alice's needs and wants seemed insatiable: "Some time when you can spare the money I saw a lovely skirt." Was Alice a gold-digger? The thought crossed Channing's mind. For stretches of time he chose not to write or send money to cover the dressmaker's bills and jeweler's payments, despite Alice's entreaties. "I have waited again in vain to day & no letter so I have now decided the trouble lies with you," Alice wrote. "Here it is going on three weeks since I saw you and you promised so faithfully to send me the money for my suit."[78]

In May 1908, when Alice wrote Channing that someone had broken into his apartment and taken a can of chicken, he accused her of unfaithfulness and prostitution while he was away. "You ask me who stayed up at the house with me," Alice wrote. "No one did. . . . Then you spoke of the hat I had on costing $8.00 as much as if I got it bad." Alice defended her honor: "Didn't I always have a nice hat. When I met you first I had a white hat I paid $17.00 for and it was mamma always gave me my hats."[79]

To confirm her own constancy and commitment, Alice plied Channing with small gifts and domestic services, offering him a comb and brush, seeing after his suits, and serving up edibles. One day she mailed a sandwich with her letter for his evening snack. Another time she brought a "box of nice things" containing the makings of a feast to Channing's apartment, only to find him gone. She left "a piece of bacon & pork 6 eggs & a can of milk in the pantry" and took the rest of the largesse—a "grand blue fish," "6 lamb chops, 12 more eggs, 2 more slices ham & a steak" to her aunt's. Given Alice's poverty and the retail price of these items—conservatively, about two dollars—they probably came from her brother John, employed at a meat and fish market.[80]

Most of all, she reported in exacting detail her efforts to make his apartment a home for the two of them. "I have just got my washing out & it looks nice and white," she wrote. "I washed the spread also the shams & bureau cover in our room so I am going to fix it up nice." Alice clearly took pride in her domestic labor and bristled at Channing's criticism of her laundering. Answering his accusations of sexual infidelity, she cataloged her domestic work as proof against the charge, a response she did not perceive as incommensurate with the allegation: "I have tried to do right & please you but it is no use. I blacked the stove & cleaned the nickel on it also the tea kettle & washed the wood work all around the sink & the towel rack."[81] For Alice, domestic labor, not contracted for but freely given, was the purview of and thus metonym for a wife, not a "tramp."

In the 1910 manuscript census schedule, one of the few official records of this relationship, Alice appeared as Channing's "housekeeper." It must have been a painful label for Alice, who wanted above all to call herself Channing's wife, a promise that Channing both held out and withheld. Occasionally she does so, signing herself "your devoted and intended," and one time, "your heartbroken wife."[82] That these words occurred together is no accident: Alice's use of the language of courtship and marriage coincided with a period of intensifying suspicion and recrimination on Channing's part.

In April 1908, when Channing landed a job as cook on a large-scale public works project, the moment filled the two with a new sense of possibility. "Write me at home & tell me all," Alice directed Channing, who had gone out to the camp at Mundale. Channing's sojourn there seems to have raised the stakes in their relationship. In light of his new job and perhaps her pregnancy,

Channing appears to have made a deeper level of commitment to Alice. He accepted her routine presence in his apartment and even entrusted her with the key. She increasingly carried out tasks on his behalf, for instance, meeting with a cook at Hubbard's restaurant, and handling the rent payment. She became part of a circle of Channing's neighbors and acquaintances—a mix of African American, Italian, and Irish working men and women—living near the Springfield armory. Most of all, Alice's thoughts turned toward creating a domestic life with Channing, as she fixed up the apartment with shelf paper, filled oil lamps, and planted seeds "so we can have flowers this summer."[83]

The circumstances of daily life cruelly conspired to betray these hopes. Alice's demands for money and her emotional neediness, Channing's withdrawal and distrust, spiraled in those months of separation. When Channing failed to write, Alice worried over the strength of his commitment. Although the *Springfield Republican* claimed women to be "an unknown quantity in this camp," Alice imagined prostitutes and sexual temptation at Mundale. "Now Chan I hope you will be true or are there any girls out there?" she asked. "Any '*French ones*'?"[84]

Each attempt Alice made to move toward her vision of domestic happiness was thwarted: by the burglary of Channing's apartment, by a neighbor's theft of the rent money, by her claims on Channing's income. She sought every opportunity to visit Channing at the Mundale construction site, but Channing, mindful of the risks to his job, put her off. "I knew you were uneasy about it so didnt say much," she wrote. By mid-June, Channing had left, or lost, his job. In a round of mutual recrimination, Channing called her a "tramp" and questioned her faithfulness, while Alice countered, "I am the one has reasons & not you." When Channing threatened to lock up the house, Alice, hurt and angry; returned the key. The turbulence culminated in an act of violence: "I know you have been good but I am afraid Chan you finished me that night you hit me." At home in Northampton, alone, she had "lots of time to think, think all the while." Did Alice see the irony in her situation, that her Irish father and black lover viewed her in similar ways, sharing a patriarchal anger and wish to govern her sexual and social life? She certainly realized with anguish and bewilderment that what gave her such pleasure—"you know my coming to your house was as natural for me as being home"—had provoked in him pain and anger. "I suppose you got tired of me coming so much," she reflected. "It is too bad it happened so but I will bear it all."[85]

ALICE articulated the practical difficulties and ethical dilemmas of her relationship in religious terms. How regular a participant Alice was in Catholic social and devotional life—whether, for instance, she belonged to a women's sodality or a "women's court" of the Ancient Order of Foresters—is unknown. But she did go to parochial school and apparently attended church. She was one of the throng at the funeral of Reverend Joseph Lynch, a young, athletic, and charismatic priest who died suddenly in May 1908.[86]

Alice also embraced certain religious teachings, including temperance. In Northampton's vigorous temperance movement in the late nineteenth century, such Catholic organizations as the Father Mathew Society and St. Mary's Society, the latter organized in Alice's church, were active and powerful. At one point Alice warned Channing that alcohol was sinful—"I hope you didnt drink anything for it would be wrong"—and impeded their chances to get ahead and be together. Temperance was a moral tenet, but it also encapsulated a set of attitudes about bodily well-being and social propriety. Whatever her commitment to the principle, in the same letter Alice yielded to another view of correct behavior, based on the sociability and mutuality of working-class culture. In celebration of her suit, Alice treated her friends to a pitcher of ale because "I didnt want them [to] think I was too cheap."[87]

Alice never explained directly how she reconciled her behavior with Catholic teachings on sexuality. The church hierarchy had little to say in these years about interracial relationships. A "mixed marriage" was, by definition, one between a Catholic and a non-Catholic. These the church opposed, warning of the "almost certain unhappiness awaiting the members of such unions." The church resolutely affirmed the sanctity of marriage and the evil of sexuality outside of it. Alice was not merely living with contradictions, she was living in sin.[88]

Alice's words may offer a few clues. When she laid bare her feelings, Alice often used a language of transcendent love that mimicked the dime novels and romance stories working-class women so avidly read. "I must be with you or I could not live," she wrote. "Dont think I am bluffing for once I love it is forever." And again, "I would be happy even in the woods with you if I only could see you every week or two." Nineteenth-century Irish American culture may have downplayed romantic love, but Alice and her peers had access to a wide range of cultural sources that celebrated it.[89]

At the same time, the repertoire of sentiments that course through Alice's letters had a religious inflection. In a statement at once formulaic and guileless, she imagined an afterlife together with Channing: "never to part until death & then after this wicked life I hope we will be together in heaven where there are no partings." If Catholic women in the latter part of the nineteenth century gained a "new freedom of religious expression," this "emotional devotionalism" may well have spilled over into the way some women understood their secular life.[90] The "wicked life" may refer specifically to her own violation of moral codes, but if she was following the teachings of her church, the statement would be inclusive, as true for those who appeared respectable as it was for herself. A woman who sinned in a "wicked" world, Alice seems nevertheless to have believed that love, fidelity, and devotion—the essence of her bond with Channing—would redeem the pair.

One lonely night in Channing's apartment, Alice read a book, "our 'Science of Life.'"[91] There are several works with this title. In 1870 Orson Squire Fowler wrote *Creative and Sexual Science*, also called *Science of Life*, a phrenological guide to sex and marriage; Robert Charles Hannon's *Science of Life and Power of Our Mind*, on mental healing, appeared in 1894. It is conceivable that Alice was reading one of these volumes: her letters offer no specific evidence of an orientation to phrenology or Christian Science, but Alice did complain frequently of physical ailments and mental uneasiness, went often to physicians, and may have turned to one of these books for guidance.

It seems more likely, however, that she was reading a book by that name written in 1904 by Pearl Mary Craigie, an Anglo-American novelist and dramatist. Addressing the problems of modernity, Craigie considered how individuals should live in a world of boundless energy, never-ending work, and new amusements and temptations. She wrote:

> Just as people never worked as they work now, they were never before so eager as they are at the present day to have luxuries and pleasures and enjoyments of every kind—and they are desperate, often without knowing it, because . . . they have this feeling . . . that if they do not get some prize here, and immediately to show for their pains, they may never get anything at all.

Craigie discussed young people whose romantic dreams clashed with the reality of life. Criticizing "sham refinement," she observed that true joy did not come from material possessions or the desire to advance beyond one's station. What then was happiness? "A good inherent in the soul, but the object that makes one happy is something outside the soul." Offering a gloss on Saint Thomas Aquinas, she reiterated, "we all have the capacity for happiness, but . . . we cannot, by ourselves, or unaided, be happy." Such happiness would come about, Craigie observed, not through large-scale social reforms, but rather through "attention to the individual."[92]

Whoever suggested she read the volume—a sibling, friend, perhaps a priest—knew the dilemmas of Alice Hanley's life. Dissatisfied with her station, absorbed with appearances, and often desperately lonely, Alice must have seen herself in Craigie's prose. Without directly attributing her thoughts to her reading *The Science of Life*, Alice goes on in the same letter to reflect upon its theme: "You know Chan that a great deal of my happiness depends on you as I know you were always ready to advise me & I think I would never be the same if I had lost your affection." Alice here restated Craigie's other-directed psychology that "you cannot have too much attention, too much care," but also imagined Channing's retort, grounded in a more Victorian view of human character: "I suppose you will say I am selfish, well perhaps I am." Alice must have considered this subject important: she composed a draft before writing this passage into her letter.[93]

ALICE imagined her future with Channing when she wrote about an omen, "something seems to be foreshown to me." Noting how "very lonesome" Channing was at the Mundale construction site, she reassured him, "I think we will be soon together forever." The actual portent, freedom from financial worry, dependency, and separation, was prosaic enough. "Perhaps after a while you could get a job some place where I could help you out even for my board & a little to help get things." Acknowledging the difficulties Channing faced in the workplace, she hoped that "perhaps some day you wont have to work like you are now." She dreamed of becoming "the proprietors of something ourself some day," a vision of small-scale ownership that permitted independence, family, and dignity to flourish. But the dream remained beyond their grasp.[94]

In the last letters, Alice's illnesses (and possibly the pregnancy), her poverty, and Channing's anger and suspicion lent a disillusioned and resentful note to her writing. Calling herself "cranky" and "nervous," Alice began to see her love almost as a mental disorder. "Oh Chan dont mind me for I know I have got to think so much of you I really think it has worked on my mind," she wrote. On several occasions she wrote about death, including a doggerel poem asking Channing to "remember me . . . when I am far above." In the summer of 1908, having returned to Northampton, she described a variety of painful symptoms, contemplated suicide (although it is difficult to say how seriously), and started to make a pillow for Channing as a token of remembrance. It may be that she was pregnant and nearing term. She now worked laundering clothes for people Channing knew. "I am so lame I can hardly stir my arms," she wrote, but "I must try & do something." Bitterly dwelling on Channing's accusations, she had set out to repay him: "Hope you are well & enjoying life while the *tramp* is gone[,] but never mind I wont always be one I hope."[95]

Although the letters cover barely thirteen months, Alice Hanley and Channing Lewis remained together for seven more years. She continued to live at home—or at least maintained that illusion—through 1912, but she spent much of her time in Springfield. In 1910 federal census takers recorded Alice Hanley both at her parents' house in Northampton and at Channing's apartment in Springfield. Stating her unhappiness when apart from Channing, Alice had conceded only one exception: "I do love to see mamma & know she is all right." In 1912 or 1913, Alice permanently "removed to Springfield." For a brief period she resided apart from Channing, who boarded

Along with the black silk stocking containing Alice Hanley's letters, other objects were found: a Catechism, an old shoe—traditionally placed inside household walls for good luck—and a catalog of modest cottage designs. Perhaps these hopes for a settled domestic life were bound up in her feelings for Channing Lewis. *Historic Northampton.*

with a relative, but from 1913 to 1915, they lived together in an apartment on Worthington Street.

These years were troubled ones for the Hanley family. James continued to work in Newton at least until 1913. John and his wife, Mary Scully Hanley, living at the Bright Avenue house, had problems early in their marriage: Mary petitioned the court in 1913 for custody of their son "as they are living apart" but the two reconciled not long after. Then Alice's mother, who had stayed at Bright Avenue as head of household, died on New Year's Day in 1914 "after a long illness." In 1916, James returned to the area, boarding with Katharine and David Hoar in Springfield.[96]

Whatever the depth of Alice's feelings for Channing—"once I love it is forever"—the two separated in 1916. Alice moved to a rooming house nearby where Thomas Brennan, a twenty-nine-year-old Irish American metal lather, also boarded. Soon thereafter the two married. Alice was now forty but, perhaps sensing an unseemliness in the marriage, they reported only a five-year age difference on the marriage license. No record reveals the nature of their union: whether, as the circumstances seem to suggest, she married on the rebound and he for convenience. Although they rented, Alice called herself a "rooming house proprietor" who presumably cooked, cleaned, and washed for boarders. In 1917, the Brennans adopted a son. Now a wife and mother, Alice achieved the form of what she had craved in her letters to Channing, but its substance eluded her. As the property and probate records indicate, Alice's father continued to shun her even after her marriage. Moreover, the pain, sickness, and gynecological problems Alice referred to in the letters probably continued through this time. In 1920 she was diagnosed with uterine cancer: a doctor began to attend her in the summer of that year, but she died in December. The contributory cause of death, the doctor noted, was exhaustion.[97]

Alice's obituary in the Springfield newspaper named her the "wife of Thomas F. Brennan." The Northampton paper, in contrast, identified Mrs. Thomas Brennan as "formerly Miss Alice Hanley of this city," survived by her father, brother, and sister, with no mention of Alice's husband or child. The funeral and Mass were held in Springfield, but she was buried in Northampton, in the family plot. Thomas Brennan waited the customary year of mourning before remarrying.[98] Alice Hanley slipped into the obscurity of history until the serendipitous discovery of her black lace stocking.

THIS may be a story of forbidden love, but it is a story framed in oddly conventional terms. As the color line was drawn more sharply, public discourses of the time cast intimacy between black men and white women as a perversion of the moral and social order. In terms of those discourses, Alice Hanley's transgressions were many, as she crossed racial boundaries, engaged in nonmarital sex, and defied the authority of her father. Seen by others, perhaps, as a "disorderly woman," Alice understood herself differently, her sins forgivable because her actions were dictated by love. We can see that for Alice, whatever questions interracial sexuality raised were deeply embedded, if not buried, in the particularities of working-class life for women. She was caught in webs of economic, familial, and psychological dependency, and she had few resources with which to extract herself from them. She felt acutely the cultural imperatives of female respectability and virtue. These considerations, and her transcendent love for Channing, were most palpable to her. Alice Hanley's letters, as difficult and ambiguous as they are, reveal some of the complex and unexpected ways people grasp and negotiate the ethical choices in sexual relationships culturally proscribed as taboo.

Notes

1. Twenty-seven letters from Alice Hanley to Channing Lewis [hereafter AH to CL], dated August 2, 1907 to August 17, 1908, and three letters from Mike Manning to Alice Hanley, November 25 to December 16, 1902, were found at 15 Bright Avenue, Northampton, and are in the possession of Pamela See.

2. Martha Elizabeth Hodes, "Sex across the Color Line: White Women and Black Men in the Nineteenth Century American South" (Ph.D. diss., Princeton University, 1991); Peggy Pascoe, "Race, Gender, and Intercultural Relations: The Case of Interracial Marriage," *Frontiers* 12, no. 1 (1991): 5–18. See also Paul R. Spickard, *Mixed Blood: Intermarriage and Ethnic Identity in Twentieth-Century America* (Madison, WI, 1989); John D'Emilio and Estelle Freedman, *Intimate Matters: A History of Sexuality in America* (New York, 1988).

3. Ida B. Wells-Barnett, *On Lynching* (1892; rpt., New York, 1969). For an example in a national women's magazine of the racist ideology Wells combatted, see Ellen Barret Ligon, "The White Woman and the Negro," *Good Housekeeping* (November 1903): 426–429.

4. Al-Tony Gilmore, "Jack Johnson and White Women: The National Impact," *Journal of Negro History* 58 (January 1973): 18–38 (quote on 32).

5. David H. Fowler, *Northern Attitudes towards Interracial Marriages: Legislation and Public Opinion in the Middle Atlantic and the States of the Old Northwest, 1780–1930 (*1963; New York, 1987), especially 215, 273–275, 285; Spickard, *Mixed Blood*, 272; Julius Drachsler, *Intermarriage in New York City*, Studies in History, Economics, and Public Law, No. 213 (New York, 1921), 43, 49–50; Olivier Zunz, *The Changing Face of Inequality: Urbanization, Industrial Development, and Immigrants in Detroit, 1880–1920* (Chicago, 1983), 245. On gay interracial interactions, see George Chauncey, *Gay New York: Gender, Urban Culture, and the Making of the Gay Male World, 1890–1940* (New York, 1994).

6. See, e.g., David Roediger, *The Wages of Whiteness* (New York, 1991); Graham Hodges, "'Desirable Companions and Lovers': Irish and African Americans in the Sixth Ward, 1830–1870," in Ron Bayor and Timothy Meagher, eds., *The New York Irish* (Baltimore, 1996).

7. Evelyn Brooks Higginbotham, "African-American Women's History and the Metalanguage of Race," *Signs* 17 (Winter 1992): 251–274.

8. This account is pieced together from public documents and Hanley family stories about their ancestors; these records are fragmentary and conflicting. See U.S. Bureau of the Census, *Ninth Census of the United States*, 1870, *Population Schedules*, Pittsfield, MA, 86; U.S. Bureau of the Census, *Twelfth Census of the United States*, 1900, *Population Schedules*, Northampton, MA, Enumeration District 630, sheet 3; Death certificate of James Hanley, May 23, 1931, Springfield City Clerk's Office. Interview with Teressia Hanley by Paul Gaffney, August 1993. No definitive information on James Hanley's emigration from Ireland has been found. The name Hanley, alternatively Handley or in Gaelic *Ohainle*, originated in Connacht, the western part of County Cork, one of the poorest regions in Ireland. See Edward Maclysaght, *Surnames of Ireland* (Dublin, 1988), 145.

Alice Ryan and her family are particularly obscure: Thomas Ryan, age twenty-five, is listed as boarding with John W. Hanley in the 1870 U.S. Census; Alice Ryan's father is also named Thomas. On the Hoosac Tunnel, see William Bond Wheelwright, *Life and Times of Alvah Crocker* (Boston, 1923).

9. Marriage Register, James Hanley and Alice Ryan, July 25, 1871, *Pittsfield Vital Statistics*, 3:2. *Pittsfield Directory for the Year* 1869 (Pittsfield, 1869), 55; *Pittsfield Directory*, 1873, 1875, and 1876; Death certificate of Alice M. Ryan Hanley, January 1, 1914, Northampton, Hampshire County; Frederick W. Beers, *County Atlas of Berkshire, Massachusetts* (New York, 1876); interview with James and Betty Hanley, June 27, 1994.

Records disagree on the age difference between Alice Ryan and James Hanley: their gravestone indicates a difference of two years; their marriage record five years. However, James Hanley's date of birth both in the 1900 U.S. Census and on his death certificate is 1854. If Alice Ryan was born in 1846, as the 1900 U.S. Census and marriage register indicate, their age difference would have been eight years. On marriage patterns among Irish immigrants, see Hasia Diner, *Erin's Daughters in America: Irish Immigrant Women in the Nineteenth Century* (Baltimore, 1983), 4–7, 46–51.

10. U.S. Bureau of the Census, *Tenth Census of the United States*, 1880, *Population Schedules*, Weston, MA, Enumeration District No. 383, 39; *Twelfth Census*, 1900, *Population Schedules*, Northampton; U.S. Bureau of the Census, *Thirteenth Census of the United States*, 1910, *Population Schedules*, Northampton, Enumeration District 695, sheet 3. Record of birth of Alice Hanley, August 25, 1875, Pittsfield, Berkshire County; Record of birth of Catherine [*sic*] Hanley, July 31, 1877, Weston, Middlesex County; F. W. Beers, *County Atlas of Middlesex County* (New York, 1875), 86. This essay spells Katharine Hanley's name as she did, although official records offer variant spellings.

11. Tercentenary History Committee, ed., *The Northampton Book* (Northampton, 1954); see especially Harold U. Faulkner, "How Our People Lived," 273–276, and Archibald V. Galbraith, "Industrial History: 1860–1900," 233–239; Phyllis Maud Freeman, "Industrial and Labor Developments in the City of Northampton, Massachusetts, 1898 to 1930" (M.A. thesis, Smith College, 1931); Massachusetts Bureau of Statistics of Labor, *Labor Bulletin* no. 16 (November 1900): 141; Charles J. Dean, "The Mills of Mill River" (1935), typescript in Forbes Library, Northampton; Albert H. Carpenter, "Northampton, Past and Present," *Western New England* 1, no. 11 (October 1911); *Daily Hampshire Gazette*, Tenth Anniversary Number, December 20, 1900. On the reform tradition, see Christopher Clark, *The Communitarian Moment: The Radical Challenge of the Northampton Association* (Ithaca, 1995).

12. Frederick D. Meehan, "The Growth and Development of the Parochial School System in Northampton, Massachusetts, 1891–1949" (M.A. thesis, Smith College, 1949), 3–4; Frederick Cusick, "The Irish: Their Settling Here Largely without Strife," *Daily Hampshire Gazette*, March 16, 1977.

13. John Francis Manfredi, "Immigration to Northampton," in Tercentenary History Committee, *Northampton Book*, 331–336; Massachusetts *Labor Bulletin* no. 21 (February 1902): 14–15. On tenements, see *Daily Hampshire Gazette*, Tenth Anniversary Number, December 20, 1900; Massachusetts Bureau of Labor Statistics, *Census of Massachusetts* 1895, 7 vols. (Boston, 1896), 4:601. On social conditions of the immigrant poor, see Chief of Police, *Twenty-fifth Annual Report*, in Northampton, *City Reports* (1908), 314; Northampton School Committee, *Twenty-fifth Annual Report* (Northampton, 1908); Overseers of the Poor of the City of Northampton,

Twenty-sixth Annual Report (Northampton, 1910); Lynn Slaughter, "The Impact of Immigration on the History of Northampton, Massachusetts" (1969), typescript in Forbes Library, 70, 75–78, 88–92. Reform efforts in Northampton are documented in the People's Institute Papers, Forbes Library, Northampton; Hampshire Regional Young Men's Christian Association Papers, Special Collections, University of Massachusetts at Amherst.

14. William W. Millett, "The Irish and Mobility Patterns in Northampton, Massachusetts, 1846–1888" (Ph.D. diss., University of Iowa, 1980), especially 162–171, 180–183, 207–213, 220–225, 274–279; Cusick, "The Irish"; Meehan, "Growth and Development," 15; Candice Conrad, "A Study of the Comparative Occupational Mobility of Five Ethnic Groups in Northampton, 1920–1962" (1969), typescript in Forbes Library. See also Katherine Ellen McCarthy, "Psychiatry in the Nineteenth Century: The Early Years of Northampton State Hospital" (Ph.D. diss., University of Pennsylvania, 1974), on the disproportionate confinement of the Irish as mental patients. For a call for religious tolerance, see *Daily Hampshire Gazette*, September 19, 1900.

15. Richard C. Garvey, "The Roman Catholic Church in Northampton" (n.d.), typescript in Forbes Library; Margaret Clifford Dwyer, *Centennial History of St. Mary of the Assumption Church, Northampton, Mass., 1866–1966* (South Hackensack, NJ, 1966); Virginia Corwin, "Religious Life in Northampton, 1800–1954," in Tercentenary History Committee, *Northampton Book*, 383–393; Meehan, "Growth and Development"; Millett, "Irish and Mobility Patterns," 259 n. 11; Slaughter, "Impact of Immigration," 116.

16. Dwyer, *Centennial History of St. Mary's; Daily Hampshire Gazette*, May 23, 1931; *Northampton and Easthampton Directory*, 1893–1894 (Northampton, 1892), 82.

17. Christopher Adams's listings in *Northampton Directory* for the years 1894 to 1898; *Daily Hampshire Gazette*, May 25, 1931. Michael J. Shea, ed., *A Century of Catholicism in Western Massachusetts* (Springfield, 1931), 270–271.

18. St. Michael's School, Northampton, Massachusetts, Register 1891–1904, Forbes Library. Millett, "Irish and Mobility Patterns," 216–217; Northampton School Committee, *Annual Report*, 1885–1886, quoted in Slaughter, "Impact of Immigration," 75.

19. Meehan, "Growth and Development," 20–22, 40.

20. On Blodgett, see *Dictionary of American Biography* (New York, 1929), 2:381–382; L. Clark Seelye, *The Early History of Smith College, 1871–1910* (Boston, 1923), 55–56. *Daily Hampshire Gazette*, May 3, 1881; July 26, 1893; Fifth Anniversary Supplement, November 30, 1895; April 30, 1904. *Atlas of the City of Northampton and Town of Easthampton* (Philadelphia, 1895); *Northampton and Easthampton Directory*, 1893–1894, 35.

21. *Pittsfield Directory*, 1873, 23, 50, 126; F. W. Beers, *County Atlas of Berkshire; St. Joseph's Parish Golden Jubilee*, 1849–1899, *Pittsfield, Mass. Souvenir* (c.1899); *Daily Hampshire Gazette*, July 26, 1893; *Newton Directory*, 1905, 278.

22. George Washington Cable, "The Home-Culture Clubs," *World's Work* 12 (October 1906): 8112.

23. Hampshire County Registry of Deeds, Book 498, May 5, 1897, 97–98; Book 498, May 6, 1897, 421–422. Mark T. Mason in Northampton and Easthampton

Directory, 1893–1894, 109; *Atlas of the City of Northampton*; Sanborn Map Company, Fire Insurance Maps, Northampton, 1884, 1889, 1895, Geography and Map Division, Library of Congress (microfilm ed., 1981).

24. *Twelfth Census*, 1900, *Population Schedules*, Northampton; *Thirteenth Census*, 1910, *Population Schedules*, Northampton; Katharine Hanley's listings in *Northampton Directory* for the years 1899 to 1910; St. Michael's School Register. On the mobility of second-generation Irish women, see Diner, *Erin's Daughters*, 77–98. For Boston wages, see Massachusetts *Labor Bulletin* no. 46 (February 1907): 77; no. 47 (March 1907): 164–165.

25. American International College, which holds the records of the Northampton Commercial College going back at least to 1902–1903, has no record for John or Katharine Hanley; before 1898; however, the commercial college offered only individual instruction and may not have kept transcripts. A Hanley descendant remembers John's diploma from the college. James and Betty Hanley interview; Roland F. Aubin to author, July 7, 1994; *250th Anniversary Guide and Business Directory* (Northampton, 1904), 15; *Northampton Directory*, 1896–1897, inside front cover; Meehan, "Growth and Development," 23.

26. Charles Forbes Warner, *Representative Families of Northampton: A Demonstration of What High Character, Good Ancestry and Heredity Have Accomplished in a New England Town*, vol. 1 (Northampton, 1917), 84–92; Home Culture Clubs, Board of Directors, Minutes 1896–1909, 1 vol., People's Institute Papers, see November 2, 1896. On women, office work, and secretarial training, see Sharon Hartman Strom, *Beyond the Typewriter: Gender, Class, and the Origins of Modern American Office Work* (Urbana, 1992); Walter Licht, *Getting Work: Philadelphia, 1840–1950* (Cambridge, 1992); and Ileen DeVault, *Sons and Daughters of Labor: Class and Clerical Work in Turn-of-the-Century Pittsburgh* (Ithaca, 1990).

27. Alice Hanley does not appear in the *Northampton Directory* for the years from 1893 to 1905; she is listed as "boarding" but without an occupation from 1906 to 1913. The 1900 to 1910 U.S Census list her in Northampton without an occupation. In her letter of April 29, 1908, she mentions that she "will go in & work to morrow & Sat.," apparently a casual or temporary job. By summer of 1908, she was earning some money washing clothes.

28. Figures calculated from *Census of Massachusetts*, 1895, 4:68–71, 578–583. See also Massachusetts Bureau of Labor Statistics, *Census of Massachusetts*, 1885, 3 vols. (Boston, 1885), vol. 1, part 2, 204–207; Massachusetts Bureau of Labor Statistics, *Census of Massachusetts*, 1905, 4 vols. (Boston, 1910), 2:207–209. Marjorie Ruzich Abel, "Profiles of Nineteenth-Century Working Women," *Historical Journal of Massachusetts* 14 (January 1986): 43–52. For a general discussion of Irish women's work, see Diner, *Erin's Daughters*.

29. AH to CL, May 17, 1908; May 6, 1908. James and Betty Hanley interview.

30. U.S. Bureau of the Census, *Tenth Census of the United States*, 1880, *Population Schedules*, Springfield, MA; U.S. Bureau of the Census, *Twelfth Census of the United States*, 1900, *Population Schedules*, Springfield, MA, Enumeration District 589, sheet 7. Records of birth of Grace C. Lewis, November 6, 1882, and Channing M. Lewis (son), March 4, 1884; Record of death of Amelia Peters Lewis, August 11, 1884, Book 1884, 71; Marriage record of Channing M. Lewis and Josephine Murphy, May 27, 1890, all in Springfield City Clerk's Office. Lewis appears in both Springfield

and Northampton in 1896–1897. *Springfield Directory* for the years 1896 to 1899 (Springfield, 1896–1899); *Northampton Directory* for the years 1896 to 1898.

31. *Springfield Directory* for the years 1902 and 1903.

32. Mike Manning to Alice Hanley, November 25, December 16, 1902; *Holyoke City Directory*, 1903 (Holyoke, 1903), 260.

33. An idea of Northampton's commercial culture can be gleaned from *Daily Hampshire Gazette* advertising and *Northampton Directory* business directories in these years. See also Tercentenary History Committee, *Northampton Book*.

34. *Daily Hampshire Gazette*, December 20, 1900; September 5, 1900. *Springfield Directory*, 1908, 777–778; Carpenter, "Northampton: Past and Present," 357. Persis Putnam, "The Trolley-Car Era: 1901–1918," in Tercentenary History Committee, *Northampton Book*, 305; Robert A. Young, "The Mount Tom Electric Railway," *Historical Journal of Massachusetts* 13 (January 1985): 43–44.

35. Chauncey, *Gay New York*, 257–267; Kathy Peiss, "Gender, Class, Race and the Geography of Urban Leisure" (paper presented at the Joint Hungarian-American Conference on New York and Budapest History, Hungarian Academy of Sciences, August 1988).

36. AH to CL, May 6, 1908; "City Items," *Daily Hampshire Gazette*, April 4, 1908; Hennessey Three Star Cigars advertisement, *Daily Hampshire Gazette*, January 27, 1906.

37. See David Hoar's and Channing Lewis's listings in *Northampton Directory*, 1907; *Springfield Directory* for the years 1896 to 1900, 1903, 1905. On Bartenders' Local #113 in Northampton, see Freeman, "Industrial and Labor Developments," 76, 81, 260. On the Nelson Hotel, see AH to CL, November 22, 1907; advertisement in *Springfield Directory*, 1902, 1053. Lewis's "connections" are suggested by the fact that he secured a job as cook to engineers and contractors overseeing a massive public works project, described in *Springfield Republican*, May 3, 1908; Pasquale A. Breglio, the contractor who supplied the unskilled labor for the project, was, not coincidentally, proprietor of a saloon and restaurant (*Springfield Directory*, 1905, 79).

38. AH to CL, August 2, 1907.

39. AH to CL, November 22, 1907; on Mary A. Ryan, see *Twelfth Census*, 1900, *Population Schedules*, Northampton; *Northampton Directory*, 1907, 158.

40. On the black population of Northampton, see Massachusetts *Labor Bulletin* no. 21 (February 1902): 14–15. *Daily Hampshire Gazette*, May 8, 1908; September 25, 1909; see also June 5, 1900; April 8, 1908; May 15, 1908.

41. AH to CL, June 1, 1908. "Lewis" listing in *Westfield Directory*, 1905 (Springfield, 1905).

42. AH to CL, August 17, 1908. Hampshire County Registry of Deeds, Book 595, April 25, 1905, 235–236; *Northampton Directory* for the years 1893 to 1923; *Newton Directory* (biannual), for the years 1905 to 1913, except 1907. *Thirteenth Census*, 1910, *Population Schedules*, Northampton, lists Alice Ryan Hanley as the head of household; James Hanley does not appear. On Blodgett's departure, see *Northampton Directory*, 1904; "Benjamin Colman Blodgett," *Dictionary of American Biography*.

43. AH to CL, December 19, 1907; May 6, 1908; May 25, 1908.

44. Hampshire County Registry of Deeds, Book 595, April 25, 1905, 235–236; Book 686, December 31, 1912, 424; Book 712, May 20, 1915, 449, 455, 461–462; Book 750, September 22, 1919, 189; Book 750, October 6, 1919, 443, 527.

45. On Alice's marriage, adoption of a son, and James's response, see Marriage record of Alice M. Hanley and Thomas F. Brennan, May 10, 1916, Springfield City Clerk's Office; Certificate of baptism and registrum of James Francis Brennan, September 16, 1923, Sacred Heart Church, Springfield; U.S. Bureau of the Census, *Fourteenth Census of the United States*, 1920, *Population Schedules*, Springfield, MA, Enumeration District 98, sheet 2; Will of James Hanley, December 26, 1925, and Probate Inventory, June 16, 1931, in Hampshire County Registry of Probate.

46. AH to CL, May 17, 1908; June 2, 1908; December 24, 1907.

47. AH to CL, June 1, 1908; May 19, 1908; May 17, 1908; August 2, 1907; April 27, 1908.

48. AH to CL, December 19, 1907. Although her language indicates that this was a pregnancy, it is possible that she had contracted venereal disease.

49. AH to CL, December 19, 1907. On working-class women and pregnancy, Judith Walzer Leavitt, personal communication, June 14, 1994. On hospital policy, see Cooley Dickinson Hospital, *Report of the Trustees* (Northampton, 1908). Also serving maternity cases in Northampton was "Mrs. Sparks' private hospital," but I have found no detailed information on it (*Daily Hampshire Gazette*, October 12, 1907).

50. James and Betty Hanley interview. Although the adoption records are closed, it does not appear that Alice adopted her own baby (which Channing fathered) in 1917. Recounting the family story, the Hanleys distinguished between the "dark" baby and the Brennan son, who is also listed as "white" in the 1920 Census Population Schedules.

51. AH to CL, July 20, 1908. On the meanings of the term "sick" in this period, Leavitt, personal communications.

52. AH to CL, April 10, 1908; August 17, 1908; June 28, 1908.

53. AH to CL, December 19, 1907.

54. AH to CL, December 19, 1907.

55. Katharine Hanley listings in *Northampton Directory* for the years 1901 to 1911; *Twelfth Census*, 1900, *Population Schedules*, Northampton; *Thirteenth Census*, 1910, *Population Schedules*, Northampton; marriage certificate of David John Hoar and Katharine Teresa Hanley, November 23, 1909, New York City. See also Diner, *Erin's Daughters*, 77–98.

56. Last Will and Testament of Oliver Smith, December 22, 1845; *Daily Hampshire Gazette*, April 30, 1907; Smith Charities, *Sixty-first Annual Report* (Northampton, 1909).

57. *Hampshire Gazette* [weekly], November 15, 1887; *Northampton Daily Herald*, February 4, 1894, clipping, in Annual Meeting Minutes, 1891–1917, YMCA Papers; *Daily Hampshire Gazette*, Fifth Anniversary Supplement, November 30, 1895.

58. See Philip Butcher, *George Washington Cable: The Northampton Years* (New York, 1959), 72–91; Cable, "The Home-Culture Clubs," 8110–8114. *Home Culture Club Letter*, 1893–1895; Home Culture Clubs [People's Institute], *Yearbook*, 1898–1910, in People's Institute Papers. *Hampshire Gazette* [weekly], February 15, 1887. In addition to Blodgett and Williston, who were founders, Edwin B. Emerson, John Hanley's first employer, was a donor and fund-raiser for the Home Culture Clubs.

59. Home Culture Clubs, *Yearbook*, 1900, 13; *Yearbook*, 1908–1909, 7–8; Cable, "Home-Culture Clubs," 8114; *Daily Hampshire Gazette*, November 27, 1899, clipping, in Home Culture Clubs, *Scrapbook*, 1889–1902, People's Institute Papers. On

Smith College students' involvement, see *Smith College Monthly*, June 1895, 24–26; Edith Brill, volume of letters, November 29, 1896, December 9, 1896, February 5, 1897, April 1, 1897, in Smith College Archives, Northampton.

60. Galbraith, "Industrial History," 238; *Daily Hampshire Gazette*, September 20, 1900, May 12, 1908; Diner, *Erin's Daughters*, 114.

61. *Home Culture Club Letter* 1 (January 1893): 1–3; *Home Culture Club Letter* 3 (October 1894): 1–3; Home Culture Club Letter 3 (November 1894): 2. Freeman, "Industrial and Labor Developments," 15, 28–37. For a view of "Florence girls" at a city celebration, see *The Meadow City's Quarter-Millennial Book* June 5–7, 1904 (Northampton, [ca. 1904]), 287, 261.

62. *Home Culture Club Letter* 1 (January 1893): 1. One People's Institute history suggests that working women had already been meeting in clubs when George Washington Cable decided to establish the organization. See "The People's Institute," 1942 typescript, box 7, folder 67, People's Institute Papers.

63. *Daily Hampshire Gazette*, September 19, 1900.

64. *Daily Hampshire Gazette*, June 2 and 6, 1899, clippings in Home Culture Clubs, *Scrapbook*.

65. *Daily Hampshire Gazette*, November 21 and 22, 1906.

66. See, e.g., Kiely-Ahearn wedding notice, *Daily Hampshire Gazette*, January 6, 1909.

67. Marriage certificate of David Hoar and Katharine Hanley. On Catholic church marriage requirements at this time, see Charles Herberman et al., eds., *The Catholic Encyclopedia*, 15 vols. (New York, 1908), 4:3.

68. My thanks to Maggie Lowe for this observation.

69. AH to CL, August 17, 1908; December 19, 1907; November 22, 1907. On working women and sexual morality, see Kathy Peiss, "'Charity Girls' and City Pleasures: Historical Notes on Working Class Sexuality, 1880–1920," in Ann Snitow et al., eds., *Powers of Desire: The Politics of Sexuality* (New York, 1983), 74–87.

70. AH to CL, December 19, 1907.

71. AH to CL, April 22, 1908.

72. Clothing advertisements, *Daily Hampshire Gazette*, April 1908; see especially April 3, 1908, 2. In 1907, weekly wages for cooks in Boston, likely higher than those in Springfield, ranged from five to seventeen dollars, with the average about eleven dollars: Massachusetts *Labor Bulletin* no. 46 (February 1907): 77.

73. There were also 310 dressmakers in Springfield. *Springfield Directory*, 1908, 633, 641–644.

74. "Among the Dressmakers," *Daily Hampshire Gazette*, June 12, 1891; "To Sew a Fine Seam: Northampton Dressmakers, 1880–1905," Historic Northampton exhibit, May 1993. Lynne Bassett provided useful information on local dressmakers, fashions, and prices in the period.

75. *Daily Hampshire Gazette*, December 31, 1908; January 8 and 9, 1909. AH to CL, May 25, 1908.

76. AH to CL, May 25, 1908; April 27, 1908, May 17, 1908. On the importance of dress to working-class women, see Diner, *Erin's Daughters*, 141; Christine Stansell, *City of Women* (New York, 1986); Kathy Peiss, *Cheap Amusements: Working Women and Leisure in Turn-of-the-Century New York* (Philadelphia, 1986), 56–87.

77. AH to CL, June 1, 1908.

78. AH to CL, May 17, 1908; May 15, 1908.

79. AH to CL, May 21, 1908.

80. AH to CL, December 24, 1907; April 10, 1908. "Retail Prices in Massachusetts for Articles of Household Consumption—October 1907," Massachusetts *Labor Bulletin* no. 55 (December 1907): 225–239, provides prices in various cities in the state, including Springfield.

81. AH to CL, April 29, 1908; May 21, 1908.

82. U.S. Bureau of the Census, *Thirteenth Census of the United States*, 1910, *Population Schedules*, Springfield, MA, Enumeration District 620, sheet 3; AH to CL, June 2, 1908; June 3, 1908.

83. AH to CL, April 10, 1908; June 2, 1908.

84. *Springfield Republican*, May 3, 1908; AH to CL, April 22, 1908. Although there may have been no "camp followers" at the Little River site, there was prostitution in the Springfield-Holyoke area. See Karen A. Terrell, "Exposure of Prostitution in Western Massachusetts: 1911," *Historical Journal of Massachusetts* 8 (June 1980): 3–11.

85. AH to CL, May 17, 1908; May 21, 1908; June 28, 1908.

86. AH to CL, May 15, 1908; *Daily Hampshire Gazette*, May 9, 1909. Interview with Margaret Clifford Dwyer by Paul Gaffney, March 4, 1994. On women in Catholic organizations, see Diner, *Erin's Daughters*, 120–137.

87. AH to CL, June 1, 1908. *Hampshire Gazette* [weekly], December 6, 1887; November 29, 1887; February 21, 1888. *Daily Hampshire Gazette*, March 19, 1907; May 31, 1907. Patrick F. McSweeney, "Old-Time Temperance Societies," *Catholic World* 62 (January 1896): 482–486. On saloon culture, see Roy Rosenzweig, *Eight Hours for What We Will* (Cambridge, 1983).

88. Joseph F. Doherty, *Moral Problems of Interracial Marriage* (Washington, 1949), 24–31. Herberman, *The Catholic Encyclopedia*, 9:698–699. See also Leslie Woodcock Tentler, "On the Margins: The State of American Catholic History," *American Quarterly* 45 (March 1993): 104–127.

89. AH to CL, June 1, 1908; May 21, 1908. On the deemphasis of romance in Irish culture, see Diner, *Erin's Daughters*, 23, 58. On romantic love in working women's culture, see Dorothy Richardson, *The Long Day* (1905), in William L. O'Neill, ed., *Women at Work*, (New York, 1972); Peiss, *Cheap Amusements*.

90. AH to CL, June 1, 1908. Tentler, "On the Margins," 116.

91. AH to CL, April 27, 1908.

92. Mrs. P[earl Mary] Craigie, *The Science of Life* (New York, 1904), 8–9, 66–67, 48–57.

93. AH to CL, April 27, 1908.

94. AH to CL, June 2, 1908; June 1, 1908.

95. AH to CL, July 20, 1908; August 17, 1908.

96. *Newton Directory*, 1913, and 1915; *Springfield Directory*, 1916. Hampshire County Registry of Probate, Box 374, September 23, 1913; Box 379, December 2, 1913. *Daily Hampshire Gazette*, January 1, 1914, 3.

97. *Fourteenth Census*, 1920, *Population Schedules*, Springfield; Marriage record of Alice Hanley and Thomas Brennan; Certificate of baptism of James Francis Brennan; Record of death of Alice Hanley, December 15, 1920, Springfield City Clerk's Office.

98. *Springfield Daily Republican*, December 15, 1920; *Daily Hampshire Gazette*, December 14, 1920; December 17, 1920. Certificate of marriage of Thomas Francis B[re]nnan and Alice Edith (Hosley) Way, December 21, 1921, Springfield.

20

By 1900, the majority of Northampton's residents were either recent immigrants or children of immigrants. This rapid influx of foreign-born mirrored the vast waves of immigrants who settled in America's urban centers. Like their counterparts nationwide, old stock Yankees in Northampton had mixed feelings about these changes. The popularity of Colonial Revival architecture during this period reflected a desire to embody traditional values in the face of the foreign and the modern. Elaborate historical pageants played out themes that enshrined the Puritan values of Northampton's early European settlers. But these symbolic representations avoided the inconvenience of actual hardship or conviction. This play-acting reassured participants of their place in civic affairs.

One such participant was a young attorney named Calvin Coolidge, whose political career owed much to these sentiments. A graduate of Amherst College, Coolidge came to practice law in Northampton in 1895. It was here that he met Grace Goodhue, a teacher of the deaf at the Clarke School. They were married in 1905. The Coolidges moved to Massasoit Street in 1906. There they raised two children. The modest two-family home remained their permanent residence until after Coolidge's return from the White House.

Although Coolidge lived simply, as the following essay argues he was not a simple man, but rather a Spartan soul who lived for politics. Coolidge held several Northampton offices, including mayor. He then served several terms in the legislature before becoming governor in 1919. Elected as Warren G. Harding's vice-president in 1920, Coolidge became president upon Harding's sudden death in 1923. At once, Coolidge became an icon. His dramatic swearing in took place by lantern light on his boyhood farm while his father, as justice of the peace, held the family Bible. But Coolidge was less a popular president than a reassuring one. His quirky Yankee ways were transformed by his campaign managers and their Madison Avenue consultants into old-fashioned virtues. Coolidge may have been born on a farm, but he never dirtied his hands at manual labor after he left the homestead, except to pose for photographers, a farmer's smock concealing the business suit underneath. Coolidge symbolized solidity in an era of national scandal and free-wheeling speculation. Though Pennsylvania Avenue may have been closer to Wall Street in the roaring twenties, it was comforting to have a president whose real home seemed to be a picture postcard of Main Street USA.

The Man Nobody Knew

*Bruce Barton and the Construction of Calvin Coolidge**

KERRY W. BUCKLEY

They can say all they want to about how President Coolidge—good old silent Cal Coolidge—isn't maybe as flashy as some of these statesmen. Maybe he isn't as much given to shooting off his mouth as certain other public figures that I could name. Maybe he isn't what my daughter would call so "Ritzy". . . He may not shoot off a lot of fireworks, but do you know what he is? He's SAFE.

Yes sir, Cal is the President for real honest-to-God Americans like us.

SINCLAIR LEWIS, *The Man Who Knew Coolidge*, 1928

BRUCE Barton and Calvin Coolidge are prominent features in the iconography of the 1920s. Accounts of that decade are likely to include, as standard fare, familiar caricatures: Barton, Madison Avenue huckster, booster of a vulgarized Christianity; and Coolidge, dour Vermonter, an accidental president whose laconic manner possessed a reassuring rustic simplicity, but belied a small-mindedness ill-equipped to deal with the complexities of modern life. There is, no doubt, more than an element of truth in these assessments. But to accept these stereotypes at face value is to risk perpetuating the myth of the twenties as a frivolous decade sandwiched between the high purpose of the Progressive Era and the seriousness of the Great Depression and to miss its significance as the epoch in which modernist America came of age.[1]

Few historians have taken Coolidge seriously as a political figure in the modern sense.[2] His administration has been characterized as lacking in leadership and initiative. Coolidge's career, wrote John D. Hicks, "was a shining example of what inertia could do for a man of patience." His apparent popularity has been explained in terms of the symbolic significance of his presidency. As a "puritan in Babylon," he seemed to those perplexed by the vast transformations in American society to stand for a simpler, more comprehensible America. Yet by the 1920s, symbols came, more and more, to be substituted for substance in American economic and political life.[3]

Nowhere was this more apparent than in the growth of advertising. By the 1920s, national advertising had come into its own, but most accounts place its advent in the political arena in the boomer economy of the 1950s. What has been little understood is the extent to which sophisticated marketing

* A version of this article appeared as Kerry W. Buckley, "A President for the Great Silent Majority: Bruce Barton's Construction of Calvin Coolidge," *New England Quarterly* (December 2003): 593–626.

strategies were in place at the highest levels of American politics in the 1920s. If one looks back to the decade after World War I, the Coolidge presidency seems almost quaint, innocent of the ballyhoo that swirled around it. Coolidge himself seems to belong to the previous century, a Vermont Yankee in the White House. But in fact, it was Bruce Barton, a popular inspirational writer and one of the greatest ad men of them all, who was responsible for creating and promoting the image that we have come to associate with Calvin Coolidge. Correspondingly, Coolidge has rarely been credited for being the shrewd player of insider politics that he was. He certainly grasped the possibilities afforded by new forms of mass communications that emerged during this period. Drawing upon the public relations expertise of professionals like Barton, Coolidge was instrumental in transforming the ceremonial role of the presidency into a vehicle of modern politics.[4]

The picture that emerges from a study of this relationship illuminates a fascinating chapter in the political history of the 1920s, but the larger issue that it suggests has to do with what Robert Westbrook has called "the commodification of American politics." In that sense, Coolidge and Barton's collaboration is illustrative of, as Westbrook has put it, the "connections between American consumer culture and the expansion of managerial power." In 1920, a war-weary nation chose Warren G. Harding, who promised a return to "normalcy," to be its president. But the politics of the '20s were not so much a reaction to Wilsonian progressivism, as they were a refinement, discarding the chaff of reformist rhetoric to reveal the hard kernel underneath: the drive for increasing precision and efficiency in management, productivity, and access to world markets and raw materials. Americans did not really want to return to the past but sought and were comforted by nostalgic talismans, the psychic salves that soothed adjustment to modernity. Advertisers were not long in recognizing these sentiments and appropriating those symbols that embodied them. Politicians soon followed, enlisting advertisers and eventually cadres of behavioral, motivational, and marketing experts as large financial interests gained control of party structure.[5] Although Barton and Coolidge were deeply ambivalent about the changes manifested by the emergence of an urban-centered, consumer-based mass society in the 1920s, they were both legitimizers and beneficiaries of this transformation. For if their concerns and anxieties mirrored those of Americans who felt their roles diminished by political and demographic change, they seemed to revitalize the old virtues only by recasting them as consumable products.

In 1919, Bruce Barton had formed his own advertising agency, Barton, Durstine and Osborn. An Amherst graduate, Barton had grown up in the genteel suburb of Oak Park, Illinois, where his father was an influential Congregational minister. But, like many Americans who came of age around the turn of the century, he struggled with conflicting impulses. He yearned for a more authentic existence exemplified by the rugged, self-reliant simplicity of an earlier America. Yet he was captivated by the glittering prospects of an emerging consumer culture.[6] After an initial period of indecision and self-doubt, Barton's flair for promotion led him into a career of public relations, writing, and editing. It was Barton who took *Collier's* moribund *Harvard Classics*—a repository of Western culture—and turned them into a commodity for self-advancement. "Let Dr. Eliot of Harvard," Barton urged, "give you the essentials of a liberal education in only 15 minutes a day."[7] As editor of *Every Week*, Barton honed a style of inspiration and uplift that proved to be enormously popular. By 1920, two collections of his editorials had been published. During World War I, Barton joined other advertisers who saw the war as an opportunity to dissipate the aroma of patent medicine that still clung to their industry by demonstrating their professionalism and effectiveness. Barton provided the Creel Committee with snappy screenplays for government propaganda films and coined the slogan: "A man may be down, but he is never out" for a successful Salvation Army fund drive.[8] The spectacular success of advertising in the war mobilization effort promised a bright future in promoting peacetime prosperity. It was at this time that he met his future partners, Roy Durstine and Alex Osborn, with whom he formed a new advertising agency in January 1919. When corporate financier Dwight Morrow and businessman Frank Stearns, Calvin Coolidge's Amherst classmates (and supporters), were looking for a public relations man to groom Coolidge for the 1920 nomination, Barton, who appeared to have fulfilled the promise of having been voted "Most Likely to Succeed" by the Amherst class of 1907, seemed a natural choice.

Before 1919, Calvin Coolidge was unknown outside of his adopted state of Massachusetts. Son of a Vermont storekeeper, Coolidge had graduated from Amherst in 1895. Settling in nearby Northampton, he read law in the local firm of an Amherst alumnus and studied for the bar. Coolidge was no less ambitious than Barton, but he almost literally never made a move without carefully considering the consequences. His decisions, even in trivial matters, were always calculated to precision. He was a man who knew how to avoid risks, but kept a keen eye for the main chance. He was also a dependable man. Reliability was his trademark as he rose through the ranks of the Republican Party. Coolidge behaved, and was hoisted up the ladder by the party blue-bloods who saw that their organization needed a bit of the common touch in order to compete with the more populist politics of the opposition.[9]

The Republican Party in the Massachusetts of Coolidge's day was a well-organized machine that worked on the "escalator" principle. One entered at the bottom and, if thought sufficiently dependable, slowly moved up. Party leadership was securely in the hands of the old Yankee aristocracy that occasionally promoted a "swamp Yankee" (one of old family, but no money) to high office in order to avoid the appearance of plutocracy. Coolidge's career advanced along these lines, partly because he was particularly adept at attracting the support of powerful mentors. As a young legislator, Coolidge benefited from the patronage of the western Massachusetts paper baron, Senator Winthrop Murray Crane. Later, he was more or less "adopted" by Frank Stearns, a Boston department store magnate and fellow Amherst alumnus. Stearns, ever seeking higher office for his protégé, never tired of promoting Coolidge. It was Stearns who poured money into Coolidge's campaigns and who enlisted other Amherst alumni like Dwight Morrow into the Coolidge camp.

As a partner in J. P. Morgan and Company, Morrow was at the center of a complex web of international finance and dollar diplomacy in the '20s. Along with his colleague Thomas Lamont, Morrow sought to stabilize long-term investment, especially in Europe, through government-sanctioned lending policies and to encourage unrestricted access to international markets. Suspicious of Herbert Hoover, this cohort of Wall Street investment bankers hoped to engineer the transfer of world financial leadership from London to New York. For this group, a return to "normalcy" meant that economic rather than political considerations should now determine the conduct of foreign affairs. Morrow saw Coolidge as one who would put no obstacles in their way. After Coolidge became governor in January 1919, Stearns and Morrow began to discuss ways to bring Coolidge to national attention. The publicity surrounding the Boston Police Strike later that year seemed to furnish just the opportunity they had been seeking.[10]

When members of the Boston police force walked off the job in September 1919, it was because their commissioner refused their right to affiliate with the American Federation of Labor. This was only part of a nationwide attempt of workers to recover from a precipitous drop in real wages due to a staggering 105 percent increase in the cost of living. But many Americans viewed the mounting labor unrest through the lens of the Red Scare of 1919 (nearing its peak that fall), which fanned deep fears of anarchy, Bolshevism, and terror. Governor Coolidge, with a weather eye out for the November elections, declined demands to intervene and kept aloof from the crisis at first, letting the mayor, a Democrat, bear the burden. After a night of violence and looting, the mayor found his bearings and ordered out the National Guard stationed in the city.

Only then did Coolidge act. By assuming command of the National Guard and issuing a strong proclamation, Coolidge, at one stroke, took center stage and relegated the mayor to the sidelines. Despite his apparent reticence, Coolidge possessed a keen sense of drama and political timing. He had seized the psychological moment, for he was lionized by the press as the defender of law, order, and as President Wilson put it, "of civilization." His now famous rebuke to an already defeated Samuel Gompers was hardly a spontaneous response, but was actually contained, along with other grandstanding remarks, in a lengthy telegram, that was simultaneously released to the press. The concept of the "soundbite" in television news certainly had its counterpart in print journalism of the pre-electronic era. Coolidge was a master of the aphorism, which he used to great effect. The excerpt that appeared in the headlines and editorial pages across the country ("There is no right to strike against the public safety by anybody, anywhere, any time.") made Coolidge's name a household word.[11]

Coolidge's victory in the November election was taken as a mandate for law and order, and his supporters were quick to press the advantage. Stearns and Morrow began to see wider political horizons for Coolidge. But they realized that today's headlines would fade from memory long before the 1920 Republican Convention, then eight distant months away. Morrow, ever sensitive to appearances, was especially concerned about Coolidge's public persona. In order for Coolidge to be considered as presidential material, he must be seen, Morrow ventured, in "a more human light."[12] Even among New Englanders Coolidge had developed a reputation for being cold, taciturn, and reclusive. In reality, he was a man charged with controlled emotion and extremely sensitive to the opinions of others. His bland exterior masked a consuming ambition. His entire life was marked by a single-minded devotion to politics and the advancement of his career. He had no other interests. The modest Northampton duplex, which he rented from the time he was a young lawyer until he retired from public life, was neither an indication of tightfistedness nor a mark of humility. He chose to live—not a *simple* life but a *Spartan* life. He was always prepared for battle.

Morrow turned to a man of proven ability—and loyalty—to cast a favorable light on some of Coolidge's more unflattering features. In November 1919, he wrote to Bruce Barton, asking for help to develop publicity, as he put it; "for our fellow Amherst man . . . up in Massachusetts."[13] Barton, with some misgivings, agreed to meet Coolidge in Boston. There he took the governor's measure. Predisposed to find Coolidge "repressed," Barton found himself surprised, and somewhat disarmed by a gracious and even relatively loquacious Calvin Coolidge. Coolidge, of course, was hardly a novice, but an old hand at dealing with the press. He could be "disarmingly friendly" at news conferences and habitually cultivated a generally approving press through frequent favors and courtesies.[14] Even his legendary reticence had its uses. When he chose, Coolidge acquired a peculiar strength from a flinty silence bereft of the usual social amenities. The hapless supplicant, desperately thrashing about for a hint of a response, soon became frustrated, then confused and eager to end the ordeal. On the other hand, Coolidge was a magnet for the powerful, which saw his silent manner as indicating a malleable personality. But Coolidge had learned the strength of keeping one's counsel. Upon the blank wall that he presented to his interviewers and favor seekers were projected their own opinions, longings, desires, and obsessions. Like Melville's character in *Bartleby the Scrivener*, Coolidge derived a perverse power from his apparent immutability.

Perhaps Barton saw in Coolidge a reflection of his own ambivalence about modern life: on the one hand, a nostalgic longing for a rural simplicity, on the other, a fascination with the dynamo of material progress. This was certainly a strain that ran throughout Barton's writing during his long association with Coolidge. Barton sensed the political potential of a Coolidge candidacy and became an intimate—as much as one could be—in the strategic circle that guided his career.

Warming to the immediate challenge of promoting Coolidge, Barton crafted an article for *Collier's* that appeared in November 1919, just weeks after his Boston interview and on the heels of Coolidge's gubernatorial election victory. It was the first feature story on Coolidge to appear in a national magazine. Barton's task, as he conceived it, was to introduce Coolidge as a political commodity, not through a discussion of issues, but through the presentation of a personality with whom Americans could identify. Certainly Coolidge had his liabilities, but through Barton's skillful handling they became not only assets, but also ennobling if not endearing qualities. Barton began by remarking that Calvin Coolidge was a nonentity before the Boston Police Strike, but since then, as he put it: "the very name inspired confidence." Like any good advertising man, Barton set great store by name recognition and brand appeal. "Calvin Coolidge," he remarked, "seems cut from granite: one could almost strike sparks with such a name, like a flint." Extending the metaphor, Barton dwelt at some length upon Coolidge's rural New England origins and ancient Yankee ancestry. This is a theme that Barton would expound upon again and again as Coolidge's principal image-maker. Certainly the nostalgic evocation of a bucolic simplicity appealed to Americans bewildered by the rapid pace of modern life. Barton's article is accompanied by a panoramic photograph of Coolidge behind a team of plow horses at his Vermont homestead. Superimposed on that homely scene is a modern portrait of the governor in business suit and soft collar—the efficient uniform for the modern executive. His roots may be in the country, the photograph seemed to say, but he resolutely faces the future.[15]

But beyond this obvious juxtaposition—a staple in American political iconography—is a more precise message for 1920 voters. An editorial commenting on Coolidge's election after the Boston Police Strike called it not only a victory of democratic over "soviet" government, but as Coolidge himself put it, the election signifies that "Massachusetts is American." Noting that Massachusetts is no longer a "Puritan State" and now had a "large foreign vote,"

Endless variations on the "farmer Coolidge" theme appeared in magazines and newspapers across the country. Posing for photographers in a farmer's smock, Calvin Coolidge, then governor of the most urban state in the Union, appeared to epitomize the rural Yankee of another century. In Bruce Barton's hands, Coolidge became a "contemporary forefather." For many voters, anxious about the future, nostalgic symbols seemed reassuring. *Historic Northampton.*

the editorial asserted that the Coolidge victory meant that Massachusetts voters are "Americans first."[16] As John Higham has pointed out, the Red Scare, then at its height, was but one aspect of a tide of nativism that continued to rise in the 1920s.[17] The enclaves of the recently arrived foreign born were feared as breeding grounds for anarchy and as a threat to the moral order. Coolidge's victory over "radicalism" in the police strike was also a victory over so-called hyphenate-America. Therefore, the portrait that Barton drew of Coolidge in that first article was doubly significant. Here was a man of unimpeachable ethnic credentials, the apotheosis of white Protestant culture. "There is no doubt," wrote Barton, "about his Yankee heritage."[18]

In a perceptive essay, "The Souls of White Folk," Walter Benn Michaels notes that Lothrop Stoddard, a contemporary popularizer of white supremacist theories, was fond of quoting Coolidge. One passage Stoddard admired read: "We have a great desire to be supremely American. That purpose we know we can accomplish by continuing the process which has made us Americans. We must search out and think the thoughts of those who established our institutions." The progressive attempt to assimilate the alien, replaced by the effort to exclude him, now resurfaced as a crusade to Americanize ethnic Americans.[19] If ethnicity itself, as some historians have argued, is not inherent but "a process of identification" constructed from a continuing dialogue between immigrant groups and the dominant society, Coolidge's remarks can be seen as an attempt to shape that dialogue and to define its content and thereby the conditions for assimilation.[20] He clearly recognized that the "desire to be supremely American" was a powerful motivator for those outside the mainstream. For Barton, a professional architect of desire, Coolidge came to embody the very idea of "American-ness," not only for those who clung to it, but also for those who aspired to it. Thus commodified, Coolidge could be promoted as an ethnic gatekeeper for white America. Lest anyone miss the point, Barton recounted a speech Coolidge made before a black audience. "He proceeded to point out to them . . . ," wrote Barton, "that the Anglo-Saxon race had been several centuries reaching its present position; and that the negro could not and must not expect in fifty years to cover that entire distance." These were "plain words," Barton admitted, but he maintained: "those who heard them liked [Coolidge] more than as if he had uttered merely sweetened platitudes." Thus Barton deftly couched Coolidge's low-keyed harangue as an example of plain speaking and candor. He was no demagogue, argued Barton, but a forthright man with "the disconcerting habit of telling the truth." It was a "truth" with which most white Americans would have agreed.[21]

In the turbulent period after the war, Americans were moving away from the idea of the "melting pot" which had served as a model of national identity in a more optimistic era. Instead, the notion of "Anglo-conformity" resurfaced as a life raft for those threatened by the flood of foreign-speaking immigrants and rural blacks to urban centers. Juxtaposed against this perception of modern life, Barton's picture of Coolidge was one that small-town white Americans, or those whose roots were rural, recognized and understood. Like Henry Ford, who collected and preserved entire buildings for his idealized nineteenth-century village in Dearborn and who encouraged folk music and square dances among his factory workers, Barton was a modernizer, an innovator who nevertheless feared the "acids of modernity" and who sought to revitalize the symbols of old Yankee culture in service to the New Era.[22]

By 1919, the reformist rhetoric of the progressives had been swallowed up by war propaganda. Wilson's lofty idealism seemed out of touch with postwar reality. But the anti-foreign hysteria that had been fanned by the Creel Committee still fueled the fears of the Red Scare, and Barton deftly cast Coolidge as the champion of the average citizen. "The great majority of Americans," Barton asserted, "are neither radicals nor reactionaries. They are middle-of-the-road folks who own their own homes and work hard, and would like to have the government get back to its old habits of meddling with their lives as little as possible." In words echoed in another election a half-century later in which a Republican candidate challenged a Democratic legacy of conflict abroad, social reform at home, and the specter of domestic radicalism, Barton distilled the essence of his message. "It sometimes seems as if this great *silent majority* had no spokesman," he wrote. "But Coolidge belongs with that crowd: he lives like them, he works like them, and understands." Thus, Coolidge's lack of social skills becomes humble virtue. Political expediency becomes patriotism. Platitudes become wisdom.[23]

Coolidge personally thanked Barton for his article and for his "kind interest."[24] But Barton had only just begun. He knew that Coolidge had to broaden his constituency, especially among a vast number of newly enfranchised women who would vote for a president for the first time in 1920. "Can you get the Governor," Barton wrote to Frank Stearns, "to send me a message to the women of the United States to be used in connection with this article [in the *Woman's Home Companion*]?" "The women have a special interest in what he did in Boston," Barton continued, "because they have more to lose even than the men if law and order break down in America." "I think," gushed Barton, "I can handle this in such a way as to make a million women feel that they have a special reason for being grateful to the Governor and for having a particular interest in him." Coolidge approved on the condition that Barton prepare the statement. "Let Barton prepare 200 words for women," Coolidge penciled across the bottom of the letter, "and submit to me." This was a role that Barton would play throughout the Coolidge presidency.[25]

Coolidge's ghostwritten "Message to Women" appeared as a full-page editorial in the *Woman's Home Companion* under a photograph of the Coolidge family posing stiffly around a Parcheesi board. The editorial praised what it called "the special gift of women to be able to divine a moral issue and respond to it." Women, it assured the reader, "are impatient of mere generalities; their test of a policy is not, 'is this expedient?' but, 'is it right?'" In an accompanying article in the same issue, Barton made it clear that Coolidge was a candidate who shared those sensibilities. Above all, he was a "spiritual leader" who "reached down beneath the material to something large, and unselfish, and eternal in men." Yet Barton was not above using the tried and true tricks of his trade. In words reminiscent of a cosmetics ad, he appealed to women as consumers. "We like novelties," he wrote, "especially do we like them in our public life." Americans were tired of the "same stuffed-shirt oratory . . . the same old exaggeration and distortion," he observed. "Only at rare intervals does something fresh and new and different break across the dull horizon." But this novelty was different indeed for it was, as Barton skillfully put it, the "old-fashioned characteristics of Coolidge" that made him "exceedingly refreshing in these ultra-modern times." For voters uncertain about the future, nostalgic about a now vanished past, Barton painted Coolidge as one who has "spent his whole life amid the traditions of the forefathers, and is himself a kind of an embodiment of those traditions, a kind of contemporary forefather."[!][26]

This conflation of opposites was classic Madison Avenue. In an era when the J. Walter Thompson Advertising Company's board of directors' suite was furnished in Colonial antiques, when "neo-colonial" was the style of choice in modern suburban housing developments, when Norman Rockwell's nostalgic illustrations began to grace the mass-produced covers of the *Saturday Evening Post*, the contradictory phrase "contemporary forefather" resonated with those ambivalent about the modern world around them. Barton's carefully crafted phrase is a prime example of advertising's role in accelerating what Jackson Lears has described as the "collapse of meaning" in American public life. Barton was drawing upon a style introduced by Albert Lasker ironically called "Reason Why" advertising. Dispensing with rational persuasion, this technique sought to create consumers by appealing to nonrational longings and desires. Words were merely tools in the business of making consumers and—as advertisers like Barton increasingly applied their skills to politics—making voters as well. In either case, the "public" no longer consisted of rational citizens, but irrational and therefore malleable consumers. When Barton employed the paradoxical phrase "contemporary forefather," he was using a strategy pioneered by legendary advertiser Claude Hopkins, whose technique of merging opposites associated products like factory-made furniture with "traditional craftsmanship" or canned goods with "old-fashioned cooking."[27]

Barton remarked to Coolidge that he believed his piece in the *Woman's Home Companion* to be "better" than the *Collier's* article, but this was just the beginning. Well connected in publishing circles, Barton boasted of his influence. "As soon as Mr. Stearns tells me what the program is to be," he wrote," I think I can do something in the *Outlook* and perhaps in one or two other places." Barton assured Coolidge that his interest was more than professional. "It is a real satisfaction," he confided, "to try to write where one can feel a real conviction." Coolidge was impressed. "You were able to do so much more," he wrote, "than I had any idea was possible."[28]

Barton plunged into the campaign. By the spring of 1920 he had become not only a publicist, but an advisor and strategist as well. Barton began to target specialized constituencies, writing pamphlets for nationwide distribution to teachers and leaflets for delegates to the Republican national convention.[29]

In the 1920 campaign, Bruce Barton carefully courted newly enfranchised women voters. Barton drafted an article under Calvin Coolidge's byline that appeared, accompanied by this homely scene, in the *Woman's Home Companion*. It is Grace Coolidge who smiles knowingly at the camera. Her husband sits in quiet approval while her sons, John and Calvin, Jr., look to her. *Historic Northampton.*

Frank Stearns had financed Houghton Mifflin's publication of a volume of Coolidge's speeches. Originally burdened with the title "Bay State Orations," the publisher managed to substitute *Have Faith in Massachusetts*, a phrase from one of the speeches. Barton assisted in the distribution of 65,000 of these books, often suggesting the wording of personal inscriptions from Coolidge to various well-placed individuals.[30] Where editorial interest flagged, Barton had ways of quickening it. The *Literary Digest* at first declined to include Coolidge in a series on presidential hopefuls. "We arranged, however," Barton wrote to Coolidge's secretary, "to have a number of letters sent to them from different parts of the country which impressed in their minds, apparently, that the Governor belonged in the series." This seemingly small victory was especially important to Barton. The piece, as he put it, would be published "at a psychological time." Barton ran a campaign finely tuned to create, manage, and sustain subtle impressions that could translate into votes.[31]

As Barton obtained precious national exposure for Coolidge, he shrewdly exploited his wide contacts for maximum effect. In a letter to Frank Stearns, for example, Barton described the interview he had arranged for Coolidge with *Leslie's Weekly*. He reminded Stearns that *Leslie's* circulation was over 500,000 and that "it has always been the organ of the business man and strongly inclined to the Republican Party." Barton had set the parameters of the interview in advance and outlined to Stearns the issues that Coolidge was to address. "Government extravagance" was a key topic. *Leslie's* publisher, coached Barton, "would like the Governor to say some pungent things on this subject." Above all, Barton as the architect of Coolidge's campaign strategy set the tone of the interview. He assured Stearns that the interviewer "understands that he will be talking to the Governor not as an avowed candidate for the Presidency but as a public man who has very definite thoughts on the problems of the hour."[32]

Barton and the other Coolidge campaigners had determined that the best strategy was to take advantage of the 'governor's natural disposition to remain aloof and above the fray, and to depict him as a hard-working public official unaffected by the lure of ambition, while they worked night and day for his nomination. As the well-financed campaigns of Hiram Johnson, General Leonard Wood, and Frank Lowden fought it out, the Coolidge camp hoped for a deadlocked convention where they might have a chance among the other dark horses: Nicholas Murray Butler, Herbert Hoover, and Warren G. Harding. Accordingly, Barton's article for *Outlook*, appearing a month before the convention was entitled "The Governor Who Stays on the Job."[33]

In June 1920, even as the convention delegates began to assemble in Chicago, the Coolidge campaign maintained the strategy of noncandidacy. Barton had been impressed with stories about Charles Evans Hughes that had appeared in the press shortly before his presidential nomination at the 1916 Republican convention. The stories described how Hughes took his usual walk in the park seemingly unconcerned that his political fate hung in the balance. Hoping to manage the same exposure for Coolidge, Barton wrote the 'governor's secretary. "If the Associated Press could carry such a story about the Governor either next Thursday or Friday morning," he argued, "it seems to me it might be very effective." First, Barton insisted, the reporter must be briefed on the governor's schedule: "seeing a delegation," Barton offered, "visiting a state hospital, pardoning some poor devil or what not." Then, Barton suggested, "the reporter might meet the Governor walking across the [Boston] Common to lunch and ask him a couple of questions. This would give the Governor a good chance to say a sentence or two in his own individual vein." Barton then instructed Coolidge's secretary to wire him in Chicago whether "proposition one" would be followed: wherein the Coolidge people in Boston would contact a "very friendly" AP man; or whether "proposition two" would be needed: in which case Barton would arrange for the Chicago AP to request the story. Barton was an innovator in transforming news into unpaid advertising by arranging events solely for the purpose of media coverage. By confining unpaid news coverage to such "pseudo-events," as Daniel Boorstin termed them, Barton was able to exercise a great deal of what today would be called "spin control" over the content of what appeared to be objective news reporting.[34]

Barton had sent his memorandum on the eve of his departure for the convention in Chicago. He and Morrow, he reported to Coolidge's secretary, were optimistic. Above all, he wrote, "it is such a *right* thing to have happen." Without a trace of irony, Barton closed by saying that Coolidge's nomination "would introduce a new era of simplicity and sincerity into our national life." Of course, with great skill and effort Barton was able to produce the *appearance* of simplicity and sincerity. Perhaps as Barton became more adapt at fusing appearances and reality, it became increasingly difficult for him to distinguish between the two.[35]

Barton, no doubt, saw his efforts to win over delegates in sharp contrast to the heavy-handed efforts of the party's old guard to control the nomination process. With a deadlocked convention and a little luck, however, he believed the Coolidge forces had an outside chance. Coolidge's prominence as a candidate, of course, was due to a very large degree to Barton's skillful public relations management. Even at the convention, Barton's campaigning continued. Each delegate was presented with a slim, leather-bound volume entitled *Law and Order*, containing speeches and proclamations designed to bolster Coolidge's anti-radical image. Each copy bore the delegate's gold-embossed name and was designed to fit neatly into a breast pocket. As the routine business and the interminable roll-calls droned on, desperate delegates across the convention floor could be seen thumbing through the little books in search of some distraction.

Their disaffection from the convention agenda was largely due to the fact that the actual decisions were being made off the floor. With Senator Henry Cabot Lodge as their spokesman, a small group of powerful senators held the balance of power at the convention. With an impasse almost inevitable, their backing of any successful dark horse would be essential. As the roll-call proceeded, it was clear that no one would gain a clear majority, and the convention looked to the relative strength of the dark horses for a compromise candidate. As their names were put into nomination, the endless parade of speeches began to have a numbing effect. Finally, about midpoint in the proceedings, Speaker of the House Frederick Gillett rose to place Coolidge's name before the convention. Coolidge had read early drafts of the speech, had fired off several telegrams suggesting last-minute changes, and finally had called Barton in for a last rewrite. Even so, Gillett received a polite, but hardly overwhelming response. There would be no bandwagon for a Coolidge presidency. After all, the convention delegates had their marching orders. They were waiting for a nod from the boys in the back room. When the convention adjourned late that night, attention shifted to the Blackstone Hotel and the legendary smoke-filled room where Harding's manager Harry Daugherty had predicted six months before that a president would be made. Lodge, a key player in the meeting, had made overtures toward Coolidge in late 1919 when the glow of the Police Strike still surrounded him. But Lodge had distanced himself from the Coolidge camp, partly because Coolidge's mentor Senator W. Murray Crane had bitterly opposed him in a platform fight on Lodge's *bête noire*: the League of Nations. Lodge also considered Coolidge to be beyond the pale of acceptable candidates. Nominate "a man who lives in a two-family house?" he once retorted, "Never!" Crane was more concerned with salvaging the League treaty than with promoting Coolidge, the result being that Coolidge had no one to speak for him among that small group of powerful senators, who were anxious to restore the party to the glory days of McKinley.

As Daugherty predicted, Harding became the man of the hour and when the convention assembled the next morning, the word quickly went out to the delegates, who fell into line and put over the nomination. All that remained was to nominate a candidate for vice-president. In a hastily assembled meeting beneath the convention platform, the same power brokers who had picked Harding now settled on Senator Irvine Lenroot of Wisconsin, whose progressive ties would balance the ticket. As Senator McCormick of Illinois put Lenroot's name in nomination, many delegates, sensing all was over, began to leave the convention, eager to make their train connections and avoid another night's stay in Chicago. But over the clash of falling chairs and the shuffle of feet, a small revolt was brewing. Shouts of "Coolidge" could be heard here and there. Finally the chair recognized a delegate he assumed would second Lenroot, but, to the astonishment of those of the old guard who remained, nominated Calvin Coolidge. A spontaneous demonstration ensued, and when the balloting was over, Coolidge had won overwhelmingly. For the first time since 1880 when the Republicans had nominated James A. Garfield, the delegates themselves, frustrated with the senatorial management of the nomination process, had broken ranks and taken control of the convention.[36]

That Coolidge was the beneficiary of this frustration was hardly accidental. Although Barton's strategy had not penetrated the inner circle of decision-makers, his message was not lost on the rank and file. It is no coincidence that the Oregon delegate who nominated Coolidge had received three copies of *Have Faith in Massachusetts*. Although no one noticed it at the time, Coolidge's nomination marked a transitional point in American politics. At one point in the convention, Uncle Joe Cannon made his farewell speech. The passing of Cannon, who connected the party to Lincoln's day, meant the end of an era. The party of James G. Blaine, Benjamin Harrison, Matthew

Quay, and William McKinley, of Mark Hanna and Nelson Aldrich was fading away. Though Lodge and the party bosses seemed to be in serene command in 1920, Barton's successful marketing of Coolidge signaled a fundamental change in the structure of American politics.[37]

Since the 1890s, as Robert Westbrook has pointed out, party politics in America had been on the decline. Professional and trade associations, labor unions and other bureaucracies increasingly became the vehicles for the pursuit of political interests. Simultaneously, progressive reforms had eroded party authority. As professional managers and planners had replaced political bosses, the spoils of patronage were wrested from partisan control. To win an election, a party could no longer simply mobilize an army of the faithful. Increasingly, political parties turned to more of what Richard Jensen has called a "merchandising" strategy. By the first decade of the twentieth century, national political campaigns were employing the services of "press agents," usually drawn from the ranks of ex-newspapermen. But it was World War I that demonstrated the effectiveness of mass advertising. By mobilizing public support for the war, advertisers gained new respect for their profession. As new forms of leisure and new styles of consumption competed for the public's attention, political parties began to draw more and more on advertisers' expertise. As a result, the first three decades of the century saw a gradual shift of power within the parties themselves, away from the political bosses and politicians to the businessmen and financiers who could raise the tremendous sums needed to mount a successful advertising campaign. Ultimately, this shift had the effect of commodifying the political process itself. Not only were political candidates "packaged" and marketed like any other product, but voters were no longer considered to be rational citizens, but merely groups of impulsive consumers deliverable as markets to those able to pay the price. As boundaries between the public arena of political discourse and the private sector of commercial advertising became less distinct, the social scientists who developed market research techniques to measure consumer preferences found a ready demand for their skills as political pollsters. Thus public opinion itself, in the jargon of these experts, became quantified and depoliticized.[38]

Barton's Coolidge campaign, with financial backing from Morrow and Stearns, is illustrative of this process. This alliance of money and expertise was able to bypass the party hierarchy and to create a viable Coolidge candidacy entirely through the mass media—without their candidate ever having to leave the state of Massachusetts. As Morrow explained to his colleague at J. P. Morgan, Thomas W. Lamont, all this was accomplished without having to dirty one's hands with the usual way of doing business in politics. "The campaign has been so purely an educational one which could stand the strictest investigation," Morrow wrote, "because no money whatever has been spent except in the very modest publicity that has been carried on. The work has all been done by volunteers and the money has been subscribed by Coolidge's Amherst friends." Though the funds may have been modest by Morgan standards, the Coolidge war chest was not insubstantial. But the beauty of this arrangement, from Morrow's viewpoint, was that a well-managed public relations campaign using mass advertising techniques could target specific audiences, making efficient use of funds on behalf of a small group of powerful backers.[39]

Stearns, a mass retailer, and Morrow, a corporate financier, were men who represented the emergence of a new managerial elite: engineers of a growing consumer economy in America and agents of economic expansion abroad. Naturally they turned to a professional like Barton, a specialist in the business of marketing and promotion. These men represented a constituency that saw Coolidge as a new kind of politician—an administrator, a civil servant whose policies would be guided neither by the democratic mass nor by political bosses, but by the advice and counsel of those like themselves, corporate managers of the nation's wealth. Though they were the shapers of modernist America, they liked to think of themselves, and to have others regard them, as revitalizers of ancient truths. "Don't hesitate to be as revolutionary as science," wrote Coolidge in one of Barton's favorite quotations, or, he continued, " . . . as reactionary as the multiplication table." Above all, the Coolidge image projected stability and predictability—reassuring qualities for the anxious investor. As Morrow observed to Thomas Lamont: "I think what America needs more than anything else is a man who will *in himself* be a demonstration of character."[40] Like the Beaux-Arts facade of a Main Street bank in the 1920s, Coolidge symbolized solidity in an era of freewheeling speculation.

Barton's association with the Coolidge campaign did not end with the vice-presidential nomination. Indeed he worked intimately with party chairman Will Hays and advertiser Albert Lasker to promote the national ticket. For Coolidge, Barton coined the slogan: "A man with a vision but not a visionary,"—a clever swipe at Wilsonian reformers. He also authored a pamphlet titled, ironically as it turned out, "Where does Senator Harding Stand on the Moral Issues?" for the Republican National Committee. Barton, however, was looking ahead. He made it clear to Coolidge that he considered his work to be merely laying the foundation for an inevitable campaign for the presidency. "We have decided to keep the [Coolidge] committee together," he wrote the governor shortly after the convention. "We think it has important work to do four years or eight years from now.[41]

After the Republican victory in November, Barton continued his association with Coolidge, occasionally writing speeches for the vice-president. But in August 1923, only three years later, Harding's sudden death made Calvin

Coolidge the thirtieth president of the United States. Coolidge assumed office amid great uncertainty. The whispers of scandal in the Harding administration were growing louder. Coolidge himself seemed reclusive and enigmatic. The public needed reassurance. Barton was immediately summoned and before the month was out, a major article appeared in a national periodical. Recycling many of the themes from the 1920 campaign, Barton added a few new twists. Shrewdly comparing Coolidge with Theodore Roosevelt, he assured his readers that time will prove that he was "no accident," but had indeed arrived where he belonged. Coolidge would reward the trust of the American people with, as he put it, "the fulfillment of their faith."[42] This was the classic Barton style. In an increasingly secular society, whole ranges of products from toothpaste to political candidates were portrayed as being able to satisfy intense private longings. Barton, a master of this technique, put his considerable gifts and influence at the disposal of the Coolidge White House. Over the next five years, and even beyond, Barton was to be the principal architect of the Coolidge image for the American people.

Scarcely two months after Coolidge's swearing-in, Barton was laying the groundwork for the 1924 campaign. With the assistance of Edward Bok, editor of the *Ladies' Home Journal*, Barton arranged for a grateful Maxwell Perkins, Scribner's legendary editor, to produce a volume of Coolidge's speeches. By March, Barton was working closely with Perkins on marketing and promotion and had placed advance copies of the book, entitled *The Price of Freedom*, in the hands of influential editors and potential campaign contributors.[43] His moment had finally arrived.

The 1924 Republican convention signaled a dramatic shift in the balance of power within the Republican Party. A new business elite had sponsored the Coolidge ascendancy: the financiers, the bankers, the corporate managers, and "new era" industrialists. Since taking office, Coolidge had quietly dismantled the old party structure dominated by bosses and politicians and had replaced them with those in whose interests they actually served. Even the setting of the convention conveyed the transformation. Gone were the billowing bunting and the carnival atmosphere of former years. The businesslike proceedings took place in Cleveland's modern civic auditorium whose vast utilitarian interior dwarfed the assembly of mere mortals below. The muted colors of the hall reflected the restrained tone of the Coolidge administration itself. Perhaps symbolic of this change was the fact that Senator Henry Cabot Lodge, a kingmaker in 1920, was virtually ignored in 1924. Chairing the convention was William M. Butler, a Massachusetts industrialist who was to become national party chairman. Lodge, whom William Allen White characterized as a "mediator of Mammon," had been deposed. Mammon itself had seized the throne.[44]

The 1924 election was also a watershed in American politics. It marked the emergence of new mass media technologies that would change both the form and content of the modern political message. With Coolidge duly nominated at the Republican convention in June and the Democratic slate selected in early July, Barton drafted a detailed campaign strategy for the Republican National Committee that took full advantage of these new developments. The president should avoid generalities and abstractions in his speeches, he recommended. "Issues are dull reading," warned Barton. Coolidge needed more of the anecdote and the homely illustration to reach the average voter. In particular, he stressed, new technologies were making not only old oratorical styles, but also old political strategies obsolete. "The radio," Barton pointed out, "has made possible an entirely new type of campaign." Barton explained what Franklin D. Roosevelt was to discover so spectacularly almost a decade later: "It enables the President," he wrote, "to sit by every fireside and talk in terms of that home's interest and prosperity. LaFollette will roar," Barton continued, "and the Democrat will pound his stuffed shirt. But if the President will only talk to the folks (not address them) he will re-elect himself." Barton advised the president to avoid the mistakes made by those unaccustomed to the new technology. "The radio audience is very different from the assembled crowd," he cautioned. "To the crowd you must reiterate; the radio audience tires quickly and can walk out on you without your knowing it." Barton understood very clearly the importance of tailoring one's political message to the contours of the new electronic media. That strategy proved to be very effective. Some historians have characterized the 1924 campaign as "the Radio election." By 1924, radio had outgrown its experimental stage and had established itself as a fledgling industry. Yet it was still controlled largely by electronics and telephone manufacturers and needed some event of great moment to demonstrate its significance as a national medium. When the political conventions and speeches of 1924 were broadcast coast-to-coast, the technological feasibility of a national network hookup was established for the first time. Sales of radio receivers boomed, and a new and powerful industry began. That Coolidge was the first president to make effective use of the new technology was due largely to Barton's understanding of its potential to communicate, not ideas, but personalities. Part of Coolidge's success, no doubt, was due to the novelty of the medium. Radio, through scientific wizardry, could bring the president himself into the living rooms and kitchens of millions of Americans. But once there, he was to act neighborly, not pretentiously. As Barton explained it: "'I,' the President, talking to 'you', Bill Jones, about the way the government affects your life, is something new and startling."[45]

As an advertising strategist, Barton tuned his messages both to shape and to reflect the growing culture of consumption in America. He sensed that traditional political party structures no longer reflected economic and demographic realities. His blueprint for the 1924 campaign called for abandoning the door-to-door pamphleteering of past elections. This method was wasteful and ineffective, argued Barton, its "principal value" being "to give the workers some work." The old military style of campaign organization was going the way of the torchlight parade. Even an army of party workers could no longer have the same effect on an increasingly diverse mass society as strategically targeted advertising. The party should adopt centralized planning and concentrate its resources only on "the doubtful states," he urged. "Obviously not in Massachusetts (which is won anyway)," he advised, "nor in Georgia (which is lost anyway)." Above all, he counseled, "the advertising copy should be very brief and very specific. We might as well recognize frankly that we have nothing to sell but Calvin Coolidge." In the wake of Teapot Dome and the scandals of the Ohio Gang, Barton warned, "the grand old buncombe of other years will not get one single vote this Fall." Steering clear of the partisan style and obscuring issues, Barton carefully crafted a campaign of personality.[46]

In early August, Barton added further refinements to the Republican battle plan. "All these campaigns run the same course," he explained: "high confidence in August, and deep gloom and apprehension in September and October. I see no reason to think that this one will be any different." Therefore, he argued, an up-to-date campaign must be run on sound managerial principles. "Advertising has to be planned far in advance to be economical and effective," Barton urged. But, above all else, professionals skilled in promoting products to a mass market must execute it. "Most political advertising of the past," he lamented, "has been mere Harrah stuff which no advertising man would endorse as of any value." In the new era of the 1920s, successful promotion substituted style for substance. Advertisers had helped create a new consumer economy where product designs, a change of product color, or even new packaging created sales that depended upon satisfying the wish fulfillment of the consumer. Image was all-important. "This is not going to be a party campaign in the old sense," Barton predicted. "I have not met anybody who is going to vote for the Republican Party. They are going to vote 'for Coolidge' or against him." Coolidge's chief liability, Barton believed, was his negative image among some voters. It was his lack of "human appeal," that Barton set out to remedy. One of his suggestions was liberal use of testimonial advertising, a technique pioneered for cosmetics products. A parade of ordinary folks would give eloquent testimony to Coolidge's common touch. With such a plan, enthused Barton, "we will build up a wonderful Coolidge legend in the country [!]" Legend indeed. As an advertising man, Barton drove his point home. "Emotions affect votes much more than logic," he concluded, "I am sure of the soundness of this plan."[47] At the end of the nineteenth century, educational campaigns with their endless streams of pamphlets had eclipsed partisan parades and spectacles, but the politics of personality had become a central feature of political strategy by the 1920s.

Barton's campaign of upbeat Coolidge imagery, however, was coupled with a coolly calculated negative strategy. As Labor Day approached, Barton drafted a campaign ad designed to play on the uncertainties and insecurities of voters. "We must convey a little worry," he explained to the Republican National Committee, "whether we honestly feel it or not." With John W. Davis the standard bearer of a deeply divided Democratic Party and Robert La Follette's formation of a third party around a progressive coalition, Barton raised the specter of an election thrown into the House of Representatives. He then planted cold fear in the hearts of conservatives by suggesting a scenario whereby the Democratic vice-presidential nominee, Charles Bryan (brother of William Jennings Bryan), could become president. "Bryanism," he wrote stood for "reaction against sound business and in favor of unsound business, government ownership, and patent medicine economics." Barton explained to his Republican colleagues that he was merely following "the Napoleonic maxim—the best way to fight a defensive battle is to attack. We are having the opprobrium of 'reaction' hung on us all the time," he complained, "Let's step out and hang it on our opponents." For LaFollette, the Republicans revived the rhetoric of the Red Scare. His supporters were depicted as, at best, radicals, probably socialists, and very possibly Bolshevist agents. Negative campaigning certainly did not begin with Bruce Barton, but he helped bring primitive mud slinging into the era of strategic political warfare.[48]

With the decisive Coolidge victory in November, Barton became a White House intimate and a key public relations strategist for the Coolidge administration. While this relationship was unofficial, that very informality proved mutually advantageous for Barton and Coolidge. Barton's highly visible White House connection gave him enormous cachet in the advertising world, bringing clients who hoped to benefit by the association to Barton, Durstine and Osborn. On the other hand, Barton not only functioned as an intermediary to the press, but—as one who served powerful financial interests—he was able to alert the White House to occasions where a timely favor would reap great rewards. He helped bring the Hearst papers, for instance, into the Coolidge camp, guided lobbyists to the Oval Office, and arranged for the president to write personal messages to selected individuals. Barton also contributed material for presidential speeches and continued to function as Coolidge's personal literary agent, negotiating additional book contracts, and arranging the most lucrative syndication rights upon the president's retirement from office.[49]

Coolidge himself was well aware of the public relations dimension of his ceremonial role as chief executive. Few have been willing to go to the lengths

Although Calvin Coolidge does not quite wrap himself in the flag, this iconic photograph succeeds in juxtaposing both images symbolically. He is shown here before the modest duplex apartment that was his home throughout his public life. Though sometimes attributed to tightfistedness or humility, Coolidge's choice of abode reflected a desire to lead not a simple life, but a Spartan life. He was always prepared for battle. *Historic Northampton.*

Coolidge routinely went to in order to please photographers. They soon learned that the president would strike any pose, don any costume—no matter how ridiculous—and endure any humiliation in order to satisfy the press's insatiable demand for novelty. It was an inside joke among the press corps. Newsreel photographers marveled at Coolidge's accessibility and made the president's image ubiquitous in darkened theaters on Main Streets all across America. But Coolidge understood the power of the visual image to affect millions of people simultaneously. If the president wearing a cowboy outfit could make a nation smile or cheer, or even feel superior, that image was worth far more at the polls than a month of exhausting stump speeches.[50]

Coolidge was far more selective with journalists, however. Although he routinely answered written queries at regularly scheduled press conferences, direct attribution was forbidden. It was Barton, therefore, who came to be Coolidge's principal interpreter and the author of the only interview with the president published during his term of office. In 1926, with the prospect of a 1928 candidacy still not ruled out, Barton, the White House, and the Associated Press conspired to bring about a sensational public relations coup. A plan was hatched whereby Barton would conduct an exclusive interview with the president. It would reveal intimate details of Coolidge's private life and career and focus on the president's personal views on issues of general interest. It was designed to counter the persistent impression of a cold, dispassionate Coolidge. Such an article would, as Associated Press chief Kent Cooper explained to the president, "adequately portray for the first time the sterling human side of a man who has been too deeply engrossed in matters of transcendent importance to give the public time to know him in any other way than as the nation's executive." It was agreed that Barton would, for the first time, quote the president directly with the understanding that he would use artistic license and his copywriting expertise to frame Coolidge's utterances in the most flattering manner. In order to give the interview an aura of casual happenstance, the Barton's were invited to be the guests of the president at his summer retreat in the Adirondacks. There, on the eve of Coolidge's departure for Washington, the two would appear to have a long, discursive chat, the resulting interview being merely an afterthought. As Barton put it to Coolidge's secretary: "Its effectiveness arises largely out of its appearance of spontaneity."[51]

Barton's arrangement with the Associated Press was mutually beneficial. The AP enjoyed exclusive copyright, and the story went out neither as a White House press release, nor as a lone correspondent's contribution to a single publication. It was distributed in a series of installments as a regular wire service feature, thereby assuring its publication not only in newspapers great and small, but also in the opposition press as well as Republican papers. Though the United Press and the White House Correspondents Association vigorously protested Barton's favorable treatment and Democratic critics denounced the interview as a "red herring across the trail of the dismal record" of the Coolidge administration, the ploy was generally successful. It certainly provoked comment and was, as some observed, "the most widely discussed story in years." Vintage Barton prose prompted some observers to declare the interview "the glimpse of a soul" or "the happiest picture of American life." "The joy of home and fireside," concluded the Harrisburg *Telegraph*, "is a gospel to which any thinking man or woman can subscribe." Others were not so sure. "As smooth and suave as it is," suggested the Baltimore *Evening Sun*, it merely tells us what Coolidge is not. "For all its creamy blandness, it is in some senses a failure." Despite all, Coolidge remained "an enigma." For H. L. Mencken's *American Mercury*, however, there was no mystery. "No man ever had a better press," it noted. "Democrat as well as Republican papers endowed him with virtues and qualities that as Vice-President everybody in Washington knew he lacked and laughed about." Unquestionably, the *American Mercury* continued, Coolidge possessed a certain "political foxiness," but that alone could not explain his success. "The answer ""is, of course, publicity—. . . the well-directed publicity of the Republican National Committee which promptly jumped in to put over by every agent it could command—including the Telephone controlled radio and the movies, the 'wise, strong, silent man' legend." There was no doubt that Barton's message had reached his intended audience. His advertising talent was highly regarded—and feared. "No man," a contemporary shrewdly estimated, "is his equal in assaying the middle-class mind and directing an appeal to it."[52]

Certainly Barton's popular inspirational writing, especially his best-selling publication *The Man Nobody Knows*, in 1925, enhanced that reputation. Repackaging mainstream Protestant Christianity, Barton sought to make the Old Time Religion palatable to a more materialistic generation by diluting the demands of its faith to greeting-card platitudes. In his hands, religion became another form of boosterism. Barton depicted Jesus in terms any twentieth-century businessman would understand. "He picked up twelve men from the bottom ranks of business," wrote Barton, "and forged them into an organization that conquered the world." Barton's Jesus was no office grind tied to dull routine, but "the most popular dinner guest in Jerusalem." He was a master at public relations whose parables Barton held up as model advertising copy. Above all, he sought and lived an active life of intense experience. Here was the key to Barton's attempt to revitalize what he saw as a weak, ineffective Protestant orthodoxy. By suffusing religious faith with therapeutic notions of "personal growth," he hoped to sanctify consumer culture through the ideology of advertising. Jesus lived a righteous life, as Barton put it, "by living more healthfully than any of his contemporaries."

Substituting "self-fulfillment" for "salvation," Barton promoted righteousness as "a happier, more satisfying way of living."[53]

In revitalizing Christianity, Barton also sought to sanctify the pursuit of profit. There was no distinction between "work and religious work," claimed Barton. After all, he argued, *credit*, the foundation of consumer-driven business culture is derived from *credo*: I believe! Jesus knew, wrote Barton, "All business is his Father's business. All work is worship. All useful service, prayer."[54]

Nowhere, Barton truly believed, did these maxims apply more than to the business of advertising. That Calvin Coolidge came to share these opinions is, perhaps, not surprising, but that the president came to express them so clearly in his speech at the 1926 meeting of the American Association of Advertising Agencies was no coincidence, but was orchestrated by Barton himself. With his partner Roy Durstine as president of the association, Barton arranged to have the annual meeting in Washington, then sought and obtained the president of the United States as keynote speaker. He then wrote the president's speech, sending Coolidge approximately two typed pages of suggested remarks, most of which were incorporated into the final version of the address. Paraphrasing Barton, Coolidge remarked that advertising "ministers to the true development of trade." "It is the method," he continued, "by which the desire is created for better things." He went on to say that it is desire itself that is the spark of civilization. "The uncivilized," Coolidge said, "make little progress because they have few desires. The inhabitants of our country are stimulated to new wants in all directions." This was no Puritan speaking. The Puritan virtues of sacrifice and self-denial, so necessary for survival in an economy of scarcity and for preparation for the Hereafter, would only bring destruction to a society based on consumerism and the fulfillment of worldly pleasures. But by bringing the Heavenly City down to earth, the prophets of plenty risked undermining the moral authority that legitimized their enterprise. Therefore it was "service," not profits, that motivated entrepreneurs. "Advertising," said Coolidge, "ministers to the spiritual side of trade." He charged the assembled advertisers with "the high responsibility of inspiring and ennobling the commercial world." Above all, he concluded, advertising "is all part of the greater work of the regeneration and redemption of mankind"[!]

Here, finally, was the golden calf, officially sanctioned, enthroned, and held up for the multitude to worship. By the Victorian era, the strength of the Puritan ethic had already been diluted. Victorians had justified their increasing preoccupation with worldly success as a means of contributing to the social good, or as a mark of superior character. Modernists had gone one step further. By the 1920s, even the pale ghost of a moral vision that had haunted Victorians had been exorcised. The pursuit of material pleasures now needed to be justified only to the extent to which they provided individual self-fulfillment. Success was no longer measured by occupational achievement, but in terms of the means it provided to satiate desires that were themselves commodified by a consumer culture.[55] Advertisers had succeeded in creating a new "symbolic universe" for consumers, one in which all desires are fulfilled, all conflicts resolved, all doubts reconciled. In such a world where there was no fear of evil, no struggle for certainty, no spiritual conflict, there was no need for salvation, no place, as Jackson Lears has suggested, for Grace. In *Babbitt* (1922) Sinclair Lewis described that world as experienced by his fictional hero: "these standard advertised wares," he wrote, "—toothpaste, socks, tires, cameras, instantaneous hot-water heaters—were his symbols and proofs of excellence; at first the signs, then the substitutes for joy and passion and wisdom."[56]

Coolidge's advertising speech symbolizes the extent of Barton's triumph. The president of the United States, partly a political commodity of Barton's own making, had, in his official capacity, declaimed what amounted to ad copy that Barton himself had written, legitimizing advertisers themselves as the new high priests of modern prosperity and implicitly acknowledging their growing influence over the political process itself.

For corporate America, advertising was more than a marketing tool. A growing awareness among businessmen and elected officials of the need for improved public relations was a powerful factor in the growth of advertising in the 1920s. Accusations of wartime profiteering had tarnished corporate reputations. The Harding scandals had linked high government officials with corporate corruption and graft. A positive public image, executives hoped, could serve to inoculate industries from threatening regulatory legislation and dilute support for unions. The Roosevelt and Wilson administrations had put corporate America on the defensive. Anti-monopoly sentiment, as it was expressed by progressives and reformers of various stripes, spawned a highly self-conscious, sustained, and largely successful public relations effort in response. In essence, its message claimed corporate America to be the embodiment rather than the antithesis of individualistic free enterprise as its critics had charged. The remarkable success of this rationale is evidenced by the fact that, even three quarters of a century later, there is scant acknowledgment by the American business community that anything but a vastly distorted resemblance to a free market economy has existed since the 1890s.[57]

It is important to note that, like many other architects of modernity, Barton was deeply ambivalent about aspects of the new era he helped to create. He was desperately trying to reinvigorate a world that he felt was irrevocably slipping from his grasp. But he served to rationalize a new era by seeming to reconcile old beliefs and values with the very forces that threatened them with extinction. Barton rejoiced in the manifestations of material prosperity, yet he feared that the pursuit of luxury would have a corrosive effect on the moral fiber of WASP elites. Like Theodore Roosevelt, he valued the strenuous life as a character-building corrective to the lassitude of modern living. Yet the authentic experience he sought from physical activity had become divorced from the necessity of labor and thus became merely another therapeutic route to self-fulfillment. Though he hoped to revitalize a languishing Protestantism, his sleek gospel of uplift only undercut its moral authority.

Barton was drawn to Calvin Coolidge because he saw in him an incarnation of those qualities that he associated with a vanished America. Here was Yankee individualism, rural independence, and cracker barrel wisdom. Yet the Coolidge administration, through figures like Herbert Hoover and Dwight Morrow, ushered in a New Era committed to the ideal of a national commonwealth of economic cooperation and to expanding U.S. economic influence abroad. Through the shrewd use of experts like Barton, Coolidge transformed the ceremonial function of the presidency into a vehicle for influencing public opinion. He saw his administrative role as more of a chief executive officer who carried out the wishes of his board of directors: the corporate and financial interests of the nation. He may have been born in rural Vermont, but Coolidge never dirtied his hands at manual labor after he left the homestead except to pose for photographs—a farmer's smock concealing the business suit underneath. It was President Coolidge, after all, who vetoed attempts to address the deepening depression of the agricultural sector in the 1920s. In fact, Coolidge's rural upbringing more closely resembled *Ethan Frome* than Norman Rockwell. He, no doubt, managed a wry smile or two at some of Barton's more sentimental characterizations, but a sentimentalist himself, he also inclined toward a nostalgic longing for a simpler, imagined past.

It is indeed this theme of lost innocence and the attempt to reclaim it that runs like a thread through the '20s. From *A Farewell to Arms*, *The Great Gatsby,* and the doubters of *The Modern Temper* to the Invisible Empire of the Klan and the Sacred Garden of the creationists, modernism had shaken foundations and loosened old moorings. Christopher Lasch has shown how the word "nostalgia" itself came to have new meaning in the twenties. Formerly a medical term for pathological homesickness, it became a way to refer to a generation's collective experience in the years after World War I. America, it seemed, had been irrevocably altered by the war. For better or worse, the modern present was measured against the backdrop of preindustrial America. Reconciling the two became the preoccupation of the decade. Much of the fuel that fired the new consumerism was the desire for authenticity in an increasingly materialist society. Fitzgerald's famous lines in the conclusion of *The Great Gatsby* crystallized this notion. "His dream," Fitzgerald wrote, "must have seemed so close that he could hardly fail to grasp it. He did not know that it was already behind him, somewhere back in that vast obscurity beyond the city, where the dark fields of the republic rolled on under the night."[58]

Other Americans who had experienced the Great War firsthand carried, like the ancient Puritans, a kind of *memento mori* with them. This consciousness of mortality was the ghost at the feast of Jazz Age consumerism, producing an ironic detachment in some, cynicism in others. A preoccupation with surfaces provided still others a certain ironic pleasure in the consumption of material goods. In *A Farewell to Arms*, the world of Ernest Hemingway's protagonist was shattered by the war. As Hemingway tells it: "Abstract words such as glory, honor, courage, or hallow were obscene beside the concrete names of villages. . . .Finally, only the names of places had dignity." But as the decade wore on, a no less jaded, but more comfortable Hemingway could dignify the brand names of products as well. The smoothness of a good scotch, the ambiance of a bistro, the heft of an Abercrombie and Fitch fly rod: the ability to distinguish "quality" in consumer goods became a mark of character in Hemingway's fiction and a preoccupation of the American middle class. There is an echo of Hemingway's Spartan prose in the terse phrases of Coolidge's speeches. It is but one of those coincidences of history that they shared the same editor at Scribner's, Maxwell Perkins. Nevertheless, the popularity of Hemingway's "strong, silent" hero and the image of "Silent Cal," rugged Vermonter, both reflect an incipient cult of authenticity in America—one which advertisers were quick to note and exploit.[59]

In Barton's hands, Coolidge, like Gatsby, became a candidate who would move forward while looking backward. He was a man of the people, yet larger than life. He had the common touch, but was a cut above the rest. Even after Coolidge's retirement from office, Barton continued to write articles about the former president and even briefly considered a "Draft Coolidge" campaign in a desperate attempt to stave off the inevitable disaster that loomed for the Republicans in 1932. But in January 1933, Coolidge died suddenly in his home in Northampton. On the day of his funeral, Barton delivered a eulogy on national radio. Characteristically, it was a highly personal tribute. "I shall say something about him," Barton announced, "that I doubt you have ever heard any man say. I *loved* him. There was a very lovable side to Calvin Coolidge. He was unique." These are strong sentiments for a relationship that was, in reality, cordial, but always formal and businesslike. Perhaps what Barton loved most of all was his own creation, his own construction of Calvin Coolidge. That image might have been a reflection of his personal needs and desires, but it was always finely tuned to the moods of a vast body of consumers. Barton's Madison Avenue office was dominated by a panoramic photograph of milling crowds at Coney Island—a constant reminder of the common denominator in his target audience. Barton's great skill as an advertiser was his ability to package commodities, from soap flakes to political candidates, so that they appeared to satisfy intense private longings. That he was able to fashion Coolidge in this way is an enduring tribute to his expertise. "The nation will remember his personality and his dry humor," Barton's eulogy continued, "long after it has forgotten most of the events of his administration." If this has been all too true, much of the credit is due to Barton himself.[60]

Barton did not invent political image-building, a skill not unknown to kings and courtiers and evidenced by the campaign biographies and slogans of nineteenth-century American politics. But his intimacy with the Coolidge administration demonstrates that in the 1920s Pennsylvania Avenue was far closer to Madison Avenue and Wall Street than it ever was to Main Street.

Far from being a throwback, a "Puritan in Babylon," Coolidge brought the presidency into the modernist era. He did not fear Mammon, but like many Americans, simply stood in awe of it. His bland pronouncements and platitudes seemed to eschew ideology while he delegated real authority to the nation's managerial elite. He shrewdly took advantage of emerging communications technologies that subtly shifted the form and content of news itself. By posing for newsreel photographers, he transformed trivial ceremonial events previously ignored by newspaper reporters into media events, today called photo-ops, witnessed by millions. A radio address was a news event in itself going directly into the nation's living rooms while bypassing the editorializing of partisan newspapers.

Certainly this merchandising or commodification of American politics worked to obscure critical issues and engendered the notion of a passive electorate, a body of consumers whose behavior could be predicted by social science and shaped by mass advertising. In reality, however, this process may have shaped the nature of political leadership itself far more than the choices of voters, whose decisions are often affected by a complex web of economic and demographic issues that have proven to be remarkably resistant to media manipulation. Despite the efforts of Barton and company, for example, voter turnout in the elections of 1920 and 1924 was the lowest of the century, reflecting, perhaps, as Robert Westbrook suggests, deep-seated "political alienation" among the electorate. "No other country in the world," noted one observer in 1924, "puts half our emphasis on 'personality'. Having lost touch, in a large measure, with our neighborhoods, we insist on recreating contact when we vote." As personality marketing came to dominate campaigns, issues blurred and party ties weakened.[61]

Contemporaries certainly viewed declining voter turnout with alarm. Most analysts believed that it was the middle-class voter who strayed from the polls. Both parties supported "Get Out the Vote" movements aimed at this group. In fact, it was the poor and working-class voters who were most disaffected by the advertised, personality politics of the 1920s. The ethnic and religious overtones of 1928 and the bread-and-butter issues of the Depression era temporarily reversed the trend of declining voter turnout. But the postwar years saw the voting curve dip again as political leaders, especially after the advent of television in the 1950s, developed a heightened sensitivity to their image—the public perception of their leadership. Preoccupation with the polls, while seeming to offer a wide range of control over the electorate, also served to narrow the scope of political decision-making and created a shadow cabinet of electoral weather forecasters who exercised a growing influence over policy decisions. As candidates became commodities, citizens became consumers, and voting, once within the sphere of civic duty, became more and more just another matter of personal choice.[62]

Coolidge's emergence on the national political scene was marked by the ascendancy of a new elite in American politics: those who had the expertise and strategic skills to wage a consumer-oriented campaign and those who could marshal the vast sums to pay for it. Bruce Barton's association with Coolidge's political triumph reveals the extent to which a consumerist ethos had permeated the very core of American institutions by the 1920s.

NOTES

1. William E. Leuchtenburg, *The Perils of Prosperity, 1914–1932* (Chicago, 1958); Frederick Lewis Allen, *Only Yesterday: An Informal History of the 1920's* (New York, 1931).

2. Exceptions are Howard Quint and Robert Ferrell, eds., *The Talkative President: The Off-the-Record Press Conferences of Calvin Coolidge* (Amherst, 1964); and John L. Blair, "Coolidge the Image Maker: The President and the Press, 1923–1929," *New England Quarterly* 46 (December 1973): 499–522.

3. John D. Hicks, *The Republican Ascendancy: 1921–1933* (New York, 1960), 81; William Allen White, *A Puritan in Babylon: The Story of Calvin Coolidge* (New York, 1938).

4. Warren Susman, "Piety, Profits, and Play: The 1920's," in Howard Quint and Milton Cantor, eds., *Men, Women, and Issues in American History,* vol. 2 (Chicago, 1980); T. J. Jackson Lears, "From Salvation to Self-Realization: Advertising and the Therapeutic Roots of the Consumer Culture, 1880–1930," in Richard Wightman Fox and T. J. Jackson Lears, eds., *The Culture of Consumption: Critical Essays in American History, 1880–1980* (New York, 1983); Leo P. Ribuffo, "Jesus Christ as Business Statesman: Bruce Barton and the Selling of Corporate Capitalism," *American Quarterly* 3 (summer 1981): 206–231.

5. Robert Westbrook, "Politics as Consumption: Managing the Modern American Election," in Fox and Lears, *Culture of Consumption* ,145–146; Lawrence W. Levine, "Progress and Nostalgia: The Self Image of the Nineteen Twenties," in Levine, *The Unpredictable Past: Explorations in American Cultural History* (New York, 1993), 190–191; Christopher Lasch, *The True and Only Heaven: Progress and Its Critics* (New York, 1991), 105–109.

6. Susman, "Piety, Profits, and Play," 203; Lears, "From Salvation to Self-Realization," 34.

7. Susman, "Piety, Profits, and Play," 206.

8. Bruce Barton, *More Power to You* (New York, 1917), and *It's a Good Old World* (New York, 1920). See also Michael O'Malley, *Keeping Watch: A History of American Time* (New York, 1990), 248; and Susman, "Piety, Profits, and Play," 206.

9. Donald R. McCoy, *Calvin Coolidge: The Quiet President* (Lawrence, KS, 1988), 50.

10. Claude M. Fuess, *Calvin Coolidge: The Man from Vermont* (Boston, 1940), 176–180; Stephen A. Schuker, *The End of French Predominance in Europe: The Financial Crisis of 1924 and the Dawes Plan* (Chapel Hill, 1976), 154; Joan Hoff Wilson, *American Business and Foreign Policy, 1920–1933* (Lexington, KY, 1971), 15.

11. McCoy, *Calvin Coolidge*,84–94; Francis Russell, *A City in Terror: 1919, The Boston Police Strike* (New York, 1975).

12. Ishbel Ross, *Grace Coolidge and Her Era* (Plymouth, VT, 1988), 52.

13. Bruce Barton, "Remarks by Bruce Barton, As a Speaker on National Broadcasting Company's Memorial Service for Hon. Calvin Coolidge, Station WEAF, Thursday, January 5, 1933, 7:30 PM," transcript contained in Bruce Barton Papers, State Historical Society of Wisconsin, Madison, cited hereafter as Barton Papers.

14. Quint and Ferrell, *The Talkative President*, 1–4.

15. Bruce Barton, "Concerning Calvin Coolidge," *Collier's*, November 22, 1919: 8.

16. "Calvin Coolidge, American," *The Outlook*, November 12, 1919.

17. John Higham, *Strangers in the Land: Patterns of American Nativism, 1860–1925* (New York, 1970).

18. Barton, "Concerning Calvin Coolidge," 24.

19. Walter Benn Michaels, "The Souls of White Folk," in Elaine Scarry, ed., *Literature and the Body: Essays on Populations and Persons* (Baltimore, 1988), 202.

20. April Schultz, "'The Pride of Race Had Been Touched': The 1925 Norse-American Immigration Centennial and Ethnic Identity," *Journal of American History* 78 (March 1991): 1267.

21. Barton, "Concerning Calvin Coolidge," 24.

22. Levine, "Progress and Nostalgia ," 193–195.

23. Barton, "Concerning Calvin Coolidge," 28. Italics added.

24. Coolidge to Barton, December 8, 1919, Barton Papers.

25. Barton to Frank Stearns, November 12, 1919, Calvin Coolidge Papers, Forbes Library, Northampton, MA, cited hereafter as Coolidge Papers.

26. Calvin Coolidge, "A Message to the Women Who Read the Woman's Home Companion," and Bruce Barton, "The Silent Man on Beacon Hill," both in *Woman's Home Companion* (March 1920): 15, 30, 88.

27. Lears, "From Salvation to Self-Realization," 18–21. Lasker himself, the owner of the Lord and Thomas Agency in Chicago, was recruited by Will Hayes, Republican National Committee chairman, to engineer the 1918 congressional campaign, which resulted in a Republican-controlled congress. Lasker and Hayes then formed a team with Harry Daughterty to manage the Harding campaign in 1920. See Michael E. McGeer, *The Decline of Popular Politics: The American North, 1865–1928* (New York, 1986), 169–171. Regarding Lasker's continuing association with the Harding committee, see Ray Bolton to Will Hays, March 20, 1923, Will Hays Papers, Indiana State Library, Indianapolis; cited hereafter as Hays Papers.

28. Barton to Coolidge, December 10, 1919, Coolidge Papers; Coolidge to Barton, December 11, 1919, Barton Papers.

29. Frank Stearns to Coolidge, March 19, 1920; Coolidge to Barton, March 19, 1920, Letterpress Book, entry #374; Bruce Barton, "Calvin Coolidge, A Close-up of a Real American," c. 1920; all contained in Coolidge Papers.

30. Barton to Henry Long, April 14, 1920, Coolidge Papers; Fuess, *Calvin Coolidge,* 236.

31. Barton to Henry Long, April 12, 1920, Coolidge Papers.

32. Barton to Frank Stearns, March 24, 1920, Coolidge Papers.

33. McCoy, *Calvin Coolidge,*114–115; Bruce Barton, "The Governor Who Stays on the Job," *The Outlook*, April 28, 1920: 756–757.

34. Barton to Henry Long, June 7[?], 1920; Coolidge's secretary cabled Barton immediately: "Will proceed in accordance with proposition number one," Henry Long to Barton, telegram, June 7, 1920, Coolidge Papers; Daniel J. Boorstin, *The Image: A Guide to Pseudo-Events in America* (New York, 1961); See also Westbrook, "Politics as Consumption,"170.

35. Barton to Long, June 7[?], 1920.

36. McCoy, *Calvin Coolidge*, 114–121; Fuess, *Calvin Coolidge*, 234–267; Henry Long to Frederick Gillett, telegram, 10:20 a.m., June 7, 1920; Long to Gillett, telegram, 10:47 a.m., June 7, 1920; Long to Bruce Barton, telegram, 11:35 a.m., June 7, 1920, Coolidge Papers.

37. Russell, *A City in Terror*, 220–222; White, *A Puritan in Babylon*, 197–215.

38. Westbrook, "Politics as Consumption,"145–173; Richard Jensen, "Armies, Admen, and Crusaders: Types of Presidential Election Campaigns," *History Teacher* 2 (January 1969): 33–50; Jackson Lears, *Fables of Abundance: A Cultural History of Advertising in America* (New York, 1994): 244; McGeer, *The Decline of Popular Politics*, 148–149.

39. Dwight Morrow to Thomas W. Lamont, May 25, 1920, Dwight Morrow Papers, Amherst College Archives, cited hereafter as Morrow Papers. On the eve of the convention, the Coolidge campaign reported that it had spent close to $70,000, as compared to, for example, Harding's $113,000. See Fuess, *Calvin Coolidge*, 248–249.

40. Barton, "Concerning Calvin Coolidge," 28; Morrow to Lamont, May 25, 1920, Morrow Papers. Italics added.

41. Barton to Coolidge, August 19, 1920, Coolidge Papers. For details on the Harding campaign's advertising strategies see *Guide to the Will Hays Papers* (Frederick, MD, 1986), vii; and McGeer, *The Decline of Popular Politics*,169–171.

42. Barton to Morrow, April 3, 1922, Morrow Papers; Barton, "Calvin Coolidge As Seen Through the Eyes of His Friends," *American Review of Reviews* (September 1923): 273–278.

43. Maxwell Perkins to Barton, October 23, 1923; Barton to Edward T. Clark, November 8, 1923; Perkins to Clark, March 14, 1924, all in Coolidge Papers; K. A. Bickel to Barton, March 14, 1924; Herbert L. Pratt to Barton, March 17, 1924, Barton Papers.

44. White, *A Puritan in Babylon*, 296–300; Hicks, *The Republican Ascendancy*, 90.

45. Barton to George Barr Baker, July 7, 1924, Barton Papers; Dave Berkman, "Politics and Radio in the 1924 Campaign," *Journalism Quarterly* (summer–autumn 1987): 422–428; Gleason Archer, *History of Radio to 1926* (New York, 1971), 316–347.

46. Barton to George Barr Baker, July 7, 1924, Barton Papers; see also: Jensen, "Armies, Admen, and Crusaders," and Westbrook, "Politics as Consumption."

47. Barton to Baker, August 6, 1924, Barton Papers; McGeer, *The Decline of Popular Politics*, 182–183.

48. Barton to Baker, August 29, 1924, enclosures, Barton Papers; Jensen, "Armies, Admen, and Crusaders," 48; Hicks, *The Republican Ascendancy*, 100.

49. Barton to Edward T. Clark, October 5, 1926; January 28, 1928; April 16, 1926; January 3, 1927; Coolidge to Barton, November 23, 1928; Barton to Coolidge, [draft] November [?], 1928, Barton Papers; Blair, "Coolidge the Image Maker," 518.

50. Blair, "Coolidge the Image Maker," 504; The Coolidge White House was also keenly aware of the growing power of Hollywood and its influence on public life. Will Hays (who, as Republican National Committee chairman, had engineered Harding's nomination with the help of Albert Lasker) had been the party's patronage czar as postmaster general, and had escaped the hot breath of the Ohio Gang scandals by becoming director of the Motion Picture Directors and Distributors Association. Hays functioned as a power broker, securing favors in Washington for his Hollywood constituents in return for industry compliance in political matters. The Coolidge forces recruited Hays, who used his influence and many contacts in the 1924 campaign. Hays was also able to ensure favorable exposure for administration policies and actively used his office to suppress newsreels critical of Republican programs. See C. Bascom Slemp to Will Hays, July 18, 1924; Paul Fuller to Will Hays, July 3, 1922, Hays Papers. See also materials in Part I, Box 24 of the Hays Papers regarding the 1924 campaign.

51. Kent Cooper to Barton, July 22, 1926; Barton to Cooper, July 26, 1926; Cooper to Coolidge, September 14, 1926; Barton to Edward T. Clark, October 5, 1926, Barton Papers.

52. Carl D. Groat to Coolidge, September [?], 1926, copy in Barton Papers; see collection of news clippings, especially "Daily Editorial Digest" summary in Coolidge file, Barton Papers; Frank R. Kent, "Mr. Coolidge," *American Mercury* (August 1924): 388. It was not only the iconoclastic *American Mercury* that held these views. That article, with the handwritten inscription "There is a germ of truth in this" scrawled across the top, was enclosed in a letter to Will Hays. See Thomas Staples Fuller to Will Hays, August 20, 1924, Hays Papers. Quote from *Judge* magazine (n.d.), clipping contained in Coolidge files, Barton papers.

53. See especially Lears, "From Salvation to Self-Realization," 29–33, and Susman, "Piety, Profits, and Play," 209–210.

54. Lears, "From Salvation to Self-Realization," 36.

55. Barton to Coolidge, October 7, 1926, enclosure; October 29, 1926, Barton Papers; Calvin Coolidge, "Address of President Coolidge Before the American Association of Advertising Agencies, Washington, D.C, October 27, 1926, at 8 PM" (Washington, DC, 1926).

56. Fox and Lears, *Culture of Consumption*, xiii; Jackson Lears, *No Place of Grace: Antimodernism and the Transformation of American Culture, 1880–1920* (New York, 1981); Sinclair Lewis, *Babbitt* (New York, 1961), 81.

57. David Brody, "The Rise and Decline of Welfare Capitalism," in John Braeman, Robert Bremner, and David Brody, eds., *Change and Continuity in Twentieth Century America: The 1920's* (Columbus, 1968), 147–178; see Richard Abrams's introduction

to the re-issue of Louis Brandeis, *Other People's Money* (New York, 1967); and Wilson, *American Business and Foreign Policy*, 6.

58. Ellis W. Hawley, *The Great War and the Search for a Modern Order* (New York, 1992), 47–82; Lasch, *The True and Only Heaven,* 105–109; F. Scott Fitzgerald, *The Great Gatsby*, reprinted in Arthur Mizener, ed., *The Fitzgerald Reader* (New York, 1963), 238.

59. Ernest Hemingway, *A Farewell to Arms* (New York, 1929), 185.

60. Barton, "Remarks . . ."; Ribuffo, "Jesus Christ as Business Statesman," 216.

61. See Christopher Lasch's discussion of "politics as spectacle" in *The Culture of Narcissism: American Life in an Age of Diminishing Expectations* (New York, 1978), 78; Westbrook, "Politics as Consumption,"170–173. In their study of "Middletown," Robert and Helen Lynd quote a young businesswoman after the 1924 election. "This time has so thoroughly disgusted me with politics," she remarked, "that I don't feel like there's much use in trying ever to vote again." Robert S. Lynd and Helen Merrell Lynd, *Middletown: A Study in Modern American Culture* (New York, 1929), 420; *Nation*, May 5, 1926: 492.

62. Arthur M. Schlesinger and Eric McKinley Erickson, "The Vanishing Voter," *New Republic*, October 15, 1924: 162–167; Harold F. Gosnell, "The Voter Resigns," *New Republic*, October 21, 1925: 224–225; McGeer, *The Decline of Popular Politics*, 184–210; Christopher Lasch, *The Revolt of the Elites and the Betrayal of Democracy* (New York, 1995).

21

THOSE who looked below the surface in Northampton during the 1920s, saw approaching shadows of things to come. The rapid expansion of industry during World War I had quickly come to a halt with the Armistice. The machine shops continued to attract those like a young Amelia Earhart, who learned engine mechanics in Northampton. But the silk industry, especially, had over-expanded. The Corticelli Mills, long a mainstay of Northampton's economy, closed their doors forever. Although other industries continued to survive, the heady optimism of the prewar years would never come again.

Depression era Northampton was not quite as hard hit as its more industrialized neighbors. But in its darkest days one quarter of its population was unemployed. Like the great floods and natural disasters of the 1930s, the tide of economic ruin was stemmed by regional planning and vigorous public works. Local boosterism and civic pride sought to paint a rosy picture of opportunity for visitors and investors. But, as in the rest of the nation, it was World War II that brought economic recovery to Northampton. A place once called Paradise now fueled the inferno. Among war materials produced were Top Secret plastic parts for the Manhattan Project.

As postwar Americans discovered a mythologized New England in the Saturday Evening Post *covers of Norman Rockwell, the still pastoral but often gritty reality inspired deeper reflection. The legendary Hampshire Bookshop published regional literary works and hosted evenings with Robert Frost. Northampton's quiet streets and parks provided settings for poets like Sylvia Plath, who lived here in the late 1950s with her husband, Ted Hughes.*

Plath described her life in the '50s as like living under a bell jar. Indeed the pressure of Cold War conformity set heavily on those who paid the price to challenge it, however privately. Newton Arvin, a distinguished writer and literary critic at Smith, lived a quiet life, keeping his sexual preferences discretely in the closet. Truman Capote, who lived with Arvin in Northampton, recalled "Newton was my Harvard." Arvin was Capote's mentor and encouraged many young writers, such as Carson McCullers. Yet government authorities raided Arvin's apartment, arresting him for possessing salacious material that would not produce a blush in today's supermarket lines. It was enough to end Arvin's career and provoke a mental breakdown. He died a broken man.

America's rehabilitation of Herman Melville in the twentieth century along with the rediscovery of Nathaniel Hawthorne's haunted tales was largely due to Arvin. Ironically the very obsessions and dark passions Arvin saw as the underside of American culture proved to be at the root of his own undoing.

Barry Werth tells the story of the Arvin case in this article reprinted from the New Yorker, *based on his recent biography,* The Scarlet Professor. *This story takes its place among others in Northampton history: the Mary Parsons witchcraft trial and the tragic Daley and Halligan hanging being the most notorious. It is a story that Hawthorne would recognize as being right in the American grain.*

The Scarlet Professor*

BARRY WERTH

ON THE afternoon of September 2, 1960, two unmarked patrol cars bearing three state troopers, a federal postal inspector, and a local policeman pulled up to a three-story brick Victorian house in Northampton, Massachusetts, where Newton Arvin lived alone in a top-floor apartment. Arvin, who was sixty years old, was the Mary Augusta Jordan Professor of Literature at Smith College and a much-honored literary biographer—renowned, in particular, for his studies of Nathaniel Hawthorne and Herman Melville. The intruders mounted the winding wooden staircase so stealthily that the tenant on the first floor failed to hear them. Hesitantly, Arvin let them in. During the next hour, the police searched Arvin's four tidy, cloistered rooms—his "cave," he called them—and confiscated a large cache of homosexual erotica. They also seized his journals, in which he had meticulously documented his sexual activities and desires.

Arvin, a timid man, who wore rubbers at the least hint of rain, was arrested on charges of possessing "obscene pictures" and of "lewdness"—offenses that carried a maximum prison term of five years and a fine of twenty-five thousand dollars. He was taken to the local police station, and there he surrendered the names of fifteen other men who, he told the police, also collected homoerotic pictures. The next day, he admitted himself to the Massachusetts state mental hospital that overlooks the Smith campus, where he remained for more than a month. On September 20, he pleaded guilty in District Court and received a one-year suspended sentence.[1]

Afterward, Arvin tried to explain himself in a letter to an old friend of his, David Lilienthal, the retired head of the Atomic Energy Commission: "It must be very difficult, if not impossible, for you to understand what has happened, or to comprehend all the behavior that led up to the crisis. For the time being, perhaps you will just have to set it down to the well-known contradictoriness, indeed perverseness, of human behavior generally."[2]

Lilienthal, who had known Arvin for fifty years, found it incomprehensible that his boyhood friend was the leader of the small-town homosexual smut

---

* From Barry Werth, "The Scarlet Professor," *New Yorker,* October 5, 1998: 57; excerpted from Barry Werth, *The Scarlet Professor: Newton Arvin, A Literary Life Shattered by Scandal* (New York, 2001).

ring described in the local headlines. Other illustrious friends of Arvin were also dismayed. "I regard Mr. Newton Arvin as one of the two or three best contemporary writers on American classical literature," Edmund Wilson wrote in a testimonial, which had been solicited by Arvin's lawyer. "I am unable to believe the charges against him . . . which sound like a fantasy of the local police distorted by an incompetent reporter."[3]

But, except for the vice-squad bluster about Arvin's being the leader of a conspiratorial ring, the charges were true. Throughout the 1950s, Arvin had collected and traded homosexual erotica, some of it hard-core but the bulk of it stylized beefcake pictures culled from muscle magazines with titles like *Adonis*, *Tomorrow's Man*, and *Physique Pictorial*. His attic apartment had provided a haven for younger men with whom he could relax and, occasionally, have sex. To his friends and colleagues, the details were shocking: his furtiveness; the relative youthfulness of the other men; and, worst of all, his betrayal of others. Suddenly, Arvin's literary and academic friends were confronted with what seemed an unbridgeable gulf between their lives and Arvin's—one that, back in 1960, made him into someone whose private self was beyond their understanding.

In researching a new book about the Arvin case, I have been struck by the depth of that gulf, and also by how effectively, both before and after his trial, Arvin was able, through his celebrated writings, to smuggle his outcast sensibility into mainstream American culture. Arvin's first great theme as a writer was the secrecy that marks so many private lives. By investigating the psychological drives of some of our most important authors through the prism of his own secret life, he was illuminating the hidden aspects of America's Puritan character.

"I know very well," Arvin wrote in an unpublished memoir, "that I did not have a wretchedly unhappy childhood of the sort that appears in some autobiographies—a childhood of utter misery and almost unrelieved distress. On the other hand, I know too that I very early began to be painfully aware of the harshness and even the cruelty of 'the world,' and to react to this in all kinds of childish and deplorable ways—by a most reprehensible habit of querulous complainingness, by fits of temper and tears, by tantrums, by the indulgence of fears, by quarrelsomeness and irritability. 'So small a boy and so great a sinner!'" He elaborated:

> I was certainly a girlish small boy, not a virile one, even in promise, and the world of boys being what it is, I was not long in being made aware of this. I was timid, shrinking, weak, and unventuresome; I had no skill in boyish games and sports, and no interest in them, and I was quickly penalized as a result—by taunts, jeers, and sometimes, though rarely, blows. . . . And from then on I was never wholly without the sense . . . of radical difference from, and inferiority to, my male contemporaries, or the sense of the inimical in the social world around me.[4]

Valparaiso, Indiana, where Frederick Newton Arvin was born in 1900, was the sort of insular midwestern farm town that was soon to be harshly memorialized in Sherwood Anderson's *Winesburg, Ohio* and Sinclair Lewis's *Main Street*. Arvin developed few boyhood friends. Instead, he immersed himself in books. In the ninth grade, he started keeping a daily journal—a discipline he maintained for fifty years—in which he wrote mainly about what he was reading. Before he could wear trousers, he had discovered in reading and writing an antidote to the Babbittry he associated with his father—a cold, overbearing insurance executive, who was away much of the time, and who Arvin was sure despised him.

Arvin early became aware of having homoerotic emotions, and he was careful not to mention them to anyone. As he reports in his memoir, at eleven or twelve he had an experience in which he and an older boy fondled each other on a fence. What he recalled most vividly, however, was the warmth and tenderness—the "undefinable element"—he felt toward another "good-looking and engaging" boy.[5]

In Arvin's senior year at Harvard, from which he graduated summa cum laude in 1921, he began sending unsolicited reviews to Van Wyck Brooks, who was then the country's best-known book critic. Brooks admired the young man's breadth and sophistication, and wrote back to him, "You are a critic by nature." At the same time, Brooks cautioned that if he was to write anything lasting he would have to experience life beyond the ivory tower. Arvin's response was to teach—first at a private school for boys in Detroit, where, desperately unhappy, he failed to finish out the year. In 1922, he became a freshman-composition instructor at Smith, the nation's premier women's college. There Arvin quickly set himself apart. At Harvard he had been a political progressive with Bolshevik leanings, and two years after moving to Northampton he chaired the local La Follette for President committee, campaigning stridently against the incumbent—Calvin Coolidge, the home-town hero, who had been a mayor of Northampton and still maintained a house in Arvin's ward. Writing to Lilienthal of Coolidge's eventual victory, Arvin noted wryly, "I think it will possibly save me from the kindnesses of a lot of respectable (and very dull) people who rather enjoy a literary radical but gag at a political one."[6]

Arvin's first book was a critical biography of Nathaniel Hawthorne that was published in 1929. Reading Hawthorne, he identified dark strains in Puritan America, which perhaps only someone who had spent much of his life in hiding could detect as fully. Like Arvin, Hawthorne had withdrawn from the world, substituting literature for life, yet that retreat had led him to discover the great theme that would pervade his most important books—what Arvin called "the dark connection between guilt and secrecy." In Hawthorne's Calvinist America—the Colonial America of *The Scarlet Letter* and *The House of the Seven Gables*—people were punished most harshly not for their acts but for their secrets.

As Van Wyck Brooks had done before him, Arvin sought to remove any trace of Victorian "femininity" from his prose. Vigorously, and with barely disguised personal urgency, he wrote, "The essential sin, [Hawthorne] would seem to say, lies in whatever shuts up the spirit in a dungeon where it is alone, beyond the reach of common sympathies and the general sunlight. All that isolates, damns; all that associates, saves."[7]

Hawthorne made Arvin's reputation as a critic and a biographer. He became a regular guest at Yaddo, the artists' colony in Saratoga Springs, New York. A shy, scholarly figure, barely thirty years old, Arvin was almost a caricature of the mousy young English professor; standing five feet eight inches tall and weighing a hundred and twenty-five pounds, he had a round face, gray-green eyes glinting behind gold, wire-rimmed glasses, a pockmarked forehead, and thinning brown hair, neatly trimmed and combed. A friend recalled that he "wore a dark suit to breakfast, sat like a furled umbrella, and buttered his toast to the edges." But because he was cordial, charming, and savagely witty and he seemed to have read everything, even Yaddo's most imposing personalities sought him out as a rising figure in the literary left. Like many other writers of the time, Arvin responded to the Depression with a keen awareness of social injustice, and in 1932 he pledged—with Lincoln Steffens, John Dos Passos, Sherwood Anderson, and Theodore Dreiser—to vote Communist.[8]

Although Arvin had turned away from his father—in college he dropped their shared first name, "Frederick"—he hoped to disprove "the official family forecast for my future," which he described as "very gloomy."[9] To that end, he married one of his former students, Mary Garrison, in 1932. A vivacious blonde, she was Arvin's opposite—"a great Valkyrian figure," Daniel Aaron, one of Arvin's closest friends on the Smith English faculty, recalled. "She could make ten meals of Newton." For both of them, the next eight years were disastrous. Arvin, who was working on a biography of Walt Whitman, gave his young wife one of the poet's ambiguously homoerotic verses, in the hope that she would understand his sexual preferences. She didn't. They divorced in 1940, but the strains of their marriage led both of them to suffer nervous breakdowns.

Arvin had male lovers—what his hospital records called "suspicious alliances with other men"—and he faithfully reported them in his journals. Like Edmund Wilson, with whom he became friends when Wilson taught at Smith for a term, he documented his sexual encounters as if they were not quite real until they were written down and pressed, like flowers, between the covers of a book. Recently, I drove to Wellesley, Massachusetts, to visit Charles Pierce and his younger sister, Barbara Arvin Pierce—two bank executives, whose mother was Arvin's niece. Sifting through a cardboard box of materials that Arvin had collected for his memoir—old letters, high school journals, lecture notes, and other faded documents—I found a tattered photograph album from the thirties, when Arvin was married to Mary Garrison. It contained only one photograph of people—a group shot of Arvin, the composer Aaron Copland, the theatrical director Harold Clurman, and the Yaddo executive director Elizabeth Ames standing on a rustic porch overlooking Lake George. All the other photographs showed buildings and monuments: four of the Grand Hotel in Saratoga; four of the Mansion, Yaddo's fifty-five-room main building; dozens of historic New England churches and houses; and pictures of the graves of Hawthorne, Emerson, and Bronson Alcott.

Arvin's torments were not assuaged by his focus on the lives of others. During the 1940s and early '50s, he tried at least three times to kill himself. One day, after watching young skaters on Smith's Paradise Pond, Arvin stumbled home, opened a bottle of liquor, put on a recording of John McCormack singing Hugo Wolf's setting of "Ganymed"—the Greek myth about a Trojan boy of great beauty who was carried away by Zeus to become cupbearer to the gods—and swallowed sixteen Nembutals. He was found the next morning by Aaron, who took him to the hospital, where his stomach was pumped.[10]

In the summer of 1946, Arvin once again left Northampton for Yaddo, where he had been elected to the board of directors. Although his place in twentieth-century American letters was now secure, the war had reversed the country's political currents. Leftist writers, like Arvin, who had dreamed of an American Socialism, found themselves out of step and in retreat from the anti-Communist New Critics on the right. All this compounded Arvin's gloom. He had failed at marriage, was in anguish about his homosexuality, had become trapped at the edge of small-town life, and was now becoming a political pariah. As he prepared to leave his apartment, he wrote in his journal, "Woke again just after five. Thoughts of death and self-destruction. 'Morning tears.'"

Truman Capote also came to Yaddo that summer. Capote was twenty-four years Arvin's junior; blond, brash, and openly salacious, he was everything Arvin was not. Within days of their meeting, Arvin was writing to a friend that he had discovered "this Thing that one can surely expect but once or twice in a lifetime." Years later, Capote, in describing Arvin to his biographer Gerald Clarke, called his new friend a "charming person, cultivated in every way, with the most wonderfully subtle mind," and went on to say, "He was like a lozenge that you could keep turning to the light, one way or another, and the most beautiful colors would come out."[11]

The two men became inseparable. At Yaddo, they ate lunch and dinner together, walked into town to the movies, took long moonlit walks around the grounds, and launched a three-year love affair that encompassed the happiest and most productive period of Arvin's life. When they were apart, they wrote each other letters every day—a passionate correspondence in which the staid Arvin even indulged in sexual joking: "LOST probably in Manhattan," he wrote from Northampton, "one peppermint-stick, beautifully pink and white, wonderfully straight, deliciously sweet. About a hand's length. Of great intrinsic and also sentimental value to owner." Arvin's shame about his sexuality seemed to melt in the younger man's flamboyant presence. As for Capote, he deepened and matured under Arvin's tutelage. Racing every second weekend by train from New York to Northampton, climbing the narrow stairs to Arvin's apartment on Prospect Street, he reveled in Arvin's donnish affection and, in the bargain, was given a crash course in the world's great books. Capote, who hadn't gone to college, would later say, "Newton was my Harvard."[12]

Capote introduced Arvin to gay New York, with what were, occasionally, troubling results. Once, during an outing to Harlem for an annual drag dance at the Celebrity Club, a mostly gay dance hall, they were caught in what seemed to be a police raid. Arvin hid in a phone booth.[13]

After that, he insisted that Capote visit him more often in Northampton. For Capote, the demand was too confining, and it contributed to their eventual breakup. In Northampton, Arvin could lovingly show off Capote—his "Little T"—to close friends like some glittering jewel. But he knew that he could never be happy in the brightly lit public arena that Capote was headed for, even though that world offered him the promise of greater companionship than Northampton ever could.

During the years of his affair with Capote, Arvin began a biography of Herman Melville. Like his earlier books, it linked the themes of his own private life with that of his subject. Through his examination of Melville's work and life, and especially Melville's relationship with Hawthorne, Arvin found a way to express his secret life. He cited an essay in which Melville wrote, "It is that blackness in Hawthorne . . . that so fixes and fascinates me. Already I feel that [he] has dropped germinous seeds into my soul. He expands and deepens down, the more I contemplate him; and further and further, shoots his strong New England roots in the hot soil of my Southern soul." Arvin went on to observe, "It is an astonishingly sexual image, but probably only such an image could adequately have expressed Melville's feeling, for the moment, of receptiveness and even passivity in the acceptance of impregnation by another mind."[14]

Herman Melville was a critical success, winning the National Book Award for nonfiction in 1951. Arvin was exultant. In his acceptance speech he celebrated Melville, who "spoke out for the 'august dignity' of the democratic man," and also Ralph Waldo Emerson, who "cried out, again and again, on behalf of the free spirit of man and against the brutal, power-hungry and inhumane forces that would enslave that spirit."[15]

Reading *Herman Melville* today, I am struck by the book's quiet brilliance. Arvin was among the first academics who occupied themselves seriously with American literature, and his chapter on *Moby Dick* remains, almost fifty years later, a textbook example of learned, finely honed criticism. Everything is there—the great gusts of Melville's genius, Arvin's exquisite parsing of the multilayered text, the erudite references to Melville's most obscure sources. There is also something prescient and modern in Arvin's recognition that the *Pequod*'s apocalyptic voyage might be the vengeance dream of a tormented, sexually injured, father-hating hero. Like Edmund Wilson and other literary critics of the era before deconstruction, Arvin was a master of discernment through descriptive fervor. He writes, "Ahab is what our wildest, most egoistic, most purely destructive malevolence could wish to be, this old Quaker skipper from Nantucket; obsessed to the point of monomania with the will to destroy the hated thing, yet free from all mere smallnesses, 'a grand, ungodly, godlike man.' He is our hatred ennobled, as we would wish to have it, up to heroism."[16]

Capote, with whom Arvin remained close, hoped that the success of the Melville book would enable Arvin to leave Smith. To David Lilienthal and his wife, Capote complained that Arvin was "surrounded by mediocrity" in Northampton and "ought to be at Harvard or Yale," but that he wouldn't "lift a finger to do anything for himself."[17] Lilienthal promised to help, but there seems to have been little he could do, even after Arvin was elected to the American Academy of Arts and Letters in 1952. The messy interruptions in Arvin's personal life—what Arvin called in his memoir the "crack-ups and breakdowns"—and the murmurs about his homosexuality had begun to trail him like a rap sheet. No elite men's college was likely to have him, no matter how distinguished his career. Besides, Arvin had become, as Aaron put it, "encysted" in Northampton—too settled, at fifty-two, in his small-town New England life, and too fearful of the outside world to live anywhere else.

After the Second World War, Arvin adapted himself to the new postwar conservatism, writing fewer pieces for the *Nation* and the *New Republic* and more pieces for *Vogue* and *Harper's Bazaar*, which also happened to pay better. When the poet Robert Lowell, drinking heavily and on the verge of a nervous collapse, attacked Yaddo in 1949 as a center of Communism, Arvin took to his bed. "Got my will, the bonds, etc. out of safety deposit," he wrote portentously in his journal.[18] Later he joined Granville Hicks, Malcolm Cowley, and the board's other leftist critics in censuring Lowell, but he had learned to keep his politics vague. Years after the end of the McCarthy witchhunt, Arvin was asked by Daniel Aaron, who was writing a book about the literary left, whether he had ever been a Communist. Arvin refused to answer, and his friend didn't press him.

Others, though, were less easily diverted. In 1954, Aloise Buckley Heath, a Smith graduate and a sister of William F. Buckley, Jr., formed a short-lived organization called the Committee for Discrimination in Giving, which appealed to alumnae to withhold donations until the college investigated alleged Communists on its faculty. The group's main targets were Arvin and four other professors. The college, conducting its own probe, contacted the U.S. attorney general's office. Although Heath alleged that Arvin had been a member of more than fifteen Communist or Communist-linked organizations, the Justice Department replied that there was "nothing of interest" in Arvin's file. Arvin panicked nonetheless. Four years earlier, under a similar threat, the brilliant Harvard professor Francis Otto Matthiessen—who was also a father of American studies, a homosexual, and a leftist—had put his affairs in order, rented a twelfth-floor room in a Boston commercial hotel, removed his Skull and Bones key from his pocket, left a note, and jumped to his death. Arvin successfully defended himself against Heath and her committee, but he was badly shaken by the ordeal.[19] "Ghastly day . . . at night took two Nembutals and fell into oblivion," he wrote in his journal on April 2, 1954.

During the 1950s, it was easier to admit to being a Communist than to admit being a homosexual, and Arvin, who was doubly vulnerable, was doubly tormented. He tried to work, but what he called "the usual terrors" increasingly made reading and writing impossible. He began a biography of Emerson, but he was now so nearly paralyzed with loneliness and fear that he wrote nothing for long periods. He received electroshock therapy for depression, which helped slightly but also impaired his short-term memory, prompting him to complain to friends that the cure was worse than the disease. He was still a major figure at Smith and was still esteemed by many of the country's best writers, but the only place that he felt truly safe was in his apartment—his own "dismal chamber" under the eaves—where he often stayed for days, barely seeing anyone and frequently drinking himself into a stupor. Van Wyck Brooks had called Arvin "a quiet man with a violent mind" who "would gladly have stood against a wall and faced a fusillade for his convictions." Increasingly, however, his friends and colleagues found him dissolute and withdrawn. "Last night . . . up the odd Gothic blind stairwell to Arvin's for drinks," Sylvia Plath wrote in her journal in 1958, when she was earning extra money by grading exams for him. "Arvin: bald head pink, eyes and mouth dry slits as on some carved rubicund mask."[20]

In his explanatory letter to Lilienthal after the arrest, Arvin referred obliquely to "all the behavior that led up to the crisis." From his journals, it seems clear that he was referring to upheavals in his private life that began in 1957.

That fall, at the age of fifty-seven and lacking family and security, Arvin began to worry about his health and his capacity for intimacy. At the same time, Daniel Aaron recalls, his sexual appetites became more voracious. "He had a very driving, passionate sexual nature," Aaron said. "He used to say to me, 'You know, Dan, you'd think with old age sexual desires would subside. But they don't. They become more and more extreme, almost as if they were raging.'" In the prevailing view of the time, he had reached that reckoning, supposedly peculiar to the conspiratorial world of the homosexual, when debasement replaces mutuality and desperation trumps precaution. The fact is, though, Arvin was the commonest of sufferers: an aging, single man looking for a young lover to rekindle his spirits.

In late 1957, Arvin thought he had found one—a classics instructor at Smith named Ned Spofford, who, at twenty-six, was nearly half his age. "A pretty serious youth, but very likeable," Arvin wrote after their first meeting. If not quite "that Thing" which he had experienced with Capote, the relationship came close, at least for a time. "He fills my spirit too full for me to feel any other need. Have [I] ever cared for anyone more?" Arvin wrote in January 1959. But the friendship with Spofford, while tender, never became sexual, and Arvin—"depressed beyond description"—compensated by indulging his taste for erotica and engaging in casual sex with partners he hardly knew. He called it "playing with deadly fire."[21]

Arvin and Spofford saw each other nearly every day, with Arvin doing his best to hide his depression from Spofford—as he did from most of his friends—for fear he might drive the young man away. They read Propertius to each other in Latin. At times, Spofford came to Arvin's apartment to watch 8-mm. black-and-white films that Arvin liked to "run off" on his projector—tame movies of "two young guys wearing briefs tumbling over each other," Spofford told me recently. But Arvin began to worry more and more that he was too "dull and jaded" to hold Spofford's affections, as he noted in a typical journal entry from the middle of 1959:

> Ned and I have lunch at Rahar's, and he comes up later in the afternoon to borrow five dollars from me. We attempt in vain to run off a new movie. The projector fails to work. He tells me of his night in Springfield. Difficult to struggle against the suspicion that I am a convenience, in part, to be used as such. Not the whole truth, to be sure, but I am afraid too much of it. Inclined at such times to withdraw from all relations with anyone under forty.[22]

By the spring of 1959, Arvin had managed to produce a truncated essay on Emerson, entitled "The House of Pain," for the *Hudson Review*. One of its central aims was to rescue the transcendentalist from what Arvin elsewhere called "the great 'glad' glow of Emersonianism," by showing that his subject's relentless optimism "was somewhat less the product . . . of a natively happy temper than it was an achievement both of intellectual and emotional discipline."[23] Some weeks after the appearance of this essay, he took the train to New York, checked into the Latham Hotel on Twenty-eighth Street, and spent the next three nights at the Everard Baths. Situated on West Twenty-eighth Street between Broadway and Sixth Avenue, the Everard was renowned among homosexuals as a steamy arena for round-the-clock sex. It was unforgettably described by Ned Rorem in his *New York Diary*:

> You enter at any age, in any condition, any time of night or week, pay early for a fetid cubicle, and are given a torn gown and a pair of mismated slippers (insufficient against the grime that remains in your toes for days). You penetrate an obscure world, disrobe in private while reading graffiti, emerge rerobed into the public of gray wanderers so often compared to the lost souls of Dante.[24]

After staying all night at the Everard, Arvin rested up, then visited a museum or two or stopped briefly in the West Village to buy books and erotica. Because he worried increasingly about receiving sexual materials through the mail, his New York trips doubled as shopping excursions. Sylvan Schendler, who taught with Arvin at Smith, remembered picking him up after a few nights at the baths and asking him how it went. "Oh, Sylvan," he'd say, "I feel so clean."

Approaching the summer of 1960, Arvin found himself in "the pit." Nervous about an abscess on his thigh, which he feared he had developed after an anonymous tryst, he swore off cruising. "This must be the last such jaunt for many weeks," he reproved himself in his journal after a fruitless afternoon at the nearby Springfield bus station. His distaste for teaching, which had always been a frustration, ripened into disgust. He wrote, "Reading student papers, blue books, etc., a form of torture . . . a matter of rubbing an iron file over one's teeth, or holding urine in one's mouth, or having the racket of a bulldozer in one's ear for an hour or two on end."[25]

Also troubling was the presidential race between John Kennedy, a staunch Irish Catholic and Cold Warrior, and "that paltry Richard Nixon," as Arvin called him, who had built his political career by attacking all forms of deviance. Congress had given Postmaster General Arthur Summerfield sweeping powers to crack down on what Summerfield called "pornographic filth in the family mailbox." Massachusetts had recently elevated possession of obscene material from a misdemeanor to a felony and had increased the maximum penalty from two years in jail to five years in a state prison. "Almost impossible to contemplate the political scene, the vulgar conventions and the like, without revulsion," Arvin wrote in his journal.[26]

The raid on Arvin's apartment was led by Sergeant John J. Regan, a blunt-spoken Irish-Catholic state trooper, who had recently been named to head the state's new anti-pornography bureau—reputedly the first such unit in the country. Regan brought a soul saver' s zeal to his mission, which had netted approximately fifty arrests since its inception four months earlier. According to press accounts of the time, Regan received a tip either from alert postal workers, who claimed that a package addressed to Arvin had broken open to reveal homoerotic pictures, or from officials in Missouri, where a raid on a pornographic mail-order house had yielded a mailing list that had Arvin's name on it. In the course of ransacking Arvin's apartment, Regan's men, according to *Newsweek*, "half filled a patrol car" with evidence.[27]

Arvin had always thought of himself as something of a coward, yet he possessed an inner steel, as was demonstrated by his extraordinary confidence in his literary judgments and by his handwriting, which was bold and slashing. Deferential and courteous in his professional relationships, he could also, according to Aaron, be "remorselessly selfish" in his private ones—for example, in his dependency on others for meals and transportation, since he seldom cooked and couldn't drive. Arvin was a survivor. Whenever he tried to kill himself, he had always managed to be discovered. He was not the type to risk success by leaping, like Matthiessen, from a twelfth-floor window.

Arvin dealt with his crisis just as he must have feared that he would and hoped that he wouldn't. He gave the police the names of a Smith colleague, Joel Dorius, an associate professor of English, and of fourteen other male acquaintances. It remains unclear whether he also gave Spofford's name to Regan or whether the investigators discovered it simply by reading his journals. In any case, after leaving Arvin at the police station Regan sent two patrolmen to Spofford's apartment. They were sorting through the young instructor's collection of erotic pictures when Spofford came home. He was brought to police headquarters, arrested, and locked in the same cell as Arvin. Recalling the event nearly forty years later, Spofford told me, "Newton suggested that we commit suicide together. I emphatically said no."

Later that afternoon, after making bail with money borrowed from friends, Arvin admitted himself to Northampton State Hospital—Dippy Hill, as the Smith undergraduates called it.

Capote, who was living on the Mediterranean coast of Spain and working on *In Cold Blood*, wrote to Arvin within hours of hearing the news:

> Well, what's happened has happened; and it has happened to many others—who, like Gielgud, took it in stride and did not let it be the end of the world. [In 1953, John Gielgud was arrested for "persistently importuning male persons" on the streets of London's Chelsea.] . . . Aside from my affection, which you already have, I will be *glad* to supply you with money should the need arise. This is a tough experience, and must be met with toughness; a calm head, a good lawyer.[28]

Lillian Hellman, who had refused to name names during the Hollywood Red hunts, wrote to Arvin:

> I would like to do anything I could, anything. And I hope you feel friendly enough toward me to tell me what I could do. . . . Please don't feel too bad. That sounds silly, but please don't. There was [a] time when I thought the world had gone to pieces for me, but it didn't, and it's our duty to see that it doesn't. Just you be very sure that many, many people admire you and respect you.[29]

These calls for toughness seemed aimed at keeping Arvin from killing himself, but apparently he was never placed on suicide watch in the hospital, and his earliest letters from the institution reveal an oddly upbeat sense of resignation. "Life here . . . is very tolerable—with some really good personal relations, as always—and I am, I believe, reasonably calm and fatalistic," he wrote to Granville Hicks. "Good may somehow emerge from all this distress, and my own personal fortune is of minor importance, even I think to me."[30]

Arvin's equanimity collapsed after his court appearance. Convicted and fined twelve hundred dollars, he was now a felon. Three weeks later, at Dorius's trial, he testified against his colleague. (Both Dorius and Spofford were eventually acquitted on appeal.) Arvin felt too mortified and too afraid to go out, but he couldn't bear to be alone in his violated apartment. He returned to the hospital.[31]

"Dear Spike," he wrote despairingly to Leonard Ehrlich, a New York novelist who was an old friend, "it is all but impossible to write to you as I should like to do; I am really too dazed and benumbed to express myself properly. . . . The torment of thinking what this has done to other people is inexpressible. . . . I am holding on grimly."[32] Helen Bacon, then the head of the classics department at Smith, who sold her war bonds to organize a defense fund for Spofford and Dorius, recalls Arvin's enveloping shame: "He thought he was wicked."

What saved him, as the Smith trustees voted to retire him at half salary ($5,800 a year), was the encouragement he received from his celebrated friends. Letters of support continued to pour in: from Lionel Trilling, Carson McCullers, even the homophobic Van Wyck Brooks. Like Capote, David Lilienthal made repeated offers of money, and Arvin accepted them, while proudly insisting that the gifts be regarded as loans. In late November, a few weeks after he left the hospital for a second time, he heard from Edmund Wilson:

> I hope that this episode will not discourage you but perhaps in the long run prove stimulating. It will not detract in the least from your literary reputation. If it is impossible now for you to teach at Smith, you ought not to have any difficulty in publishing reviews and articles. Would you like me to speak to *The*

> *New Yorker* and [The] *Nation.* I have always thought you didn't write half enough. . . . Goddam all this interference with people's personal affairs![33]

Arvin replied: "I feel very much as if I had been involved in a violently destructive automobile accident that had no intelligible meaning, only a shattering one."[34]

Arvin hoped that Hicks and others could arrange for him to spend a quiet winter at Yaddo; the Yaddo administration replied that he was welcome but requested his resignation from the board of directors. Arvin was devastated.

He returned to the state hospital for a third time on December 2, 1960. As had happened previously, he was assigned to the newest building, a low-slung three-story red brick box with locked wards and barred windows, and there he was surrounded by shuffling, chain-smoking, mostly indigent new patients—all of them male, in obedience to the hospital's policy of separating patients by sex. Former staff members remember Arvin as extremely quiet and refined, always impeccably groomed and dressed, although his belt and ties had been taken from him. He kept to himself, asking for little, socializing with two or three other patients who made him feel comfortable. "He wouldn't get any judgment here," Pat Carr, a nursing supervisor, recalls. "He was just accepted for what he was." Two weeks later, he emerged from the hospital, somewhat strengthened. In January, a month after his discharge, he wrote to Hicks:

> I have ventured more and more into public places, including the college library, and though it is painful enough sometimes, I gain a little strength by doing so. So far as I can intuit peoples' attitudes, they are mostly friendly or at least tolerant: I have not yet encountered any real rebuff anywhere, and some people have gone out of their way to be kind—sometimes surprising people. So in one sense I may "live it down" ultimately—though in another sense, subjectively, I never can. The imagery for a nightmare will always be there.[35]

At the end of January, Arvin returned to the hospital once again, too depressed to receive visitors. His handwriting—which always clearly marked the degree of his resolve—was shaky and barely legible. "I am sorry to be (or rather seem) so unfriendly and unhospitable now but I am in the hospital again and feeling too miserable to talk," he wrote to Ehrlich. He scarcely felt better two months later, when he wrote, again to Ehrlich, about his disappointment at having the first book review he'd been able to write since his arrest rejected by *Commentary*: "I have little or no news beyond this. I get through the days as best I can, seeing almost no one and reading until the pages swim before my eyes. I hardly know how the time passes but looking back on it, as usual, it seems to have flown. . . . I need you worse than ever."[36]

But as long as Arvin worked, he could keep going. He began a critical biography of Longfellow, whose poetry he had first read fifty years earlier, and, to his surprise, he was able to write well and cleanly and without a trace of bitterness. By July, he had written the first chapter and he could even cluck dismissively at people who might be outwardly tougher than he but had lost the will to soldier on. He wrote to Hicks: "Hemingway's suicide knocked me for a loop when I read of it, and has haunted me ever since. Yet in a sense it was a characteristic and almost a predictable thing for him to do, wasn't it? That lifelong preoccupation with death."[37]

By the following fall, Arvin—like his hero, Emerson—had discovered the great healing force of optimism as a moral imperative, a necessary antidote to the pain of American life. "Things are a little less bleak, now that college has begun," he wrote to Ehrlich in late September 1961. He added, "I have long since found that, little as one may like it, one can *live* through ages of loneliness. What has kept me sane, perhaps, is that, to my delight, I have found that I can *work*."

"He was at the flood tide of his energy and power; never more enthusiastic about what he planned to do, or more eager to set about doing it," the critic Louis Kronenberger recalled of Arvin.[38] One of Arvin's closest friends, Madeline Fisher, told me, "Nobody could do anything that would hurt him anymore. The blows had been dealt."

Arvin seldom left his apartment except to go to the library. He worked hard on his Longfellow book and on his memoir; read voraciously, not only in English but also in French, German, Italian, Spanish, and Latin; and plotted several new projects, including an ambitious history of literary ideas in America. The fact that he had brought trouble to his friends seemed no longer to plague him, nor did he acknowledge responsibility for their suffering. He mourned his estrangement from Spofford, but coldly, numbly, without remorse, as he noted in a letter to Hicks in 1962:

> You have no doubt heard the news of Ned's acquittal by the state court. . . . Of course it is wonderfully good news, and I "really" rejoice. But I was shocked at myself to find how little, honestly, it really elated me. I *knew* that it was a happy fact, but somehow I could hardly *feel* anything. Perhaps my capacity for feeling, at least in that connection, is frozen once for all. And there is the thought that, acquitted or not, Ned will never be the same person again that he was before; that he will be lamed by the whole ghastly episode for life; and that our really exquisite friendship was utterly annihilated by it.[39]

Arvin's health problems—always a worry—persisted throughout the Kennedy years. Prostate surgery resulted in months of painful incontinence. In the middle of 1962, he finished *Longfellow*. Then, in early 1963, he was found to have pancreatic cancer. Arvin didn't complain, nor did he seem dismayed. Perhaps, as some of his friends surmised, he felt that he deserved the disease as a form of punishment. Again, he seems to have been well prepared. He had written Daniel Aaron a decade earlier:

> The *staple* of life is certainly suffering, though surely not its real meaning; and we differ mainly in our capacity to endure it—or to be diverted from it. I myself never found it consoling to have this denied or minimized; it seems to me to give one *some* strength just to know that pain is normal, and disappointment the rule, and disquiet the standard—and that the things that have the other quality (work, friendship, the arts) are the wonderful, incredible exceptions and mitigation.[40]

Arvin lived just long enough to see *Longfellow* published and to have the pleasure of reading Edmund Wilson's glowing review in the *New Yorker*. Wilson wrote, "Among the writers who have really devoted their lives to the study of our literature . . . I can think of only two who can themselves be called first-rate writers: Van Wyck Brooks and Newton Arvin."[41] In the days before Arvin died, on March 21, 1963, in Northampton's Cooley Dickinson Hospital, he studiously excised with a razor dozens of potentially embarrassing passages from his journal. Shortly before his death, Capote telephoned him, for the last time. Arvin consoled him with the remark "never mind, at least I've grown up at last."[42]

Twenty-one years later, Capote died, leaving a will that established that an annual award for excellence in literary criticism be given "in memory of Newton Arvin."[43]

THE deep clipped voice of Joel Dorius sounded frail when I reached him, not long ago, by phone at his home, in San Francisco. He is seventy-nine, has retired from teaching English literature, and is crippled by intractable back pains that have left him housebound since the 1980s. When I asked him how Arvin's betrayal had affected him, he told me that after thirty-four years of being so filled with hate that he felt "numb" he begun to write an autobiography, and it was now nearly finished. "I've been plunged back into the white-hot cauldron," he said.[44]

When I first approached Dorius for an interview, he had been reluctant to talk. He told me that he was worried about reopening old wounds and was nervous that it would preëmpt the material in his book. He changed his mind when I mentioned that Arvin's last years had not been grim but productive.

"That that strange, mysterious, bland man had become so serene and happy was absolutely unthinkable to me," he said in a subsequent telephone conversation. Dorius's fall had been uncushioned. He had refused to inform on friends, and—along with Spofford—he was fired from Smith. Dorius told me that, because of the disgrace, he had felt forced to leave the United States; he had taught in Germany for two years before returning to finish his career, at San Francisco State College.

He said that he had been hospitalized for depression in 1961. Nearly forty years after the event, his rage at Arvin was undiminished. In a halting voice, he said, "his being so very chipper and hale after he did us in. . . . I can't imagine anyone that morally neutral, or detached from life."[45]

Ned Spofford, who agreed to an interview by phone and correspondence, told me a slightly different story. He is sixty-seven, and he lives in Palo Alto, an hour from his close friend Dorius. Whereas Dorius was in mid-career at the time of their arrest, Spofford was twenty-nine, and was more resilient—or so it seemed. He left Northampton for further graduate studies, at Harvard, then studied classical poetry in Rome for two years on a fellowship. From 1964 to 1971, he taught at Cornell and received tenure, but he found Ithaca so lonely that he moved to San Francisco. Until his retirement in 1988, he was a classics professor at Stanford.

Like Dorius, Spofford told me that he had tried to put the past behind him by maintaining a public silence about the Arvin affair. Like Dorius, he had been hospitalized—in his case, three times—for depression. But Spofford didn't seem to share his friend's bitterness. In a letter to me, he wrote, "Joel tends to speak in the plural: 'It devastated our lives, and that's that.' It didn't devastate my life. With a lot of help from friends, before and after The Event, I have had a fairly happy life."[46]

Even today, he has continued to cling to the belief that his was not among the names that Arvin gave to the police. "I suppose I've just tried not to think about it," he said. Spofford added that when Arvin was dying, he had had a friend write to Spofford, asking the younger man to call him. At the time, Spofford had been too angry to pick up the phone, but he didn't feel that way anymore. When I pressed him on the matter, Spofford replied, simply, "Newton and I were each other's closest friend."

NOTES

1. Press accounts include "2 Smith Teachers Held in Vice Case," *New York Times*, September 4, 1960; "Suspended Jail Term Given 4; 2 Others Appeal," *Daily Hampshire Gazette*, September 20, 1960; and "3 At Smith Accept Finding of Guilt," *New York Times*, September 9, 1960. See also Stacey Sklar, "Scandal at Smith College: The Newton Arvin Case" (bachelor's thesis, Amherst College, 1989), 10–11.

2. Newton Arvin to David Lilienthal, November 3, 1960, David E. Lilienthal Papers, Seeley G. Mudd Manuscript Library, Princeton University.

3. Edmund Wilson testimonial, September 12, 1960, Newton Arvin Papers, Mortimer Rare Book Room, William Allen Neilson Library, Smith College.

4. Newton Arvin, "The Past Recaptured," Arvin Papers, 102, 81.

5. Arvin, "The Past Recaptured," 136–137.

6. Dean Flower, "Newton Arvin," in John A. Garraty, ed., *Dictionary of American Bibliography, Supplement Seven, 1961–1965* (New York, 1981), 18–19; Brooks to Arvin, June 8, 1921, Arvin Papers. See also Margot Cleary, "Newton Arvin's Fall from Grace," *Daily Hampshire Gazette*, October 11, 1991: 10; Arvin to Lilienthal, June 12, 1924, Lilienthal Papers.

7. Newton Arvin, *Hawthorne* (Boston, 1929), 59.

8. Flower, "Newton Arvin," 19.

9. Arvin to Lilienthal, September 6, 1920, Lilienthal Papers.

10. Gerald Clarke, *Capote: A Biography* (New York, 1998), 113.

11. Clarke, *Capote*, 105.

12. Clarke, *Capote*, 117–119.

13. Clarke, *Capote*, 148.

14. Newton Arvin, *Herman Melville* (New York, 1950), 138.

15. Arvin, "Speech of Acceptance on Receiving the National Book Award for Non-Fiction," February 1951, Arvin Papers. See referenced also in Sklar, "Scandal at Smith College ," 36 and Flower, "Newton Arvin," 18.

16. Arvin, *Melville*, 171.

17. *The Journals of David E. Lilienthal*, 4 vols. (New York, 1964–1969), 3:274.

18. Newton Arvin journal, February 28, 1949, private collection.

19. Sklar, "Scandal at Smith College," 37, citing "Heath Chronology," March 5, 1954, William Allen Neilson Library, Smith College; Matthiessen's suicide reported in "Professor F. O. Matthiessen Dies in Boston Plunge," *New York Times*, April 1, 1950, and "Professor's Leap Laid to Worries," *New York Times*, April 2, 1950.

20. Van Wyck Brooks quoted in Flower, "Newton Arvin," 18–19; Sylvia Plath journal, March 8, 1958, William Allen Neilson Library, Smith College, also published in Ted Hughes and Frances McCullough, eds., *The Journals of Sylvia Plath* (New York, 1982), 203.

21. Arvin journal, December 14, 1957; January 25, 1959; April 11, 1959.

22. Arvin journal, April 28, 1959.

23. Newton Arvin, "Ralph Waldo Emerson," in Arvin, Daniel Aaron and Sylvan Schendler, eds., *American Pantheon* (New York, 1966), 10, 23.

24. Ned Rorem, *The New York Diary* (New York, 1967), 189.

25. Arvin journal, July 22, 1960.

26. "Obscenity in the Mails—Who Sends It, Who Gets It," *U.S. News and World Report*, September 14, 1959: 88–89; Arvin journal, July 27, 1960.

27. Emilie Tavel, "Bay State Drives on Pornography," *Christian Science Monitor*, September 17, 1960. See also Sklar, "Scandal at Smith College," 10–11. "Morals: Scandal on the Campus," *Newsweek*, September 10, 1960: 43–44.

28. Capote to Arvin, September 6, 1960, Arvin Papers.

29. Hellman to Arvin, September 1960, Arvin Papers.

30. Arvin to Hicks, September 15, 1960.

31. Sklar, "Scandal at Smith College," 25. See also "Morals Case Is Lost By Smith Professor," *New York Times*, October 12, 1960. Arvin's testimony appears in Commonwealth of Massachusetts v. Joel R. Dorius, "Report," Hampshire County Superior Court No. 5655, 4–8 (October 1960).

32. Arvin to Ehrlich, September 23, 1960.

33. Wilson to Arvin, November 26, 1960, Arvin Papers.

34. Arvin to Wilson, December 1, 1960, Beinecke Rare Books and Manuscript Library, Yale University.

35. Arvin to Hicks, January 11, 1961.

36. Arvin to Ehrlich, April 13, 1961. See also Arvin to Hicks, April 14, 1961 on *Commentary* incident.

37. Arvin to Hicks, July 8, 1961.

38. Louis Kronenberger, "A Memoir," in Arvin, Aaron, and Schendler, *American Pantheon*, xxv.

39. Sklar, "Scandal at Smith College," 49, citing letter from Arvin to Hicks, March 5, 1962.

40. Arvin to Aaron, April 23, 1953; see also Daniel Aaron, "Introduction," in Arvin, Aaron, and Schendler, *American Pantheon*, xvii.

41. Edmund Wilson, "Arvin's Longfellow and New York State's Geology," *New Yorker*, March 22, 1963: 174–181.

42. Clarke, *Capote*, 186–187.

43. Hilton Als, "A Capote Legacy," *New Yorker* January 22, 1996: 31–33.

44. Joel Dorius, telephone interview with author, June 15, 1998.

45. Joel Dorius, telephone interview with author, July 6, 1998.

46. Ned Spofford, letter to author, July 7, 1998.

Notes on Contributors

David W. Blight is Professor of History at Yale University. His books include *Frederick Douglass's Civil War: Keeping Faith in Jubilee; Race and Reunion: The Civil War in American Memory;* and *Beyond the Battlefield: Race, Memory, and the American Civil War.* He has edited and co-edited five other books, including *When This Cruel War Is Over: The Civil War Letters of Charles Harvey Brewster* and *Union and Emancipation: Essays on Politics and Race in the Civil War.*

Margaret Bruchac, Abenaki, is currently researching the colonial erasure and contemporary recovery of Connecticut River Valley Native histories, in the Anthropology Department at the University of Massachusetts, Amherst. She is co-author of *1621: A New Look at Thanksgiving.* Her "Earthshapers and Placemakers: Algonkian Indian Stories and the Landscape" will be published in the forthcoming *Indigenous Archaeologies: The Politics of Practice,* edited by H. Martin Wobst and Claire Smith.

Kerry W. Buckley is Executive Director of Historic Northampton. He is author of *Mechanical Man: John Broadus Watson and the Beginnings of Behaviorism,* and co-editor, with Christopher Clark, of *Letters from an American Utopia: The Stetson Family and the Northampton Association, 1843–1847.* His articles and reviews have appeared in the *New England Quarterly* and the *Journal of American History.*

Christopher Clark is Professor of North American History at the University of Warwick, England. He is author of *The Roots of Rural Capitalism, Western Massachusetts, 1780–1860,* which won the Frederick Jackson Turner Award of the Organization of American Historians, *The Communitarian Moment: The Radical Challenge of the Northampton Association,* co-editor, with Kerry W. Buckley, of *Letters from an American Utopia: The Stetson Family and the Northampton Association, 1843–1847,* and (with Nancy Hewitt) the second edition of *Who Built America: Working People and the Nation's Economy, Politics, Culture, and Society,* vol. 1.

John Putnam Demos is Samuel Knight Professor of American History and Professor of American Studies at Yale University. He is the author of many books and essays, including *A Little Commonwealth: Family Life in Plymouth Colony* and *The Unredeemed Captive: A Family Story from Early*

America. His *Entertaining Satan: Witchcraft and the Culture of Early New England* was awarded the Bancroft Prize.

DEAN FLOWER is Professor of English Language and Literature at Smith College. He has published articles and reviews in the *New England Quarterly*, the *Massachusetts Review*, *Essays in Criticism*, and the *Hudson Review*, where he has also served as advisory editor since 1982.

JILL A. HODNICKI has lectured on the Connecticut River Valley and on the history and architecture of Holyoke, Massachusetts. She was curator of "Locks, Stocks, and Barrels: The South Hadley Canal at 200 Years" at the Mount Holyoke College Art Museum, and was an advisor for that museum's exhibit "Changing Prospects: The View from Mount Holyoke".

MARTHA HOPPIN is an art historian, recently co-curator and essayist of *Changing Prospects: The View from Mt. Holyoke*. She is editor of *Arcadian Vales: Views of the Connecticut River Valley* and has published articles in *American Art Journal* and *American Art Review*. She is currently researching a book on the American nineteenth-century painter John George Brown.

HELEN LEFKOWITZ HOROWITZ is Professor of American Studies at Smith College. She is the author of *Rereading Sex: Battles over Sexual Knowledge and Suppression in Nineteenth-Century America; Culture and the City: Cultural Philanthropy in Chicago from the 1880s to 1917; Alma Mater: Design and Experience in the Women's Colleges from Their Nineteenth-Century Beginnings to the 1930s; Campus Life: Undergraduate Cultures from the End of the Eighteenth Century to the Present; The Power and Passion of M. Carey Thomas*, and co-editor, with Kathy Peiss, of *Love across the Color Line: The Letters of Alice Hanley*.

MARLA R. MILLER is Associate Professor of History at the University of Massachusetts, Amherst, where she is Chair of the Public History Program. She is recipient of the Organization of American Historians' Lerner-Scott Prize for outstanding work in women's history. Her articles have appeared in the *New England Quarterly*, the *Proceedings of the Dublin Seminar on New England Folklife*, and the *William and Mary Quarterly*.

STEPHEN NISSENBAUM is Professor of History at the University of Massachusetts, Amherst. Major publications include *The Battle for Christmas*, a Pulitzer Prize finalist; *Sex, Diet, and Debility in Jacksonian America: Sylvester Graham and Health Reform*, and *Salem Possessed: The Social Origins of Witchcraft* (with Paul Boyer), which won the American Historical Association's John H. Dunning Prize.

GREGORY H. NOBLES is Professor of History in the School of History, Technology, and Society at Georgia Tech, where he specializes in early American and environmental history. He is the author of *Divisions throughout the Whole: Politics and Society in Hampshire County, Massachusetts, 1740–1775*. His most recent book is *American Frontiers: Cultural Encounters and Continental Conquest*. He is currently at work on a book entitled *Naturalist Nation: The Art and Science of Birds in Audubon's America.*

NELL IRVIN PAINTER is currently the Edwards Professor of American History at Princeton University. She was Director of Princeton's Program in African-American Studies from 1997 to 2000. As a scholar, Professor Painter has published numerous books, articles, reviews, and essays, including, *Sojourner Truth: A Life, a Symbol*. Her most recent book is *Southern History across the Color Line*. Six earlier books are also still in print.

KATHY PEISS is the Roy F. and Jeannette P. Nichols Professor of American History at the University of Pennsylvania. She is the author of *Cheap Amusements: Working Women and Leisure in Turn-of-the-Century New York; Passion and Power: Sexuality in History* (co-edited with Christina Simmons); *Men and Women: A History of Gender, Costume, and Power* (co-authored with Barbara Clark Smith), *Love across the Color Line* (co-edited with Helen Horowitz); and *Major Problems in the History of American Sexuality*. Her most recent book is *Hope in a Jar: The Making of America's Beauty Culture.*

LEONARD RICHARDS, is Professor of History at the University of Massachusetts, Amherst. He won the American Historical Association's Albert J. Beveridge Prize in 1970 for his *"Gentlemen of Property and Standing": Anti-Abolition Mobs in Jacksonian America*. Other books include *The Life and Times of Congressman John Quincy Adams*, a finalist for the 1987 Pulitzer Prize for biography. His most recent book is *Shays's Rebellion: The American Revolution's Final Battle.*

RONALD STORY is Professor of History at the University of Massachusetts, Amherst. He is author of *The Forging of an Aristocracy: Harvard and the Boston Upper Class, 1800–1870* and co-author of *Generations of Americans: A History of the United States.*

KEVIN SWEENEY is Professor of History and American Studies at Amherst College, author of *The River Gods and Other Minor Deities: The Williams Family and the Culture of the Connecticut River Valley, 1637–1790* and co-editor, with Evan Haefeli, of *Captors and Captives: The 1704 French and Indian Raid on Deerfield.*

PETER A. THOMAS is former director of the Consulting Archaeology Program at the University of Vermont. He has published numerous papers on various topics in ethnohistory, archaeology, and anthropology. His research has focused on the Indian trade and cultural process in the middle Connecticut River Valley from 1635 to 1665.

BARRY WERTH is the author of *The Billion-Dollar Molecule; Damages;* and *The Scarlet Professor*. He has written for the *New Yorker*, the *New York Times Magazine,* and other national publications. He lives and works in Northampton.

Index

A Farewell To Arms, 485–486
Aaron, Daniel, 497, 498, 500, 502, 504, 507
Abercrombie and Fitch, 486
Adam, Phebe Grant, 309, 311, 334
Adam, William, 301–302, 307–309, 311–314, 322–323, 327, 334
Adams, Christopher, 426
Adams, John, 179–180, 186–187, 258
Adirondacks, 481
Aitken, Alexander, 380
Alcott, Bronson, 498
Aldrich, Nelson, 474
American Academy of Arts and Letters, 500
American Association of Advertising Agencies, 483
American Federation of Labor, 463
American Mercury, 482
American Scene, 398, 401
Ames, Elizabeth, 497
Ames, John W., 416
Amherst College, 404, 459, 461–463
Ancient Order of Foresters, 426, 446
Anderson, Sherwood, 496–497
Arvin, Newton, 493–511
Assellaquompas, 5
Associated Press, 471, 481
Atomic Energy Commission, 494
Awonusk, 25

Babbitt, 484
Bacon, Helen, 505
Baltimore Evening Sun, 482
Barry, Rev. Michael, 425
Bartleby the Scrivener, 465
Bartlett, Mary Bridgman, 63–65
Bartlett, Robert, 44
Bartlett, Samuel, 63–65
Bartlett, Solomon, 201, 203–204
Bartlett, William Henry, 235–237, 270
Barton, Bruce, 460–492
Barton, Durstine and Osborn, 461, 479
Beecher, Henry Ward, 273
Benson, George W., 301–304, 306–309, 313–315, 319–320, 322–323, 326–328, 330, 334–335, 344, 346–347, 355, 359
Berenson, Senda, 411
Berkshires, 398
Bierce, Ambrose, 366, 381
Billings, Joel, 169
Bishop, Will, 369
Blackstone Hotel, 473
Blaine, James G., 389, 473
Bliss, George, 369
Bliss, Margaret, 44, 50–51, 54–55
Bliss, Thomas, 50–51, 54–55, 62, 65
Blodgett, Benjamin Colman, 427–429
Boltwood, William, 204–205
Bok, Edward, 476
Boorstin, Daniel, 472
Bosanquet, Theodora, 401
Boston Police Strike, 463, 465
The Bostonians, 398
Boughton, Alice, 401
Bowdoin, James, 169, 173, 180, 186–187, 217
Boyle, James, 349, 359
Brady, Matthew, 399
Brennan, Thomas, 449–450
Brewster, Charles Harvey, 365–394
Brewster, Harvey, 370
Brewster, Martha Russell, 370
Brewster, Martha, 369–370
Brewster, Mary Katherine, 369–370, 389–390
Bridgman, James, 43–49
Bridgman, Sarah Lyman, 43–49, 55–63
Briggs, Col. Henry S., 368
Briggs, George N., 368
Brocklesby, William C., 411, 414
Brooks, Samuel, 302, 306
Brooks, Van Wyck, 496–497, 500, 505, 508
Broughton's Meadow, 301, 305, 323, 334
Bryan, Charles, 479
Bryan, William Jennings, 479
Bryant, William Cullen, 270, 277
Buckley, William F., Jr., 501
Burleigh, Charles, Jr., 253–255, 350
Burt, Henry M., 276–277
Burton, Marion LeRoy, 414
Butler, Gen. Benjamin F., 383
Butler, Nicholas Murray, 471

Butler, William M., 476
Byrne, Susan, 320

Cable, George Washington, 399, 419, 438
Camp Brightwood, 370, 375, 383, 385
Cannon, Uncle Joe, 473
Carnegie, Andrew, 414, 419
Capote, Truman, 493, 498–500, 502, 504–505, 508
Celebrity Club, 499
Chaffee, Orwell S., 305–306, 314
Chicago, Illinois, 471–472
Chickahominy Creek, 382
Chickwallop, 5, 8, 26
Child, David Lee, 331–333
Child, Lydia Maria, 332–333, 365
Clapp, Warham and Sophia, 28, 30
Clark, Fred, 369
Clark, Samuel, 169
Clarke School for the Deaf, 403, 459
Clarke, John, 403
Clarke, Gerald, 498
Cleveland, Grover, 389
Clurman, Harold, 498
Coe, William, 304–306, 320, 322, 334
Cole, Thomas, 231–235, 237, 266, 396
Collier's, 462, 469
Commentary, 506
Committee for Discrimination in Giving, 501
Comstock, Ada Louise, 404, 414, 416
Conant, Joseph, 301–302, 305–309, 314–315, 322, 334
Coney Island, 486
Connecticut River, 232–233, 235
Cooley Dickinson Hospital, 508
Coolidge, Calvin, 459–492, 496
Coolidge, Grace Goodhue, 459
Cooper, Kent, 481
Copland, Aaron, 498
Cornell University, 509
Corticelli Silk Company, 493
Cosmian Hall, 403
Couch's Brigade, 370
Cowley, Malcolm, 500
Craigie, Pearl Mary, 447
Crandall, Prudence, 304, 323, 345–346, 355
Crane, Stephen, 378
Crane, Winthrop Murray, 463, 473
Creel Committee, 462
Cutchamaquin, 8

Daley and Halligan, 494
Daughterty, Harry, 489N
Davis, John W., 479
Day family, 188
Day, Luke, 170–174, 189
Dearborn, Michigan, 467
de Grailly, Victor, 237
Dewey, Charles A., 408
Dickens, Charles, 265–266
Dickinson family, 187
Dickinson, Oliver, 185
Dickinson, Rebecca, 222
Dickinson, Reuben, 176, 189
Diner, Hasia, 438
Dixon, Ella Hepworth, 401
Dodge, Edwin Sherrill, 416
Dorius, Joel, 504–505, 508
Dorsey, Basil, 349
Dos Passos, John, 497
Douglass, Frederick, 301, 344, 347–349, 351, 355, 358
Dreiser, Theodore, 439, 497
Durstine, Roy, 462, 483
Dwight, John S., 333
Dwight, Theodore, 234, 237, 259–261, 269–270
Dwight, Timothy, 231–232, 257–261, 265–266, 276

Earhart, Amelia, 493
Eden, John, 261, 274–276
Edwards, Jonathan, 79, 82, 85, 91–105
Edwards, Sarah, 96
Ehrlich, Leonard, 505–506
Ellison, Ralph, 386
Ely family, 188
Ely, Reuben, 188
Ely, Samuel, 168, 175–176, 215
Emerson, Ella, 416
Emerson, Ralph Waldo, 257, 267, 498, 500–502, 507
Ethan Frome, 485
Everard Baths, 503
Every Week, 402

Fair Oaks, battle of, 371, 377, 380
Farrer, Thomas Charles, 238, 240, 241
Father Mathew Society, 438, 446
Fisher, Madeline, 507
Fitzgerald, F. Scott, 485
Forbes Library, 414
Forbes, Judge Charles Edward, 403

Ford, Ford Madox, 401
Ford, Henry, 467
Fort Hill, 20, 26
Forward, Justus, 205
Fowler, Orson Squire, 447
Fredericksburg, battle of, 378
Free Congregational Society, 347
Frémont, John C., 383
French, J. W., 275–276
Frost, Robert, 493
Fur Trade, 5, 10–14, 52
Fussell, Paul, 366, 380

Garfield, James A., 473
Garrison, Mary, 497–498
Garrison, William Lloyd, 301, 303–304, 312, 328, 344, 346–347, 355, 358–359
Gere, Isaac, 197
Germany, 508
Gettysburg, battle of, 365, 372
Gielgud, John, 504
Gilbert, Olive, 354–358, 360–361
Gillett, Frederick, 472
Glatthaar, Joseph, 382
Gompers, Samuel, 464
Goodrich, Ansel, 197, 209
Gosse, Edmund, 398, 401
Graham, Sylvester, 282–298, 344, 351
Grand Army of the Republic, 389
Gray family, 187–188
The Great Gatsby, 485
Green, John Morton, 406

Hale, Enoch, 216
Halleck, Gen. Henry W., 383
Hall, Basil, 233–235, 262, 264–266
Hampshire Bookshop, 493
Hampshire Gazette, 168, 216, 218, 219, 399, 432, 439, 443
Hancock, John, 186, 217
Hanley, Alice, 419–458
Hanley, James, 423, 426, 429, 434
Hanley, John, 431
Hanley, Katherine, 428, 437
Hanley, Mary Scully, 449
Hanna, Mark, 474
Hannon, Robert Charles, 447
Hannum, Honor, 45–46, 48, 61
Hannum, William, 45–46, 48
Harding, Warren G., 459, 461, 471, 475, 484, 489N
Harlem, 499
Harper's Bazaar, 500
Harrisburg *Telegraph*, 482
Harrison, Benjamin, 473
Harvard Classics, 462
Harvard University, 416, 496, 500, 509
Have Faith In Massachusetts, 470, 473
Hawley, Joseph, 80, 140, 149, 212
Hawthorne, Nathaniel, 267, 308, 493, 494, 496, 498–499
Hays, Will, 475, 489N, 491N
Hazen, Charles Downer, 399
Heath, Aloise Buckley, 501
Hellman, Lillian, 505
Hemingway, Ernest, 486, 507
Hicks, John D., 460
Hicks, Granville, 500, 505–507
Higginbotham, Evelyn Brooks, 422
Higham, John, 466
Hill, Samuel L., 302, 304–305, 308–309, 313–315, 320, 322–323, 325–327, 330, 334–336, 346, 348, 359, 403
Hillyer, Winthrop, 413
Hines, Joseph, 169
Hitchcock, Edward, 234, 261
Hitchcock, Orra White, 234
Hoar, David, 431
Hockanum, 234–235, 260
Holland, Josiah G., 273, 275, 276
Home Culture Clubs, 419, 427, 429, 438–439
Hoosac Tunnel, 424, 427
Hoover, Herbert, 463, 484
Hopkins, Claude, 469
Hospital Hill, 18, 30–32
Houghton Mifflin Company, 470
The House of the Seven Gables, 497
Howe, Samuel Gridley, 407
Howells, William Dean, 397
Hudson, Erasmus Darwin, 301–302, 307–309, 319–320, 322–323, 325–328, 330, 334
Hudson Review, 502
Hughes, Charles Evans, 471
Hughes, Ted, 493

In Cold Blood, 504
Irving, Washington, 257, 267

J. P. Morgan and Company, 463, 474
J. Walter Thompson Advertising Company, 469
Jackson, "Stonewall," 365

James, Henry, 257, 273, 395–402
James, William, 395
Jensen, Richard, 474
Jewett, Milo, 406
Jewett, Sarah Orne, 397
Johnson, Hiram, 471
Johnson, Jack, 421
Jordan, Elizabeth, 401
Jordan, Mary Augusta, 494
Judd, David, 197
Judd, Frances Birge, 307
Judd, Hall, 302, 306–309, 313–314, 320, 322–323, 326–327, 334
Judd, Jonathan, 147, 149, 212, 218, 219
Judd, Sylvester, 21, 307
Judson Female Seminary, 406

Keegan, John, 381
Kelley, Abby, 317, 320
Kellogg, Daniel, 223–224
Kelton and Company, 428
Kennedy, John F., 503
Kenney, John, 426
King Philip's War, 18, 26–27
King, Franklin, 416
King, Rufus, 187
King, Titus, 27–28
Kingsley, Will, 369
Kronenberger, Louis, 507

Ladies' Home Journal, 476
LaFollette, Robert, 477, 479, 496
Lamont, Thomas, 463, 474–475
Langdon, George, 44
Langdon, Hannah, 44, 61
Lasch, Christopher, 485
Lasker, Albert, 469, 475, 489N, 491N
Latham Hotel, 503
Law and Order, 472
Lead mine, 58
League of Nations, 473
Lears, Jackson, 469, 484
Lee, Gerald Stanley, 276
Leed, Eric, 375
Lenroot, Irvine, 473
Leonard family, 188
Leonard, Reuben, Jr., 188
Leslie's Weekly, 471
Lewis, Channing, 419–458
Lewis, Sinclair, 460, 484, 496
Lilienthal, David, 494, 496, 501, 505
Lincoln, Abraham, 382–383
Lincoln, Benjamin, 169–170, 173, 184
Lind, Jenny, 231, 252
Linderman, Gerald, 377
Literary Digest, 470
Lodge, Henry Cabot, 472, 473, 476
Longfellow, William Wadsworth, 506–508
Lowden, Frank, 471
Lyman, John, 57–60
Lyman, Joseph, 216
Lyman, Richard, 56–58
Lyman, Richard, Jr., 57–60
Lyman, Robert, 58–59
Lynch, Rev. Joseph, 446
Lynd, Helen, 492N
Lynd, Robert, 492N
Lyon, Mary, 404–405

Mack, David, 302, 307–308, 322, 326, 334
Mack, Maria Brastow, 308, 334
Main Street, 496
Maminash family, 18, 28–31
Maminash, Elizabeth, 28, 31
Maminash, Joseph, 28, 31
Maminash, Sally, 28–31
Manchester, William, 377
Manhattan Project, 493
Mann Act, 421
Manning, Mike, 430
Martin, Joseph C., 326
Mason, Jonathan, 183–184
Mason, Minnie, 428
Matthiessen, Francis Otto, 501, 504
Mattoon, Ebenezer, 189, 217
May, Samuel J., 304
McCarthy, Joseph, 500
McClellan, Gen. George B., 383
McClellan, Katherine, 399, 401
McCormack, John, 498
McCormick, Medill, 473
McCullers, Canson, 505
McKinley, William, 473, 477
Melville, Herman, 465, 493–494, 499–500
Mencken, H. L., 482
Metacom, 26
The Metaphysical Club, 395
Michaels, Walter Benn, 466
Middletown, 492N
Mill River, 19, 26, 33, 346
Miller, John, 216, 219, 223
Millerites, 355–358
Minot, George, 214, 217
Mitchell, Reid, 375

Moby Dick, 500
The Modern Temper, 485
Morrow, Dwight, 462–464, 472, 474–475, 484
Motion Picture Directors and Distributors Association, 491N
Mount Holyoke, 231, 233, 235, 237–238, 257–277
Mount Holyoke College, 404
Mount Tom, 276–277, 431
Murphy, Josephine, 430

Nally, Edward, 369
Napier, Thomas, 333
Narrative of Sojourner Truth, 353–360
Nassicohee, 5
National Book Award, 499
Nation, 500, 506
Native Americans, 5–16, 18–34
Neessahalant, 5
Neilson, William Allan, 404, 416
Newsweek, 504
New Republic, 500
New York, 499, 503
New York Diary, 503
The New Yorker, 506, 508
Nichols, Edward, 238, 239
Nixon, Richard, 503
Nonotucks, 5, 18, 22–24
North American Review, 396
Northampton Association of Education and Industry, 301–336, 343–353, 355, 403
Northampton Cooperative Bank, 428
Northampton Commercial College, 428
Northampton Silk Company, 301–302, 304–306, 315–316, 334, 346
Northampton State Hospital, 252, 282, 424, 504
Northampton Street Railway, 431

Oak Park, Illinois, 461
O'Donnell, John B., 425
Ohio Gang, 478, 491N
Osborn, Alex, 462
Outlook, 469, 471

Palo Alto, California, 508
Pancake Plain, 28, 30–31
Paqualant, 5
Paradise Pond, 498
Parsons, Catherine Phelps, 107, 109, 111, 113, 119–123, 125, 127–128
Parsons, Col. Joseph B., 370, 379
Parsons, Henry W., 375
Parsons, Joseph, 10, 39, 43–66
Parsons, John, 64
Peabody & Stearns, 408, 413
People's Institute, 438
Pequod, 500
Perkins, Maxwell, 476, 486
Peters, Amelia, 430
Pierce, Barbara Arvin, 497
Pierce, Charles, 497
Pine Laws, 139
Phelps, Charles, 210
Phillips, William, 184
Plath, Sylvia, 402, 493, 501
Poll taxes, 185–186
Polley, George F., 387
Pomeroy, Medad, 53
Population, Hampshire County, 208
Preston, Enos L., 314
The Price of Freedom, 476
Putnam, Karl S., 416
Pynchon, John, 5, 10–12, 25–27, 47–48, 52, 62, 64, 66
Pynchon, William, 5, 8–10, 23–24, 48, 51–52

Quequelatt, 26
Quay, Matthew, 473–474

Rahar's, 502
Railroad, 263, 273–276
The Red Badge of Courage, 378
Red Scare, 463, 466–467, 479
Regan, John J., 503–504
Renwick, James, 406
Republican National Committee, 475, 477, 479
Republican Party, 382, 462, 476
Revolutionary War, 137–163
Riants, 5
River Gods, 75–86
Rhodes, Elisha Hunt, 370, 387
Rockwell, Norman, 395, 469, 485, 493
Roderick Hudson, 395, 397, 399
Rogers, John F., Jr., 395
Roosevelt, Franklin D., 477
Roosevelt, Theodore, 399, 476, 484–485
Rorem, Ned, 503
Round Hill Road, 398
Rowell, James, 390
Ruggles, David, 349, 351–353, 359

Rust, Alvin, 369
Ryan, Alice, 424, 427
Ryan, Mary, 432
Ryan, Thomas, 424

St. Joseph's Society, 438
St. Mary's Temperence, Abstinence and Benevolent Association, 438, 446
St. Michael's School, 426, 429
Salvation Army, 462
Sampson, Joseph, 21
San Francisco, 508–509
San Francisco State College, 508
Saratoga Springs, New York, 497–498
Sargent, John Singer, 399
Saturday Evening Post, 469, 493
Scales, Laura, 416
Scarborough, Theodore, 301–304, 322
The Scarlet Letter, 496
Schendler, Sylvan, 503
Sedgewick, Catherine Marie, 268
Seelye, L. Clark, 407
Seventh Massachusetts, 370
Shays, Daniel, 159, 172–173, 187–188, 216
Shays's Rebellion, 168–189, 213–218
Shepard, Levi, 137, 197, 199, 200–202, 217, 220
Shepard, William, 170, 173–174
Shepherd Woolen Manufacturing Company, 197
Shurtleff, Flavel, 379
Silk Production, 314–316
Smith College, 19, 22–23, 254, 398, 403–418, 424, 427, 429, 438, 493, 496, 500, 505
Smith Charities, 437
Smith, DeWitt, 415
Smith, Sophia, 403, 406–407
Spofford, Ned, 502, 504–505, 507–509
Spotsylvania, battle of, 381
Springfield *Republican*, 445
Springfield, MA, 503
Stearns, Frank, 462–464, 468–470, 474–475
Stebbins, Giles, 349
Steffens, Lincoln, 497
Stetson, Dolly Witter, 310, 343
Stetson, George R., 348
Stetson, James, 310, 314
Stoddard, Esther, 78
Stoddard, John, 80–82, 85
Stoddard, Lathrop, 466
Stoddard, Solomon, 75, 77–79
Storrs, Nathan, 197, 223
Strong, Caleb, 168, 197, 216, 218–219, 223
Strong, Sarah, 60
Summerfield, Arthur, 503
Swift, Earl Dwight, 301–302, 305–306, 309

Tappan, Benjamin, 220–221
Tappan, Lewis, 317
Teapot Dome, 478
Tenth Massachusetts Volunteers, 365–394
The Man Nobody Knows, 482
Thirty-sixth New York, 370
Thomas, Robert B., 205
Tontine Building, 120, 209
Trilling, Lionel, 505
Trumbull, James Russell, 21
Truth, Sojourner, 301, 343–361
Twain, Mark, 386

Umpanchela, 25–26
United Press, 481

Wampum, 12, 25
Washington, Booker T., 419
Washington, George, 258
Weatherell, Capt. James H., 379
Wellesley, MA, 497
Wells-Barnett, Ida B., 421
Wells, Hiram, 301–302, 304–305
Westbrook, Robert, 461, 474, 486
Wharton, Edith, 398
White House Correspondents Association, 481
White, William Allen, 476
Whitman, Walt, 497
Whitmarsh, Samuel, 315–316
Whitmarsh, Thomas, 316
Wilderness Campaign, 378
Wilderness-Spotsylvania campaign, 372
Wiley, Bell, 367, 382
Williams, Anna P., 388
Williams family, 76–86, 143, 147
Williams, Israel, 81, 83, 85–86, 140, 147, 149–157, 210, 212
Williams, Rev. John, 77–78
Williams, Rev. William, 77–79
Williams, Sidney, 388
Williams, Stephen, 158–162
Willis, Nathaniel Parker, 235–237, 259, 261, 270

Williston, A. Lyman, 429
Wilson, Edmund, 495, 497, 500, 505, 508
Wilson, Martha, 416
Wilson, Woodrow, 463, 467, 484
Winesburg, Ohio, 496
Witchcraft, 39–66
Wolf, Hugo, 498
Woman's Home Companion, 468–469
Wood, Leonard, 471
World War I, 365, 461–462, 474, 493
World War II, 493
Worthington, John, 147, 156–157
Wright, Chauncey, 395
Wulluther, 5

Yaddo Artist's Colony, 497–498, 500, 506
Yale University, 500

Valparaiso, Indiana, 496
Vassar, Matthew, 406
Vermont, 485
Vinovskis, Maris, 366
Vogue, 500

Yerrinton, George Brown, 358–359

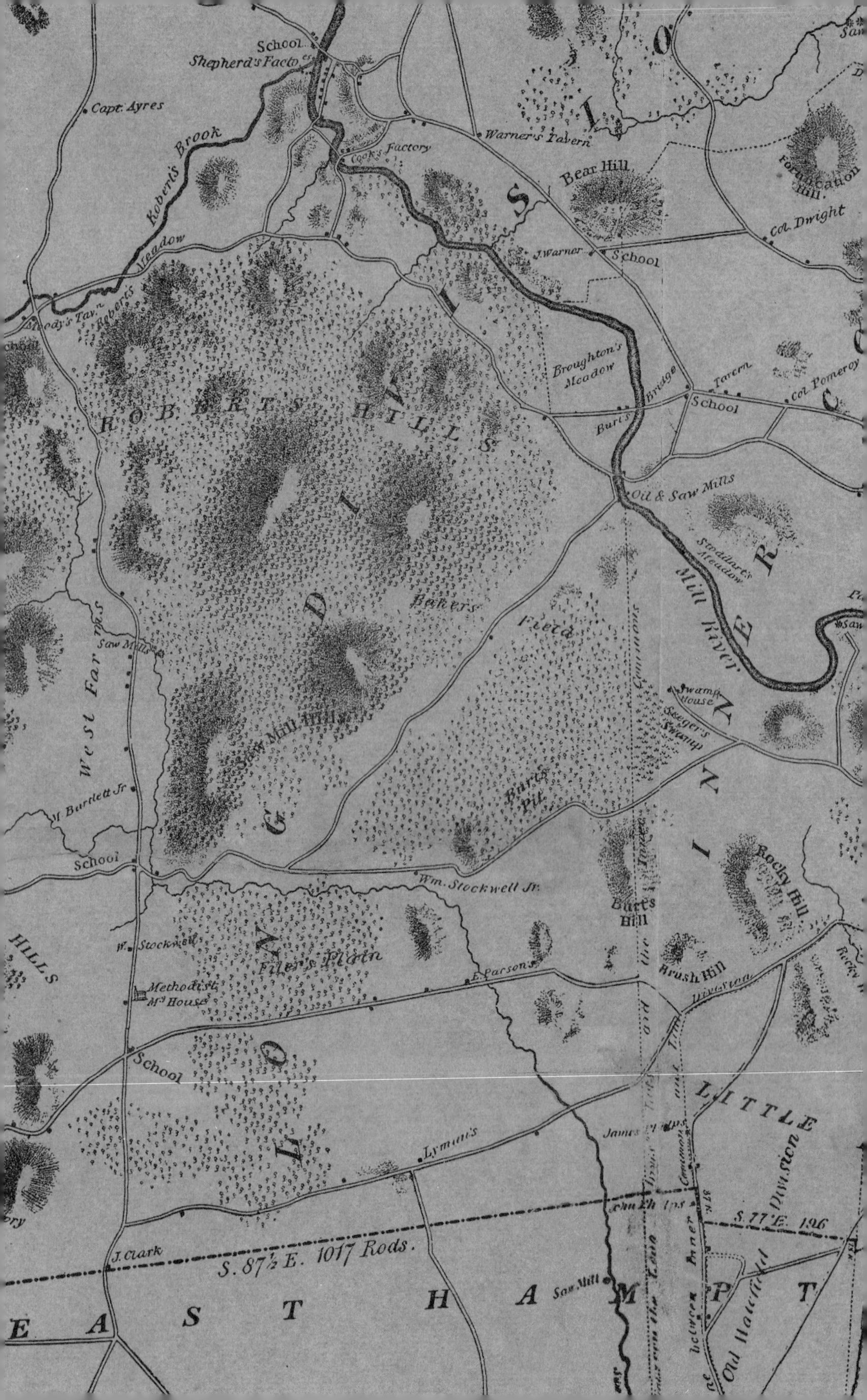

School
Shepherd's Factories
Capt. Ayres
Robert's Brook
Warner's Tavern
Cook's Factory
Bear Hill
Fornication Hill
Col. Dwight
J. Warner
School
Robert's Meadow
Moody's Tavn
Roberts
Broughton's Meadow
Burt's Bridge
Tavern
School
Col. Pomeroy
ROBERTS HILLS
Oil & Saw Mills
Stoddart's Meadow
Mill River
Bakers
Field
Saw Mills
West Farms
Swamp House
Seeger's Swamp
Saw Mill Hill
Burt's Pit
M. Burtlett Jr.
School
Wm. Stockwell Jr.
Rocky Hill
Burt's Hill
W. Stockwell
Filer's Plain
E. Parsons
Brush Hill
Methodist Mg House
School
LITTLE
Division
Lymans
S. 77°E. 196
J. Clark
S. 87½ E. 1017 Rods.
Saw Mill
E A S T H A M P T
Old Hatfield
GOODWIN
NORTH
HILLS